**WITHDRAWN** JUL  2007

*Accordions, Fiddles,
Two Step & Swing*

# ACCORDIONS, FIDDLES, TWO STEP & SWING

## A Cajun Music Reader

*edited by*
Ryan A. Brasseaux & Kevin S. Fontenot

*with a foreword by Wayne W. Daniel*

Center for Louisiana Studies
Lafayette, LA
2006

Front and rear cover designed by Ryan A. Brasseaux and Jennifer R. Cooper

Front photograph of Nathan Abshire holding his accordion courtesy of Elemore Morgan, Jr.

Rear photographs of women dancing from Center for Louisiana Studies, University of Louisiana at Lafayette, accession number 66; musicians on band wagon during a traditional *courir de mardi gras*, ca. 1980s, courtesy of James Edmunds.

ISBN (paper): 1-887366-71-7
ISBN (cloth): 1-887366-72-5
Library of Congress Catalog Number: 2006932813

Book design and layout by Jennifer R. Cooper

Copyright © 2006
Center for Louisiana Studies
University of Louisiana at Lafayette
PO Box 40831
Lafayette, LA 70504-0831
http://cls.louisiana.edu

## DEDICATION

Ryan A. Brasseaux
*To my maternal grandparents, Norris and Evon Melancon,
who imparted their love of Cajun music to me*

Kevin S. Fontenot
*In memory of my grandmother, Eliza Fontenot Carpenter*

# CONTENTS

Foreword .................................................................................................. 1

Preface .................................................................................................... 3

Acknowledgements ............................................................................... 7

Introduction .......................................................................................... 9

### *Under the Green Oak Tree: Origins and Locales of Cajun Music*

Excerpts from Louisiana French Folk Songs ..................................... 35
*Irène Thérèse Whitfield*

Acculturation in Cajun Folk Music .................................................. 47
*Harry Oster*

The Socio-Cultural Traits of the French
Folksong in Louisiana ........................................................................ 55
*Elizabeth Brandon*

The Public and Private Domains of Cajun Women
Musicians in Southwest Louisiana .................................................... 77
*Lisa E. Richardson*

Grand Texas: Accordion Music and Lifestyle
on the Cajun Frontière ....................................................................... 83
*Carl Lindahl*

Let the Good Times Unroll: Music and Race Relations
in Southwest Louisiana ...................................................................... 97
*Mark Mattern*

Introduction and Use of Accordions in Cajun Music ................... 107
*Malcolm L. Comeaux*

Heritage, Tradition, and Travel:
Louisiana French Culture Placed on a California Dance Floor ..... 115
*Mark F. DeWitt*

The Cajun Dancehall ........................................................................ 139
*Malcolm L. Comeaux*

Une 'Tite Poule Grasse ou la Fille Aînée [A Little Fat Chicken
or The Eldest Daughter]:
A Comparative Analysis of
Cajun and Creole Mardi Gras Songs ................................................................. 153
Rocky L. Sexton and Harry Oster

The Cajun French Music Association:
The Development of a Music-Centered Ethnic Organization ...................... 179
Rocky L. Sexton

## The Water Pump: Commercialization of Cajun Music

Cajun Music ........................................................................................................... 197
Barry Jean Ancelet

Louisiana Folk and Regional Popular Music
Traditions on Records and the Radio:
An Historical Overview with
Suggestions for Future Research ....................................................................... 229
Stephen R. Tucker

"Colinda:" Mysterious Origins of a Cajun Folksong .................................... 251
Shane K. Bernard and Julia Frederick

How Y'all Are: Justin Wilson, Comedy,
and Ethnic Identity .............................................................................................. 265
Kevin S. Fontenot

Country Chameleons:
Cajuns on the Louisiana Hayride ..................................................................... 273
Tracey E.W. Laird

J.D. Miller and Floyd Soileau:
A Comparison of Two Small-Town Recordmen of Acadiana ...................... 279
Shane K. Bernard

Twisting at the Fais Do-Do:
The Roots of South Louisiana's Swamp Pop Music ..................................... 291
Shane K. Bernard

The Cajun Music Festival: Genesis and Legacy ............................................. 301
Barry Jean Ancelet

## "He Decided a Song About That:" Profiles of Cajun Artists

Joseph C. Falcon, Accordion Player and Singer:
A Biographical Sketch .................................................................. 321
*Lauren C. Post*

"Mama, Where You At?:"
The Chronicle of Maius LaFleur .................................................. 339
*Donald Lee Nelson*

Playing in the Shadows:
Obscure Early Cajun Recording Artists ....................................... 347
*Ron Brown*

Acadian Fiddler Dennis McGee and Acadian Dances .................. 363
*Brenda Daigle*

Moonshine and Mosquitoes:
The Story of Dewey Segura .......................................................... 379
*John H. Cowley*

Leo Soileau ................................................................................... 383
*Tony Russell*

The Hackberry Ramblers .............................................................. 389
*Ben Sandmel*

Brief History of the Hackberry Ramblers ..................................... 399
*Luderin Darbone*

The Bayou Buckaroo:
LeRoy "Happy Fats" LeBlanc ........................................................ 407
*John Broven*

Harry Choates: Cajun Fiddle Ace ................................................. 419
*Mike Leadbitter*

Iry LeJune .................................................................................... 423
*Mike Leadbitter*

King of the Dancehalls:
Accordionist Lawrence Walker .................................................... 425
*Kevin S. Fontenot and Ryan A. Brasseaux*

Aldus Roger: King of the Cajun Accordion ................................. 431
*Ann Allen Savoy*

Jimmy C. Newman and His Cajun Country Roots ............................................. 435
*Douglas B. Green*

People Buy the Feel:
Cajun Fiddle Master Rufus Thibodeaux ......................................................... 439
*Kevin S. Fontenot*

Vin Bruce ............................................................................................................ 443
*Michael Hurtt*

Dewey Balfa: A Cultural Ambassador ............................................................. 453
*Barry Jean Ancelet*

The Cajun Mick Jagger ..................................................................................... 459
*Richard Baudoin*

Hawaiian Shirts and Cajun Power:
Basking in the Sunshine of Michael Doucet and Beausoleil .......................... 467
*Ryan A. Brasseaux and Erik Charpentier*

Never Mind the Bowties—Here's the Bluerunners ........................................ 477
*Michael Tisserand*

Fabricating Authenticity:
The Cajun Renaissance and Steve Riley & the Mamou Playboys ................. 487
*Ryan A. Brasseaux and Erik Charpentier*

Get Lost: The Lost Bayou Ramblers ................................................................ 495
*Erik Charpentier*

*Saving Culture with a Song:*
*Cajun Music and the Twenty-First Century* ..................................................... 501

*Appendix: An Evolutionary Chronology of Cajun Music* ............................... 507

Recommended Readings .................................................................................. 513

Index ................................................................................................................... 519

# Foreword

CAJUN IS ONE OF the most engaging and infectious of America's roots musics. Once heard, it is never forgotten. Both its language and its cadence, like lusty sirens, are irresistible, and few are those who, even though they may be endowed with the thinnest shred of musical sensibility or the slightest terpsichorean inclination, can resist the urge to wish for more. Although Cajun music can be enjoyed without knowledge of its background, awareness of its lineage greatly enriches the listening experience. The history of the culture in which Cajun music was born and nurtured is a unique and fascinating story that serves as a perfect example of how folk music develops. Like other forms of American vernacular music, Cajun music attracted the attention of twentieth-century mass media moguls, with the result that this captivating cultural expression, once confined to a relatively small geographic area of the country, became known to radio listeners and buyers of phonograph records all across America. In the process, talented performers of Cajun music achieved recognition as ambassadors of the genre and became known and revered far beyond their native environs. These and other aspects of Cajun music are addressed in this publication.

As the reader of *Accordions, Fiddles, Two Step & Swing* will learn, Cajun music has been the subject of serious scholarly investigation for three-quarters of a century. In this informative book, two scions of the Cajun culture, Kevin Fontenot and Ryan Brasseaux, have brought together a collection of interesting and important reports from the extant body of research in the area of Cajun music. Fontenot and Brasseaux are eminently qualified to assess the quality of available investigative findings and to select those most relevant to their goal of defining "Cajun music scholarship as a distinctive field of study with a rich genealogical heritage." Between the two of them, their credentials include their own documented studies of the subject, a life-long, first-hand acquaintance with Cajun culture, and Cajun music performance skills.

*Accordions, Fiddles, Two Step & Swing* should find an audience among ethnic music scholars, performers of Cajun music, and fans of the genre. The book will likely become required reading in college courses in ethnomusicology and kindred disciplines, while the general reader will be thankful for the ability to learn about Cajun music without having to search for information, topic by topic and article by article, in scattered and often difficult to access sources.

Wayne W. Daniel
Professor Emeritus
Georgia State University

# Preface

THE IDEA FOR THIS project germinated at the 2004 Louisiana Historical Association's (LHA) conference. After years of collaborating at annual LHA meetings, we decided to share our respective Cajun music bibliographies in book form. The articles featured in this volume profoundly impacted our perception of the genre. Some explore the traditional and commercial contexts that nourished musical expression in south Louisiana, while others offer details concerning the lives of the artists. These essays traverse academic disciplines, span historical eras, and tap into those resources published in respected popular music magazines. All of these materials remained scattered across North America and Europe in journals, out-of-print manuscripts, and defunct magazines until we embarked on this project.

Our motivation to compile this reader stemmed directly from a desire to outline Cajun music studies' genealogy—from its earliest inceptions to its latest incarnations—by surveying influential meditations on the ethnic musical expression in hopes of stimulating further research. The articles featured here stand as representative examples of the literature available dealing with the subject. We have also taken the opportunity to include here newly composed essays to help realize our objective. Although *Accordions, Fiddles, Two Step & Swing* focuses primarily on music, some basic terminology should be addressed regarding the information covered in these essays.

The term Cajun is an Anglo American corruption of the French ethnic label *Acadien* (Acadian). In this study Cajun refers to a white bilingual ethnic group whose cultural orientation reflects the transnational character of south Louisiana's cultural landscape. Cajun culture is a synthetic New World product—an amalgamation of the cultural influences that converged in varying degrees within the region as the group absorbed persons of German, Creole, Irish, French, French Canadian, Native American, Anglo American, Italian, and Spanish ancestry. By the twentieth century, this cultural and linguistic group's particular brand of folk music had come under the microscope of academic analysis.

Cajun music is broadly defined in this study as the range of musical expression generated by this predominately French-Catholic ethnic group. One of America's most diverse forms of vernacular music, the tradition encompasses *a cappella* French ballads, accordion-based dance music, fiddle tunes, French-inflected country and western, and local interpretations of rhythm and blues and rock and roll known as swamp pop.

According to historian Shane Bernard,[1] swamp pop is a synthetic blend of New Orleans rhythm and blues, Cajun and black Creole music, and country and western music, particularly popular during the 1950s and 1960s. Unlike

---

[1] Shane K. Bernard, *Swamp Pop, Cajun and Creole Rhythm and Blues* (Jackson, MS, 1996).

Cajun and zydeco, which have traditionally carried distinct racial connotations, swamp pop boasted both black and white musicians performing in the same style. It should be noted that swamp poppers of color, like zydeco musicians, generally identified with Afro-Creole (Franco-Catholic) culture, as opposed to African American (Anglo-Protestant) culture.

During the territory's colonial history, settlers defined *Creole* as "born in Louisiana." This ethnic label applied to people of European descent born in Louisiana (*Créole blanc* or white Creole) and to enslaved peoples of African descent born in the colony (*nègre créole* or black Creole). Over time, the French language and Catholicism also factored into the term's definition.

Before the thirteenth amendment abolished slavery in the United States, Louisiana law recognized a group of landowners, merchants, and artisans known as *gens de couleur libre*, or free women and men of color. Free people of color became part of south Louisiana's Afro-Creole aristocracy and adopted the title "Creole of Color" after the Civil War to distinguish themselves from newly freed bondsmen. The word Creole also applies to an indigenous Louisiana cuisine, native produce (e.g. Creole tomatoes), language, and music, among other things. Creole music is an umbrella term that sometimes addresses musical forms such as historic Afro-Creole music—*juré* and *la-la*—and its contemporary form zydeco.

Zydeco is an accordion-based black Creole musical tradition indigenous to southwest Louisiana and east Texas. This syncopated dance music has been greatly influenced by Afro-Caribbean rhythms, New Orleans rhythm and blues, Cajun music, country and western, and mainstream African American popular music. Musicians traditionally rendered songs in Creole French, often improvising lyrics, though English has become the preferred linguistic medium, particularly among younger groups. In contrast to the popular misconception perpetuated outside of French Louisiana, zydeco is not a traditional form of Cajun music, but rather a complementary and parallel style maintained by south Louisiana's Afro-Creole community. While Afro-Creole music has profoundly affected the sounds and stylings of its Cajun cousin, we have limited the parameters of this project to include only articles specifically addressing Cajun music, though several articles acknowledge the genre's intersection with zydeco.

The historiographical development of the study of Cajun music has followed several lines. Academics initially expressed interest in the traditional ballads and folksongs following the lead of such scholars as Francis James Child.[2] Their approach was informed by the idea that the ballads were a form of folk poetry and they eagerly collected and studied the variants of songs rooted in the European past. Early scholars were also interested in ritual songs, such as

---

[2] Francis James Child, *The English and Scottish Popular Ballads* (Boston and New York, 1883-98).

those linked to Mardi Gras and other holidays. These studies focus on the literary nature of ballads and the influence of outside factors on folksong development.

Academic studies tended to ignore dance music, particularly the vital commercial tradition that emerged during the 1920s. Before the 1990s, when a flurry of reissued recordings originally issued on 78 rpm became widely available on compact disc, scholars had to rely on scant discographic information and private record collections to make assumptions about commercial dance music. During the 1950s and 1960s, Harry Oster and Lauren Post became the first academics seriously interested in dance music and recording artists. Their fieldwork resulted in important studies such as Post's ground-breaking interview with Joe Falcon, the first published academic work on a commercial Cajun artist. Oster and Post were joined in their study of individual musicians by a host of record collectors, many from Europe, who came looking for the artists behind the names on 78 labels. Tony Russell, Mike Leadbitter, and John H. Cowley sought out aging artists and gathered important biographical information from Leo Soileau, Dewey Segura, and others. This group published some of the first profiles of Cajun artists in such journals as the *John Edwards Memorial Foundation Quarterly* and Russell's *Old Time Music*. These sketches formed a strong base, expanded upon by later researchers such as John Broven. Collecting the life stories of musicians remains one of the most active and enlightening areas of research. It is also one of the most diverse as it attracts the talents of academics, journalists, and pure enthusiasts.

We have tried to draw on a representative range of the best writings on Cajun music. We have also tried to show the development of the field by including examples of early material and some hard to find pieces. Some sketches presented here were the first steps toward understanding important artists. For example, Mike Leadbitter's Harry Choates profile forms the basis upon which extended treatments, such as the liner notes to Bear Family's reissue,[3] grew. Other early artists such as Iry LeJeune, Leo Soileau, and Lawrence Walker await similar treatment. Interesting work on the environment of Cajun music, such as Malcolm Comeaux's singular study of the dancehall, continues to expand and the role played by Cajun women needs serious attention. In some cases, essays presented here are parts of larger studies. Shane Bernard has fully explored the swamp pop genre and Tracey Laird places Cajun-Country performers in context in her recent study of the Louisiana Hayride.[4] We hope that the essays presented here help to inspire greater research in the area of Cajun music and allied fields. In addition, the other motivating factors behind this

---

[3] Andrew Brown, *Devil in the Bayou*, Bear Family.

[4] Tracey E.W. Laird, *Louisiana Hayride* (Oxford, 2005).

volume also include stimulating a greater interest in Louisiana's musical traditions by shedding some light on the underlying cultural and historical complexities that generated one of America's richest musical legacies.

*Note on Recordings*
The compact disc revolution has finally reached classic Cajun music. Many of the recordings mentioned in Barry Ancelet and Steve Tucker's surveys of Cajun and Louisiana music are now available on compact disc. Due to the often ephemeral nature of reissues, it would be almost foolhardy to provide a listing of CDs that might go out of print nearly as soon as they appear. We would however like to offer some advice on building a collection of classic Cajun music. The European labels JSP and Proper have recently released excellent box sets of early Cajun music. These sets offer a broad overview of the major recording artists and styles of early Cajun music. Arhoolie and Yazoo have produced excellent artist-oriented collections focusing on such performers as Leo Soileau, Amédé Ardoin, and Blind Uncle Gaspard. Arhoolie, Swallow, and Ace offer a wide range of classic Cajun recordings and interested collectors should pay attention to these labels' catalogs. Recordings from these labels are the backbone of any solid collection of Cajun music.

*Note on Spelling of French and Cajun Names*
Many people discussed in this book appear in different articles with different name spellings. For example, Iry LeJeune's last name is alternately spelled as LeJune, Lejune, and Lejeune; Amédé Breaux's first name also appears as Amidie and Amédée. Such spelling variants are often due to the phonetic nature of the Cajun French language as well as to the fact that recording companies sent people from elsewhere to Louisiana to record these artists, and they did not always clarify the spelling of artists' names. We have made every effort to standardize spelling throughout the essays to avoid confusion, but also have retained certain name spellings in order to remain faithful to the original publication of some articles.

# Acknowledgements

THE EDITORS WOULD LIKE to thank all the colleagues, friends, and family that who facilitated and supported this project. Many thanks are extended to Carl A. Brasseaux, Director of the Center for Louisiana Studies at the University of Louisiana at Lafayette for expressing an interest in publishing a Cajun music reader; to the authors who agreed to contribute new materials—Ron Brown, John Broven, Erik Charpentier, Mike Hurtt, Ben Sandmel, Rocky Sexton, Michael Tisserand; to all of the authors and publishers who graciously granted permission to reprint their materials in this volume; to Tony Russell for generously helping obtain permissions from the British authors included here; to Associate Professor Sandra Himel and Cajun and Creole Music Collection at the University of Louisiana at Lafayette; and to Jennifer Cooper of the Center for Louisiana Studies for guiding this book through completion.

Ryan Brasseaux would like to thank professors Jay Edwards, Carolyn Ware, and Helen Regis; his grandparents Norris and Evon Melancon for regaling him with stories about attending dances featuring some of Cajun music's legendary artists such as Iry LeJeune, Harry Choates, and Lawrence Walker; and with much gratitude his wife, Jessika Ducharme Brasseaux, and their children, Anne Elise and Joseph Emile, for their unwavering support, encouragement, and tolerance during the long nights he spent behind a computer screen.

Kevin Fontenot would like thank his parents Nolton and Barbara Fontenot, Amy Trepagnier, Bill C. Malone, and the late Ralph T. Carpenter, who introduced him to Jimmie Rodgers and the Saturday broadcasts from Fred's Lounge.

# Introduction

"**T**HEY LOVE TO DANCE most of all, more than any other people in the colony," French immigrant C.C. Robin wrote of the Cajun community in 1803. "There may be only a couple of fiddles to play for the crowd, there may be only four candles for light, placed on wooden arms attached to the wall; nothing but long wooden benches to sit on, and only exceptionally a few bottles of Tafia [cheap rum] diluted with water for refreshment. No matter, everyone dances."[1] Thanks to Robin's astonishment with the vibrancy of folk musical traditions in south Louisiana, Cajun music scholars have some inkling of the contexts that accompanied Cajun music at the moment of the Louisiana Purchase.

Since the colonial period, enchanted travel writers generated numerous first-hand accounts describing Cajuns and the ethnic group's exotic brand of folk music. These fragmented depictions, ranging from French governmental correspondence to fictional backdrops created by nineteenth-century authors like Kate Chopin and Sidonie de la Houssaye, collectively represent the forerunner to a Cajun music studies' genealogical lineage that emerged during the twentieth century.[2] Between the 1930s and the 1950s, an interdisciplinary group of students and faculty at Louisiana State University (LSU) helped to generate the first generation of Cajun music scholarship. Though grounded in folkloric and anthropological fieldwork methodology, the collective works of Irène Whitfield, Lauren Post, and Harry Oster took place across disciplines and placed the university at the forefront of the field. Other camps soon emerged. A parallel Franco-oriented school of thought surfaced at the Université Laval during the 1940s and 1950s, through the efforts of Corinne Saucier and Elizabeth Brandon, two graduate researchers interested in the French texts entwined in the Cajun ballad tradition. In the early 1970s, Catherine Blanchet helped to establish Cajun music studies at the University of Southwestern Louisiana[3] with her Master's thesis "Louisiana French Folk Songs Among Children in Vermilion Parish, 1942-54" (1970), before professor Barry Ancelet almost single-handedly made the university the epicenter of Cajun music studies. Ancelet explored the dynamics of Cajun musical expression, sketching in broad strokes the history and evolution of Cajun music from a late-twentieth-century perspective. Over time scholars and music writers developed a lit-

---

[1] C.C. Robin, *Voyage to Louisiana by C.C. Robin, 1803-1805*, trans. by Stuart O. Landry, Jr. (New Orleans, 1966), 115.
[2] DeClouet to Miró, October 8, 1785, AGI, PPC, 198A: 237; R.L. Daniels, "The Acadians of Louisiana," *Scribner's Monthly* 19 (1879-1880): 390; "A Trip to the Teche," *Frank Leslie's Popular Monthly*, Vol. 12 (November 1881) 563-66; Alexander Barde, *The Vigilante Committees of the Attakapas* (Lafayette, LA, 1981); Kate Chopin, *Bayou Folk and A Night in Acadie* (New York, 1999) 146; Sidonie de la Houssaye, *Pouponne and Balthazar*, trans. J. John Perret (Lafayette, LA, 1983) 75.
[3] In 2000, the university changed its name to the University of Louisiana at Lafayette.

erature based on the Bayou Country's musical traditions. These investigations found a warm reception in a handful of journals, magazines, and university and popular presses.

Journals and magazines such as the *Louisiana Folklore Miscellany, Journal of American Folklore, Old Time Music, John Edwards Memorial Foundation Quarterly, Revue de Louisiane,* and the Louisiana Folklife Festival booklet frequently published essays pertaining to Cajun music, thereby enriching and sustaining the field of study. Academic presses sporadically published manuscripts focusing on Cajun Country's musical traditions following Louisiana State University Press' printing of Whitfield's *Louisiana French Folk Songs* and Macmillan Press' issue *Our Singing Country*, which included samples of John and Alan Lomax's Louisiana fieldwork, publications only took the form of articles and theses. By the end of the twentieth century, studies published by the University of Texas Press, the Center for Louisiana Studies at the University of Louisiana at Lafayette, the University Press of Mississippi marked the beginning of Cajun music studies most prolific era. In the late twentieth century independent Louisiana publishers like Swallow Publications in Ville Platte, Pelican Publishing Company in Gretna, and Ann Savoy's Bluebird Press in Eunice released important popular materials that subsequently gave a voice to non-academic writers. These periodicals and publishing houses stimulated a dialogue that shaped both the Cajun community's and the world's perception of Cajun music, though no one study acknowledges the richness of the field's literature or the scholars who keenly constructed meaning around Louisiana's indigenous musical forms.

This project began as an effort to recognize the efforts of those scholars and music writers who contributed to the understanding of this unique form of American music. *Accordions, Fiddles, Two Step & Swing* attempts to outline the evolution of the field of study. The essays contained in this volume represent the broadest spectrum of Cajun music studies taken from landmark and influential publications to little known research papers tucked away in obscure journals on dusty university library shelves. The editors gave careful consideration to each of the entries here in hopes of presenting the cultural dynamics and historical currents that shaped Cajun music, such as the relationship between women and song, the genre's popularity on radio and record, and Cajun music's role beyond the parameters of south Louisiana, while highlighting some of the theoretical and methodological approaches that informed the literature through time. This publication strives ultimately to define Cajun music scholarship as a distinctive field of study with a rich genealogical heritage.

As Cajun music scholarship began in earnest during the 1930s, the earliest surveys provided a wealth of information and transcribed texts without much analysis. Following in the footsteps of early anthropologists and folklorists like

# Introduction

Frans Boaz, Cecil Sharp, and John Lomax, who helped to make "salvage ethnography"[4] standard practice in the behavioral sciences, field workers combed through southwest Louisiana's musical landscape in hopes of locating and identifying what they viewed as eroding cultural phenomena, such as *a cappella* musical traditions. Text-heavy ballads were of particular interest to two Acadia Parish women studying language and music in separate romance language departments, because these unaccompanied arrangements represented a sort of oral literature for the largely non-literate Cajun society.

Irene Petitjean conducted the first academic study to focus specifically on Cajun music. Her Master's thesis "Cajun Folk Songs of Southwest Louisiana," completed in January 1930 at Columbia University, compiled 144 song transcriptions taken from an unpublished late-nineteenth-century manuscript by Mrs. Arthur Aléman, a collection of songs from Petitjean's field expeditions in her native Rayne, Louisiana, and selected 78 rpm Cajun recordings issued after the genre's 1928 commercial debut. Without substantive analysis, her efforts went largely unnoticed. Irène Thérèse Whitfield, on the other hand, following closely on Petitjean's heels and completed her ground-breaking Master's thesis "Louisiana French Folk Songs" in 1935 at Louisiana State University.[5]

Irène Thérèse Whitfield was born on La Belle Savanne (Beautiful Prairie) Plantation in Acadia Parish on October 26, 1900. She developed a deep appreciation for Louisiana's Francophone culture in which she grew up and went on to pursue and academic career in education and French. In 1919 and 1920, Whitfield received diplomas for two year's academic college work and the teacher's-training course respectively from Southwestern Louisiana Institute in Lafayette. In 1924, she received a Bachelor of Philosophy in Education from the University of Chicago with departmental honors in French before graduating from the Department of French and Italian at Louisiana State University.[6]

Whitfield's scholarly reputation bestowed the musicologist with the honorary designation as gatekeeper and unofficial spokesperson for Cajun music. She went readily into the field, defying the conventional male-dominated contexts generally associated with Cajun musical traditions, to observe musical performances and to transcribe folk material during her salvage ethnographic excursions. Visiting scholars followed Whitfield's lead and relied heavily on her intimate knowledge of southwest Louisiana's cultural landscape.

In 1939, Louisiana State University Press published a revised edition of her thesis, the landmark book *Louisiana French Folk Songs*, which included an

---

[4] Salvage ethnography equated to the documentation of what field researchers perceived as endangered cultural traits. Researchers hoped to collect and document folk and vernacular cultural materials—language data, stories, folk songs, legends, etc.—before mainstream culture completely wiped out these traditions.
[5] Irene M. Petitjean, "'Cajun' Folk Songs of Southwestern Louisiana" (M.A. thesis, Columbia University 1930).
[6] Irène Thérèse Whitfield, *Louisiana French Folk Songs* (Baton Rouge, 1939), 226; Malcolm Comeaux, personal correspondence to Ryan A. Brasseaux, February 16, 2005.

account of her song-hunting expeditions with John and Alan Lomax during her thesis research.[7] Whitfield's revolutionary publication was the first extensive exploration of Cajun music in the academic literature, and a novel interdisciplinary study straddling the boundaries of Francophone studies, ethnography, literary analysis, musicology, and folklore. In turn, her work immediately captured the imagination of folklorists, folk music enthusiasts, and New Deal affiliates who were swept up in the nation's burgeoning interest in indigenous America.

In 1934, Whitfield opened a weird and mysterious Cajun world unto ballad hunters John and Alan Lomax, who came to south Louisiana to collect indigenous American music for the Archive of Folk Song at the Library of Congress. The Lomaxes arrived in Cajun Country with a three-hundred-pound portable aluminum disc recorder, a relatively new form of technology that gave concrete form to ephemeral musical performances, and documented the cross-cultural musical interaction that took place across racial and ethnic boundaries in Depression-era Louisiana. The musicologists found the ballads they were searching for and much more. The sounds of Afro-Creole *jurés*, community brass bands, cowboy and English folk songs, and French accordion dance numbers etched their way into history by way of the Lomaxes' aluminum discs. In their 1941 publication *Our Singing Country*, however, John and Alan Lomax analyzed only *a cappella* ballad performances by a handful of Louisiana musicians. The folklorists portrayed the arrangements as Old World compositions still performed in the New World:

> the ballad singers are still singing their ancient Norman ballads at country weddings, the fais-dodo [sic] bands creating their wild and fertile music at the rural dances. The songs in this section, the second collection of the kind, so far as we know, that has been published anywhere, will indicate, better than we can, what a rich storehouse of folk music is the Cajun country of southwestern Louisiana.[8]

The Lomaxes only published material that contributed to their rigid definition of the "folk"—impoverished people who lived beyond the corrosive influence of American popular culture.[9] Music historian Benjamin Filene believes that academics like the Lomaxes, the commercial record and radio industries, and publicists acted as "cultural middlemen," who presented to the public an interpretation of authentic American folk culture. In *Romancing the Folk* (2000), Filene examines American folk music and the middlemen who worked to create a romantic image of performers and musical styles. "These folklorists, record

---
[7] Whitfield, *Louisiana French Folk Songs*, 24-27.
[8] Alan Lomax and John A. Lomax, *Our Singing Country: A Second Volume of American Ballads and Folk Songs* (New York, 1941), 179.
[9] Nolan Porterfield, *Last Cavalier: The Live and Times of John A. Lomax, 1867-1948* (Urbana and Chicago, 1996), 77.

company executives, producers, radio programmers, and publicists 'discovered' folk musicians, recorded them, arranged concert dates for them, and, usually, promoted them as the exemplars of America's musical roots," writes Filene. "In doing so, they did more than deliver 'pure' music: they made judgments about what constituted America's pure musical traditions, helped shape what 'mainstream' audiences recognized as authentic, and, inevitably, transformed the music that the folk performers offered."[10] These judgments resonated through the end of the twentieth century, as fiddler Michael Doucet and folklorist Barry Ancelet respectively reintroduced the folklore preserved by the Lomaxes as representative examples of the authentic roots of Cajun music through contemporary musical interpretations and through scholarly publication.[11] The Lomaxes' Southern field expeditions also helped to encourage folklore methodology and salvage ethnography among song hunters and academicians, particularly as recorded sound technology became more widely available to the general public.

In 1936, a literature major at the University of Texas named William Owens took time off from his studies to work as a stage manager at the National Folk Festival and Texas Centennial celebration in Dallas. Between acts, the curious student explored the fair grounds and stumbled across Irène Whitfield and a Cajun dance band, who were part of the Louisiana delegation represented at the festival. Whitfield insight into Louisiana's musical traditions and an impromptu jam session by the accordion band's captivated Owen's imagination.[12] He reminisced in his memoirs,

> I often sat with them listening to a kind of singing and playing that never got on the stage—too spontaneous, not professional enough. In them was the beat of the bayou I had heard in Port Arthur [Texas], in them meanings that came to me not through language but through the emotions of love and laughter, in them the story of a people full of the overtones that had been edited out of the canned version they presented on stage.[13]

Owen's fascination with Cajun culture stemmed from his love of music and Texas' cultural landscape. He wanted to understand better the people and Francophone culture embedded in the Golden Triangle—the area between Orange, Beaumont, and Port Arthur, Texas, where thousands of Cajuns migrated to work in petroleum-related industries during the first half of the

---

[10] Benjamin Filene, *Romancing the Folk: Public Memory and American Roots Music* (Chapel Hill and London, 2000), 5.
[11] Barry Jean Ancelet, *The Origins and Development of Cajun Music* (Lafayette, LA, 1989); Barry Jean Ancelet, Jay Edwards, Glen Pitre, *Cajun Country* (Jackson and London, 1991). The band Beausoleil's interpretations of the Lomax collection can be heard on releases like *Déjà vu* ("Belle" and "Je m'endors"), *Vintage Beausoleil* (live version of "Belle"), *L'Amour ou la Follie* ("Boudreaux"). The original field recordings are featured on the Rounder Records release *Cajun and Creole Music Vol. I & II: The Classic Louisiana Recordings, 1934/1937*, Rounder Records 11661-1843-2 (Cambridge, MA, 1999).
[12] William A. Owens, *Tell Me a Story, Sing Me a Song: A Texas Chronicle*, (Austin, 1983), 118-122.
[13] Ibid., 119.

twentieth century—that helped to shaped the sounds of the Lone Star State. Forty-six years following his initial foray into Louisiana's musical traditions, the Columbia University English professor published a chapter entitled "Cajun French: Lapping Over From Louisiana" in the third installment of his autobiographical writings *Tell Me a Story, Sing Me a Song*. The essay chronicles the author's adventures in Cajun Country and provides one of the best descriptions in the scholarly literature of the Depression-era context in which Cajun music thrived.

Between Christmas and New Year in 1937, William Owens and friend Calvin Vaughn embarked from Texas for the Bayou Country with a Vibromaster recorder in tow. The researchers traveled throughout Cajun Country, exploring, recording, and documenting what they considered the authentic roots of French Louisiana's musical traditions through the guidance of Whitfield, whom Owens and Vaughn sought out at the Whitfield family plantation near Duson, Louisiana. Not only did these young Texans experiment with the latest sound recording technology, their salvaging expedition paralleled the innovative ethnographic methodology of more famous collecting excursions by the Lomaxes. In essence, the Lomaxes, Owens, and Vaughn validated only ballad traditions, thereby ignoring both current trends in Cajun music and the expanse of the Cajun repertoire in lieu of perceived European cultural survivals. Owens and Vaughn had already established in their minds the parameters Cajun folk music before stepping foot in the Bayou Country, despite their limited knowledge of the south Louisiana repertoire. The Texans wanted non-professional singers, who sang antiquated compositions at home or within the community, not commercially. "I found records with Joe Falcon singing 'Allons à Lafayette,'" Owens explained, "I could enjoy his records but not use them."[14] When the researchers made their first Cajun field recording in Scott, Louisiana, they solicited an elderly woman, who accommodated the fieldworkers' request for "old" French songs by launching into "La Marseillaise," much to the chagrin of Owens and Vaughn. They quickly modified their query to compile exclusively an assortment of French ballads that expanded the available information on Cajun *a cappella* song texts during the 1930s and complimented the material collected by their contemporaries.

In the late 1940s and early 1950s, the Université Laval in Québec City, Canada, cultivated young scholars interested in French North American cultural expressions. Two graduate students in particular, Corinne Saucier and Elizabeth Brandon, focused their attention on ballad traditions in Louisiana to examine both linguistic and cultural phenomenon in the Bayou Country. As a Master student under Ralph Steele Boggs, Corinne Saucier explored ex-

---

[14] Joe Falcon and his wife Cléoma Breaux Falcon recorded the very first Cajun record "Allons à Lafayette"/"The Waltz That Carried Me To My Grave" in 1928. Ibid., 122.

tensively the musical traditions in her native Avoyelles Parish, recording folk ballads by elderly singers with her "old-fashioned" disc-cutting recorder. In 1947, Saucier presented much of her collection in her dissertation "Histoire et Traditions de la Paroisse des Avoyelles en Louisiane." "It was her intention, shortly before her death in 1960," write Louisiana State University at New Orleans faculty Marie-Louise Lagarde, William S. Chute, and George F. Reinecke in a tribute to Saucier's Cajun music research, "to publish the texts and at least some of the musical notations of the songs she had collected; however, Dr. Saucier was somewhat handicapped by an acquaintance with music less thorough than her knowledge of the language and the people of Avoyelles Parish."[15] Nonetheless, Saucier's disc recordings, her dissertation, her publication *Traditions de la Paroisse des Avoyelles en Louisiane*, along with Lagarde, Chute, and Reinecke's article "Six Avoyelles Songs from the Saucier Collection" shed light on the often ignored musical traditions from the northern fringe of Cajun Country.[16] Elizabeth Brandon probed the folk and musical customs of Vermilion Parish in her 1955 study "Moeurs et langue de la paroisse Vermilion en Louisiane," directed by French Canadian folk song expert Luc Lacourcière. Laval's French Language and Literature program steeped Saucier and Brandon in traditional folklore ideology and salvage ethnography. Both researchers emphasized the textuality and linguistic intricacies of individual ballads through their analyses of song lyrics. Indeed, Laval's Cajun music scholars rightfully viewed the texts that gave form to ballads as an illiterate population's folk literature. The Québecois camp, however, stood in contrast to the socio-cultural oriented research conducted at Louisiana State University in the wake of Irène Whitfield's graduation.

"Well, I'm not an Acadian," cultural geographer Lauren Post once remarked, "but I am an American stewed in Cajun gravy."[17] Lauren Chester Post grew up on a homestead near Duson in Acadia Parish, directly across the Southern Pacific railroad tracks from the Whitfield family's La Belle Savanne. Born only one year before Irène Whitfield, the two relatives developed a close bond first as childhood playmates and later as colleagues. Whitfield remembered her friend in a memoriam published in the *Louisiana Folklore Miscellany*. "[H]e could speak Cajun French fairly well when he was ten years old," she recalled, "having learned it through association with the boys of the families of Bouillon, Sensat, Sonnier, Gautreaux, and Thibodeaux. Moreover, he had noticed many of their ways of life and even their little folk songs, the latter of which he con-

---

[15] Marie-Louise Lagarde, William S. Chute, and George F. Reinecke, "Six Avoyelles songs from the Saucier Collection," *Louisiana Folklore Miscellany* 11 (April 1965): 1.
[16] Corinne L. Saucier, *Traditions de la Paroisse des Avoyelles en Louisiane* (Philadelphia, 1956), 147-54; Lagarde, Chute, and Reinecke, "Six Avoyelles songs from the Saucier Collection," 1-26.
[17] Irène Whitfield Holmes, "In Memoriam: Lauren Chester Post," *Louisiana Folklore Miscellany* 4 (1976-1980): 8.

sidered catchy, cute, and different."[18] Each summer, he returned to his native Acadia Parish with his wife, dramatic soprano singer Valeria Postnikova Post, to photograph and record Cajun bands in an effort to document the evolving musical traditions that the scholar fell in love with as a youth.

Well known for his contributions as a geographer and historian, particularly through his 1962 publication *Cajun Sketches*, Post's legacy within Cajun music studies has not been fully realized in the academic community. For instance, the current academic literature rarely mentions, and then only in passing, that the scholar is responsible for the first Cajun musical performance at a national festival. In 1936, Post (then at Louisiana State University) chaired the Louisiana delegation at the National Folk Festival held in Dallas, Texas. The thirty-six-person entourage consisted of Post, Whitfield (interpreter and folk music critic), vocalist Elmore Sonnier, two Cajun textile weavers, a six-member accordion-based Cajun dance band, the Evangeline Band (a nineteen member song and dance troupe from St. Martinville), and a vocal quartet from Southern University. Rather than presenting *a cappella* ballad singers, the chairman hand-picked what he considered the best talent selected from three popular Acadian dance bands: Lawrence Walker of Scott—leader, accordion player and singer; Sidney Broussard, Sr. of Lake Arthur—fiddler; Sidney Broussard, Jr. of Lake Arthur—guitar player and singer; Ardus Broussard of Rayne—fiddler and singer; Evelyn Broussard of Lake Arthur—singer; Norris Mire of Rayne—triangle player and substitute accordion player. Post included in his "Report on Louisiana's Part in the National Folk Festival," submitted to Louisiana State University's Dean James F. Broussard, Pres. James M. Smith, and Louisiana Gov. Richard Leche, that the dance band left a deep impression on those in attendance at their performances:

> This band, composed of the best talent selected from three different Acadian dance bands, performed on five programs, one of which was a broadcast over KRLD, a Dallas Columbia broadcasting station. This band had been selected by the chairman himself with the greatest of care and was rehearsed in the typical Acadian music with every precaution to render a real Acadian folk program. On every program in which it participated this band proved a decided success and won the highest compliments of the officials of the [Texas] Centennial, the officials of the Folk Festival, and of such as Alan Lomax, an authority on folk singing.[19]

Post did not restrict his definition of folk music to ballad singers, as did many of his contemporaries. The researcher saw fit to incorporate on the National Folk Festival program the fashionable sounds thriving in local dancehalls and on commercial recordings during the 1930s, thus expanding the clas-

---

[18] Ibid., 7.
[19] Lauren Chester Post Papers, accession number 2854, 7:11-19, Box 2, Folder 58, Special Collections, Hill Memorial Library, Louisiana State University, Baton Rouge, LA.

sification of folk expression to include lyrically austere dance music and folk-rooted popular culture. Lauren Post helped to promote the state's indigenous music and validate Cajun music studies at Louisiana State University, meanwhile laying the groundwork for the most prominent scholars to emerge in the field during the 1950s and 1960s.

Louisiana State University English professor and musicologist Harry Oster interjected a new direction in Cajun music studies with his 1958 article "Acculturation in Cajun Folk Music." Though his fieldwork built on the foundation laid by Whitfield and the Lomaxes, Oster decidedly shifted his attention away from ballad traditions in lieu of contemporary expressions that reflected the changing cultural and musical landscape in Cajun Country. The Ivy League alum was also keenly aware of the country's evolving academic climate, and, in a novel approach, examined Cajun music through a lens colored by the latest theoretical developments in anthropology.

In the United States, interest in acculturation grew from the concern for "salvaging" folk cultures that social scientists and folklorists perceived as vanishing in the wake of industrialization and modernization. Anthropologist Richard Thurnwald introduced the concept in his 1932 publication "The Psychology of Acculturation," where he defined the cultural phenomenon as an adaptive process by which people acclimate to new situations and conditions.[20] Six years later, Louisiana State University's influential sociologist T. Lynn Smith became the first academician to apply the model to French Louisiana in his 1938 collaboration with Vernon Parenton, "Acculturation among the Louisiana French," published in the *American Journal of Sociology*. The sociologists argued that the social mechanism was at play when south Louisiana's Acadian and French population absorbed extraneous population elements over time—German, Spanish, Anglo-Saxon, etc.—thus creating a dynamic regional Francophone culture. The theory of acculturation was, however, still in its infancy when Smith and Parenton noted that, "Louisiana is unexcelled as a laboratory in which to study the process."[21]

One generation later, acculturation had become anthropological gospel as evidenced by the 1953 Social Science Research Council Summer Seminar at Stanford University, where the field's top theorists attempted to develop a concise definition of the construct. "[A]cculturation," they declared, "may be defined as culture change that is initiated by the conjunction of two or more autonomous cultural systems."[22] That is, a "donor" culture transfers cultural

---

[20] Richard Thurnwald, "The Psychology of Acculturation," *American Anthropologist* 34 (1932): 557-69.
[21] T. Lynn Smith and Vernon J. Parenton, "Acculturation Among the Louisiana French," *The American Journal of Sociology* 44 (November, 1938): 355. Also see T. Lynn Smith and Lauren C. Post, "The Country Butchery: A Co-operative Institution," *Rural Sociology* 2 (1937): 335-37.
[22] Bernard J. Siegel, Evon Z. Vogt, James B. Watson, and Leonard Broom, "Acculturation: An Exploratory Formulation," *American Anthropologist* 55 (1953): 974.

information, thereby modifying the cultural integrity of a "receptor" culture. Indeed, by the time Harry Oster accepted his appointment at LSU in 1955, the theoretical concept was widely circulated in social science circles. In contrast to the Smith and Parenton's sociological study, though, Oster chose to apply the model to empirical musical evidence of the Americanization process underway during the late 1950s. He explicated his premise to the Baton Rouge *Morning Advocate* in 1959:

> Numerous factors—the speaking of English in public schools, the road building of the '30s, the invasion of the phonographs, radio, movies, and TV; the industrialization of Southwestern Louisiana—have united to pull the Cajun communities out of their isolation and into conformity with the nation. As they have emerged, French traditions have weakened. It is the older community members who know and sing the folk songs; today's young Cajuns prefer and warble hit parade tunes.[23]

For the first time in Cajun music studies, an academician acknowledged the Cajun-American voice. Oster referenced "hybrid" folksongs featuring Cajun French interpretations of southern mountain music, African American blues and jazz, and country-and-western numbers. He cites Cajun classics like Leo Soileau's jazz-inflected recording "Grand Mamou" (1935) and his field recording of Mrs. Rodney Frugé and Savy Augustine's version of "Eyoùss Que T'es Parti," a French adaptation of the English folk ditty "My Good Ol' Man," as a pertinent examples of the region's evolving musical landscape.[24] The musicologist did not publish on Cajun music again until his 2001 collaboration with his understudy Rocky Sexton, when the *Journal of American Folklore* posthumously issued Oster's final work "Une 'Tite Poule Grasse ou la Fille Aînée [A Little Fat Chicken or The Eldest Daughter]: A Comparative Analysis of Cajun and Creole Mardi Gras Songs."[25]

Harry Oster's contributions to Cajun music studies extended beyond journal publications. Within four years of his appointment at LSU, Oster recorded more than 700 folksongs, over 400 of which were in French. His most famous Cajun field recordings were collected between 1956 and 1959 between Mamou and Eunice, Louisiana, with the aid of community gatekeepers Revon Reed, Paul Tate, and Kenneth Fuselier of Mamou.[26] His ethnographic expeditions documented a slice of Louisiana's diverse repertoire, introduced and sustained by Evangeline Parish's large French (non-Acadian) population. In 1959, Oster

---

[23] Baton Rouge *Morning Advocate*, June 7, 1959.
[24] Harry Oster, "Acculturation in Cajun Folk Music," *McNeese Review* 10 (Winter 1958): 17-19.
[25] Rocky Sexton and Harry Oster, "Une 'Tite Poule Grasse ou la Fille Aînée [A Little Fat Chicken or The Eldest Daughter]: A Comparative Analysis of Cajun and Creole Mardi Gras Songs," *Journal of American Folklore* 114 (2001): 204-24.
[26] The record is currently available in compact disc format as *Folksongs of the Louisiana Acadians*, Arhoolie CD 359 (1994). Other Oster releases included "A Sampler of Louisiana Folksong Jambalaya," an album featuring the musicologist performing folk material on his guitar, and "Angola Prisoners' Blues" recorded at Louisiana's Angola State Penitentiary.

collaborated with Arhoolie Records to produce his landmark *Folksongs of the Louisiana Acadians* long-play record, a title that perpetuated the misconception that the repertoire in Evangeline Parish was of Acadian origin.[27] Following in the Lomaxes' footsteps, the researcher attempted to capture ballad and fiddle performances, dance numbers, and harmonica ditties in a context similar to the country dances in which these musical forms thrived naturally. "The singers came from Mamou and the countryside," he explained to the *Morning Advocate* upon release of the album. "Some are cotton growers as Wallace 'Cheese' Reed, fiddler and singer; some grow rice like Savy Augustine, spoon player, and Cyprien Landreneaux, fiddler and father of 11 children. Chuck Guillory, fiddler and singer, alternates as a merchant seaman and oil field worker. Harmonica player and singer, Isom J. Fontenot, is 63 and a former carpenter."[28] Oster's legacy continued to influence Cajun music scholars, not in LSU's English department, but in the university's cross-pollinated geography-anthropology department.

Historical and cultural geographer Malcolm Comeaux was born into the royal family of Cajun music studies. Following in the footsteps of his aunt Irène Whitfield and cousin Lauren Post, Comeaux earned his doctorate in geography from Louisiana State University, where he received the interdisciplinary training that allowed this meticulous scholar to apply cultural analysis to historical data, particularly concerning the contexts and material culture associated with Cajun music. The geographer indulged his penchant for material culture and his fascination with the diatonic Cajun accordion in two articles entitled "The Cajun Accordion" and "Introduction and Use of Accordions in Cajun Music."[29] Comeaux also explored the broader contexts and social implications that shaped the music and dance in south Louisiana with his ground-breaking analysis entitled "The Cajun Dancehall," an examination of the space in which music, courtship, and community interaction transpired.[30]

LSU's geography-anthropology department continued to produce Cajun music scholars following Malcolm Comeaux's departure. Cultural anthropology alumni Ray Brassieur (M.A. 1980) and Rocky Sexton (M.A. 1990)—who also apprenticed under Harry Oster at the University of Iowa during his doctoral studies—developed fine reputations for their extensive ethnographic research in Cajun Country and their knowledge of the historical structures

---

[27] A large number of ex-French militiamen and white Creoles settled Evangeline Parish in the eighteenth century. Over time other groups, including Scots-Irish, African Americans, and a small number of Acadians relocated to the region. Though the parish rightfully boasted a large Francophone Cajun population, the number of families claiming Acadian ancestry is dramatically lower when compared to Acadia, Vermilion, and Lafayette parishes' demographics.

[28] Baton Rouge *Morning Advocate*, June 7, 1959.

[29] Malcolm L. Comeaux, "The Cajun Accordion," *Revue de Louisiane/Louisiana Revue* 7 (1978): 117-28; Malcolm L. Comeaux, "Introduction and Use of Accordions in Cajun Music," *Louisiana Folklore Miscellany* 14 (1999) 27-40.

[30] Malcolm L. Comeaux, "The Cajun Dancehall," *Material Culture* 32 (2000): 37-56.

that shaped and informed contemporary traditions in south Louisiana. Their interdisciplinary research frequently interwove an historical perspective with anthropological theory and methodology. Brassieur's and Sexton's research complimented, though sometimes contrasted, the folkloric and Franco-oriented research generated by affiliates of the Cajun Renaissance movement who created a parallel scholarly corpus within the field in Lafayette, Louisiana, sixty miles west of Baton Rouge.

The Cajun Renaissance (1964-present) began as a socio-political movement based on the notion that Cajuns could reclaim an idealized version of their language and culture to replace perceived hegemonic English-based cultural institutions. Scholars associated with the Renaissance defined French as the symbolic foundation of Cajun ethnicity and culture, and the criterion for authenticity, sometimes reducing the ethnic group's socio-historical complexities to one-dimensional characterizations by portraying the Cajuns as a homogenous Francophone society. The movement was informed by America's struggle for minority and civil rights, cultural activism in New Brunswick, and Québec's *Revolution Tranquille*.[31] The Renaissance encouraged Cajuns to generate an introspective literature that in essence validated their own customs and musical expressions.

The Cajun Renaissance took many forms. The Council for the Development in Louisiana (CODOFIL) gave political clout to the movement under the direction of politician James Domengeaux, while French authors began to publish articles, poems, and books in Cajun French. Musicians like Dewey Balfa, Zachary Richard, and Michael Doucet of Beausoleil collectively gave a musical voice the faction. Their performances, and in some instances their compositions, were an emotional reaction to the tempo of change within and around the Cajun community, particularly as the number of monolingual Francophones in the region began to dwindle dramatically.[32] Cultural activism also manifested through literature, as Renaissance authors like Revon Reed, Barry Jean Ancelet, and Ann Savoy created general introductory overviews of Cajun music's evolution through a Francophone lens. These activists, music writers, and scholars built on the foundation laid by the head of the Division of Arts and Crafts at the Smithsonian Institute during the 1960s, Ralph Rinzler.

Festival coordinator and ethnographer Ralph Rinzler worked to generate a greater consciousness of Louisiana's folk musical traditions on the national and local levels. In the early 1960s, Newport Folk Festival board member Alan Lomax deployed Rinzler to Cajun Country in search of folk performers that

---

[31] The *Revolution Tranquille* (Tranquil Revolution) is the popular moniker for the French province's fervent confrontation with Anglo Canadian society's historic repression of Francophone culture. The separatist movement in the province is perhaps the clearest manifestation of the cultural "revolution."
[32] Shane K. Bernard outlines the decline of native French speakers in Louisiana after World War II in *The Cajuns: Americanization of a People* (Jackson, 2003).

# Introduction

might be appropriate for the festival. The public folklorist secured the services of fiddlers Louis "Vinesse" LeJeune and Dewey Balfa, triangle player Revon Reed, and accordionist Gladius Thibodeaux and escorted the ensemble to the 1964 festival. The experience spurred Balfa's career as a grass roots cultural activist, and launched Rinzler's love affair with the Cajuns of south Louisiana. Rinzler and Balfa continued their collaboration in 1974 by joining forces with the Louisiana Folk Foundation and CODOFIL to create one of the most pivotal manifestations of the Cajun Renaissance, the first annual *Hommage à la musique Acadienne* (Tribute to Cajun Music festival, now *Festivals Acadiens*). On the academic front, Ralph Rinzler and folklorist Ralph Abrahams, then president of the American Folklore Society, convinced the president of the University of Southwestern Louisiana to establish the Center for Acadian and Creole Folklore to compliment the Center for Louisiana Studies.[33]

Like the Lomaxes and Harry Oster before him, Rinzler made field recordings between 1964 and 1966 that captured a sonic snapshot of contemporary musical trends. Performances by musicians like accordionist Austin Pitre, the Balfa Brothers, the Creole duo Bois Sec Ardoin and Canray Fontenot, and harmonica master Isom Fontenot[34] were subsequently released as *Louisiana Cajun French Music from the Southwest Prairies Vol. 1 and Vol. 2* on the Rounder Record label.[35] In addition, Rinzler's field recordings feature some of the only recorded interviews with the two most important innovators of commercial Cajun music Joe Falcon and Leo Soileau.[36]

In 1972, CODOFIL launched the journal *Revue de Louisiane/Louisiana Revue* dedicated to the study of French language and culture in Louisiana. The interdisciplinary quarterly frequently featured articles analyzing Cajun music, including essays like "La musique traditionnelle des francophones de la Louisiane" (Traditional Francophone Music in Louisiana) by French Canadian documentary filmmaker André Gladu, Malcolm Comeaux's first treatise on the Cajun accordion, and Elizabeth Brandon's exploration of the contexts surrounding Cajun music. Brandon, who continued to explore the linguistic subtleties of song variants within Louisiana's ballad traditions for much of her career, expanded her repertoire in *Revue de Louisiane* and foreshadowed the direction of Cajun music studies at the end of the twentieth century with an inquiry into the socio-cultural traits that shape musical expression in Cajun

---

[33] Barry Jean Ancelet, "Research on Louisiana French Folklore and Folklife," in Wolfgang Binder ed., *Creoles and Cajuns: French Louisiana—La Louisiane Française* (Frankfurt am Maim and Berlin, 1998), 85.

[34] Fontenot is also featured on Oster's "Folksongs of the Louisiana Acadians."

[35] Ralph Rinzler, *Louisiana Cajun French Music From the Southwest Prairies, Vol. 1*, Rounder CD 6001 (1989). David Evans, "Louisiana French Music," *Journal of American Folklore* 97 (April-June, 1984): 247.

[36] Joe Falcon interview conducted by Ralph Rinzler, October 10, 1965, accession number RI1.024, Ralph Rinzler Collection, Archives of Cajun and Creole Folklore, Center for Louisiana Studies, University of Louisiana at Lafayette, Lafayette, LA (hereafter ACCF); Leo Soileau interview conducted by Ralph Rinzler, October 20, 1965, accession number RI1.025, Rinzler Collection, ACCF.

Country in her 1972 publication "The Socio-Cultural Traits of the French Folksong in Louisiana."

1972 also witnessed the publication of *Tears, Love, and Laughter: The Story of Cajuns and Their Music* by Cajun cultural activist and educator Pierre Varman Daigle. The manuscript presented a compilation of short biographical vignettes that sought to document and acknowledge the creative forces behind the contemporary sounds of Cajun music. Daigle drew on his experiences at house dances and dancehalls when considering the criteria for inclusion in the manuscript. Contrary to the studies conducted during the 1930s and 1940s, which only analyzed ballad texts and less frequently ballad singers, the educator featured accordionists, fiddlers, vocalists, and other entertainers who enjoyed lucrative careers as commercial recording artists, and obscure musicians who never set foot into a studio, but performed at local dances. Daigle's popular publication encouraged other local writers and activists to pen their own manuscripts, while setting the stage for two landmark Cajun Renaissance publications—Ann Savoy's *Cajun Music* and Barry Ancelet's *Makers of Cajun Music*—that, like *Tears, Love, and Laughter*, compiled biographical sketches and transcribed interviews outlining the careers of specific performers. Daigle hoped to preserve historical data concerning the Cajuns and their music for posterity. Meanwhile, his contemporary in Mamou, Revon Reed, began writing to validate publicly both the Cajun experience and the ethnic group's mother tongue.

Grass roots cultural activist Revon Reed was an important proponent of the Cajun Renaissance movement in the Evangeline Parish town Mamou. With academic credentials including a Bachelor of Arts from St. Mary's University and a Master of Education from Boston University, Reed championed Louisiana's French language, working-class Cajun culture, and musical traditions as a French radio announcer on the "Mamou Cajun Hour" and as author of the French-language manifesto *Lâche Pas la Patate* (which included a chapter dedicated to the development of Cajun music), published in Québec in 1976 at the height of the province's ethnic and linguistic independence movement. Ironically, working-class Cajuns, to whom the book was dedicated, transmitted French orally across generational lines. High illiteracy rates and the oral nature of French among the ethnic group made the book an ineffective communicative medium in Louisiana, though the publication added fuel to the fire in Québec, where activists lashed out at Anglophone culture's stranglehold on Francophone communities in North America. Then again, *Lâche Pas la Patate* did not go completely unnoticed in the Bayou Country. Reed's speculations about the eighteenth and nineteenth-century developments of Cajun music left an impression on Cajun music scholar and activist Barry Ancelet.

# Introduction

During his travels, musician and cultural activist Dewey Balfa encountered recorded sound collections at folklore repositories around the United States. The fiddler realized that these invaluable resources served as virtual libraries for oral-based cultures like his own, and encouraged a charismatic French student at the University of Southwestern Louisiana named Barry Ancelet to establish a Cajun-oriented archive. Motivated by Corinne Saucier's claim that the thirty-three folktales published in her book *Folktales from French Louisiana* stood as "representative, if not all inclusive, of our southern Louisiana form of oral literature known as folklore,"[37] the maverick began his quest to document and understand the dramatically underestimated material that constituted some of the most dynamic manifestations of the Cajun imagination—the literary volumes contained in orally transmitted folktales, yarns, and the poetry and verse woven into south Louisiana's musical fabric. The Cajun ethnographer based his approach to fieldwork and scholarship on a simple premise, to validate French oral traditions from a Cajun perspective, "to have something that left a paper trail to officially declare that we exist."[38] His cultural activism, in turn, attempted to promote and perpetuate this French orality.

Barry Ancelet's field recordings constituted the initial contributions to the landmark Archives of Cajun and Creole Folklore at the University of Louisiana at Lafayette, before Balfa persuaded the ethnographer to seek out and organize Cajun music's fragmented documentation scattered throughout North America. The folklorist helped to assemble for the first time an inclusive field recording collection amassed from the collective works of John and Alan Lomax, William Owens, Elizabeth Brandon, Harry Oster, and Ralph Rinzler. As the collection grew, so did Ancelet's comprehension of Cajun music. The scholar remembered in an interview with archivist and curator of the Archives of Cajun and Creole Folklore's Ancelet Collection, Erik Charpentier, "We could understand things concerning our culture and our history that we had never realized, because it was so departmentalized."[39]

The budding ethnographer's education continued outside of Cajun Country. Barry Ancelet earned a Master's degree from Indiana University's Folklore Institute before becoming a doctoral student at the Université de Provence (Aix-Marseille I). Upon completing his doctoral studies in 1984, Ancelet published his first book-length work on Cajun music, *The Makers of Cajun Music*, featuring complimentary photojournalistic images by Elemore Morgan Jr. Following an introductory overview that briefly outlined the development of Cajun music and a summation of Cajun music studies, the folklorist presented bilingual transcriptions of his ethnographic research that focused

---

[37] Barry Ancelet interviewed by Erik Charpentier, October 28, 2004 (English translation of French interview by Ryan A. Brasseaux, copy of interview in editor's possession).
[38] Ibid.
[39] Ibid.

on a handful of extant performers whom Ancelet defined as the purveyors of Francophone musical traditions within the Cajun community. Ancelet's publications, and his efforts as organizer and moderator for the *Hommage à la musique Acadienne*, subsequently honored a handful of musicians such as Dennis McGee, Nathan Abshire, Varise Conner, and Dewey Balfa, who joined legendary Cajun musicians Joe Falcon and Iry LeJeune in the Cajun music pantheon.

In 1988, the researcher produced a two-disk long-play album featuring French selections taken from John and Alan Lomax's Louisiana field recordings. One year later, Ancelet opened a new line of inquiry into the development of the genre by publishing a monograph entitled *The Origins and Development of Cajun Music*, a generalized survey of French music's evolutionary course within the Cajun community.[40] This study led to a parallel essay featured in his book-length collaboration with Louisiana State University anthropologist Jay Edwards and documentary filmmaker Glen Pitre entitled *Cajun Country*,[41] and an overview of commercial Cajun music available in the mid-1990s entitled simply "Cajun Music" published in the *Journal of American Folklore*.[42] As Ancelet helped establish the University of Southwestern Louisiana as the hub of Cajun music studies, a handful of women with connections to Lafayette, including Lisa Richardson, Laura Westbrook, and Carolyn Ware, began to explore the feminine side of Cajun music by probing the dynamics of home music and ballad traditions among Cajun women, and the motifs that subjugate women in song. In nearby Eunice, musician Ann Savoy extensively researched south Louisiana's musical landscape and presented her findings through her own concert performances and in print.

Virginian-*cum*-Cajun musician and music writer Ann Allen Savoy first encountered Cajun music and her future husband Marc Savoy in 1976 at The Barns at Wolf Trap near Washington, D.C. The experience transformed the early American music aficionado and former French student, who began a life-long love affair with Cajun music and those performers who created the art form. In 1984, she published a complimentary study to Ancelet's *Makers of Cajun Music* entitled the *Cajun Music: A Reflection of a People*, a massive influential volume containing short biographical sketches and transcribed interviews of Cajun music's most important figureheads. Savoy's historically oriented encyclopedia contained lyric transcriptions (in French, English phonetics, and English translations), musical notation, discographic information (based on Richard Spottswood's invaluable Cajun discography published in his *Ethnic Music on Records* series),[43] and hundreds of historic photographs

---

[40] Ancelet, *The Origins and Development of Cajun Music*.
[41] Ancelet, Edwards, Pitre, *Cajun Country*.
[42] Barry Jean Ancelet, "Cajun Music," *Journal of American Folklore* 107 (Spring, 1994): 285-303.
[43] Richard Keith Spottswood, *Ethnic Music on Records: A Discography of Ethnic Recordings Produced in the United States, 1893 to 1942* (Urbana and Chicago, 1990).

# INTRODUCTION

illustrating the men and women who created Cajun music. With little analytical substance, her collection of raw data served both researchers exploring historical biographical information on particular artists and budding literate musicians learning songs and lyrics. Her study helped blaze a path for other photographic compilations like Johnnie Allan's *Memoires: A Pictorial History of South Louisiana Music* (1988), and the song transcription compendium *Yé Yaille, Chère* (1990) by Raymond François.[44]

Ann Savoy is but one of many Cajun music enthusiasts who came to appreciate the genre through shellac and vinyl records. Across the Atlantic Ocean, Frenchman Gérard Dole, and later Belgian Robert Sacré, became leading proponents of Cajun music studies in Francophone Europe. In the United Kingdom during the 1960s and 1970s, important articles pertaining to traditional Louisiana music, swamp pop and Cajun recording artists found a home in magazines like *Blues Unlimited* and *Old Time Music*, which catered to Britain's increasing infatuation with indigenous American music. These publications frequently explored genres and popular artists generally neglected by folklorists who often perceived such cultural expression as evidence of assimilation into the American mainstream. Pioneering British writers like Mike Leadbitter, Tony Russell, and John Broven, on the other hand, offered a different perspective that recognized Cajun-inflected western swing, Cajun rock and roll, and swamp pop as viable indigenous expressions that were unlike their Anglo-American counterparts. John Broven's 1983 publication *South to Louisiana* represented the culmination of the English contributions to Cajun music studies.[45] The book was the first attempt to outline the history of commercial Cajun music, influential artists in subgenres like swamp pop, and the Afro-Creole contributions to south Louisiana's musical landscape.

On American soil, country music scholars offered a novel approach to the study of Cajun music by defining the tradition as a subcategory of country-and-western. Bill Malone first proposed the notion in his influential *Country Music, U.S.A.* and persuaded his understudies like Stephen Tucker to acknowledge the dialogue that transpired between French musical expression in south Louisiana and Anglo Southern traditions, thus placing the music into a larger regional context.[46] As Tucker devoted three chapters to Cajun music in his doctoral dissertation at Tulane University, contributors to the *John Edward Memorial Foundation Quarterly* helped to acknowledge the genre as a viable southern and country musical expression. These publications coincided with the burgeoning Cajun Renaissance movement that continue to dominate the

---

[44] Johnnie Allan, *Memoires: A Pictorial History of South Louisiana Music* (Lafayette, LA, 1988); Raymond E. François, *Yé Yaille, Chère!: Traditional Cajun Dance Music* (Ville Platte, LA, 1990).
[45] John Broven, *South to Louisiana: The Music of the Cajun Bayous* (Gretna, LA, 1983).
[46] Bill C. Malone, *Country Music, U.S.A.: A Fifty Year History* (Austin, 1969); Stephen R. Tucker, "Louisiana Saturday Night: A History of Louisiana Country Music" (Ph.D. dissertation, Tulane University, 1995).

public's perception of Cajun music in Louisiana despite the most recent post-modern trend in Cajun music studies.

In the mid-1980s, Louisiana's economy virtually collapsed when the state's oil industry bottomed out, resulting in a massive Cajun exodus that dispersed and fragmented the cohesiveness that once solidified musical traditions in Bayou Country. The fragmentation of the Cajun community coincided with the rise of post-modern theory in academe, a style of analysis that sought to de-contextualize cultural information to generate new meaning. During the 1990s, post-modern scholars from a wide range of disciplines produced studies that ran the spectral analytical gamut. Shane K. Bernard, son of pioneering swamp pop musician Rod Bernard, built on John Broven's work and countered arguments about the authenticity of the musical form and validated swamp pop as a legitimate category within the framework of Cajun music. Bernard's study also underlined the transnational nature of south Louisiana's musical traditions, by acknowledging the culturally diverse components that informed the genre. Freida Marie Fusilier, Jolene Adam, and Mark DeWitt's examinations of Cajun transplants in the San Francisco Bay-area and the region's thriving Cajun and zydeco music scene helped shed light on the fragmentation of the Cajun community beyond the parameters of south Louisiana. *Disenchanting Les Bon Temps* (2003), Charles Stivale's delusions of becoming Cajun via dance and music as explored through the theoretical machinations of Gilles Deleuze and Felix Guattari, represents the most extreme example of the post-modern tendencies within Cajun music studies. And, indeed, this collection of essays is yet another example of the post-contemporary perspective.

The editors have extracted significant and influential articles, essays, and book chapters from the Cajun music studies literature, and organized them into a commentary on the evolution of thought in the field through time. In addition to previously published materials, new articles by popular writers and music scholars who are actively working to develop a new Cajun music literature through their frequent publications in journals and magazines are given prominence in this volume. These authors have contributed mindful reactions to contemporary and historical problems concerning the evolution of Cajun music. Such new material includes: Ryan A. Brasseaux and Erik Charpentier, "Hawaiian Shirts and Cajun Power: Basking in the Sunshine of Michael Doucet and Beausoleil," and "Fabricating Authenticity: The Cajun Renaissance and Steve Riley & the Mamou Playboys;" John Broven, "The Bayou Buckaroo: LeRoy 'Happy Fats' LeBlanc;" Ron Brown, "Playing in the Shadows: Obscure Early Cajun Recording Artists;" Erik Charpentier, "Get Lost: The Lost Bayou Ramblers;" Kevin S. Fontenot, "People Buy the Feel: Cajun Fiddle Master Rufus Thibodeaux" and "How Y'all Are: Justin Wilson, Comedy, and Cajun Ethnic Identity;" Kevin S. Fontenot and Ryan A. Brasseaux, "King of the Dancehalls:

Accordionist Lawrence Walker;" Mike Hurtt, "Vin Bruce;" Ben Sandmel, "The Hackberry Ramblers;" Rocky L. Sexton, "The Cajun French Music Association: The Development of a Music-Centered Ethnic Organization;" Michael Tisserand, "Never Mind the Bowties, Here's the Bluerunners."

The materials featured in this volume are organized into categories based on their thematic focus—socio-cultural context, commercialization, and artist biographies. The articles in the contextual category appear in chronological order by date of publication to create an evolutionary sense of thought and theoretical orientation in the field over time. Those materials comprising the commercialization component begin with sweeping surveys that give way to essays dealing with specific instances of Cajun music's emergence on radio and record. Biographical information is arranged in chronological order based on an artist's historical provenance to parallel the socio-cultural evolution presented in the contextual component of the manuscript. A bibliography containing studies not included in this volume appears at the end of the book to encourage further reading, and, we hope, future scholarship.

*Accordions, Fiddles, Two Step & Swing* is designed with scholars, students, and Cajun music aficionados in mind. The articles included here represent the spectrum of Cajun musical expression as interpreted by authors from all walks of life. Materials ranging from instrumentation to information dealing with specific artists and social contexts demonstrate that Cajun music is defined more by ethos and social context than a delimited set of stylistic features.

# UNDER THE GREEN OAK TREE

## Origins and Locales of Cajun Music

The ancestors of the Cajuns brought with them from France and Acadie a storehouse of ballads and folksongs. In North America the Acadians added songs both newly composed and borrowed from their European and Indian neighbors. This oral literature traveled with them during the *Grand Dérangement* and formed the basis of Cajun folksongs in Louisiana. Music and song were integrated into everyday life of the Cajuns, and eclecticism informed the ever expanding repertoire of the Cajun people.

Ballads, dance tunes, and folksongs served as the core of the Cajun musical tradition before the advent of commercialization. Ballads tended to be sung in the home and were often passed down by mothers. The ballads recounted the lives of famous individuals or tales of lost love. Many were parts of a larger European ballad tradition documented by scholars as diverse as Sir Walter Scott and the Harvard academic Francis James Child. Some folksongs were linked to specific ritual activities, Mardi Gras most notably. Mardi Gras songs and drinking songs were largely the realm of men and reflected the rough frontier existence of the region. This "folk poetry" was the first area of Cajun folklore to attract academic scrutiny, which focused almost entirely on the text of the ballad.

Dance tunes and instrumental music were rarely documented with any clarity. Travelers' accounts of Cajun dances often focus on the setting and the liveliness of the music but seldom mention much beyond instruments used. The darling of Cajun instruments was the fiddle, an easily portable instrument that appears early in records of Cajun music. The fiddle's stature as the primary Cajun instrument was challenged in the late nineteenth century by the accordion. The accordion was firmly established as the central instrument for Cajun dances by the time of commercialization in the 1920s. Other stringed instruments also entered the Cajun band—guitars and mandolins—primarily through mail order catalogs and in local dry goods stores.

Initially Cajun dances were held in private homes and were called *bals de maison*. But near the dawn of the twentieth century, community dancehalls emerged where dancers danced to the sounds of the newer accordion-based bands. In the dancehalls Cajun musicians could demonstrate their prowess, and some gained reputations as excellent players. Within this context they found a ready economic supplement to their work on the farm or in the oil fields. The coming of the oil industry early in the century also encouraged the professionalization of Cajun music as men with disposable income from the oil fields could pay to hear music.

Work in the oil fields and in World War II defense plants enticed Cajuns to leave Louisiana for jobs in Texas and California. Cajuns who left home took their music with them and it increasingly became a vital part of their ethnic identity. In the "far-off" realms of Texas and California, new fusions occurred and non-Cajuns were attracted to the dancehalls. Thus began a battle over definition and identity over exactly what Cajun music "in exile" was. In California, Cajun music and zydeco were often merged and presented in the same venues, an act that did not occur in southwest Louisiana until late in the century. Even then it was met with resistance as locals understood that the two styles were separate genres. Swamp pop—Cajun rock and roll—flourished along the Gulf Coast and often shared the stage with its cousins Cajun music and zydeco.

Questions of exactly what constituted Cajun music and identity were closely linked as Cajuns saw the music as one of their defining characteristics. Like many ethnic groups in the 1970s and 1980s, they formed groups, like the Cajun French Music Association, to promote "traditional" music and language. These groups often drew lines that respected older boundaries, seeing Cajun music and zydeco as separate genres. For these groups, it was dance music that constituted the foundation of Cajun music. Old ballad traditions faded and became academic performances on the stages of the nearly innumerable festivals that sprang up in Acadiana. In those festivals music and food became the central symbols of the culture. And Cajun French, which was in protracted decline as a language, was preserved as a musical voice.

Margie Lamperez Ford Breaux and an unidentified partner dancing at a local dancehall, ca. 1948.
*Photo courtesy of the Margie Lamperez Breaux Collection, Center for Louisiana Studies, University of Louisiana at Lafayette, accession number 4043.*

# *Excerpts from* Louisiana French Folk Songs[1]

## *Irène Thérèse Whitfield*

### *Experiences Collecting the Louisiana French Folk Songs*

To state exactly when I began collecting Louisiana French folksongs is impossible. Some of my earliest childhood memories are those of singing *Hier après-midi* and *Pas loin de chez moi* with playmates, and it seems I can hear yet, mingled with the rumble of wagon wheels, the fais-dodo songs played on the accordion and the singing and yells by the tenants as they went to the "*bal.*"[2]

Then, in my memory, there is a little country school where on Mardi Gras during the regular routine of the day's activities a band of maskers break in, dance over the floor, and sing repeatedly with a sort of tune: "*Mardi Gras! Chick à la pas.*"[3]

Later as the school term closes there is the annual picnic at which the country orchestra of accordion, triangle, and violin accompanies a screechy voice singing *Fais do-do, mignonne* while the oversized "smarties" of the school, freshly shoe-shined, shaved, and powdered, dance with the schoolteachers, whom they have pestered all year. The words of that song say "the more you turn, the more I love you."[4] If true, there must have been some ardent lovers by sundown, for many a turn was made in the shade of the moss-festooned oaks by the dancers refreshed only by lemonade from the new galvanized iron washtub.

It seems almost difficult to steer clear of French folksongs in some parts of Louisiana, whether you learn them or not. The man who says he learned his songs "on the road"[5] is about correct. He may add truthfully as some do, "I don't know really where I took that" or he may claim, "I always knew that." Nevertheless, some time far back in his childhood his grandmother perhaps sang to him her cherished *Joli tambour* or *Malbrough s'en va-l-en guerre*; or his big brother, proud of his new accomplishment of singing and full of the idea of his own importance in going to dances, sang *Jolie blonde* or *Quoi je t'ai fait, malheureuse?* At any rate, the fact is that he knows his songs just why he does is hard to say. The conversation of two girls in New Iberia may help explain: "How's that you know-all those songs? I guess I heard 'em, me, but I never learned 'em.... I dunno, why I know 'em. I heard 'em like that. Don't you learn 'em when you

---

[1] This article is composed of two book chapters, "Experiences Collecting the Louisiana French Folk Songs" and "Cajun Folk Songs," originally published in *Louisiana French Folk Songs* (Baton Rouge, 1939), 12-23, 68-73.
[2] Dance.
[3] In some parishes, "Chick à la paille."
[4] "Plus tu tournes, plus je t'aime."
[5] Quoted from Mr. Julien Hoffpauir, New Iberia, LA.

Cajun music studies matriarch, Irène Thérèse Whitfield ca. 1939.
*Courtesy of Malcolm L. Comeaux.*

hear 'em?" Some people may be gifted in remembering enough to add to other words or melodies that they know and develop what they think is the song they heard.

Amusing is the way Louisiana French people have of using English and French combined. At the home of a good singer of folksongs, in answer to the question "Where is your father?" his child replied, *"Il est gone. J'crois il est up town. Hein, mom?"*[6] While hunting for the home of another singer, the following instructions were given. *"Vous go ahead au coin. Là, vous turn à droite, et la maison est droit in front."*[7]

It is, however, mainly the children who are so unaffected, as grown people quickly sense that they are talking to a stranger (in that part of the country) and try to speak properly, as though ashamed of their own dialect.

Particularly do people seem ashamed of their dialects while singing, and if not thoroughly unsophisticated, when repeating a song they will change to a correct form if they know it. *Marilier* will become *marier; ya, il y a;* and *il na, il y en a*. Just as these people are ashamed of the Louisiana dialects, they are proud of good French when they know it. They say, "But now, that is real French, not Cajun. There is no gumbo to that." Strange as it may seem, nowhere were these old country folks able to show a printed publication of French folksongs, though they sang them. They claimed they had never seen such a book, wouldn't know how to read one if they saw one, had never been to school a day in their lives, and that their parents who sang these songs had never been to school.

It has been said that money talks. A friend and I saw this fact clearly demonstrated one day. We were in the home of a singer who stood near the stove against the wall in his two-room cabin, twiddling his thumbs, and claiming all the while that he could not remember either words or melody, that he had no accordion, that there was none near by, and that he was able to borrow one only when he played for dances. Prospects seemed poor. I concealed my paper and pencil as well as I could and in my friendliest manner attempted to coax from the man some faint acknowledgment of his ability to recall something of songs I had heard him sing at a dance the night before. Two children played unconcernedly on the floor, but the wife and the mother-in-law nodded approval occasionally to the man's denials of being able to sing that day. Prospects seemed poor. My friend, whom I had made custodian of the quarter and five nickels to be given the man, unconsciously began playing with the coins. She noticed as soon as I did that as the man perceived these coins, he began to recall songs. She knocked one coin on the other, slipped them from hand to hand, tossed them from one hand to the other, and finally lifted them high in one hand and

---

[6] "He is gone. I believe he's up town. Huh, mamma?"
[7] "You go ahead to the corner. There you turn to the right, and the house is right in front."

let them drop one by one into the other. From higher and higher fell the coins; louder and louder they sounded; and more the man remembered. He was able to put together with little difficulty the words and melodies of the songs he had sung so easily the night before. Presently the wife and mother-in-law chimed in, supplying missing lines and suggesting different songs. The afternoon was profitably spent. Money talks. The following morning I saw the man sent money by a little boy for a package of tobacco.

Ordinarily I found people very willing to sing if they were able, and if mourning did not prevent. I knew one man at a watering place who was very amusing. He told French jokes and said he could sing French songs. I was told he had been at this resort the summer before with his wife—his third wife. Both were old and decrepit and walked with canes. The summer I knew him he had become a widower and he was walking without a cane. He was the "life of the crowd," and I know he asked one woman, "*Madame, vous êtes pas veuve?*"[8] Yet this man would not sing. He admitted he could sing, but he said he should not. "*Non*," he said, "*J'ai un devoir à faire.*"[9] Another singer told me he knew lots of songs and would sing after the service held one year after the death of his father. Sometime later I met him in the road and asked when he was coming to sing for me. He answered, "*Mais là, on a eu le service de pape et j'vas v'nir chanter dimanche.*"[10] He was true to his word, just as he had been faithful to his principles.

One of the more willing singers was a colored woman, Tizabel. She had a severe cold and lay in a heavy wooden bed canopied with a red cambric tester. She had called a doctor that morning, and had been told to remain in bed, and not "go in the air." She consequently had the single wooden window of the room closed, making the interior quite dark. I sat by the open door and listened to her talk and sing. She said she was seventy-seven years old, that she had been a slave in the home of a well-to-do family, had remained with the family after the slaves were freed, and had rocked to sleep the seven children with the lullaby *C'est la poulette blanche*. If she started another song the children would say, "*Non, non, pas ça, pas ça—la poulette blanche.*"[11] Many years have passed since Tizabel sang for the children, and yet the face of this old slave lighted up with the memory of by-gone years as she sang her beloved songs. Her head bobbed up and down swinging the gold earrings, her eyes brightened, and her breath came faster.

Possibly her home might be of interest. It was a two-room unpainted shack, plain-walled except for newspapers at places. The doors and windows were of six-inch flooring put together with bars. The chimney was made of

---

[8] "Madam, are you not a widow?"
[9] "I have a duty to perform."
[10] "Well now, we have had the service for papa and I'll come sing Sunday."
[11] "No, no, not that, not that—the white hen."

bricks which came from a kiln on an old plantation nearby. On the mantel, which was fringed with newspaper cut into lacework, were a few pictures, including a photograph of a priest. Above the mantel hung a huge, over-ornate frame in which there was a marriage certificate. In the fireplace rested an iron skillet apparently ready for the preparation of the evening meal. The hatchet, used for splitting kindling for firewood, hung next to the fireplace which was the sole means of heating and cooking in this humble dwelling in which Tizabel lives.

Another interesting colored woman I encountered was "Tante Marguerite," who sang for me the "onliest" French song she knew. She seemed old and said she did not know her age. She explained that at one time she had had a "sort of paper" telling her age, but that all the papers in her house had been destroyed when her house burned. A great deal of coaxing was required to get "Tante Marguerite" to sing, as she was choir leader for a sect that thought singing was sinful except for church and school songs. When asked to sing she refused, saying, "Non, non; priez bon Dieu; mais pas des chansons."[12] A piece of sweet olive tree, a bunch of roots of vetiver, and a nickel finally caused her to give the little song *Fais do-do, Colas, mon p'til frère*, a lullaby, against which no evil can be said.

On one occasion I was out "song-hunting" with Mr. Alan Lomax.[13] He had in his automobile the machinery for making phonograph records for the Library of Congress, while I was armed with paper for writing songs. We first went to Crowley, where we secured for the day the services of a man who posed to know everyone in the Marais Bouleur district, northeast of Crowley, a place reputed to have good Cajun singers.

This young man proved quite a relief from the staid, conventional people with whom Mr. Lomax and I were usually associated. He was a handsome Creole type with a true Creole name, but first claimed to be of Irish descent, and later he was Spanish. He said he had been shot at on several occasions, served three sentences in jail, and had been cut twice with a razor by a woman attempting murder. Scars which he showed attested to the razor slashes; but the man did not need any proofs, as his own *naïveté* and sincerity, and his constant references to "God's truth" and "God A'mighty" should have been adequate proofs of his statement.

He entertained us awhile talking of his marital relations. He was divorced from his first wife, having let her go when she became "more interested of someone else" than she was "of" him. Now in his early twenties he was married to a second wife but hoped to get enough money "roughnecking" in the Bosco Oil Fields the following week to leave her and go somewhere else to live. He

---

[12] "No, no; pray to God; but no songs."
[13] Author of "Collecting Folk-Songs of the Southern Negro," *Southwest Review* 19 (1934): 105-31.

seemed to know everything about making money, saying he bet he had made more in a week in the past years than Mr. Lomax had in the full year, notwithstanding all the heavy machinery he had in his car. "But, of course, you must go into a business that pays money," he kept repeating. By questioning we did find the best paying of all businesses, but as prohibition no longer exists, even this gateway to wealth is closed.

When we arrived in the Marais Bouleur district, our guide took us through a series of sharp turns in dirt roads and crop headlands to a house in which lived the best of the Cajun accordion players of the neighborhood. At every bump in the road Mr. Lomax feared for his recording machinery. We found the most famous of all the accordion players seated in the center of a room surrounded by admiring listeners. He had just been asked to play for a wedding in that vicinity, was cleanly shaven, well powdered, and was practicing his repertoire of songs for the occasion. He was enough of an artist to enjoy his playing, and prefaced each song with some such remark as, "I just made this song last week; I like this song better than that one; I heard my grandfather play this one; this a beautiful waltz," or some similar comment.

The father of the bride arrived in his new car to take the player to the wedding. When he heard that Mr. Lomax made records, he cordially invited us to go to the wedding and record the songs there. We accepted the invitation; but since we had a few other people to hunt that day, we said that we would go later in the afternoon. Then the problem of finding the house arose. Mr. Lomax and I would have been willing to rely on remembering the name, but the father wanted us to have it in writing, though he could not sign his name. Fortunately, then, some man drove up who could write, and who for pencil and paper, went to the hood of the car, and started the slow process of forming eleven letters. The car, which had been standing in the sun while we were in the house, had become so hot that the heat over the hood was uncomfortable. Consequently the man chose as a table for writing the hood of a car that was in the shade and returned triumphantly some minutes later with the paper bearing the name written faultlessly and apparently with much care.

Before long Mr. Lomax, the guide, and I were hunting for "a white house back of three chinaberry trees, at the first turn after the little store." By the combination of asking for the home of the man whose name we had in written form, and following the directions given us for finding the house, we arrived in ample time for the wedding.

According to plans, the little bride dressed in a tenant's house near her father's home. She intended to come at four o'clock to take her seat near her groom in chairs set aside for them and draped in white cotton; but at twenty minutes after three, she came streaking across the pasture, holding her train up out of the cockleburs and grass, and picking her steps in the spots that were not too thickly piled with dust. Some one in jest had advanced the clock at the tenant's house. The young bride was not in the least disconcerted by being forty minutes early; she sat quietly in her chair, cast a sweet gay smile on her assembled girl friends, as she glanced around the room occasionally, and chewed gum contentedly. I heard her described as a blonde who would fade young; but on this her wedding day, she was superb. Her complexion was fresh and fair; her eyes bright; and her lips picturesquely arched with just the correct shade of lipstick to match the pink paper of the flowers of her bridal bouquet. As to her costume, one might say that it left nothing to be desired in a combination of white crepe, satin, and tulle.

Except for chairs and benches and a dresser with a heavy marble top, the furniture had been removed from the room, leaving the center vacant. The reason for this was soon apparent. At four o'clock the musicians and gentlemen guests strode into the room and the wedding march began. A violinist and our friend the accordion player led, followed by a player of the triangle, next the bride and groom, and then the other young people of the community in couples. The groom was unmistakable; he wore a dark suit, black gloves, and a worried look, and beads of perspiration had formed on his temples and forehead. He was perfectly groomed, and with his little bride made a picture justly admired by the assembled friends.

Around and around the march continued for several minutes. The musicians seemed to have an endless supply of tunes while they walked around with measured steps. When finally they did stop, some lady advanced to the bride suggesting that she and the groom not dance because of the heat. She led them off the floor to their chairs from where they viewed the dances. The musicians sat on a bench reserved for them in one corner of the room. They played with all their strength, shrieked occasionally, passed among themselves their much-loved bottle, and placed it on the floor beside them between swigs. As the dance progressed they became gayer and gayer, the shrieks more and more numerous and high-pitched, but the dancers less and less enthusiastic because of the great heat.

When the number of dancing couples had dwindled considerably, the bride's father went to her, led her to his car, and tried placing her and her bouquet first in the front seat of the car, but not finding enough space transferred her and her flowers to the rear seat. A bridesmaid climbed in beside her. Meanwhile, the guests were preparing to follow the car, and the musicians had lined up on a bench in the yard and were playing for the departure while Mr. Lomax was recording. At first there was only the instrumentation interspersed with yells, but as the bride's car traveled forth bearing its little burden so willing to try another life, the accordion player broke spontaneously into song—something like:

"Tite fille, tu quittes ton papa et ta maman pour aller dans la misère. Bye-bye tite fille, ton papa et ta maman..."[14]

I rushed over to the singer, thinking that as soon as he stopped playing I should ask him for his words. I had understood them but had not been able to write them all as he sang them. Try as I might, I could not make him even believe he had sung. He looked at me blankly. The triangle player came to my rescue telling him that I wanted the words of his song. He answered very willingly but hopelessly, "Question me Monday, I'm too damn drunk today." When we left him Mr. Lomax remarked that it would be a long day before we saw him again. The day is not yet over. I have tried since to distinguish the words on the record. They are indistinct, as the music is heavy and the articulation poor.

We did not wait until the married couple returned, but while Mr. Lomax recorded more orchestra music I went to the back of the house and became acquainted with the ladies who had remained, and played with the babies lying on pillows on the dining-room floor. The people were friendly and hospitable. One lady offered me cake and even after my refusal handed me a plate with slices of several kinds. I ate some and enjoyed it. The house was immaculately clean, and rags, soaked with coal oil and wrapped around the legs of the safe, kept ants off the food. From the conversation I learned that the real wedding dance was to take place that night in a rented hall at which time a freewill offering was to be taken. The custom is to give the money received to the groom to begin housekeeping. Some man came into the dining room asking where his wife was, complaining that she had left him only twenty-five cents for the dance.

When Mr. Lomax had finished recording what he wanted, we thanked our friends and left. We passed through Crowley to take our guide home. He had certainly been worth our while. He had guided us, entertained us, made announcements on records, coaxed singers, and pacified drunkards. Memory of him might have been perfect had he not, as we put him down in Crowley, bolted into a saloon from which he emerged later quite intoxicated. It was then that he addressed me for the first time, and to the best of his memory I was "Mrs. Bergeron." With all respect due the honorable name of "Bergeron," I have always been thankful that it must have figured some way in the life of this man.

## Cajun Folksongs

The modern Cajun-French folksongs are probably indigenous to Louisiana. They seem endless in length, because they are played over and over again until they run on and on and on like the flat country of the southern part of the state

---

[14] "Li'l girl, you are leaving your papa and your mamma to go into wretchedness. Bye-bye li'l girl, your papa and your mamma..."

which developed them. They fit the "pulling and pushing" of the accordion, having been made so to speak "of the accordion," "by the accordion," and "for the accordion." No other instrument seems to have quite the quality that makes the Cajun tune so appealing. One might say of them as they are played on the accordion that they are *ces airs dont la musique a l'air d'être en patois*.[15]

The music of the Cajun folksong is generally characterized by a flexibility of form manifested in its impure tones, some quarter-tone intervals,[16] the portamento style of singing,[17] irregular location of pulse,[18] and irregular number of lines to the stanzas to songs.[19] With the accordion to fill in gaps a fifth line may be added to any ordinary four-line stanza; and any number of "mais," "oh," "chère," and "la belle"[20] may be diffused throughout the stanzas by an extra push-pull of the same instrument. There is in many of these folksongs no semblance of scientific rules of composition, nor of development according to a plan of preconceived ideas. Topsy in *Uncle Tom's Cabin* claimed, "I 'spect I growed. Don't think nobody never made me."[21] So it is with this Cajun music. It grew from spontaneous outbursts of emotions and varies with them. Even the same song may be quite different before and after a dance.

The melodies of this music that sprang from the Louisiana Cajuns sometimes show the wide range of tones and the large intervals between notes found in standard French folksongs;[22] but, on the other hand, many show little variance in tones;[23] and some, a few wailing melodies, use only the pentatonic, five-note scale.[24] Miss Helen L. Gunderson of the School of Music of the Louisiana State University informed me that she had found this pentatonic scale in the folksongs in China. Possibly it adapts itself readily to the weird, primitive sort of music found in wails.

The language used in this group of French folksongs is the Cajun-French, the dialect spoken by the descendants of Acadians, and by some Creoles. It is very much like that spoken by the peasants in certain provinces of France. Instead of saying *elle* the peasant says *a*:[25] he says *je vas* for *je vais*;[26] he rarely uses

---

[15] Edmund Rostand, *Cyrano de Bergerac* (New York, 1927), act IV, sc. 3, p. 121, 1. 15. "Those melodies of which the music seems to be in dialect."
[16] Cf. *Ma belle m'a donné un capot*, and *Quoi je t'ai fait, malheureuse?*
[17] See note 16.
[18] See note 16.
[19] Cf. *J'ai passé devant la porte; French blues; Enterre-moi dans la cour;* and *Jolie blonde*.
[20] Cf. *Un pauvre hobo* and *Cajun blues from near Morse, Louisiana*.
[21] Harriet Beecher Stowe, *Uncle Tom's Cabin* (New York, n.d.), 90.
[22] Cf. *La valse des Créoles; Bye-Bye, Fédora;* and *J'ai passé devant la porte*.
[23] Cf. *Madame Baptiste* and *Ton ti bec est doux*.
[24] Cf. *Mon amour est barré* and *Quoi je t'ai fait, malheureuse?*
[25] Cf. *Quand je suis parti pour le Texas*.
[26] Cf. *Enterre-moi dans la cour*.

*ne* in negation;[27] and says *hier au soir* for *hier soir*;[28] *plombeau* for *pommeau*;[29] and *quoi sta fait?* for *qu'est-ce que to as fait?*[30] On the whole, however, this dialect is easily understood by one who knows French.

Like all folksongs, these songs express simple ideas in few themes. The unsophisticated person represented sings his life and publishes what fate has done to him. He makes no attempt to conceal any of his misfortune; nothing is his fault anyway. Like the romantic heroes of the nineteenth century in France, he enjoys his suffering enough to want to tell the world about it.[31]

From a study of these dialectic songs an interpretation of the character of the Louisiana Cajuns can be made. This interpretation, while not perhaps psychologically complete, does serve as a means of understanding a part of their character. Folksongs are usually echoes of the incidents of life. These songs portray the young man as primarily interested in the girl loved, *la belle*. He loves her;[32] he tells her good-bye when she marries someone else;[33] he wants to know what he has done to make her treat him so mean;[34] he blames her because he is poor;[35] he thinks of suicide when she does not love him;[36] he flatters her;[37] he dreams of her;[38] he regrets her when she sends him away;[39] he reproaches and threatens her for leaving him;[40] he begs her to make her little package and go to his house with him;[41] or promises to feed her upon *pain perdu*,[42] *pain de mais*,[43] or *caillé*,[44] or other food which in his own estimation is most delectable;[45] he asks her mother for her, which shows the persistent French tradition of marriage contracts;[46] he advertises that he wants to marry and states impediments to the marriage;[47] he weeps with a broken heart when she dies before he does;[48]

---

[27] Cf. *C'est pas la bague*.
[28] Cf. *Mon amour est barré dans l'armoire*.
[29] Cf. *La valse des Créoles*.
[30] Cf. *Jolie blonde*.
[31] See note 30.
[32] Cf. *La valse de la Grand Chénier*.
[33] Cf. *Bye-Bye, Fédora*.
[34] Cf. *Quoi je t'ai fait, malheureuse?*
[35] Cf. *Un pauvre hobo*.
[36] Cf. *Toutes les larmes que j'ai versées*.
[37] Cf. *Ton ti bec est doux* and *T'es petite, mais t'es mignonne*.
[38] Cf. *Mon amour est barré dans l'armoire*.
[39] Cf. *Ma belle m'a donné un capot* and *C'est pas la bague*.
[40] Cf. *Jolie blonde*.
[41] Cf. *Faites votre paquet, allons à la maison*.
[42] Lost bread or French toast. William A. Read, *Louisiana-French* (Baton Rouge, 1931), 55.
[43] Corn bread.
[44] Clabber.
[45] Cf. *La valse des Créoles* and *Enterre-moi dans la cour*.
[46] Cf. *Madame Fardeuil*.
[47] Cf. *Je veux me marier*.
[48] Cf. *J'ai passé devant la porte*.

and if he dies before she does, he begs to be buried in the corner of her father's yard so that he may look at her dear little eyes throughout eternity.[49]

Probably the ardent wooer is attentive after marriage. Only once is he accused of leaving his wife and sick baby on Sunday night to go to a gambling joint. Then the wife complains that days which were rosy for her, before marriage have become as green as cabbages.[50]

If the Cajun is no longer in the good favor of his *belle*, or if he thinks of faraway lands, the main place he sings of is Texas.[51] This is attributed to the fact that during the early days in Louisiana, Texas represented the far-off country of the unknown, the country of great adventure. Consequently, when a young maiden gave a "coat" to her lover (*a donné un capot*), signifying in the Cajun that he was to leave her house never to return,[52] he went to Texas to face his destiny and forget his *belle*.

When the Cajun is not being worried by amorous difficulties, he is thrilled with the joy of living. His carefree manner makes him seek pleasure in cards, whiskey, and dances. He is the sort of cavalier who rides a dashing steed with *la djog au plombeau*.[53]

The characteristic of lightheartedness and mirth also causes the Cajun to sing of animals, often in foolish predicaments.[54]

Possibly still another phase of the characteristic of this lightheartedness is shown in the Cajun's apparent lack of worry about the Lord. These songs show neither shouts of joy at getting religion nor the low, moaning, minor note, both so characteristic of the English Negro spirituals. Different theories have been given me explaining this absence of religious element, but I have not found any written ones. Consequently, I cannot quote. Opinions vary. Is the Cajun irreligious? Is he just non religious? Is he too happy to moan? Is he too sad to make "a joyful noise unto the Lord?"[55] Does he throw the responsibility of his salvation on a church? Is he too frivolous to be concerned with matters of another life? Or is he too full of the joy of living to be concerned with the supernatural? Regardless of the reason, the fact remains that in the Cajun songs of Louisiana apparently the religious element is absent.

Besides showing great love for the *belle*, a carefree nature, lightheartedness, and an absence of the religious element, the Cajun songs show the Cajun as

---

[49] Cf. *Enterre-moi dans la cour*.
[50] Cf. *Mon bébé est malade*.
[51] Cf. *A waltz from Calcasieu Parish*.
[52] Jay Karl Ditchy, *Les Acadiens Louisianais et Leur Parler* (Baltimore, 1901), 68 if., *donner un capot, éconduire un jeune homme qui a cessé de plair d'une jeune fille*.
[53] The jug of alcohol on the pommel of the saddle as in: *J'ai fait tout le tour du grand bois; J'ai fait trois tours du grand bois; Les filles du Mamou; French blues; La valse des Créoles*.
[54] Cf. *Saute crapaud; Câilletle; Si la paille ne coûtait pas si cher; Un carrosse bien attelé; Les maringouins ont tout mangé ma belle*.
[55] Psalm 100, verse 1.

frank and unafraid.[56] He names places and people;[57] he says just what he means. He is romantic and adventurous; he makes love ardently and if he loses out, he is willing to *aller au Texas*,[58] the far-distant country of the great unknown, there to drown his sorrows, to seek forgetfulness, and probably to love again. He is sentimental and knows all the sentimental appeals to reach the heart of his lady love. He is intensely jealous. In *fais-dodos*,[59] his country balls, undue attention shown his fiancée by another inevitably brings about a quarrel—sometimes a fatal fight.

In the music as well as the words of the folksongs, one reads the character of these simple folk who live close to the earth, who are rather elemental in their passions and feelings, and yet who have inherited all the romantic tendencies of the nineteenth century.

Allen C. Redwood's sketch of "Cupid on horseback" from the prairie country of southwestern Louisiana; ca. 1879.
From R. L. Daniels, "The Acadians of Louisiana," *Scribner's Monthly* 19 (1879-1880): 388.

---

[56] Cf. *Les filles de Mamou; Allons d Lafayette; Les gens de Crawley* in French blues; *Marais Bouleur* waltz.
[57] Cf. *Bye-Bye, Fedora; Qui est-ce qui passe? Madame Baptiste, tirez-moi pas; Marais Bouleur* waltz.
[58] Go to Texas.
[59] In 1937 the admission charges for one of these dancehalls read: Gents 25¢, Married men 15¢.

# Acculturation in Cajun Folk Music[1]

## *Harry Oster*

Because of isolation from the rest of the world and because of pride in their French heritage, descendants of the Acadians, now usually called "Cajuns," have retained a fundamentally French culture for most of the two centuries of their stay in a dominantly English-speaking nation. A generation ago, a French visitor to southwest Louisiana, the area along the Lafourche, Teche, and Vermilion bayous, could easily have imagined himself in a province (somewhat tropical) of France itself. He would have noticed that the people spoke French almost exclusively, a dialect much like that of the provinces, that they still practiced many French customs, and that some of the people sang ancient French folksongs.

During the past thirty years, however, the strength of the French influence has been waning because of a variety of forces. When the public schools came into general existence, many of them forbade the speaking of French on the premises. The purpose was to force the children to speak English. The widespread building of roads during the nineteen thirties brought these communities into more easy contact with the rest of the world. The rise of the phonograph, radio, motion pictures, and most recently television has had the double effect of (1) changing the tastes of this traditional people in the direction of conformity and (2) substituting mass produced, homogeneous entertainment for the old folk dances and songs. In addition, the return of veterans of World War II after years elsewhere, the discovery of oil on many Cajun farms, industrialization and the consequent influx of executives and workers from other states have badly upset the ancient ways which were so traditionally a part of an agricultural and fishing way of life.

The changes that took place in the Cajuns' choice of music constitute a particularly interesting example of acculturation, in this case, the modification of a minority culture as a result of the influences of a majority culture. As Cajun culture is in a highly transitional state, one can still find music representing the three most important stages of development of the Cajun community. The music now being performed includes (1) the folk music of seventeenth-century France, still circulating in a relatively pure form; (2) hybrid folksongs which combine lyrics in Cajun French with elements from one or more outside sources (southern mountain folksongs, commercial popular music of the country-and-western type, and Negro folk music of the blues variety); and (3) current popular music of the times.

For the most part those who sing songs in the direct French tradition,

---
[1] This article first appeared in the *McNeese Review* 10 (1958): 12-24.

songs which traveled from France to Acadie in Canada during the early seventeenth century, then to Louisiana in the eighteenth century, are among the older members of the community, those over forty-five—grandparents and great-grandparents, many of whom learned these songs from their parents before the phonograph came into wide use in southwest Louisiana. Typical of this ancient French tradition is this courtly lyric which I recorded near Abbeville in 1957 as sung by seventy-five year old Caesar Vincent.

### Mon Aimable Catin

Oh, dites-mois donc, mon aimable catin,
Quoi fais-tu dans ton jardin?
Oh, dites-mois donc, mon aimable catin,
Quoi fais-tu dans ton jardin?
J'suis après cueillir des fleur de toutes couleurs,
C'est pour mon serviteur.
Mais encore donc, mon petit Coeur,
Je t'en ferai ton bonheur.
Oh, dites-moi donc aimable beauté,
Quand vas-tu bien partager?
Entre les étoiles, de mes bons oeillets
Qui sont double bien fins,
Vous prendriez celles
Plus doux qu'ils paraîteront.

Mademoiselle, c'est pas de tes beaux oeillets,
Mais qu'ils y a qui me charmaient;
Ce sont ces jolis yeux doux,
Tout remplis d'amour,
M'a rendu z amoureux,
Mais encore donc, mon petit coeur,
Je t'en ferai ton bonheur.

Mon bon monsieur, je crois que vous badinez,
Mais ainsi que vous riez,
Moi, qui n'as de rien
Que mon jardinage
Pour mon entretient,
Je le jure sur mon honneur,
L'enfant de plus au siegneur.

Mademoiselle, je coris que vous badinez,
Moi, aussi que vous riez.
Tiens, violà mon diamant
Qui me coûte mille francs;
Je le jure sur mon honneur,
L'enfant de plus au seigneur.

### My Dear Sweetheart

Oh tell me, dear sweetheart
What are you doing in your garden?
Oh tell me, dear sweetheart
What are you doing in your garden?
I am picking flowers of all colors.
It is for my master.
But then, my little darling,
I will bring you your happiness.
Oh, tell me, my kind beauty
When are you going to share them?
Under the stars you would take
Those of my carnations
Which are especially fine,
Those which appear sweetest to you.

Miss, it is not your beautiful carnations
Which have charmed me;
But your two pretty eyes,
Full of love
Have made me amorous;
My little darling,
I will bring you your happiness.

My good sir, I think you are joking,
That you are laughing.
I have nothing except my gardening
For my support,
Which cost me a thousand francs.
I swear it on my honor
As a most devoted child of the Lord.

Miss, I believe that you are joking,
I also believe that you are laughing.
See, here is my diamond
Which cost me a thousand francs.
I swear it on my honor
As a most devoted child of the Lord.

Another example of the pure French tradition is a song which used to be a traditional feature of Cajun weddings. It was a song performed by the bride in which she wept for her carefree, happy maidenhood, which was being exchanged for the heavy responsibilities of marriage. She would find consolation in the idea that she and her sweetheart would spend the rest of their days together. The use of this song in its traditional functional setting has all but disappeared. This was sung for me in 1957 by Mrs. Éli Landry, a young grandmother from Abbeville, Louisiana.

| | |
|---|---|
| J'avais promis dans ma jeunesse | I had promised in my youth |
| Que j'm'aurais jamais marillié | That I would never marry. |
| J'avais promis dans ma jeunesse | I had promised in my youth |
| Que j'm'aurais jamais marillié | That I would never marry. |
| Adieu, la fleur de la jeunesse, | Good-bye flower of youth, |
| la noble qualité de fille, | Noble quality of girlhood |
| la noble qualité de fille. | Noble quality of girlhood |
| C'est aujourd'hui je veux la quitter. | Today I wish to leave it. |
| C'est aujourd'hui que ma tête est couronnée | Today my head is crowned |
| Et que mon coeur es t orné d'un bouquet. | And my heart is ornamented with a bouquet. |
| Adieu, la fleur de la jeunesse, | Good-bye flower of youth, |
| La noble qualité de fille. | Noble quality of girlhood |
| C'est aujourd'hui je veux la quitter. | Today I wish to leave it. |
| C'est aujourd'hui que je porte le nom de dame. | Today I carry the name of lady. |
| C'est par l'anneau que je porte au doigt. | It is through the ring I wear on my finger. |
| Adieu, la fleur de la jeunesse, | Good-bye flower of youth, |
| La noble qualité de fille. | Noble quality of girlhood |
| C'est aujourd'hui je veux la quitter. | Today I wish to leave it. |
| C'est aujourd'hui que je vieux faire le serment. | Today I make the promise |
| C'est de finir mes jours avec toi. | To finish my days with you. |
| Adieu, la fleur de la jeunesse, | Good-bye flower of youth, |
| La noble qualité de fille. | Noble quality of girlhood |
| C'est aujourd'hui je veux la quitter. | Today I wish to leave it. |

Similarly, pure French folksongs have lost their functional role as a basic source of entertainment in the community. Usually the older people themselves turn for their diversion to the phonograph, radio, motion picture, and television. Even if they wished to do otherwise, they would find it difficult to oppose the enthusiasm of the younger members of the household for such modern entertainment.

As to the hybrid type of Cajun folksongs which results from an interaction of French culture, or at least the French language, and other cultural influences in which such influence is in its style of performance or its general form, the popular "Grand Mamou" is a pertinent example. While the words are by Joe Falcon, the tune itself is probably of folk origin. As Terry Clement of Evangeline, Louisiana, recorded it for me in 1957, accompanying himself on the accordion, his performance embodies a great deal of syncopation, no doubt influenced by current jazz trends. The rhythm is a product of Negro folk music either directly or indirectly, and the words and the wailing style of singing are quite close to the Negro blues tradition.

**Grand Mamou**

Eh, jolie p'tite fille, mais malheureuse
Qui m'a quitté pour s'en allerz à Grand Mamou
Parce qu'on est pas comme moi-même, moi, j'vas faire
Moi j'vas faire, moi, tout seul à la maison.

Eh, tu m'as quitté pour t'en aller,
Pour t'en aller t aussi loin z avec un aut',
Moi, j'connais j'mérite pas ça, mais chère 'tite fille,
Moi, j'connais tu vas pleurer pour ça qu' t'as fait.

Oh, mais quoi faire, mais chère, mais t'as fait ça,
Moi, j'connais j'mérite pas ça mais malheureuse
Tu vas pleurer, chère 'tite fille, mais sera trop tard,
Sera trop tard, j'veux plus t'voir dans la maison.

**Big Mamou**

Eh, pretty little girl, you poor dear,
Who left me to go to Grand Mamou
Others are not like me
For I'm going to get along by myself at the house.

Eh, you left me to go away
To go away so far with another.
I know I don't deserve that, but dear little girl,
I know you're going to cry for what you did.

Oh, but my dear, but you did just that,
I know I don't deserve that, but unhappily
You're going to cry, dear little girl, but it will be too late.
I don't want to see you anymore at the house.

When settlers from the southern mountains, inheritors of the tradition of the British Isles, made their way into the Cajun country, they often brought with them Anglo-Saxon and southern mountain songs. Some of these found so much favor with the Cajuns they translated them into the French idiom. Some followed the original quite closely with little or no modification to make the French words rhyme. For example, "A Paper of Pins" became "Un Paquet d'Épingles" and "Billy Boy," "Billy Garçon."

However, variant versions that are typically Cajun will be found as in the song "My Good Ol' Man" which appears as "Eyoùss Que T'es Parti." In the original, it begins comically, but ends mockingly supernatural as follows:

## My Good Ol' Man

Where are you a goin', my good ol' man?
Where are you a goin', my honey, my lam'?
    *Spoken*: Huntin!

When will you be back, my good ol' man?
When will you be back, my honey, my lam'?
    *Spoken*: "Saturday."

What do you want for supper, my good ol' man?
What do you want for supper, my honey, my lam'?
    *Spoken*: "Eggs."

How many of 'em do you want, my good ol' man?
How many of 'em do you want, my honey, my lam'?
    *Spoken*: "Bushel."

Why! A bushel'll kill you, my good ol' man?
Why! A bushel'll kill you, my honey, my lam'?
    *Spoken*: "I don't mind."

Where d'ye want to be buried, my good ol' man?
Where d'ye want to be buried, my honey, my lam'?
    *Spoken*: "In a chimney corner."

Why! The ashes'll fall on yuh, my good ol' man?
Why! The ashes'll fall on yuh, my honey, my lam'?
    *Spoken*: "Don't care if they do."

What'll ye do then, my good ol' man?
What'll ye do then, my honey, my lam'?
    *Spoken*: "I'll haint yuh."

A haint cain't haint a haint, my good ol' man?
A haint cain't haint a haint, my honey, my lam'?

"The pot-hunter," by E. W. Kemble.
*In George Washington Cable, "Au Large,"* Century Illustrated Monthly Magazine *35 (November, 1887-April, 1888): 89.*

Except for a difference in rhythm, the opening bars of the Cajun variant are identical with those of the southern mountain one. While the supernatural element, wherein the wife answers that he cannot haunt her because she is already a ghost, has disappeared in the Cajun version, love, liquor, and food are given strong emphasis instead because the typical Cajun has no inclination to sing about the supernatural. Here is that version.

## Eyoùss Que T'es Parti

Eyoùss que t'es parti, oué, mon bon vieux mari?
Eyoùss que t'es parti, ce qu'on appelle l'amour.
Eyoùss que t'es parti, oué, mon bon vieux mari?
Le meilleur buveur du pays?
*Spoken*:
Parti m' souler!

Eyoùss que tu vas r'venir, oué, mon bon vieux mari?
Eyoùss que tu vas r'venir, ce qu'on appelle l'amour.
Eyoùss que tu vas r'venir, oué, mon bon vieux mari?
Qu'il est le meilleur buveur du pays?
*Spoken*:
Demain ou un aut' jour!

Qui tu vas ram'ner, oué, mon bon vieux mari?
Qui tu vas ram'ner, ce qu'on appelle l'amour.
Qui tu vas ram'ner, oué, mon bon vieux mari?
Qu'il est le meilleur buveur du pays?

*Spoken*:
Cinq douzaine d'oeufs et un gallon d'couche-couche!

J'ai peur ça va te tuer, oué, mon bon vieux mari?
J'ai peur ça va te tuer, ce qu'on appelle l'amour.
J'ai peur ça va te tuer, oué, mon bon vieux mari?
Qu'il est le meilleur buveur du pays?
*Spoken*:
Oh, ça! J'veux mourir comme meme!

Eyòuss tu veux j't'enterre, oué, mon bon vieux mari?
Eyòuss tu veux j't'enterre, ce qu'on appelle l'amour.
Eyòuss tu veux j't'enterre, oué, mon bon vieux mari?
Qu'il est le meilleur buveur du pays?
*Spoken*:
Enterre-mon dans l' coin d' la cour et tous les temps en temps passé-mon une patate chaude!

## Where Are You Going

Where are you going, my good old husband?
Where are you going, the one they call love?
Where are you going, my good old husband?
The best drinker in the country?

Going to get drunk!

Where are you coming back, my good old husband?
Where are you coming back, the one they call love?
Where are you coming back, my good old husband?
The best drinker in the country?

Tomorrow or another day!

What are you going to bring back, my good old husband?
What are you going to bring back, the one they call love?
What are you going to bring back, my good old husband?
The best drinker in the country?

Five dozen eggs, and a gallon of porridge!

I'm afraid that will kill you, my good old husband?
I'm afraid that will kill you, the one they call love?
I'm afraid that will kill you, my good old husband?
The best drinker in the country?

Makes no difference. I want to die anyway!

I'm afraid that will kill you, my good old husband?
I'm afraid that will kill you, the one they call love?
I'm afraid that will kill you, my good old husband?
The best drinker in the country?

Bury me in the corner of the yard and every so often pass me a hot potato!

Another significant example of a Cajun variant of a popular commercial hit by means of translation is the version of a song of the nineteen forties, "I Hear You Knocking, but You Can't Come In." When this song was being widely played by swing bands on the radio, apparently a bilingual Cajun liked it enough to put it into translation. The performance I recorded was very similar in style to that of dance bands of about fifteen years ago.

| Tu Peux Cogner Mais Tu Peux Pas Rentrer | You can knock but you can't come in. |
|---|---|
| Tu peux cogner mais tu peux pas rentrer. | You can knock but you can't come in. |
| J'ai la clef desus la porte d'en avant; | The front door is locked. |
| Tu peux cogner mais tu peux pas rentrer. | You can knock but you can't come in. |
| Tu peux cogner mais tu peux pas rentrer. | You can knock but you can't come in. |
| J'ai la clef desus la port du côté; | The side door is locked. |
| Tu peux cogner mais tu peux pas rentrer. | You can knock but you can't come in. |
| Tu peux cogner mais tu peux pas rentrer. | You can knock but you can't come in. |
| J'ai la clef desus la porte d'en arrière; | The back door is locked. |
| Tu peux cogner mais tu peux pas rentrer. | You can knock but you can't come in. |

There have also been translations of hillbilly popular hits like "They Cut Down the Old Pine Trees."

| The original words are as follows: | Here is the Cajun translation: |
|---|---|
| They cut down the old pine tree, | Il' ont coupe le vieux arb' de pin |
| And they hauled it away to the mill | Ils l'ont halé là-bas au moulin |
| To make a coffin of pine | Faut faire ein cerceuil de pin |
| For that sweetheart of mine. | Pour ma jolie catin. |
| They cut down the old pine tree. | Il'ont coupé le vieux arb' de pin. |
| But she's not alone in her grave tonight. | Mais elle n'est pas tout seule dans sa fosse ce soir, |
| For it's there my heart will always be. | Car c'est là mon coeur sera laissé. |
| Though we'd drifted apart, | Oh, on peut s' séparer, |
| Still they cut down my heart | Eh mon coeur est cassé, |
| When they cut down the old pine tree. | Car le vieux pin a été coupé. |

This is a very literal translation in which the lyrics follow an American rather than a French idiom; e.g., "mon coeur est cassé" is an American turn of phrase. Also, the performance which I recorded in 1957 was in the standard commercial hillbilly style, which is highly popular in the Cajun area.

From the foregoing examples, the impact of popular music on the Cajun world is clear. The final stage, following that of the creation of hybrid Cajun songs, is already well advanced. Whereas the oldest people in southwest Louisiana speak only French and the next generation speaks both French and English, the current generation of teen-agers for the most part speaks only English, and perhaps understands the French of their parents. Without a natural perpetuation of the language, most of the folklore is doomed. The forces of Americanization will within the next decade or two completely swallow up the old

French and Cajun folk music. Typical of the trend is the career of Terry Clement, a young accordionist and singer, one of whose performances was described earlier in this article. Mr. Clement, who a few years ago performed hybrid Cajun songs professionally at dances, now plays rock-and-roll for teen-age groups. Although he himself prefers Cajun music, the teen-age paying public insists on the music which is currently popular throughout the rest of the United States. Thus the process of acculturation is rapidly approaching the point where the music of the Cajun country will be indistinguishable from the popular hits disseminated by the mass media of entertainment.

Radio provided new performance opportunities for Cajun musicians and brought the sounds of America into Cajun homes.
*Image adapted from 1923 Sears Roebuck catalog, courtesy of Jennifer Cooper.*

# The Socio-Cultural Traits of the French Folksong in Louisiana[1]

*Elizabeth Brandon*

The French Louisiana folksong is the expression of blending of various cultural strains which influenced the people inhabiting Lower Louisiana. A comparison of published and manuscript songs collected in Canada and in France with the songs of French Louisiana shows, in the latter, the adoption of new elements and the process of borrowing in three essential areas: musical, linguistic, and socio-cultural. This essay will treat the socio-cultural aspect of a representative selection of songs and will discuss the evolution of certain traits in these songs.

Most of these songs were brought to Louisiana by various groups of settlers, the majority of them French speaking: the first colonists coming directly from France, colonists, explorers, *voyageurs* and *coureurs de bois* from Canada, and the Acadians from Nova Scotia. The latter group, of sturdy peasant stock stemming originally from the northwestern provinces of France, colonized Nova Scotia (Acadia) in the seventeenth century. After France lost this territory to England, as per the Treaty of Utrecht in 1713, the fate of the Acadians became precarious. For political and ideological reasons the English governor of Nova Scotia, Charles Lawrence, issued a decree exiling the Acadians from their homeland. Uprooted by the deportation, known as the "Grand Dérangement" of 1755, close to 4,000 of these French Catholics were unloaded in the English American colonies where, due to political complications of the period, they were treated as alien enemies of the crown. The majority of these displaced people started drifting into Louisiana after the end of the Seven Years War. The Treaty of Paris of 1763 stipulated that the Acadians be permitted to leave the English colonies in order to join their relatives and friends in French speaking territories. Most of the newcomers settled west of the Mississippi, along the bayous: Lafourche, Teche and Vermilion.

Other French-speaking newcomers kept arriving through the remainder of the eighteenth century. Waves of Canadians, who left New France after the fall of Québec, were followed by other contingents of former Acadians. Numerous families reached the shores of Louisiana after having spent several years in the French possessions of the Caribbean. An important group of 1,600 people of deported Acadians came to Louisiana in 1784, after a thirty-year odyssey. Many changes occurred among these people during the years of wandering through the ports of England, north-western maritime ports of France, and

---

[1] This article first appeared in *Revue de Louisiana/Louisiana Review* 1 (1972): 19-52. Erik Charpentier kindly translated the French lyrics included in this article.

the unsuccessful stay in the two colonies created for them within the borders of France, in Poitou and Belle-Isle-en-Mer. The older people died out, children were born and raised in pre-revolutionary France, young people took spouses whose roots were deep in France. The arrival of these colonists almost doubled the French-Acadian population in Louisiana and the linguistic and cultural impact of this addition must have been dramatic.

In the last decade of the century two other groups of importance reached the shores of Louisiana: many families of noblemen fleeing the French Revolution and the refugees from Saint-Domingue fleeing the uprising of the slaves. The aristocratic newcomers from France established themselves in and around Saint Martinville where they mixed eventually with the Acadians, which was not always the case with the Creole noblemen in and around New Orleans.[2]

There were two contingents of exiles from Saint-Domingue. The first, consisting of about 4,000 people, came directly from the Haitian island in 1792. The second contingent of former Saint-Domingue inhabitants came after a seventeen year stay in Cuba, where they had sought refuge from the slave revolution. When Napoleon invaded Spain, the governor of Cuba declared its allegiance to the Spanish mother country and, as a reprisal, drove the French nationals from the island. In 1809, several boats left Havana and unloaded almost 6,000 French refugees in New Orleans. In the years to come, the 10,000 Haitians composed of whites, black slaves, and "gens de couleur libres" exercised a notable influence on the folklore of French Louisiana.

In the nineteenth century, Louisiana welcomed still other émigrés from France: Napoleonic soldiers and Bonapartists after the fall of Napoleon, republicans fleeing the Bourbon Restoration and the Second Empire, and the royalists leaving the Second and Third French Republics. After the Louisiana Purchase, the non-French-speaking settlers from the southern mountains and the seaboard states of English, Scottish, Irish, and German descent joined the French inhabitants.

---

[2] The Creoles, descendant of the original French colonists, in and around New Orleans, the French "fonctionnaires" and proprietors of large stretches of land granted them by the kings of France, continued living on the same grand scale in Louisiana as they or their ancestors used to live in France. When the Acadian peasant deportees reached Lower Louisiana, the Creoles who had nothing in common with this social class of Frenchmen, assumed an indifferent or even a haughty attitude and did not mingle with the newcomers. The situation was different when the younger generation of Creoles moved away from New Orleans and made a new life in the southwestern plains of Louisiana. These young people who did not have large plantations and were in more modest circumstances found themselves close to the Acadians. Away from their families and the influence of the social life among the noblemen in a big city, they changed gradually their attitude and soon became a part of the community.

The conditions in which the French émigrés from the Revolution found themselves in and around Saint Martinville were different from those in New Orleans. True, in the beginning, thinking that their exile would be temporary, they continued the mode of life to which they had been accustomed before the Revolution. However, when their funds were exhausted, they had no other alternative but to toil the land and earn a living like their humble neighbors, the Acadians. In these circumstances they mixed freely with the Acadians, intermarried and became eventually completely absorbed by them.

Of all these heterogeneous groups, the Acadians, colloquially called "Cajuns,"[3] constituted the strongest unit which finished by assimilating all the rest. Because of their isolation and closely integrated family and community life, the Cajuns continued to cling to their language,[4] their customs, and their Catholic religion. Through their marriages to Cajun girls, the young American bachelors became thoroughly assimilated. Their descendants continued the pattern of life of the bayou country without any change until the beginning of the twentieth century.[5] The newcomers adopted the language, religion and customs of the Cajuns, and, in turn, made substantial contributions of their own cultural elements which blended into existing patterns. The French folksong in Louisiana is a reflection of this acculturation.

Until the First World War singing was a feature of the daily life of the French Louisianian and had a functional importance. The lack of roads and means of transportation, and the homogeneous character of the closely knit, rural community, was conducive to the preservation of the original forms of entertainment, *les veillées* and *les fais-dodo*[6] during which songs were sung. In the second quarter of the century, building of the roads, economic, industrial and educational progress, shifting of the population, and, above all, a strong policy of Americanization brought enormous changes. For many years French was discouraged by the public schools and people who spoke French "were looked upon as backward and un-American." Due to this attitude English started gradually replacing French in many areas of daily life and the French influence has been declining. In the last few years, the concerned and enlightened citizens of Louisiana, alarmed over the fact that the French language is becoming

---

[3] "Cajun"—corruption from the French word "Acadien." The pronunciation of "di" having undergone the process of palatalization became "dj."
[4] The language spoken by the modern Cajun is a combination of French and of recently acquired anglicisms. The Cajun French has retained many seventeenth-century archaisms, as well as regional expressions stemming from the original provinces of the colonists. To this were added many agricultural and nautical words from the occupational vocabulary of the Acadians most of whom were peasants and fishermen. Due to the influence of modern American ways, the oral traditions of the bayou folk represent a fusion of the French and American heritages in the environment of contemporary progress and uniformity of modes of existence.
[5] T. Lynn Smith and Vernon J. Parenton, "Acculturation among the Louisiana French," *American Journal of Sociology* 44 (1938): 363. "These Acadian people until a quarter of century ago had preserved one of the purest examples of a seventeenth century folk culture to be found in the United States."
[6] "La veillée"—an evening spent socially, especially among the peasantry during the winter months. The "fais-dodo" (literally "go-to-sleep" in children's language) in Louisiana is a dance or a country ball that lasted into the morning hours. Since the whole family used to attend these events, the babies and children brought by the parents used to be put to bed in the "parc-aux-petits," a special section reserved for them. The term possibly originated because of this fact.

In the olden times, when each family was isolated and lived far away from neighbors, when the only means of transportation were pirogues and buggies, these gatherings were important happenings in the life of the bayou population. The younger, unmarried people danced, the older ones discussed their affairs, told yarns, sang songs, played cards or just visited. Today it is a public dance in one of the many dancehalls in the country-side of southern Louisiana. In Vermilion Parish ("parish"—county) where I did my folklore research I have never heard the expression "fais-dodo" used by my informants. Everyone has always referred to it as "bal" or "danse."

extinct, formed the Council of the Development of French in Louisiana, which succeeded in reversing the former school policy of discouraging the speaking of French in the classrooms of southern Louisiana. Henceforth French will be taught in all public schools in the state.[7]

Although the traditional entertainment in the form of "veillées" has all but disappeared, it is interesting to note the survival of French songs in the area. The songs collected in Cajun French may be divided into four groups:

1. French songs indigenous to Louisiana, composed by local musicians.
2. Songs from American folklore translated into French.
3. French Negro Spirituals indigenous to southern Louisiana.
4. Traditional French songs stemming from three sources: France, Nova Scotia and Canada.

Lithographer A.R. Waud's notorious 1866 sketch.
From "Wash Day among the Acadians," *Harper's Weekly*, October 20, 1866.

The fun-loving Cajun, whose characteristic "joie de vivre" separates him from his northern neighbors, produced the "Cajun music" which is extremely popular in Louisiana as well as in the adjoining areas of Texas, where many Cajuns moved to work in industrial centers. The countryside of southern Louisiana is dotted with barn-like structures where a few times a week, especially on Saturday evenings, the inhabitants gather to dance and drink. The musicians who play in these dancehalls are often the composers of this music. These dance bands can be heard at various festivities and festivals in

---

[7] Act No. 408, House Bill No. 437. The Louisiana Legislature voted unanimously on July 20, 1968, "to further the preservation and utilization of the French language and culture of Louisiana...and requirement that the French language...shall be taught for a sequence of years in the public elementary and high school systems of the State."

different parishes,[8] as well as over the radio, broadcast by disc jockeys from stations in the French-speaking regions. The music and the lyrics of these songs present a striking example of acculturation. The lyrics of these compositions are a mixture of fragments taken out of traditional French songs and vocabulary and syntactical structures of the Cajun's daily language. An analysis of the texts of these songs is revealing because it reflects the thinking and the preoccupations of the local people. The hybrid music, as described by researchers, has elements from one or more outside sources: southern mountain folksong, Tin Pan alley hits, country-and-western music, cowboy and hillbilly, Negro Jazz and blues.[9]

> However French they may be in origin, Cajun folksongs have in some cases a definite Negro flavor to be found in the super-imposed elementary rhythms which give them sort of a "jazzy" atmosphere, nowhere else to be found in folksongs derived from France other than in the Caribbean.[10]

Some of the well known titles of the Cajun songs are: *J'ai passé devant ta porte, La valse de la Grande Chênière, Jolie Blonde, Tu peux cogner mais tu peux pas rentrer, J'aime une petite fille, Grand Mamou*,[11] etc.

The existence of this indigenous music has been of enormous importance since it created the climate in which the traditional songs could be better preserved. The repertory of any older folk performer consists of a heterogeneous assortment of songs; he does not discriminate and sings with the same zest a modern Cajun song, a medieval French "complainte" along with a pseudo-literary hit of a Parisian café-concert of Toulouse-Lautrec's time.

Folksongs from the American folklore, with roots in England, Scotland, and Ireland, translated into French, are known by all the singers, young and old.

---

[8] Most of the parishes have their festivals once a year. There are shrimp, crawfish, sweet potato, sugar cane, rice, dairy festivals, etc.
[9] Harry Oster, *Folksongs of the Louisiana Acadians* (Recorded in Grand Mamou), Folk-Lyric Recording Co., Baton Rouge, LA, 1958, Notes, 4.
[10] Lucie de Vienne, *Introduction and Texts to Cajun Songs from Louisiana*, Ethnic Folkways Library Album No. P. 438, 1957, 3.
[11] *J'ai passé devant ta porte* may serve as an example of a Cajun song.

> J'ai passé devant ta porte
> J'ai crié baï-baï la belle
> 'l ya personne qui m'a répondu
> Oh yé yaï mon coeur fait mal,
>
> J'ai passé devant ta porte
> J'ai vu tout le monn' après pleurer
> J'ai pensé y avait que'qu' chose
> Oh yé yaï mon coeur fait mal.
>
> J'ai passé devant ta porte
> J'ai vu tous les chandelles allumées
> A l'entour de ton cercueil
> O yé yaï mon coeur fait mal.
>
> Sung by Lucille Saltzman, Gueydan, 1972

The favorites are *Billy Boy*, often called *Billy Garçon*, *Et où c'que t'es parti, mon bon vieux mari?*—translation of *My Good Old Man*, *Un papier d'épingles*, the English *Paper of Pins*, *La fille d'un boucher* taken from the well known British broadside ballad *The Butcher Boy*, etc. The latter may have also come by way of Canada since many versions of this song in French translation were collected there.

The French Louisiana spiritual has not been collected extensively, but studied only in brief by Harry Oster.[12] An analysis of these songs is particularly interesting for they represent a fusion of Afro-American and French elements. The French traits were transmitted to the blacks by the Cajuns and by the French missionaries. The Cajuns have always maintained close and friendly contacts with their Negro neighbors.

> As landless immigrants the Acadians had a lower social status than the old French settlers: and as persecuted minority in their former northern homeland, they were not standoffish with the Negro slaves. Their relations were not tempered by a master slave attitude...[and] there seems to have been a considerable cultural exchange in some areas between the Negroes and Cajuns. As a result, numerous Negroes in proximity to the Cajuns today sing Cajun songs in Cajun dialect and play Cajun tunes without any suggestion of foreign intrusion.[13]

This, of course, does not preclude the fact that many Negroes speak the Creole patois and sing Creole French songs, reminiscent of those sung in the Congo Square in New Orleans during the nineteenth century.

Music played an all-important role in the African slave's communal life and ritual, and his descendants had a continuous need to carry on, wherever possible, this tradition. The French Negro spiritual in Louisiana is a religious song that had a specific function from the time of emancipation through the first quarter of the twentieth century. It started as a counterpart of the Negro American spiritual. During the Reconstruction period, many Catholic Negroes turned to Protestant religions primarily because of the influence of the Baptist and Methodist missionaries who had come from the North. An important factor that attracted the Catholic Negroes to the Protestant faith was the opportunity of oral self-expression. One of Lyle Saxon's informants explained to him that he joined the Protestant church because he wanted to participate more actively in the service:

> The Catholic preachers from France would not let us shout and the Lawd done said you gotta shout if you want to be saved. That's in the Bible.[14]

---

[12] Harry Oster, "Negro French Spirituals of Louisiana," *Journal of the International Folk Music Council* 14 (1962): 166-67.
[13] Harold Courlander, *Negro Folk Music, U.S.A.* (New York, 1963), 1, 64.
[14] Lyle Saxon, Edward Dreyer, and Robert Tallant, *Gumbo Ya-Ya* (Boston, 1945), 242.

The priests in Catholic Louisiana understood the black parishoners' need for vocal expression which was so freely practiced by some Protestant churches. They made concessions by permitting Negroes to sing during the mass some hymns, songs for the dead, and hallelujahs. But the spiritual was not a part of the Sunday service in the Catholic church. It was sung in private homes throughout the parishes where on designated Sundays the community gathered for group singing. During Lent especially, when there was no other form of amusement available, these singing sessions served as an entertainment as well as an outlet of religious fervor. The preceptor who was the priest or a chosen elder, taught the words to the participating audience. He gave out one line at a time which the group repeated. The texts used in these "cantiques," as they were called by the singers, were taken out of French religious canticles or sacred songs. A few singable words or phrases were chosen and repeated over and over again. Refrains were particularly favored because everybody learned them fast and enjoyed repeating them. The entire energy of the performers was devoted to the music rather than to the meaning. The description of the gathering was reported to me by one of my informants:

A black child at the holy water font, St. Louis Cathedral, New Orleans, Louisiana, 1874. From Edward King, "The Great South," *Scribner's Monthly* 7 (November 1873-April 1874): 4.

> Everyone gathered in one house at 3 o'clock Sunday. The house had been cleaned, the furniture moved out. The men fixed the seats; they were benches made of two or three thick pieces of wood, usually trunks of trees, and the benches were covered with sheets made of sacks.
>
> The young people sat in front, the older ones in back to pray and sing. The leader was a priest or an old man and he stood in front of the altar. The altar was made out of a table covered with a sheet. On the altar there was a cross or a crucifix, sometimes flowers or green leaves. There were also candies in empty bottles. There were rarely candlesticks. If there were candlesticks it is because the whites gave it to them, or to their parents, or grandparents.
>
> The leader recited the rosary and we repeated after him. Then the singing started. They called it cantiques or prayers. One person was saying the line and everybody sang together. The Catholics did not sing in church. No hand clapping, no foot tapping, no instruments. Between songs we recited the rosary. We had about one hour of singing. We didn't sing songs for the dead.

The next Sunday we went to another house. The man was going from house to house. He had everything in his head, he did not know how to write. His name was Nicolas, Nicolas Bérard. My father-in-law told me that 55 years ago there was a priest, Father Zachary, who taught him the cantiques.[15]

The subjects treated in the "cantiques" are easily recognizable from the titles. In *La Passion de Jésus-Christ*, instead of the developed story of the Passion, the Louisiana version repeats only a few lines:

> Et avec vos voeux 'l est attaché su' ein croix Avec des clous de quarante
> *And with your wishes he is tied to a cross with forty nails*
> Avec vos voeux son côté percé
> *With your wishes his side pierced*
> Avec un coup de lancette
> *Struck with a lance*
>
> Et avec vos voeux sa tête couronnée
> *With your wishes his head is crowned*
> Avec des fleurs en aspique
> *With lavender flowers*

The refrain which is repeated after every stanza is:

> Oh! la passion de not' Saint-Jésus Ah! 'l est trist', adorable.
> *Oh! The passion of our Holy Jesus Ah! He is sad, adorable*

The text of the refrain is not always stable. Instead of "Saint-Jésus" the performer sang on occasion "not' Jésus," or "Jésus-Christ."[16]

Another "cantique" about the death of the Christ:

> On me demand: Donc qui qu'c'est mort?

---

[15] Edna Solomon, fifty-one years old, Negro, illiterate, bilingual, speaks Cajun French, Houston, Texas, 1971. Mrs. Solomon was born in Lafayette Parish, Louisiana, and lived there and in Vermilion Parish until 1951 when she moved to Houston. She tells me that today in Houston, where many French Catholic Negroes moved from Louisiana, prayer gatherings are still being practiced at private homes. On Sunday the priest usually announces where and when the next get-together is to be held. It resembles a prayer meeting and is conducted in English. This tradition may be the continuation of the old custom of singing the "cantiques."

[16] Sung by Laurent Solomon, Negro, illiterate, Cajun French speaker, knew a little English, now deceased. He sang this "cantique" in 1953, in Kaplan, Louisiana, when he was sixty-four. He was the father-in-law of Edna Solomon. Mr. Solomon was a remarkable performer and had a large repertoire of excellent folktales. He was also a good singer, but did not specialize in singing. He was born in Broussard, Lafayette Parish, and moved with his family to Kaplan, Vermilion, in the early twenties. When I knew him he was working as a gardner and cotton picker. Whenever he could not remember a tale I asked for, or when he could not recall a detail or a motif, he used to promise me to do some thinking ("jongler") about it as soon as the cotton picking season came and he went into the fields. There he could meditate about it without being disturbed. He always kept his word and usually came through with a perfectly developed narrative which he recited to me on my following visit. He was a great actor which could be particularly seen when he was telling a dialog. He acted out each part and changed his voice, from a falsetto when representing children, to a low voice when he took the parts of adults, and a rasping voice when he imitated a sorcerer or "la bête à sept têtes." He was one of the most respected citizens of the black community in Kaplan and in the vicinity and his death was deeply mourned.

*They ask me: "So who's dead?"*
On me répond: L'Enfant Jésus.
*They answer: "The child Jesus"*

Apporte-moi ce drap mortel
*Bring me this mortal sheet*
Pour ensevelir l'Enfant Jésus.
*To bury the child Jesus*
Flambeau du Ciel est éclairé
*Torch in the sky is lit up*
Pour éclairer l'Enfant Jésus.[17]
*To illuminte the child Jesus*

The topics treated in the other religious songs pertain to the Virgin Mary, the sinners called to meet the Lord, Mary Magdalene, saints or apostles. Many of the words although corrupted are still recognizable, others no longer make any sense. Shouting and foot tapping are noticeably absent from the performance of these French spirituals. Although our recording sessions were often gay, the performers behaved like in church when they sang their "cantiques".

The traditional songs collected in Louisiana in the last thirty-five years have their counterparts in France and in Canada. A musical comparison of these bodies of songs elicited the following statement from the French ethnomusicologist, Marguerite d'Harcourt:

> The collection of the Louisiana songs that you sent me is extremely interesting from the linguistic as well as from the musical point of view. In comparison with the Canadian songs I find yours simpler and somewhat lacking in the lyrical ornate style so prevalent in Canada. On the other hand, though, your songs are of great musical value for the old modes are numerous and the pentatonic scales, so seldom found in France or Canada, are frequent in your collection. As a whole, the songs are very good and form a very important part of the French folklore across the Atlantic.[18]

The mention of the prevalence of the pentatonic scale, common to both Anglo-American and African traditions, testifies to the important influence of the Southern United States on the French songs in Louisiana. This element of acculturation is not only reflected in music but also in the texts, as will be seen from the analysis that follows.

---

[17] Sung by Célestine Morton, Negro, illiterate, Cajun French speaker, did not know English. Now deceased. She sang the "cantique" in 1953, in Kaplan, LA, when she was seventy-nine. Mother-in-law of Laurent Solomon. Born in Youngsville, LA, moved to Kaplan in the early twenties. She remembered vividly the Reconstruction period and told me about the hard times her mother, an emancipated slave, went through. She was an old lady with a great sense of humor and a twinkle in her eye, especially when she was telling naughty stories. She was not known as a "raconteuse" and did not have an extensive repertory of songs and tales, but her rendition of whatever she related was good, precise and animated. She spoke an unusually good and correct French which she learned from the Creole family with whom her mother was living. She used to smoke a corncob pipe with the dignity of a queen. Her family revered her and referred to her as "einne grande dame."
[18] In a personal letter of March 31, 1957. The translation was made by the author.

The usual subjects are treated in the folksongs. There are songs of courtship, love and marriage, songs of soldiers and sailors, songs narrating adventure and death, songs to amuse and songs to satirize. The two themes lacking in the Louisiana repertoire are those pertaining to occupations and to religion. The dearth of songs describing various trades had been also noticed in Canada. This phenomenon is explained by the fact that this type of work songs did not develop in the French provinces which sent colonists to the New World.[19] Songs like *Bruits de Métiers*, *Les Charpentiers*, *Il nous faut des Tondeurs*, or *Plantons la Vigne*, relative to occupational activities have not been encountered in this hemisphere. The authors of the French Louisiana *Danse Rondes* quote a possible remnant of a trade song.[20] It is surprising that in agricultural Lower Louisiana, where the Cajun's main occupation has been the cultivation of sugar cane, cotton, and rice, not a single song describing these chores has been recorded. In a few of the slave songs in Creole patois there is mention of working in the fields and cutting sugar cane, but neither of these activities is treated as the central theme of the songs.

It is known that any song may be used as a work song. Tiersot and Van Gennep reported that their French informants stated that they used various tunes and lyrics, including rounds and sentimental romances, so long as the rhythm was suited to the execution of a given task. In French Canada the "voyageurs" and the canoe-men adjusted the cadence of familiar songs to the rhythm of their paddling. Negro slaves in the South sang spirituals and love songs when working in the fields, loading cotton bales on steamboats, building levees and railroads, or rowing on the rivers. And yet, trade songs are plentiful in the United States. The lumberjacks, miners, wagoneers, canallers, railroad men, river boatmen, laborers, and sailors created occupational ballads.

> Folk song in the United States is unusual for the number of songs created by wandering workers.... They worked in logging camps, in construction camps, in mine patches and coal camps, and on shipboard.... Each trade developed its own folklore—stories, songs, and heroes.[21]

Songs like *Cotton Needs Pickin'*, *The Boll Weevil Song*, *The Erie Canal*, *The Lumberman's Alphabet* give us an idea of what the preoccupations of the people were. In this respect the Cajun song is lacking.

The religious element is also absent from the collections of French songs in Louisiana. The one song that has a religious text and that is known by many

---

[19] Marguerite et Raoul d'Harcourt, *Chansons folklorique au Canada* (Québec, 1956), 55:

> ...nous de donnons aucun chant de labour.... Ici la carence est imputable au Canada. Les chants de labour y sont inconnues; il est vrai qu'ils s'étaient surtout développés en France dans des régions qui n'ont guère fourni d'émigrants au Nouveau Monde.

[20] Marie del Norte Thériot and Catherine B. Blanchet, *Les Danses Rondes, Louisiana French Folk Dances* (Abbeville, 1955), 12n30.

[21] Russell Ames, *The Story of American Folk Song* (New York, 1955), 171.

singers is *La Sainte Catherine* (or *Sainte Marguerite*). It recounts the story of the martyrdom of a christian princess whose pagan father tortures and kills her with a sword for having embraced the Christian religion. It is sung in a boisterous and often comical tone, and its refrain and rhythm suggest a dance or a march. The refrain is invariably Tara or Bara or *Para bourn, bourn, bourn*, with an additional *Ha, ha, ha!* or *A y yai, Ay yai!* In France and in Canada it is known as both a religious song and a round, while in Louisiana it has been known as a *danse ronde*, although it is not danced now too often.[22] Its character reflects a custom known in French tradition where many tragic or solemn religious songs were often sung on an air of gaiety. The practice of using profane melodies with sacred words was frequent in France. Some of the well known Christmas carols are still sung to tunes of jovial drinking songs and have refrains which are farcical and often licentious.[23]

One can occasionally hear some religious canticles in Louisiana. They are usually sung by elder ladies who learned them from French nuns during their school years in French convents. These songs, however, never achieved oral currency. In contrast to Louisiana, many known sacred songs and "miracles" have been collected in Canada.

The characteristic lack of religious songs in Louisiana may point toward the conflict which has confronted the Cajun in the matter of religious beliefs. Whitfield discussed in her *Louisiana French Folksongs* the "light-heartedness of the Cajun and his apparent lack of worry about the Lord."[24] In an article of the eighteen eighties, "The Teche Country of Fifty Years Ago," the following is stated:

> They were not a pious people, the men at any rate, in the estimation of the orthodox American. Indeed it was a common sentiment among them that "religion was a good thing for the wife and children, but for the man, no use," and in this respect they acted out their convictions by going with their families to church and waiting patiently outside until mass was over....[25]

Such an attitude is reminiscent of the traditional anti-clerical attitude in France. Although the men did not actually protest or fight against religion, it is probable that in any group situation, the men's obvious indifference to religion did not encourage singing of hymns or songs on religious subjects. And yet, religion was an extremely important factor in the life of a Cajun family and it was not a laughing matter. The early bayou folk were deprived for a long time of ministering of a priest for which they felt a great need. The women were

---

[22] Thériot and Blanchet, *Les Danses Rondes*, 20-21, 31.
[23] Julien Tiersot, *Histoire de la Chanson populaire en France* (Paris, 1889), 257. No French *Noels* have been recorded in Louisiana with the exception of those that have been learned in convents or from books.
[24] Irène Thérèse Whitfield, *Louisiana French Folk Songs* (Baton Rouge, 1939), 72.
[25] F.D. Richardson, "The Teche Country of 50 Years Ago," *Southern Bivouac* 4 (1885-1886): 595.

particularly sensitive to this situation and they did what they could to give their children a religious upbringing. There were never enough priests in the area even after the establishment of the first churches. Ambulant missionaries came from time to time, but could not reach all the families in the wilderness. Such conditions were propitious to adopting the custom practiced by the slaves of "jumping over the broom" ("sauter le manche à balai") as a symbol of getting married. In the absence of a priest, the young couple who contemplated marriage, held hands and jumped together over the broom that had been placed on the floor. This was considered a real marriage ceremony in the eyes of God and witnesses. When the priest finally arrived, months later, he performed the religious ceremony.[26] Many were the times when the missionary had to perform two ceremonies at once: the marriage and the baptism.

Abuse or irreverence toward clergy in such conditions would be unthinkable. The satirical type of song, mocking the man of the cloth, is not known in Louisiana. *Le petit Moine qui mignonnait* can serve as an example of transformation of lyrics that occurs. It is a known French song about a monk who helped his favorite "belle" milk a cow. The cow kicked the helpful monk, turned over the bucket and spilled the milk which spotted his black cassock in the process. The song usually starts:

> C'était un petit moine
> *It was a small monk*
> Qui d'amour vivait
> *Who lived for love*
> Qui allait voir sa belle (sa mie, les filles)...
> *Who would visit his belle (his friend, the girls)...*

In Louisiana the whole beginning disappears and the interest centers only around the action of milking the cow. Neither the monk nor the black cassock are mentioned. It becomes a simple little story of a frisky cow who spills the milk and whitens with it the black clothing of an unknown wearer; or the victim is whitened with milk and blackened with mud:

> elle m'a blanchi de lait
> *she whitened me with milk*
> elle m'a noirci de boue.
> *She blackened me with mud*[27]

---

[26] "Sauter le manche à balai" means today to start a common law marriage.

[27] The statements made by me pertaining to any comparative study of French and Canadian songs in this paper stem from my work in the Archives de Folklore of Laval University, Québec, Canada, where I spent many months doing research in preparation for my forthcoming book of songs collected in French Louisiana. In the Archives, under one roof, are gathered tape, manuscript, and printed French Canadian sources, a large collection of printed and manuscript microfilmed materials from France, a sizable tape and manuscript collection of Louisiana materials, and most important, an analytical card index of the materials. This card index is accompanied by transcribed texts of about 60,000 versions of 6,000 types of songs, classified and cross-filed according to Conrad Laforte's *Catalogue de la Chanson folklorique française* (Québec, 1958). I am

The fact that the Cajun does not sing songs ridiculing the clergy may point to the tolerant attitude of the priest toward his flock in French Louisiana. Satirical songs developed usually in places where the clergy exercised a strict control over their congregation. In such conditions, a biting song, aimed at the oppressor, serves to make the situation more bearable for the parishoner, and offers him an emotional release.[28]

The French priests who chose to minister to the colonists across the Atlantic were prompted to make this decision by a strong commitment to the cause of priesthood and by deep humanitarian convictions. There were practically no adverse reports about their conduct in Louisiana. The critical and mocking attitude that people assumed toward the men of cloth in France stemmed also from the fact that many clerics, because of their lack of calling for the priesthood, did not lead exemplary sacerdotal lives. Under the existing system in France during the "ancien regime," the estate and the title of the noble family was inherited by the eldest son, leaving nothing to the other children. Thus the younger sons, "les cadets de la famille," were often forced to embrace professions for which they were not suited and opted for the army or the ministry, where as a result, their services left much to be desired.

The Cajun may not worry too much about the Lord, but he does not scorn the Lord's protection. A Louisiana version of a well known marriage song invokes the Lord's blessings and arranges the text to read:

Que Dieu bénisse les amoureux
*May God bless the lovers*
Qui se mettent en ménage.
*Who get married*

No mention of the Lord was ever recorded in the variants collected in France. This substitution has already been noted in many versions in Canada and may have reached Louisiana in this way.

In another case, a Louisiana singer's imagination chose to end a song of a jilted girl, who killed her perfidious lover and then took her own life, with the admonition: "Recommandez-vous à Dieu," where the end of the European version offers a mere advice:

Restez, belle jeunesse, Fidèle à vos amours.
*Pretty young ones, remain faithful in love*

When the young men of English-Scottish-Irish extraction moved into the area and married young Cajun women, some of their attitudes left an imprint

---

greatly indebted to the Director of the Archives, Professor Luc Lacourcière, and to Professor Conrad Laforte for granting me access to the collection and for giving me their constant assistance without which my work would not have been possible.

[28] Mary Ann Griggs, *The Folk-Song in the Traditional Society of French Canada* (Sudbury, 1969), 18.

on the French Louisiana folk mores. The moral code of pioneer America was based on Calvinist and Puritan ideas. Any activity of the population was judged by the criteria of right and wrong according to the precepts of Puritanical protestant religion.

> The Protestant catalog of sins included love-making, drinking, gambling, playing fiddle, singing worldly songs, dancing, fishing on Sunday, and anything else a hysterical preacher could think of.[29]

The Cajun rejected almost all of the above taboos: he loves to drink, gamble, dance, sing, play the fiddle and fish on Sunday, but in the discussion of love-making he has undergone the Puritanical influence of his American neighbors. The freedom with which a French song treats matters of sex is missing in Louisiana. French song tradition on the American soil has been "censored both conscientiously and consciously."

Examples of this Puritanical attitude abound in the French Louisiana song, however, it would not be just to attribute the restrictive customs of the Cajuns to the American Puritan tradition only. This characteristic can be observed in the songs that came to Louisiana from French Canada. Coirault discusses this evolution as occurring in Canadian songs and he ascribes it to the chaste mores of the Canadian singers…or the first Canadian folksong collector.[30] He is obviously alluding to Gagnon who says the following in his *Chansons populaires du Canada*, published in 1865:

> Many of our songs are sung in France with lewd variants that are unknown in Canada. It is obvious that the work of expurgation must have been done….[31]

Gagnon states further that according to history only people of sterling character and exemplary mores were permitted to emigrate to Canada from France, and that "those whose virtue was questionable, seemed to have undergone purifying influences during the crossing" so as not to mar the early colony, which he compares to "a vast religious community."[32] A scrutiny of songs collected in the last half of our century in French Canada shows that only a part of the songs have been expurgated. Many songs have not undergone any changes and are conveyed with the same candour as in France. The censorship was due, as some writers have charged:

---

[29] Alan Lomax, *The Folk Songs of North America* (Garden City, 1960), 17.
[30] Patrice Coirault, *Formation de nos Chansons folkloriques*, 4 vols. (Paris, 1953), 1:105.
[31] Ernest Gagnon, *Chansons populaires du Canada* (Montréal, conforme à l'édition de 1880), P.X. The translation was done by the author.
[32] Ibid.

...[to] many constricting forces operating to limit the feeling of freedom and strength. Foremost of these was the Church which...pressured the peasant class with a Jansenist fear of sin and death. Many songs attest to this charge.[33]

Some substitutions may have been circumstantial. Since many of the collections in Canada have been made by priests or members of religious orders, it is entirely possible that the performers found it necessary to introduce changes so as not to offend the collectors' feelings.

Illustrations of expurgation occurring in Louisiana songs are abundant. The previously quoted song, about the jilted girl, *La Délaissée*, is startling in its naivete. Disappointed, sweet, young love that ends in murder and suicide is extremely farfetched under the circumstances, in which a young man forsakes a sixteen-year-old girl. Most of the French ballads of that type end in tragedy because the man grows tired of his sweetheart after he has taken advantage of her, particularly after he discovers that she is pregnant, and he abandons her. In that case the bereft girl's actions are the direct result of her desperation and/or vengeance. Nothing in the text of the Louisiana versions of *La Délaissée* justifies the violence of the ending. The strongest misdeeds of the suitor that the text mentions are "tes baisers trompeurs" and "tes fausses promesses" after which comes the shock:

> Elle est partie furieuse
> *She left furious*
> Elle a tué son amant
> *She killed her lover*
> Après, la malheureuse
> *Afterwards, poor lady*
> Z elle s'en a fait z autant.
> *She did the same*

Another ballad of jilted love, *The Butcher Boy*, which in many British and in some American variants alludes to the "babe that was not born" and to the "apron strings that are worn high" or "under the chin," makes no mention of pregnancy in Louisiana. In the same song when, before committing suicide, the young girl leaves a note to her parents and places it on her "poitrine," which may mean chest, bosom, or breast, the word is often replaced by "coeur." In some Canadian variants the singers went even further to replace "poitrine" by "estomac" which injects a ludicrous streak into the tragedy.

As a general rule, the Louisiana song does not mention any uncovered parts of the body. In an eighteenth-century literary song the young man sings to his beloved:

---

[33] Griggs, *Folk-Song in the Traditional Society of French Canada*, 12-13.

Si j'étais hirondelle
*If I was a swallow*
Que je puisse voler
*And I could fly*
Sur votre sein mam'selle
*On your breast, miss*
J'irais me reposer.
*I will rest*

In Louisiana this stanza became:

Si j'aurais des ailes
*If I had the wings*
De toutes les hirondelles,
*Of the swallows*
J'irais me reposer
*I would go and rest*
Sur le coeur de ma belle.
*On the heart of my love*

Or:
J'irais me reposer
*I would go and rest*
Près de toi, ma belle.
*Near you, my love*

The song *Le Galant qui voit mourir sa Mie* illustrates many instances of censorship. The young man comes to see his sweetheart early in the morning and finds her deathly ill. When after her death his mother sees him grieving, she tries to console him by telling him that he can find other girls to marry, namely the president's daughters who are rich. To this the bereaved cavalier answers:

J'aimerais mieux ma mie
*I would prefer my friend (girl)*
Nue dans sa chemise (or Nue sans sa chemise)
*Naked in her shirt (or Naked without her shirt)*
Que les filles du président
*Instead of the president's daughters*
Avec leur or et leur argent.
*With their silver and their gold*

The American folksinger went to great length in order to avoid discussion, the sweetheart's bedroom attire or lack of it. Some versions avoid the issue completely by having the young man say that he will never marry and will remain faithful to his lost love, other versions dress up the young girl in *her clothes* (son habit), or in a *chintz dress* (robe d'indienne). Three Louisiana variants situate her simply *in a house*:

> Maman, j'estimerais mieux
> *Mom, I'd rather see*
> De voir ma mi'dans sa (ma) maison-ze.[34]
> *My friend (girl) in my house*

One courageous singer finishes the song by:

> J'aime mieux la mienne,
> *I like mine better*
> La mienne qui est sans *chemise*,
> *The one who wears no shirt*

but he had taken the precaution to legalize the situation by adding this revealing verse in the beginning: "*Le premier soir des noces.*" This last example shows that the expression "sans chemise" was known by performers, but its use was obviously avoided.

In their *Chansons folkloriques françaises au Canada* the d'Harcourts discuss the Canadian version of this song as compared to some of the French variants, state that often the lovers spend the night together before the girl becomes gravely ill the next morning. This element is consistently rejected by both the Canadian and the Louisiana singers. As for the ending, the d'Harcourts note that the "galant" uses the same or a similar phrase in *all* the French versions: "J'estimerais mieux ma mie *nue en chemise*...."[35] The Canadian versions of this song are in this instance more faithfully reproduced and retain very often the classical French ending.

Very popular in Louisiana are the songs of "maumariés," mismatched or bad marriages, a genre which originated in medieval France and has remained typically French. One of these songs, known in Louisiana, *Le Mari de Quatre-Vingts Ans*, has been found in as early a source as a fifteenth-century French manuscript.[36] It tells the story of an unhappy young girl who is forced to marry an old man of eighty (or ninety) for his money. The day after the wedding the young bride complains to her father that during the wedding night her old bridegroom turned away from her. To her father's remark that such an old man will soon die and will leave her a rich widow, she answers:

> Au diable la richesse
> *To hell with riches*
> Quand le plaisir n'y est pas.
> *When there is no pleasure (joy) involved*

---

[34] The singers are careful to add the "ze" to "maison" in order to maintain the same ending of the verse as in "chemise."

[35] D'Harcourt, *Chansons folklorique au Canada*, 122.

[36] Gaston Paris, *Chansons du xv$^e$ Siècle*, publiées d'après le Manuscrit de la Bibliothèque Nationale de Paris [No. fr. 12744 (anc. suppl. fr. No. 168)], Paris, Société des Anciens Textes Français, 1885, p. 5, No. V. Music for the song is found on plate 3. The Louisiana versions follow closely the text quoted by Paris. The d'Harcourts, in *Chansons folklorique au Canada*, 261, mention this fifteenth-century song as recorded in the *Manuscrit de Bayeux*, Chanson XVII, Conti 6 and published by Théodore Gérold in *Chansons populaires des xv$^e$ et xvi$^e$ siècles avec leurs mélodies* (Strasbourg, 1910), 36.

When sung by white informants in Louisiana no reference is made to the scene during the wedding night, nor to the girl's answer. However, when collected from black informants, the two important motifs are retained. The explanation for this is furnished by Alan Lomax:

> The full weight of Puritanism did not fall upon the Negroes who came largely from cultures which placed a high value on erotic and aggressive behavior and which provided vivid outlets for them in song, dance and ceremonial. As slaves and later, as second-class citizens in the South they were not expected to conform rigidly to the conventions of harrassed whites.[37]

Related to the genre of "maumariés" are the lampooning songs treating the May-December marriage of a rich old widow with a young man, a type of song virtually unknown in American folklore. A few days after the wedding the old bride dies and the widower marries a young girl with the inherited money. The moral of the story is:

> Et quand on se marie avec des vieilles
> *And when you marry older women*
> On se marie bien plus souvent.
> *You marry well more often*

This type of song is a survival of the extremely popular subject in folk traditions of France. It retains the satirical and droll character, reminiscent of the *Fabliaux*, which is compatible with certain tendencies of the French temperament, but not American. The American custom approaching in mood this type of song is the "shivaree" which also comes from French traditions.

> "Charivari," American "shivaree." A French marriage-baiting custom dating from the Middle Ages. Originally common after all the weddings, then directed at unpopular or unequal matches as a form of public censure.... The constant element of shivaree has been the noise-making instruments.... Introduced to America by the French of Canada and Louisiana, where the name was corrupted into shivaree, the custom fitted into the frontier and backwoods pattern of rough horseplay and wild sports, especially in the South and the Middle West.[38]

In the description of the old woman who marries the young man there is neither charity nor pity; there is ridicule and derision in the enumeration of her old age infirmities. Every song quotes invariably the fact that she has only two or three teeth left in her mouth, which the intended demands to see. The singers seem to take a particular delight in describing vividly and with precision the condition of the old lady's remaining teeth:

---

[37] Lomax, *The Folk Songs of North America*, 19.
[38] *Standard Dictionary of Folklore, Mythology and Legend*, 2 vols. (New York, 1949), 1:212.

L'une branle, l'autre penche
*One is shaking the other is bending*
Et l'autre ne tient aucunement.
*And one can't stand at all*

Y en a une qui balance
*One is swinging*

L'autre qui fait gardin, gardin (garin, garon).
*The other does see-saw*
Une qui hausse et l'autre qui baisse
*One rises the other lowers herself*
Et l'autre qui garoche (branle, grouille), quand il fait vent.
*One throws when it is windy*

The misfortunes of old age are viewed in their comical aspect rather than sad or tragic and these descriptions are supposed to elicit laughter rather than understanding. The predilection for this type of song attests to the persistence of this trait of French character in the modern Cajun.

This tradition was greatly reinforced by the influence that came to Louisiana from the French islands in the Caribbean.

> ...on the plantations where Latin influences were dominant, in New Orleans and the urban communities of the Antilles, the satirical song was greatly in vogue...there is scarcely a doubt in my mind but that the penchant for musical lampooning which is marked among the black Creoles of the Antilles is more a survival of a primitive practice brought by their ancestors from Africa than a custom borrowed from their masters.[39]

> At their merry meetings and midnight festivals, they [the slaves] are not without ballads of another kind, adapted to such occasions, and here they give full scope to a talent for ridicule which is exercised not only against each other, but also, not infrequently, at the expense of their owner or employer.[40]

The fusion of French and African traditions left a permanent imprint in the form of satirical songs in French Louisiana.

There still remain in Louisiana marriage songs which used to have a function during the marriage ceremonies of yesteryear. These songs are an example of the blending of both cultures, American and French. Typically American is the concept of love, happiness, and hope in marriage. Although romantic love discovered in the age of medieval chivalry stems from Europe, marriage as a culmination of romantic love does not represent the point of view of French tradition. Among the upper classes and the bourgeoisie, as well as among the French Creoles in the colonies, the concept of marriage was a proper match which gave the couple material stability and social status, and assured the future of their

---

[39] Henry Krehbiel, *Afro-American Folksongs* (New York, 1914), 140-41.
[40] Ibid., 144.

children. For the French peasant marriage did not augur any happiness and this feeling is expressed in his songs. Van Gennep discusses lines of wedding songs addressed to the young couple enumerating worries, misery, and sadness that are awaiting them.[41] Tiersot states that in the folksong love and marriage are foreign and incompatible notions.[42] "Avoid marriages" is the refrain that Rossat heard over and over.[43] Another collector, Servettaz, reports:

> In our folksongs marriage is considered from a very pessimistic point of view. Thus only two out of about fifty songs of this type that we collected, refer to happiness in marriage. In all the others it is a regrettable event…more sorrow, grief, and trouble than joy or happiness. No longer any love in marriage; marriage killed all this.[44]

In the Louisiana songs pertaining to marriage all this was toned down or changed. Most of the lines predicting doom and spelling pessimism disappear. Statements of unhappiness are replaced by expressions of hope. The texts of the French songs which speak invariably of the unhappiness of the newlyweds have been changed. Statements of gloom have been replaced by expressions of hope. The following stanza:

> J'entends le rossignol chanter
> *I hear the nightingale sing*
> Qui dit dans son langage
> *In his tongue he is saying*
> Malheureux sont les amoureux
> *Sad are the lovers*
> Qui se mettent en ménage.
> *Who get married*

has become:
> J'entends le rossignol chanter
> *I hear the nightingale sing*
> Qui dit dans son langage
> *I hear the nightingale sing*
> Que Dieu hénisse les amoureux
> *May God bless the lovers*
> Qui se mettent en ménage.
> *Who get married*

This substitution is also very noticeable in the Canadian variants of the song. Verses promising love and lifetime devotion appear. However, the tune has not changed in Canada nor in Louisiana. Instead of the joyful and gay rhythms of a wedding song that we usually expect in the American culture, the melodies

---

[41] Arnold Van Gennep, *Manuel de Folklore français contemporain* (Paris, 1946), 515.
[42] Julien Tiersot, *Chansons populaires recueillies dans les Alpes françaises* (Grenoble, 1903), 260.
[43] Arthur Rossat, *La Chanson populaire dans la Suisse Roniande* (Bâle, 1917).
[44] Claudius Servettaz, *Vieilles Chansons savovardes* (Annecy, 1963), 18. The translation was done by the author.

are sad and dejected. Some collectors have interpreted it as the expression of the passing sadness of the bride in the moment of her departure. She seems to regret leaving her home, family and friends, and she is apprehensive about closing the door on her carefree youth and assuming the burden of responsibility that marriage represents. Doubtless these feelings are present, however, the doleful, melancholy music of the songs should be considered rather as a survival of the French folk tradition which reflected the misgivings and concern of a young couple in rural France of two centuries ago. The hard life of a peasant in France, the meager livelihood that the family anticipated, military service lasting many years, general privations and political insecurity that awaited the bride and groom, were not conducive to singing joyous wedding songs.

It was said that the European peasant did not compose protest songs. The mournful melody of the marriage song, while not an outspoken protest, seemed nevertheless to make known to all those who would listen, the "inferior and precarious position of the French peasant class"[45] during the "ancien régime." The contrast between this social class of French citizens of the past and the hardy and energetic Frenchman who found a home in the New World is striking. The latter had the initiative to reject anything which was conflicting with his psychology and to retain, adopt and/or develop customs that he found attractive. Thus the heritage of the New and the Old Worlds created a new personality which has taken its rightful place in the American culture.

*A wedding at New Iberia, ca. 1925. Courtesy of I. A. Martin Collection, Center for Louisiana Studies, University of Louisiana at Lafayette, accession number 1107.*

---

[45] *Standard Dictionary of Folklore, Mythology and Legend*, 2:1036.

# The Public and Private Domains of Cajun Women Musicians in Southwest Louisiana[1]

## Lisa E. Richardson

Until the women's movement brought gender issues into the limelight, the course of music history was often presented as an exclusively male domain. Women's role in creating, shaping, and performing music was largely overlooked. But within the past twenty years, women's music that was previously unknown to researchers, or undervalued and taken for granted by cultural insiders, has increasingly piqued interest. This rediscovery has yielded some unexpected and illuminating results for all involved.

The traditional music of southwest Louisiana's Cajun culture has also exploded into national attention within the past twenty years. Although most of the publicly accessible music is composed and performed by men, some Cajun women participate both in the private, home-based musical tradition and in an increasingly audible public side.

### The Private Domain of Cajun Music

Since the time of the *Grand Dérangement* when the Acadians were expelled from Nova Scotia, there have been French Louisiana songs and ballads which were sung, usually unaccompanied, for pleasure within the home among family and friends. Older relatives taught these songs directly to the younger generation, or children picked them up as they were performed as entertainment during family soirées. These include songs that recall the terrible hardships of the trip from Acadie, social drinking songs, call-and-response children's songs, and humorous epics about the various predicaments of romantic love. These "home songs" are basically a separate repertoire from Cajun dancehall music, although some dance band pieces naturally cross over into the private domain.

Various aspects of home songs, such as their rhythmic subtlety, subject matter, or length, make them more appropriate for intimate performances than for performances with a band at large gatherings. For example, many of these songs are in modes other than the usual major or minor, or may change mode mid-song—something a band does not usually do. Since these were usually solo performances, singers could take rhythmic liberties and stretch out or quicken a phrase according to their feelings. These were songs to be listened to rather than danced to, so the poetry was in some cases more elaborate and descriptive and the songs were often longer than their counterparts in the dance repertoire.

---

[1] This article first appeared in the 1991 Louisiana Folklife Festival booklet.

One genre of traditional songs provided a link between the dance band and home songs: the "reels à bouche," similar to Celtic "mouth music." These were tunes that were sung to accompany round dances during Lent when instrumental performances were not allowed. The verses and meters of these pieces are generally simpler than those of the home music, but they are still a more private mode of expression than the dancehall numbers.

Both home songs and round dance songs were orally transmitted. The only people who learned these pieces were those who had the opportunity to hear them in person repeatedly, usually from a relative. In this way, the songs were given a kind of personal ownership within families. For instance, Tante Emedine might sing the epic love song "Isabeau," one or two musically inclined nieces might learn it, and although other versions may exist, no one outside of the extended family would know it in quite the same form. The shared knowledge of these songs acted as a glue which strengthened family and cultural bonds.

Although women dominated the home music repertoire, it was not always exclusively their domain. Older performers in their seventies and eighties have cited many examples of men enthusiastically joining in the singing of home songs, although not as often as women. Unfortunately, members of this older generation of singers were rarely documented during their lifetimes. Today, however, some men, like Sullivan Aguillard of Oberlin, continue to sing traditional ballads and help to keep the tradition alive.

Social pressure has played an important role in women's performance of music. Cajun men have always had the option of public performances without risking much social stigma. Women, on the other hand, have usually been emphatically discouraged, in both subtle and overt ways, from bringing their musical

Allen C. Redwood's sketch of "a young matron" from the prairie country of southwestern Louisiana, ca. 1879.
From R. L. Daniels, "The Acadians of Louisiana," *Scribner's Monthly* 19 (1879-1880): 387.

talents into a public arena. This may be one reason that the home songs flourished particularly among women as an outlet for artistic expression. Cajun women have, more often than not, chosen to express their musicality in the most socially acceptable manner available to them, among family and friends.

These home songs provided both entertainment and a way of reciting oral history. With the advent of mass media, however, these purposes began to fade in importance. Unlike dance music which thrived along with the phonograph and radio, home songs' popularity declined as technological advances offered new possibilities for entertainment in less time-consuming, less energy-taxing ways. Only as these songs have teetered on the edge of extinction have they begun to receive the attention they deserve.

Up until around the 1930s to 1950s, the home songs and the dancehall songs existed as complementary repertoires within the culture—the home songs acting as an ancient base anchoring Cajun culture in the past and providing some material upon which modern Cajun composers could draw. It seems this anchor is slipping away with each passing generation. Perhaps these songs are no longer relevant to modern life in the context in which they were originally performed.

Some notable women performers, however, have continued the tradition of home music, sometimes bringing their songs into the public arena through recordings and performances at festivals. For example, the late Lula Landry of Abbeville had an incredible repertoire of home songs, most of which she learned before the age of fifteen from her Tante Olympe who would sing to Lula during their catechism lessons. Lula was a musical sponge and could learn a piece on first hearing no matter who or what the source was. In fact, her husband's big band used to use her as a human tape recorder when they went to clubs to hear other bands. On the way home, Lula would sing the tunes that they had heard that evening to the members of the band, and in this way they could learn new pieces without having to invest in sheet music.

Inez Catalon is a Creole woman from Kaplan and is another wellspring of home music with a repertoire and a style completely different than Lula's. Inez learned many of her songs from her mother at the hearth of their home—the same home Inez resides in today. Inez is a chameleon of style. Not only can you hear her mother's heart-wrenching voice through hers, but she can also become the voice of Jimmie Rodgers and many of the popular radio stars of the early part of this century. Inez is a vibrant tell-it-like-it-is character with a wealth of music, jokes, and stories within her. (Inez died in November 1994).

Other cultures, such as those in Bulgaria and England, have rescued much of their time-honored music from extinction by reinterpreting it for modern society and reclaiming it as their own. Perhaps families no longer have the inclination to entertain each other with song. But the lyrics—about love, pain, loss, struggle, joys—are still pertinent to modern life, and the melodies, with their modal complexities and non-standard meters, are still as beautiful as ever. It is time to unearth this buried treasure. Today, there is an increased interest in women singers and their home-based music. For example, Ann Savoy's upcoming volume two of her series of books on Cajun musicians will focus on women performers.

### The Public Domain

Historically, Cajun women have been discouraged from public performance. According to many men and women in French Louisiana, the dancehall stage of the past was not considered a place for "decent" women to be. As has been the case in many other societies throughout time, certain false assumptions and misconceptions have arisen concerning the morals of women who perform in public. There have been exceptions, the most famous of which is Cleoma Breaux Falcon who performed with her husband Joe Falcon from the late 1920s until her death in 1941. She was a curiosity, yet she was considered "safe" since she was with her husband.

Only in recent times have women ventured into the spotlight to be the center of a group's attention on a solo instrument, or even the leader of a group instead of an innocuous part of the whole. Becky Richard, for example, is a young Cajun guitarist and singer from Church Point who has regularly performed with her accordionist father Pat over the past several years. It was actually Becky who was the motivating force behind reviving her father's musical talent. She convinced him to dust off the accordion in his closet and join her in performing the music of their heritage. Becky has a beautiful, soulful voice and a talent for songwriting.

Cankton accordionist Sheryl Cormier has been a pioneer for the cause of Cajun women's public performance for years. She is a powerful and exciting performer who was a natural on her instrument at an early age, a talent she believes was inherited from her father. In the mid-1980s, she formed the first all women Cajun band. Since then she has been the leader of a band including her husband, Russell on vocals and their son, Russell Jr., on drums.

Guitarist and singer Ann Savoy, although not a native of Acadiana, is another champion of Cajun music, not only on stage but on paper. She performs across the country at festivals and in clubs with her husband, Eunice accordionist Marc Savoy, and is also the author of the book *Cajun Music: A Reflection of a People*. The Savoys prefer to perform a style of Cajun music older than the styles used by many of the dancehall bands of today. They usually choose to perform in a trio format of accordion, guitar, and fiddle, and avoid electric instruments altogether.

Sheryl Cormier avec les Musicians Cajuns at Cankton, Louisiana, dancehall, 1985. From left to right, Emily Moore, Sheryl Cormier, Bonnie Smith, Teddie Meche, and Becky Richard.
*Courtesy of Johnnie Allan.*

The women performers of Cajun music have struggled with their art—struggled to be taken seriously as musicians and struggled through the suspicions of others. Through this struggle they are paving the way, hopefully, for future women performers to follow the path that they have opened.

*A Brief Discography*
Inez Catalon:
> *Zodico: Louisiana Creole Music* (Rounder Records)
> *Louisiana Creole Music* (Folkways Records)
> *J'Etais au Bal: Music from French Louisiana* (Swallow Records)

The Hoffpauir Family and others:
> *Louisiana Creole and Cajun Music 1934: The Lomax Recordings* (Swallow Records)
> Odile and Solange Falcon, *J'ai ete au Bal, vol. 1* (Arhoolie Records)

Recordings of women dancehall performers:
> Becky Richard, several 45s on Lyric Records
> Sheryl Cormier, *La Reine de Musique Cadjine* (Swallow Records)
> Ann Savoy, many recordings with the Savoy-Doucet Band (Arhoolie Records)

Zydeco recordings of female performers:
> Ann Goodly, *Miss Ann Goodly and the Zydeco Brothers* (Maison de Soul)
> Queen Ida, *Queen Ida and the Bon Temps Band in New Orleans* (GNP Crescendo)
>> *Zydeco a la Mode* (GNP Crescendo)
>> *Zydeco* (GNP Crescendo)

Queen Ida was one of the earliest female zydeco artists to experience broad success through her recordings.
*Courtesy of Cajun and Creole Music Collection, Edith Garland Dupré Library Special Collections, University of Louisiana at Lafayette.*

# Grand Texas: Accordion Music and Lifestyle on the Cajun Frontière[1]

## Carl Lindahl

Twice exiled—from France and from Canada—the Cajuns (or Cadiens or Acadiens) began arriving in Louisiana in the second half of the eighteenth century. A tradition current among contemporary Cajuns holds that their ancestors chose the swamps of Louisiana and the desolation of its prairies because they were determined not to be exiles again: with no neighbors, one has no enemies. But eventually, inevitably, as they fanned westward across the plains of the United States, the Cajuns crossed paths with English speakers. This happened near the Sabine River which marks the present-day border of Texas and Louisiana.

Many contemporary anthropologists hold that we learn most about a culture from its borders with other cultures. Threatened with an alien lifestyle, a people will tend to reinforce its own. If this is true, the experience of Cajuns and Texans—and particularly that group of people who call themselves Texas Cajuns—will ultimately reveal not only something of the history and nature of the conflicts between the two groups, but also something otherwise extremely difficult to grasp concerning the nature of Cajun culture as a whole.

At first glance Texas seems to figure purely as an evil force in Cajun culture. Along the Sabine River, the Texas-Louisiana equivalent of the Rhine, incendiary words have been exchanged about who is and who isn't Texan, who is and who isn't Cajun. In 1981, when I first visited this *frontière*, being Cajun was just beginning to be chic with the American population at large, and it was just beginning to be acceptable to many of the Anglo-Americans in East Texas, who leaned heavily on the expletive "coon-ass" to describe Cajuns. This term carries approximately the same force as "nigger" or "wetback;" it's something one Cajun may sometimes call another and get away with, but outsiders who are respectful don't use it. About that time, the legendary Cajun fiddler Dewey Balfa was performing in Texas, and someone in the audience called out to him, "Get down, Coon-ass!" Dewey shot back, "The only difference between a Coon-ass and a horse's ass is the Sabine River!" This, my first impression of Texan-Cajun relationships, was memorably negative.

Looking more closely at the Texas-Louisiana *frontière*, I found a good deal of resentment and rivalry from the Louisiana side. Texas has its reputation for

---

[1] This article first appeared in *The French American Review* 62 (1991): 26-36. The author wishes to thank Pat Jasper and Texas Folklife Resources for convening the conference on Texas's accordion traditions, where this paper was first presented; Clyde Vincent and Les Acadiens de Texas for putting up with many stupid questions; and Barry J. Ancelet for providing ten years of insight into the nature of Cajun culture.

size and boasting about size, and Louisiana Cajuns—like Arkansawyers and Oklahomans and other people who have to live next to Texans—have their jokes about that too. The Cajun jokes carry an added vehemence, however, because the French American minority tends to view giant Texas as representing all English-speaking Americans—thus as a powerful and unsympathetic force. Older Cajuns remember when they called all English speakers, "Américains," as if to say that they themselves were not, that the Cajuns were as much exiles in Louisiana as they had earlier been exiles from France and Canada. In one tall tale told by the great Cajun narrator Tanis Faul—and recently published in Barry Ancelet's book *Cajun Country*—

> there were two friends, but one of them was a terrible liar. So [of course] the big liar went to Texas. He decided he would go to live in Texas. So he tells the other one, "Come live with me. Let's go live in Texas. There's good land there. Great crops are possible there." [The liar eventually came back to visit Louisiana and he told the Louisiana man] "Come to Texas, that's where the good land is.... I'll tell you one thing.... There's a man who grew a head of cabbage...he has one hundred sheep and the hundred sheep sleep in the shade under that big head of cabbage."
>
> The Louisiana man said to him, "Well that's surely a nice head, I imagine." [But he is growing tired of the liar and he wants to go home; so he says,] "I saw fifty men making a pot...each with a hammer so far apart that they couldn't hear each other striking the pot."
>
> The Texas liar asks, "why the hell did they waist to build such a big pot?"
>
> "Well," he said, "to cook your head of cabbage!"
>
> That gave him a chance to go [home].[2]

This is a far milder putdown than Dewey Balfa's horse's ass remark, but it too betrays a sense of rivalry.

I hadn't yet heard anything good about Texas in Cajun culture when I was told of a Louisiana Cajun who had a pond on his farm. In the middle of that pond he'd made a little island shaped like Texas. It seemed to me that I'd finally found a positive Cajun image of Texas until I was told that the pond itself had been dug in the shape of Louisiana. In one farmer's visible compensation fantasy, the much smaller state had surrounded and overwhelmed the Anglo giant.

Something is going on with these stories and instills and images, something more than a friendly rivalry, but also something more than a rivalry. Texas Cajuns have a long history of their own, a history with some very special cultural weight, a history that has created a mystique—both in their minds and in the minds of the kin they've left behind in Louisiana.

---

[2] In Barry Jean Ancelet, Jay Edwards, and Glen Pitre, eds., *Cajun Country* (Jackson, 1991), 205-06.

One place to discover the roots of the mystique is its folksong. Although until recently the Cajuns were illiterate in then native French, they were far from unartistic. They created a rich body of oral poems sung to traditional tunes. The older ballads were sometimes performed by solo voice, but the songs that people danced to were accompanied by instruments: often the fiddle, but most notably the accordion, which has provided the signature sound of Cajun music. Within a generation of the invention of the diatonic accordion (in Vienna in 1828), these ponderous but durable instruments had found their way into Cajun Louisiana. By the end of the nineteenth century, the accordion was essential to Cajun musical style.

One of the four or five most popular songs of the great Cajun accordion revival was Aldus Roger's *Grand Texas*. Pumped at a furious pace with Roger's legendary precision, it is perfectly representative of the "new" accordion sound that hit Cajun music in the 1950s. But more of that later. First, consider the words:

| | |
|---|---|
| Tu m'as quitté pour t'en aller au Grand Texas | You've left me to go away to Big Texas |
| t'en aller aussi loin avec un autre; | to go so far away with another man; |
| Criminelle, comment je vas faire moi tout seul? | No-good-woman, how will I manage all alone? |

The theme of the Cajun girl lost to a Texan lover is widespread—and not entirely true. Louisiana men I've talked to insist that they've lost few if any Cajun women to Texas men. But there is a certain reality imbedded in the song's romantic imagery. This song, like many of its time, presents Texas both as a land of opportunity and a place of painful separation. Those who go there may do well; those left behind inevitably mourn. This mixed message reflects a long history of the Cajun settlement of East Texas.

Consider these lyrics from another Cajun folk song about Texas[3]—

| | |
|---|---|
| Quand j'ai quitté la Louisiane | When I left Louisiana |
| Pour aller dans le Texas | to go to Texas |
| Ma pauvre maman s'est mise à pleurer. | My poor mother started to cry. |
| A m'a tant demandé a dit: | She begged me and begged me. |
| "Mon cher garcon fais pas ça; | "My dear boy, don't do that; |
| ça va finir de me tuer. | that will end up killing me. |

—and a third song:[4]

---

[3] Irene Thérèse Whitfeld, *Louisiana French Folk Songs* (Baton Rouge, 1939), 93-94.
[4] Whitfield, *Louisiana French Folk Songs*, 94-96.

| | |
|---|---|
| J'ai pris ce char ici, belle, | I took this car, belle, |
| pour m'en aller au Texas belle; | to go to Texas belle; |
| Il y avait just trois jours, belle, | I'd just been there, belle, |
| que j'étais là-bas, belle, | three days, belle. |
| J'ai reçu une lettre de toi, belle, | When I received a letter from you, belle, |
| que tu étais bien malade belle… | saying you were very sick belle… |

These songs depict Texas as the force that tears women away from men, parents, from children, condemning those left in Louisiana to die of sorrow. Not good press for Texas—but not altogether inaccurate as a description of families divided by migration across the Sabine River.

Cajuns didn't come to Texas for men, but in stages for the two things that outsiders most strongly associate with Texas: cattle and oil. As early as the 1830s, before there was a Republic—let alone a state—of Texas, Cajuns were expanding their settlements from the marshy prairies of Louisiana to similar terrain in Texas. The people who first came were most often males, members of working communities—people whose presence in Texas meant that they'd left Louisiana families behind.

The Texas frontier, like other American frontiers, offered great economic opportunity at the cost of community. Because Cajun Louisiana was—and remains—one of the most family centered cultures imaginable, economic gain can never fully compensate for loss of family. The songs reflect such a philosophy. Just as in the romanticized film, *Belizaire the Cajun* (which tells the story of a nineteenth-century Cajun who fled to Texas for refuge from the law), Texas was both the home of the outlaw and the site of abandonment. Clearly, these sung images possess real-life historical roots.

The second Cajun exodus also began with male workers. With the discovery of oil at Spindletop in East Texas in 1901, there was an immediate demand for dirty oil field work, and Cajuns were among the most numerous of the populations that moved in to take advantage of the situation. Though this began a workers' migration, it led to a greater degree of family settlement than ranching had before. Many families were split up in this and subsequent settlements, but now there were established populations of Cajuns on both sides of the Sabine: in moving from Louisiana to Texas, settlers were joining a newborn Cajun community as well as leaving one behind.

This history made it clear to me why in Lafayette—situated as it is at the center of Louisiana Cajun culture—people called Texas "Cajun Lapland," and considered it a place where people occasionally disappear and from which they never return.

Such was the alienating image of Texas I took with me. In 1982, when I went for the first time to visit "Les Acadiens de Texas," a group based principally in Beaumont and Port Arthur that meets once a month in the small town of Nederland. I'd expected they'd feel like waifs or refugees. But that simply was not the case. When I started asking them how it felt to live in Cajun Lapland, they looked at me curiously. And one of them told me, "We're not Cajuns first and Texans second. We're not Texans first and Cajuns second. We're Texas Cajuns. Period." There is a palpable pride in both affiliations.

As we talked on, I found that most of them still had family in Louisiana, but many had been Texans all their lives, and some traced their Texas roots well back into the nineteenth century. They found Texas acceptable in every respect, except one: unlike Louisiana, whose French population and New Orleans Mardi Gras tradition are sufficiently strong to affect state law, Texas has no legal Mardi Gras holiday. "It's a damn shame to have to call in sick, then drive to the next state to celebrate Mardi Gras. That's unholy," one man told me. Even in the midst of community solidarity, there is the continual knowledge that Texas Cajuns are a minority culture whose values and habits, work and play schedules will never be reflected in the surrounding culture.

For their part, Texas Cajuns have their own mystique about Louisiana—though its not as overwhelming or forbidding as the reverse image. Louisiana is the motherland—revered, respected, but not often mythologized. Like urban

Wildcatters at an oil derrick near New Iberia, Louisiana, ca. 1930. Courtesy I.A. Martin Collection, Center for Louisiana Studies, University of Louisiana at Lafayette, accession number 1296.

ethnic populations throughout the United States, Texas Cajuns talk at length about the towns across the water where their parents were born. Yet I've found little impulse among Texas Cajuns to visit those sites, unless living relatives were there. As one older Cajun told me, "I'd just as soon stay at home as see the world, but there's no place I wouldn't go to see my son." Family more than statehood, more than language, is the glue of Cajun social relations.

Leaving behind the song lyrics and the migrations for a moment, consider some cultural and musical influences that worked the other way, riding the winds of acculturation from Texas to Louisiana. One more reason why Cajuns might view Texas not merely as alien, but as antagonistic: Texas was known as the place that nearly took the French language and the accordion out of Cajun music. In the 1930s and 1940s Cajun musical culture went through a period of serious assimilation. As modern paved roads carved up the prairies and bayous, as teachers in the state-supported school systems began to teach exclusively in English, it was no longer acceptable to be French. Deeply influenced by the English-speaking majority, Cajuns began to perform and record their songs in English. The greatest outside influence of all was Texas Swing. As the entire nation fell under the influence of Texas "cowboy" music, Bob Wills and his Texas Playboys became such a presence among Cajuns that bands all over Louisiana paid the Playboys the ultimate tribute of taking their name: there were the Lafayette Playboys, the Duson Playboys, the Evangeline and Eunice and Ville Platte Playboys.

At first all the Playboy bands were string bands. The fiddle dominated, the accordion disappeared. While Cajun violin was easily integrated into the country sound, the accordion was not. The accordion produced a marked sound, a sonic symbol of all that was backward, all that didn't fit in—all those parts of Cajun culture that many now wished to leave behind. Cajuns started to call accordion music chanky chank: "trivial" or "irritating noise." And, at least for awhile, most Cajun musicians abandoned it. Joe Bonsall, one of the great *joueurs d'accordeon* (accordion players) who played Texas halls, recalls a time in the 1940s when there were no more than three men regularly playing the accordion in East Texas—"and I was one of them," he remembers proudly.

The fiddle so dominated the Cajun music of the forties that, to this day, most Texans think of Cajun music especially as fiddle music. They think of Harry Choates, Frenchie Burke, Doug Kershaw. In any East Texas dancehall where the strains of Western Swing predominate and the "Cotton-Eyed Joe" is danced, the band is likely to play at least a couple of Cajun waltzes. If the band knows only one Cajun number, it is *Jolie Blonde*.

Often called the Cajun national anthem, *Jolie Blonde* became nationally popular when played by Texas Cajun Harry Choates. Choates was an immigrant: born in Rayne, Louisiana, he moved to East Texas in the 1940s and began to compose tunes named after the towns where he so often played, tunes like the "Austin Special" and the "Port Arthur Blues." Choates did something with the music that would have been unthinkable two decades earlier. His version of *Jolie Blonde* had no accordion part. Recorded for Houston-based Gold Star Records, this fiddle-dominated *Jolie Blonde* has stayed in the East Texas repertoire for nearly half a century. But Choates' French singing did not. Along with the accordion, it disappeared. Moon Mullican, who could make no sense out of the French lyrics, recorded his own strange English version in 1946, and that one is still sung today at Western Swing dances.

The accordion had been nearly banished from the dancehalls and was entirely absent from recordings by 1948, when Louisiana legend Iry LeJeune recorded *La Valse de pont d'Amour* (Love Bridge Waltz), which brought Cajuns of the postwar generation—growing finally and rapidly tired of cultural assimilation—back to the accordion. If *Jolie Blonde* is the Cajun national anthem, the "Love Bridge Waltz" is the Cajun accordion national anthem. Accordion players on the *frontière* still feel a particular debt to Iry LeJeune and a special regard for that particular waltz.

Now the accordion has re-entered Texas, sounding the forceful signal that Cajuns—or at least some of them—wish to practice their culture on their own terms, rather than on those defined by dominant Anglo trends. At the Elks Club in Beaumont and the Rodair Club outside Port Arthur, it has been years since anyone suggested that it would be possible to have Cajun music without the accordion. Without the accordion, Cajun music is now simply called Country Music. Diris Thibodeaux has been taking tickets and waiting tables at the Rodair for twenty-six years. When I asked her if any bands had played there without accordions, she answered, "We booked a couple of country bands some years back; but nobody came to listen. People expect to hear *Cajun* music here." The accordion has become one of the surest measures of Cajun culture on its Texas frontière.

Asked to describe Cajun accordion music in one phrase, the best I could do is to call it music that works—in just about every sense of the term. In terms of projecting sound through a crowded noisy dancehall, the accordion works—one of its greatest assets in the days before electronic amplification was its ability to deliver pure, raw, loud sound.

In terms of taking punishment, the accordion works. There is a famous scene in a film titled "French Dance Tonight" in which Louisiana accordion maker Mark Savoy throws his accordion on the ground and stands on it, kicking some sheep dung on it in the process, as he says, "These things are...

indestructible.... Oh, I got a little bit of sheep shit on it. I guess that won't hurt it either."[5]

In terms of making musicians sweat as much as frenzied dancers, the accordion works. A macho image follows the Cajun accordion. I've seen older players point to their arm muscles and smile. The late Nathan Abshire would make a great point by playing an enormous accordion for hours while standing up and without a shoulder strap. The esthetic for such young players as Wayne Toups of the ZydeCajun band is to play in an undershirt or muscle shirt, with a sweat band around the forehead and to work the accordion until the player has driven himself and the dancers to the verge of exhaustion.

And in terms of making people who work hard play hard, the accordion works. It works especially well for people who do almost everything to the limit—and that's the way that a great many Cajuns describe their lifestyle.

The association between the accordion and hard work is one that's been well cultivated by many of the players I have talked to. The first story ever told me by one accordion player about another illustrates what I mean.

Felix Richard was talking about his personal hero, Iry LeJeune, the man whose *Valse de Pont d'Amour* returned the accordion to Cajun music: Iry was poor, like most of the great musicians. And parents didn't want their kids to be musicians, they wanted them to work, to grow up to make an honest living. But Iry was almost blind—and he couldn't see well enough to pick cotton well. While grabbing for the cotton he'd leave too many of the fibers clinging to the boles. So the family finally let him play because he couldn't do any other work. Playing became his work. He'd play while they worked—and of course he went on to be the greatest player there was.

Often parents frowned deeply on their sons' attempts to play accordion. Children would have to work and scheme very hard just to find the time to practice. In Barry Ancelet's and Elemore Morgan's masterful study of *The Makers of Cajun Music*, Nathan Abshire tells of his struggle to play the accordion.

> I was six years old. I started playing on an accordion that cost three and half dollars. It wasn't mine. It was for one of mine uncles. He lived at home, and there was this little old armoire, but there were these marks that he would put it between, and I didn't know that. I couldn't see those marks, and when he left to go to work, I'd get it to play. When he'd come back at noon, he'd take off his belt, Jack. He'd give me a licking, and he really could whip! Listen! But I never gave up. At noon, he'd leave again and I'd grab it again. At night, when he came hack home he'd check it again. When it wasn't in the same place, he'd give me another licking. Then he finally gave up and gave it to me.[6]

---

[5] Les Blank, director, *French Dance Tonight*, PBS television program broadcast 1990; condensed from Blank's longer film, *J'ai Été au Bal*.
[6] Barry J. Ancelet and Elemore Morgan, *The Makers of Cajun Music: Musiciens cadiens et créole* (Austin, 1984), 101.

One reason why families made their children work so hard to get to play the accordion lies in its role as chaperone. In traditional Cajun culture, dance music and courtship went hand and hand. There was no courtship without dancing. But the men who made the music were paradoxically excluded from the courtship process. They were the only single adults who were not courting. As much as his music was respected, the musician often was not—to the point that he remained single. In more conservative Cajun communities, married men weren't supposed to make music. A newly married musician would put up the accordion and might not play it again until decades had passed and his children had grown.

Thus Cajun music has led a curious double life. In some senses music is a member of the family: learned at home, passed down from parents and uncles to sons and nephews, always in the background during courtship, always playing at the wedding dance. The music is always honored. The amateur family musician is always honored. But the professional musician was the exception—he could become an outsider, and as long as he remained a professional he was likely to remain unmarried, a man without a family.

These old conceptions have not entirely died out. The best and most traditional of today's Cajun bands, like those of the past, are filled with great musicians who really don't make a living playing music. It remains part of country Cajun lifestyle to be a jack of all trades—and master of all. The culture prides itself on how highly successfully it adapted to both the extremes of Nova Scotia cold and Louisiana heat, both the landless world of the bayous and the endless plains of the prairies.

By the same token, Cajun men value versatility and resourcefulness in making a living. It is more common than not for country Cajuns to have more than one occupation. A man who is a car mechanic may also farm a crop, flood his field to raise crawfish after the harvest, and play accordion at a local dancehall every Saturday night. As one Cajun told me, "I've got one employer. That's enough for any man. But I've got a dozen jobs—and I'm my own boss on all the rest." To give one further example, the great accordion player Don Montoucet of Scott, Louisiana, is a master mechanic, carpenter, electrician, welder, plumber, mason, and school bus driver.[7]

Cajun musicians pride themselves in being survivors. Perhaps the idea of the professional musician is offensive to some, not because there's anything wrong with being a musician, but because there's something wrong with being exclusively a musician. It's not smart to put all your money on one horse.

Accordion music remains a major factor in the lives of many of the hundreds of thousands of Cajuns who now live in Texas, most of them along the Gulf Coast between the Sabine River and Houston. Just as the accordion

---

[7] Ibid., 62.

has long served to divide Cajuns from non-Cajuns, it can reveal certain things about the ways in which people have retained or failed to retain their Cajun traditions. Speaking very generally, it's possible to divide music-loving Texas Cajuns into two groups, recreation Cajuns and full-time Cajuns.

The former are more numerous. These are people of Cajun origin who are very proud of their ethnicity, but who no longer live in Cajun communities. They make Cajun music part of their play lives, but by and large they don't speak French. Pressured by their parents into the melting pot, they were brought up with the goal of assimilating with mainstream American culture, and many of them succeeded beyond their wildest dreams—sometimes, as well, far beyond their real hopes. Because Cajun culture has always been an essentially rural culture, Cajuns migrating to the larger cities lost their community identity rather quickly.

The center of recreational Cajun culture in Texas is Houston, where more than 100,000 people of Cajun descent may be found. Unlike French-speaking blacks, who maintained their community identity—at least for awhile—in the urban setting, Cajun Houstonians did not create extensive urban neighborhoods. For many, just coming to the city was a commitment to a new lifestyle—a lifestyle that abandoned many traditional values.

Martha C. is one of the many Houstonians of Cajun descent whom I have gotten to know. Born in Port Arthur around 1940, she heard her parents speak French often, but they refused to speak it to her. In their minds, being Cajun was two strikes against their daughter. They had hopes for her education and success. Therefore, not only French, but merely speaking English with a Cajun accent was forbidden. And taking part of the Cajun musical culture was associated with the same cultural stigma. Martha heard about the Rodair Club often, but in her parents' opinion it wasn't a place where the better people went, and to this day she's never gone.

In many respects she remained a Cajun. Martha married and divorced a Cajun man, and on her second marriage joined another Cajun family. [Family ties are the last things to go, if one is Cajun.] But her husbands, like her, felt embarrassed about certain aspects of the Cajun tradition. It was only in the 1980s, when being Cajun became not only acceptable but enviable to Americans at large, that Margaret turned back to her roots, started seeking out accordion bands, listening to the music, asking her older relations to speak to her in French. Now she is both excited and mournful about the past that she wishes she hadn't left so far behind.

There are many Houston Cajuns like Martha, who are now being more Cajun than they ever have before. Many of them can be found any given Saturday afternoon at P T's (or *Petit's*) Cajun Bar-B-Q House, just south of Houston, near Ellington Air Force Base. This is the club closest to the center of

Houston that plays Cajun music regularly, but it only hosts Cajun bands once a month. Far more frequently, at least once a week, P T's presents a non-Cajun French-American musical tradition from Louisiana: zydeco, a mixture of blues, jazz, and French folksong performed by African Americans.

What happens at P T's every Saturday is in many ways typical of the recreational Cajun lifestyle. Established in an area where many Cajuns had migrated during World War II to work in the petroleum and shipbuilding industries, P T's has always had a core of French-speaking, rural, old-time Cajun clients. But its proximity to Houston cast an urban influence on it, and attracted so many recreational Cajuns, as well as outsider fans of Louisiana music, that the black zydeco tradition, which has always had a stronger hold on Houston, came to dominate the entertainment. Zydeco, with its obvious blues and jazz connections, lured many younger Cajuns, just as had been the case in Lafayette and New Orleans, where many fans simply don't distinguish between Cajun and zydeco music. To them, it's all French music, it's all good. And as much as the musicians themselves know the difference between the two styles, it simply doesn't matter to most of the urban crowd.

On a typical Saturday afternoon at P T's Cajun Bar-B-Q you will hear L.C. Donato or Wilbert Thibodeaux playing zydeco for a crowd perhaps one quarter Cajun, one quarter black Creole, and half fans with no French background who simply love the music. On the dance floor both Cajun and zydeco two-steps can be seen, along with much free-form wriggling by those who haven't mastered the two-step. There are line dances, shuffles, and circle dances in which blacks and whites join together, in a way that one won't find in the rural Cajun dancehalls. There's something very exciting going on here, a process of fast-paced cultural-blending, or creolization. Yet the Cajun accordions are missing, as in traditional Cajun music.

Of Texas' enormous Cajun population, there is a relatively small percentage that I would identify as full-time Cajun, but it is an extremely vital group. Full-time Cajuns are concentrated in far East Texas, an area called the Golden Triangle, in the countryside and in the three cities of Orange, Beaumont, and Port Arthur. The southern half of Jefferson County, where the majority is French-American, marks the heart of Texas Cajun country. Traditional Cajun music is often heard at the Elk Lodge in Beaumont or, most especially, the Rodair Club in Port Arthur which to my mind is the hub of Cajun music in Texas.

Two migrations from the second quarter of this century created the backbone of the Rodair's clientele. The earlier influxes had consisted principally of working men, but from the 1930s forward, whole families formed the bulk of the migration. The Great Depression drew many Louisiana farmworkers, sharecroppers who grew and harvested cotton and rice. It was still a frontier adventure to cross the Sabine River in the 1930s. The trail from Louisiana to Port Arthur followed many dirt roads. Many of the women and men who visited the Rodair Club on a Sunday afternoon took those dirt roads to a new life in East Texas back in the 1930s.

A number of these families came to join relatives and friends who had settled here earlier, swelling the French-speaking population in the process. From the mid-thirties into the early 1950s, Ben Benoit recalls, it was possible for a Texas Cajun to go for weeks on end without hearing English spoken—unless one turned on the radio. As Ben said, "Your family was speaking French. So were your friends, and the people you worked with. And the people you worked for. We were all Cajuns then, out around Port Arthur."

The second, larger wave started during World War II and may not have ended yet. This swell consists mainly of Louisiana people from farming backgrounds looking for city work in Texas. In the past, the petroleum refineries of the Gulf Coast have provided most of their jobs.

Full-time Cajuns were the clientele of the Rodair when it first opened more than thirty years ago, and that same population can be found any Sunday afternoon in that long low-ceilinged wood hall just outside of Port Arthur. Some of the older men gathered at the bar will tell you that though the owners rake in the money on Saturday night, they take a loss on Sunday. Yet the Rodair will always be open on Sunday because as the man behind the bar told me, "the older people won't let us stop doing those Sunday dances."

On Sunday the full-time Cajuns are out. This is a group for whom accordion music is more than entertainment: it is a natural and inescapable part of life. The older people did all their dancing to it, fell in love to it, got married to it. And the accordion is still setting the pulse of their lives. There are families that have been going to the Rodair every Sunday afternoon for thirty years. They bring their spouses, their children, their grandchildren, their friends from out of town. They meet their friends, talk to the same people every Sunday, do their catching-up. They do this with an intensity that can be disconcerting to outsiders. When I first went to a Sunday dance at the Rodair and tried to meet the men around the bar, I had trouble breaking into the conversation—the talk was so concentrated, so animated, so personal. I was invisible. When I did manage to get the attention of some of the patrons, one at a time, acceptance and involvement were total. The men spoke with passion about what this music did for them. A simple question would spark two hours of frank reminiscence.

For me, the work-hard-play-hard ethic of the old timers at the Rodair is best summed up by Ben Benoit, a man I was lucky enough to visit with one Sunday. Mr. Benoit seems to do everything for keeps. Sixty-six, he has been married forty-eight years. Though his four children live all over Jefferson County, he tries to see them every day. He has family in Church Point, Louisiana, where he was born, and he visits them every week when possible. Every Saturday night, he takes his wife to the Rodair. Every Sunday afternoon he comes alone to visit with his men friends. Twice a weekend, every weekend, he listens to the accordion, and it never bores him and it never makes him tired.

Ben came to Texas from Louisiana in the 1930s to sharecrop.

He remembers working very hard for low pay. In the 1940s, when he quit farming and went to work for M.W. Kellogg in Port Arthur, he made forty dollars a week:

> I had four children, took care of all of them, brought them all up speaking French, and brought them all here.
>
> They all got married to [the accompaniment of] French bands too.
>
> My kids don't believe I ever worked for that little money. But they do believe it when I tell them that the Cajuns got the jobs in the refineries around here because they were willing to work so hard. The Texas people wouldn't work like that. That's how we got these jobs. That's why we stayed here.

Like Ben Benoit, the accordion players at the Rodair play hard. Almost all of the musicians work two or three others jobs for a living. By and large, they learned to play at home from family, and many of them are teaching their children or grandchildren at home.

The musical tradition, like the clientele, is old-fashioned. Unlike Lafayette, Louisiana, the only city in United States where the urban concentration of Cajuns is great enough to support such "wild" innovations in Cajun music as Zachary Richard's Fatras band and Wayne Toups ZydeCajun, the Rodair Club sticks to the old-fashioned songs and styles.

But on the floor the dancers are all ages. Children are dancing with grandparents. And something similar is happening on stage. In a one-hour period one Sunday at the Rodair, I saw the accordion change hands six times. All the players played well. There were an older man, two middle-aged men, a young man trying to look and sound like Wayne Toups, and two kids under fifteen. The young boys played with flair and precision.

At these Sunday afternoon dances men and boys who have previously played only at home come forward to entertain their neighbors. Some will never play in any other public setting. A few will go on to play accordion at other Cajun dancehalls.

The older men at the bar watch the boys and encourage and furiously applaud them. At other times, they give more than encouragement. Many belong to a group titled the Cajun French Music Association that meets monthly at the Rodair to raise funds for contests and apprenticeships and other means of supporting young Cajun musicians. They are so intent on keeping accordion music alive that it sometimes seems to outsiders like myself that the future life or death of Texas Cajun culture is bound up in the bellows and reeds and buttons of that instrument.

People like Ben Benoit spend a great deal of time talking about how the world's changed, about how their grandchildren neither can nor care to comprehend what it used to mean to be Cajun. Ben doesn't understand the young people's video games, and he has a hard time accepting that they can reach the age of fifteen without learning how to do farm or factory work.

But Ben does understand the way that the boys at the Rodair play the accordion. Just as the accordion accompanied him through childhood, courtship, and marriage and accompanied the marriage of his own children—it is now the major thread connecting him to the youngest generation at the Rodair.

"You can make me cry when you play that thing," he tells a fourteen-year-old jouer named Thibodeau.

"But why would I want to do that?" Thibodeau jokes back.

Ben pats him on the back. Thibodeau looks up, genuinely proud of the compliment, but a little bewildered, because he knows these older men just well enough to know that when he's playing for them he's giving them something very powerful that he himself doesn't yet understand.

# Let the Good Times Unroll: Music and Race Relations in Southwest Louisiana[1]

## Mark Mattern

*Laissez les bon temps roulez,* or "Let the good times roll," is often heard at musical events, parties, festivals, and other upbeat events of both black Creoles and Cajuns living in southwest Louisiana. Black Creoles are black persons living in the area whose contemporary identity reflects strong French and African roots as well as other ethnic and cultural influences. Their music is widely known as zydeco music. In this article, the term "black Creole" will be used rather than "African American" since it is the preferred term among most residents of southwest Louisiana, including among most black Creoles. The term "Cajun" is an anglicized rendition of "Cadien," which is a shortened version of "Acadien," the French word for Acadian. It refers to the white, Francophone people and culture of southwest Louisiana.

In this article, I use music as a window into relations between black Creoles and Cajuns, interpreting music as a social arena in which relations between the two groups are partly determined.[2] As the title of this article suggests, musical practices in recent times have been the source and site of some discontent between black Creoles and Cajuns. Beginning in the 1960s, Cajun musicians led a Cajun cultural revival that succeeded in drawing attention to some of the problems of Cajuns, such as cultural assimilation, poverty, and ethnic stigma. It also succeeded in helping to partially overcome these problems. Many black Creoles believe that at least some of this resurgence of Cajun culture has come at their expense. They charge that Cajuns have profited from the use of black Creole cultural property, that black Creole contributions to cultural vitality in southwest Louisiana are too frequently overlooked, and that the Cajun revival represents a bid for cultural dominance. Much of this controversy has been generated by, or around, musical practices.

---

[1] This article first appeared in *Black Music Research Journal* 17 (1997): 159-68.
[2] A more extensive treatment of some of the themes raised in this article, along with additional case studies, can be found in Mark Mattern, *Acting in Concert: Music, Community, and Political Action* (New Brunswick, N.J., 1998). For a history of Cajuns, see especially Carl Brasseaux, *The Founding of New Acadia: The Beginnings of Acadians Life in Louisiana, 1765-1803* (Baton Rouge, 1987); Brasseaux, *Scattered to the Wind: Dispersal and Wanderings of the Acadians 1755-1809* (Lafayette, 1991); Brasseaux, *Acadian to Cajun: Transformation of a People, 1803-1877* (Jackson, 1992). For histories of Cajun and zydeco music, see especially Barry Jean Ancelet, *The Makers of Cajun Music* (Austin, 1984); Ancelet, *Cajun Music: Its Origins and Development* (Lafayette, 1989); Ancelet, Introduction to *Cajun Music and Zydeco* by Philip Gould, (Baton Rouge, 1992); and Ann Allen Savoy, *Cajun Music: A Reflection of a People* (Eunice, 1984).

## Music as a Social Arena of Communication and Interaction

Taken together, zydeco and Cajun music represented a social arena of communication and interaction. This arena is defined by the musical texts themselves and also by the complex of associated practices that define the context in which musical texts circulate. In other words, it encompasses the people and sites involved in the production, consumption, and use of zydeco and Cajun music. Within this arena, black Creoles and Cajuns share experiences, communicate with each other, and partly determine their mutual relations. This can be seen more clearly by briefly examining the overlapping histories of zydeco and Cajun music.

Both zydeco and Cajun music have absorbed many different influences, especially elements drawn from French and African roots. Historically, musicians in both traditions sang almost entirely in French, and both traditions emphasized waltz and two-step dance forms derived primarily from Europe. Today, many musicians continue to compose and sing in French, and the waltz and two-step remain popular among both groups. Cajuns brought their French heritage with them when they emigrated from French Canada during the latter half of the eighteenth century. Black Creoles acquired their French heritage from their Acadian neighbors, from immigrants and slaves arriving from Haiti, and from their parents and grandparents who were themselves immigrants and slaves from Haiti. The African influence in Cajun and zydeco music can be seen in blues sentiments and expressions, percussive and rhythmic techniques, syncopation, and vocal and instrumental improvisation.

"In the store," sketch by E.W. Kemble. From Eugene V. Smalley, "Sugar-Making in Louisiana," *Century Illustrated Monthly Magazine* 35 (November, 1887-April, 1888): 109.

The African precursors of zydeco music include slave music in the form of rhythmic stomping, field hollers, *juré* singers, and hand clapping accompanied by rhythm instruments such as spoons, washboards, and sticks. Later precursors include "la la" music, fast French dance music with a rhythm-and-blues influence developed in southwestern Louisiana in the early and mid-twentieth century.

In modern times, zydeco reflects the strong influences of African American blues, soul, jazz, and rhythm and blues. Different zydeco musicians incorporate different influences. For example, the zydeco of Clifton Chenier and Stanley "Buckwheat Zydeco" Dural reflect a strong rhythm-and-blues influences, and the zydeco of Terrence Simien, while incorporating elements as diverse as reggae, is most obviously influenced by soul music.

Cajun and zydeco musicians draw from similar and sometimes identical individual musical sources. Early twentieth-century black Creole musicians who provided the foundations for zydeco music included Amédé Ardoin (accordion), Freeman Fontenot (accordion), Alphonse "Bois Sec" Ardoin (accordion), Canray Fontenot (fiddle), Claude Faulk (accordion), and Bébé Carriere (fiddle). These are the same musicians often cited as important early influences for Cajun music.

During the late nineteenth and early twentieth centuries, poor Cajuns (the vast majority) interacted closely with black Creoles, their fellow tenant farmers, despite concurrent pressure for segregation. Cajun musicians acquired some of their Africa-inspired musical elements from this interaction. This influence is apparent in abundant testimonies by Cajun musicians, such as Octa Clark, who states that he composed blues songs after hearing black Creoles singing in the fields. His longtime music partner, Hector Duhon, acknowledges a similar debt to black Creoles: "Tenant farmers would come up to the store. My old daddy would give them something to play. You'd also hear them singing in the fields, spirituals, hollers and yells. It was beautiful the way they sang."[3]

Although there are significant differences between Cajun and zydeco music, there are also many striking similarities. Both rely heavily on the accordion, for example. Cajuns and some zydeco musicians prefer the single-row diatonic accordion, whereas other zydeco musicians such as Clifton Chenier and Stanley "Buckwheat Zydeco" Dural replaced the diatonic accordion with the more versatile piano accordion. While the fiddle continues to play a central role in Cajun music, it has largely been dropped from use by contemporary zydeco musicians.

The legendary black Creole accordionist Amédé Ardoin is often cited as the primary influence in the development of traditional Cajun accordion playing as well as contemporary zydeco music.[4] Ardoin often played for dances at white homes and dancehalls as well as black Creole events. This, along with the recordings he made in the late 1920s with the Cajun fiddler Dennis McGee, challenged strict segregationist codes of his day. Many of Ardoin's compositions remain in the contemporary Cajun repertoire.

---

[3] Nicholas Spitzer, liner notes, *Octa Clark and Hector Duhon: The Dixie Ramblers-Ensemble Encore*, Rounder Records 6011, 1982.
[4] Savoy, *Cajun Music*, 152.

The musical sensibilities and lyrical themes of Cajun and zydeco music also have much in common, reflecting similar experiences and lives. Both, for example, contain strong blues inflections such as blues scales and vocal breaks evoking crying or sadness. Their lyrical themes emphasize economic marginalization, lost love, and unrequited love. Both zydeco and Cajun music nearly disappeared under pressure from Anglo assimilationist influences, going "back-porch" during the lean years of the 1930s, 1940s, and 1950s although not disappearing entirely. Both have also experienced revivals within the last thirty years, albeit with significant differences, discussed below.

The affinities between zydeco and Cajun music suggest a history of at least partially shared experiences and of overlapping points of identity. The similarities of musical expression reflect common and shared experiences that, significantly, occurred in a context of near-absolute social segregation. Cajuns and black Creoles had frequently played together for dances and house parties during the eighteenth, nineteenth, and early twentieth centuries.[5] Certain prominent musicians in the twentieth century played key bridging roles. As already noted, Amédé Ardoin, Canray Fontenot, and Alphonse "Bois Sec" Ardoin are frequently cited for their contributions to both Cajun and black Creole musical traditions.[6] Cajun musician Dewey Balfa was noted for his willingness to cross the rigid racial lines in southwest Louisiana. Clifton Chenier, popular with white as well as black audiences, regularly played white clubs, and whites sometimes braved racial segregation to hear him perform at black Creole clubs such as Richard's in Lawtell and Slim's Y Ki Ki in Opelousas. Chenier and "Good Rockin'" Dopsie also sometimes recorded with whites.

Social interactions between black Creoles and Cajuns still occur through the music and musical practices. The contemporary repertoire of Cajun and zydeco music reflects a lively, ongoing cross-fertilization. For example, many of Amédé Ardoin's compositions remain in circulation in Cajun music, and popular Cajun bands such as Beausoleil and Wayne Toups' ZydeCajun both experiment widely with zydeco rhythms and instruments such as the *frottoir* (rub board). Some of the most popular zydeco bands now playing in southwest Louisiana, such as Beau Jocque's Zydeco Hi-Rollers and Zydeco Force, use the same single-row diatonic accordion as Cajun accordionists and perform slower waltzes and two-steps in a style similar to Cajun bands. Blacks and whites still mingle occasionally at festivals and other musical venues. Festivals Acadiens, an annual music festival held in Lafayette, always includes representative black Creole musicians. Festival International de Louisiane, an annual event also held in Lafayette that attracts crowds as large as one hundred and fifty thousand, showcases both black and white musicians from various French-speaking parts

---

[5] Ancelet, interview with the author, Lafayette, LA, October 2, 1993.
[6] Savoy, *Cajun Music*, 66-78, 320-41; Ancelet, *The Makers of Cajun Music*, 73-87.

of the world, including southwest Louisiana.

Direct social interaction through musical practices, however, has always been and remains limited. Although musicians could sometimes cross racial barriers, non-musicians found it much more difficult. Everyday social life, including and especially in musical venues, remains very segregated even though workplaces and schools are desegregated.[7]

Creole fiddler Canray Fontenot, ca. 1976. *Courtesy of Center for Louisiana Studies, University of Louisiana at Lafayette, accession number 2611.*

*Musical Practices as a Cause of Racial Conflict*
Many black Creoles believe that the contemporary promotion of Cajun music and culture partially erases black Creole contributions to the culture of southwest Louisiana.[8] They argue that the Cajun promotion, some of it funded by local, state, and federal governments, unfairly singles out Cajuns as representative of all of southwest Louisiana, involves a claim of dominant status for Cajuns among the many ethnic and racial groups in the area, and entails a colonization of black Creole culture. One result is increased racial tension, already at high levels due to economic competition, white support for David Duke, and lingering resentments over the perceived failure of desegregation. There is "widespread disapproval" among black Creoles of the promotion of Cajun music and culture. While black Creoles "speak in even tones about perceived white racism and discrimination…voices become angry when talking about the Acadian renaissance of the last 20 years." Much of this anger and mistrust is fueled by musical practices.[9]

The contemporary roots of the tension between black Creoles and Cajuns can be found in early organizing efforts for the Cajun revival. In attempting to acknowledge their cultural debts to black Creoles and honestly portray their own roots, Cajun music festival organizers usually included black Creoles. The 1974 First Tribute to Cajun Music, the forerunner to today's annual Festivals Acadiens, included black Creoles Clifton Chenier, Alphonse "Bois Sec" Ardoin, and Canray Fontenot. Subsequent "Cajun" music festivals have followed a simi-

---

[7] Pat Watters, "Different Worlds," *The Times of Acadiana*, September 29, 1993, 12-13; Ancelet interview.
[8] David Chretien, "In a diverse culture: 'Cajuns' and 'Creoles' should be promoted," *Creole Magazine* 3 (1992), 26-27; Watters, "Different Worlds," 13-14.
[9] Watters, "Different Worlds," 12-14.

lar pattern, including and even honoring black Creole musicians. While these may be "steps in the right direction"[10] toward acknowledging black Creole contributions to Cajun music and culture, the perception among black Creoles remains that there exists a concurrent process of incorporating black Creole cultural expressions into the category of Cajun, including and especially zydeco music.

There are many examples of this incorporation process. In addition to the festivals already noted, various publications, recordings, legislative initiatives, and other public documents and pronouncements routinely subsume black Creole contributions to the culture of southwest Louisiana under the label Cajun. For example, Ann Savoy entitled her book on the music of the area *Cajun Music* even though it also discusses zydeco music. She states in her introduction that Cajun music "is the rubboard and the triple row accordion driving to the beat of an electric bass in a black club in a creole community" as well as fiddle and single-row diatonic accordion music.[11] She also includes an entire section on "Old Style Creole and Modern Zydeco."[12]

Barry Ancelet's *The Makers of Cajun Music* (1984) also addresses both Cajun and zydeco music. Since Cajun and black Creole music are both so intimately tied to their respective communities, subsuming zydeco music under the category of Cajun implicitly subsumes black Creole communities under Cajun communities, which, in turn, places the category of Cajun in a dominant position relative to black Creole.

In his book *South to Louisiana: The Music of the Cajun Bayous*, John Broven describes zydeco music as music sung by "black Cajuns."[13] Chris Strachwitz, owner of the California-based Arhoolie record label, which helped bring the music of southwest Louisiana to a national and international audience, calls Amédé Ardoin "The First Black Cajun Recording Artist."[14] In 1981, KEUN radio in Eunice, Louisiana, began broadcasting an hour of zydeco music on Saturday mornings, announcing that "zydeco, traditional black Cajun music, has been neglected by southwest Louisiana radio stations for years."[15]

These examples of references to zydeco music as music of "black Cajuns" make the incorporation of black Creoles into the category of Cajun explicit. The reference to Amédé Ardoin as a "black Cajun" especially grates on black Creoles for whom he represents a revered cultural godfather. Finally, according to the liner notes for a recording by Queen Ida and the Bon Temps Band, "Zydeco music is of Cajun origin and brought to Louisiana from French Canada by the

---

[10] Ancelet, Introduction to *Cajun Music and Zydeco*, xviii.
[11] Savoy, *Cajun Music*, xi.
[12] Ibid., 300-413.
[13] John Broven, *South to Louisiana: The Music of the Cajun Bayous* (Gretna, LA, 1983), 101.
[14] Chris Strackwitz, liner notes, *Amédé Ardoin: The first blalck Cajun recording artist* (1991) Arhoolie Records OT124.
[15] Broven, *South to Louisiana*, 116.

Acadians.... The Creoles adopted the music and added their cultural flavor."[16] This explanation of the origin of zydeco music implicitly condones a primary valuation of the French contribution and concurrent devaluation of the African influence. It also distorts history, since African influences, which hardly originated in French Canada, primarily define zydeco music. It is especially unfortunate since Queen Ida (Guillory) is a black Creole.

This incorporation process sometimes appears to encompass the entire culture of southwest Louisiana. Responding to tourist interest, the Louisiana legislature designated southwest Louisiana as "Cajun Country," as billboards announce upon travelers' arrival. The University of Southwestern Louisiana recently rechristened its sports teams the "Ragin' Cajuns" despite the fact that a large number of the athletes are African American. The city of Lafayette now calls its bus system, used primarily by people of color, the "Ragin' Cajun Busline." Throughout the area, one can now buy just about anything carrying a "Cajun" label, from McCajun fries to Cajun fishing bait to Cajun lingerie. Ancelet rightly notes that "Creoles are left to wonder what happened to their contribution to the French Louisiana cultural gumbo."[17]

The significance of this incorporation process in the world of music can further be appreciated by examining the roots of the term "zydeco." The phrase *les haricots sont pas salé* (the snapbeans are unsalted), a reference to hard times that is found on an early Clifton Chenier recording, is usually cited as the source of the term "zydeco."[18] Although the reference to hard times may be appropriate as a metaphor for this bluesy music of black Creoles, this popular understanding of the term's origin tells only part of the story. Chenier himself offered a different explanation. According to Chenier, the term was already circulating when he began playing music: "See, the old people used to say 'Let's go to the zydeco,' meaning the dance. And I kept that in mind, and when I started playing music I called my music 'zydeco.'"[19]

Clarence Carlow's "Bon Ton Roula," recorded in the late 1940s, contains a direct reference to zydeco as an event: "At the church bazaar or the baseball game,/ At the French La La, it's all the same,/ You want to have fun, now you got to go/ Way out in the country to the Zydeco./ Well, let the Bon Ton Roula."[20] The social event to which Chenier and Barlow refer included a com-

---

[16] *Zydeco: Cajun/Creole/Bayou Music*, liner notes (1976) GNP Crescendo 2101.
[17] Ancelet, Introduction to *Cajun Music and Zydeco*, xxi.
[18] "Zydeco," so the story goes, is the phonetic rendering of the last three syllables of *les haricot*. The Creole French spoken by many black Creoles in southwest Louisiana was until recently strictly an oral language. In attempting to turn into a written language, spellings for various words had to be invented. The term "zydeco" has been in circulation for a long time, but only in the early 1960s did ethnomusicologist Mack McCormick attempt to render it in writing. Barry Jean Ancelet, "Zydeco/Zarico: Beans, blues and beyond," *Black Music Research Journal* 8 (1988): 33-49.
[19] As quoted in Savoy, *Cajun Music*, 373.
[20] Broven, *South to Louisiana*, 105.

munal feast with a gumbo to which all participants contributed, as well as music and dancing. It played a central social and celebratory role in the life of rural black Creoles in southwest Louisiana. Its cooperative, communal, and celebratory dimensions both revealed and reshaped the characteristics of black Creole communities. Given the historical significance of zydeco as a community-affirming social event, calling zydeco music "black Cajun" music and placing it under the label of Cajun implicitly involves not only an incorporation of music but of whole communities of black Creoles.

Since the early 1980s, black Creoles and others have responded with criticism to this incorporation and with attempts to develop a cultural revival paralleling the Cajun revival. Some, such as Takuna El Shabazz, openly criticize Cajuns for indiscriminately incorporating black Creole cultural expressions into the category of Cajun. He calls the Cajun promotion in southwest Louisiana "a form of white colonialism," since it involves a new form of domination of black people by white people.[21] Making matters worse, in his view, black Creoles must help *pay* for their own colonization, since tax money is now routinely asked to promote Cajun tourism. This, he says, "is taxation without representation, and misuse and abuse of public funds."[22]

El Shabazz and others in the Lafayette area formed the Un-Cajun Committee in 1982 in order to draw attention to their concerns and organize a response. Although attacked for being anti-Cajun, for organizing in order to "bash Cajuns," and for attempting to stir up hatred between whites and blacks,[23] El Shabazz insists that the Un-Cajun Committee exists not to oppose or disparage Cajuns but to counter the colonization of black Creole cultural expressions and identities and to highlight the differences between Cajuns and others in southwest Louisiana. El Shabazz and other members of the Un-Cajun Committee frequently draw criticism for allegedly focusing on an inconsequential issue and for failing to focus on the real issues of education, jobs, drugs, and crime that plague some black Creole communities. El Shabazz responds that these criticisms imply that "one has nothing to do with the other."[24] At the heart of these problems, in his view, is that black Creoles "have no real sense of [their] own history and culture" and that the Cajun promotion exacerbates this problem. Robbing black Creoles of their cultural foundations contributes to the social and economic problems that plague their communities by "contributing to the self-hatred syndrome of black people in Southwest Louisiana" and by "killing the desire for self-determination." Efforts by El Shabazz and oth-

---

[21] Takuna Maulana El Shabazz, "Promotion of 'Cajun/Acadiana' is colonialism" *Creole Magazine* 3 (1992): 43-45.
[22] Ibid., 43.
[23] Barry Jean Ancelet, "Ragin' Cajuns: What's in a name?," *Creole Magazine* 3 (1992): 42; Shabazz, "Promotion of 'Cajun/Acadiana' is colonialism," 45.
[24] Shabazz, "Promotion of 'Cajun/Acadiana' is colonialism," 45, 43.

ers have promoted awareness among black Creoles of the problem of cultural incorporation. Many black Creoles now believe that implicit in the process of Cajun expansion and promotion is a bid for cultural dominance.[25]

Black Creole activists in southwest Louisiana have also attempted to foster a revival comparable to the Cajun revival. Like the Cajun revival, music provides a cornerstone. Prominent annual zydeco festivals now include the Southwest Louisiana Zydeco Music Festival held in Plaisance and the Zydeco Extravaganza held in Lafayette's Blackham Coliseum. The Plaisance festival, organized initially in 1982, now routinely attracts more than twenty thousand fans. Organizers call it "a celebration of Creole culture," a "revival," a "rebirth," and a "rubberstamp" of Creole culture.[26] Their efforts are helping to return zydeco to its original sense of a communal event and to revitalize the communities in which it is set.

Black Creoles now host radio and television programs on zydeco music and black Creole culture. Black Creoles also now host their own music awards program for zydeco musicians, the Zydeco People's Choice Awards. Efforts are underway to promote tourist interest in black Creole music and culture by collaborating with organizations such as the Greater New Orleans Black Tourists Commission. This organization attempts to link interest in New Orleans jazz with interest in zydeco music in southwest Louisiana.

Two other organizations have emerged that occasionally promote zydeco music: CREOLE, Inc. (Cultural Resourceful Educational Opportunities for Linguistic Enrichment) and *Creole Magazine*. CREOLE, Inc. was formed in 1988 to create an awareness of cultural differences in southwest Louisiana between black Creoles and Cajuns and to promote black Creole culture. *Creole Magazine* covers many issues of concern to black Creoles in southwest Louisiana, including cultural expressions such as zydeco music. It promotes black Creole political, social, economic and cultural interests, offers Creole French lessons, and serves as art information vehicle.

### Music as a Catalyst for Change?

In spite of current racial tensions, Cajun and zydeco musicians continue to borrow freely from each other, albeit generally not through face-to-face interactions. The two musics continue to overlap at multiple points. This signals the persistence of a communicative arena in which black Creoles and Cajuns share at least some social experiences and where difficult cultural and racial issues can be raised. Social segregation between whites and blacks has been an accepted fact of life in south Louisiana for a long time. Its very mundaneness

---

[25] David Chretien, "In a diverse culture: 'Cajuns' and 'Creoles' should be promoted," *Creole Magazine* 3 (1992): 26-27.
[26] Wilbert Guillory, Liz Savoy, and Paul Scott, Brochure, "The Original Southwest Louisiana Zydeco Music Festival (Plaisance, 1993).

may legitimize and perpetuate it. The barriers erected by social segregation prevent progress on mutual problems such as the endemic poverty that affects many Cajuns and black Creoles alike. The conflict stirred up by musicians has brought this impasse into sharper relief. While regrettable, it may be a necessary prelude to change.

# Introduction and Use of Accordions in Cajun Music[1]

## Malcolm L. Comeaux

The history of the accordion begins with the invention of the "free reed" in either southern China or Laos, where instruments using this reed date back to 1000 B.C.[2] In the free reed, the tongue (lamella) fits in a frame, whereas the beating reed, so common in European instruments, fits on top of the frame. The concept of free reeds was slow to arrive in Europe, and it was not until the late 1700s that they began to be used in instruments there.[3]

The accordion's history begins about 1800 when Europeans began the rapid development of instruments using free reeds. The *"handaeoline"* was developed in Berlin in 1822 by C.F.L. Buschmann, and its major advance was that, rather than having a human lung force air over the reeds, it used a mechanical one.[4] It had only five buttons on the treble side, but Buschmann realized it could hold more. In Vienna organ builder Cyril Demian improved on the *handaeoline* by placing fixed chord buttons for the left hand, and on June 6, 1829, patented his *"akkordion,"* the first use of the word.[5] Invention of the accordion thus dates back to either of these two dates. Demian's *akkordion*, however, was little more than a toy. A month after the *akkordion* was patented, Charles Wheatstone in England patented the concertina,[6] at the time a much more advanced instrument than the *akkordion*. This led to rapid development and evolution of the accordion, to the point that it was soon accepted as a true musical instrument and no longer only a toy or curiosity. By 1835 there were at least six varieties of accordions available.[7] Manufacturing of these instruments began quickly, and to avoid the question of the patent, some manufacturers who copied the *akkordion* called their instrument *"handharmonika,"* a word by which it now is known in some parts of the world.[8] Many were manufactured and shipped around the world. In some way or another accordions made their way to south Louisiana and were accepted by the Cajuns. It will probably never be known when the first accordion came to Louisiana, or when the first Cajun acquired or played one, nor does it really matter. What is important is that they

---

[1] This article first appeared in *Louisiana Folklore Miscellany* 14 (1999): 27-40.
[2] Sibyl Marcuse, *A Survey of Musical Instruments* (New York, 1975), 730-31.
[3] Ibid., 734.
[4] Joseph Macerollo, *Accordion Resource Manual* (n.p., 1980), 8-13.
[5] Ibid., 13.
[6] Macerollo, *Accordion Resource Manual*, 13-15.
[7] Sibyl Marcuse, *Musical Instruments: A Comprehensive Dictionary* (Garden City, NY, 1964), 2.
[8] Marcuse, *A Survey of Musical Instruments*, 742.

did come to Louisiana and were accepted by musicians in southwest Louisiana. This fact greatly changed the music of this area.

The primary musical instrument used in Canada by Acadians prior to expulsion (1755) was the fiddle (or violin), and it remains the main instrument among Acadians in the Maritime Provinces.[9] Acadian refugees coming to Louisiana either brought fiddles with them, or much more likely, acquired fiddles soon after their arrival (either homemade or purchased). The fiddle was widely used at house dances after Louisiana settlement, and house dances remained popular well into the twentieth century. House dances were undoubtedly crowded and noisy. Although only six to twelve couples danced at a time,[10] there were many people in and around the house, and they were all talking, laughing, and in general enjoying themselves. In order to be heard above the din, Cajun violinists developed a playing style that required them to bear down hard on bows in order to play as loud as possible.[11] It gave this music a unique sound, but acceptance of the accordion was to bring many changes to the music.

### Introduction of the Accordion into South Louisiana

There is definite proof of an accordion in Louisiana in 1871. Documenting this is a picture of an old German lighthouse-keeper near the mouth of the Mississippi River playing an accordion.[12] This is appropriate, since accordions were probably exported from Germany to French Louisiana via the lower Mississippi River.

There is other evidence of accordions very early in south Louisiana. Tisserand[13] illustrates a copy of a daguerreotype, dated "circa 1850," that is located in the Louisiana State Museum in New Orleans. A very old type of accordion, only vaguely resembling modern ones (for example, there are twelve buttons on the treble side), is held in the hands of a black musician, but there is no proof that it is truly from mid-century. Another early view of a black

---

[9] Anselme Chiasson, Charlotte Cormier, Donald Deschenes, and Ronald LaBelle, "Le Folklore Acadien," in *L'Acadie des Maritimes*, ed. Jean Daigle (Moncton, N.B., 1995), 699-701.
[10] John Broven, *South to Louisiana: The Music of the Cajun Bayous* (Gretna, LA, 1987), 12.
[11] Barry Jean Ancelet and Elmore Morgan, Jr., *The Makers of Cajun Music*/Musiciens cadiens et créoles (Austin and Québec, 1984), 22.
[12] Ralph Keeler and Frank Waud, "On the Mississippi," *Every Saturday*, June 3, 1871, 524-26.
[13] Michael Tisserand, *The Kingdom of Zydeco* (New York, 1998), 44-45. There is no proof or evidence that this photo was taken at mid-century. It could have been taken much later, with a musician holding an old instrument. Also, if it was taken in Louisiana (and it probably was), it was probably taken in New Orleans, and not in southwest Louisiana.

Tisserand reported on a WPA interview where an accordion was mentioned long ago, but it stretches credulity in some respects. It was from a woman reportedly born in 1827, who as a young girl went to dances where an accordion was played by a black musician. It would thus have probably been prior to 1847. But, if the interviewee was truly born in 1827, that would have meant that she was well over one hundred at the time of a WPA interview, and 1847 is terribly early to find the accordion in south Louisiana. This was reported for the lower Teche, an area today not noted for accordion players.

accordionist in Louisiana was in 1877 when a black prisoner is shown playing for fellow prisoners and guards (and another has a banjo) along the Cane River in central Louisiana.[14] If a black prisoner can have an accordion, and knew how to play it, it should be assumed that accordions were rather widely available by the 1870s.

Blacks, as seen above, had access to accordions, and probably played a major role in acceptance of accordions in south Louisiana. Canray Fontenot, a black Creole fiddle player, related how he had been told that during the days of slavery some blacks learned to play the accordions of their masters,[15] and in a short story by Kate Chopin, published in 1897, three black musicians, two fiddlers, and an accordionist, play at a dance for whites.[16] Canray, born in 1922, also states that his father, his mother, and his father's father all played the accordion.[17] Thus, the accordion in Creole culture goes rather far back. In the early twentieth century some of the most influential and innovative musicians were black Creoles.[18] Several were accordionists, such as Amédé Ardoin and Adam Fontenot (father of Canray),[19] and many older Cajun musicians mention Amédé Ardoin as having a major influence on their music. There was much cooperation between white and black musicians,[20] and many blacks played at white dances, so their influence was probably not insignificant.[21]

Although accordions were in Louisiana at an early date, their acceptance by Cajuns came later. In a book published in 1861 on a series of controversial incidents on the prairies of southwest Louisiana, a Frenchman often mentioned fiddles (and fiddle players, although never in a positive light), as well as other instruments, such as mandolin, banjo, and guitar. No accordion or accordion player, however, was ever mentioned.[22] Twenty years later, a visitor on the prairies encountered a settlement of 150 Cajun families, and found "no less than sixty fiddlers," an amazingly large number for a relatively small settlement.[23] But, again, there was no mention of accordion players. Although the accordion was introduced in the latter half of the nineteenth century, and was probably widely

---

[14] *Frank Leslie's Illustrated Newspaper*, December 22, 1877, 264.
[15] Tisserand, *The Kingdom of Zydeco*, 44.
[16] Kate Chopin, *The Complete Works of Kate Chopin*, 2 vols, ed. Per Seyersted (Baton Rouge, 1969), 1:490.
[17] Ann Allen Savoy, *Cajun Music: A Reflection of a People* (Eunice, LA, 1984), 326.
[18] Barry Jean Ancelet, *Cajun Music: Its Origins and Development* (Lafayette, 1989), 19.
[19] Ancelet and Morgan, *The Makers of Cajun Music*, 23.
[20] Barry Jean Ancelet, Jay Edwards, and Glen Pitre, *Cajun Country* (Jackson, 1991), 150-51; Ancelet and Morgan, *The Makers of Cajun Music*, 74; Rick Olivier and Ben Sandmel, *Zydeco* (Jackson, 1999), 130.
[21] Barry Jean Ancelet, *Cajun Music: Its Origins and Development* (Lafayette, 1989), 19-20; Shane K. Bernard, *Swamp Pop: Cajun and Creole Rhythm & Blues* (Jackson, 1996), 12; Nicholas Spitzer, "Zydeco and Mardi Gras: Creole Identity and Performance Genres in Rural French Louisiana" (Ph.D. dissertation, University of Texas, 1986), 316-21. Accordionists in black Africa also play in a highly syncopated style, and while not identical to that found in Cajun music, it is rather close.
[22] Alexandre Barde, *The Vigilante Committees of the Attakapas*, eds. David Edmonds and Dennis Gibson, trans. Henrietta Guilbeau Rogers (Lafayette, LA, 1981).
[23] *Frank Leslie's Popular Monthly* 12 (1881): 566.

available, one scholar maintains that fiddles remained the main instrument of choice on the prairies of southwest Louisiana until the 1920s,[24] and this was undoubtedly the case.

One way accordions may have been acquired was through the mail. *Frank Leslie's Illustrated Newspaper*[25] had an advertisement of accordions for sale in 1886. Such a magazine, however, would have been read only by local upper classes, a group that typically had disdained accordions. Accordions were also offered for sale in various early catalogs. The Montgomery Ward Company was distributing catalogs by the early 1870s, and the first Sears, Roebuck catalog was issued in 1894.[26] In a reproduction of a 1908 catalog, twenty accordion types manufactured by five companies are offered for sale.[27] Those who accepted the accordion were the largely under-educated Cajuns on the prairies of southwest Louisiana, with many being illiterate. While it is possible for them to have seen such early advertisements, they probably would not have ordered them by mail, and certainly not before they had acquired some prior knowledge of accordions and how to play them. Accordions made by the Hohner Company were very popular, and any Hohner accordion sold through the 1908 catalog included a free carrying case.[28] Older musicians, however, always mentioned carrying accordions in sacks, not cases.

I believe that German-Jewish merchants were important in the sale of accordions. There were Jewish merchants with stores in all Cajun towns, and probably the best example was the Mervine Kahn store in Rayne, established in 1884,[29] only four years after the railroad arrived. Many Cajuns bought their accordions from Mervine Kahn prior to World War II. How the first accordions arrived at these stores is unknown. The first ones may have been imported in a speculative fashion by Jewish merchants. More probably Cajuns began requesting accordions, and

Accordions sold in many catalogs, such as these from a 1923 Sears-Roebuck catalog. These sold for $2.95 and $3.45, respectively. Image adapted from 1923 Sears Roebuck catalog, courtesy of Jennifer Cooper.

---

[24] Rocky Sexton, "Cajuns, Germans, and Les Americans: A Historical Anthropology of Cultural Demographic Transformations" (Ph.D. dissertation, University of Iowa, 1996), 157-59.

[25] *Frank Leslie's Illustrated Newspaper*, May 15, 1886, 206.

[26] Frank Brown Latham, *A Century of Serving Consumers: The Story of Montgomery Ward* (Chicago, 1972), 6-12; Gordon Lee Weil, *Sears, Roebuck, U.S.A.: The Great American Catalog Store and How it Grew* (Briarcliff Manor, NY, 1978), 11.

[27] Sears, Roebuck and Company, *The Great Price Maker, Catalog Number 117, 1908*, ed. Joseph J. Schroeder, Jr. (Chicago, 1969), 243-44.

[28] Ibid., 244.

[29] Mary Alice Fontenot and Paul B. Freeland, *Acadia Parish, Louisiana: A History to 1900*, 2 vols. (Lafayette, 1997), 1:139, 324.

Jewish merchants found they could import and sell them for a profit. These merchants, with close connections to Eastern firms, and possibly directly with German manufacturing companies, began importing accordions to their rural, unsophisticated, French-speaking customers.

*Early Acceptance of the Accordions by Cajuns*
We will never know the name of the first person to bring an accordion into south Louisiana. Since the accordion evolved in German-speaking lands, it is usually assumed that it was a person from this region who first brought an accordion to south Louisiana. Germans were constantly filtering into New Orleans and from there into southwest Louisiana. The only organized settlement of Germans in southwest Louisiana, in Roberts Cove, did not occur until 1881, well after the accordion was in Louisiana.[30] Also, German Americans from this community were never noted for playing accordions, so they played no roll in acceptance of the accordion. German American wheat farmers from the Midwest came to Cajun country to become involved in the rice industry soon after 1880, and one researcher states it is "probable" that one of these introduced the instrument.[31] Another source states that the accordion "entered South Louisiana by way of Texas and German settlers."[32] There is simply no proof for any of these theories at this time. It must further be noted that accordions were manufactured in places other than Germany, such as in France, and accordions were exported around the world at a very early date. The first accordion could have arrived here in any number of ways, and by whom, when, and how is not important. What is important is that it came, was accepted, and made a major impact on Cajun music.

It will probably never be known when the first Cajun began to play the accordion or who this person was, but it seems that the first individual to bring an accordion to south Louisiana did not teach Cajuns or black Creoles to play it. People on the prairie of southwest Louisiana developed a style of playing that was not smooth and easy, as was done in Europe, but rather they began playing with fast choppy rhythms in a syncopated style that had many fast runs. It evolved into a style not found elsewhere in the world, and based on the style, probably first developed by black Creoles and then taught to Cajuns. The first Creoles to develop accordion skills were probably descendants of small independent black farmers who lived on the prairie west of Opelousas. This is the only large settlement of small independent black farmers on the prairie, and it is in this area where many of the early black accordionists originated, and where many, especially those using the old diatonic accordion, are now found.

---

[30] Stanley Joe McCord, "A Historical and Linguistic Study of the German Settlement at Roberts Cove, Louisiana" (Ph.D. dissertation, Louisiana State University, 1969), 70.
[31] Catherine Blanchet, "Acadian Instrumental Music," *Louisiana Folklore Miscellany* 3 (1970): 72.
[32] Ancelet and Morgan, *The Makers of Cajun Music*, 22.

This region has always been a "hotbed" of accordion players, both white and black.

Although there were undoubtedly accordions in south Louisiana at an early date, they at first did not make an impression on Cajun musicians. One reason is that the first ones imported were in the keys of A and F.[33] The fiddles could not be tuned to those keys (the strings would have to be strung too tight, and thus tended to break), so the accordion had to be played as a solo instrument. It did not receive much local attention. Good quality accordions, made with excellent reeds and good quality bellows, began to be imported in the early 1900s. The first of these was the "Monarch" brand, and later the "Sterling" and "Eagle" were introduced, and they were widely accepted by Cajuns. These were called *les tit noirs* ("the little blacks") by their users because of their color, and they became the basic model for all Cajun accordions after this time (except for the color). It was in the 1920s that accordions in the keys of C and D began to be imported.[34] These could be played with the fiddle, and now the accordion, already well known and widely used, exploded in popularity. Accordions lost popularity in the 1930s, and when they again came in vogue in the 1940s, none were to be had from Germany.

No accordions were imported during World War II, and few were imported for many years after the war because German factories were devastated, and some accordion factories were located in the Russian sphere of influence. Since no new accordions could be purchased for a considerable time, local Cajuns began repairing and refurbishing old accordions, and soon began making accordions.[35] The quality of these first accordions was not particularly good (because the reeds and bellows were often taken from Hohner accordions, or from very old accordions). Quality, however, has improved greatly since 1980, and now the accordions are made by true craftsmen using the finest of imported bellows, reeds (both from Italy), and woods. They cannot be called truly "homemade." There are at present twenty-nine persons in southwest Louisiana making accordions (and one in Texas and another in New Orleans), and their accordions are sold around the world.

Unfortunately, Cajun music was often derogatorily called "chank-a-chank," and throughout the first half of the twentieth century (at least until

---

[33] Malcolm L. Comeaux, "The Cajun Accordion," *Louisiana Review* 7 (1978): 118; Savoy, *Cajun Music: A Reflection of a People*, 13. According to Larry Miller, an accordion maker from Iota, it was Mr. John J. Mrnustik, an owner of a music store in Houston and an immigrant from Eastern Europe, who first began making accordions some time in the 1950s. He would only make them when he had an order for five or more, and he sold them locally and to Cajuns in southwest Louisiana. His widow told Mr. Miller that he made "over ten accordions." Mr. Sidney Brown, of Lake Charles, is the person recognized as making the first accordions in Louisiana. He had been repairing accordions, and may have picked up the idea of making accordions from Mr. Mrnustik.

[34] Savoy, *Cajun Music: A Reflection of a People*, 13.

[35] Comeaux, "The Cajun Accordion."

the mid-1960s) this music was not valued by the local intelligentsia. It was considered the music of unsophisticated, rural, under-educated whites. Anyone who played it, or listened to it, received ridicule by the educated and the press. It was not until this music was accepted on the national level, particularly at national folk festivals, that the educated in Louisiana realized that it was a unique music style and worthy of respect. This national recognition also gave local Cajun musicians respect and pride in their music and their skills, and acceptance grew rapidly among all people in south Louisiana.

Some black Creoles from southwest Louisiana, steeped in French culture and tradition, also accepted the accordion, but took the music along different lines. This Creole music was first called "la-la," but now it is universally known as zydeco. Many of the black zydeco musicians use large piano accordions or triple-row button accordions (especially those living along Bayou Teche), but the small diatonic accordion was always popular with black Creoles on the prairies, and several of these folks in recent years have received recognition in the zydeco community. Zydeco music is thus played on all types of accordions, but small diatonic accordions, similar to the ones made and used by Cajuns, seem to be gaining in popularity in zydeco music.[36]

Unidentified Creole accordion player. Image courtesy of the Center for Louisiana Studies, University of Louisiana at Lafayette, accession number 3836.

Although accordions were dependable and did not tend to get out of tune, probably the main reason they were accepted by Cajuns and Creoles was the fact that they were loud instruments—in fact very loud when compared to other folk instruments. Even when fiddlers bore down hard on their bows, they could not make it play loud enough to be heard over a large crowd. Fiddles were acceptable in a confined place, such as a room at a house dance,

---

[36] The best studies of zydeco are by Tisserand, *The Kingdom of Zydeco*; and Spitzer, "Zydeco and Mardi Gras," 300-410.

but when dancehalls began to gain acceptance in the late 1800s, dancers could only hear music from the fiddle when they were immediately in front of the band (they went in a counter-clockwise fashion on the dance floor). Electric amplification of music began in the early 1930s.[37] At that time fiddle players began to change their style to a lighter one, but by then the accordion was firmly entrenched, and fiddles (although quite loud with amplification) had taken a back seat to accordions in Cajun and Creole music in southwest Louisiana. Other instruments were added to Cajun bands, and today it is common to hear drums, guitars, steel guitars, a small triangle, and the like, but accordions remain the main instrument that defines a "Cajun" band.

*Conclusion*

The accordion goes back to the latter half of the nineteenth century in south Louisiana. How, when, and by whom it was first introduced is unknown, but the influence of black musicians cannot be discounted. The accordion was accepted on a limited scale by Cajuns sometime at the end of the nineteenth century, and became very popular by the 1920s when accordions were imported in keys that were compatible with fiddles. It is the instrument by which most Cajun music is identified, especially that from the prairies of southwest Louisiana, and this music has had an impact on the national scene.

Limited in keys and notes, the diatonic accordion's acceptance greatly simplified old Cajun songs, and those songs it could not play were abandoned.[38] Cajun music lost much, but gained in other ways, as it continued to grow and evolve. There was a brief time in the 1930s when the accordion, and Cajun music in general, began to lose favor, but it was revived in the 1940s, and today is growing in popularity and recognition, not only in south Louisiana, but around the country, and indeed around the world. It is no longer considered "chank-a-chank" music, and rarely is this derogatory term used today. Many very young musicians are learning to play the accordion, and bands now are having a hard time finding fiddle players. Many Cajuns now play the accordion as if to make a political statement—"I am a Cajun."

Older Cajun tunes are still being played, and new sounds are constantly evolving. Excellent quality accordions are being hand-made by local artisans (and inferior copies are made and sold by German manufacturing firms), and many youngsters are learning to play it. The future of the accordion in south Louisiana, and in Cajun music, is firm.

---

[37] Savoy, *Cajun Music: A Reflection of a People*, 115-16, 118; Lauren C. Post, "Joseph C. Falcon, Accordion Player and Singer," *Louisiana History* 11 (1970): 46ff.
[38] Ancelet and Morgan, *The Makers of Cajun Music*, 23; Savoy, *Cajun Music: A Reflection of a People*, 13.

# Heritage, Tradition, and Travel: Louisiana French Culture Placed on a California Dance Floor[1]

## Mark F. DeWitt

*Where Are We?*
Where are we and where could we be? These two fundamental questions, which imply a potential for movement, can be asked at any moment. Their import and immediacy provide leverage for many kinds of public persuasion, including preaching, advertising, tourism, folkloric performance, and ethnographic presentation. In advertising for tourism, for example, an emphasis of difference between where we are and where we could be creates a motivation for action. In other contexts, the goal is not to highlight differences between what is and what could be, but rather to conflate these two conditions as much as possible. This question of "where" implies a notion of distance that encompasses both space and time. A successful tourist destination lets the tourist know in no uncertain terms that she has *arrived*, that the gap between where she is and where she wants to be has disappeared. The act of arrival may get manufactured purely inside the tourist's mind, but in those places that cultivate a tourism industry, it is better to project a strong and distinctive sense of place than to leave such matters to chance.

When, in a manner of speaking, the destination travels to the tourists rather than the other way around, the importance of establishing a sense of place is in no way diminished. This essay addresses one such instance. In a region of California stretching from the San Francisco Bay Area south to Santa Cruz, east to Sacramento, and north to Sonoma County, live Cajun or zydeco music and dancing take place several times a week. According to some touring Cajun musicians, it is the largest such scene outside of the music's home region of southwestern Louisiana and eastern Texas. The activity has grown from music played at house parties of Louisiana Creole migrants in the 1940s to the development of local bands that play primarily in public clubs and dancehalls. A substantial pool of dancers supports a dozen or more bands, a handful of dance teachers and venues that feature regular dances, informal house parties and jam sessions, and a few outdoor festivals each year.[2]

---
[1] This article first appeared in *The World of Music* 41 (1999): 57-83.
[2] Explicit recognition of California's notable if limited role in the history of zydeco music has grown in recent years. In an article on the "geography of zydeco music," San Francisco and Los Angeles appeared on maps showing cities where prominent zydeco musicians live and where venues that regularly feature zydeco music are located. A self-published history of Cajun and zydeco music on the West Coast-based on interviews

A fifty-year history and contemporary profusion of Cajun and zydeco dance music in urban northern California, separated from Louisiana by over half the continent invites further explanation. Three related theoretical perspectives are brought to bear on the familiar question of what happens to music (and dance) when it becomes recontextualized. Clifford's "traveling cultures" metaphor provides a point of departure for viewing this phenomenon that has been the work both of (mostly Creole) immigrants and of cultural outsiders. Second, the essay discusses how musical and dance practices contribute to "a sense of place." These observations lead to the main discussion, in terms of "heritage" and "tradition" as Kirshenblatt-Gimblett has refined them, of how the scene for Louisiana French music and dance in California both fulfills and exceeds its surrogate roles as reminder of the past for immigrants and "virtual tourism" for others. The conclusion reviews how these various theoretical approaches fit together, based on the experience of applying them to this case.

### Louisiana "Traveling Culture"

Cajun music and zydeco have traveled to California both in live and mass-mediated forms over the years. Clifford's ideas about traveling culture encompass the study of music-making of relocated ethnic populations and the dissemination of musical styles across national and ethnic boundaries, but they do not stop there. He sketches images of informants and ethnographers as travelers and proposes the metaphor of travel as an alternative to more traditional ethnographic notions of culture based on isolated dwelling-places. He recommends "travel" as a unit of comparative analysis in order to reexamine various modes of human movement (e.g., tourism, pilgrimage, migration, and fieldwork) that have received less attention in anthropology than have stationary communities.[3]

Migration has been one key ingredient of the northern California Cajun and zydeco scene, specifically the movement of Cajuns and Creoles from Louisiana to California.[4] Louisiana French people, especially Creoles, began

---

and including profiles of several Louisiana-born California "pioneers" received some attention in Louisiana as well as in California, and a more recent history of zydeco music devoted a chapter to expanding on this history. Robert Kuhlken and Rocky Sexton, "The Geography of Zydeco Music," *Journal of Cultural Geography* 12 (1991): 27-38; Freida Marie Fusilier and Jolene M. Adams, *Hé, La-Bas! A History of Louisiana Cajun and Zydeco Music in California* (Sacramento, 1994); Michael Tisserand, *The Kingdom of Zydeco* (New York, 1998), 203-19.

[3] James Clifford, "Traveling Cultures," in *Cultural Studies*, Lawrence Grossberg, Cary Nelson, and Paula Treichler, eds., (New York, 1992), 96-116.

[4] A basic understanding of their ethnicity is required. Cajuns and Creoles, whom I call Louisiana French when referring to them as a single group, themselves distinguish between their two cultural groups, as well as between themselves and *les américains*. Broadly defined, "*Cajun*" refers to a white person with some relation by blood or marriage with French-speaking ancestors who were deported from their *Acadie* in eastern Canada at the hands of the British in 1755. In southwestern Louisiana, "Creole" refers to a person of color descended from French speakers with some mixture of European, African, and Native American ancestors. Cajuns and Creoles alike apply the term "American" to outsiders not to disavow their citizenship to

to immigrate to California in significant numbers during World War II due to military assignments and wartime industry employment opportunities.[5] From the early 1960s, Creole parishioners organized zydeco dances in Catholic parish social halls as church fund-raising events. This practice had already been in place among Creoles in Houston, Texas, since the 1950s,[6] when Clifton Chenier, the chief innovator of zydeco music, lived there. Chenier subsequently discovered the California Catholic church hall audiences of Creoles in Los Angeles[7] and San Francisco in the 1960s. His performances there increased ex-Louisianians' enthusiasm for their own music at the same time that he was introducing "Americans" to it through his appearances at blues festivals. Creole musicians who relocated to northern California and subsequently helped to meet the demand for music among their fellow immigrants have included John Simien, Danny Poullard, and 1980s national zydeco star Queen Ida.[8]

This music and dance might have remained largely in migrants' homes and at church dances had it not been for a growth in interest among outsiders—musicians and dancers—about Cajun and Creole cultures. The money that maintains the frequency of events (from a minimum of four in a week up to ten or more in northern California) comes mostly out of the "American" dancers' pockets, in the form of expenditures on cover charges, beverages, and sometimes food. Contexts for Louisiana French music and dancing now include public dancehalls, bars, business district lunch hours, festivals of various themes (including Louisiana-specific ones), voluntary association potlucks, and so on.

The social mixing of Cajuns, Creoles, and others in California provides a case study of a traveling culture, illustrating how "unresolved historical dialogues between continuity and disruption, essence and positionality, homogeneity and differences (cross-cutting 'us' and 'them') characterize diasporic articulations."[9] The hundreds of Louisiana French music and dance events that take place in northern California each year present us with examples of contexts in which

---

the United States, but rather to mark differences in language and culture. Barry Jean Ancelet and Elmore Morgan, Jr., *The Makers of Cajun Music/Musiciens Cadiens Et Creoles* (Austin, 1984), 16.

[5] Mark DeWitt, *The Cajun and Zydeco Music and Dance Scene in Northern California: Ethnicity, Authenticity, and Leisure* (Berkeley, CA, 1998), 58-68.

[6] John Minton, "Houston Creoles and Zydeco: The Emergence of an African American Popular Style," *American Music* 14 (1996): 480-526.

[7] It should be noted that this article addresses itself specifically to northern California, leaving aside the question of how Louisiana French music and dance have "traveled" to southern California. While the Los Angeles area probably has a larger population of Louisiana Creoles than San Francisco, as well as a history of church dances and Louisiana French festivals, the current situation is decidedly different. Informants who have spent significant time in southern California have reported to me that there is no "scene" there, referring both to the frequency of events held and, I believe, to a critical mass of dancers either inside or outside of the Creole community who would support dances scheduled on a weekly, or more frequent, basis.

[8] Fusilier and Adams, "Hé, La-Bas!;" Queen Ida Guillory with Naomi Wise, *Cookin' With Queen Ida* (Rocklin, CA, 1990).

[9] Clifford, "Traveling Cultures," 108.

notions of "us" and "them" are greatly complicated in the process of traveling. In the ensuing identity confusion, role reversals are as often a cause of amusement as of dismay. A white couple from California travels to Louisiana to enjoy a zydeco festival, enters a dance contest on a whim and wins it. A married couple from Louisiana, long-time residents of the San Francisco Bay Area, sometimes stays in hotels when they go to visit their home state so that they are free to go out dancing at the public clubs with their friends from California. They would not be able to do so were they to stay with their more socially conservative, class-conscious relatives.

Who attends Louisiana French dance events in northern California? Without the benefit of a demographic study, it is still possible to say that, outside of the church dances, Louisiana French people and their families are in the minority, and occasionally may be absent altogether. Whites and blacks predominate, with a few scattered Latinos and Asian Americans; women often outnumber men,[10] and the majority are single or divorced persons over thirty-five years of age. A few bring their children to festivals and other, mostly daytime, events. Some possess a considerable disposable income, others very little. Approaches to dress vary widely, and present little in the way of an income barrier.

Among the musicians, I have counted approximately thirty different California-based bands over a four-year period from 1994 to 1998, of which about half have at least one member of Cajun or Creole descent. The number of bands is misleading, however, as their lineups typically consist of various combinations of the same musicians. Interracial band membership is common enough to be the rule rather than the exception. Women on the bandstand are somewhat less common, although there have been five groups led by women in recent years to augment Queen Ida's earlier example. The musicians fall mostly in the same age range as the bulk of the dancers.

When culture "travels" via immigration, do places or a sense of place "travel" with it? To answer with an illustration: a Californian not from Louisiana once under-took to organize a special dance event in honor of a Creole community member. He booked a hall for the event, one of the regular venues for Cajun and zydeco dances in the Bay Area, and set about to spread the word among Creole families and other dance regulars for what he was hoping would be a family-oriented event. His Creole contacts informed him that he had erred in his choice of location: few if any Creole women and children would be likely to attend his otherwise laudable affair. He was told that, just as in Louisiana, there were some clubs in California where it was all right for Creole families to go, and others where "respectable" people (women especially) did not go. This follows a typically Caribbean dichotomy between respectability and reputa-

---

[10] It should however be observed that women tend to leave a dance earlier than men, so that by the end of an evening women are often in the minority.

tion[11] that Spitzer has identified as operational also among black Creoles in Louisiana:

> Respectability is the female-centered value associated with homelife, marriage, child-rearing, stability, modesty, loyalty and, most of all, the ideal order. Home and kin networks as well as church settings are the primary "social matrices"[12] where this value is acted out. Reputation is the male-centered value associated with men joining with the cohorts in groups away from the home in bars, clubs, and on street corners to assert their personal worth and manhood through bragging and tales of conquest of women.[13]
>
> However, clubs are not automatically places of reputation.... There are clubs that are known for drinking, gambling, boasting, toasting, pool playing and men's reputation behavior in general.... There are also clubs that function as dancehalls for zydeco music on weekend nights. These tend to be more respectable places patronized by family groups where a single woman can attend without being stigmatized as "loose."[14]

This "American" organizer had unwittingly run afoul of the Creole distinction between reputation and respectability by scheduling his family event at a place that the Creoles considered to be a place of reputation. The concept of such a place had survived the transition from Louisiana to California, even though certain activities, such as heavy drinking, pool-playing, and gambling, were not present at the club in question. Moreover, "American" woman informants tended to hold a contrasting view of this same club as one where, going alone, they felt safe and relatively free of harassment.

Not to be ignored is the travel of Louisiana French culture in the opposite direction, from California and elsewhere back to Louisiana. Zydeco is now sufficiently popular across the United States that festival weekends in Louisiana have become, among other things, rites for the expression of regional identities among dancer-tourists. At these events, dancers from Seattle, Minneapolis, northern California, and other metropolitan areas of the United States all have some awareness of their own and of others' group identities. They constitute smaller, distinct social units within the mass of tourists. After attending a Louisiana event in 1999, one California newsletter writer wrote:

> This trip started off, as always, with a Thursday night visit to Rock 'N Bowl in New Orleans. Geno Delafose & French Rockin' Boogie played a great, high energy set to 1:30 in the morning without a break. Throughout the night, new dancers from all over the country kept showing up. These first pre-festival dances have come to feel like a

---

[11] Roger D. Abrahams, *The Man-of-Words in the West Indies: Performance and the Emergence of Creole Culture* (Baltimore, 1983).
[12] Peter J. Wilson, "Reputation Vs. Respectability: A Suggestion for Caribbean Ethnology," *Man* 4 (1969): 81.
[13] Nicholas R. Spitzer, *Zydeco and Mardi Gras: Creole Identity and Performance Genres in Rural French Louisiana* (Austin, 1986), 226.
[14] Ibid., 258-59.

ritual evening, "The Gathering of the Zydeco Dance Tribes," and the weekend's kick-off party-reunion atmosphere has always been a delight to participate in.[15]

At the 1997 Festivals Acadiens in Lafayette (south-central Louisiana), some musicians attempted to appeal to the tourists in the audience by asking over the microphone how many people were from particular places such as Atlanta. One woman, a Creole and longtime California resident who was visiting her home state in part to attend the festival, hailed a friend on the dirt dance "floor" simply by yelling, "Hey, California!" Another Californian confided to me that whenever she saw someone dancing in a strange manner, she assumed that they were from Washington, DC.

Many but not all tourists find that their California dance floor experiences have adequately prepared them for dancing in Louisiana. Upon returning to California from their first trip to Louisiana, a pair of "American" women dancers forthrightly admitted to me a moderate letdown, in spite of social pressures to say the opposite. The two of them agreed that the dancing was better in California. When I asked why, they both offered that the *music* was better in California, an unusual statement. One of them reasoned that it was a mistake to expect that the fun of going to a dance in California, where she knows many people, would be duplicated in a strange place where she didn't know anyone and no one asked her to dance. In their early forties, a typical age for California dancers, they found themselves significantly younger than the average dancers at the Louisiana Cajun events they attended and older than average at the zydeco events. They said that next time (which would not be any time soon), they would go to Louisiana for a major festival so that they would be sure at least to see some other people that they know from California.

## Space and Place

The basic question of where we are is continually answered using our notions of place. Since culture conditions those notions, places belong to culture. Martin Stokes has made a distinction between a physical space and how a musical event, as we say, takes place: music "evokes and organizes collective memories and present experiences of place" that may be far from the site of the event, ef-

---

[15] Andrea Rubinstein, "Zydeco Extravaganza Weekend," *California Friends of Louisiana French Music Newsletter* 4 (1999): 8. New Orleans, as the author of these remarks is well aware, lies outside of the home region of Cajun and Creole culture. This home region (to some Creole consternation) has become known as "Cajun Country" and "Acadiana" in newspapers and tourism guides. However, an "oil bust" of the 1980s affected all of Louisiana and led to cultural tourism initiatives both in Acadiana and in New Orleans, which in turn paved the way for the regular appearance of Cajun music and zydeco in New Orleans itself. Dancer-tourists on their way to Acadiana via the New Orleans airport incorporate these urban venues into their travel plans. Barry Jean Ancelet, "Cultural Tourism in Cajun Country: Shotgun Wedding or Marriage Made in Heaven?," *Southern Folklore* 49 (1992): 256-66; Connie Zeanah Atkinson, "Whose New Orleans? Music's Place in the Packaging of New Orleans for Tourism," in *Tourists and Tourism: Identifying With People and Places*, Simone Abram, Jacqueline Waldre and Donald V.L. Macleod, eds., (Oxford, 1997), 91-106.

fecting a "relocation" of those present.[16] In writing of anthropological notions of "the field" (as in "field research"), Clifford uses the phrase "spatial practices" to acknowledge that spaces do not exist without their interlocutors and inhabitants, that they are always "discursively mapped *and* corporeally practiced."[17]

Taking my cue from Stokes, Clifford, and others,[18] I focus here on the following meaning of "sense of place:" one that is grounded in bodily experience of particular physical places and conditioned by personal history and cultural expectations. The examples in the previous section illustrate this sense of place. Two different groups of people hold contrasting views, stemming from cultural differences, of the same dance club. The two women who visited Louisiana for the first time were not uniformly disappointed with the place—they enjoyed their swamp tour—but they were most disappointed with the dance floor as a place for social and physical interaction, for which their expectations were created from their experience as dancers in California. This is not to ignore, of course, another meaning of "sense of place" as an indexical function, for example in the advertising for tourism that I mentioned at the outset. For music to serve as an index for a place, no physical experience aside from hearing the music is necessary for an association to be created. The two meanings can operate simultaneously: when immigrants play music from their previous home, they can bring to mind the place both for those who have a personal experience of it and for those who do not. This second meaning of sense of place as index has been discussed at length with respect to the entwined histories of romantic nationalism and folk music[19] and has some bearing on Kirshenblatt-Gimhlett's notion of heritage, to be discussed below.

Despite the frequency with which northern Californians use Louisiana French music and dance to celebrate ethnicity, satisfy curiosity about another culture, or to make money by touristic association, they also participate in it for its own sake. Voicing a sentiment that other dancers have also expressed, late Berkeley club owner David Nadel once enthused to the press:

> I always look forward to Cajun-zydeco nights because I never have any problems. No arguments, no hassles. People come to boogie. It's like a social meeting. The regulars are fanatical.... So it's not a fact at all. It's even more than a scene. It's a cultural phenomenon on the West Coast.... Back in the Queen Ida days people didn't know how to do two-steps, waltzes and shuffles. They did the old Berkeley jiggle-around step. Once dance teachers began to give lessons to the locals, Cajun-zydeco music found its sustaining power.[20]

---

[16] Martin Stokes, ed., *Ethnicity, Identity, and Music: The Musical Construction of Place* (Oxford, 1994), 3.
[17] Emphasis added, James Clifford, *Router: Travel and Translation in the Late Twentieth Century* (Cambridge, 1997), 54.
[18] Notably Steven Feld and Keith H. Basso, eds., *Senses of Place* (Santa Fe, 1996).
[19] Philip V. Bohlman, *The Study of Folk Music in the Modern World* (Bloomington, 1988), 52-68.
[20] Quoted in Dan Oullette, "Ragin' Cajun," *The Monthly* 25 (1994): 7.

According to Nadel, himself a revivalist of a wide variety of traditional and popular dance through the programming at his club, the "regulars" have gone beyond the stage of media consumption and superficial fascination with an exotic culture. They keep coming back because they have established a new "cultural phenomenon," centered around a certain cluster of musical and dance practices and a social group that maintains them.

On the role of quality in creating the sense of place, Stokes has written:

> What is important is not just of musical performance, but of good performance, if music and dance are to make a social event 'happen.'... Without these qualities, however they are conceived in the particular society, the ritual event is powerless to stake the expected and desired connections and transformations.[21]

Stokes' comments corroborate David Nadel's observation on the skills of California dancers, that once they learned how to waltz and two-step, "Cajun-zydeco music found its sustaining power." The equivalence between a food booth in California and one in Louisiana or between musical performances or dance floors, relies not only on discourse about heritage but also on myriad details of "corporeal practice" in order to achieve acceptance. Of course, the nature of "quality" can change from Louisiana to California.

At a typical event, the dance floor is for most people the final destination and center of attention, and therefore it is the quintessential performance site. The following observations on dance and music, which hold true for most Cajun and zydeco dance events in northern California, describe both the patterns of physical movement of bodies through space and the social conventions that guide them. I shall also address quality, not only in terms of the "good performance" that is necessary "to make the expected and desired connections and transformations," but also simply in terms of properties of typical dance events in this regional context that make them what they are. Clearly, the quality and selection of the music are part of this, affecting the enthusiasm of the dancers as well as the selection of dance steps.

For most songs, aside from the occasional line dance, dancers form couples to dance a two-step, "Cajun jitterbug,"[22] or waltz. The configuration of dancing bodies on the floor is punctuated by the musicians, who play one song at a time and put a clear ending on one before beginning another. Partnerships almost never change in the middle of a song. Dancers far outnumber bystanders while live music is being played, but the reverse is true during band breaks, when recorded music at a lower volume can be heard.

---

[21] Stokes, *Ethnicity, Identity, and Music*, 5.
[22] A modified jitterbug with the "limping step" footwork is a Louisiana innovation that appeared around 1970 and features intricate twirling and spinning moves using the arms. Ormond Plater, Cynthia Speyrer, and Rand Speyrer, *Cajun Dancing* (Gretna, 1993), 36-37.

While there is a wide range of skill levels and interpretations of the basic dance steps, the degree of fundamental intersubjective agreement among dancers on the dance heat is obvious when compared to a floor full of dancing people who have little familiarity either with zydeco music or with the dance style. Agreement evidences itself not only in a tactile fashion, as when a couple in physical contact synchronize with each other and the music, but also visually. Although neither dancers nor dance teachers explain it this way, the movements of the two step, "Cajun jitterbug," and line dance all entail a slightly deeper knee and ankle bend on the second and fourth beats of each measure, cued by the backbeat usually played on the snare drum. The net effect of this characteristic, distributed over most of the couples on a dance floor, is a sea of heads gently bobbing together in time to the music, regardless of variations in footwork and arm orientation. In the two-step, many dancers also execute the so-called "double bounce," in which smaller sinking movements on beats one and three are added to the pronounced sinking movements on beats two and four, which means that all of the dancer's upward movements happen between the beats, in constant syncopation with the music.

The basic steps of Louisiana French social dancing are simple, but the role of skill on the dance floor is not a straightforward one to address. While many dance teachers and others who carry an ethos of achievement from other styles of dance aim for creativity and sophistication, these tendencies are kept in check by some values widely held in Louisiana French dancing. Such values include the importance of having fun, though not at the expense of others (especially one's partners, who may not know or be able to follow more advanced moves), and of adhering to the basic step patterns. A "better" dancer may be recognized for a variety of reasons, including not only a repertoire of flashy moves but also gracefulness, partner communication, improvisational spontaneity and emotional expressiveness. Although some dancers are recognized for their superior skills, and for a time a demonstration Cajun and zydeco dancing troupe was active, formal dance competition has never been part of the scene.

At any given moment on the dance floor, there are three physical stances with respect to the dancing that each have their own social entailments: some people are actually dancing, some are seated at the tables around the perimeter, and some are standing between those dancing and those seated. This range of physical distances from the center of dancing activity can reflect one's level of current engagement with it: those immersed in the activity, those seeking to enter it (standing), and those who are simply watching or resting (seated). There is enough truth in this simplistic classification to help the newcomer, fresh from a dance class and eager to practice, to identify potential dance partners. While it is generally understood that the man in the couple leads the moves on the dance floor, it is common enough for a woman to invite a man to dance. Also widely understood are conventions that facilitate the incorporation of new members into a constantly changing social group: to circulate among partners (two dances maximum per partner) and politely to accept (or decline) invitations from strangers.

With continued attendance at these events, a more complex social topography to the dance floor naturally emerges which I can only superficially describe here. While everyone is a potential dance partner in theory, this is obviously not so in practice. The viability of a partnership is determined in part by a match of dancing skills, attitudes of both parties towards dancing with strangers or with someone of vastly inferior (or superior) skills, and past experiences of dancing with each other. There are usually not enough tables for the number of dancers in the room; those who arrive early enough to claim them are usually established groups of friends or extended families, but the tables also serve as havens for newcomers who are less comfortable with dancing. When the floor is full of dancers and the tables are deserted, it is acceptable to sit at one until its occupants return. In general, a sense of place on the dance floor resides in each individual's negotiation of the social spaces contained in it as well as the physical environment of an open floor containing nothing but other dancers and bystanders.

While there has been recognition from Louisianians that some California musicians and dancers have achieved a reasonable facsimile of Louisiana practices, there are also some clear differences. Few dance in the counterclockwise circle around the perimeter of the floor that is customary especially at Cajun dances in Louisiana and is also seen at Creole dances. Neither do many in California adjust their dancing style according to whether Cajun or zydeco music is being played. The six-count "Texas two-step" popular in country music (slow, slow, quick-quick), used by many Cajun couples in Louisiana in place of the four-count version (slow, quick-quick), is almost never seen on the California dance floor. Tisserand has observed that line dances are somewhat more popular in California than in Louisiana.[23] Furthermore, in contrast to Louisiana, drinking to excess at California dances is socially frowned upon, and smoking indoors is generally prohibited altogether.

Styles of dancing, as already noted, have diverged somewhat (but only somewhat) in California from their Louisiana French models, and in ways that I would argue amount to a new tradition.[24] These practices are reasonably consistent within the population of regular California dancers. No one set out to create a distinctively Californian style of zydeco dancing; it simply happened

---

[23] Tisserand, *The Kingdom of Zydeco*, 218.
[24] I have heard much less general discussion about a distinctively California style of zydeco or Cajun music, outside of my suggestion above that the two genres are more often mixed or confused into one than they are in Louisiana. Further discussion of musical change is beyond the scope of this paper.

over a period of time. Indeed, the differences are not strongly marked nor are they universally recognized, but from time to time they are discussed as a part of cultural politics that so often arise around issues of authenticity. From a preservationist point of view espoused by a handful of Louisiana French immigrants and others, those who dance should respect the culture enough to adhere closely to how it is done in Louisiana: no Cajun jitterbugging to zydeco, for example, and "ladies do not stomp." To this argument arises the rejoinder that respect is being shown, that the couple dances and especially the two-step have not been abandoned,[25] but rather that California now has its own style of zydeco dancing. One promoter who has made this response reinforced it by telling me how someone from Seattle, Washington, had asked permission to videotape one of his events. The reason? The person allegedly wanted to study the tape for innovative California dance moves to teach in Seattle zydeco classes. The request was refused.

If dance is central to these events, how important then is musical quality? Music permeates the place even when the musicians themselves and their equipment occupy only a corner of it. For some, the musical requirements are basic: the performance should be live rather than recorded; the band's instrumentation should establish a suitable acoustic signifier pointing to Louisiana (i.e., an accordion, usually also either a rubboard[26] or a violin); and the band should provide stimulating rhythms and tempo suitable for dancing waltzes, two-steps, and line dances. For others whose musical sensibilities have been refined by collecting recordings, living in or traveling to Louisiana, or playing the music themselves, further criteria come into play. These include: Does the band play songs from the existing stock of Cajun and zydeco repertoire? Does the singer sing songs in French where it is customary to do so and, if so, how well is he or she able to sing and pronounce the lyrics? Do the instrumental solos exhibit skill at embellishment or are they the same every time? Those who ask these sorts of questions differentiate themselves from the majority, whose attitude they characterize as: if it has a beat you can dance to, it's good enough. These two contrasting aesthetic attitudes do not seem to split cleanly along lines of ethnicity, travel time spent in Louisiana, or any other identifiable factor.

---

[25] Tisserand confirms that dancers outside of southwest Louisiana are, if anything, more conservative in their dance preferences. This group "states a preference for steady dance rhythms.... More Louisiana musicians are seeing a market for traditional two-steps and waltzes" while touring than on their home turf (Tisserand, *The Kingdom of Zydeco*, 338).

[26] The rubboard (Louisiana French: *frottoir*) is a scraped metal idiophone. A descendant of the domestic washboard used for cleaning clothes, the contemporary musical instrument is cut and formed from a single piece of sheet metal into a corrugated vest that hangs from the shoulders down the front of the player to the waist or sometimes lower. Scrapers are generally made of metal but otherwise vary according to player preference: spoons and bottle openers are common choices. Except for the occasional solo, the rubboard usually plays relatively fixed rhythmic patterns.

While participants continue to recognize distinctions between Cajun and zydeco styles,[27] they are often blurred in practice. An emphasis on zydeco over Cajun music began with the predominance of Creoles who migrated to California relative to the number of Cajuns. As a partial consequence, musical repertoire, performance practice, and dance styles influenced by zydeco music tend to dominate the northern California events schedule. This picture is complicated by present-day Creole musicians, especially Danny Poullard and Andrew Carrière, whose performances sound more like Cajun music than zydeco, as did those of earlier generations of musicians in their families who called what they played simply "French music." Further complicating the question of what to call the music made in California is a tendency by certain bands to play in both Cajun and zydeco styles in a single night. In addition, the context of ethnic identity politics between Cajuns and Creoles, which in Louisiana tends to maintain the boundary between the two related styles of music, is largely missing in California. Therefore, throughout this paper I prefer to use the two in conjunction, as in the compound modifier "Cajun and zydeco" or "Cajun-zydeco."[28]

California bands have found many strategies to identify themselves with Louisiana French culture by name, in which the Cajun and zydeco labels figure prominently and do have some significance in indicating what style of music the band plays most. To some extent band names also reveal marketing strategies, many of which refer to heritage of some sort (see next section). Aside from simply using the words "Cajun" (e.g., California Cajun Orchestra, Cajun Bandits, Cajun Classics, Cajun Coyotes), "Creole" (Creole Belles), or "zydeco" (Bad Boy Zydeco, Zydeco Flames, Zydeco Magic, Zydeco Slim), some have used other references to Louisiana French life, such as favorite songs (Motordude Zydeco, Bayou Pon Pon, Frog Legs), wildlife (Crawdaddy, Gator Beat), food (Mumbo Gumbo), and geography (Bayou Brothers, Swamp Dogs). Still others have adopted French or French-looking names tailored to their own identities:

---

[27] Briefly, Cajun and zydeco share some repertoire and basic dance steps but are distinguished from each other in terms of instrumentation (use of violin and electric steel guitar in Cajun music but not in zydeco, use of *frottoir* in zydeco but not in Cajun) and in terms of borrowing repertoire and performance practices from either rhythm and blues (zydeco) or American country music (Cajun). Much more has already been written on this subject. Mark F. DeWitt, *The Cajun and Zydeco Music and Dance Scene in Northern California: Ethnicity, Authenticity, and Leisure* (Berkeley, CA,1998), 176-228; Rick Olivier and Ben Sandmel, *Zydeco!* (Jackson, 1999), 22-29; Nicholas R. Spitzer, "Zodico: Louisiana's Black Créole Music," *Sing Out!* 27(1979): 2-7; Spitzer, *Zydeco and Mardi Gras*, 300-410.

[28] In contrasts that informants make between California and Louisiana, the subject of mixing—of musical styles, of dance styles, of race—surfaces repeatedly. The musical mixing of Cajun (associated with whites) and zydeco (associated with blacks) is not the result of ignorance. I believe, as most people who attend events regularly for a few months learn the basic differences between these two styles. Furthermore, some of the mixing of styles is carried out by Louisiana French natives themselves. Many express a preference for zydeco, suggesting that the distinction has been learned and a choice made. What the mixing of the musics and, perhaps to a greater degree, the dance styles does seem to echo is an avowed apathy towards racial distinctions, a belief that racial identity should not dictate cultural practices.

Tete Rouge, named after its red-headed leader; the Aux Cajun-als, a group that plays occasionally in public; Tee Fee (from *petite fille*, Cajun French for 'little girl' or 'girlfriend'), a band led by two women; Delta Cajun, named after the region where its musicians live (the Sacramento River Delta) as well as the kind of music they play; and Miss Freida and the Cajun Fusiliers, a name formed from the leader's full name, her ethnicity and style of music (Cajun), and the form of address that people "back home" might use for her ("Miss Freida"). Although not all Cajun and Creole names sound French, band leaders who do have French-sounding names (Andrew Carrière and the Cajun Classics, R.C. Carrière Zydeco, Gerard Landry and the Cajun Bandits, Kent Menard, André Thierry and Zydeco Magic) also tend to use them.

Suzy Thompson, Afro-Creole Danny Poullard, and Eric Thompson of California Cajun Orchestra.
*Photo courtesy of Suzy Thompson.*

Edward S. Casey argues that our perceptions of physical space and time derive from culturally contextual, bodily inhabited places rather than the other way around. For him, a place is an active rather than a passive entity, with a life distinct from that of the human bodies that pass through it. Proceeding from the assertion that places actively gather things and living beings together. He postulates that "...a place is its midst, being in the midst of its own detailed contents; it is what lies most deeply amid its own constituents, gathering them together in the expressive landscape of that place."[29] While I do not take Casey literally as to the active agency of places, I find that he powerfully evokes the subjective experience of place. All that has been discussed thus far—travelings of Louisiana French culture through immigration and mediation, selective importation of values and practices, notions of quality and distinctiveness—has been gathered together to create a distinctive place for music and dancing, "a California dance floor." What remains to be discussed are some of the underlying cultural concepts that have facilitated the production of this place via both tacit agreement and explicit contention among its participants.

---

[29] Casey, "How to Get From Space to Place," 28.

## Heritage and Tradition

Kirshenblatt-Gimblett has theorized that the terms "heritage" and "tradition" refer to distinct "modes of production" of cultural practices. She defines "heritage" as a quality that "gives buildings, precincts, and ways of life that are no longer viable for one reason or another a second life as exhibits of themselves; it also produces something new."[30] "Tradition," by contrast, is that which is transmitted as a matter of course and taken for granted, that which is self-evident rather than self-conscious.[31] The prominence of places in these definitions is noteworthy.

From my research, the contrast between the self-evident and the self-conscious is exemplified in two signs for the same event, a so-called "dance ranch" weekend outside of Vacaville, California. The first sign that one saw, a piece of white cardboard hand-lettered with "DANCE RANCH 1–8 PM TODAY," directed automobile traffic to the parking lot in a self-evident, actual (i.e., not virtual) fashion. The second sign, "Entering Louisiana" hand-painted on a white cloth, announced the first "exhibit" that most visitors saw, a small dance floor named "The Cajun Back Porch." A plastic crawfish caught in a net hovered above the sign, while a patched-up wooden plank wall formed the backdrop for the band and suggested the front of a modest dwelling. This stage set conflated where we were (Vacaville) and where we could be (Louisiana). Compared to the main stage, the "Cajun Back Porch" was designed to project a more intimate atmosphere appropriate for storytelling and informal music-making. The stage set illustrates "relocations" both in space—from California to Louisiana—and in time—from the age of television and air conditioning back to the era of Cajun *bals de maison* (house dances) and *veillées* (evening social gatherings).[32]

On the surface, and despite its author's stated intentions, the theorization of tradition and heritage appears to reinscribe an older pairing, that of authenticity and alienation. Consider the alignment of oppositions that she does make (Table I).

---

[30] Barbara Kirshenblatt-Gimhlett, "Theorizing Heritage," *Ethnomusicology* 39 (1995): 370.
[31] Barbara Kirshenblatt-Gimhlett, "Sounds of Sensibility," *Judaism* 47 (1998): 54.
[32] Barry Jean Ancelet, Jay Edwards, and Glen Pitre, *Cajun Country* (Jackson, 1991), 46-50.

Table I. Sources of Heritage/Tradition Opposition[33]

| Source | Domain | Opposition | |
|---|---|---|---|
| Raymond Williams, *Marxism and Literature* (New York, 1977), 132–33. | literature/ cultural studies | feeling | ideology |
| Haym Soloveitchik, "Rupture and Reconstruction: The Transformation of Contemporary Orthodoxy," *Tradition* 28 (1994): 64-130. | religion | impulse, tradition | ideology |
| Barbara Kirshenblatt-Gimblett, "Sounds of Sensibility," *Judaism* 47 (1998): 49-78. | folklore | tradition | heritage |

Impulse, feeling, and freedom from the "contamination" of ideology all prepare the way to an accurate outpouring of an individual's inner emotional and musical life, an authenticity of individual expression that has been highly valued since the Romantics.[34] The distinction between heritage as self-conscious and tradition as self-evident also harks back to earlier European thought: "The continued craving for experiences of unmediated genuineness seeks to cut through what Rousseau called the wound of reflection, a reaction to modernization's demythologization, detraditionalization, and disenchantment."[35] This valuation of the genuine is itself, of course, an ideology, one that still has many subscribers despite the advent of postmodernism. It is because these Romantic attitudes persist, perhaps, that Kirshenblatt-Gimblett needs to make the case for heritage as something worthy of study, to defend the legitimacy of those cultural expressions that are more or less obviously "made not found."[36]

Heritage as a mode of production is indeed worthy of study in explaining the maintenance of the Cajun and zydeco scene in northern California. Heritage productions attract newcomers to take part via media exposure, especially via the marketing of Louisiana tourism, food, and music. The current status of Louisiana French culture as a national popular novelty in the United States contrasts sharply with its previous reputation for backwardness in the American South. A number of global trends have contributed to this reversal of perception, including folk revival, civil rights, and "new ethnicity" trends in the 1960s,[37] and attention from the tourism industry following a downturn in regional oil production in the 1980s.[38] These developments led to the repre-

---

[33] Kirshenblatt-Gimblett, "Sounds of Sensibility," 54-56.
[34] Regina Bendix, *In Search of Authenticity: The Formation of Folklore Studies* (Madison, 1997), 38-44.
[35] Ibid., 8.
[36] Kirshenblatt-Gimblett, "Theorizing Heritage," 369.
[37] James H. Dorman, *The People Called Cajuns: Introduction to an Ethnohistory* (Lafayette, 1983).
[38] Barry Jean Ancelet, "Cultural Tourism in Cajun Country: Shotgun Wedding or Marriage Made in Heaven," *Southern Folklore* 49 (1992): 256-66.

sentation of Cajun and zydeco music as heritage both in and outside of Louisiana.

In the northern California scene, preservationist impulses of heritage provided an outlet for some (though not all) Creole immigrants from Louisiana to host their own dances. A common refrain among Cajun and Creole musicians who relocated to California is that they did not care much for "French music" when they lived in Louisiana or eastern Texas, but they found they wanted to hear it and even play it themselves once the music had disappeared from their immediate environment.[39] Once these practices were established among the immigrants, then they became a drawing card for other Californians who came initially to Cajun and zydeco dances essentially as tourists and then helped dances to happen with greater regularity through their reliable attendance. Heritage has also had a formative influence, I believe, through the imagining of a "Cajun zydeco community"[40] of dancers and musicians, despite the highly heterogeneous, urban environment of northern California. This community has occasionally coalesced for memorial services. Benefits for musicians with health problems, and fund-raising to keep a dancehall operating, but otherwise I would assert that its existence is largely symbolic (in the sense of "symbolic ethnicity"),[41] and its main benefit is to provide a sense of belonging. Heritage concepts of authenticity in music and dance have given Cajuns, Creoles, and Americans some incentive to pool their efforts through a shared image of the communal folk.

Voluntary member associations dedicated to the promotion of Cajun and zydeco music have contributed to the production of Louisiana French heritage in California. The two women who produced the Cajun Back Porch as part of a for-profit enterprise have also run a non-profit group that sponsored annual awards-of-recognition ceremonies and other events. These events have often honored musicians and dancers of Louisiana French descent, sometimes with speeches offered in both French and English. Another non-profit organization was formed with the mission of fostering understanding and appreciation of Cajun and Creole music and dance. In keeping with this educational emphasis, this second organization hosts occasional "jams," dance events in which an experienced musician is hired to lead a group of volunteers who may already play in a band or who need more practice playing for dancers. It has also assembled a festival booth, consisting of books and photographs about Cajun and Creole culture culled from members' personal collections, which members operate during the organization's own festivals and also at some commercial ones.

---

[39] Fusilier and Adams, *Hé, La-Bas!*.
[40] Benedict R. Anderson, *Imagined Communities: Reflections on the Origin and Spread of Nationalism*, rev. and ex. ed. (London, 1991).
[41] Herbert J. Gans, "Symbolic Ethnicity: The Future of Ethnic Groups and Cultures in America," *Ethnic and Racial Studies* 2 (1979): 1-20.

It is apparent to anyone involved that heritage productions can have destructive as well as creative consequences. At the same time that he noted success in certain Louisiana touristic productions such as the "Rendezvous des Cajuns" radio show, Cajun folklorist Barry Jean Ancelet expressed ambivalence by the early 1990s at changes in Louisiana French culture wrought by the very self-consciousness that makes heritage possible:

> There are important issues to be considered, such as cultural ecology and the interaction between visitors and the community.... There are inherent problems. such as self-consciousness and misinformation. On a recent fishing trip with a friend, I found myself sitting in a Cajun-brand boat, using Cajun-brand crickets and grabbing a Cajun-brand beer from a Cajun-brand ice chest filled with Cajun-brand ice.... Recently, Burger King featured something called a Cajun whaler (its usual fish patty dipped in crab boil) and Pizza Hut offered a New Orleans-style Cajun pizza (whatever that is). Cajun musician Marc Savoy was asked recently if he regretted that the Cajuns had been discovered. He answered, "What's worse is that the Cajuns have discovered themselves."[42]

Implied in Ancelet's commentary is the suggestion that "misinformation" has been bred from profit-driven motives to slap the Cajun label on anything sold in southern Louisiana, either through the suggestion of some ethnic difference in design or use where none exists (crickets, beer, ice chest, ice) or through the fabrication of Cajun folklore (in this case, foodways) for consumption by people who either don't care or don't know any better. The "made not found" quality of heritage here has been conflated with fakelore. Hovering in the background is an irony arising from the contemporary use of the word "Cajun" as a positive attribute, whereas earlier in the twentieth century it was regarded as an ethnic slur. Also suggested is that self-consciousness—Savoy's remark recalling Rousseau's "wound of reflection"—itself breeds misinformation during the process of creating a market for Cajun products, in which historical truth is the first casualty of economic warfare.

A heritage approach to Cajun and zydeco music in northern California has also carried some disadvantages with it, in the form of exoticism and identity politics. The explosive potential of exoticizers and exoticized dancing cheek to cheek and playing together on the bandstand is considerable. For example, Cajuns and Creoles who participate in the scene politely endure, as a rule, statements made by beginners in ignorance but will spring to corrective action when beginners who become regulars are seen to appoint themselves experts on dance style or some other aspect of Louisiana French culture. The question of who has more of a right to play the music can also figure occasionally in the constant tension among bands competing for jobs. Authenticity issues have fanned the flames of controversies that have led to schisms in the form of

---

[42] Ancelet, "Cultural Tourism in Cajun Country," 264.

multiple voluntary associations and clubs.

In discussing heritage and authenticity, the role of simulation deserves further attention. Addressing the Society for Ethnomusicology at its 1994 Annual Meeting in Milwaukee, Wisconsin, Kirshenblatt-Gimblett observed:

> The production of hereness, in the absence of actualities, depends increasingly on virtualities. The frenzy of memory in downtown Milwaukee requires the instruments of historic walks, plaques, historical societies, museums, tours, and exhibitions because Old Milwaukee is a phantom. It hovers in the spaces cleared by freeways, parking lots, hotels, and convention centres.[43]

There is much rhetorical and physical work that goes into the construction of a heritage site. For example, despite its co-location with the old city, Old Milwaukee is a virtual place: it refers to an historical and/or geographical context other than its own. Virtuality operates as a powerful principle both in tourism and in folkloric performance; indeed they often appear in tandem, and both depend on the establishment of an imagined time and space.

Consider Valone Smith's loose definition of tourism as visiting a place away from home in order to experience a change[44] in conjunction with music's power to transport metaphorically, to a place far from its physical location. For an Oakland, California, resident to make the short drive next door to Alameda for the Friday night zydeco might therefore also be considered a form of tourism. One might also say that the power that makes this possible derives not only from the music but more generally from the quality of heritage that is exploited in the tourism business. Artifacts that are "disappearing" or "gone" can be given "a second life" as exhibitions of themselves[45] at Eagles' Hall in Alameda, California, more or less as readily as they can at Mulate's Cajun Restaurant in Breaux Bridge, Louisiana. Furthermore, regardless of where a festival of Cajun music is held, a food booth is a food booth, a stage is a stage, a dance floor is a dance floor, and a two-step is a two-step. With some collective attention to quality, i.e., to details such as food preparation, musical performance practice, and dance style, the illusion of a virtual time and place appears.

What I am suggesting—call it "virtual tourism"—is not exactly a new idea: popular music of the world beat variety has been called "sonic tourism,"[46] while the Smithsonian Festival of American Folklife

> ...may be said on one level to have more thoroughly realized, through bureaucratic organization and planning.... the principle of tourism: in effect it collapses the cultural

---

[43] Kirshenblatt-Gimhlett, "Theorizing Heritage," 376.
[44] Valene L. Smith, *Hosts and Guests: The Anthropology of Tourism* (Philadelphia, 1977).
[45] Kirshenblatt-Gimhlett, "Sounds of Sensibility," 52.
[46] Timothy D. Taylor, *Global Pop: World Music, World Marker* (New York, 1997), 19.

universe, formerly diffused on the margins of the social center, into a culturological garden whose margin is the touristic or the social scientific gaze.[47]

In contrast to the Smithsonian Festival, however, the margins of the garden of Cajun and zydeco music in northern California are not nearly so well-trimmed nor are they maintained by any central bureaucracy. Rather, "the principle of tourism" has emerged from the confluence in one place of the migration of Louisiana French people, a local (that is to say, northern Californian) appreciation for folklife of various origins, and entrepreneurial and curatorial energies of certain individuals. Kirshenblatt-Gimblett's characterization of heritage is evident in Cantwell's notion of "framing devices,"[48] conventions that insulate "participants" (musicians and artisans) from "visitors" (tourists) and that maintain the Smithsonian's "garden paths." Framing devices may appear in some California contexts such as the Vacaville Dance Ranch event but are largely absent at the more routine weekly dances. One social interaction at a time, individuals in California negotiate boundaries among groups of visitors and participants (borrowing Cantwell's typology). These fluid boundaries do not align automatically along racial or ethnic lines. It may take a new California dancer one or two years to learn, if she is even interested, who among the people she sees regularly are from Louisiana families, for the "participants" have formed an informal folk group[49] based on music and dancing, not on ethnic affiliation.

Following an idea of rootlessness suggested by virtual tourism and traveling cultures, the "field" of my fieldwork in a sense has been a free-floating dance floor, a "hotel" where traveler-informants come and go,[50] where a sense of place is achieved more by the convening of like-minded people than by geographical location. This is a field that "hovers in the spaces" (as Kirshenblatt-Gimblett puts it), it "exists in the midst" (as Casey might say) of the dancers, musicians, sights, sounds, tastes, and built environments that comprise it.

One of the most sustained and concerted efforts to create a virtual tourism context for live Louisiana French music and dancing literally embodies the hotel metaphor. The Berkeley Marina Marriott Hotel, which has since changed ownership, sits on waterfront property looking across the bay to San Francisco and the Golden Gate Bridge. For two years beginning in the summer of 1995, the hotel hired local Cajun and zydeco bands to play from 6:15 to 8:15 p.m.

---

[47] Robert Cantwell, *Ethnomimesis: Folklife and the Representation of Culture* (Chapel Hill, 1993), 276.
[48] Ibid., 274-75.
[49] Alan Dundes, *Interpreting Folklore* (Bloomington, 1980), 7-14.
[50] In his "Traveling Cultures" essay, Clifford introduces the hotel metaphor for the fieldwork site and then rejects it for a number of reasons, mostly having to do with associations of socioeconomic class that it brings. I have chosen to use it here in any case because it so effectively emphasizes (perhaps overly so) the transience of the population that attends these events, and it also reinforces the notion of the California dance floor as a virtual tourist site. James Clifford, *Router: Travel and Translation in the Late Twentieth Century* (Cambridge, 1997), 30-36.

on Fridays in the bar for the benefit of both bar customers and patrons of the adjoining restaurant. According to the food and beverage manager, the music served as part of a "total package" for Friday nights that included a Cajun buffet and other dinner specials in the restaurant, as well as a "Ragin' Cajun Happy Hour" in the bar, with "specialty cocktail menus featuring Blackened Voodoo Lager, Rattlesnake Beer, Hurricane Cocktails."[51] Neither anyone in the kitchen nor the manager was from Louisiana, but because he had some experience in producing Mardi Gras events at a hotel in Hawaii, the manager felt "comfortable" with overseeing the Friday evening theme. The program was conceived as an alternative to the restaurant's previous generic Friday seafood buffet, to run for a year or two and then be replaced by something else. On some Fridays, dancers from the regular Cajun and zydeco scene filled half of the bar, and on others very few patrons paid any attention to the music.

After we give heritage its due, acknowledging the kind of cultural construction it is and its intrinsic interest as an object of study, the adumbrated category of "tradition" awaits further attention. If, as summarized in Table 1, heritage represents some sort of ideology (as in a Romantic idea of pre-modern utopia), then tradition must reside in unanalyzed feelings, impulses, and cultural practices. If there is such a thing as authentic experience, it resides on the side of tradition, not heritage, despite the many claims of purveyors of the latter that theirs is the purest, the oldest, the most essential. In the context of exhibiting taonga (Maori treasure) in a New Zealand museum, Kirshenblatt-Gimblett appears to be saying the same thing when she opposes heritage ("second life as an exhibit") to "the truly alive."

> The lifelike is not to be confused with the truly alive. For taonga Maori the issue is not a second life as an exhibit. What is at stake is restoration of living links to taonga that never died…. The life force of taonga depends not on techniques of animation, but on the living transmission of cultural knowledge and values. What is at stake is not the vividness of a museum experience, but the vitality, the survival, of those for whom these objects are taonga. And that depends on intangible cultural property, which lives in performance.[52]

The Louisiana French dance scene in northern California, when it is at its best, accomplishes a "living transmission of cultural knowledge and values" through the Cajun and Creole immigrants and their families who attend the events and the "Americans" who have absorbed and promulgate some of these values, such as the importance of fun over virtuosic display and the incorporation of children in adult activities.

Note that in my application of these terms heritage and tradition, the presence of one does not deny the possibility of the simultaneous presence of

---

[51] Text taken from a glass display case posted on a hallway wall leading to the bar.
[52] Kirshenblatt-Gimblett, "Theorizing Heritage," 378.

the other. What is self-evident tradition for one person may be approached by another, as commonly happens in the California scene, either as one's own long-lost heritage or as someone else's. Moreover, an individual's orientation to a cultural form may change with time, from heritage to tradition or vice versa.

Music and dance no longer function as ethnic markers to those outsiders who through bodily practice, have come to regard these cultural forms as self-evident tradition *without* assuming a Louisiana French ethnic identity themselves. The coupling between this expressive culture and its ethnic sources has loosened considerably in this context, even as acknowledgement of those sources continues to he made. Heritage criteria, such as the ethnicity of the performers or conformance with orthodox performance practices, cease to hold strong sway over many of the musicians and dancers in the scene. Concern for performance quality, however an individual construes it, remains.

There is more to the California scene than virtualities: it has actualities that also matter. Questions of authenticity do arise, but I would like to sidestep them with one observation.[53] On one hand, Rousseau's "wound of reflection" has been somewhat healed, to the (partial) extent that musicians and dancers can go about their business without having to think about what they are doing in terms of heritage. One might say that it has become possible to experience these forms of expressive culture in an intuitive, unreflective, "authentic" fashion. On the other hand, the performances that result in such a context do not necessarily reproduce their Louisiana models faithfully, and in such instances authenticity in another sense is lost. Belying its "deceptive promises of transcendence,"[54] authenticity, in its multiple meanings, offers in the end only conflicting interpretations.

## Conclusion

This examination of the presence of Louisiana French music and dance in northern California began with some observations about culture on the move when accompanied by culture-bearers themselves.[55] An emerging body of work by phenomenologists, anthropologists, and ethnomusicologists suggests that, regardless of who uses it, expressive culture achieves a "sense of place" through performance and other bodily practices.[56] Evocations of place are intensified in heritage productions which employ principles of virtuality to simulate a specific place and time. Standing in contrast to such productions are traditions which

---

[53] Authenticity and its many contradictory meanings have been much discussed elsewhere—Bendix, *In Search of Authenticity*; DeWitt, *The Cajun and Zydeco Music and Dance Scene*; Peter Kivy, *Authenticities: Philosophical Reflections on Musical Performance* (Ithaca, 1995); Timothy D. Taylor, *Global Pop: World Music, World Markers* (New York, 1997).
[54] Bendix, *In Search of Authenticity*, 7.
[55] Clifford, "Traveling Cultures," 91-116.
[56] Casey, "How to Get From Space to Place," 13-52; Stokes, *Ethnicity, Identity, and Music*.

remain (or resume their place in) the fabric of everyday life.[57] To conclude, I propose how these various theoretical constructs dovetail and how they have illuminated the subject of this research.

There are connections to be made among all of the three perspectives that I have used: between traveling culture and sense of place; between sense of place and heritage: and between traveling culture and heritage. Clifford does well to question the privileged status of the remote village as the preferred place for anthropological research, for example with his call for a "focus on hybrid cosmopolitan experiences as much as on rooted, native ones."[58] What his reverse emphasis on traveling over dwelling does not address, however, is that even as they are "traveling," the bodily practices of music and dance tend to evoke some kind of place. The appearance of stability, at least, remains important. Indeed, as music and dance travel elsewhere from where they are created, their powers as signifiers of place have the greatest potential to intensify.

To say that music and dance help to create a sense of place, of course, is one way of acknowledging their powers of virtuality, of evoking another place and/or time. Whether consciously perceived or not, there is an element of illusion in any sense of place. The strength of that illusion results both from discourse and from performance, in which the quality of details matters. Regarding quality, above I made some intentionally outrageous statements inspired by the concept of virtuality: "a food booth is a food booth," for example, but perhaps only until one tastes the food! The detailed description contained herein of northern California dance practices, in contrast to ad hoc reception by dancers of the music in other regions (such as Ohio, where I live now), drives this point home. Furthermore, we cannot say that "a dancehall is a dancehall," with the Louisiana tourist stop on the one hand and a Berkeley landmark, complete with Jewish heritage markers and radical political slogans, on the other. Yet Ashkenaz, David Nadel's club, has been one of the most important public venues for Cajun and zydeco music in the Bay Area, where the performance of music and dance transforms a building remodeled after a *synagogue into a virtual* Louisiana dancehall.[59]

Given the origins of Kirshenblatt-Gimhlett's concept of heritage in her work with museum displays, it is no surprise that heritage is ready-made for travel. Once something has been turned into a display of itself, broken off from its original surroundings, it can be displayed anywhere. The exhibition is available for touring. Even a display such as the Cajun Back Porch, in its attempts to imitate the context for casual Cajun music-making with its visual props and

---

[57] Kirshenblatt-Gimhlett, "Theorizing Heritage," 367-80; Kirshenblatt-Gimhlett, "Sounds of Sensibility," 49-78.
[58] Clifford, "Traveling Cultures," 101.
[59] On other nights, the same club evokes other places, as its programming includes music from Africa, the Caribbean, the Middle East, Eastern Europe, India, and so on.

costumed Cajun emcee, of course represents only a fragment of the life and times in which the music was created.[60] Tradition, on the other hand, is not so portable. It represents, in the definition I am exploring here, a whole cultural environment prior to ethnographic reification of some part of it. And, in California, the life and times in which Louisiana French music actually *is* created is the hybrid cosmopolitan experience of which Clifford wrote.

Where are we? At times when I have found myself under the stained glass and wooden beams at Ashkenaz, or in the hot sun at a Vacaville ranch, or at a bar in Richmond, or a church hall in El Cerrito, or dancing with California friends at a club in Louisiana, the same "sense of place" has emerged, what I am calling a California dance floor. Where could we be? This dance floor simultaneously points to its counterparts in southern Louisiana (as heritage) and offers the possibility of sufficiency unto itself (as tradition). We could be virtually there or actually here. The meaning of attending a Louisiana French dance in California exists in a field of tension between the self-conscious practice of heritage production and the self-evident practice of an ongoing tradition. In some instances, as with newcomers at the Vacaville Dance Ranch event, heritage dominates, while in others, as with the attendance of regulars at Friday night zydeco dances at Eagles' Hall in Alameda, (recently established) tradition continues with an air of unremarkableness. In the latter case, "virtual tourism" is no longer an apt description. The importance of virtuality gives way to a new actuality, and some traveling culture comes to rest, however fleetingly.

---

[60] Barbara Kirshenblatt-Gimhlett, *Destination Culture: Tourism, Museums, and Heritage* (Berkeley, 1998), 17-23.

# The Cajun Dancehall[1]

*Malcolm L. Comeaux*

Cajun dancehalls are mentioned in the writings of various authors, but only in a passing way, and nothing has been published that focuses on this topic. Many questions can be asked about Cajun dancehalls. Are they similar to dancehalls found elsewhere in America? Are they different, and if so, how? A large number of researchers have studied various aspects of Cajun music, and one newspaper recently gave a rather good listing of former dancehalls,[2] but the dancehall itself, where much of the music is played and where much of the music evolved, remains an unknown.

There were many Cajun dancehalls when I was in high school in the mid-1950s, and at that time I began going to them. Webb's Neighborhood Lounge was about a mile from where I was raised north of Lafayette, and I often went there, if nothing more than to listen to music from the outside until I was eighteen and could legally enter. After discharge from the Army in 1960, I continued visiting Cajun dancehalls through most of the 1960s. After leaving Louisiana to teach in 1969, I continued to enjoy Cajun dancehalls every summer. I have been to dancehalls elsewhere in America, and contend that those in south Louisiana are unique. Their uniqueness is not just the result of cultural factors (Cajun music being played, food consumed, card playing, and the like), but the fact that the very form, use, and shape of the dancehall is different. Most of the old Cajun dancehalls are now gone, but a few still survive in their traditional shape, function and form. Although few Cajun dancehalls survive, ideas and concepts behind them not only still survive, but are thriving in the restaurant/dancehalls now popular in south Louisiana.

Ancestors to the Cajuns first came to America in the seventeenth century, establishing a homeland in the Maritime Provinces of Canada. These people became known as Acadians (from whence comes the word Cajun), and their descendants in the Maritime Provinces of Canada are still known by that name. Dances were popular among Acadians. With time, however, the "civilizing" effect of clergy was felt, and changes occurred in the culture. Foreign priests, usually from France or Belgium (or sometimes Québec), played a major role in lives of these Catholics, and dancing was frowned upon, except in some situations where clergy had control.[3] An example of this is a description of a conversation in the early twentieth century where a priest "gave everyone permission

---

[1] This article first appeared in the journal *Material Culture* 32 (2000): 37-56.
[2] Jim Bradshaw, "Louisiana French Music," *The Daily Advertiser's History of Acadiana*, December 29, 1998, newspaper supplement.
[3] Anselme Chaisson, Charlotte Cormier, Donald Deschnes, and Ronald Labelle, "Le Folklore Acadien," in *L'Acadie des Maritimes*, ed. Jean Daigle (Moncton, N.B., 1993), 701-02.

to dance" after a barn raising.[4] In some areas house dances were popular, but by the middle of the twentieth century some Acadians had never danced for fear of condemnation by clergy.[5] It was not until some time in the twentieth century before Acadians in the Maritimes began to have dances, and then usually in church halls. Dancing and public dancehalls were not a large part of their culture. The Cajuns of Louisiana were quite different, as their culture evolved along different lines.

Cajun culture evolved differently compared to their cousins in the Maritime Provinces. The biggest reason was the very physical environment settled by those who went to Louisiana. The semi-tropical climate encouraged an adjustment to new crops, house types, clothes and the like.[6] There were other influences as well, in particular, contact with other peoples. Many blacks lived in and among the Cajuns. There were also Frenchmen coming directly from France, and French Americans arriving from the Gulf Coast and the Illinois country. In Louisiana there was also a strong Spanish influence originating coming from the time Spain controlled the Louisiana colony, as well as Spanish influences entering from Texas. Southern white settlers certainly influenced Cajuns, and they were a people with very different values when compared to the New Englanders in close contact with the Acadians in the Maritimes. Contact with these various peoples greatly influenced the evolution of the culture.[7]

The Cajuns lived in a very dispersed pattern, and without nearby priests. Many lived isolated in swamps, others lived on narrow fingers of high lands scattered throughout south Louisiana, while a significant number lived in scattered and isolated places on the prairies of southwest Louisiana. Although Catholic, there was little influence from clergy during the latter half of the eighteenth or all of the nineteenth centuries.[8] As an example, in 1834 there were only twenty-six churches and twenty-four priests in all of Louisiana.[9] Among Cajuns, dancing remained an important part of their culture.[10] Although Catholic, many Cajuns took the church lightly. This writer remembers attending masses in the late 1940s where women and children were inside the church,

---

[4] Sally Ross and J. Alphonse Deveau, *The Acadians of Nova Scotia: Past and Present* (Halifax, 1992), 146.
[5] Chiasson et al., "Le Folklore Acadien," 649-705.
[6] Malcolm L. Comeaux, "The Acadians of Canada and the Cajuns of Louisiana: Cultural Change over Distance and Time," in *Ethnic Persistence and Change in Europe and America: Traces in Landscape and Society*, eds. Klaus Frantz and Robert A. Sauder (Insbruck, 1996), 29-45.
[7] Carl A. Brasseaux, *Acadian to Cajun: Transformation of a People* (Jackson, 1992); Jacques Henry, "From Acadian to Cajun to Cadien: Ethnic Labelization and Construction of Identity," *Journal of American Ethnic History* 17 (1998): 29-62; Cécyle Trepagnier, "The Cajunization of French Louisiana: Forging a Regional Identity," *Geographical Journal* 157 (1991): 161-71.
[8] Carl A. Brasseaux, *The Founding of New Acadia* (Baton Rouge, 1987), 153-66.
[9] Roger Baudier, *The Catholic Church in Louisiana* (New Orleans, 1939), 382.
[10] One researcher (Marcia Gaudet, *The Folklore of St. John the Baptist Parish* [Lafayette, 1984], 18) found where one priest along the Mississippi River, probably in the early twentieth century, would not give absolution to anyone who went dancing. So, young folks would row across the river to go to confessions with a more liberal priest.

while most of the men were outside, talking, joking and smoking (and that was where I wanted to be).

### House Dances in South Louisiana

The earliest dances were in homes, and called "house dances." House dances were mentioned in the early Maritime Provinces,[11] so may have been an idea brought to Louisiana from there. House dances, however, were also popular throughout the South[12] so could have been an idea accepted from Anglo neighbors.

There is little published on the house dance (or *bal de maison*), but there are two good published interviews on the topic[13] as well as several passing references to them in Savoy, and in other sources, but all of them for house dances of the early twentieth century. There is one good description of what was probably a house dance somewhere near the Mississippi River in 1803:

> Ordinarily their manner is reserved, but they are no strangers to gaiety. They love to dance most of all; more than any other people in the colony. At one time during the year, they give balls for travelers and will go ten or fifteen leagues to attend one. Everyone dances, even grand-mère and grand-père no matter what the difficulties they must bear. There may be only a couple of fiddles to play for the crowd, there may be only a couple of candles for light, placed on wooden arms attached to the wall; nothing but long wooden benches to sit on, and only exceptionally a few bottles of tafia diluted with water for refreshment. No matter, everyone dances. But always everyone has a helping of gumbo, the Creole dish par excellence; then "Good Night," "Good Evening," "So Long," "See you next week" (if it isn't sooner). One shoves off in his pirogue, his paddle in his hand; another gallops off on horseback, others who live nearer walk home singing and laughing.... The women wear a simple cotton dress and often in the summer they wear only a skirt. They go to the dances barefoot, as they go to the fields, and even the men only wear shoes when they are dressed formally.[14]

When someone was to hold a house dance, a rider would go among neighbors waving a flag[15] or firing a gun informing them of the dance and where it would be held. Participants would come from miles around in family units, and never as courting couples (although this is where most courtship occurred), and unescorted ladies were not welcome.[16] Furniture was usually cleared from the largest room in the home, benches and chairs were placed along walls, and

---

[11] Anselme Chaisson, *Chéticamp: Histoire et Traditions Acadiennes* (Moncton, N.B, 1961), 210.
[12] For a humorous example of this in south Arkansas, see Arthur W. Bergeron, Jr., ed., *The Civil War Reminiscences of Major Silas T. Grisamore, C.S.A.* (Baton Rouge, 1993), 16768; in north Louisiana see John Q. Anderson, "Folkways in Writing about Northeast Louisiana before 1865," *Louisiana Folklore Miscellany* 1 (1960): 19-22.
[13] Lauren C. Post, "Joseph C. Falcon, Accordion Player and Singer," *Louisiana History* 1 (1970): 63-79; Brenda Daigle, "Acadian Fiddler Dennis McGee and Acadian Dances," *Attakapas Gazette* 7 (1972): 124-43.
[14] C.C. Robin, *Voyage to Louisiana 1803-1805*, trans. Stuart Landry (New Orleans, 1966).
[15] George W. Cable, Notes on Acadians in Louisiana, Manuscript Division, Tulane University Library, New Orleans, 155.
[16] Ann Allen Savoy, *Cajun Music: A Reflection of a People* (Eunice, 1984), 45.

cornmeal or sawdust spread on the floor. Someone at the front door would allow dancers to enter. The rooms were small, so only a few dancers were allowed in at a time.[17] Some men, wishing not to dance, would gather to play cards, often in a back room. The band was usually paid by requesting donations. House dances were almost always on weekends.[18]

Food and alcohol were important at house dances. A large pot of gumbo was cooked and served. This was not an expensive meal, as it was often quite watered down, with only little chicken and served with much rice. Beer and hard liquor were always seemingly consumed, as well as coffee and perhaps juice. Alcohol was served outside, and away from the dance floor. And, if anyone got too rowdy, he was not allowed in to dance.

Entire families went to house dances. Children, once they had spent their energy, were put to sleep, sometimes on the floor protected by a grandmother's feet and shins,[19] or more usually in a rear or side room, called the *parc aux petits*.[20] This tradition led to these dances being called *fais-dodo* (baby-talk for "go to sleep"), a term still sometimes used to define a dance, or sometimes the dancehall itself (though not by all Cajuns), and street dances associated with festivals are also sometimes called *fais-dodo*. Young ladies were very closely supervised and watched by their mothers, and a tradition developed of dancing where bodies of couples were not touching (there is a popular song that discusses this, "Colinda,"[21] and everyone understands the meaning, even today). Everyone took part in the dance, from very young to elderly. As long as someone could dance, and wanted to dance, they were welcome, and it was very common to find dancers crossing several generational lines. It was always considered a family affair. Many mention that house dances among the Cajuns ended at midnight, while others state they lasted through the night.

## Dancehalls (Salles de Danse)

Dancehalls began to be built in southwest Louisiana in the nineteenth century. The first mention of a dancehall this writer found was in 1861,[22] when a writer (who was quite opinionated) mentioned dancehalls, and states that they were used on Saturday evenings. There are two good descriptions of dancehalls given by travelers in the late 1880s. One described a dancehall this way:[23]

---

[17] John Broven, *South to Louisiana: The Music of the Cajun Bayous* (Gretna, 1987), 12.
[18] Post, *Cajun Sketches*, 176.
[19] Lauren C. Post, "Acadian Folkways," *Louisiana State University Alumni News* 12 (1936): 7-9, 26-27.
[20] Lyle Saxon, Edward Dreyer, and Robert Tallent, *Gumbo Ya-Ya* (Boston, n.d.), 197, 199; Barry Jean Ancelet, Jay Edwards, and Glen Pitre, *Cajun Country* (Jackson, 1991); *Louisiana: A Guide to the State* (New York, 1941), 93.
[21] This song and its meaning is discussed at length by Shane Bernard and Julia Girouard, "Colinda: Mysterious Origins of a Cajun Folksong," *Journal of Folklore Research* 29 (1992): 37-52.
[22] Alexandre Barde, *The Vigilante Committees of the Attakapas* (Lafayette, LA, 1981), 39, 106.
[23] Charles Dudley Warner, Charles Dudley. "The Acadian Land," *Harper's New Monthly* 74 (1887): 353.

in front, on the bayou, Mr. Le Blanc had erected a grand ballroom, which gave an air of distinction to the place. This hall, which had benches along the wall, and at one end a high dais for the fiddlers, and a little counter where the gombo [sic] file (the common refreshment) is served, had an air of gayety by reason of engravings cut from the illustrated papers, and was shown with some pride. Here neighborhood dances take place once in two weeks.... The other traveler in the late 1800s not only described a dancehall, but in great detail described what occurred at the dance.[24]

The ballroom was a large hall with galleries all around it. When we entered it was crowded with persons dancing to the music of three fiddles. I was astonished to see that nothing was asked for entrance, but I was told that any white persons decently dressed could come in. The man giving the entertainment derived his profits from the sale of refreshments.... We went together to the refreshment room, where were beer and lemonade, but I observed that the favorite drink was black coffee, which indeed was excellent. At midnight supper was served; it was chicken gombo [sic] with rice, the national Creole dish.

After supper my friend asked me if I wanted to see le parc aux petits. I followed him without knowing what he meant, and he took me to a room adjoining the dancing hall, where I saw a number of little children thrown on a bed and sleeping. The mothers who accompanied their daughters had left the little ones in the parc aux petits before passing to the dancing room, where I saw them the whole evening assembled together in one corner of the hall and watching over their daughters. Le parc aux petits interested me very much, but I found the gambling room stranger still. There were about a dozen men at a table playing cards. One lamp suspended from the ceiling threw a dim light upon the players who appeared at first sight very wild, with their broad-brimmed felt hats on their heads and their long untrimmed sunburnt faces. There was, however a kindly expression on every face, and everything was so quiet that I saw that the men were not professional gamblers. I saw the latter a little later, in a barn near by where they had taken refuge. About half a dozen men, playing on a rough board by the light of two candles. I understood that these were the black sheep of the crowd, and we merely cast a glance at them.

I was desirous to see the end of the ball, but having been told that the break-up would only take place at 4 or 5 o'clock in the morning, we went away at one o'clock. I was pleased with my evening, and I admired the perfect order that reigned, considering that it was a public affair and open to all who wished to come, without any entrance fee. My friend told me that when the dance was over the musicians would rise, and, going out in the yard, would fire several pistol shots in the air, crying out at the same time: le bal est fini.

It must be remembered, however, that house dances and dancehalls continued to co-exist well into the twentieth century. By 1960, however, the tradition of house dances was almost completely gone, although a few have been held in recent years by those trying to revive old traditions. Dancehalls became important in the early twentieth century, but they retained many traditions of house dances,[25] such as free food being served. Drinking remained impor-

---

[24] Alcée Fortier, "The Acadians of Louisiana," *Attakapas Gazette* 26 (1991): 139.
[25] Rocky L. Sexton, "Passing a Good Time in Louisiana: An Ethnohistoric and Humanistic Approach to the

tant and no drinking was done inside dancehalls. Families continued to attend, even children, for the tradition of the *parc aux petits* remained, while parents, especially mothers, continued to closely supervise daughters. And, gambling at cards remained. There were also some differences, the major one being that now some dancehalls were known for their violence—it was a public event, and not only neighbors or family groups attended.[26] There was less screening of undesirables, and young, rowdy men from neighboring communities sometimes attended. There also was no need to notify neighbors of a dance, because they were always held at dancehalls at a pre-set time. Another change was that bands were paid, and a cover charge imposed on those who entered the dance area (probably a reflection on a developing cash-oriented economy linked to wage labor in agriculture and the oil industry).[27]

A description of a dancehall in 1950 is given in Savoy:[28]

> Imagine that you are walking into this big building. Ninety percent of the time you could see the rafters. Along the walls there were benches; sometimes two, sometimes three levels high, like you would have in school. The mothers would escort their daughters to the dancehalls [sic] and they would bring along their little children and they would sit there on these bleachers as long as the dance went on. As you walked in, there was a fence with a gate where you could come in and watch the people dance and listen to the music if you didn't have any money to go into the dancehall [sic].

Something mentioned by many musicians, and certainly confirmed by this writer, was the heat in older dancehalls.[29] The heat of a Louisiana summer, combined with many very active people in a building with a low ceiling, combined to make dancehalls very hot places. Once electricity became available, large exhaust fans were installed that drew heat and smoke from buildings, and they helped somewhat. Dancehalls now are all air-conditioned.

---

Study of Cajun Bars/Clubs as Place" (M.A. thesis, Louisiana State University, 1990), 27-28.

[26] It must be noted, however, that lawlessness swept through south Louisiana, beginning with the late antebellum period. At this time there were vigilante and anti-vigilante organizations that led to violent confrontations. The Civil War followed with two major Union invasions that caused havoc, along with violence by Jayhawkers, all of which contributed to an embracement of violence as a way to settle personal disputes (and not with fists as had been the case prior to 1850). The acceptance of violence continued throughout Reconstruction, and did not end until the early twentieth century (Carl Brasseaux, *Acadian to Cajun: Transformation of a People* [Baton Rouge, 1992], 112-49). As a result of this violence, dancehall owners held almost dictatorial powers and often sanctioned force to insist upon an acceptable code of conduct for patrons.

[27] Dancehalls (as were house dances years ago) are also common to black Creoles (blacks with a strong French cultural heritage). I have visited many of the well-known ones (Richard's Club, Slim's Zydeco Y-Ki-Ki, Gilton's Club, El Sido's Zydeco and Blues Club, and others), and while they have some of the physical features of traditional Cajun dancehalls low—nondescript buildings with low ceilings—on the inside they are simply large rooms. They are patronized mostly by black Creoles and feature zydeco music (see for example Robert Kuhiken and Rocky Sexton, "The Geography of Zydeco Music," *Journal of Cultural Geography* 12 [1991]: 27-38).

[28] Savoy, *Cajun Music*, 240.

[29] Broven, *South to Louisiana*, 17; Savoy, *Cajun Music*, 116; Post, "Joseph C. Falcon," 71.

All traditional weddings called for a dance as part of the celebration.[30] In earliest days they were held in houses,[31] but since advent of dancehalls they were commonly held there. Dancehall owners always liked to have wedding dances since they were relatively wild times, were well attended, and patrons tended to spend money more freely than otherwise. Owners went so far as to pay couples to hold dances at their establishments.[32] Wedding dances are still sometimes held in dancehalls, and all are welcome to attend. Relatively few Cajun dancehalls are left. Many young reject traditional Cajun music (though this trend made a significant turnaround in the 1970s), and they want to hear modern and very loud music. Plus, they do not like having the close supervision of parents. Most people attending dancehalls today are thus middle-aged or elderly, with only a few young folks. All dancehalls are owned by individuals, and if they do not make money, they are closed. Economics will probably close most remaining dancehalls within twenty years, unless the middle-aged of today begin to emulate their elders as they age—something that might happen. Dances at these establishments are almost always on Friday and Saturday nights, and Sunday afternoons.

Bourque's Club, Lewisburg, Louisiana.
Photo courtesy of Paul Harris Photography.

Cajun dancehalls are relatively large buildings. I found them throughout Cajun country, from the bayous of south Louisiana to reach the restroom the prairies of the southwest (where they survive in much greater numbers), and there is even one in east Texas.[33] Typically, Cajun dancehalls are older wooden buildings, built low to the ground, and many seemingly on verge of collapse.[34]

---

[30] Ancelet, *Cajun Country*, 51-52.

[31] A description of one is given by Irène T. Whitfield, *Louisiana French Folk Songs* (Baton Rouge, 1939), 18-23.

[32] Post, "Acadian Folkways," 26.

[33] Carl Lindahl, "Grand Texas: Accordion Music and Lifestyle on the Cajun Frontière," *French American Review* 62 (1991): 34-36; Carl Lindahl, personal communication, January 5, 2000.

[34] Guidry's Club, in Lewisburg, Louisiana, southwest of Opelousas, started as a blacksmith shop in the early 1900s, and the building was converted into a dancehall and cockpit in 1926. When used for a dance, the cockpit was hoisted into a recess in the ceiling, and the recess is still there, but cockfights are no longer held here. The present owner bought the building in 1961 and ran the dancehall until 1998, when someone else took over the operation. Blacks were at one time served alcohol in a room at the rear (the door to the left), but it is now used for bourré, and this is one of the few dancehalls where cards are still played, and here almost daily.

The Bon Chance Club, a dancehall located in the eastern zone of French Louisiana, along a ridge of high land barely above the plane of the swamp, north of the town of Pierre Part. It is not in southwest Louisiana, and today they no longer exclusively have Cajun music, but more commonly country and western.

Bourque's Club, Lewisburg, Louisiana.
Photo courtesy of Paul Harris Photography.

Floors are of wood, and except for the dance area, are quite uneven. Lauren Post[35] described dancehalls of the 1930s in a similar manner:

> The fais-dodo [dancehall] as a building was far less impressive than the fais-dodo as an institution. It might be taken for a barn or a warehouse. It had a reasonably good pine floor, wooden benches all the way around, wooden shutters for the windows on all sides, and not much else except a room with a bed or two for babies, a card room for the men who were not dancing, and a refreshment stand.

This description probably dates from the 1930s when Post did most of his research. By the early 1960s I had visited many Cajun dancehalls, and in all the "refreshment stand" mentioned by Post was a bar on one end of the dancehall. In his early era, however, pop was sold inside and liquor was drunk outside.[36]

All old traditional Cajun dancehalls, unless modified, have a bar at the entrance, with a partition separating it from the dance floor. Origin of the bar area comes from the tradition of young unmarried men being separated from dancers. Old timers often mention that this is where young men not dancing would stand. Between dances, men could leave this area and ask ladies for the next dance. This area was at the entrance, and was referred to as *la cage aux chiens*[37] or the "bull pen."[38] This area became a fixed feature in all Cajun dancehalls, and evolved into the bar area, probably starting as the "refreshment stand" mentioned above by Post. The idea of young un-attached males being separated from dancers undoubtedly began in the era of house dances. Indeed, one

---

[35] Post, *Cajun Sketches*, 156.
[36] Ibid., 154.
[37] Ancelet, *Cajun Country*, 48-49.
[38] Savoy, *Cajun Music*, 80, 240. Keyes mentions the "bull pen" at one end of the dancehall, the bandstand on the other, a bar was along one side, and the other side held benches for the very old or very young. This writer never saw such, and certainly by 1960 the bull pen and bar had merged into one. Frances Parkinson Keyes, *All This is Louisiana: An Illustrated Story Book* (New York, 1950), 248.

author writing in 1881 states that young men and women were "kept pretty well apart until dancing began."[39]

There is a cover charge on leaving the bar (the former *cage aux chiens*) to enter the dance floor area. This arrangement allows people entering to drink, watch dancers, and listen to music, but not pay a cover charge. To identify those who paid the cover charge, it was customary to staple a ticket to the clothes (usually a collar), although now a hand stamp is generally used. All dancehalls today have tables along edges of the dance floor, not benches as mentioned in earlier dancehalls or house dances. The halls are larger now, and space for tables is available. Family groups or groups of older friends sit at tables, while it is still customary for young unattached men to stay in the bar area, the former *cage aux chiens*, except when dancing. Waitresses bring drinks from the bar area to those at tables. It is now, at the turn of the century, rare to see small children in the dance floor area—the *parc aux petits* no longer exists. However, as late as the 1970s it was not unusual to find several children sleeping on tables, on mats on the floor, or in play pens along one side of the building, and it is still occasionally seen in some dancehalls.

There is a railing, or narrow counter, about four feet high on which a person can lean to watch dancers or listen to music from the bar area (or, *la cage aux chiens*). Below the counter is solid wood, while above it, it is usually open, or has a wire mesh between the counter and ceiling. Several of these establishments use a solid moveable partition above the railing, allowing owners to heat or air condition only the bar area when the dancehall is not being used. At such times large dancehalls become simply small bars.[40]

The dance area is a large open space. Ceilings are low, rarely much over eight feet, but with the open space it seems even lower to a viewer. Posts are often found along edges of the dance floor as they are needed to support ceiling and roof, as the span is very wide. The band plays on one end, usually opposite the bar. There was sometimes a wire enclosure to protect the band from patrons,[41] but this writer has not seen such. The dance floor is immediately in front of the band, and tables for those attending are on three sides of the dance floor. A person sits just inside the dance floor area to collect cover charges and be sure those who enter have paid. This job reflects back to the house dance era, when someone in charge would only allow a limited number onto the dance

---

[39] "A Trip To The Teche," *Frank Leslie's Popular Monthly* 12 (1881): 566.

[40] Surprisingly, the concept of a bar area separate from the dance floor, is found in all cockpits in French Louisiana. One enters a bar and food area at no cost, but to see the cockfights, one pays to enter that section of the building (unlike the dancehall, where one may see the action from the bar area). One of these (as done in the dancehalls of the 1950s) staples a ticket to the lapel when you pay, rather than using a hand stamp, claiming it is easier to check who has paid as patrons wander between cockpit and bar area. Also like dancehalls, some have card games (especially bourré) held in the food/bar area next to the cockpit.

[41] Savoy, *Cajun Music*, 91; Broven, *South to Louisiana*, 13, 27; Post, *Cajun Sketches*, 155; and as seen in the movie *Blues Brothers*.

floor. There is an excellent photograph from the 1930s of a *cage aux chiens* in the book by Ancelet et al.[42] and in the foreground is the employee who collects fees, and checks to be sure each person who enters the dance floor has paid the cover charge.[43]

One enters the restroom directly from the bar if one is male. Owners make much money on those drinking beer, whether there is a dance or not, and usually menfolk are the main patrons. It is common for the only entrance to the women's restroom to be from the dance floor area. Thus, if it is winter, and only the bar is heated, a woman would have to walk through a large cold room to reach the restroom.[44] There is often a pool table in the bar area, as well as a juke box for when there is no band, although it is sometimes used when a band is on break.

Group celebrating Joe LaTour's birthday, OST Club, Rayne, Louisiana, ca.1949. Joe LaTour, the club's owner, is the first person on the left.
Photo courtesy of Johnnie Allan.

There is relatively little variation in the model presented. Sometimes today the wall separating dancers from drinkers is eliminated, resulting in everyone paying a cover charge to enter the building. In such a situation, the dancehall is usually open only when there is a dance, and it is not used as a bar. Several older dancehalls are converted to now resemble this style, and most of the newer ones are built this way. In making this change, however, they resemble dancehalls found elsewhere in America. I did, however, find one new and very large aluminum building built as a dancehall that resembles old dancehalls, in particular since it has *la cage aux chiens*, but the ceiling is very high, destroying much of the ambiance of old dancehalls.

There are relatively few changes in dancehalls at the turn of the twentieth century. A room for gambling with cards can still be seen in some dancehalls, but this is no longer an important part of the dancehall scene. Card playing re-

---

[42] Ancelet, *Cajun Country*, 48.
[43] Dancehalls (as were house dances years ago) are also common to black Creoles (blacks with a strong French cultural heritage). I have visited many of the well-known ones (Richard's Club, Slim's Zydeco Y-Ki-Ki, Gilton's Club, El Sido's Zydeco and Blues Club, and others), and while they have some of the physical features of traditional Cajun dancehalls low, nondescript buildings with low ceilings—on the inside they are simply large rooms. They are patronized mostly by black Creoles and feature zydeco music (see for example Robert Kuhlken and Rocky Sexton, "The Geography of Zydeco Music," *Journal of Cultural Geography* 12 [1991]: 27-38.
[44] On the other hand, while at a dance, a lady would not have to walk through the bar area in order to reach the restroom.

OST dancehall, Rayne, Louisiana, ca. 1949.
*Photo courtesy of Johnnie Allan.*

mains important in south Louisiana, but mostly it is done in the small clubs and bars found scattered across the landscape.[45] The card game played is bourré—a game developed in south Louisiana from French roots, and largely unknown to outsiders.[46] Also no longer an important part of the dancehall scene, but still sometimes encountered, would be free food (usually gumbo), and children in the dancehall. Development of Cajun dancehalls resulted in changes to the music of Cajuns. In house dances the primary instrument was the fiddle—but the fiddle was not a loud instrument. House dances often had only six to twelve couples dancing at a time,[47] but houses were usually crowded and the sound of a fiddle did not carry well above the noise. As a result, Cajun fiddlers developed a style of playing that required players to bear down hard on bows in order to be heard, and the singing was usually in a shrill voice that could be heard over the din.[48] It is still common to hear this singing style, and voice quality is not important to Cajuns. A person with "too pretty" a voice will generally not be accepted by traditional audiences. In dancehalls, however, dancers could hear fiddlers only when dancing immediately in front of the band (dancers go in a counter clockwise fashion on the dance floor, passing in front of the band several times during a typical song).[49] Accordions began to be accepted by Cajun musicians in the late 1800s, and it changed the music, for it was exceptionally

---

[45] The best description of this is found in Rocky L. Sexton, "Passing a Good Time in Louisiana: An Ethnohistoric and Humanistic Approach to the Study of Cajun Bars/Clubs as Place" (M.A. thesis, Louisiana State University, 1990), 46, 50, 60-62.

[46] Preston Guidry, *Official Rules and Techniques of the Cajun Card Game Bourré* (Lafayette, LA, 1988); Roy J. Nickens, *Bouré: That's the Name of the Game* (Baton Rouge, 1972).

[47] Broven, *South to Louisiana*, 12.

[48] Barry J. Ancelet and Elmore Morgan, Jr., *The Makers of Cajun Music/Musiciens cadiens et creoles* (Quebec, 1980), 22-23; Sharon Arms Doucet, "Cajun Music," *Journal of Popular Culture* 23 (1989): 93; Chris Strachwitz, "Recording Louisiana Folk Music for Arhoolie Records," in *Louisiana Folklife: A Guide to the State*, ed. Nicholas Spitzer (Baton Rouge, 1985), 243.

[49] Savoy, *Cajun Music*, 116.

loud and could be heard from the rear of dancehalls, in spite of the noise. Accordions became an integral part of most Cajun music in southwest Louisiana in the early twentieth century, and in the 1920s became firmly entrenched. Electronic amplification was first used in Louisiana in the very early 1930s and since then Cajun fiddlers developed a lighter style of playing. By the 1930s, however, accordions were found in all Cajun bands, and it remains an important part of almost all Cajun music.

### The Restaurant/Dancehall

Although relatively few Cajun dancehalls survive, many concepts found in house dances and traditional dancehalls are found in modern Cajun restaurant/dancehalls in south Louisiana. Several of these exist in Lafayette and the neighboring region, and one, Mulates, has other dancehall/restaurants in New Orleans and Baton Rouge. The oldest dancehall/restaurant is Mulate's.[50] The original owner, Mr. Mulate Guidry, moved an even older dancehall to the present location in Breaux Bridge in 1952.[51] New owners in 1980 enlarged this dancehall and converted it into a dancehall/restaurant, and it was an immediate success. Not surprisingly, this restaurant/dancehall bears a striking resemblance to older dancehalls, especially with the very low ceiling. All other restaurant/dancehalls are new structures, and are more open and with higher ceilings.

Similarities between these new restaurants and old dancehalls are many: there is a Cajun band playing (but not just on weekends as at house dances or dancehalls); entire families attend—even children; there is dancing, much of it cross generational; food is consumed; there is a bar area (*la cage aux chiens*); and one restaurant even has a small set of bleachers on one side of the dance floor and benches on two others, like at house dances or at dancehalls of the 1920s and 1930s. None, however, have card rooms.[52]

Many Cajuns consider these restaurant/dancehalls nothing more than tourist traps, and some are, but they are still frequented by Cajuns because they can afford to hire the best Cajun bands. One, however, in a more rural area, is an honest continuation of the dancehall tradition, with all the parts and pieces that made up the traditional dancehall, except for the card room. Old traditions are surviving, but in an altered form.[53] These restaurant/dance-

---

[50] The outside of Mulate's, the first of the Cajun restaurant/dancehalls. So many tourist busses arrive in fall and spring months, that often locals cannot get reservations to come in to eat and dance.

[51] Goldie Comeaux, owner of Mulate's, personal interview, March 23, 1999; Kenneth P. Delcambre, *Lords of the Basin, History of the Lost Village...: Atchafalaya, Louisiana* (n.p., 1988), 28.

[52] The restaurant/dancehalls try to emphasize a more family-oriented atmosphere, and it continues the trend started in dancehalls in the 1970s of card games played elsewhere.

[53] It is interesting to note that there is now at least one black Creole restaurant (Café Creole in Lafayette) that hosts Sunday afternoon zydeco performances, although the physical setting is different from Cajun dancehalls/restaurants.

halls are also an important venue for bands. There is a Cajun band employed every night at most of these establishments, and on the slow nights (as a Monday or Tuesday) newer less-expensive bands are hired, and they can hone their skills. They are an important source of income for many bands.[54]

## Conclusions

Cajun dancehalls are unique, and certainly different when compared to dancehalls elsewhere in America. Their roots begin with the house dances of long ago, and they changed through time into dancehalls, and continue to evolve. Those found today closely resemble dancehalls of the late 1800s, except for lack of a *parc aux petits*, and the evolution of the bar area from *la cage aux chiens*. A few old dancehalls still exist, and many old traits of dancehalls survive in restaurant/dancehalls that are today quite popular.

Some traditional dancehalls, still used for dancing, are today found on the landscape, but they are fading fast. None of them were substantial buildings to begin with, and many others stand abandoned, never again to be used. Change is inevitable, and while it is disheartening to see the passing of this tradition, it is comforting to see development of dancehall/restaurants and survival of so many older traits, albeit in an altered form. There is a general resurgence and a growing vitality and respect for Cajun music. It remains popular at existing dancehalls, at restaurant/dancehalls, and at music festivals, and not just those in Louisiana, but at festivals around the world. This growth and respect for the music, however, is not reflected in greater attendance at traditional dancehalls, as young folk apparently find too much competition for time in our modern society, and they look elsewhere for entertainment. Change has been the only constant.

The Cajuns have survived, and much of their culture remains strong. Cajuns have always been willing to adjust and adapt as situations and conditions changed through time and space.[55] Their culture has thus changed and evolved, but they, as a people with a unique culture, have survived. This is clearly reflected in changes in their dances, their music, and in places where they dance.

---

[54] Among other places where bands could receive paying gigs would be at church halls, Veterans of Foreign Wars and American Legion Posts, local bars, and at festivals that occur almost weekly from early Spring to late Fall.
[55] Comeaux, "The Acadians of Canada and the Cajuns of Louisiana," 29-45.

# *UNE 'TITE POULE GRASSE OU LA FILLE AÎNÉE* [A LITTLE FAT CHICKEN OR THE ELDEST DAUGHTER]: A COMPARATIVE ANALYSIS OF CAJUN AND CREOLE MARDI GRAS SONGS[1]

## Rocky L. Sexton and Harry Oster

In recent years, there has been a growing body of research on various aspects of the Louisiana Cajun and Creole country Mardi Gras celebration that is characterized by a begging quest.[2] The songs associated with this manifestation of the celebration are a topic that has received little attention. This article explores the origins and evolution of Louisiana country Mardi Gras song texts by examining their relationship to continental French and North American French song traditions. It outlines scenarios for textual transformations linked to inevitable changes that occur in the oral transmission of songs, the conscious desire to develop new variants, and modifications stimulated by a new socio-cultural and physical environment. Contemporary Mardi Gras songs fall into two categories: songs derived from generic French drinking songs and modified to fit the theme of Louisiana Mardi Gras, and similarly modified songs with connections to French and French Canadian begging songs and begging quest customs. There are, however, similarities across these types because of borrowing among traditions in France and North America.[3]

---

[1] This article first appeared in the *Journal of American Folklore* 114 (452): 204-24.
[2] See for example, Barry Ancelet, *Capitaine Voyage ton Flag: The Traditional Cajun Country Mardi Gras* (Lafayette, 1989); Carl Lindahl, "The Presence of the Past in Cajun Country Mardi Gras," *Journal of Folklore Research* 33 (1996): 125-53; Carl Lindahl, "Bakhtin's Carnival Laughter and the Cajun Mardi Gras," *Folklore* 107 (1996): 49-62; Carl Lindahl and Carolyn Ware, *Cajun Mardi Gras Masks* (Jackson, 1998); Rocky Sexton, "Cajuns, Germans, and Les Americains: A Historical Anthropology of Cultural and Demographic Transformations in Southwest Louisiana, 1880 to Present" (Ph.D. dissertation, University of Iowa, 1996); Rocky Sexton, "Cajun Mardi Gras: Cultural Objection and Symbolic Appropriation in French Tradition," *Ethnology* 38 (1999): 297-313; Rocky Sexton, "Ritualized Inebriation, Violence, and Social Control in Cajun Mardi Gras," *Anthropology Quarterly* 17 (2001): 28-38; Nicholas Spitzer, "Zydeco and Mardi Gras: Creole Identity and Performance Genres in Rural French Louisiana" (Ph.D. dissertation, University of Texas, 1986); Nicholas Spitzer, "Mardi Gras in L'Anse Prien Noire: A Creole Community Performance in Rural French Louisiana," in *Creoles of Color of the Gulf South*, ed. James Dorman (Knoxville, 1996), 87-125; Carolyn Ware, "Reading the Rules Backwards: Women and the Rural Cajun Mardi Gras" (Ph.D. dissertation, University of Pennsylvania, 1994). Far more Cajun Mardi Gras song texts have been collected than Creole Mardi Gras song texts. This unequal distribution is unlikely to change given that there are very few remaining Creole Mardi Gras groups. This analysis attempts to consider the song texts of both groups, although this disparity results in a heavier emphasis on Cajun song texts.
[3] The research for this article included field research in Grand Marais and Tee Mamou, Louisiana, and Prairie du Rocher, Illinois. Comparative archival data was located in the Laval University Folklore Archives, The University of Moncton; Center for Acadian Studies; The University of Maine, Fort Kent, Center for Acadian Studies; and the Brest University, Center for Breton Studies. We are grateful to Jean-Pierre Michelin, Brenda Ornstein, Fanch Postic, and Ellen Badone for their assistance in locating various song texts. Special thanks are extended to C. Ray Brassieur for sharing his unpublished data on Guignolée songs and his insightful

The roots of Mardi Gras (Fat Tuesday) lie in pre-Christian rites of winter. Bahktin suggests a genetic link between celebrations like Mardi Gras and ancient pagan festivities that included comic elements in their rituals.[4] By the Middle Ages, many such celebrations were loosely associated with the Catholic liturgical calendar.[5] Mardi Gras is now popularly viewed as a time of excess before Ash Wednesday ushers in Lent, a forty-day period of abstinence and solemnity, during which music, dancing, eating, and drinking are curtailed among devout Catholics. Mardi Gras in Louisiana, as in France, the Caribbean, and Brazil, is generally associated with urban carnival. In Louisiana, this atmosphere dominates in New Orleans where Mardi Gras, in much of its current form, developed in the late nineteenth century as a season characterized by lavish parades and balls extending over weeks and culminating on Fat Tuesday.

Aerial view of Rex, King of Carnival, New Orleans, Louisiana, ca. 1980s.
Photo courtesy of the Center for Louisiana Studies, University of Louisiana at Lafayette, accession number 1083.

The Louisiana country *Courir du Mardi Gras*, with a begging quest as a defining element, is different from its urban counterpart, although both versions of the holiday derive from the same broad carnival tradition. It has been postulated that the rural Mardi Gras is merely an extension of the New Orleans celebration,[6] but it is impossible to ignore its connection to continental French and French Canadian celebrations that were characterized by a begging quest. In order to understand the development of Louisiana Mardi Gras songs, it is necessary to understand the socio-historical contexts in which songs associated with begging quests originated in both France and North America. Begging quests occurred primarily within a carnival season that began as early as Christmas and lasted until the onset of Lent.[7] In France, begging quests associated with Mardi Gras (also called "carnival") occurred on one or more of *les jours gras* (the fat days), generally the Sunday, Monday, and Tuesday preceding Ash Wednesday.[8] Other holidays with associated begging quests included

---

comments on Mardi Gras songs.
[4] Mikhail Bakhtin, *Rabalais and His World* (Bloomington, 1984).
[5] Spitzer, "Zydeco and Mardi Gras."
[6] Lauren Post, *Cajun Sketches from the Prairies of Southwest Louisiana* (Baton Rouge, 1962).
[7] Arnold Van Gennep, *Manuel de Folklore Francais Contemporain*, 4 vols. (Paris, 1947).
[8] Ibid.

l'Eginane/Guignolée. This tradition was not linked to a particular Catholic holiday and it could occur anytime between Christmas and Mardi Gras. However, it was staged much more frequently between Christmas and New Year's Day.[9] La Chandeleur (Candlemass) commemorates the presentation of Christ at the temple in Jerusalem and the purification of the Virgin Mary. It is celebrated on February 2 and is known as "Chandeleur" because it is a day for the blessing of candles in church ceremonies.[10] Mi-Careme (Mid-Lent) falls outside of the carnival season and seems to have evolved as a brief suspension of Lenten restrictions.[11] However, the structure and theme of its begging quest were the same as the above mentioned traditions.[12]

Although constituting different holidays, these events often featured begging quests that could be known as *a courir* (run) in reference to the highly mobile tour that occurred. This was especially true in Mardi Gras/Carnival, for example, Van Gennep noted the phrase *faire courir carnaval* (run carnival) in reference to nineteenth-century begging quests in areas of France. In some portions of France such as Anjou, the participants were specifically referred to as Les Mardi Gras (the Mardi Gras).[13] Begging quest participants traveled house-to-house where they sang, danced, and performed comical acts in exchange for meat, flour, butter, grease, chickens, eggs, candy, and money.[14] These items were consumed on the spot, accumulated for a communal feast to climax the holiday, or in some instances of the Guignolée celebration, they benefited the poor of a community.[15]

Costumes included grotesque masks, blackface, ragged clothing, clothing worn inside out or backwards, and outrageous hats and bonnets. Also common was cross-dressing by both sexes. Disguise ensured the anonymity of participants and promoted an atmosphere of inversion and disruption of notions of everyday or normal behavior. This carnivalesque imagery is articulated by Bahktin "We find here a characteristic logic, the peculiar logic of the 'inside out,' of the 'turnabout,' of a continual shift from top to bottom, from front to rear, of numerous parodies and travesties, humiliations, profanations, comic crownings and uncrownings."[16]

---

[9] Fanch Postic and Donatien Laurent, « Eginane, au Gui l'An Neuf?: Une Enigmatique Quete Chantee,» *Armen* 1 (1986): 42-56.

[10] George Arsenault, *Courir La Chandeleur* (Moncton, 1982). There does not appear to be mention of begging quests in association with continental French Chandeleur celebrations. Arsenault suggests that a begging quest was linked to La Chandeleur after its diffusion to the Canadian Maritimes.

[11] Van Gennep, *Manuel de Folklore Francais Contemporain*.

[12] Cross-cultural parallels to French begging quests include German Fastnacht and Christmas season mumming in the British Isles.

[13] Ibid.

[14] Ibid.; Maguy Gallet-Villechange, *Fêtes Traditionelles et Rejouissances Publiques en Poitou de Rabalais a Nos Jours* (Poitiers, n.d.).

[15] Postic and Laurent, « Eginane, au Gui l'An Neuf?, » 42-56.

[16] Bakhtin, *Rabalais and His World*, 11.

These celebrations included outrageous behavior by the participants; for example, using whips or sticks to discourage overly curious spectators who might attempt to un-mask them, or carrying muddy brooms to soil the clothes of innocent passersby.[17] One seventeenth-century continental French description of a Guignolée celebration portrayed the conduct of overzealous celebrants as approaching extortion when they went to extremes in obtaining food and money from reluctant households.[18] However, begging quests often had participants with honorific titles such as *capitaine* (captain) and *chef* (boss) who provided leadership. These leaders often carried a long staff or walking stick decorated with ribbons as a symbol of their status.[19] A common feature of these festivities was begging songs with humbly worded lines that alluded to the group being hungry or which articulated the group's quest for particular foodstuffs. These songs were performed as bands of beggars sought entry into households where they would entertain the hosts in exchange for offerings of food and drink.

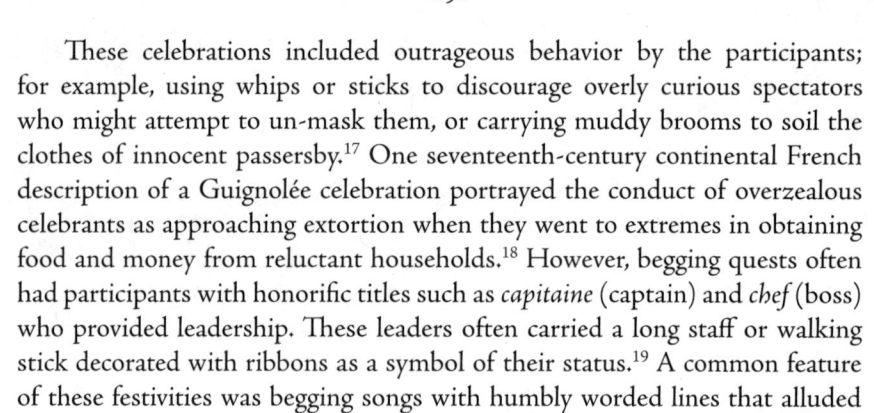

These holidays were introduced to North America and survived in various forms well into the twentieth century, if not into the present. As in France, French North American communities often celebrated only one holiday with a begging quest. This varied distribution of North American begging quests was undoubtedly linked to the different regional origins of French colonists who settled North America. For example, the Guignolée celebration was widespread in Québec, although Mardi Gras and Mi-Careme were common to many districts.[20] Guignolée was also the primary celebration in the French settlements of present day Missouri, Illinois, and Indiana.[21] Begging quests associated with Mardi Gras/Les Jours Gras, La Chandeleur, and Mi-Careme were prevalent in different portions of Acadia.[22] However, Mardi Gras is the only celebration with a begging quest that took root in Louisiana.

Tracing the introduction of Mardi Gras to Louisiana to a specific time or wave of French settlement is problematic considering Louisiana's complex settlement history and incomplete historical documentation of the subject. A

---

[17] Van Gennep, *Manuel de Folklore Francais Contemporaine.*
[18] Postic and Laurent, « Eginane, au Gui l'An Neuf?, » 42-56.
[19] Ibid.
[20] Lucie Dallaire, « Le Mardi Gras, » *Culture et Tradition* 6 (1982): 32-39; Anne-Marie Desdouits, *La Vie Traditionelle au Pays de Caux et au Canada Français* (Québec, 1987).
[21] C. Ray Brassieur, "Expressions of French Identity in the Mid-Mississippi Valley" (Ph.D. dissertation, University of Missouri, 1999).
[22] George Arsenault, *Courir La Chandeleur* (Moncton, 1982); Jean Daigle, *Acadie Des Maritimes* (Moncton, 1993); Gerald Thomas, "Noel, La Chandeleur, Mardi Gras: Begging Rituals in French Newfoundland," in *Fields of Folklore: Essays in Honor of Kenneth S. Goldstein*, ed. Roger Abrahams, (Bloomington, 1995), 300-10.

Guignolée does not appear to have been present in the Canadian Maritimes prior to the late twentieth century when it was introduced to some communities as a means of raising funds for civic organizations (Desdouits, *La Vie Traditionelle*; Ronald Leblanc, personal communication, May 9, 1995).

large component of early Louisiana settlers came directly from various regions of France. However, many of the French involved in the earliest exploration, colonization, and trade in Louisiana were from Québec and French settlements in the upper Mississippi Valley.[23] There was also contact between upper and lower Mississippi Valley French settlements throughout the colonial era. The later colonial era was characterized by a large influx of Acadians (the ancestors of contemporary Cajuns) who had been deported from what is now Nova Scotia and New Brunswick during the Seven Years' War.[24] A significant number of French refugees from the Haitian Revolution relocated to Louisiana in the first decade of the nineteenth century. Additional continental French immigrants arrived in Louisiana throughout the nineteenth century.[25]

There is little written record of rural Mardi Gras celebrations in Louisiana prior to the early twentieth century, but oral history indicates that Mardi Gras and Mardi Gras songs were a long-standing tradition by the mid-nineteenth century. One story from southwestern Acadia Parish (in the heart of the southwest Louisiana prairie region) relayed to the authors, tells of Jayhawkers (outlaw marauders) singing the Mardi Gras song when approaching a farmstead to commandeer food during the Civil War. Another account was given by a very elderly gentleman from northwestern Acadia Parish who was taught the Mardi Gras song as a young child by his then-elderly grandfather, who learned it as a boy during the Civil War era.

By the early twentieth century, the annual Mardi Gras run was found in rural Cajun and Creole communities throughout French Louisiana, especially in southwest Louisiana.[26] The tradition declined sharply by the mid-twentieth century but it was revived or revitalized in many communities as part of a broad, late twentieth-century Cajun French ethnic revival movement. Since then, the custom has been most associated with Cajun French ethnicity although it is still found in a few Creole (Afro-French) communities.[27]

---

[23] Gwendolyn Hall, *Africans in Colonial Louisiana* (Baton Rouge, 1992); Louis Hebert, unpublished copybook located in the Laval University Folklore Archives [circa 1865]; Arthur Leblanc, « La Chandeleur Chez Les Acadiens de l'Isle du Cap Breton » (M.A. thesis, Laval University, 1954).

[24] Carl Brasseaux, *The Founding of New Acadia* (Baton Rouge, 1987).

[25] Carl Brasseaux, *The "Foreign French:" Nineteenth Century French Immigration into Louisiana*, vol. 1, 1820-1839 (Lafayette, 1992).

[26] Barry Ancelet, *Capitaine Voyage Ton Flag: The Traditional Cajun Country Mardi Gras* (Lafayette, 1989); Corinne Saucier, *Traditions de la Paroisse Des Avoyelles en Louisiane* (Philadelphia, 1956); Sexton, "Cajuns, Germans, and Les Americains: A Historical Anthropology of Cultural and Demographic Transformations in Southwest Louisiana, 1880 to Present;" Ware, "Reading the Rules Backwards: Women and the Rural Cajun Mardi Gras." The Creole has historically been linked to the Francophone descendants of colonial-era Louisiana inhabitants both black and white. In contemporary southwest Louisiana, the ethnic label *Creole* is most commonly linked to the Afro-French. However, in the New Orleans area, "ownership" of the label is a matter of debate between blacks and whites.

[27] Sexton, "Cajun Mardi Gras: Cultural Objectification and Symbolic Appropriation in a French Tradition," 297-313.

The contemporary Mardi Gras run unfolds as a rowdy band of costumed characters,[28] known individually and collectively as Mardi Gras, travel house-to-house on horse-back and/or in wagons soliciting *charité* (charity)—provisions for a communal gumbo to be served at an evening *bal de Mardi Gras* (Mardi Gras dance).[29] Hence, basic gumbo ingredients like flour, oil, rice, sausage, and chickens were collected. Live chickens are the most desired item of charity; they are thrown into the air by the host, resulting in a wild chase by the Mardi Gras.[30] As with many rites of reversal, Mardi Gras entails considerable alcohol consumption and non-normative behavior. Hence, each Mardi Gras group is headed by an unmasked capitaine, a highly respected member of the community who often carries a flag as a symbol of his considerable authority. The capitaine usually approaches homes and asks permission for the Mardi Gras to visit. He also maintains order within the group with the help of assistants, also called captains, and he serves as a responsible mediator between the Mardi Gras and the community.[31]

There is significant variation in Mardi Gras groups from community to community. This is reflected, for example, in the many differences between the Cajun Mardi Gras runs of Tee Mamou and Grand Marais, rural communities that are only a short distance apart.[32] Tee Mamou is completely mechanized as the group uses a large modified livestock trailer for transportation. The group has a pair of intermediate characters known as the *nègre* (black man) and *négresse* (black woman), a clear instance of racial and gender inversion. These characters fall midway in the hierarchy of the Mardi Gras, between the captain and rank and file members (known individually and collectively as Mardi Gras, who wear clownlike suits, tall peaked hats, and highly decorated screen masks). The Grand Marais Mardi Gras, on the other hand, is half mechanized while the remainder of the group is mounted on horseback. The group is led by a captain but also utilizes four or five whip-wielding men in blackface *(les nègre)* who are responsible for much of the begging and for maintaining order among the other members known as *soldats* (soldiers) who dress in ragged clothing,

---

[28] The Mardi Gras run was traditionally a male endeavor, although some children's groups could be found. In the last few decades, various communities have organized female runs as well as children's runs.

[29] Gumbo is a souplike dish served over rice. Its ingredients and preparation style represent a blending of African, European, and Native American practices.

[30] It is interesting to note that Louisiana Mardi Gras visits occurred outdoors, so the groups sought only access to the host's yard where activities like singing, dancing, the chicken chase, etc. took place. In Europe, Canada, and the upper Midwest, begging quest groups sought entrance to the host's house. The regional inside/outside dichotomy is probably due to Louisiana's mild climate which permitted considerable outdoor activities.

[31] Ancelet, *Capitaine Voyage Ton Flag*; Saucier, *Traditions de la Paroisse Des Avoyelles en Louisiane*; Harry Oster and Revon Reed, "Cajun Mardi Gras in Louisiana," *Louisiana Folklore Miscellany* 1(1060): 1-17; Ware, "Reading the Rules Backwards: Women and the Rural Cajun Mardi Gras."

[32] Tee Mamou is the locally accepted spelling of '*tite* which is derived from the French term *petite*. It refers to the narrow southern end of Mamou Prairie and is not to be confused with the town of Mamou (often called *Grand Mamou*) located at the broad northern end of Mamou Prairie.

hats, and wear face paint. Other groups are eclectic in costume styles and the use of intermediate characters.[33]

Further variation can be seen in the structure of visits by Mardi Gras groups. In Tee Mamou, after the capitaine receives permission for the Mardi Gras to visit a home, the group slowly advances in ranks toward the hosts while singing the Mardi Gras song under the leadership of the nègre and négresse. In Grand Marais, les nègre range ahead of the group in order to approach households and beg. If a host offers a substantial gift such as a live chicken and requests a visit, then the entire group will slowly approach the house. The Grand Marais song is sung after the soldiers have entered the host's yard and have formed a circle while seated on the ground.

The Mardi Gras run is climaxed by a *bal de Mardi Gras* held in a central location in each community. Traditionally, a communal supper of gumbo made from the various ingredients collected by the Mardi Gras was served as a final feast before Lent ushered in forty days of austerity. However, fewer households maintain chicken flocks, so contemporary groups use the money collected the previous year to purchase food for the supper.

*Variation in Mardi Gras Song Texts*
A common feature of the Mardi Gras run is the performance of a Mardi Gras song. The diversity in Louisiana country Mardi Gras runs is paralleled by variation in Mardi Gras song texts and performance styles. The first category consists of texts derived from drinking songs. This type is now limited to three Cajun Mardi Gras groups, Lacassine, Tee Mamou, and Grand Marais, the latter two of which will be discussed in this paper. Of the Tee Mamou and Grand Marais songs, the Tee Mamou song is the best known and it has been transcribed and transliterated to facilitate its transmission to non-French speaking participants. It is now in a highly standardized form. The Grand Marais song is still transmitted orally and, therefore, is more open to interpretation and improvisation by participants. Neither the Tee Mamou or Grand Marais song is accompanied by music. Tee Mamou, however, does utilize a lively instrumental called the "Hee Haw Breakdown" as part of the group's entrance into the evening dance.

---

[33] For example, Oster and Reed and Post discuss a character called the *Paillease* whose disguise suggests a scarecrow.

*Tee Mamou Mardi Gras Song*
Les Mardi Gras et où viens tu,
tout à l'entour du fond d'hiver?
On vient de l'Angleterre,
oh mon cher, oh mon cher
On vient de l'Angleterre,
tout à l'entour du fond d'hiver.
Les Mardi Gras quoi porte tu,
tout à l'entour du fond d'hiver?
(repeat)

On porte que la bouteille,
oh mon cher, oh mon cher
On porte que la bouteille,
tout à l'entour du fond d'hiver.
Et la bouteille est bu,
tout à l'entour du fond d'hiver.
(repeat)

Il reste que la demi,
oh mon cher, oh mon cher
Il reste que la demi,
tout à l'entour du fond d'hiver.
Et la demi est bu,
tout à l'entour du fond d'hiver.
(repeat)

Il reste que la plein verre,
oh mon cher, oh mon cher
Il reste que la plein verre,
tout à l'entour du fond d'hiver.
Et la plein verre est bu,
tout à l'entour du fond d'hiver.
(repeat)

Il reste que la d'mi verre,
oh mon cher, oh mon cher
Il reste que la d'mi verre,
tout à l'entour du fond d'hiver.
Et la d'mi verre est bu,
tout à l'entour du fond d'hiver (repeat)

Il reste que la rinçure,
oh mon cher, oh mon cher.
Il reste que la rinçure,
tout à l'entour du fond d'hiver.
Et la rincure on la bois pas,
tout à l'entour du fond d'hiver. (repeat)

Bonjour, le maître et la maîtress
dans la maisson.
On vous demande un peu de chose;
On vous demande la fille aînée;
On va la faire faire une bonne chose;
On va la faire chauffer ses pieds.

*Translation*
Mardi Gras, where do you come from,
all around the end of winter?
We come from England,
oh my dear, oh my dear
We come from England,
all around the end of winter?
Mardi Gras what do you carry,
All around the end of winter?
(repeat)

We carry (only) a bottle,
oh my dear, oh my dear
We carry (only) a bottle,
all around the end of winter.
And the bottle has been drunk,
all around the end of winter.
(repeat)

Only half a bottle is left,
oh my dear, oh my dear
Only half a bottle is left,
all around the end of winter.
And the half bottle has been drunk
all around the end of winter.
(repeat)

Only a full glass remains,
oh my dear, oh my dear
Only a full glass remains,
all around the end of winter.
And the full glass is drunk,
all around the end of winter.
(repeat)

Only a half glass is left,
oh my dear, oh my dear
Only a half glass is left,
all around the end of winter.
And the half glass is drunk
all around the end of winter (repeat)

Only the dregs are left,
oh my dear, oh my dear.
Only the dregs are left,
all around the end of winter.
We do not drink the dregs,
all around the end of winter (repeat)

Greetings (to the) master and mistress of the house.
We ask of you a small favor;
We ask for your eldest daughter;
We'll make her do a nice thing;
We'll make her warm up her feet.

*Grand Marais Mardi Gras Song*
Mardi Gras, d'où viens tu, tout à l'entour du fond du verre. (repeat)
Je viens de l'Angleterre, oh mon cher, oh mon cher;
Je viens de l'Angleterre, tout à l'entour du fond du verre.
Mardi Gras, comporter-tu, tout à l'entour du fond du verre. (repeat)
Je porte que la bouteille, oh mon cher, oh mon cher
Je porte que la bouteille, tout à l'entour du fond du verre.
Oh, la bouteille est bu, tout à l'entour du fond du verre.
(repeat)
Il reste que la demi bouteille, oh mon cher, oh mon cher;
Il reste que la demi bouteille, tout à l'entour du fond du verre.
Oh, la demi bouteille est bu, tout à l'entour du fond du verre. (repeat)
Il reste que le plein verre, oh mon cher, oh mon cher;
Il rest que le plein verre, tout à l'entour du fond du verre.
Oh, le plein verre est bu, tout à l'entour du verre. (repeat)
Il reste que le demi verre, oh mon cher, oh mon cher;
Il reste que le demi verre, tout à l'entour du fond du verre.
Oh, le demi verre est bu, tout à l'entour du fond du verre. (repeat)
Il reste que la rinçure, oh mon cher, oh mon cher;
Il reste que la rinçure, tout à l'entour du fond du verre.
Oh, la rincure est bu, tout à l'entour du fond du verre. (repeat)
Oh, ringy rangy mon bouteille, mon bouteille;
Oh, ringy rangy mon bouteille, qui s'en va.
Les Acadiens sont pas si fou, de se laisser sans boire un coup;
Tous chansons qui perdre son fin mérite un peu 'tite coup a boire.

*Translation*
Mardi Gras, where do you come from, all around the bottom of the glass. (repeat)
I come from England, oh my dear, oh my dear
I come from England, all around the bottom of the glass.
Mardi Gras, behave yourself, all around the bottom of the glass. (repeat)
I carry only a bottle, oh my dear, oh my dear
I carry only a bottle, all around the bottom of the glass.
Oh, the bottle is drank, all around the bottom of the glass.
(repeat)
There remains only a half bottle, oh my dear, oh my dear;
There remains only a half bottle, all around the bottom of the glass.
Oh, the half bottle is drunk, all around the bottom of the glass. (repeat)
There remains only a full glass, oh my dear, oh my dear;
There remains only a full glass, all around the bottom of the glass.
Oh, the full glass is drunk, all around the bottom of the glass. (repeat)
There remains only a half glass, oh my dear, oh my dear;
There remains only half a glass, all around the bottom of the glass.
Oh, the half glass is drunk, all around the bottom of the glass. (repeat)
There remains only the dregs, oh my dear, oh my dear;
There remains only the dregs, all around the bottom of the glass.
Oh, the dregs are drunk, all around the bottom of the glass. (repeat)
Oh, ringy rangy my bottle, my bottle;
Oh, ringy rangy my bottle, which is gone.
The Acadians are not so crazy, to leave to leave themselves without a drink;
All songs that lose their end deserve a little shot of drink.

Although currently found only in three communities, this form of Mardi Gras song was traditionally used in other areas of Louisiana. For example, in 1936 Lauren Post recorded the following "Acadian Mardi Gras Song" in Lafayette Parish approximately forty miles east of Tee Mamou.[34]

| An Acadian Mardi Gras Song | Translation |
|---|---|
| O, Mardi Gras, de ou tu viens, toute alontour du fond du verre. | Oh, Mardi Gras, from where do you come, all around the drinking glass. |
| (repeat three times) | (repeat three times) |
| Je viens de l'Angleterre, oui je viens, oui je viens; | I come from England, yes, I come, yes, I come; |
| Je viens de l'Angleterre, oui mon cher, oui mon cher. | I come from England, yes my dear, yes my dear. |
| O, Mardi Gras, quoi tu portes dan la bouteille? | Oh, Mardi Gras, what have you in your bottle? |
| Je portes du vin dans la bouteille. | I have wine in my bottle. |
| La bouteille du vin est bu, | The bottle of wine is drunk, |
| Il reste que la plein verre, | Only a glassful is left, |
| Il reste que le fond du verre, | Only the bottom of the glass is left, |
| Il reste que le rinçure, | Only the rinsings are left, |
| Le rincure du vin est bu. | The rinsings have been drunk. |
| Il reste que le bouchon, | Only the cork is left, |
| Le bouchon on boira pas. | The cork, we shall not drink. |

The Tee Mamou, Grand Marais, and Post songs have the same basic structure. Like the Tee Mamou song, the Grand Marais and Post versions ask from where the Mardi Gras come and the reply is England. There are slight differences in wording, for example, the use of *Je* (I) as opposed to *On* (we), the use of *et où* (where) instead of *d'où* (from where), and *oh mon cher* (oh my dear), as opposed to *oui mon cher* (yes my dear). The body of all these Mardi Gras songs narrate the gradual consumption of a bottle of beverage. However, a significant deviation among the Mardi Gras songs occur in that the Tee Mamou and Post variants ask what the Mardi Gras carries, whereas the Grand Marais version states, "Mardi Gras behave yourself." Another distinction is the reference to the dregs/rinsings which are consumed in the Grand Marais song but not in the Grand Marais song, whereas in Post's version, reference is made to the bottle's cork as the remnant of a once full bottle.

These Mardi Gras songs are presented within the context of a begging ritual, but no reference is made to charity or the items associated with it. The only request which occurs is in the last verse of the Tee Mamou variant when the Master and Mistress are asked for their eldest daughter whose feet the Mardi

---

[34] Lauren Post, "Acadian Mardi Gras," *Louisiana State University Alumni News* 12 (1936): 10. Post reported that various lines of this song involved repitition; however, he was not specific as to the number of times each line was repeated.

Gras wish to warm up, presumably by dancing.[35] The Grand Marais song, on the other hand, is rounded out with lines that will be discussed shortly.

Because Tee Mamou, Grand Marais, and Lacassine lay directly west of the area where Post recorded "An Acadian Mardi Gras Song," one could assume a westward diffusion of the basic song through time in conjunction with the historical westward movement of Louisiana French. Also, similarities in the Tee Mamou and Grand Marais Mardi Gras songs could occur because the groups are geographically close. In the past, as well as the present, there were individuals who participated with both groups or lived in both communities during their lifetime. For example, the father of Drozin Sonnier, a long-serving Grand Marais captain in the early decades of the twentieth century, was raised in the area where the Tee Mamou variant is performed. He later moved to the Grand Marais area, where Drozin was born, and eventually assumed leadership of the Grand Marais Mardi Gras group.[36]

These forms of the Mardi Gras song demonstrate slight to moderate deviations from generic French Canadian drinking songs such as "Ami, Ami, d'où reviens-tu?" (friend, friend, from whence do you return?),[37] and "Je Reviens de la Guerre" (I return from the war).[38] Both songs were collected in early twentieth-century Québec, but similar variants are found in the Canadian Maritimes.[39]

*Ami, Ami, d'où Reviens-Tu?*
Ami, ami d'où reviens-tu?
Ami, ami d'où reviens-tu?
Je reviens de la guerre, Ma lon lon la;
Je reviens de la guerre, Lan lir lan la;
Ami, ami, m'en donneras tu?
Ami, ami, m'en donneras tu?
Je t'en donnerai plein ton verre.
Ami, ami, le verre est bu (repeat);
Je t'en donnerai la moitié de ton verre.
Ami, ami, la moitié du verre est bu; (repeat)
Je t'en donnerai le quart de ton verre.
Ami, ami, le quart du verre est bu; (repeat)
Je t'en donnerais garni le fond de ton verre.
Ami, ami, le fond du verre est bu;
Va t'en, Je ne t'en donnerais plus.

*Translation*
Friend, friend, where do you come from?
Friend, friend, where do you come from?
I come from the war, Ma lon lon la;
I come from the war, Lan lir lan la;
Friend, friend, what will you give?
Friend, friend, what will you give?
I will give you a glass of wine.
Friend, friend, the glass is drunk (repeat);
I will give you half a glass.
Friend, friend, half the glass is drunk; (repeat)
I will give you a quarter of a glass.
Friend, friend, the quarter of the glass is drunk; (repeat)
I will cover the bottom of your glass.
Friend, friend, the bottom of the glass is drunk;
Go away, I won't give you any more.

---

[35] There is a separate Tee Mamou women's run that was created in the early 1970s. It has the same capitaine and overall organization minus the *nègre* and *négresse*. The only change in the song text is that the eldest son rather than the eldest daughter is requested.
[36] Sexton, "Cajuns, Germans, and Les Americains: A Historical Anthropology of Cultural and Demographic Transformations in Southwest Louisiana, 1880 to Present."
[37] Hebert, unpublished copybook located in the Laval University Folklore Archives.
[38] C.M. Barbeau, Ms. No. 7, recorded at Isle d'Orleans, Laval University Folklore Archives, Québec, 1925.
[39] See for example, Suzie Leblanc, *Ami, ami, d'ou Reviens—Tu?*, collected from Cecile LeBlanc, Isles de la Madeleine (Québec, 1977).

*Je Reviens de la Guerre*
Je reviens de la guerre, o ma chère, o ma chère. (repeat)
Soldat, soldat, qu'emporteras-tu?
Soldat, soldat, qu'emporteras-tu?
Une bouteille pleine o ma chère, o ma chère, o ma chere,
Une bouteille pleine, o ma chere petite enfant.
Soldat, soldat, que me donneras-tu?
Soldat, soldat, que me donneras-tu?
Je t'en donnerai pleine un verre,
o ma chère, o ma chère,
Oh ma chère, je t'en donnerai pleine un verre, o ma chère infant.
Soldat, soldat, mon verre est bu.
Soldat, soldat, mon verre est bu.
Encore la moitié du verre, o ma chère,
O ma chère, o ma chère
Encore la moitié du verre, o ma chère enfant.
Soldat, soldat, la moitié du verre est bu.
Soldat, soldat, la moitié du verre est bu.
Encore le quart du verre,
o ma chère, o ma chère,
Oh ma chère, encore le quart du verre, oh ma chère.
Soldat, soldat, le quart du verre est bu.
Soldat, soldat, le quart du verre est bu.
Encore la queue du verre, o ma chère,
o ma chère, o ma chère,
Encore la queue du verre, o ma chère enfant.
Soldat, la queue du verre est bu.
Soldat, la queue du verre est bu.
Encore le robinet,
o ma chère, o ma chère, o ma chère,
Encore le robinet, o ma chère enfant.
Soldat, soldat, Le robinet est bu.

*Translation*
I return from the war, oh my dear, oh my dear. (repeat)
Soldier, soldier, what are you carrying?
Soldier, soldier, what are you carrying?
A full bottle, oh my dear, oh my dear, oh my dear,
A full bottle oh, my dear child.
Soldier, soldier, what are you going to give me?
Soldier, soldier, what are you going to give me?
I am going to give you a full glass,
oh my dear, oh my dear,
Oh my dear, I am going to give you a full glass, oh my dear child.
Soldier, soldier, my glass is drank.
Soldier, soldier, my glass is drank.
There is still half a glass, oh my dear,
Oh my dear, oh my dear,
There is till a half a glass oh my dear child.
Soldier, soldier the half a glass is drank.
Soldier, soldier the half a glass is drank.
There is still a quarter of a glass,
oh my dear, oh my dear,
Oh my dear, there is still a quarter of a glass, oh my dear child.
Soldier, soldier, the quarter of a glass is drank.
Soldier, soldier, the quarter of a glass is drank.
There is still the tail of the glass,
oh my dear, oh my dear, oh my dear,
There is still the tail of the glass, oh my dear child.
Soldier, the tail of the glass is drank.
Soldier, the tail of the glass is drank.
There is still the spigot, oh my dear,
oh my dear, oh my dear,
There is still the spigot, oh my dear child.
Soldier, soldier, the spigot is drank.

The textual and thematic similarities among Louisiana Mardi Gras songs and drinking songs are striking. For example, Mardi Gras singers state that they come from *l'Angleterre* (England). Post (1936) suggested that because the Mardi Gras wished to convey an image as potential troublemakers they used England as a place of origin because of that country's responsibility for deporting the Acadians from Canada. However, it is far more likely that the textual transformation occurred because *de l'Angleterre* (from England) sounds like *de la guerre* (from the war) and it conveys the notion that the Mardi Gras have come from a long distance—an important theme of Louisiana Mardi Gras in other songs. The phrase, *du fond du verre* (from the bottom of the glass) from drinking songs slips easily into *le fond d'hiver* (the end of winter), and although some Mardi Gras participants insist that *du fond du verre* is the correct line, others propose that *le fond d'hiver* is more appropriate because of the season in which Mardi Gras occurs. However, given the obvious connection to drinking songs and the reference to the bottle, glass, etc., *le fond du verre* seems more likely to be the original line.

Some minor transformation of Mardi Gras song verses across the Tee Mamou and Grand Marais songs, and in relation to other versions such as Post's, is attributable to the nature of the French language in Louisiana. Because most French speakers were not literate in the language, songs were transmitted orally, hence the potential for changes in wording across generations, a universal feature of folk songs. Changes may also be attributed to the preference of a particular captain or even individual singers even though they may not be shared by the entire community. A good example of this is the perspective of a former Grand Marais captain who stated that *du fond du verre* is the proper line, whereas his wife stated that she always thought that the verse was *du fond d'hiver*.

Major differences in the Mardi Gras song texts must also be considered. The phrase "Mardi Gras what do you carry" in the Tee Mamou and Post variants differ considerably from the statement "Mardi Gras behave yourself" in the Grand Marais song. The former Grand Marais captain is the most adamant in proposing that this is the proper line rather than "What do you carry?" He interprets "behave yourself" as indicating that the soldiers must form a neat circle and perform the song in an orderly manner as part of each visit. This perhaps reflects his responsibility for maintaining order in the group. It seems clear, however, that at one time the Grand Marais song, or at least the song from which it derived, actually included the question "Mardi Gras what do you carry?" Considering that the next line carries the same response as the Tee Mamou variant and drinking songs: "I/we carry a bottle."

The Tee Mamou and Grand Marais songs differ most in their endings. The final lines of the Tee Mamou song make reference to the eldest daughter of the household. This verse is almost identical to portions of the Guignolée song, especially variants from the upper Mississippi Valley and Québec. For example, the Guignolée song currently performed in Prairie du Rocher, Illinois, includes lines, which apart from differences in dialect, convey the same image as the end of the Tee Mamou Mardi Gras song:

| | Translation |
|---|---|
| Nous vous demandons seulement | We only ask of you, |
| La fille aînée. | The eldest daughter. |
| Nous lui ferons faire bonne chère, | We will make her be a good girl, |
| Et nous lui ferons chauffer les pieds. | And we are going to warm her feet |

The song used in the now-disbanded LeJeune Cove Cajun Mardi Gras near Tee Mamou had additional lines that are nearly identical to Guignolée songs. There, the greeting to the hosts and household: *Bonsoir le maître and la maîtresse, Et tout le monde du logis* (good evening to the master and mistress, and everyone in the household) precedes the request for the eldest daughter.[40]

It has been suggested, although certainly not substantiated and indeed over fanciful, that the request for the eldest daughter is in reference to pre-Christian customs of human sacrifice. Supposedly, within the context of Christianity, the reference was transformed into a request for a dancing partner.[41] However, it is more likely that this request originated because the singers wished access to the eldest (and hence most eligible) daughter for dancing and courtship. The similarity between the Guignolée song and the Tee Mamou Mardi Gras songs suggests a direct integration of begging song themes into drinking songs. Unfortunately, the specific process of textual borrowing can probably never be satisfactorily documented and, hence, only possible linkages can be proposed. Portions of the Guignolée song could have been introduced to Louisiana in the course of eighteenth-century contact between the French settlements of the upper and lower Mississippi Valley. In fact, some contemporary Louisiana French families can trace their ancestry to settlers who migrated from upper Mississippi Valley communities where Guignolée was celebrated. Or, equally plausible, these verses could have been introduced as a song fragment by a later settler from an area of France or Canada where Guignolée songs were common.[42] The mystery remains, however, as to why only this line from the Guignolée song was incorporated into the Tee Mamou song, although as will be discussed shortly, the conscious desire to selectively borrow fragments from other songs may be a factor.

In contrast to Tee Mamou, the conclusion of the Grand Marais Mardi Gras song is similar to French Canadian (and by extension continental French) drinking songs and toasts. One example of this genre of toast is the following excerpt from Québec called "Les Canadiens ne sont pas des Fous" (the Canadians are not fools).[43]

---

[40] Brassieur, "Expressions of French Identity in the Mid-Mississippi Valley."
[41] Ernest Gagnon, *Chanson Populaire du Canada* (Québec, 1955).
[42] Brassieur, "Expressions of French Identity in the Mid-Mississippi Valley."
[43] Joseph Tache, *Forestiers et Voyageurs* (Montreal, 1946).

| | |
|---|---|
| Ah les Marquis, boum | *Translation* |
| Sont pas des fous, boum | Ah the Marquis, boum |
| Partiront pas, boum | Are not fools, boum |
| Sans prendre un coup. | Don't leave, boum |
| | Without having a shot [drink] |

Versions of this toast diffused to Louisiana where they survived in forms which refer to "Les Acadiens" (the Acadians). Two variants of these texts are reported from Vermilion Parish (a relatively short distance from Grand Marais) but they do not appear to be associated with Mardi Gras songs in that area. The first, reported by Brookshire Blanchet in 1970 is as follows:

| | *Translation* |
|---|---|
| Les Acadiens sont pas si fou | The Acadians are not so |
| de nous laisser à boire | crazy to leave us to |
| un gout, à boire, | drink a taste, to drink, |
| à boire un petite gout. | to drink a little taste. |

A more developed text was recently recorded from the same general area.[44]

| | *Translation* |
|---|---|
| Les Acadiens sont pas si fou | The Acadian are not so crazy |
| de se laisser sans boire un coup | as to leave themselves without a drink |
| Que le diable leur casser les côtes | May the devil break his ribs |
| Toutes les unes après les autre | One after another |
| Les petite comme les grosses. | The little ones like the big ones. |

It is interesting to note that the Post variant is much closer to drinking songs because it has no colorful ending. If the Tee Mamou and Grand Marais songs were derived from a song like the Post variant, or that exact song, it is highly plausible that these communities chose to round out the original song with lines taken from other songs. These changes indicate a conscious choice to transform texts in order to differentiate them from neighboring variants.

A parallel to this scenario can be found in the contemporary Prairie du Rocher, Illinois Guignolée celebration. The current song leader stated that earlier this century when there were various active Guignolée groups in the same area, each utilized the same basic song text but they added a few lines to the ending in order to distinguish it from other groups. If the Mardi Gras song did, in fact, diffuse westward from Lafayette Parish to Tee Mamou and then to Grand Marais, the Guignolée example could serve to illustrate how the Mardi Gras songs came to differ in many respects particularly the endings. Related to this theme, Lindahl[45] proposes that each Mardi Gras group creates its own

---

[44] The authors are grateful to Marc David for providing the text of this song.
[45] Carl Lindahl, "The Presence of the Past in the Cajun Country Mardi Gras," 125-53.

identity by elevating one or more of the basic elements of Mardi Gras above all others.

A similar process may be assumed for the development of community-specific song Mardi Gras texts through time. For example, Tee Mamou has always emphasized dancing with female members (as indicated in its song text, ideally the eldest daughter) of households during visits whereas this does not occur in the Grand Marais performance. However, the Grand Marais group does emphasize a mini-ritual for consuming whiskey during the run. In order to be given a shot of whiskey (i.e., "a little shot of drink") by those charged with distributing alcohol, participants must kneel and remove their hat.

## Mardi Gras Begging Songs

The second category of Mardi Gras songs is specifically phrased as "begging songs" and they are associated with most contemporary Mardi Gras groups. Two such variants were first documented in the Cajun Grand Mamou Mardi Gras;[46] however, similar texts can be found in Cajun Mardi Gras groups in Basile, Church Point, and Elton, and in the Creole Mardi Gras groups of Basile and Anse Prien Noire. Because of subsequent commercial recordings and distribution of the Grand Mamou songs, they are the best known in the region. In fact, in most communities, including Tee Mamou and Mardi Gras, the Grand Mamou versions are performed by musicians who accompany some Mardi Gras groups or recordings of the song are played over a loudspeaker as the groups travel the countryside. However, local variants of the Mardi Gras song are performed, generally without musical accompaniment, during actual visits to homes.

*La Danse de Mardi Gras (variant A)*
Les Mardi Gras ça vient qu'eine fois par an tout enl'entour du moyeu.
Les Mardi Gras c'est tout des bons jeunes gens.
Les Mardi Gras ça demande quand meme eine 'tite charité.
Les Mardi Gras ça demande quand meme eine 'tite charité.
Les Mardi Gras ça vient juste eine fois par an.
Les Mardi Gras ça demande eine 'tite poule, quand même c'est eine vieille couvasse.
Les Mardi Gras ça demande quand meme eine 'tite bouche d'sucre.
On va passer mais porte en porte demander la charité a maître et la maîtresse.

*The Mardi Gras Dance Translation*
The Mardi Gras come only once a year, all around the hub.
The Mardi Gras are all good people
The Mardi Gras ask for at least a little charity.
The Mardi Gras ask for at least a little charity.
The Mardi Gras come just once a year.
The Mardi Gras ask for a little fat hen even if it is an old sitter.
The Mardi Gras ask for at least a little mouthful of sugar.
They pass from door to door to ask for charity from the master and mistress.

---

[46] Oster and Reed, "Cajun Mardi Gras," 1-17.

Capitaine, capitaine, voyage ton flag, la belle est loin.
Les Mardi Gras ca vient eine fois par an demander la charité au maître et la maîtress.
Les Mardi Gras ça vient juste eine fois par an demander au maître et la maîtress la charité.
Les Mardi Gras ça d(e)vient de l'Angleterre
Capitaine, capitaine, voyage ton flag, la belle est loin.
Les Mardi Gras ça vient qu'eine fois par an demander la charité.
Les Mardi Gras ça vient de l'Angleterre demander la charité au maître et la maîtresse.
Les Mardi Gras ça devient tout juste eine fois par an.
Et ça que j'trouve plus mauvais, la bouteille alle est proche sec.

*Variant B*
Capitaine, capitaine, voyage ton flag. Allons se mettre dessus le chemin.
Capitaine, capitaine, voyage ton flag. Allons aller chez l'autre voisin.
Les Mardi Gras se rassemblent une fois par an, pour demande la charité.
Ca va-z-aller-z-en porte en porte. Tout à l'entour du moyeu.
Les Mardi Gras devient de tout partout. Oui, mon cher bon camarade,
Mais tout à l'entour du moyeu.
Les Mardi Gras devient de tout partout; mais
Principalement de Grand Mamou.
Les Mardi Gras devient de tout partout; mais à l'entour du moyeu.
Voulez-vous recoir mais cette bande de Mardi Gras?
Mais voulez-vous recoir mais cette bande des grands soûlards?
Les Mardi Gras demandent mais la rentrez au maître et la maîtresse.
Ca demande mais la rentree-z-avec tous les politesses.
Donnez-nous autres-z-une tite poule grasse, Pour q'on se fait un gombo gras.
Donnez-nous autres une 'tite poule grasse; Mais à l'entour du moyeu.
Donnez-nous autres un peu de la graisse, s'il vous plaît,

Captain, captain, wave your flag, the beloved is far away.
The Mardi Gras come once a year to ask for charity from the master and the mistress.
The Mardi Gras come just once a year to ask the master and the mistress for charity.
The Mardi Gras come from England.
And what I find most troubling, the bottle is nearly dry.

*Translation*
Captain, captain, wave your flag. Let's get on the road.
Captain, captain, wave your flag. Let's go to the other neighbor's place.
The Mardi Gras riders get together once a year to ask for charity;
They are going from door to door. All around the hub.
The Mardi Gras riders come from everywhere. Yes, good old comrade;
All around the hub.
The Mardi Gras riders come from everywhere,
But mainly From Grand Mamou.
The Mardi Gras riders come from everywhere,
Now, all around the hub.
Will you welcome this band of Mardi Gras riders?
Will you welcome this band of big drunks?
The Mardi Gras riders ask permission to come in from the Master and Mistress.
They ask permission to come in with all politeness.
Give us a little fat hen, so that we can Make a fat gumbo.
Give us a little fat hen. All around the hub.
Give us a little bit of lard, if you please, my friend.

| | |
|---|---|
| Mon carami. | Now give us a bit of rice. All around the hub, my friend. |
| Mais donnez-nous autres un peu du riz; Mais tout à l'entour, mon ami. | The Mardi Gras riders thank you a lot for your good will. |
| Les Mardi Gras vous remercient bien, Pour votre bonne volonté. | The Mardi Gras riders thank you a lot for your good will. |
| Les Mardi Gras vous remercient bien, Pour votre bonne volonté. | We invite you all to the dance tonight, Over there at Grand Mamou. |
| On vous invite tous pour le bal a ce soir; Mais la-bas a Grand Mamou. | We invite you all to the big dance. All around the hub. |
| On vous invité tous pour le gros bal; Mais tout à l'entour du moyeu. | We invite you all for the big gumbo, over there in the kitchen. |
| On vous invité tous pour le gros gombo; Mais la-bas a la cuisine. | We invite you all for the big gumbo, Over at John Vidrine's place. |
| On vous invite tous pour le gros gombo; Mais la-bas chez John Vidrine. | Captain, captain, wave your flag. |
| Capitaine, capitaine, voyage ton flag, Capitaine, voyage ton flag. | Captain, wave your flag. |
| Allons aller chez l'autre voisin. | Let's go to the other neighbor's place. |

As mentioned earlier, many Creole communities staged Mardi Gras runs, but in the present, only a few have maintained or revived the tradition. One of the best known Creole Mardi Gras songs is found in Anse Prien Noire located west of Grand Mamou:[47]

| | |
|---|---|
| *Anse Prien Noire* | *Translation* |
| (Lead) Oh Mardi Gras allons-nous. | (Lead) Oh Mardi Gras let's go. |
| (Chorus) Ouais mon/bon cher camarade. | (Chorus) Yes my good dear friend. |
| (chorus is repeated after every line but is not printed hereafter) | (chorus is repeated after every line but is not printed hereafter) |
| On est bon des politessiens q'reviennent beaucoup de loin. | We are polite people who return from far away. |
| Mardi Gras est miserab'. | The Mardi Gras is poor. |
| Une poule par an c'est pas souvent. Not 'gombo est réellement faible. | One chicken a year is not much. Our gumbo is really weak. |
| Nous t'invité a manger un bon gombo. | We invite you to eat a good gumbo. |
| Mardi Gras t'a 'mande po' nous recevoir. | The Mardi Gras has asked you to receive us. |
| Mardi Gras t'a 'mande po' nous recevoir. | The Mardi Gras has asked you to receive us. |
| Mardi Gras t'a 'mande po' nous recevoir. | The Mardi Gras has asked you to receive us. |
| Une poule par an c'est pas souvent. Notre gombo is réellement faible. Notre gombo is réellement faible. Mardi Gras allons-nous en. | One chicken a year is not much. Our gumbo is really weak. Our gumbo is really weak. Mardi Gras let's go away. |
| Mardi Gras est beaucoup satisfaits. | The Mardi Gras is very satisfied. |
| On vous invité pour gran bal au soir chez Monsieur A\_\_\_\_. | We invite you for a big dance tonight at Mr. A\_\_\_\_'s place. |

---

[47] Spitzer, "Zydeco and Mardi Gras," 420–21.

| | |
|---|---|
| Mardi Gras allons-nous en. | Mardi Gras let's go away. |
| Capitaine voyage ton flag. | Captain wave your flag. |
| Mardi Gras allons-nous en. | Mardi Gras let's go away. |
| On n'a pas souvent beaucoup fait ca. | We do not often do that. |
| Mardi Gras allons-nous en. | Mardi Gras let's go away. |
| Allons-nous en de l'autre paroisse. | Let's go away to another parish. |
| Allons-nous en de l'autre voisin. | Let's go to another neighbor. |

These songs share numerous textual similarities. The Mardi Gras identify themselves as participating in a great voyage that occurs only once a year. They state that the groups come from far away or, more specifically, in the first Grand Mamou song, England is identified as the point of origin. The refrain "all around the hub" in the Grand Mamou variants suggests a circular tour with the site of the evening's ball in the center. A key component of all these variants is the reference to the captain. The singers specifically request charity: chickens, grease, rice, and sugar, or they mention these items with the connotation that the impoverished group needs them for food. The beggars emphasize that they are *des bons jeune gens/des politessiens* (good/polite people). In keeping with the theme of a quest, the Mardi Gras songs emphasize that the group must continue on its route by urging the captain to wave his flag thus signaling the group to move on to another site; for example, *Capitaine, capitaine, voyage ton flag, la belle est loin* (captain, captain, wave your flag, the sweetheart is far away), or *Capitaine, capitaine, voyage ton flag, allons aller chez l'autre voisin* (captain, captain, wave your flag, let's go to another neighbor's place). Lastly, all three Louisiana variants (as well as other related songs) share the theme of inviting the hosts to the evening gumbo and dance which benefits both the Mardi Gras and the greater community.

The Anse Prien Noire Mardi Gras song text is obviously adopted from the Cajun-French. However, the manner in which it is performed is indicative of the retention of African performance style. For example, Spitzer (1986) notes a major stylistic difference among the begging songs of Grand Mamou and L'anse Prien Noire. He differentiates the Creole variant in that, "this call-response chant, with partially improvised text, marks the Creole Mardi Gras as different from the Cajun Mardi Gras which emphasizes the repetition of a more standardized text to a more elaborated melody by one voice [human or instrumental]."[48] At least one Cajun group, the counterpart to the Basile Creole Mardi Gras, performs the Mardi Gras song in similar fashion, perhaps an indication of African American call and response performance influences on Cajun performance style in that community. However, it must be noted that call and response is found in other North American French traditions, for example the Prairie du Rocher, Illinois Guignolée song.

---

[48] Spitzer, "Zydeco and Mardi Gras," 484.

Capitaine of a rural courir de Mardi Gras, southwest Louisiana.
*Photo courtesy of the Louisiana Tourist Development Commission.*

These Mardi Gras songs are clearly related to earlier European begging songs. Two factors suggest this connection. First, as Oster and Reed (1960) noted in a pioneering article on Louisiana Mardi Gras, both variants of the Grand Mamou Mardi Gras song are "sung to the same melody, which is ancient since it has a gapped and modal scale."[49] Thus, the indication is that, at least stylistically, these songs can be traced to France of several centuries ago.

Secondly, many lines from these variants of the Mardi Gras song are strikingly similar to continental French Mardi Gras and Guignolée songs as well as nineteenth-century French Canadian Guignolée and twentieth-century La Chandeleur songs. For example, the notion of an annual visit is present in many Upper Mississippi Valley and Québec Guignolée songs. The reference to a captain hearkens back to nineteenth-century Guignolée celebrations in Brittany, France, which mention a leader called "capitaine" or "chef."[50] The portrayal of the Mardi Gras as being in need of food is found in continental French Mardi Gras songs, for example, one nineteenth-century song text states *Mardi Gras n'a pas soupé* (Mardi Gras hasn't eaten),[51] whereas another variant informs the hosts that *c'est Mardi Gras qu'est à la porte. Qui demande des crêpes molles* (It's Mardi Gras who is at the door. Who requests soft pancakes).[52] Such statements are also very similar to continental French Guignolée songs which emphasize that the beggars *Chercher de la viande....* (Seek meat).[53] This theme is also present in upper Mississippi Valley and Québec variants that request *une chignée/echinée* (pork backbone) to make *a fricassée* (stew).[54] Requests for foodstuffs also occur in some twentieth-century Acadian La Chandeleur songs of the Canadian

---

[49] Ibid.
[50] Postic and Laurent, « Eginane, au Gui l'An Neuf?: Une Enigmatique Quete Chantee, » *Armen* 1 (1985): 42-56.
[51] Van Gennep, *Manuel de Folklore Francais Contemporain* (Paris, 1947), 1:897.
[52] J. Noques *Les Moeurs D'Autrefois en Saintonge et en Aunis* (Marseille, 1891), 57.
[53] Postic and Laurent, « Eginane, au Gui l'An Neuf? » 42-56.
[54] Brassieur, "Expressions of French Identity in the Mid-Mississippi Valley;" Gagnon, *Chanson Populaire du Canada.*

Maritimes; for example, *Monsieur Marie a pas encore dine. Va-t-en dans ton quart me chercher du lard, va dans ta potchine me chercher d'la farine* (Mister Marie has not yet eaten. Go bring me some bacon, go bring me some flour).[55] Assurances about the good conduct of the beggars are also made in continental French Guignolée songs stating that *Nous ne somme pas des malfaiteurs* (We are not troublemakers).[56] The sense of urgency in continuing the route after each visit appears in French Guignolée songs such as the lines: *Au nom de Dieu, depechez, depechez. Car nous avons encore très loin à aller* (In the name of god, hurry. We still have far to go), *La route est longue et le terme est loin* (The route is long and the end is far), and *Allons dans une autre maison nous promener. Chercher une autres maison comme celle-ci* (Let's go to another house. Find another house like this one).[57]

Despite continental French origins, these songs are not simply pristine survivals of an earlier era but rather they demonstrate considerable in situ modification. For example, the dish gumbo, an example of cultural creolization in Louisiana, features prominently in Mardi Gras songs, a reflection of its importance as the last extravagant meal before the onset of Lent. Correspondingly, chickens, the primary ingredient of gumbo, are the item of charity most emphasized in these songs. The mention of chickens is rare in accounts of continental French Mardi Gras with the exception of begging quests in nineteenth-century Marne which were started after the end of communal cockfights, and Champagne where the collection of live chickens was a component of Mardi Gras.[58] Chickens are a significant element of Acadian Chandeleur. For example, the leader of nineteenth- and early twentieth-century Acadian Chandelur groups often carried a staff topped with the carved figure of a chicken.[59] The evening meal associated with the *courir du Chandeleur* included chicken *fricot* (soup). However, no continental French or French Canadian song texts that refer to chickens were located.

With the exception of some continental French Guignolée songs, reference to a captain seems to be found only in Louisiana Mardi Gras songs, and mention of the *capitaine's* flag seems to be unique to Louisiana Mardi Gras. Reference to the *capitaine* and his flag is a dominant theme in Louisiana Mardi Gras begging songs; this is perhaps indicative of the paramount authority wielded by Louisiana begging quest leaders in contrast to their French and French Canadian counterparts. Another Louisiana-specific distinction occurs in the variant of the Grand Mamou song stating that the group comes from England; this is most likely a local borrowing from a drinking song-derived

---

[55] Arsenault, *Courir La Chandeleur*.
[56] Postic and Laurent, « Eginane, au Gui l'An Neuf?, » 42-56.
[57] Ibid.
[58] Van Gennep, *Manuel de Folklore Francais Contemporain*.
[59] Arsenault, *Courir La Chandeleur*.

Mardi Gras song.[60] And the use of the refrain "all around the hub" does not appear in any of the numerous continental French or French Canadian songs surveyed. Likewise, an invitation to the communal gumbo and dance is found in all Louisiana begging songs but seems absent elsewhere.

*Additional Mardi Gras Songs*

In the past, there were additional songs associated with Mardi Gras runs regardless of the form of Mardi Gras songs utilized. These were sung during the play that accompanied visits. For example, Post (1936) reported the Ridelle, whose verses called for "the successive touching of the foot, knee, stomach, head and back to the ground in unison with the words." This was a parallel custom to holidays elsewhere. For example, *Que Sais-Tu Bien Faire*, performed as part of La Chandeleur visits on L'Isle du Cap Breton in Acadia earlier this century, is similar to La Ridelle.[61]

Other songs were performed as Mardi Gras groups departed a location and these were verses of thanks or reproach depending on the generosity of the hosts or the lack thereof.[62] For example, Lindahl[63] reports that in Basile, the Cajun Mardi Gras sang verses stating that it was hoped that the chickens of uncooperative households would die. This practice is also related to parallel French and French Canadian traditions: for example, in some continental French Guignolée songs and Acadian Chandeleur songs, cooperative hosts were informed in verse that God would reward them, while inhospitable hosts were insulted or threatened with some sort of punishment.[64] Few, if any, of these songs are still performed. This is due to the decline of the French language in Louisiana, which makes learning and maintaining a repertoire of French songs difficult.

*Discussion*

Louisiana Mardi Gras songs fall into two categories. The first genre discussed in this paper obviously have origins in continental French and French Canadian drinking songs. The second type, begging songs, share themes with continental French and French Canadian Mardi Gras, Guignolée, and Chandeleur songs. The similarities among these songs is due to several factors: probable borrowing across traditions in France and in Canada, or, considering their com-

---

[60] The area around Grand Mamou once supported numerous Mardi Gras groups, however, at the time of the Oster and Reed article the Grand Mamou run was the dominant run in the area. Although the song texts collected by Oster and Reed are linked to Mamou, the texts (or variants of them) may have originally belonged to other communities.
[61] LeBlanc, *Ami, ami, d'ou Reviens-Tu?*
[62] Sexton, "Cajuns, Germans, and Les Americains: A Historical Anthropology of Cultural and Demographic Transformations in Southwest Louisiana, 1880 to Present;" Ware, "Reading the Rules Backwards: Women and the Rural Cajun Mardi Gras."
[63] Lindahl, "The Presence of the Past in the Cajun Country Mardi Gras," 125-53.
[64] Postic and Laurent, « Eginane, au Gui l'An Neuf?, » 42-56; Arsenault, *Courir La Chandeleur*.

## Analysis of Cajun & Creole Mardi Gras Songs

*The Mardi Gras chase a chicken for their gumbo, southwest Louisiana.*
*Photo courtesy of Louisiana Tourist Development Commission.*

mon theme, parallel developments in song texts. The begging songs used in Louisiana Mardi Gras, or portions of them, diffused from France to Louisiana, or equally plausible, from Canada or the upper Midwest. Because Mardi Gras was the only holiday that developed with a begging quest in Louisiana, it could have served as a mixing pot of song texts from different customs introduced at different times. Elements of these songs could be adopted by different communities and then changed through oral transmission or they were consciously changed for a unique sound just like the Mardi Gras songs derived from drinking songs. Other changes reflect adaptation to Louisiana, for example, the reference to gumbo and correspondingly a strong emphasis on chickens in begging songs.

Why some communities became distinguished by begging songs and others by those derived from drinking songs is difficult to ascertain. However, this distinction may be linked to the desire to develop a new Mardi Gras song based on the modification of a drinking song rather than directly borrowing an existing begging song. The geographical origin of French settlers must also be considered. For example, the northern prairie region of Louisiana, where begging songs are so common, was initially peopled by non-Acadian French settlers.⁶⁵ The southern and central portion of the prairie region where drinking song texts are/were utilized have historically had high concentrations of inhabitants of Acadian descent.⁶⁶ Also, as proposed earlier, communities may have purposely modified Mardi Gras songs found in other settlements in order to distinguish their custom. This is perhaps the best explanation for differences between the Mardi Gras songs of Tee Mamou and Grand Marais and it also offers insight into why begging songs differ from community to community. Of course, some differences in song texts also occurred through the course of oral transmission of the songs. Despite the great contrasts between the two types of

Mardi Gras capitaine, chiropractor R.L. Savoie of Church Point, leads his riders, southwest Louisiana.
*Photo courtesy of Louisiana Tourist Development Commission.*

---

⁶⁵ Brasseaux, The *"Foreign French,"* vol. 1.
⁶⁶ Ibid.; Sexton, "Cajuns, Germans, and Les Americains: A Historical Anthropology of Cultural and Demographic Transformations in Southwest Louisiana, 1880 to Present."

Mardi Gras songs, there was obviously some borrowing across these categories, for example, the theme that the Mardi Gras come from England.

Song texts obviously exhibit change through time, but communities often assume that their songs have persisted in an unchanged form. This assumption should not be surprising. As Lindahl notes,[67] a community will acknowledge that their Mardi Gras tradition is of great antiquity, but specific knowledge of the tradition is based on the Mardi Gras practices of recent generations. Thus, subtle changes become codified through time. Unfortunately, because of the oral nature of these songs and the dearth of historical information on the subject, the specific details of these various musicological transformations may never be fully documented. However, the analysis provided clearly demonstrates the complex processes behind the evolution of the various songs that still echo across southwest Louisiana during Mardi Gras.

---

[67] Lindahl, "The Presence of the Past," 125-53.

# The Cajun French Music Association: The Development of a Music-Centered Ethnic Organization[1]

## Rocky L. Sexton

The Cajun French Music Association (CFMA) is a grassroots organization with ten chapters in south Louisiana and Texas and a membership of approximately 3,000 families. This essay examines three aspects of the Cajun French Music Association. First, the development of the organization within the context of broader post-World War II cultural preservation in French Louisiana is charted. Next, the structural organization of the CFMA is outlined. Lastly, the CFMA's activities devoted to the preservation and promotion of Cajun music and other aspects of Cajun culture are described. These efforts are sometimes complicated by concerns and debates over defining traditional culture.[2]

### Cajun Cultural Decline and Preservation

The twentieth century has been recognized as a time of significant cultural decline among the Cajun French. The implementation of mandatory education in 1916 and increasing stigmatization of the French language contributed to gradual linguistic erosion.[3] There was a dramatic population shift from small rural agricultural communities to towns and cities in Louisiana and east Texas for work in the oil industry and manufacturing.[4] Language shift, dislocation from traditional settlements, and socioeconomic transformations among Cajuns facilitated the decline of traditional customs, including accordion-led Francophone music and the rural Mardi Gras celebration, in favor of mainstream American entertainment.[5]

Awareness and concern about Cajun cultural decline became pronounced in the 1950s. Conscious efforts were set in motion to counter the trend toward assimilation that many feared would destroy local culture. Up until the 1980s, cultural preservation and promotion fell into two categories: formal, elite-led organizations devoted to French language promotion and links to the Fran-

---

[1] The editors kindly thank Rocky L. Sexton for preparing this article for publication here.
[2] Unless otherwise indicated, much of the content of this essay is derived from firsthand observation of CFMA activities and interviews and informal conversations with CFMA members.
[3] Rocky L. Sexton, "Cajun French Language Maintenance and Shift: A Southwest Louisiana Case Study to 1970," *Journal of American Ethnic History* 19 (2000): 24-48.
[4] Rocky L. Sexton, "Cajuns, Germans, and Les Americains: A Historical Anthropology of Cultural and Demographic Transformations in Southwest Louisiana, 1880 to Present" (Ph.D. dissertation, University of Iowa, 1996).
[5] Barry Ancelet, *Cajun Music: Its Origins and Developments* (Lafayette, 1989); Sexton, "Cajuns, Germans and Les Americains."

cophone world; and informal individual and community-level efforts oriented toward various aspects of local culture associated with the Cajun French.

Francophone interest groups emerged in the mid-twentieth century, but they were not necessarily representative of the Cajun population or concerned about contemporary Cajun culture.[6] For example, Esman identifies an "old elite" of upper-class Louisiana French planters and merchants that included white Creoles and upper class whites of Acadian descent, the latter often referred to as "Genteel Acadians."[7] Both groups had marked class-based and cultural differences with Cajuns. Representatives of the upper-class white Francophone population formed *France-Amerique de la Louisiane Acadienne* in 1951. It emphasized higher formal education, standard French, and connections with Francophone nations, or at least their intellectual, economic, and political elite representatives.[8]

A similar, but much broader elite-led effort was initiated in 1968 with the founding of the Council for the Development of French in Louisiana (CODOFIL). Its purpose was to develop and preserve French in Louisiana for tourism and cultural benefits. Like *France-Amerique*, CODOFIL was founded and directed by socioeconomic elites including those of non-Acadian descent. It also emphasized forging links with various Francophone nations. CODOFIL's efforts at linguistic revival were focused on limited teaching of standard French in public schools, a large-scale endeavor often dependent on instructors recruited from various Francophone nations. The group also provided financial support for university-level French language study abroad.

Elite-led organizations placed a strong emphasis on the label Acadian. It was manipulated as a historicized, romanticized image of simple pastoral eighteenth century Francophone peas-

CODOFIL founder, James Domengeaux, center, with unidentified dignitaries, 1969.
Photo courtesy of the Center for Louisiana Studies, University of Louisiana at Lafayette, accession number 234.

---

[6] Gerald Gold, "The French Frontier of Settlement in Louisiana: Some Observations on Culture Change in Mamou Prairie," *Cahiers de Geographie du Québec* 23 (1979): 263-80.
[7] Marjorie Esman, interview with the author, circa 1983; Carl Brasseaux, *Acadian to Cajun: Transformation of a People, 1803-1877* (Jackson, 1993).
[8] Esman interview.

ants victimized by British aggression, as documented in Longfellow's (an Anglo-American writer) *Evangeline*. This retrospective approach to cultural affiliation and promotion often ignored many elements of contemporary Cajun culture and identity, for example, accordion-led Cajun music and the rural Mardi Gras celebration, that were viewed by some as low class and unsophisticated.[9] Nonetheless, Trepanier has argued that during the racial upheaval of the Civil Rights era, promotion of Cajun identity, despite the elite misgivings about Cajun culture, assured a white identity for the region given Cajun's unquestioned linkage to the term Acadian with its respected pedigree.[10]

By the 1970s, the efforts of old line Francophone elites were increasingly merged, albeit sometimes reluctantly, with those of a new Cajun middle class that Esman suggests emerged in the mid-twentieth century because of the flourishing oil industry.[11] Elements of this group joined the small traditional class of rural and small town middle class Cajun merchants who had served as mediators between the mass of lower class Cajuns and local Francophone elites and Anglo-Americans.[12] To this class one could add the increasing number of Cajuns, the children of farmers and blue-collar workers, who sought upward mobility in blue-collar occupations or who took advantage of higher education and white-collar employment.

Some economic brokers, and upwardly mobile children of modest Cajun families, became culture brokers as they identified traditional Cajun culture as worthy of preservation and they served as local cultural experts.[13] In contrast to historicized perspectives on Cajun identity promoted by their elite counterparts, these activists emphasized various aspects of Louisiana French cultural content (often elements not of strictly Acadian provenience) specific to their childhoods that they felt were endangered.[14] Thus, they provided initiatives and leadership for early loosely organized grassroots revival activities.

Cajun-oriented revival efforts represented various levels of organization and agendas. For example, in the 1950s, individuals in the town of Mamou began working to revive the traditional Mardi Gras run which had declined in recent years. They also promoted Cajun music and the public use of French, for example, in radio shows that featured Cajun music and Cajun French lan-

---

[9] Barry Ancelet, *Cajun Music: Its Origins and Development* (Lafayette, 1989); Barry Ancelet, "Mardi Gras and the Media: Who's Fooling Whom?," *Southern Folklore* 46 (1989): 211-19; Rocky Sexton, "Cajuns, Germans, and Les Americains."

[10] Cecyle Trepanier, "The Cajunization of French Louisiana: Forging a Regional Identity," *The Geographical Journal* 157 (1991): 161-71.

[11] Marjorie Esman, interview with the author, circa 1981.

[12] Gold, "The French Frontier of Settlement in Louisiana."

[13] Ibid.

[14] Ibid.; Rocky Sexton, "Cajun Mardi Gras: Cultural Objectification and Symbolic Appropriation in a French Tradition," *Ethnology* 38 (1999): 297-313.

guage various customs through cooperation with applied folklorists. Such cooperation provided a degree of legitimacy for revival efforts given that previously ignored cultural elements were increasingly deemed worthy of scholarly inquiry. Some scholars involved in this work made efforts to promote Cajun music at regional and national festivals.[15] In recent decades, a multitude of local festivals, often devoted to specific aspects of Cajun culture, have been organized to stimulate ethnic tourism, an important endeavor given past low points in the local oil industry.[16] Therefore, various elements of Cajun culture have been increasingly showcased publicly for reasons ranging from sincere interest in cultural preservation to exhibitions for cultural tourism, or a combination of the two goals.

Cajun activists, including culturally aware college students, also played a role in pressuring CODOFIL to include a focus on Cajun culture, in particular Cajun music, in its efforts by the mid-1970s.[17] In fact, by the early 1990s, Cajuns began to assume key positions in CODOFIL. These leaders attempted some degree of outreach to Cajun organizations and individuals and cooperation with them.

### *The Cajun French Music Association*

The Cajun French Music Association was founded in the southwest Louisiana town of Basile in 1984. Charter organizers were mostly middle-aged and elderly Cajun musicians from the general area. The association emerged partially in response to feelings that CODOFIL, despite its increasing support of Cajun culture, was elitist and did not adequately represent Cajun interests.[18] The CFMA's stated purpose is to "Promote and preserve, not only Cajun music, but also various aspects of the Acadian heritage." Its membership is described as mostly, "Grass roots Cajuns who want to preserve their heritage by teaching authentic Cajun language and the traditions of their Acadian ancestry."

Original CFMA chapters were founded in towns like Church Point, Lafayette, New Iberia, Houma, and Lake Charles that are located within the French Louisiana culture region. Additional chapters represent the expansion of the organization both geographically and through the growing involvement of non-Cajuns who share the interests and goals of the CFMA. Consequently, the CFMA now consists of ten chapters distributed from New Orleans to San Antonio Texas (see figure 1). The CFMA stresses membership by entire

---

[15] Ancelet, *Cajun Music: Its Origins and Development*.
[16] C. Paige Gutierrez, *Cajun Foodways* (Jackson, 1992).
[17] Barry Ancelet, *The Makers of Cajun Music* (Austin, 1984).
[18] N.R. to J.S., March 21, 1989; L.M. to Music-Culture Enthusiasts, June 14, 1989; J.S. to the President, Vice President, and Members of the Governing Body, CFMA, March 23, 1989.

families rather than individuals, and therefore places its membership at approximately 3,000 families.

*Structural Organization*

All CFMA chapters have the same organization (see figure 2). Individual chapters are charged with local affairs, including monthly meetings and activities, and the organization of local annual festivals. The structure of chapters is replicated and expanded in a national governing body that establishes guidelines for the entire association (see figure 3). The association works collectively to stage an annual weekend-long awards ceremony and festival called *Le Cajun*. The CFMA publishes a newsletter *La Voix Des Cajuns* (LVDC) with sections allotted to each chapter for reporting news and advertising activities.

*Language*

The CFMA is concerned with preserving Cajun French, efforts that it portrayed as different from CODOFIL's language promotion. For example, in an untitled, undated internal correspondence, a CFMA member stated, "If we desire and want to bad enough, we can educate ourselves and our children in the language we speak here, not the French used in France or Canada, but our very own Cajun." To this end, the organization strives to promote Cajun French through various efforts. *La Voix des Cajuns* is printed in English, but French words and expressions are interspersed throughout each issue. The newsletter also includes brief lessons in French. As one such example, the Baton Rouge Chapter provides samples of traditional Cajun French expressions along with a discussion of their origin.[19]

Various chapters have organized and/or sponsored weekly and bi-monthly French classes.[20] These are often informal gatherings where interested parties meet with fluent Cajun French speakers to learn basic conversational Cajun French.

Some CFMA members are involved with local French choir groups.[21] Performances by these choirs, as well as French language Catholic Masses, are often scheduled in conjunction with chapter-sponsored festivals and the national *Le Cajun* festival.[22]

The CFMA has also been involved in informal language outreach to public schools. For example, members of the Houma Chapter distributed Cajun French dictionaries to several schools in St. Mary Parish, while another member of that chapter reported efforts at teaching Cajun French to her elementary school students.[23]

---

[19] *La Voix des Cadjins*, August 2001.
[20] *La Voix des Cadjins*, October 1991, November 1991, March 1991, April 1992, July 1992, October 1996.
[21] *La Voix des Cadjins*, November 1991.
[22] *La Voix des Cadjins*, May 1991, April 1992.
[23] *La Voix des Cadjins*, December 1991.

The CFMA assists other efforts to promote French education in public schools, a process originally initiated and spearheaded by CODOFIL. The most recent fruit of regional language promotion efforts in general is French immersion programs in selected schools. As an indication of the CFMA's support for formal French education, a writer from the Lafayette Chapter argued that the CFMA should set up a scholarship fund for college students majoring in French. The same writer stated that the public school system should be supported in its effort to continue teaching French.[24] Later, members of the Lafayette Chapter forwarded a petition in support of the French immersion program to the Lafayette Parish School Board. The chapter also urged parents to contact school officials and politicians to voice their support of the immersion program. The Lafayette Chapter has subsequently included French speaking demonstrations by immersion students at its activities.[25] Formal cooperation between the CFMA and CODOFIL for language promotion among children has occurred. The Acadiana Chapter, for example, now sponsors an annual children's conversational French contest between the CFMA and CODOFIL at the Church Point Cajun Day Festival.[26]

### Dance

Cajun dance lessons are frequently given following chapter meetings and at monthly and bi-monthly classes. Every chapter has an official adult dance troupe. These groups perform at official CFMA functions and they also provide demonstrations at non-CFMA events upon request. A *Joie de Vie* children's dance troupe was also created which now performs many times annually at various CFMA functions or other events requiring Cajun French dance demonstrations.[27]

### Music

The preservation and promotion of Cajun music is obviously the central goal of the CFMA. As with the promotion of other aspects of Cajun culture, this effort occurs at various levels. CFMA chapters advertise the schedules and performance venues for local Cajun bands in their portion of the newsletter. Also, the newsletter frequently provides listings of local radio stations that broadcast Cajun music. The CFMA works proactively to advocate for the public presentation of Cajun music. For example, individual chapters have urged members to write letters of protest to radio stations that cut or eliminate Cajun music programming.[28] The CFMA has awarded plaques to several

---

[24] *La Voix des Cadjins*, October 1991.
[25] *La Voix des Cadjins*, November 1996.
[26] *La Voix des Cadjins*, June 1997.
[27] *La Voix des Cadjins*, November 1996.
[28] *La Voix des Cadjins*, October 1991.

radio stations in recognition of their support of Cajun music programming.[29] On one occasion, the association also organized a convention to honor radio DJs who are active in broadcasting and promoting Cajun music.[30]

Teaching Cajun music commonly occurs within chapters and as an organization-wide effort. The Houma Chapter, for example, has advertised violin lessons for a "small fee," while other chapters have provided free or fee-based accordion, violin, and guitar lessons at informal classes and formal workshops.[31] Other chapters devote considerable resources to teaching Cajun music. As one such example, the New Orleans chapter allotted $1500 at one point to purchase accordions for music instruction.[32] The Acadiana Chapter developed the Lee Manuel-Dewey Balfa Fiddle Apprenticeship program.[33] In this program, young violinists with some formal training work under the tutelage of a noted Cajun violin player. According to conversations with one of its organizers, this program was developed to address a growing shortage of Cajun violin players.

The CFMA cultivates opportunities for fledgling musicians to practice and demonstrate their skills. For example, jam sessions are organized at the end of official chapter meetings and incorporated into chapter functions like picnics.[34] Various CFMA chapters also sponsor jam sessions in settings ranging from bars to community centers. There are specific forums developed for the performance of Cajun music by youngsters. For example, in addition to offering accordion, violin, and guitar lessons, the Lafayette Chapter also sponsors a Newcomers Festival for child musicians at Vermilionville, a living history museum in Lafayette.[35] The CFMA also sponsors a children's music contest at the annual Cajun Day Festival in Church Point, and assists in sponsoring accordion contests for youngsters at other non-CFMA affiliated events.

### Le Cajun Award Ceremony and Festival

The CFMA's priority on various Cajun cultural elements is reflected in its national awards ceremony. The first annual *Le Cajun* award ceremony and festival was organized in 1991. It has been referred to by CFMA officials as the "Cajun Grammys," and, "the most important thing being done by the CFMA to influence the guidance or what is and is not good Cajun music." The first event drew a crowd of several thousand to Blackham Coliseum in Lafayette,

---

[29] CFMA, General Meeting, January 7, 1991.
[30] CFMA Governing Body, January 21, 1991.
[31] *La Voix des Cadjins*, May 1992, October 1996, June 1997.
[32] *La Voix des Cadjins*, April 1992.
[33] *La Voix des Cadjins*, October 1996.
[34] *La Voix des Cadjins*, June 1997.
[35] *La Voix des Cadjins*, December 2000.

since the ceremony's regular venue, and it attracted considerable regional media coverage.

The CFMA awards selection process is well-structured. Each chapter selects representative for the nominations committee. Every year the committee solicits recordings from record companies. Out of this pool, a short list of ten nominees is selected for each category. The committee then reduces the nominees in each category to three. Finalists are voted on by the general CFMA membership.

Award categories include best male and female performer, best song, best album, and a New Horizon award presented to the best new young musician. The CFMA also developed the *Prix Dehors* to honor Cajun bands (often consisting of non-Cajuns) outside of Louisiana that are viewed as performing in a traditional style. This award has been presented to bands from areas ranging from Minnesota to Scandinavia.

The awards ceremony takes place on a Friday evening. Awards are given to Cajun musicians as well as others such as DJs and scholars of Cajun culture who are acknowledge for their contributions to preserving and promoting Cajun culture. Each award is co-presented in English and French by a pair of presenters, often consisting of a CFMA official paired with a local celebrity. Winners give acceptance speeches in French and/or English.

The Saturday and Sunday following the awards ceremony are devoted to a festival. Several prominent bands are scheduled throughout both days and evenings. Arts and crafts booths, including those by craftsman like accordion builders, are situated throughout the coliseum. A large concessions area sells various traditional Cajun foods.

### *Defining Cajun Culture*

The CFMA has various rules regarding what it will promote as traditional Cajun music. Acceptable forms of the genre are generally described as accordion-led music accompanied by the violin and guitar. However, additional instruments like the steel guitar, drums, and keyboard are also approved. Ideally, lyrics are entirely in Cajun French, and in fact, songs must be performed in French to be eligible for awards.

Given geographical variation in Cajun music, differing intergenerational perspectives on music style, and even personal idiosyncrasies, there have been concerns and controversies over acceptable musical forms. In particular, the fear of Cajun music being confused with Afro-French zydeco music or overly influenced by it or country music has been voiced.[36] Discussions about defining Cajun music and acknowledgement of the difficulties in such efforts have occurred. In particular, tensions sometimes develop between tradition-

---

[36] CFMA Board of Directors Meeting, May 22, 1991; CFMA, General Board and Cajun Festival Update meeting, Houston Heritage Chapter, May 9, 1991; CFMA, Governing Body, Meeting, August, 20, 1990.

alists, especially older members, and those who feel that including "progressive" forms of Cajun music is necessary to appeal to younger generations or a broader membership.

*Conclusion*

The Cajun French Music Association has emerged as the first formal, region-wide grassroots organization specifically devoted to the preservation and promotion of Cajun music. It contrasts with earlier formal efforts, such as CODOFIL, that focus on French language promotion and links to the Francophone world. However, the CFMA's efforts are also directed toward other aspects of Cajun culture, including Cajun French language, dance, and foodways. In fact, these practices are generally interwoven within the context of events like chapter festivals and the national awards ceremony.

Many CFMA activities are directed toward transmitting various cultural elements to children as well as educating adults. In addition to activities within the organization, the CFMA has also taken a proactive and often public role in promoting what it perceives to be traditional Cajun music and culture. This involves outreach to public schools and universities, efforts to support and honor those are involved in publicly promoting Cajun music and culture, and efforts to educate the public in general about Cajun culture.

As with any effort to establish guidelines for cultural elements or musical style, the CFMA has been involved in discussions and debates over acceptable cultural forms. In some instances, these are ongoing dialogues. However, such episodes highlight the geographical, generational, and idiosyncratic diversity within contemporary Cajun culture. Therefore, the CFMA is an interesting case study in ethnic revival and it may serve as an interesting model for other ethnic groups who wish to develop formal institutions to negotiate and promote their culture and identity.

**Figure 1**
**CFMA Chapters**

| Name | Headquarters |
|---|---|
| Acadiana Charter Chapter | Eunice, LA |
| New Orleans Chapter | Metairie, LA |
| Baton Rouge Chapter | Baton Rouge, LA |
| Lake Charles Chapter | Lake Charles, LA |
| Chapitre de Lafayette | Lafayette, LA |
| Bayou Cajun Chapter | Houma, LA |
| Houston Heritage Chapter | Houston, TX |
| Golden Heritage Chapter | Nederland, TX |
| De Fa Tras Chapter | San Antonio, TX |
| Les Cadiens de Teche | New Iberia, LA |

**Figure 2**
**CFMA Chapter Organization**

President
Vice-President
Secretary
Treasurer/Membership
Sergeant-at-Arms
Representatives to National Board
Local Board

**Figure 3**
**CFMA National Governing Body**

President
Vice President
Secretary
Treasurer
Membership Chair
National Board Members

**Figure 4**
**CFMA National Committees**

Festival Dates & Security
CFMA Constitution and Bylaws
Le Cajun Awards and Festivals
Le Cajun Dance Troupe
Le Cajun Queens
CFMA Hall of Fame and Museum
Cajun Lyrics Authenticity Advisory
Publisher
Membership Mailing Committee
HOF Nominating Committee
Legal Accounting and Income Tax
Historian Committee Chairman
Internet Webmaster

# THE WATER PUMP

## Commercialization of Cajun Music

RADIO AND COMMERCIAL RECORDING elicited the greatest change on Cajun music during the twentieth century. Both mediums brought outside influences into Acadiana and opened doors for aspiring musicians. The opportunities provided by radio and recording gave musicians the chance for regional fame and a career in music. The results invigorated Cajun music, moving it beyond its traditional base and forging new styles of expression.

As radio spread across the country during the 1920s, it presented two opportunities to the Cajun community. First, the new medium provided performance outlets for local musicians who used radio shows to promote local appearances. This allowed for greater professionalization of Cajun music as performers could now advertise concerts and dances far beyond the local area. The resulting exposure then increased demand for radio performers. Radio performances also exposed audiences outside of Acadiana to Cajun music. Secondly, radio brought new sounds into the region, and Cajuns eagerly consumed the sounds of jazz, blues, and country music, particularly the Western Swing version of the latter. Musicians fused these new styles into Cajun music and produced such genres as Cajun swing and, later during the rock and roll era, swamp pop.

Likewise, recording gave musicians opportunities to both make money and to enhance their local reputations by advertising themselves as "recording artists." Recordings helped to standardize Cajun songs as hit versions by famous artists displaced personal or regional variations of standards. A good example is the classic "Jole Blon" which moved out of the folk tradition first as "Ma Blon Est Parti" by Amédé Breaux, then saw life under the name "Gueydan Waltz" by Leo Soileau before being given its now accepted name by the Hackberry Ramblers. In the mid-1940s Harry Choates recorded a regional hit version that spawned innumerable copies and "answer" songs, most of which took off on Choates' fiddle-driven version. By the 1950s playing "Jole Blon" inevitably meant working off the now standardized Choates version. The same trajectory can be traced with songs such as "Colinda" and Nathan Abshire's "Pine Grove Blues," which began life (at least on record) as "Petit Chien Blues" by Amédé Breaux. Recordings also raised listeners' expectations that live performances needed to sound like the recorded performance, even down to the three or so minute time limit of the early 78s.

Local entrepreneurs saw the value and profitability of recording. Early Cajun recording artists often received the push to record from local furniture salesmen, who hoped to enhance sales of record players by offering recordings by local favorites. Soon some of these entrepreneurs entered the recording business themselves, becoming the masters of the south Louisiana scene. These recordmen exhibited catholic tastes and a willingness to take chances on experimental artists. As a result, such individuals as J.D. Miller and Floyd Soileau helped shape the very nature of Cajun music.

Recordings also brought the outside world to Acadiana. The personal record collections of Cajuns often contained more recordings by Jimmie Rodgers, Bob Wills, and Hank Williams than those by Cajun artists. Cajun musicians replayed their heroes' records, studied the styles of those artists, and incorporated the new sounds into their own reporitores. Artists willing to experiment and move into other styles, such as Cajun-country artists Jimmy C. Newman and Vin Bruce and rockers Rod Bernard and Joe Barry, enjoyed national success.

Radio and recording provided not only outlets for Cajuns to express themselves and expand their audience, these media brought outside influences to Acadiana and expanded the horizons of Cajun people. As well, radio and recording threatened to homogenize the Cajuns by exposing them to Anglo-American culture and standardizing certain aspects of their world. By the 1950s, however, the rise of local independent record companies and the emergence of French-language radio led to a revitalization of culture and the language around the music. Revon Reed's broadcasts from Fred's Lounge in Mamou and the success of the labels owned by such recordmen as Soileau and Miller ensured at least partial survival of the language and a renewed interest in both traditional and experimental Cajun music. Commercialization proved to be both homogenizer and savior.

The first Cajun record, Joseph Falcon's "Lafayette."
Courtesy of the Cajun and Creole Music Collection, Edith
Garland Dupré Library Special Collections, University of
Louisiana at Lafayette.

# Cajun Music[1]

## Barry Jean Ancelet

Cajun music has often been studied and presented as a folk music, and in many respects it is. But the traditional process that produced what we now call Cajun music is neither very old nor complete. Most of what is heard today in dancehalls and at local festivals, as well as on records, has developed since the turn of the century. Cajun musicians continue to produce new songs and adapt new styles, keeping the tradition contemporary. Although some songs come from anonymous sources, in many cases we know exactly who composed and first recorded songs and who developed popular styles. In fact, these composers and stylists are highly regarded within the community of Cajun musicians.

Joseph and Cléoma Falcon were the first to record Cajun music, in 1928. Their first release on Columbia, "Lafayette," was not an old song. The tune is closely related to an older dance song entitled "Jeunes gens de la compagne," but the Falcons rearranged the tune and improvised a new set of words that had nothing to do with the song on which it was loosely based. The Falcons apparently thought that, because they were covering new ground by making the first record, they ought to do it with new material.

The process that led to "Lafayette," now better known as "Allons à Lafayette" from the first line of the song, is typical of the way Cajun music has developed over the years. The Falcons borrowed a little from here, a little from there, and added something new. The recording industry helped to fix in the Cajun repertoire this song and many of the others that followed in those early years of recording between 1928 and the late 1930s. Improvisation was as important to early Cajun music as it has been to other typically American music forms that resulted from the combination of European and African influences that met in the New World, such as jazz and the blues. Musicians improvised countless songs during dance jobs, but now a lucky few could freeze their improvisations in the grooves of those old 78s. Consequently these recorded versions of what had long been a rather fluid song tradition stuck in the popular mind and became the "right" way to sing those songs. Also, the musicians on record became well known and in demand for dances beyond their neighborhoods.

The decade or so following 1928 can be thought of as a sort of classic period. Arhoolie's Old Timey label covers this early period, as well as the major developments in Cajun music through the 1950s, in its excellent series, *Louisiana Cajun Music: Vols. 1-5* (OT 108-111, 114, 1971-73); unless otherwise not-

---

[1] This article first appeared in the *Journal of American Folklore* 107 (1994): 285-303.

Cléoma and Joe Falcon, ca. 1928.
Photo courtesy of Johnnie Allan.

ed, all recordings cited are LPs). Recently Arhoolie/Old Timey added to its already excellent coverage of early Cajun music with *Pioneers of Cajun Accordion Music, 1926[sic]-1936* (OT 128, 1989), which features more recordings by the major players born around the turn of the century. *Le Gran Mamou: A Cajun Music Anthology, Vol. 1* (CMF 013-D), a CD released in 1990 by the Country Music Foundation, further documents the early history of Cajun music. While some of the songs of this early period are included on these anthologies primarily for their historical importance (the fact that they were recorded at all), others, such as those of Joe and Cléoma Falcon, the Breaux Brothers (Amédé, Ophé, and Cléopha, all brothers of Cléoma), and Angelas LeJeune, have more lasting cultural value and are still part of today's active dance-band repertoire. Some of the most influential figures of this period were meteoric, such as Mayuse LaFleur who was killed in a barroom brawl before he could hear his first record. Others, such as Nathan Abshire and Lawrence Walker, were around for much longer. Among these, perhaps the most important were white Cajun fiddler Dennis McGee and black Creole accordionist Amédé Ardoin, who played and recorded together regularly in contradiction to the segregationist social codes of the times and who were forced to improvise a social relationship, as well as a musical style.

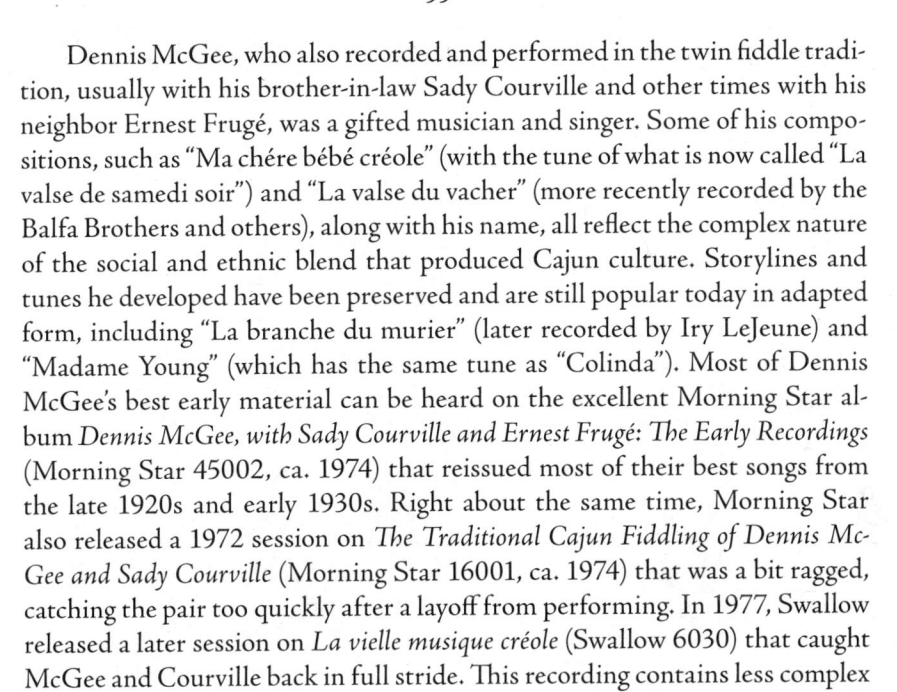

Dennis McGee, who also recorded and performed in the twin fiddle tradition, usually with his brother-in-law Sady Courville and other times with his neighbor Ernest Frugé, was a gifted musician and singer. Some of his compositions, such as "Ma chére bébé créole" (with the tune of what is now called "La valse de samedi soir") and "La valse du vacher" (more recently recorded by the Balfa Brothers and others), along with his name, all reflect the complex nature of the social and ethnic blend that produced Cajun culture. Storylines and tunes he developed have been preserved and are still popular today in adapted form, including "La branche du murier" (later recorded by Iry LeJeune) and "Madame Young" (which has the same tune as "Colinda"). Most of Dennis McGee's best early material can be heard on the excellent Morning Star album *Dennis McGee, with Sady Courville and Ernest Frugé: The Early Recordings* (Morning Star 45002, ca. 1974) that reissued most of their best songs from the late 1920s and early 1930s. Right about the same time, Morning Star also released a 1972 session on *The Traditional Cajun Fiddling of Dennis McGee and Sady Courville* (Morning Star 16001, ca. 1974) that was a bit ragged, catching the pair too quickly after a layoff from performing. In 1977, Swallow released a later session on *La vielle musique créole* (Swallow 6030) that caught McGee and Courville back in full stride. This recording contains less complex tunes than the earliest material, but it swings nevertheless with the seemingly boundless energy of this remarkable man who lived and played well into his nineties, including a roaring two-week stint at the 1985 Smithsonian Festival of American Folklife.

Almost every song that Amédé Ardoin recorded, in the beginning of his career with Dennis McGee and later alone, has become part of what could be described as the core repertoire of Cajun music. Many of his tunes were later revived by Iry LeJeune after World War II, including "The Eunice Two Step" ("Jolie Catin"), "La valse de l'orphelin" ("Viens me chercher") and "La valse à Abe" ("La valse de quatre-vingt-dix-neuf ans"). His bluesy, improvised lyrics and highly percussive accordion style also served as the basis for zydeco, which would hit full stride when Boozoo Chavis and Clifton Chenier retooled it with a rhythm-and-blues lathe in the 1950s. Many of Amédé Ardoin's best songs are on Arhoolie/Old Timey's *Amédée Ardoin, Louisiana Cajun Music Vol. 6, The First Black Zydeco Recording Artist: His Original Recordings, 1928-1938* (OT 124, ca. 1981), as well as on others of its Old Timey series.

The string-band era of the late 1930s and early 1940s first bumped the accordion and eventually the traditional sound of Cajun music from popularity. This period was characterized by the smoother, lighter touch of musicians playing for the first time with electrical amplifiers and strong influences from other American traditions, especially country and swing. The Hackberry Ramblers, and bands led by Leo Soileau and J.B. Fusilier, dominated the first half of this period; Harry Choates almost single-handedly dominated the second. The best of this material is available on the Arhoolie Old Timey series mentioned earlier and on its re-release, *Harry Choates: The Fiddle King of Cajun Swing, Original 1946-49 Recordings* (Arhoolie 5027, 1982).

After World War II, Cajuns began to rethink the drift away from their cultural and social values that had begun during this "Americanization" period. Musicians were among the first to announce this trend. Iry LeJeune appeared to be going directly against the grain in 1948 when he recorded "La valse du Pont d'Amour," after hitching a ride to the studio with Virgil Bozman's Oklahoma Tornadoes Band. Yet the traditional sound that informed his music had never completely disappeared. It had simply gone underground. It was no longer recorded, but it continued to be played for private house dances and family gatherings throughout south Louisiana. LeJeune revived many of Amédé Ardoin's songs, even preserving Jouline, Ardoin's recurring mythical mistress. LeJeune recorded songs from his own family tradition, such as the "Bayou Pon Pon" and "La fille de la veuve" (which has the same tune as "Jolie Blonde"), both recorded earlier by his uncle, Angelas LeJeune. He also composed a few new songs with obvious influences from country and bluegrass tradition, such as "Bosco Blues" (its tune and some of its lyrics are from Jimmie Rodgers's "Blue Yodel #7" ["Anniversary Blue Yodel"]) and "J'ai fait une grosse erreur" (clearly inspired by country music). Iry LeJeune was a powerful accordion player and helped to revive that instrument's waning popularity.

Ivy Mire, Steve Doucet, Sing Abshire, Simon Schexnider, a Cajun string band from 1940. *Photo courtesy of Johnnie Allan.*

Yet his main contribution was as a lyricist and a stylist. Though many of the songs he recorded came from older sources, his cuts are generally regarded by contemporary Cajun musicians as the definitive versions. It is LeJeune's words and arrangements that survive today, performed by every Cajun band in south Louisiana and southeastern Texas. A few of his songs are on the Arhoolie/Old Timey releases, but the mother lode is on the two albums that compiled previously issued singles, published about 1968 by Goldband and then leased by Swallow in 1970—*The Legendary Iry LeJeune, Vols. 1 and 2* (LP 7740 and 7741). Recently these two were combined on a single CD, Goldband CD-7741 (1991). Though primitively recorded, these records capture the emotional power and poetry of this extraordinary singer and accordion player.

In the same period immediately following World War II, several Cajun musicians emerged to perform for the renewed demand. Some of them, such as Austin Pitre, Nathan Abshire, and Lawrence Walker, had been popular before the accordion had faded from the scene. Like Iry LeJeune, Austin Pitre revived several of Amédé Ardoin's songs, such as "Two step de la prison." He also released several "original" versions of songs that had been in the tradition in looser forms, such as "Les flammes d'enfer" and the "Opelousas Waltz," both also inspired by black Creole tradition. Some of Pitre's songs can be found on Arhoolie's Old Timey series. More recently, Swallow released *The Evangeline Playboys* (Swallow 6041, 1981), which reissued some of Pitre's most popular 45 recordings.

The titles of some of Nathan Abshire's best compositions leave little doubt as to one of the major influences in his music: "The Pine Grove Blues," "The Service Blues," "The Offshore Blues," "The French Blues," and "The Popcorn Blues." He also recorded some the tradition's hottest two steps, such as "Courtableau," "Fifi Foncho," and "La queue de tortue," as well as some of its most-moving waltzes, such as "La valse de Kaplan" (whose tune was first recorded by Angelas LeJeune as "La valse de Pointe Noire"). He adapted tunes from country songs to produce memorable Cajun songs, such as "La valse de Bélizaire" (from Roy Acuff's "The Precious Jewel") and "Mon coeur fait plus mal" (from Hank Snow's "I Don't Hurt Anymore"). Swallow has released two fine compilations of Abshire's singles, *Pine Grove Blues* (Swallow 6014, 1974; cassette) and *The Good Times Are Killing Me* (Swallow 6023, 1976; cassette), both of which capture the magic combination of Nathan and the Balfa Brothers before their unfortunate breakup in the early 1970s. Recently, Swallow gathered some of Abshire's best material on *A Cajun Legend: The Best of Nathan Abshire* (Swallow SW-CD-6061, 1991). In the 1970s, La Louisianne released *Nathan Abshire: A Cajun Tradition, Vols. 1 and 2* (LL 139, ca. 1975; LL 144, 1978). These recordings featured the south Louisiana equivalent of studio musicians, because Nathan did not maintain a regular band after his breakup with the Balfa Brothers. This backup band included two well-known Cajun/country fiddlers, Merlin Fontenot on fiddle and Rufus Thibodeaux on bass, and former swamp-rocker Bessyl Duhon on guitar. These two records are a bit slick, more tightly wound than Abshire's usual rambling, emotion-packed, bluesy recordings, but they contain some exuberant performances nevertheless.

Lawrence Walker is credited by many for developing what came to be called "new style" Cajun music in the 1950s. A demanding bandleader, he tightened arrangements and smoothed the sound of his Wandering Aces, especially reducing the syncopation in his own accordion style. He also composed several Cajun classics, including "The Reno Waltz" and "La valse du malchanceux," and gave a definitive version to "Chère Alice," which had been known as "La valse à Petit Dom Hanks." His early recordings were with several local companies, but La Louisianne's *Tribute to the Late, Great Lawrence Walker* (LL 126, ca. 1969) and Swallow's *Lawrence Walker: A Legend at Last* (Swallow 6051, 1983) feature his best cuts. He is also included with an eclectic Cajun/country/bluegrass band on *French Music and Folk Songs of Le sud de la Louisianne* (LL 103, 1961) along with Happy Fats, Doc Guidry, and Alex Broussard.

Another important group to emerge after World War II was Alphé Bergeron's aptly named Veteran Playboys. Alphé was a fine-enough accordion player, but the band was especially distinguished by the singing and songwriting of his son, Shirley. His crystal-clear high-pitched vocals enhanced the soulful new lyrics that he sang to traditional songs such as "Quelle étoile," "La valse de la belle," and "J'ai fait mon idée," giving these and others what has come to be considered their final poetic form. The band's best album, a collection of their best 45s, is *Alphé and Shirley Bergeron and the Veteran Playboys: The Sounds of Cajun Music* (Lanor 1000, 1968, leased by Swallow in 1970 and reissued in 1992 by Ace records on a CD, with the addition to the title of *French Rocking Boogie*).

The next major development in Cajun music was the music of Aldus Roger and the Lafayette Playboys in the 1960s. His hard-driving and tightly arranged sound shocked audiences in local dancehalls. The band's sound was criticized by some for its lack of emotion and improvisation. Some felt Roger was a good technician but too mechanical. Yet he quickly became immensely popular in the region, performing weekly on the CBS-affiliate television station in Lafayette. Roger built one of the first big Cajun bands that included a steel guitarist, drummer, electric bass player, electric rhythm guitarist, and as many as three fiddlers at one point, in addition to Roger on accordion. His singers, such as Fernice "Man" Abshire and Philip Alleman, have been called crooners by some who think they lacked the emotional edge that char-

Aldus Roger and the Lafayette Playboys in the early 1960s. From left to right, Phillip Alleman, Tunice "Bee" Abshire, Roger, Harry Lee Bat, Doc Guidry, Louis Foreman, and David Abshire.
*Photo courtesy of Johnnie Allan.*

acterized early singing styles. The new smoothness was undoubtedly the result of the same influences that also had expanded and electrified the band—Americanization and the western swing and country sounds that came with it. Roger's Lafayette Playboys were recorded by several of the local recording companies that emerged after the national companies turned their attention to broader markets, but his best recordings are those released by La Louisianne: *Aldus Roger Plays French Music* (LL 107, 1964), *Aldus Roger: King of the French Accordion* (LL 114, ca. 1966), and *Aldus Roger Plays Cajun French Classics* (LL122, 1968).

When rock was born in the 1950s, Cajun musicians had a front-row seat. Several of rock's early giants, including Jerry Lee Lewis and Antoine "Fats" Domino, were from nearby in the state, and their influence was inevitable. The new names of some swamp-pop performers indicate what was happening: Warren Shexnayder became Warren Storm, Clinton Guillory became Clint West, John Allen Guillot became Johnny Allen, and Elwood Dugas became Bobby Page. Some of these, such as Rod Bernard, Joe Barry (Josef Barrios), and Grace Broussard (of Dale and Grace), had considerable success with hits beyond south Louisiana. One of the best examples of this period's influence on Cajun music is Belton Richard and his Musical Aces. His songs show the same cross between rhythm and blues and country that characterized early rockabilly performers. Some songs, like "Un autre soir ennuyant" (Another Lonely Night), are basically swamp pop but in French, and others, such as "Les cloches de noce" (Wedding Bells), are translations of popular country hits. He was Swallow Records' hottest Cajun recording artist in the 1970s, with albums such as *Belton and the Musical Aces* (Swallow 6010, 1968), *Good 'n Cajun* (Swallow 6021, 1975), *Louisiana Cajun Music* (Swallow 6032, 1980), and *Belton Richard: At His Best* (Swallow 6043, 1981).

Belton Richard was one of the most popular Cajun musicians of the late 1960s and early 1970s. His polished rock- and country-influenced sound was representative of the trend in south Louisiana to modernize the music. Popular bands, such as Blackie Forrestier's Cajun Aces, followed his lead away from the unadorned roots of Cajun tradition. The older styles from which these new developments departed were in grave danger of fading completely. In 1964, when Gladdy Thibodeaux, Louis "Vinesse" LeJeune, and Dewey Balfa were invited to perform at the Newport Folk Festival, even people who attended dancehalls faithfully would have been surprised at the choice of fieldworker Ralph Rinzler, had they known about it. Most did not and continued to dance to the sounds of bands such as the Lafayette Playboys and the Musical Aces. At Newport, however, the three Cajun musicians were overwhelmed by the standing ovations they received for playing their old-time music. Even more important, though, Dewey Balfa returned to Louisiana determined to bring home the echo of those standing ovations. In addition to his tireless efforts to organize festivals and school presentations, he also eventually convinced local record producer Floyd Soileau to release a few recordings of his family's traditional Cajun music. Soileau was reluctant at first, but Dewey eventually wore him down. One of the first of these, a 45 featuring the ancient "La Valse du bambocheur," was a surprise local hit and proved that there was a growing interest in the root sound.

The Balfa Brothers' first releases were soon gathered together on their first Swallow album *The Balfa Brothers Play Traditional Cajun Music* (Swallow LP-6011, 1965), often called the yellow album. Dewey was a perfectionist and had the band fine-tuned and right on the beat. The first Balfa recordings had drive and an emotional edge that gave new life to the old traditional material they were playing. There were also a few surprises, new compositions such as the "Newport Waltz," named in honor of the turning point not only in Dewey's life but also in the recent development of Cajun music. Their first album featured friend and neighbor Hadley Fontenot on accordion. The second Swallow release, *The Balfa Brothers Play More Traditional Cajun Music* (Swallow LP-6019, 1974), featured accordion virtuoso Marc Savoy. A traditionalist well known as an accordion maker, he has also contributed significantly over the years to the effort to reenergize old songs. In 1990 Swallow reissued both Balfa albums on a single CD, *The Balfa Brothers Play Traditional Cajun Music* (SW-CD-6011).

Over the years, Dewey Balfa made dozens of records, all of them with the same basic goals as these first two. Swallow's compilation, *The Best of Nathan Abshire*, cited earlier, also features the Balfa Brothers on most cuts. The all-too-brief collaboration of the Balfas and Nathan Abshire is considered by many Cajun music scholars and fans alike as one of the high points in recorded Cajun music. This version of the band was featured in several films including Jean-Pierre Brunot's *Dedans le sud de la Louisiane* and Les Blank's *Spend It All*. Unfortunately the band blew apart because of internal tensions; Dewey and Nathan agreed not to play together in order to preserve their friendship. Several attempts to reconcile the group failed, but their personal relationship endured until Nathan's death in 1981. After Dewey's brothers Will and Rodney died in 1979, he continued to make music and records. *The New York Concerts* (Swallow 6037, 1980) featured the Balfa Brothers live on the folk-festival circuit. *The Balfa Brothers* (Rounder 6007, n.d.) was an interesting personal statement by the band, an acoustic musical album of the family's musical heritage. Dewey made two Cajun-fiddle instructional albums. He also appeared on several albums with friends such as Bois-Sec Ardoin and Canray Fontenot, on *The Ardoin Family Orchestra, with Dewey Balfa* (Sonet 873, 1981), with Rockin' Dopsie on *Rockin' Dopsie and the Twisters*, which included Tony Balfa and J.W. Pelsia (Sonet 872, n.d.), and with Marc Savoy and D.L. Menard, on *Under the Green Oak Tree* (Arhoolie 5019, 1977), which featured the first recording of the title song by D.L. Menard. On his last Swallow album, *Souvenirs* (Swallow 6056, 1985), Dewey demonstrated convincingly that he was no antiquarian and that creation within tradition was not only possible, but that it could be a beautiful affirmation of the life of the tradition. The album features a burst of "brand-new old songs" he had composed with his late brother Rodney. One of these, "Quand j'étais pauvre," has become a dancehall standard performed by just about every Cajun band.

D.L. Menard recorded in the 1960s as a member of Eliard Badeaux's Louisiana Aces. In fact, D.L. composed some of the band's most popular songs. "La porte d'en arriére," easily D.L.'s most memorable song, was composed in 1962. It was considered unusual at the time, so unusual in fact that D.L. had to pay for the session himself to get the band to record it. It was an immediate local hit and became his signature song. He went on to compose several other standards, including "The Jolly Roger's Waltz," "I Can't Forget You," "Rebecca Ann," "Un homme marié," "A Bachelor's Life," "The Water Pump," and "Under the Green Oak Tree," among others. He sang them all in his characteristic Hank Williams-influenced nasal vocals. Most of his best early material can be found on Swallow's compilation *The Back Door* (Swallow 6038, 1980). Members of the original Louisiana Aces were gathered together once more after the band had

Legendary Cajun singer D.L. Menard performing on a festival stage.
Photo courtesy of Acadian Museum, Erath, Louisiana.

retired to record *D.L. Menard and the Louisiana Aces* (Rounder 6003, 1974) for Dick Spottswood in 1972. The band was a little out of sync by then, but the recording does capture much of the spirit of the old band. Since then, D.L. has preserved the Louisiana Aces name in several new versions, in recordings such as *No Matter Where You At* (Rounder CD-6021, 1988), which featured Eddie LeJeune and Blackie Forrestier on accordion and Ken Smith on fiddle. This album has a variety of songs, including a couple of Cajun music classics, "J'ai passé devant ta porte" and "Petits yeux noirs," one of D.L.'s own classics "The Water Pump," and a dizzying translation of the country standard "Wildwood Flower." D.L. also realized a life-long dream when he recorded *Cajun Saturday Night* (Rounder 0198, 1984), with a few old-time country songs, including "Wedding Bells," "House of Gold," "Why Should We Try," and "My Son Calls Another Man Daddy," by his hero Hank Williams, as well as "The Banks of the Old Pontchartrain," a couple of his own French classics "Bachelor's Life" and "Underneath the Green Oak Tree," and a few original English compositions, such as "This Little Girl" and "The Judge Did Not Believe My Story." He received all-star support from the likes of former members of Williams's band the Drifting Cowboys, Jerry Rivers and Don Helms, as well as from Buck White, Ricky Skaggs, Jerry Douglas, and his own son Larry Menard from the local pop/country band Atchafalaya. More recently, D.L. joined forces with Ken Smith on fiddle and Eddie LeJeune on accordion for *Cajun Soul* (Rounder 6013, 1988) and *Le Trio Cadien* (Rounder CD-6049, 1992), both of which feature mostly new versions of older songs, as well as a few new songs by Eddie and D.L. This trio has been especially popular in Europe, where they have had several successful tours.

Eddie LeJeune also recorded an excellent album, *It's in the Blood* (Rounder CD-6043, 1991), with the members of his regular Morse Playboys band (at the time). Compared to the trio's recordings, this album has a less tightly produced, more natural and spontaneous feel to it, and it is a pleasure to hear featured Lionel Leleux on fiddle and Hubert Maitre on guitar, both underappreciated veterans of many Cajun bands, including Lawrence Walker's Wandering Aces. Eddie nails the songs to the wall with his piercing LeJeune-clan vocals, including the most rousing version of "Donnez-moi-la" (also known as "Petite ou la grosse") ever recorded, a few new songs such as "Je l'ai rencontrée" [I Met Her], "Les conseils j'ai écouté" [The Advice I Listened To], and "J'ai quitté ma famille dans les miséres" [I Left My Family in Misery], and a few of his father Iry LeJeune's classics. The only unfortunate thing about Eddie's vocals is that they are sometimes hard to understand, and he often does not preserve the rich lyrics of his father's songs.

Marc Savoy recorded several popular 45s in the 1960s with an electric Cajun band, but his most memorable recordings are those he has made with his wife Ann and with Michael Doucet in what has become known as the Savoy-Doucet Cajun Band: *Savoy Doucet Cajun Band* (Arhoolie 5029, n.d.), *Savoy-Doucet Cajun Band: With Spirits* (Arhoolie 5037, n.d.)—combined in a 1992 CD reissue as *Home Music with Spirits* (Arhoolie CD-389)—and *Savoy-Doucet Cajun Band: Two Step d'Amédé* (Arhoolie CD-316, 1989). This unusual combination of a staunch traditionalist, Savoy, and an eclectic experimentalist, Doucet, has produced some of the most exciting old-time Cajun music on record. The Savoy-Doucet Band has influenced contemporary bands by re-injecting old songs into today's repertoire. The band's recordings of revved-up traditional material is based on intense and complex performances. They have composed lyrics for traditional instrumentals, such as the much-imitated "Johnny Can't Dance," and invented whole new configurations, such as their "Amédé Two Step," inspired by the music of the late Amédé Ardoin. Marc Savoy also released a version of his earlier electric band sound, complete with steel guitar, on the second side of *Oh What a Night!* (Arhoolie 5023, 1981). The only sure thing about Savoy and Doucet, beyond their inspired musicianship, is their shared unwillingness to be predictable.

Image of Coteau during the filing of French Candian filmmaker André Gladu's documentary, *Réveille*.
Photo courtesy of Center for Louisiana Studies, University of Louisiana at Lafayette, accession number 2610.

    Michael Doucet first approached Cajun music in a highly experimental rock-country-Cajun fusion band called Coteau, the first band to attract the young hip university crowds around the relatively urban Lafayette area. Unfortunately Coteau never released a record, although they were once recorded live in Québec. After Coteau fell apart from internal tensions, Doucet turned to his hobby-band Beausoleil and, as they say, the rest is history. His newfound cultural and historical awareness is evident in the band's name, after Joseph Broussard *dit* Beausoleil, the leader of a small band that fought against the British when they exiled the Acadians from Nova Scotia in 1755. The group's first album, *The Spirit of Cajun Music* (Swallow 6031, 1977), was an eclectic tour de force that reflected on the roots of contemporary Cajun music, combining traditional, classical, rock, and jazz elements in classy, experimental, and somewhat self-conscious arrangements, including some of Alan Lomax's 1930s field recordings learned by Doucet before he had had a chance to hear them, having only seen transcriptions of the songs in Irène Whitfield's *Louisiana French Folk Songs* (Baton Rouge: LSU Press, 1939). The first album featured Françoise Schaubert (from France) on vocals and original Beausoleil accordionist Bessyl Duhon. The second, *Les Amis Cadjins* (Modulation 33000, 1980), later re-released as *Zydeco Gris Gris: Highly Seasoned Cajun Music* (Swallow 6054, 1985), featuring Joel Sonnier on accordion and Annick Colbert (from Belgium) on vocals, was less experimental, though there is still a saxophone and piano, both played by Steve Conn. It was also obviously dedicated to some of the formative influences in Doucet's still-developing style: the Balfas, Canray Fontenot, Varise Conner, and Dennis McGee, although credit to their compositions is sometimes unclear or lacking.

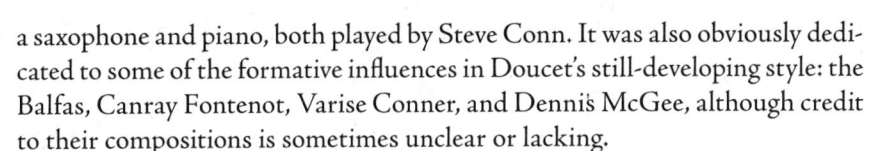

Subsequent Beausoleil albums were more spontaneous as Michael Doucet's fusion began to take shape. *Michael Doucet dit Beausoleil* (Arhoolie 5025, 1982) features the more laid-back accordion-style of Errol Verret, who would stay with the band for several years. This recording also features Michael's brother David on guitar. Traditionally, the guitar was limited to percussive accompaniment in Cajun music (sometimes locally referred to as the "boom-chick" sound, the result of stopping the ring of the strings on alternating strums). Certain Cajun guitarists, such as Rodney Balfa and D.L. Menard had already begun to develop more-complex accompaniment styles, but David applied his knowledge of old-timey and bluegrass guitar styles to create an innovative flat-picking lead style. This development is so new and so relatively complex that it has not yet been widely imitated, although it certainly is envied by many. *Michael Doucet with Beausoleil: Parlez-nous à boire* (Arhoolie 5034, 1984) had basically the same personnel. *Allons à Lafayette* (Arhoolie CD-308, 1989) featured Creole fiddler Canray Fontenot on some of his original tunes, such as "Shoo, Black," "La table ronde," and "Blues à Canray." Michael also continued his ingenious use of old material, including "J'ai marié un ouvrier" from the Lomax collection and Will Balfa's "Mon vieux wagon." This album also includes Beausoleil's version of Lawrence Walker's "Johnny Can't Dance," with the new lyrics that Michael Doucet developed for the Savoy-Doucet Band's earlier recording. Somewhere along the way, Michael Doucet joined forces with Pat Breaux and Jono Frishberg and former Coteau drummer Kenny Blevins in a wild experiment with a fusion of the sounds that we all grew up with in south Louisiana in the 1960s and 1970s, especially Cajun music, swamp pop, and rock. *Cajun Brew* (Rounder CD-6017, 1987) included Belton Richard's French swamp-pop classic "Un autre soir ennuyant," as well as "Wooly Bully" and "Louie Louie" from top-forty radio. The experiment was fun, but it did not capture the attention of the Cajun population and was too weird for Cajun music enthusiasts outside of Louisiana.

By *Hot Chili Mama* (Arhoolie 5040, 1987), Jimmy Breaux replaced his older brother Pat, who had temporarily replaced Errol Verret, as Beausoleil's regular accordionist. This version of the band has become relatively stable; with Jimmy on accordion and Michael and David Doucet, the band regularly features Tommy Alesi on drums and Billy Ware on percussion. Tommy Comeaux joined them on bass and mandolin when he could, until recently when his duties as a medical doctor forced him to leave the band. On *BeauSolo* (Arhoolie CD 321, 1989), Michael Doucet and brother David flex their considerable musical talents in a simpler setting, with retooled ballads such as "Isabeau" and "Sept ans sur mer" and fiddle tunes from Michael's lesser-known mentors, Wade Frugé and Varise Conner.

The band did a couple of albums for Rounder that tested the waters of change. *Bayou Boogie* (Rounder CD-6015, 1987) included a bilingual version of "Zydeco gris gris" and Sonny Landreth's English-language "The Flame Will Never Die," in addition to a few retooled old tunes like "Kolinda" and "Mama Rosin Boudreaux," many of which were vaguely reminiscent of something Zachary Richard had done a few years before. *Bayou Cadillac* (Rounder CD-6025, 1989) reconsidered the *Cajun Brew* experiment with Beausoleilized versions of "Iko Iko," "Baby, Please Don't Go," "Bo Diddley," "Not Fade Away," and the title song, "Bayou Cadillac" [Buy You a Cadillac], as well as "Bunk's Blues" (after south Louisiana jazz pioneer Bunk Johnson). These experiments were interesting but again not always enthusiastically received in south Louisiana's Cajun heartland. It is perhaps because of this drift from traditional sources that David Doucet and Jimmy Breaux elected to record their own more-rooted albums. David's *Quand j'ai parti* (Rounder CD-6040, 1991) featured his buddies from Beausoleil, as well as Josh Graves on dobro and John Stewart on upright bass, playing straight stuff like "Coulée Rodair" and "J'ai fait le tour." The title of Jimmy's album *A Little Bit More Cajun* (La Louisianne CD-1003, 1991) clearly states his intentions. In addition to his Beausoleil pals, he invited Richard Comeaux on steel, Mike Dugas on bass, and brother Gary Breaux on drums. U.J. Meaux, a veteran of Lawrence Walker's Wandering Aces and current fiddler in Walter Mouton's Scott Playboys, adds a fine, old-style fiddle and heartfelt vocals on "Tu vas jamais casser mon coeur" [You'll Never Break My Heart] and Doc Guidry's "La valse d'amitié" [The Waltz of Love]. Beausoleil released two more albums on Rounder before switching labels. *Hoogie Boogie* (Rounder CD-8022, 1992) is an album with songs and rhymes intended for children. *Live! from the Left Coast* (Rounder CD-6035, 1989) is perhaps the band's best-received album ever among Cajuns back home in Louisiana. It has enjoyed lots of local sales and radio airplay, probably because it includes some of the most mainstream-sounding tracks ever recorded by the group. The live-ness and the groove of the album, on songs such as "Cajun Groove/The Scott Playboys Special" and the "KLFY Waltz," are infectious.

*Cajun Counja* (RNA CD-70525, 1991) marked Beausoleil's debut on what might be considered a major label, Rhino Records' RNA series. The band seems to have made the transition without forgetting why they were signed in the first place. The album featured old songs, such as "Sur le Pont de Lyon," imported from France, new compositions, such as "Le Chanky-chank français," and more evidence of Michael Doucet's early heroes, including "Tasso/McGee's Reel." Guests Richard Thompson, Sonny Landreth, and Steve LaCroix and an intense production effort give this album a rich, carefully crafted sound.

Nominated for a 1994 Grammy in the progressive folk music category, Beausoleil's *Danse de la vie* (Rhino R271221, 1993) is the group's most original album to date. It features several original compositions by Michael Doucet, including the title song with lyrics about the good life. "Dans le grand brouillard" describes a dream of lost love; "Zydeco X" was inspired, one supposes, by Malcolm X in a style resembling "Zydeco gris-gris;" "Ouragon" is a haunting and complex blues instrumental; and "Attrape mes larmes" is an instrumental tribute to the late Dewey Balfa. Bandmate Jimmy Breaux collaborated on "R.D. Special." Michael's wife, Sharon Arms Doucet, contributed the lyrics to the lullaby "Chanson pour Ezra" and collaborated on the lyrics to "Dis-moi pas," which has roots in both county and swamp-pop styles. The band's country connection is also evident in the guest appearance of Mary Chapin Carpenter, returning the favor for Beausoleil's performance on one of her albums. Also included are "Quelle belle vie," a swinging bilingual version of Roy Hayes's "Oh What a Life," as well as retooled versions of a few traditional classics: Angelas LeJeune's "Jeunes filles de la campagne," the ballads "La fille de quatorze ans" (which Zachary Richard also recorded on one of his first records) and "Je tombe au genoux," and a medley of Dennis McGee and Sady Courville reels, "Ménage à trois reels." The album features close harmony vocals by the Doucet Brothers and some fancy flat-picking by David Doucet, now integral parts of Beausoleil's contemporary sound.

A recent reissue of Doucet and Beausoleil, *Déjà vu* (Swallow 6080, 1990), offers a good sampling from the group's early Swallow albums, updated with live cuts from *La musique chez Mutate's, le restaurant cajin* [sic], and something from their Christmas album, *Christmas Bayou* (Swallow CD-6064, 1986), itself a combination of translated Christmas standards and traditional gems such as "Bonsoir, Bonne Année" and "Fais trois tours de la table ronde," both learned from the legendary Creole fiddler Canray Fontenot. *Déjà vu* also includes "The Arc de Triomphe Two-step" from their very first album, *Beausoleil la nuit* (Pathé Marconi EMI 2-C666-14352, 1976), and two previously unreleased cuts. Virtually unknown in this country, it was recorded while the group was on its inaugural tour in Paris during Louisiana's bicentennial exhibition there in 1976 and released exclusively in France. This early album, incidentally, though difficult to find, provides a rare example of the original

Beausoleil sound, featuring Bessyl Duhon on accordion, Bruce McDonald on acoustic guitar, the Richard brothers Kenneth and Sterling, as well as Michael Doucet on fiddle. The only other cut from the original group is "La valse du pont d'amour" on *The Spirit of Cajun Music*, recorded live at Jimmy Carter's inaugural ceremonies in Washington in January 1977.

Zachary Richard was one of the first young musicians to emerge from the Louisiana French movement. A graduate in history from Tulane, Richard had become conscious of the mournful plight of his own people and made a career shift from English-language folk rock and country to French-language Cajun music in the early 1970s. He returned home to learn about the language and music of his own ancestors. He learned accordion from a friend and neighbor, Felix Richard (no relation), who has since recorded a live album with his band, the Cankton Express, *Traditional Cajun Music Live Chez Mulate's* (Swallow 6073, 1988) featuring Felix's lively, driving accordion style and son Sterling Richard's Iry LeJeune-influenced singing. Zachary sharpened his focus even further during a trip to Québec and to the Acadian parts of the Canadian maritime provinces. Upon his return to Louisiana, Richard refused to speak English in public and challenged others to do the same. But the politics of confrontation he encountered in Québec were foreign to his native south Louisiana. His angry, politicized performance at the second annual Hommage à la musique acadienne festival in Lafayette in 1975 baffled the eight thousand or so Cajuns in attendance. They had no idea why he was so visibly upset. His first album, *Bayou des Mystéres* (Kébec Disc KD 913, reissued on RZ CD-1017, 1991) represented this early stage of his musical transformation. It included a mixture of ballads that he learned from Whitfield's *Louisiana French Folksongs*, contemporary Cajun dance songs, and original compositions such as "Réveille," one of the first songs in the Cajun music repertoire to refer directly to the exile.

Richard's next album, *Mardi Gras* (reissued from the earlier CBS version as RZ CD-1005 in 1989), was less politicized and more focused on reinvigorating old songs such as the Mardi Gras song with intricate new pop-influenced arrangements. This recording also included poetic new country and rock-influenced compositions. The original record was all in French. A subsequent re-release, the only version now available, has several of the songs translated into English, presumably for a larger audience. Richard has sometimes been described as a musical chameleon. *Allons Danser* (CBS PFC 80032, 1979; reissued as RZ CD-1007, 1989) featured more traditional and original songs, this time in a South Louisiana swamp pop and New Orleans R & B-influenced style. Richard's popularity soared in Québec and France, where he represented ethnic and linguistic survival in defiance of the American mainstream. He gained an enthusiastic following, received several awards, and sold lots of records there. *Live in Montréal* (RZ CD-1003, 1991) captured the excitement of a Richard performance in that context, with perhaps the best Louisiana band he ever assembled, featuring Sonny Landreth on slide guitar. At the same time, Richard remained a marginal figure in Louisiana. The young, hip crowd knew of his accomplishments and the more danceable of his songs played on the radio, but many were still unnerved by the fiery lyrics of his protest songs and others found his dance songs too unfamiliar-sounding to accept. *Vent d'Été* (Kébec Disc KD 541, reissued on RZ CD-1019, 1992) and *Migration* (CBS PFC 80009, ca. 1978, reissued on an RZ CD in 1992) were more introspective and the albums played well in France and Québec, but they were virtually unplayed in south Louisiana, though by now some young Cajuns had discovered his earlier material and developed a taste for it. He continued to strain against the edges of Cajun music.

Richard, who had long been earning a living with his music, needed to continue finding new sounds and new directions. When he broke with Kébec Disc/CBS, he bought his part of the catalog, which he later reissued on the RZ label, and recorded one album completely on his own, *Zack Attack* (Apache 240506, 1984, reissued as RZ CD-1009, 1989) that included some shocking rap-influenced sounds. He then signed with Rounder to do two albums. Both of them, *Zack's Bon Ton* (Rounder CD-6027, 1988) and *Mardi Gras Mambo* (Rounder CD-6037, 1989), represented an attempt to capture a part of the American market with an eclectic blend of styles, including Cajun and New Orleans rhythm and blues, and songs sung mostly in English. Soon after the first Rounder release, he was approached by A&M Records to do more of the same. He managed to slip a version of Rick Michot's moving waltz "La Ballade de Howard Hébert" and the traditional "Aux Natchitoches" among the mostly good-time English material on *Women in the Room* (A&M CD-75021 5302 2, 1990) and *Snake Bite Love* (A&M CD-75021 5387 2, 1992). Yet he did not completely shy away from cultural and political statements. "No French No More," on the first, is a powerful and lucid indictment of the turn-of-the-century policy of punishing children for speaking French on the schoolgrounds. "Sunset on Louisiane," on the second, is a daring exploration of the relationship between the economic opportunities provided by the petrochemical industries and the threat to health and the environment caused by industrial pollution.

Not all Cajun music is accordion-driven. In fact, during the late 1930s and through most of the 1940s, the accordion completely faded from the commercially recorded scene. As noted earlier, during this period string bands were the order of the day, as Cajuns imitated their English-speaking

American neighbors in earnest. Leo Soileau's Four Aces, J.B. Fusilier's Jolly Boys, Luderin Darbone's Hackberry Ramblers, and Happy Fats's Rayne-Bo Ramblers were the dominant bands of the period. They all can be heard on Arhoolie's Old Timey collection (Vols. 2 and 3), and on the Country Music Foundation's *Le Gran Mamou: A Cajun Music Anthology*. Arhoolie also gathered some of Leo Soileau's best material on *Leo Soileau: Original 1930s Recordings* (OT 125, n.d.) in its Old Timey series. Principal heir to this legacy was Harry Choates, who easily went back and forth between western-swing-influenced Cajun music and Cajun-influenced western swing. Arhoolie included some interesting material on *Volume 4* of its Old Timey series and re-released more of his regional hits from 1946-1949 on *Harry Choates: The Fiddle King of Cajun Swing*. Notably missing from this otherwise fine collection is Choates's classic remake of "Jolie Blonde," unavailable from Starday Records. This historic cut does appear, however, on La Louisianne's *French Music and Folk Songs of Le Sud de la Louisianne*.

An often-neglected heir to the swing fiddle-led tradition of the string band era was Adam Hebert. He usually performed and recorded with an accordion player, first with Alphé Bergeron while he was a member of the Veteran Playboys and then with Claby Richard while running his own Country Playboys band. Hebert is best known for his own compositions, some of which are heavily based on country songs, including "La Pointe au Pain," "Cette là j'aime" [The One I Love], "Mon tour va venir un jour" [My Turn Will Come], and "J'aimerais connaître" [I'd Like to Know]. His songs, characterized by strident vocals and a piercing fiddle line, remained dormant until recently when several popular contemporary bands, including McCauley, Reed, and Vidrine, as well as Steve Riley and the Mamou Playboys, gave them new life. Now many of his compositions have be-

Julius C. Lamperez, "Papa Cairo," steel guitar innovator and band leader. Photo courtesy of Margie Lamperez Breaux Collection, Center for Louisiana Studies, University of Louisiana at Lafayette, accession number 3991.

come part of the standard repertoire for weekend dance bands throughout south Louisiana. His most important recordings are gathered on *The Best of Adam Hebert* (Swallow 6065, 1987).

Another important fiddle stylist is Hadley Castille, who grew up with Cajun music, but also played country and bluegrass along the way. His first few Cajun music albums, including *Hadley J. Castille* (Kajun 5010, 1981) and *Cajun Fiddling and Singing, Now and Tomorrow* (Kajun 5020, 1983) were recorded with a group he called the Cajun Grass Band. Castille's early recordings focused on the sound of Cajun music without the accordion, with obvious influences from the swing era of Cajun music, such as guitar leads and piano rides. *Going Back to Louisiana* (Swallow 6057, 1985) featured visits by Doug Kershaw, a Cajun musician who pursued a minor career out of Louisiana and into Tennessee and California, and Ann Savoy, author of *Cajun Music: A Reflection of a People* (Eunice: Bluebird Press, 1985), a Richmond, Virginia, native who married Marc Savoy and plays with him in their family band. In *Along the Bayou Teche* (Swallow 6078, 1989), Castille turned his attention to the composition of original songs based on events in the life of Hadley and his neighbors in the Pacaniére region south of Opelousas. "Faire whiskey" is a lighthearted song about the bootlegging operations once common in the area, and "Maudit Bayou Teche" is the mournful description of an accidental drowning and its effects on family and community. Castille went a step further on "*200 Lines: I Will Not Speak...*" (Swallow 6088, 1991), bravely confronting in the title song the linguistic discrimination he and most members of his generation experienced when they arrived in school for the first time as children.

On the eastern side of the Atchafalaya Basin, the accordion faded and did not come back like it did on the western prairies after World War II. There Cajun music continued to follow a country-influenced string-band tradition. The dominant performer from the Terrebonne/Lafourche region is Vin Bruce. His rich bass vocals are unusual in Cajun music, which has traditionally preferred a high-lonesome singing style. But Bruce's vocals are perfectly suited to his country-flavored songs such as "Dans la Louisiane" and "Dans le c'ur de la ville." A very shy person, Bruce turned down a shot at Nashville to stay close to home. His best early material is gathered on *Jole Blon* (Swallow 6002, 1962), *Vin Bruce: Greatest Hits* (Swallow 6006, 1965), and *Cajun Country* (Swallow 6015, 1972). La Louisianne Records brought him back into the studio to remake some of his best songs for *Cajun Country's Greatest* (LL 134, 1972). Another fine Cajun country-style singer from the wetlands is L.J. Foret, who can be heard on *Cajun Country Singer* (LL 138, 1973). A more recent product of this region is Waylon Thibodeaux, who first emerged as a fiddler in Bruce Daigrepont's band and now has struck out on his own with *Best of Cajun: The Traditional Songs* (Mardi Gras CD-5007, 1992) and *Cajun Festival: Live from the Bayou* (Mardi Gras CD-5008, 1993).

In the late 1950s and 1960s, the groundwork was laid for what would eventually be a renaissance of Cajun music. Between 1956 and 1959 Harry Oster, then at Louisiana State University in Baton Rouge, made several fieldwork forays into Cajun country. The results appear on *Folksongs of the Louisiana Acadians, Vols. 1 and 2* (Arhoolie 5009 and 5015, n.d.), volume one comprising material originally issued on his own Folk-Lyric label (LFS-A-4, ca. 1960) under the same title, and volume two mixing unissued cuts with portions of *Cajun Folk Music* (Prestige International/Documentary Series 25015, 1962). Oster focused primarily on music from Vermillion Parish and the Mamou area, including the Deshotels brothers, Milton Molitor, Isom Fontenot, and Shelby Vidrine. There are ancient unaccompanied ballads and fiddle tunes, as well as more recent dance music. Oster avoided the slicker side of Cajun music to focus on its older, less-public side. The two volumes have a raw, uncompromising power. Many of the songs have been spit-shined and put back into circulation by contemporary performers such as Zachary Richard and Michael Doucet.

When the Newport Folk Festival was looking for roots musicians to present alongside revivalists such as Bob Dylan, Joan Baez, and Peter, Paul and Mary, board member Alan Lomax, who had done field work in the area in the 1930s with his father, suggested sending someone down to Louisiana to find some Cajun musicians. Ralph Rinzler and Mike Seeger were among those who came to do the initial fieldwork. *Cajun French Music from the Southwest Prairies*, Vols. 1 and 2 (Rounder CD-6001, 1989; CD-6002, 1992), contains recordings made by Rinzler between 1964 and 1967. Again, these recordings represent the gutsy, rural sound of Cajun music. The searing, emotion-laden vocals of singers such as Austin Pitre and Cyprien and Adam Landreneau are not for the faint of heart. The haunting ballads of Isom Fontenot and Edius Naquin had just about faded from the scene, except when a folklorist asked for them. These records also feature some of the earliest recordings of the Balfa Brothers and the Ardoin Family Band with Canray Fontenot. Both groups went on to become leaders, both in Louisiana's cultural renaissance and on the national folk-arts scene. Dewey Balfa, Alphonse Ardoin, and Canray Fontenot were eventually recognized for their efforts by the National Endowment for the Arts Folk Arts Program, with National Heritage Fellowship awards. Unfortunately, these historically important records were released before the booklets intended to accompany them were ready. Thus, important documentation is missing from the package. But the recordings themselves are an important part of the history of the rekindling of interest in Cajun music and zydeco. More recently, Ann Savoy compiled another collection based largely on Rinzler's fieldwork from the 1960s: *Edius Naquin: Ballad Master* (no number, n.d.), a cassette collection with accompanying booklet. The project was supported by a grant from the New Orleans Jazz and Heritage Foundation.

*J'étais au bal: Music from French Louisiana* (Swallow 6020, 1980) was recorded by Ron and Fay Stanford in the early 1970s with support from a National Endowment for the Humanities Youth grant. It was issued with an accompanying booklet of information on the culture and the music. The Stanfords worked under the tutelage of Newport vet Dewey Balfa. Together they were responsible for making the University of Southwestern Louisiana [now the University of Louisiana at Lafayette] aware of its role in continuing this work from the inside. They were also instrumental in helping to establish the first Tribute to Cajun Music festival in Lafayette, a turning point in the revitalization of the culture and the music. The album contains definitive performances, from ballads to old-time fiddling to Cajun dance music to zydeco to swamp pop, by a range of singers and musicians, both Cajun and black Creole, from Agnes Bourque to Clifton Chenier, and from the Lawtell Playboys to the Dixie Ramblers. This album remains one of the best and tightest anthologies of Cajun music and zydeco ever compiled.

Ironically, material from the Louisiana French fieldwork of Alan Lomax, who influenced all three of the fieldworkers mentioned above, was not released as a collection until 1987, although several individual songs had appeared earlier on Library of Congress compilations of the Lomax material. Lomax first recorded in south Louisiana in 1934, six years after the first commercial records were made. But while the record companies documented what was developing as contemporary Cajun music in the first third of this century, Lomax concentrated on songs and music that were considered old at that time, thus reaching even further back. Copies of the original recordings were obtained from the Library of Congress by the University of Southwestern Louisiana's Center for Acadian and Creole Folklore, and we convinced Swallow records to release a limited edition of *Cajun and Creole Music: The Lomax Recordings, 1934* (Swallow 8003-2, 1987). The release provided old songs to recycle into new material. Michael Doucet made particularly good use of this resource, rearranging several songs, such as "Pierrot Grouillet and Mademoiselle Josette," "Belle," "Je m'endors," and "J'ai marié un ouvrier," for his group Beausoleil.

Not all field-recorded albums are successful. *Cajun Social Music* (Smithsonian/Folkways CD SF 40006, 1990; originally Folkways FA 2621, 1977), features such greats as Nathan Abshire, Mark Savoy, and

Hector Duhon, yet its raw, warts-and-all documentary style makes it unpleasant to listen to. It sounds like what it was: a candid recording of great musicians and not-so-great musicians playing together for their own pleasure and with no notion that what they were doing might be made available to the public. Many of the performers included here were surprised and somewhat dismayed to find these private sessions on record.

One of the many bands revived with the renewed interest in Cajun music during the early 1970s was Octa Clark, Hector Duhon, and the Dixie Ramblers. First "rediscovered" by fieldworkers Ron and Fay Stanford and Nick Spitzer, they were invited to perform at festivals and eventually to record their turn-of-the-century sound that featured Hector's parallel-fiddle lead and Octa's smooth accordion and soulful singing. Their releases *Old Time Cajun Music* (Arhoolie 5026, ca. mid-1980s), with Michael Doucet, and *Ensemble Encore* (Rounder 6011, 1983) were the band's first albums, although they had played together for decades. Duhon and Clark careen through complex melodies, following each other note for note as though each could read the other's mind. And Clark nails the high vocals like few other singers in Cajun music. His lyrics are sometimes plaintive, sometimes witty. He takes daring chances with the phrasing, refusing to play it safe. Sometimes he gets caught out of step, but most times he makes it just under the wire. This practice has an interesting side effect as knowledgeable listeners find themselves engaged in the effort, rooting for him to find a way to cram too many syllables in not enough beats.

Another often overlooked musician who recorded late in life is Ambrose Thibodeaux, who began playing again decades after putting his accordion aside as a young man to raise his family. All of his major releases were on La Louisianne records. *Authentic French Acadian Music* (La Louisianne 112, 1963) featured his son-in-law Merlin Fontenot on fiddle. Originally from Eunice, Louisiana, Merlin spent years in Florida, where he added country and bluegrass styles to his repertoire. His lighter, fancier fiddle style was criticized by purists but was popular among Cajun music fans. One of the reasons Thibodeaux was often overlooked is that he never sang. Vocals were provided by Preston Manuel, a veteran from the country- and western-swing influenced string-band era of Cajun music, who also played guitar. Preston Manuel's English exhortations during the recording session bothered Thibodeaux, a staunch traditionalist, and he was not included on subsequent recordings. *More Authentic French Acadian Music* (LL 119, ca. late 1960s) had Leon Doucet on fiddle. Gervis Quebedeaux's powerful vocals and deft phrasing are reminiscent of Iry LeJeune. For *Ambrose Thibodeaux* (LL 133,

1974), Thibodeaux went back to Merlin Fontenot on fiddle and tapped young Reggie Matte to sing. By his fourth album, *Authentic Cajun French Music and Folk Songs* (La Louisianne 143, 1977), Thibodeaux had finally settled on his first string, which included Gervis Quebedeaux on vocals and son-in-law Merlin on fiddle. Unfortunately, by then, the song list was getting a little short. The albums that feature Quebedeaux are the best of the lot, although the others are certainly worth consideration.

Paul Daigle is one of the young musicians who emerged from the effort to inspire kids to play the music of their heritage. A native of the Acadia Parish area, he won one of the early Church Point Cajun Days young accordion players contests in the mid-1970s. His first album was not recorded until later, however, when he and Michael Doucet collaborated on *The Cajun Experience* (Swallow LP-6058, 1985). They were joined by Robert Elkins on guitar and vocals. Paul soon formed his own tight, high-energy band called Cajun Gold and began a meteoric career that would produce nearly an album a year between 1985 and 1990, fueled in large part by the prolific songwriting of Pierre Varmon Daigle. Their first album *Cajun Gold* (Swallow LP-6060, 1986) featured Rufus Thibodeaux's cousin Tony Thibodeaux on fiddle. *La lumiére dan ton chassis* (Swallow LP-6068, 1987) is perhaps the band's best effort, with a few Cajun music classics and several new and interesting songs by Varmon Daigle. Robert Elkins's soulful performances enhanced the ambitious, sometimes complex storylines of these songs. Louisiana fiddle champion Ken Smith replaced Tony Thibodeaux. *Coeur farouche* (Swallow LP-6077, 1988) and *Est-ce que to pleure?* (Swallow LP-6082, 1990) were vehicles for more Varmon Daigle songs that eventually began to sound self-conscious and a little repetitious. The band and their recordings were immensely popular in south Louisiana during their brief tenure, packing dancehalls on the tough Saturday night schedule, as well as playing actively on the local festival circuit. They finally broke up soon after their last release, at what many would have described as the height of their popularity, probably due to burnout. Paul Daigle retired for a while to reassess his own personal priorities. He recently unpacked his accordion again to tour with D.L. Menard. The band has had a few emotional and memorable reunions but not on record.

A break in his country music career provided south Louisiana native Joel Sonnier an opportunity to record a collection of mostly Cajun music, *Cajun Life* (Rounder CD-3049, 1991). His mastery of the accordion reminded listeners of why he was considered Iry LeJeune's heir in his youth, especially on a ninety-nine-mile-an-hour version of the "Perrodin Two Step" that has fiddler Merlin Fontenot struggling to catch up, and with his uncanny vocal phrasing on classic Cajun waltzes and two-steps such as "La valse du grand bois," "Chère Alice," "Lacassine Special," and "Allons à Lafayette." He takes wild chances with his vocals, loading them with emotion, and never fails to nail them and his listeners to the wall. He even sings "Petits yeux bleus" in the same sky-high key that he first recorded it as a preteen, never missing a note. A few out-takes from the album proved to be hits as single releases, including a French translation of "Jambalaya" (Hank Williams originally borrowed the tune from an old Cajun two-step variantly named "L'anse couche-còuche" and "Grand Texas") and what may be the best recording of "Jolie Blonde" since the Breaux Brothers' original version from the late 1920s. These are included on the CD. Fortunately for Joel Sonnier and unfortunately for Cajun music fans, his country career soon took off again with the release of *Come On, Joe* (RCA CD-6374-2-R, 1987), but he has not completely forgotten his roots; he managed to sneak an exciting cut of the "Evangeline Special" on *Have A Little Faith* (RCA 9718-4-R, 1989).

One of the most exciting new singers to emerge on the contemporary Cajun music scene is Johnny Sonnier, whose clear, soulful vocals are reminiscent of Belton Richard. His two albums, *Tous les dimanche après-midi* (Lanor 1010, 1989) and *Send a Message to My Heart* (Vidrine CD-91004-2, 1993), feature some original songs such as Sonnier's own "La lettre," Hubert Vidrine's "Dans le magasin," and Ken Vallot's "Image dans le miroir" and "Dernière, dernière chance" (which won the Cajun French Music Association's song-of-the-year award in 1992). Sonnier's recordings are also liberally sprinkled with translations of country songs, such as "Sept anges de Cajuns" (from Willie Nelson's "Seven Spanish Angels"), Kostas and Louvin's "Send a Message to My Heart," and Rice and Price's "Till a Tear Becomes a Rose." Unfortunately, the poor recording quality of these recordings does not do justice to this excellent singer and musician.

Nancy Tabb Marcantel singing the national anthem at the Superdome, New Orleans, Louisiana, 1978.
*Photo courtesy of Johnnie Allan.*

Women have long been involved in making Cajun music. The first songs most children heard were sung by their mothers, grandmothers, and aunts. Cléoma Falcon accompanied her husband, Joseph, on the first Cajun record, "Lafayette," and provided the vocals for several of the records they eventually made together. Yet men have undeniably dominated the public performance of Cajun music over the years. Recently, however, a few women have begun to change things. Sheryl Cormier and Becky Richard formed an all-women Cajun band that was popular for the short time they stayed together. Sheryl now plays the accordion and runs her own band that features mostly men, including her husband Russell, on vocals. Their "Mon coeur et mon amour" is one of the most popular songs in recent Cajun music history. Cormier's *La Reine de Musique Cadjine (Queen of Cajun Music)* (Swallow LP-6081, 1990) gathered some of her best material. Becky Richard, who briefly pursued a career in country music, returned to Cajun music to form her own band, joining forces with her father Pat (on accordion). They recently released *Southern Belle* (Kajun 5042, 1991) that includes some moving original songs, especially Larry Lemaire's "Vieux chapeau de paille," as well as a few Cajun classics.

Jambalaya is one of the most popular dance bands in South Louisiana and has been called the hardest working band in Cajun music. The original band, featuring Larry Picard on accordion, Terry Huval on bass, Tony Huval on drums, and Richard Comeaux on steel guitar, released *Buggy Full of Cajun Music* (Swallow 6035) in 1979. The sound was good but a little too intense at times. After Picard bailed out, the band was drastically reorganized by Terry Huval, who switched to fiddle, passed his bass on to Ken David, got Reggie Matte to join them on accordion and Bobby Dumatrait on guitar. This more traditionally based lineup released *Le nouvel esprit de la musique cadien* (Swallow LP-6075, 1988) and *C'est Fun* (Swallow LP-6085, 1990). The latter offers an interesting blend of traditional songs, such as "La Pointe aux Pins" and a swinging version of the old Creole blues "La Coulée Rodaire;" original compositions, including "C'est fun" and Reggie Matte's moving autobiographical waltz "Gone, Gone, Gone;" and a borrowing from country music, "J'aimerais avoir cette danse" [Can I Have This Dance]. They followed this fine release—Chef Paul Prudhomme is quoted on the liner as saying "This one's going in my collection in my truck!"—with *Instrumental Collection* (Swallow SW-CD-6094, 1992), intended, according to Terry Huval, for those "who enjoy Cajun music but can't understand the lyrics," that may in fact work best for radio deejays who need to fill the ends of hours and commercial backgrounds with instrumentals.

The work of McCauley, Reed, and Vidrine could perhaps best be described as regressive Cajun music, a trip back in time. They are in no way interested in experimenting with the music or pushing the limits of the tradition. They just enjoy playing the old the stuff the old way, unadorned and uncluttered, straightforward and sitting down. This purity is clearly evident on their first album *1929 and Back: Traditional Cajun Music* (Swallow LP-6090, 1991), which features a collection of songs from the likes of Amédé Ardoin, Angelas LeJeune, Joseph Falcon, and Cyprien Landreneau. Ironically, this old stuff sounds hot because it bypasses the smoother influences of the 1950s and 1960s to feature instead the syncopated, percussive sound of the turn of the century, a sound that is similar to the hard-driving style of many contemporary bands. Philip Alleman recently replaced Cory McCauley on accordion in the group, renamed Tasso (Cajun French for "smoked meat"). The first effort of this version, *The Old Timey Way* (Swallow CD-6103-2, 1993), features classics as well as a few tunes rescued from obscurity, all played in a deliberately regressive style. Alleman's jumpy accordion style and warbly vocals are reminiscent of Moïse Robin, who recorded with Leo Soileau in the late 1920s and early 1930s after Mayus Lafleur was killed in a barroom shootout.

Wayne Toups raced to the top of the Cajun music scene in 1984 with an electrifying performance at the annual Festival de musique acadienne in Lafayette. He had, however, paid considerable dues by then, coming up through the ranks, playing on the weekly dance-hall circuit. His first album, *Wayne Toups and the Crowley Aces*, a fieldwork project by Sam Charters on the Sonet label, was not released in this country and went virtually unnoticed here, except by particularly assiduous fans, although it contains some interesting material from a formative period in Toups's development, as he was still imitating his heroes, notables such as Walter Mouton, Iry LeJeune, and Belton Richard. Toups's lusty vocals and his southern rock-influenced arrangements, featuring keyboards, an electric lead guitar, and a hard-driving bass and drum line have since made him one of the most imitated accordion players and singers in Cajun music today, especially among young musicians. His early material on the Crowley-based MTE label was highly experimental but still firmly based in the tradition. On *ZydeCajun* (MTE CD-5032, 1986), he recorded two of the most beautiful waltzes in Cajun music, his own "Mon ami" and Paul Marx's "Soigne mes enfants," as well as what has become the new definition of Iry LeJeune's classic "J'ai été au bal," characterized by a break that Toups learned from Walter Mouton and accentuated even further. (Mouton has taken his own Scott Playboys band in the studio only once, to record a 45, although he recently provided the title song for the soundtrack of Chris Strachwitz's film *J'ai été au bal* [Arhoolie CD-331 and 332, 1992].) *Johnnie Can't Dance* (MTE CD-5035, 1988) further established Toups as a new cultural phenomenon. While Michael Doucet should properly be credited with innovating lyrics for the title song, a classic instrumental by Lawrence Walker, it is Wayne Toups's rollicking new arrangement of the song which pasted it onto the playlists of just about every dance band in Cajun country.

Toups's ZydeCajun band has undergone many personnel changes over the years and now includes few others who grew up with Cajun music like he did. Consequently, the band now plays set arrangements. His two major label releases, *Blast from the Bayou* (Polygram CD-8365181, 1989), which included several cuts from *Johnnie Can't Dance,* and *Fish Out of Water* (Mercury-Master Trak CD-848 289-2, 1991), are well produced and feature original songs in both English and French. The pressure of signing with a national label has caused him to drift somewhat from the Cajun music core of his raising, as Toups courts a wider, English-speaking American audience. Nevertheless, he managed to place more French songs with a traditional base on his second Polygram album than his first, including "Night at the Wheel," "Late in Life," and "Rocking Flames." "Ooh La La" is a natural blend of English and French lyrics. And both Mercury releases have won regional Cajun French Music Association awards, indicating that he has not yet lost his connection to home. MTE has also released *Down Home Live* (MTE CD-5043-2, 1992), which captures a memorable performance at the Crowley Rice Festival.

Steve Riley and the Mamou Playboys are the most recent force to emerge on the Cajun music scene. Their first album, *Steve Riley and the Mamou Playboys* (Rounder CD-6038, 1990), produced by Zachary Richard, clearly demonstrated the focus of the band: to breathe new life into the Cajun classics, such as "La valse de Eunice" and "La Pointe au Pin" with tight but traditional arrangements, excellent vocals, and virtuoso instrumental performances. Bandleader Steve Riley's apprenticeship (and devotion) to Dewey Balfa and Marc Savoy is clear throughout. He pulls off daredevil maneuvers on the accordion without disturbing the traditional feel of the music. David Greely's fiddle style is an interesting combination, heavy on the smoother old masters such as Dewey Balfa, Varise Conner, and Lionel Leleux, but with a little Michael Doucet thrown in as well. Kevin Berzas preserves Rodney Balfa's bass-running accompaniment style on guitar. Michael Chapman's drumming is solid but understated. And Christine Balfa's triangle gives the group's sound a high-end snap that sounds both comfortably traditional and exhilarating. Riley's second Rounder release *Petit Galop pour Mamou* (Rounder CD-6048, 1992) includes some interesting new developments. The vocals are more solid and mature. A few more contemporary songs, such as Aldus Roger's "Lafayette Playboys Waltz" (from the 1960s), appear, and there is some interesting experimentation, including "La petite Anna à Mogène Meaux," which is the traditional instrumental "Fife Foncho" with lyrics from ballad singer

Lula Landry, and a wild-ride medley combining the single-key "Mardi Gras Jig" and Walter Mouton's "Scott Playboy Special," one of Cajun music's complicated fancy tunes that Steve Riley manages to modulate on his single-row diatonic accordion. Fiddler David Greely also recorded an excellent solo cassette album *La talle des ronces* (Swallow 6031, 1991) featuring his silky fiddle sound and some classics from old masters such as Dennis McGee, Varise Conner, and Dewey Balfa. The Mamou Playboys' third album, *Trace of Time* (Rounder CD-6053, 1993), is another excellent production, nominated for a 1994 Grammy award in the traditional folk music category. Its somewhat cosmic title may indicate that the band is growing in self-awareness. The music is still inspired by the old stuff (complex harmonies revive Shirley Bergeron's nearly forgotten "Old Home Waltz"), but there are a few new compositions. Of these, two are by non-Cajuns: Peter Schwartz's "Corner Post," and Jay and Molly Ungar's "The Lover's Waltz." "La valse de regret" is a remake of an old Cleveland Crochet song, with searing new lyrics by fellow Balfa protégé Robert Jardell. "La Pointe-au-Pic" was borrowed from Québec by way of Philippe Bruneau and Marc Savoy. The album opens with a hot medley, now a trademark of the Mamou Playboys sound, this time a flawless and inspired merger of the traditional "Bayou Noir" and Octa Clark's instrumental "Back of Town." It closes with a rocking version of "Zydeco est pas salé," featuring Sonny Landreth on slide guitar and showing influences from Wayne Toups as well as Aldus Roger. Up to now, the Mamou Playboys' most important innovations have been stylistic. Some of their south Louisiana audience is eager to see how they might do at creating their own original material within the tradition.

The Basin Brothers' very first album, *Let's Get Cajun* (Flying Fish FF 70539, 1990), was nominated for a Grammy in the folk music category. Although the album did not win, its nomination gave a shot in the arm to this interesting band. While most Cajun musicians are from the western prairies of South Louisiana, the Basin Brothers hail from St. Martin Parish, in the eastern wetlands, where the dialect is Creole rather than Cajun and the musical style tends to be softer and sweeter. Their second album, *Stayin' Cajun* (Flying Fish FF 70581, 1992), confirmed the creative talents of the group, featuring several interesting and original songs, again sung in Creole. The group recently switched accordion players, with Beausoleil veteran Errol Verret replacing Danny Collette. Their third album, *The Louisiana Music Commission and Mulate's Present the Basin Brothers* (Bayou Teche [no number], 1993), is their best effort yet, with a smoother, more solid sound, and still more interesting and original lyrics.

Bruce Daigrepont fell in love with the music of his own culture at the Cajun Music Festival, in Lafayette. He was playing banjo in a bluegrass band at the time and shifted to the accordion and Cajun music after seeing Terry Huval's original Jambalaya band perform there. Since then he has produced some of the best original Cajun music around. His *Stir Up the Roux* (Rounder CD-6016, 1987) and *Coeur de Cajun* (Rounder CD-6026, 1989) feature lots of original songs with pop arrangements that are more complex than most old-time Cajun music. Some of these, such as his "Marksville Two-step" and "Valse de la Riviére Rouge," have nevertheless become dance-hall standards performed every weekend by many other bands. Some, such as "Acadie à la Louisiane" and "Disco fais do do," are thought-provoking yet danceable explorations of historical and contemporary issues.

Mamou's highly experimental *Mamou* (Jungle CD-1010, 1988) was quite a shock to most local sensibilities. Billing themselves as "the band that rocks Cajun music," Steve LaFleur and his group incorporated the sounds of traditional Cajun music and heavy metal as though it were obvious that they were compatible. Oddly enough, the combination seemed to work as rock. They attracted the attention of a younger generation that grew up assuming that it should hate the Cajun music of its predecessors. At the same time, mainstream Cajun music fans were less than wild about the raucous sounds produced by the unlikely marriage, such as their version of "Balfa's Waltz," with digital delay, wa-wa pedals, and a scorching lead line from LaFleur's Fender Stratocaster. Yet there is something brutally real about this stuff. It comes from the same out-all-night, wrong-side-of-town kind of crowd that had produced some of Cajun culture's greatest musicians. LaFleur and Mamou laid all their cards on the table the first time out. By the time they got around to doing *Ugly Day* (Rounder CD-6050, 1992), which represented a return to the roots but with the same outlaw feeling of the first album, they had nothing left to prove. The plugs and gadgets are absent from most of the songs, but the core of this sound is still hard.

The growing popularity of Cajun music, especially on the American folk festival scene, has generated interesting questions. What happens when musicians from other cultures fall in love with Cajun music and begin to play it? Is this still Cajun music? Like the blues and bluegrass and old-time country, Cajun music seems to be taking a place in the American music scene. In many cases, the outsiders play a brand of Cajun music that is more historically "authentic-sounding" than that of some contemporary Cajun groups that can, of course, afford to experiment within their own tradition. For example, a group from Minnesota called The Bone Tones that developed undoubtedly out of a Prairie Home Companion connection, recently released *Queue de Tortue* (BTRI, CD, 1992). The collection rings surprisingly true, relatively speaking. All cuts are in French and are packed with the emotional quality of hardcore Cajun music. This album has been receiving lots of air play on south Louisiana Cajun music radio shows, with the announcers rarely failing to point out how surprising it is to hear such music from Minnesotans. The *California Cajun Orchestra* (Arhoolie CD-3562, 1991) represents a San Francisco Bay Area connection. Chris Strachwitz's Arhoolie Records and Les Blank's Flower Films, both of which have long featured Cajun music and culture, are in El Cerrito near Berkeley. Also lots of Creoles and some Cajuns have migrated to the Left-Coast for jobs and new opportunities. There are native Louisianians in the California Cajun Orchestra; Danny Poulard leads on accordion and Andrew Carriére keeps time on *frottoir*. But the rest of the gang includes Suzy and Eric Thompson, Charlie St. Mary, Bill Wilson, Sam Siggins, and Kevin Wimmer. This album has also received lots of local radio airplay. The influence of Dewey Balfa is palpable on both of these releases.

Ironically perhaps, Balfa, whose primary interest was the preservation of his own Cajun culture by and for Cajuns, also influenced lots of outside musicians in festival workshops, seminars, and special concerts throughout the country. And Balfa was on record as defending the rights of outsiders to play Cajun music. He even featured a few on his own albums, including longtime friends Tracy and Peter Schwartz on *Les quatre vieux garçons* (Folkways FA 2626, 1984) and *Souvenirs*. But the questions remain. Just what is Cajun music? Is it music played by Cajuns? If so, then English-language swamp pop would qualify. Is it the repertoire that has come to be recognized as Cajun music? If so, then can anyone play it? This would include Emmylou Harris's cut of Iry LeJeune's "Lacassine Special" on her album *Thirteen* (Warner Brothers 25352, 1986). Other traditional music forms have experienced similar expansions. White guys and gals play the blues, and urban intellectuals play country and bluegrass. In the case of Cajun music, the phenomenon is still new enough to be unsettling to many south Louisiana purists who consider the really real thing to be Cajun music played by Cajun musicians. Yet the repertoire and style continue to expand from within, and it is sometimes difficult to make the call blindfolded.

The disappearance of vinyl has changed the Cajun music recording scene in interesting ways. Companies that have long been the major suppliers of Cajun music, including Swallow, Arhoolie, and Rounder, have switched to CDs along with everyone else. This switch has filtered out some bands that might have otherwise been able to muster a limited album release. On the other hand, there has been an increasing use of cassette tapes to relieve this strain, so that newer, less well known bands can still get their music recorded and distributed (even if some have to do it themselves, just as they once did with 45s and albums). Consequently, there is just as much mediocre recorded Cajun music available now, maybe even more. But some solid recordings continue to appear, as do innovative new steps taking the tradition forward into the future. In fact, there is even some pressure to produce appropriate new material as some companies are less and less interested in releasing yet another version of the classics. This pressure contributes to the ongoing vitality of the tradition; Cajun musicians cannot afford to stagnate. And those who like Cajun music are lucky that Cajun musicians regularly refuse to listen to folklorists and ethnomusicologists. They have a better, innate sense of what works and what does not. Though there is sometimes some weird and inappropriate experimentation, everyone involved knows when it is right and when it is wrong. And somehow they rarely fail to relieve and even pleasantly surprise us.

# Louisiana Folk and Regional Popular Music Traditions on Records and the Radio: An Historical Overview with Suggestions for Future Research[1]

## Stephen R. Tucker

The genesis and subsequent evolution of the commercial exploitation of the folk music traditions of the American South is by now a familiar story.[2] Detailed examinations of various ethnic groups, subgenres and geographic entities continue to emanate from the pens of journalists, folklorists, literary scholars, anthropologists, musicologists, discographers, sociologists, historians and others.[3] That large gaps continue to exist in documentary recordings as well as in descriptive and analytic literature is undeniable. Many areas of research concerning the musical traditions of Louisiana can illuminate, extend and deepen larger ongoing scholarly endeavors. Louisiana has, along with Texas, a musical heritage as rich and dynamic as any of the United States.

The modern commercialization process began with radio. Whether or not the earliest radio station in the state, WWL of New Orleans, was the first to employ folk-style musicians has not been determined. What seems most likely is that the second station to broadcast, KWKH of Shreveport, became the first to be publicly identified as a dependable medium for folk music, specifically the style known as "hillbilly." KWKH began its broadcasting life as WGAQ in July 1922. The earliest evidence of the scheduled programing of folk music comes from a newspaper reference listing the forthcoming performance of the Old Fiddlers Club of north Louisiana on Friday evening, March 14, 1925.[4] What then of the intervening two-and-one half years? A diligent search of station records and newspaper files might well uncover earlier information.

Valuable work of a general nature has been done on KWKH and its flamboyant owner, W.K. Henderson, perhaps the key nonperforming figure

---

[1] This article first appeared in Nicholas R. Spitzer, ed., *Louisiana Folklife: A Guide to the State* (Baton Rouge, 1985), 223-40.

[2] There will be no attempt made in the ensuing discussion to fully define such terms as "folk," "popular," "pre-commercial," or "commercial." It is hoped that their meanings will become clear as various contexts within the essay emerge. One should note that the terms "media documentation" and "commercial exploitation" will be used synonymously.

[3] The best introduction to the literature of Southern folk music and its commercial extensions is found in Bill C. Malone, *Southern Music*, American Music (Lexington, 1979), 164-90.

[4] *Shreveport Times*, March 8, 1925.

in the early commercial period.[5] Still, there is a great deal to be learned about programming practices and decisions, audience and community attitudes, advertising ploys, and, especially, the identities, back styles and repertoires of the musicians themselves. As an example of this approach might view Tony Russell's study of one of the popular early groups, the Taylor-Griggs Louisiana Melody Makers, as a model of initial research. Through interviews with the sole surviving member of the group and the subsequent publication of a brief article, Russell has done much to identify and document some important participants in the commercialization process.[6]

The brief radio and recording career of Taylor-Griggs ensemble was quite typical of most hillbilly performers during the early commercial period. Originally consisting of six members of the Robert C. Grigg family from the remote north Louisiana community of Bear Creek and a fiddling attorney from the small town of Arcadia, Foster R. Taylor, the group gained professional experience through countless appearances in their home area, at house parties, school plays, civic banquets, and the like. Thus they were seasoned entertainers by the time they were hired by W.K. Henderson to appear on KWKH during the summer of 1928. Though they clearly were heirs of the southern Anglo-Celtic folk music tradition, like almost any contemporary stringband of the 1920s, they also enjoyed playing songs from Tin Pan Alley. For their inaugural appearance on KWKH, they performed Democratic presidential candidate Al Smith's campaign song, "The Sidewalks of New York."

An even more popular hillbilly act employed by Henderson during the early years of KWKH went by the name of the Lone Star Cowboys. Led by a pair of brothers from East Texas named Bob and Joe Shelton, the group generated a loyal following throughout the Mid-South region. Subsequent incarnations as the Sunshine Boys and as simply the Shelton Brothers brought them and KWKH a measure of popular acclaim unmatched in Louisiana and neighboring states.[7] Along with the Sheltons, numerous other well-known hillbilly artists peppered KWKH programming. Around 1928, a brother trio from the Macon, Georgia, area, the Newman Brothers, began a six-year tenure as featured entertainers.[8] Still another popular brother act was the

---

[5] C. Joseph Pusateri, "The Stormy Career of a Radio Maverick: W.K. Henderson of KWKH," *Louisiana Studies* 15 (1976): 389-407; C. Joseph Pusateri, *Enterprise in Radio: WWL and the Business of Broadcasting in America* (Washington, DC, 1980).

[6] Tony Russell, "Music in Arcadia: The Story of the Taylor-Griggs Louisiana Melody Makers," *Old Time Music* 24 (1977): 8-16.

[7] The Shelton Brothers appeared regularly on numerous other radio stations including WSB, Atlanta; WWL, New Orleans; and WFAA, Dallas. For a necessarily superficial review of their complex careers, see my forthcoming essay on the history of country music in Louisiana.

[8] Ivan Tribe, "Georgia Crackers in the North: The Story of the Newman Brothers," *Old Time Music* 30 (1978): 9.

Rice Brothers, brought to Shreveport from Atlanta by Bob and Joe Shelton in 1934.[9]

Probably the most representative artist of the early commercial period was Jimmie Davis. Steeped in rural Protestant culture, but enamored of the blues style, Davis began his musical career as a street singer in Alexandria in 1927. By 1929, like the Taylor-Griggs group and the Shelton Brothers, he had gravitated to W.K. Henderson's station, the first crucial step in a career that would last for over half a century and culminate in election to the Louisiana governorship in 1944 and 1960, and enshrinement in the Country Music Hall of Fame in 1973.[10]

KWKH was temporarily matched as a forum for hillbilly music by WWL of New Orleans. Chiefly as a result of the work of business historian C. Joseph Pusateri, we can learn a great deal about the commercial use of folk music on the state's other radio giant. It is difficult to point to any date or artist as marking the beginnings of country music on WWL, but Pusateri has noted that programming from the period 1924-1928 was characterized by "decorum" rather than "popular appeal."[11] By the early 1930s however, country acts dominated the station's broadcasts. In 1934, for example, WWL featured comedian musician Lew Childre; Childre's partner, Wiley Walker; Jerry Behrens, a yodeling guitarist in the mold of country music idol Jimmie Rodgers; the Four Crazy Hickory Nuts; J.E. Mauny and his Caroline Ramblers; the Country Breakdowns; the Fiddling Bees; Smiling Henry Berman's Village Barn; and the Pickard Family, one of the most traveled singing groups in country music history.[12] From 1933 to 1934, the Shelton Brothers (now minus Leon Chappelear) and virtuoso fiddler Curley Fox also appeared regularly on the station.[13]

WWL's tenure as a haven for hillbilly talent was actually quite brief. WWL was owned by Loyola University, an institution whose authorities had long winced at the station's growing reputation as the "ache and pain station of the nation." Attainment of network status in 1935 undoubtedly encouraged the gradual removal of almost every hillbilly musician from the air. By 1938, 75 percent of evening and 50 percent of daytime programming was network-based.[14]

Despite Pusateri's groundbreaking study, the full story of the New Orleans station's contribution as a purveyor of country music is untold. A figure

---

[9] Joe Shelton, interview with Bill C. Malone, Yantis, Texas, July 31, 1974.

[10] Jimmie Davis, author interview Baton Rouge, Louisiana, February 12, 1980; Gordon Bellcase, "Governors' Mansions, Halls of Fame, and Streets of Gold," Typescript, Country Music Foundation Library and Media Center, Nashville, n.d.

[11] Pusateri, *Enterprise in Radio*, 57.

[12] Ibid., 126-27.

[13] Shelton, interview with Bill C. Malone.

[14] Pusateri, *Enterprise in Radio*, 125, 174-76, 189-95.

such as Jerry Behrens, about whom almost nothing is known, deserves to be rescued from historical anonymity, if only as an example of the tendency of solo stars to emerge in the wake of Jimmie Rodgers after 1927. Behrens may well be alive today; should an enterprising researcher discover his whereabouts and interview him, many of the existing gaps in the documentary record would begin to close. And what of even more obscure entertainers like the Fiddling Bees? What were their names? Where did they originate? How did they gain airtime on WWL and what became of them? What tunes did they perform? The industrious scholar will search for patterns and configurations which give order and shape to the large complex problem of the commercialization of folk culture. Finally, it is a great irony indeed that radio, clearly the most important medium in the early commercial period, should be the most difficult to document. The fact that many pioneer artists and executives are still around, even if unlocated, is encouraging, to those interested in learning more about a crucial era in the development of American regional and national culture.

Recordings have long been the most common resource for studying folk music and its commercial outgrowths. And it is accurate to add that blues recordings have attracted more attention than those in parallel musical traditions such as country and Cajun. Recordings allow the assignment of chronological and historical landmarks with a high degree of certainty. The discographical labors of English record collectors has been particularly valuable in this regard.[15]

When was the first commercial recording made in Louisiana and what was it? In his book, *Country: The Biggest Music in America* (1977), journalist Nick Tosches offered a tantalizing clue to early recording activity in the state. Tosches cited a catalogue put out by the Louisiana Phonograph Company of New Orleans in 1892.[16] After identifying "two groups of recordings by a man named Louis Vasnier," Tosches speculated that the company may have produced "some real country, blues, and jazz records" almost three decades before the flowering of commercial recording in the 1920s.[17] Certainly any further evidence of the activities of the Louisiana Phonograph Company would be most welcome.

Within two years of the inaugural radio broadcast in Louisiana, the first commercial recording unit traveled to New Orleans. It was there in March 1924, that the Okeh Record Company recorded several blues and gospel

---

[15] Unless otherwise noted, the following discussion of blues recordings made in Louisiana is taken from John Goodrich and Robert M. W. Dixon, *Blues and Gospel Records, 1902-1942*, 2d. rev. ed. (Nashville, 1969 and 1970).

[16] Tosches does not indicate the location of the catalogue. He misidentifies the address of the company as 128 Cravier Street. The correct address, according to *Soards' New Orleans City Directory, 1892*, was 218 Gravier Street. This directory also identifies the company's officers.

[17] Nick Tosches, *Country: The Biggest Music in America* (New York, 1977), 245-46.

performers. The first person to cut a record in the state seems to have been a female vocalist named Lela Bolden. Accompanied by Armond J. Piron on violin and Steve Lewis on piano, Bolden cut two sides, "Southern Woman Blues" and "Seawall Special Blues." Thereafter, record companies in search of folk music of all kinds—gospel, blues, hillbilly, Cajun—made New Orleans a semi-regular stopping place for field units. From 1924 to 1936, New Orleans was the site of thirteen field sessions, ranking it third in terms of gospel and blues activity behind Atlanta and Dallas. In addition many hillbilly and Cajun sessions took place in the Crescent City, producing at least two landmark recordings.[18]

While this is not the place for a definitive examination of records made in Louisiana, it is possible to survey the topic, with emphasis on especially significant artists and sessions.

The Okeh Company returned to New Orleans in January 1925, where two blues duets by Billy and Mary Mack were recorded. In April 1926, a Columbia unit cut several gospel performers, including one of the most popular artists of the prewar years, J.M. Gates. Victor held its first New Orleans session in the early spring of 1927, followed by another Columbia field unit it few weeks later. A year later Columbia returned to the city. Then, near the end of 1928, Brunswick entered the field with the recording of four acts, including Bo Chatman. Chatman was an excellent blues performer from Mississippi who often fronted a string band named the Mississippi Sheiks. Chatman, who also recorded under the name of Bo Carter, was the most prolific musician to record in New Orleans, cutting more tunes over a longer time span than any other individual or group.

Recording activity resumed in February 1929, when Brunswick's Vocalion subsidiary cut numbers by a blues singer and a gospel ensemble. Near the end of 1929, Vocalion returned to record four additional sides of gospel music. About a month later, both Columbia and its recently acquired subsidiary, Okeh, sent field units to the Crescent City, with Okeh again recording J. M. Gates.

Columbia and Okeh sessions of 1929 were the last commercial field recordings held in New Orleans for over five years. The only other field trip elsewhere in Louisiana from late 1929 to early 1935 took place in February 1930, in Shreveport. There the Mississippi Sheiks made eight records for the Okeh label, including their classic version of "Sitting on Top of the World," a

---

[18] There is no equivalent discographical study of country or Cajun music to the works of Goodrich and Dixon. Tony Russell is currently working on a comprehensive discography of country music before World War II, of which some preliminary sections have been produced, notably relating to Jimmie Davis and the Shelton Brothers. There are literally dozens of discographies concerning specific artists scattered throughout the literature. Richard K. Spottswood has begun a major discographical study of ethnic recordings from 1895 to 1942.

song that not only became a blues standard, but entered the hillbilly tradition as well.

The obvious explanation for the long hiatus in recording activity in the state was the onset of the Great Depression. Scarcely had record companies begun to compete with radio as a medium of musical expression when the national economic collapse threatened the destruction of the industry. Particular damage was done to ethnic music of all kinds, since it was assumed that such styles had an automatically narrow appeal. A few statistics will highlight the devastating impact of the Depression on the record business. In 1929, record companies made 1,250 hillbilly recordings and released 800; by 1931, the respective totals were down to 975 and 575; by 1934, 825 and 375. Corresponding figures for race recordings (jazz, blues, and gospel) were: 1929, 800 and 500; 1931, 1,575 and 400; 1934, 375 and 225.[19] Clearly the cutback in actual numbers recorded reflected an almost complete termination of field recordings. As the Depression deepened, fewer and fewer excursions into the hinterlands were financially feasible. Those few artists whose commercial potential allowed them the luxury of continued recording activity were forced to go to the companies. Only Atlanta, Dallas, and San Antonio were visited more than once by recording companies from 1931 to 1934.

The ramifications of such radically revised policies may be briefly summarized. First, the record industry necessarily became more centralized, and competition was minimized. Second, since only established acts continued to record, new talents, perhaps even some very great performers, were denied the opportunity to be permanently documented. Third, and by extension, certain styles and substyles, each dependent upon a specialized audience, vanished from company logbooks. That is why fewer hillbilly artists were recorded than popular ones, fewer race than hillbilly and fewer ethnic than race. Most telling of all regarding the folk heritage of Louisiana was the absolute dearth of Cajun recordings made during this time.

Cajun musicians had never been recorded in substantial numbers even before hard times further limited their access to recording studios. The first Cajun recording was *Allons à Lafayette* by accordionist Joe Falcon, cut for Columbia in New Orleans on April 27, 1928.[20] Leo Soileau, an innovative fiddler, followed Falcon by three months, cutting four sides for Victor in Atlanta. Soileau was the leading Cajun musician of his generation, certainly the most talented to record during the first wave of commercialization. He was also the most prolific and widely traveled. During the summer and fall of 1929, he

---

[19] Norm Cohen, "America's Music: Written and Recorded," *John Edwards Memorial Foundation Quarterly* 16 (1980): 128-29.

[20] Tony Russell, personal communication, March 18 and March 29, 1980; *Louisiana Cajun Music*, volume 1, Old Timey 108, liner notes by Chris Strachwitz, 1970; Lauren C. Post, "Joseph C. Falcon, Accordion Player and Singer: A Biographical Sketch," *Louisiana History* 11 (1970): 63-79.

recorded for Paramount in Richmond, Indiana, for Victor in Memphis, and for Vocalion in New Orleans.[21]

New Orleans was also the likely site of the first recording of black French musicians. According to Tony Russell, the honor should go to Douglas Bellar and Kirby Riley, who first recorded for Vocalion in the Crescent City in early October 1929.[22] The next black French artist to record was accordionist Amédée Ardoin, who cut his earliest sides for Brunswick in 1930, accompanied by a Cajun fiddler named Dennis McGee. Ardoin was by all accounts the greatest of the pioneer black French-speaking artists. He later made records for Bluebird, Decca, and Melotone before his death in a Pineville mental asylum in the 1940s.[23]

Ardoin's partner, Dennis McGee of Eunice, has had the longest career of any Cajun musician; he still performs on occasion, well into his eighth decade. McGee's fiddle style has always reflected the nineteenth-century folk roots of Cajun music. Other Cajun pioneer recording artists, about whom much is yet to be learned, included Cléoma Breaux Falcon, Joseph's first wife; the Breaux Brothers (Cléoma's brothers, Amédée, Clifford and Ophy); the Segura Brothers; and Roy Gonzales, who was a Cajun Jimmie Rodgers imitator.[24]

Cajun artists had just begun to record when the Depression intervened. Following the Brunswick sessions of November 1930, no Cajun records were made for almost four years.[25] And even as the Depression waned, more traditional Cajun performers continued to be shunned in favor of those such as the Dixie Ramblers and Darbone's Hackberry Ramblers, who had adopted a more mainstream hillbilly string band sound or, later, the new jazz-influenced approach called western swing.

Through the lean years of the early 1930s, only one Louisiana native, Jimmie Davis, regularly recorded. Not even Davis, however, made records in his home state. Davis participated in sessions for Victor in Memphis in May 1930; in Charlotte in May 1931; in Dallas in February 1932; in Camden, New Jersey (Victor headquarters) in November 1932 for Victor's Bluebird subsidiary; in Chicago in August, 1933 and September 1934. For the Chicago sessions, Davis was backed by Bob and Joe Shelton and Leon Chappelear.[26]

---

[21] Leo Soileau, interview by Bill C. Malone, Ville Platte, Louisiana, June 15, 1974; Russell, "Leo Soileau," 5-9; Tony Russell, "Music in Arcadia: The Story of the Taylor Griggs Louisiana Melody Makers," *Old Time Music* 24 (1977): 8-16; Tony Russell, "Backtrack: The First Recording of Black French Music," *Old Time Music* 29 (1978): 20.

[22] Russell, "Backtrack," 20.

[23] Pierre V. Daigle, Tears, Love and Laughter: The Story of the Acadians, (Church Point, LA, 1972); Graham Wickham, "Cajun Music on Brunswick," *Blue Yodeler* 20 (1968): 3-4; *Louisiana Cajun Music*, vol. 1.

[24] Russell, "Music in Arcadia," 8-16; Russell, "Backtrack Music," 20; Wickham, "Cajun Music on Brunswick," 3-4; *Louisiana Cajun Music*, vol. 1; *Louisiana Cajun Music*, vol. 5, Old Timey 114, liner notes by Chris Strachwitz, 1973.

[25] Russell, "Music in Arcadia," 8-16; Russell, "Backtrack," 20.

[26] Tony Russell, "Jimmie Davis Discography" typescript, Country Music Foundation Library and Media

Davis's recording schedule was quite exceptional due in part to the fact that he popularized many folk styles from gospel and blues to hillbilly, and also because of his non-folk crooning style as a solo entertainer. By contrast, even popular hillbilly radio performers like the Taylor-Griggs group found themselves bereft of recording opportunities. They had managed to gain an audition with head Victor scout and producer Ralph Peer during the same summer in which they first appeared on KWKH. The Peer audition led to their first recording session for Victor in Memphis in September 1928. A year later they again journeyed to Memphis to cut several times, but with a new, more polished lineup. Before the group's recording career could fully begin, however, economic exigencies forced them to disband late in 1929.[27]

After 1934 there was a gradual resumption in recording activity for all but traditional sounding Cajun musicians. In January 1935, Bluebird made the first field trip to New Orleans since 1929. Bo Carter and the Mississippi Sheiks headed the coterie of blues performers who participated in the sessions, but it was the hillbilly and country artists that made the most significant recordings in the city prior to World War II. Three acts who made the trip to New Orleans to record under the direction of Victor's Eli Oberstein came from Nashville, where they were regularly featured on the Grand Ole Opry—fiddler Arthur Smith, brothers Alton and Rabon Delmore, and banjoist-comedian Uncle Dave Macon. The most memorable single cut was Arthur Smith's modern version of "Listen to the Mockingbird," the nineteenth-century chestnut which was given new life and destined to influence an entire generation of country fiddlers. Accompanying Smith were the Delmore Brothers, who also cut several numbers on their own, including "Brown's Ferry Blues, Part 2," "Alabama," "I Know I'll Be Happy in Heaven," and "The Fugitive's Lament." The final artist to record was probably the best

The Riverside Ramblers, the Hackberry Rambler's English-language alter ego, in uniform, ca. 1937. From left to right, Joe Werner, Luderin Darbone, Lennis Sonnier.
Photo courtesy of Luderin Darbone.

---

Center (Nashville, n.d.).
[27] Russell, "Music in Arcadia," 8-16.

The Hackberry Ramblers performing a KVOL broadcast at Montgomery Ward's in Lafayette, ca. 1937. From left to right, Joe Werner, unidentified store representative, Luderin Darbone, unidentified store representative, Lennis Sonnier. *Photo courtesy of Luderin Darbone.*

known of all, the Grand Ole Opry's first solo star. Uncle Dave Macon cut six tunes, each of which suggested key elements in the southern folk music tradition: "Over the Mountain," "When the Harvest Days Are Over," "One More River to Cross," "Just One Way to the Pearly Gates," I'll Tickle Nancy," and "I'll Keep My Skillet Good and Greasy."[28]

The year 1936 had its significant moments of recording history as well. Both Bluebird and Decca made field trips to New Orleans. The Decca field sessions were historic for the simple reason that they were the only ones held by the company before World War II. The Bluebird sessions produced a recording of major proportions in "Wondering" by the Riverside Ramblers.

The Riverside Ramblers were a group of Cajun musicians who did not record in an identifiable Cajun style. Their approach was heavily influenced by the dominant sound of their region and generation, an eclectic amalgam of hillbilly string band music, blues, jazz and pop called western swing. The Riverside Ramblers were, with a slightly expanded lineup, best known by the name Hackberry Ramblers. Along with Leo Soileau and his Three Aces, the Rayne-Bo Ramblers, and Beethoven Miller's Merrymakers (all of

---

[28] Alton Delmore, *Truth is Stranger Than Publicity: Alton Delmore's Autobiography*, Charles Wolfe, ed. (Nashville, 1977), 95, 99-103, 108; Charles K. Wolfe, *A Good Natured Riot: The Birth of the Grand Ole Opry* (Nashville, 1970), chapter six.

whom recorded for Bluebird), the Hackberry-Riverside Ramblers were in the vanguard of south Louisiana musicians who favored the newer sounds over traditional songs with accordion accompaniment and French lyrics. Thus it was that the Riverside Ramblers (Luderin Darbone, Lennis Sonnier and Joe Werner) whose first records were made in New Orleans in September 1935 (under the name of the Hackberry Ramblers) came to record the decidedly pop-sounding "Wondering" in 1936.[29]

Western swing highlighted the Decca sessions of 1936. From March 3-5, one of the most talented aggregations ever to record in the style, Milton Brown and his Musical Brownies, cut almost fifty sides, including such classics as "Hesitation Blues," "Stay on the Right Side Sister," and "Baby Keep Stealin.'"[30] What made the sessions even more significant was the fact that they were the last for the pioneer western swing, bandleader Milton Brown. Just over a month after Brown and his group left New Orleans, he was killed in an automobile accident in Texas.

Some of the most creative western swing artists concentrated their careers in Texas and Louisiana, particularly the southern border area bounded by Houston on the west and Lafayette on the east. Ted Daffan was born in Louisiana, reared in Texas, and went on to become an influential steel guitarist, bandleader, and songwriter (best remembered for his honky-tonk standard, "Born to Lose"). Fiddlers Cliff Bruner and Link Davis were highly regarded performers from the Beaumont-Port Arthur area. Hank Penny, a fine guitarist, singer, and comedian, and progressive steel guitarist Noel Boggs both had a brief tenure at WWL in New Orleans. Jimmie Davis also readily adopted the pervasive western swing style, recording with the Musical Brownies in 1937 and employing several talented sidemen, including pianist Moon Mullican, Cajun fiddler Doc Guidry, steel guitarist Charles Mitchell, guitarist Jimmie Thomasson, and vocalist-songwriter Buddy Jones.[31] The entire question of the relationship between New Orleans-based Dixieland jazz and the subsequent development of western swing has never been adequately explained.[32]

Blues and gospel artists had also resumed recording activity in New Orleans by the mid-1930s, though not with the same frequency as before. In August 1935, Victor recorded three blues men in the Crescent City: Monkey Joe, Harry Carter and an outstanding pianist, Little Brother Montgomery. Montgomery was an exemplar of indigenous piano blues style that had been

---

[29] Luderin Darbone, telephone interview, February 10, 1981; *Louisiana Cajun Music*, vol. 5; Nicholas R. Spitzer, "The Louisiana-French Connection in Country and Western Music on the Texas Border," paper read at the American Folklore Society Convention (Philadelphia, 1976), 5.

[30] *Western Swing*, vol. 4, Old Timey 119, liner notes by Tony Russell.

[31] Cliff Bruner, interview with Bill C. Malone, League City, Texas, June 19, 1976; Spitzer, "The Louisiana-French Connection in Country and Western Music on the Texas Border," 5-8; *Western Swing*, vol. 5.

[32] Charles Townsend, *San Antonio Rose: The Life and Times of Bob Wills* (Urbana, 1976); Nick Tosches, *Country: The Biggest Music in America* (New York, 1977); and Malone have all discussed the problem.

forged in the sawmill and levee camps along the Mississippi River.[33] In February 1936, the company returned to record Bo Carter. The Decca sessions of 1936 yielded, in addition to cuts by Milton Brown's Musical Brownies recordings by blues singer Walter Vinson (yet another of the Mississippi Sheiks) and several Cajun acts. Then in October 1936, Victor made the last commercial field recordings in Louisiana, cutting numbers by a large variety of artists: the Chatmon Brothers, Mississippi Matilda, Sonny Boy Nelson, Robert Hill, Bo Carter, Tommy Griffin, Annie Turner, Little Brother Montgomery, Creole George Geusnon, and Walter Jacous.

Field recordings of Louisiana folk musicians did not cease with the withdrawal of the record companies. Substantial documentation had been undertaken by the Library of Congress beginning in July, 1933. Field workers John, Ruby, and Alan Lomax traveled extensively throughout Louisiana in search of blues, gospel, and Cajun musicians. Again, with the aid of Goodrich and Dixon, a chronological outline of the Lomaxes' work may be sketched.

John and Alan Lomax made the first of their many field trips to Louisiana in 1933. One of their first stops was the state penitentiary in Angola on July 16. There they discovered a wealth of material and a number of interesting singers whom they hastened to document. Among the inmates to record were Rudolf Thomson (five sides), Ernest Rogers (one side), Jimmy Otis (one side), Roy McDaniels (three sides), and most importantly, a twelve-string guitarist named Huddie Ledbetter, better known as Leadbelly. Leadbelly was an incomparable discovery; in time he became the best known black folk musician in the country. His repertoire, documented in a series of recordings for the Library of Congress and a succession of folk-oriented labels such as Biograph and Folkways, projected an amalgam of Louisiana's folk music heritage to a national audience. The Lomaxes were quite taken with Leadbelly from the beginning; the initial Angola sessions consisted of eight numbers, including "The Western Cowboy," "Frankie and Albert," "Honey, Take a Whiff On Me," and an early version of his most famous song, "Goodnight Irene."

From Angola, the Lomaxes traveled to New Orleans where in late August, they recorded a vocalist named Sullivan Rock. In July 1934, they returned to Louisiana, recording blues singers and songsters in New Iberia, Amelia, Lafayette, Lloyd, and Baton Rouge; gospel artists and Afro-French *juré* singers on Avery Island, near False River, and in Lafayette and Lake Arthur; and a black church service on a plantation outside Baton Rouge. Another visit to Angola resulted in thirteen more tunes by Leadbelly (many of which were repeated from the previous year's sessions). In September, following a pardon from Gov. O.K. Allen, Leadbelly cut one song in Shreveport and served as an

---

[33] Zur Heide, Karl Gert, *Deep South Piano: The Story of Little Brother Montgomery* (London, 1970); Robert Shaw, *Robert Shaw: Texas Barrelhouse Piano*, Almanac 10 (1978), liner notes by Mack McCormick, 27-35.

accompanist for other musicians during field trips to Little Rock, Pine Bluff, Gould, and Tucker, Arkansas.[34]

A brief excursion to New Orleans in 1937 resulted in one session at the Lafont Catholic Old Folks Home, two years later a more extensive tour was made. The 1939 sessions, held in Knight and Merryville, yielded fourteen recordings, all either gospel songs or sermons. In September and October 1940, the last Library of Congress field trips took place. These sessions were, next to the Leadbelly sessions of 1933 and 1934, the most fruitful of any held in Louisiana. In September, gospel singers were documented in Merryville, and in Baton Rouge, bluesman Burley Mayberry cut one number. A month later, John and Ruby Lomax headed for the Shreveport area, where they struck a rich vein of folk music. In Oil City they found and recorded Noah Moore, one of Leadbelly's cousins, and his Uncle Bob Ledbetter, who furnished his version of "Irene."[35]

The Lomaxes had come to Oil City from Shreveport proper where they had recorded Oscar Woods, a singer and guitarist, and Kid West and Joe Harris, a mandolin-guitar duo. Woods Harris and West were well-known street singers in the Shreveport area, performing on corners, in front of theatres and inside what Woods characterized as "little hop joints."[36] Shreveport and vicinity had long been a region alive with music, especially that of the folk variety. Oscar Woods had in fact been recorded before. He had backed Jimmie Davis on some early recordings, cut some solo numbers under the pseudonym of "The Lone Wolf" for Decca in New Orleans in 1936, and at the behest of Davis, fronted a band called the Wampus Cats at sessions for Vocalion in San Antonio in 1937 and Dallas in 1938.[37] West and Harris were older musicians but novices at recording. Like Leadbelly they reflected the nineteenth-century background in both style and repertoire.

Among the many folk performers documented by the Lomaxes were Louisiana French musicians. Less is known about this aspect of their field work, but the same tours which yielded examples from the Afro-American tradition also uncovered Cajun and Creole French-speaking artists (Alan Lomax, liner notes). The most productive sessions may have been those that were held during the summer of 1934. In New Iberia, members of the Hoffpauir family were recorded. In Crowley and Delcambre, respectively, fiddlers Wayne Perry

---

[34] Leadbelly continued his association with the Lomaxes for several years and made numerous subsequent field trips with them.

[35] *Jerry's Saloon Blues*, Flyright Matchbox LP260, brochure notes by Paul Oliver, 1978; Tony Russell, *Blacks, Whites and Blues* (New York, 1970), 81-85.

[36] *Jerry's Saloon Blues* notes.

[37] Russell, *Blacks, Whites and Blues*, 81-85; Jimmie Davis was the central figure on the Shreveport folk music scene at least until his election as governor in 1944. He was, after Jimmie Rodgers, the first country artist to record with black musicians. Besides Woods, Davis was often backed by an excellent guitarist named Ed Shaffer.

and Eddie Segura played several dance tunes. At Angola, Odgel Carrier, a black accordionist, also performed a dance number.[38]

Radio, of course, provided most of the commercial opportunities for aspiring folk musicians throughout (and well after) the prewar period. Hillbilly music undoubtedly dominated programming among folk-derived styles as stations proliferated in all sections of the state. Unfortunately, the history of radio in Louisiana, with the major exceptions of Pusateri's work and Lillian Jones Hall's 1959 dissertation, remains unwritten.

Papa Cairo's band at KPLC radio station. Photo from the back of Papa Cairo's business card. Photo courtesy of Margie Lamperez Breaux Collection, Center for Louisiana Studies, University of Louisiana at Lafayette, accession number 4006.

When did radio first appear in places like Alexandria, Monroe, Crowley, Lake Charles, Lafayette, New Iberia, and Natchitoches, each of which has produced significant artists? When and where did black artists begin to perform and in what manner? How was music advertised and programmed? These and related questions must be addressed in order to understand the implications for commercialization of indigenous folk styles. We do know that KWKH continued to be a stronghold of country music, with regular appearances by old favorites like the Shelton Brothers and the Rice Brothers and newer acts like Harmie Smith and a popular gospel quartet the Blackwood Brothers.[39] Other radio stations in the state which were likely places to hear hillbilly and or Cajun music before World War II were KALB (Alexandria), WWL (New Orleans), WNCE (New Orleans), KSIG (Crowley), KPLC (Lake Charles), KVOL (Lafayette), KMLB (Monroe), and WJBO (Baton Rouge).

At least one important survey of radio audiences in Louisiana appeared during World War II. Based upon census figures, opinion polls and other data from 1940, LSU scholar Edgar Schuler produced a detailed examination of the listening habits and preferences of thousands of Louisianians. Many of his findings shed light upon the status of folk music in the state's general population had radios. 72.6 percent of urbanites, 52.5 percent of rural non-farm and 27.3 percent of farm residents had radios. As to types of music,

---

[38] Also see the article by F.A. de Caro and the Library of Congress Archive of Folksong Listings in Louisiana for information on the Lomaxes' work in Louisiana.

[39] Lillian Jones Hall, "A Historical Study of Programming Techniques and Practices of Radio Station KWKH, Shreveport, Louisiana, 1922-1950" (Ph.D. dissertation, Louisiana State University, Baton Rouge, 1959), 100-30; Horace Logan, author interview, Monroe, Louisiana, August 22, 1981.

The cast of Happy Fats Show on KSLO, ca. 1948.
Happy Fats is seated, second from right.
Photo courtesy of Johnnie Allan.

"hillbilly and rural" was included under the broader category of "Popular and Folk Music." Hillbilly was listed as the first preference for 2.4 percent of Schuler's respondents; secondly, 3.3 percent; third by 2.2 percent; and fourth by 2.6 percent. For "Popular and Folk Music" in general, however, the figures were somewhat higher: first, 16.3 percent; second, 17 percent; third, 17.9 percent; fourth, 17 percent. In terms of all types of programming, "Popular and Folk Music" ranked as fourth choice behind "Entertainment," "Drama," and "News." When broken down even further, hillbilly music ranked twelfth. The most popular radio stations in the state were WWL, WSMB (New Orleans), WDSU (New Orleans), and KWKH. In the North Louisiana region, KWKH ranked first, followed by KTBS and KRMD (all located in Shreveport). Thus, on the eve of World War II, Schuler's survey indicated that audiences were only mildly interested in folk music and almost completely disinterested in country music. Even a cursory reading of the results of the study, however, reveals a clear bias in favor of educated, urban listeners. There was no attempt to classify listeners by income or any other index of class or status. Nor were black audiences clearly delineated. Still, the LSU study provides a rare look into radio audiences in Louisiana near the end of the early commercial period.

World War II was a watershed in the commercialization of American folk music, as it was in many ways for the society as a whole. Among the most important postwar developments were the rise of Top 40 radio and the overwhelming dominance of rock'n'roll (later, rock) music; the synthesis of musical styles, of which rock'n'roll was a culmination of sorts; the emergence of television as a competitive medium to both records and radio; the immediate decentralization of the recording industry which helped spawn a bewildering number of new companies, many of which catered to specialized audiences; and the thoroughgoing re-examination of America's traditional cultures, especially those of ethnic origins, by entrepreneurs scholars and audiences.

The most dramatic general development in the postwar years was the emergence of local independent record companies which catered to specialized audiences. Thus, within the framework of the society marked by increasing centralization and standardization in industry, government, transportation and communication, there arose across the country a series of new companies, each locally owned and operated and each directed at a discrete market. In Louisiana, such companies drew upon possibly the richest and most variegated pool of musical talent in the nation. Even when the Louisiana independents had no more complex a design than uncovering the latest rock'n'roll teen idol in the mold of Elvis Presley, certainly with the national mass market in clear view, they managed to tap into an incredible wellspring of creativity. The companies were above all extensions of the personalities and tastes of their owners, entrepreneurs who often served as producers, agents, managers, engineers, distributors, salesmen, publicists, and in some cases, even songwriters and side men. From the late 1940s to the present, men like Bill Quinn of Houston, Huey P. Meaux of Winnie, Texas, George Khoury and Carol Rachou of Lafayette, Stan Lewis of Shreveport, Cosimo Matassa of New Orleans, Floyd Soileau of Ville Platte, and, in terms of longevity and sheer output, especially Jay D. Miller of Crowley and Eddie Shuler of Lake Charles were responsible for the most extensive commercial documentation of folk music traditions a single geographic area in the entire country. The subject deserves more attention than it can be given here; for present purposes only, the activities of Shuler and Miller will be touched upon.

Eddie Shuler formed Goldband Records in Lake Charles in 1949, having moved to the city seven years earlier. From 1942-1945, Shuler had served as vocalist and guitarist with the Hackberry Ramblers. In 1945, he formed his own group, the All-Star Reveliers, and also went to work as a disc jockey and announcer for KPLC radio. It was in the latter capacity that Shuler met a young Cajun accordionist from Church Point named Iry LeJeune.[40]

LeJeune was a musician of incredibly raw power, whose style of playing harked back to the pioneer generation of Amédé Ardoin, probably his chief influence. LeJeune was destined to lead a revival of interest in the traditional Cajun sound, especially accordion music.[41] His earliest recordings were issued on the Houston-based Opera label in 1948. It was as a Goldband artist, however, with songs like "Love Bridge Waltz" and "Lake Charles Special," that LeJeune achieved his greatest popularity. Only his death in a roadside accident in 1954, prevented him from becoming even more widely known. As it was, the "Cajun Hank Williams," as he is sometimes called, left an endur-

---

[40] Mike Leadbitter and Eddie Shuler, *From the Bayou: The Story of Goldband Records*. Blues Unlimited (London, 1969); Eddie Shuler, author interview, Natchitoches, Louisiana, July 27, 1981; Allan Turner, "The Cajun Crusader," *Austin (Texas) American-Statesman*, November 27, 1977.

[41] Mike Leadbitter, "Iry LeJune," *Old Time Music* 14 (1974): 21; Daigle, *Tears, Love and Laughter*, 86.

ing legacy: he had helped reclaim prestige for Cajun culture and encourage a reawakening of interest in the accordion which continues to the present.[42]

By 1952, due in large part to the success of Iry LeJeune, Shuler built his first recording studio. Besides LeJeune, he released country records by his own group, the All-Star Reveliers, and then, in 1953, began to branch out into the rhythm and blues market with black artist James Freeman's "Big Leg Mama." Soon thereafter he recorded Boozoo Chavis, who specialized in an exotic sounding style of music called zodico or zydeco.[43] Zydeco was an indigenous south Louisiana sound, described by one writer as in part consisting of a mingling of "Acadian or Afro-American blues tunes placed in an Afro-Caribbean rhythmic framework."[44] It is perhaps best understood as bearing a similar (though slightly closer) relationship to rhythm and blues as modern Cajun music does to the mainstream country sound. In any event, zydeco, as heard in songs like Boozoo Chavis's 1954 hit on Goldband, "Paper in My Shoe," reflects the cultural syncretisms often found in Louisiana folk music.

From the folk style rhythm and blues and zydeco, it was only a short step to popular, regional rock'n'roll, and Eddie Shuler eagerly recruited an outstanding lineup of black and white singers who performed in the style forged by Elvis Presley: Gene Terry, Larry Hart, Guitar Jr., Jay Nelson, Billy Earl, Sticks Herman, and Al Ferrier.[45] Probably the best of the lot was Ferrier, a native of the Natchitoches area. Ferrier was and is in exceedingly powerful vocalist whose career never quite matched his talent. He has recently recorded for the European label, Sonet Records.

Still it was Cajun music on which Shuler built his reputation. Artists like Leroy Broussard, Sidney Brown, Hobo Bertrand, Aldus Roger, Lionel Cormier, Luderin Darbone and Lennis Sonnier have provided the bulk of Goldband's sales over the years, in spite of forays into country music,[46] rhythm and blues, and rock'n'roll.

J.D. Miller began his recording activities in Crowley in 1946 as an outgrowth of his work as an electrical contractor and appliance store owner. Recognizing the unsatiated postwar demand for Cajun music. Miller, soon moved to meet the demands of the local record-buying public. Over the course of better than two decades, he would gain notice as a discoverer and producer of rhythm and blues artists, but his first clients were Cajun and hillbilly performers.[47] The third artist to record for Miller was a young singer from the

---

[42] Leadbitter, "Iry LeJune," 21; Turner, "The Cajun Crusader;" Shuler, interview, July 27, 1981.
[43] Leadbitter and Shuler, *From the Bayou*, 12-18.
[44] Nicholas R. Spitzer, "Zodico: Louisiana's Black Creole Music," *Sing Out!* November/December (1979): 3.
[45] Leadbitter and Shuler, *From the Bayou*, 21.
[46] Among the performers who have recorded on Goldband at various times are Dolly Parton, Freddy Fender and Mickey Gilley.
[47] Mike Leadbitter, *Crowley, Louisiana Blues* (Sussex, England, 1968), 6-8.

Mamou vicinity, Jimmie C. Newman. With Newman came substantial local success, and due at least in part to Miller's Nashville connections with the huge Acuff-Rose publishing company and their subsidiary, Hickory Records, eventual national acceptance followed.[48]

Another possibly more significant figure who first recorded for Miller in 1947 was Al Terry (born Alison Theriot) of Kaplan. Like Newman, Terry had grown up in a small, predominantly French-speaking community. Through access to the recordings of early, country music pioneers like Vernon Dalhart and Jimmie Rodgers and the films of Gene Autry, both developed an affinity for musical styles that had little direct connection with Cajun traditions.[49]

In the early 1950s, Miller followed his successes with Newman and Terry by recording a group from Jennings called the Continental Playboys. Led by three brothers, Pee Wee, Doug and Rusty Kershaw, the group favored an eclectic repertoire featuring Cajun, hillbilly, and rockabilly tunes. Miller recorded the brothers in several styles, but he eventually settled on a rockabilly approach for Rusty and Doug, who continued their careers after Pee Wee retired from music. Regardless of the prevailing style, the Kershaw brothers generated quite a following in south Louisiana and ultimately in Nashville and the nation at large. Their combined skills marked them as dynamic and original interpreters of Louisiana's folk music traditions.[50]

Miller entered the rhythm and blues field in 1954 with a release by Otis Hicks ("Lightnin' Slim"). Thereafter, a stream of rhythm and blues talent flowed through Miller's studio. "Lightnin' Slim" was followed in turn by Leslie Johnson ("Lazy Lester"), Lonesome Sundown, Slim Harpo and a superb

Hadacol radio broadcast, ca. 1949. From left to right, Happy Fats, Al Terry, Senator Dudley J. LeBlanc, and Doc Guidry. Photo courtesy of Johnnie Allan.

---

[48] *Jimmy C. Newman and Al Terry*, Flyright LP573, liner notes by Bruce Bastin, 1981.
[49] Al Terry, author interview, Lafayette, Louisiana, October 17, 1980; *Jimmy C. Newman and Al Terry*, Flyright LP573, liner notes by Bruce Bastin, 1981.
[50] Doug Kershaw, author interview, New Orleans, Louisiana, November 20, 1979; Doug Kershaw, *Louisiana Man*, Robin Nelson, music ed. (New York, 1971), 18-27; Rusty and Doug Kershaw with Wiley Barkdull, Flyright LP571, liner notes by Bruce Bastin. Legendary Jay Miller Sessions, vol. 22, 1981.

pianist from Houston, Katie Webster. By the late 1950s, Miller was also producing an astounding array of rock'n'rollers: Terry Clement, Johnny Jano, Al Ferrier, Pee Wee Trahan, Dale Houston, Erwin Babin, Arnold Broussard, Warren Storm, and J.P. Richardson (the "Big Bopper"). Over the course of approximately two decades, Miller recorded and released music on a number of labels—Fais Do Do, Feature, Kay, Spot, Action, Zynn, Kajun Classics, Kajun Rocket, Ringo, Tribute, French Hits—in the process documenting the sounds of Louisiana more fully than any individual.[51] Finally, Miller has also gained notoriety as a producer and distributor of mail-order racist records on the Rebel and other labels; even this side of folk-derived music failed to escape his attention.

Each of the other independent producers—Lewis, Rachou, Meaux, Soileau, Matassa—could easily serve as subjects of extended study. Most remain active in the record business, continuing to document, in a commercial fashion, music front Louisiana. Floyd Soileau, in particular, operates a highly successful mail order and retail business in Ville Platte. His Swallow label (and its subsidiaries such as Jin and Maison de Soul) tends to dominate the south Louisiana market.[52]

The most important out of the state company to make extensive use of Louisiana talent, especially Cajun musicians, was California-based Arhoolie Records. Begun in the early 1960s by Chris Strachwitz, Arhoolie has featured some of the best performers of the past and present, including Joe Falcon, the Hackberry Ramblers, and Clifton Chenier. The traditional music of the British Florida Parishes is represented in the Arhoolie catalogue by a group called the Louisiana Honeydrippers. Strachwitz has also produced a definitive historical anthology series of Cajun music on 78's (seven volumes as of 1984).

Following the essentially non-commercial, academic course marked out by the Lomaxes in the 1930s was an LSU folklorist named Harry Oster. Oster did extensive fieldwork throughout the state during the 1950s as well as founding the Louisiana Folklore Society. Through a spate of publications and record albums, Oster did more than any academician of his day to preserve, display and interpret the folk music heritage of Louisiana.

The performers most active in the presentation and preservation of traditional Cajun culture in Louisiana were the Balfa Brothers from Basile. Originally semi-professional musicians who played the south Louisiana dance

---

[51] Leadbitter, *Crowley, Louisiana Blues*, 7-67; J.D. Miller, interview with Bill C. Malone (field notes), Crowley, Louisiana, June 24, 1974.

[52] Jim O'Neal, "Louisiana Wax Facts: The Blues and Record Scene, 1973," *Living Blues*, Summer (1973): 9-12; Joe Nick Patoski, "Huey Meaux's Bathtub Sound," *Rolling Stone* (July 13, 1978): 18; Nick Patoski, "Freddy Fender and Huey Meaux," *Country Music* (1978): 40-43; Ryan Bernard, "The Cajuns," *Houston City* (1980): 40-46ff; "Cash Register Rings for Recording Company," *Acadiana Profile* (1974): 16; John Broven, *Rhythm and Blues in New Orleans* (New Orleans, 1978); Soileau letter, October 9, 1980.

circuit in the 1940s, the group, led by fiddler Dewey Balfa, became highly visible folk performers as a result of an appearance at the 1964 Newport Folk Festival and subsequent work with various cultural agencies like the Smithsonian Institution. It was the Balfas, in fact, who persuaded Floyd Soileau to establish his Cajun music-oriented Swallow label.[53] Following the tragic 1979 death of his brothers, Will and Rodney, Dewey has continued to crusade for traditional Cajun folk culture.

In radio one postwar development overshadowed all others—the establishment of a KWKH radio and stage show known as the Louisiana Hayride. Begun in 1948, the Hayride in its heyday could claim a roster of talent second to none, including the more publicized Grand Ole Opry. Not surprisingly, the artists who gave the show its reputation as the "Cradle of the Stars" represented almost the entire spectrum of Anglo-American folk song style and its modern derivatives. Among the dozens of important performers associated at one time or another with the Shreveport program were Hank Williams, its first great star; the Bailes Brothers, exemplars of the religious song tradition; Kitty Wells, the original "Queen of Country Music;" Charlie Monroe, brother of bluegrass patriarch Bill Monroe; comedian Cousin Wilbur, an heir to the minstrel and medicine show traditions; possibly the preeminent brother duo in Country music history, the Blue Sky Boys; blind singer-composer Leon Payne; smooth-voiced crooner Jim Reeves; singing cowgirl Patsy Montana; yodeler Slim Whitman; hillbilly boogie virtuosos, the Maddox Brothers and Rose; Red Sovine, who became best known for his recordings of truck-driving songs; honky-tonk stylist George Jones; Johnny Horton, the master of the saga song; and, of course, Elvis Presley. Among Louisiana natives who made their breakthrough on the Hayride were Clyde Baum, Margie Singleton, Werley Fairburn, Claude King, Merle Kilgore, David Houston, Floyd Cramer, James Burton, Jerry Kennedy, Faron Young, Buddy Attaway, Jimmie C. Newman, and Webb Pierce. Certainly a key element in the show's success was the professional staff headed by producer-announcer Horace Logan and aided by top announcers like Ray Bartlett and Frank Page, who actually put the Hayride together. For approximately ten years, from 1948 to 1958, the Louisiana Hayride was a focal point for country music enthusiasts and performers in the Southwest and across the nation. Not the least of the program's legacies was its role as a showcase for rockabilly performers, beginning with Elvis.[54]

The rockabilly phenomenon represented much more than a threat to other musical styles; it was a synthesis of various traditions, most importantly,

---

[53] Barry Jean Ancelet, "Dewey Balfa: Cajun Music Ambassador," *Louisiana Life* (1981): 78-85; Floyd Soileau (letter).

[54] Stephen R. Tucker, "The Louisiana Hayride, 1948-1954," *North Louisiana Historical Association Journal* 8 (1977): 187-201; Horace Logan, author interview, Monroe, Louisiana, August 22, 1981.

rhythm and blues and country music. Elvis was a true catalyst for the new sound; his stint on the Louisiana Hayride helped focus attention on Shreveport and the rest of Louisiana. The state rested in the center of the mid-South region which, with its imaginary boundaries at Lubbock, Texas on the west and Jackson, Tennessee on the east (the homes of Buddy Holly and Carl Perkins, respectively), also formed the heartland of rockabilly music. Included within the area were the hometowns of most of the artists who gave shape to the controversial style. Louisiana alone contributed such key figures in the movement as Dale Hawkins (Shreveport), Jimmy Clanton (Baton Rouge), Bobby Charles (Abbeville), Roy "Boogie Boy Perkins" Suarez (Lafayette), and Jerry Lee Lewis and Mickey Gilley (Ferriday). Hayride alumni who either flirted with or wholly embraced rock'n'roll included Merle Kilgore, George Jones, Sonny James, Faron Young, Bob Luman, and Tommy Sands. As mentioned previously, the studios of Miller and Shuler produced some of the most dynamic performers in the field: Al Ferrier, Terry Clement, Johnny Jano, Rusty and Doug Kershaw, and J.P. Richardson. Three latter-day artists who clearly showed direct rockabilly influence were Johnny Rivers of Baton Rouge, Tony Joe White of Oak Grove, and Joe Stampley of Springhill. James Burton went from the Louisiana Hayride to Los Angeles, where he played lead guitar in turn for Ricky Nelson, Elvis Presley, and Merle Haggard. Another Louisiana native to gain a measure of success in Los Angeles was Opelousas native Gib Guilbeau, who figured in the creation of country-rock during the late 1960s.

Of all the Louisiana natives to emerge in the wake of Elvis Presley, the most renowned talent was Jerry Lee Lewis. Lewis's individualistic piano style (derived in part from great Louisiana boogie and blues pianists like Little Brother Montgomery, who once lived in Ferriday, and country pianists Merrill Moore and Moon Mullican, and catalyzed by a constant exposure and immersion in Pentecostal religion), his visceral personality, his unsurpassed repertoire, all marked him as a unique artist and synthesizer of folk tradition. If one characteristic of the great musicians from Louisiana (Leadbelly, Jimmie Davis, Professor Longhair, Fats Domino, Doug Kershaw) stands out, it is an eclectic temperament which feeds upon the various folk musical traditions found in the state, which in turn produces an intensely personal performance style. Certainly Jerry Lee Lewis epitomizes such a process.

If any one Louisiana city or community can legitimately claim to have been involved in the creation of rock'n'roll, it was, of course, New Orleans. The New Orleans story has been detailed by at least one writer, John Broven, who traced the recorded contributions of most of the city's great rhythm and blues and rock'n'roll artists, a list that would have to include Professor Longhair (Henry Oreland Byrd), Roy Brown, Dave Bartholomew, Fats Domino, Lloyd Price, Clarence "Frogman" Henry, Little Richard, Lee Dorsey, Jessie Hill,

Frankie Ford, Tommy Ridgeley, Ernie K-Doe (Chador), Allen Toussaint, Mac Rebennack (Dr. John), and the Neville Brothers. Certainly the city's role as a center for rhythm and blues and rock'n'roll compares favorably to its more popular perceived status as the birthplace of jazz.

Louisiana's folk heritage as a source of musical activity has generated more attention in recent years than at any previous time. Commercial in-state record companies and labels like Goldband, Jin, Swallow, La Louisianne, Paula and Chillier, along with other national and international labels such as Arhoolie, and, especially, Flyright and Sonet, are quite active in issuing and reissuing a myriad of recordings which feature almost every style which has developed in the state within the last six decades. Country music, of course, has become a national mania, and Louisiana has remained fertile ground, producing such recent stars as Mickey Gilley and Joe Stampley. Cajun music is more popular than ever. It would be accurate to say that more Cajun music is available on records than at any time in the past. Harry Oster's groundbreaking work of the 1950s has been carried on by collectors, field workers and producers like Chris Strachwitz, Samuel Charters, Gerard Dole, and Nicholas Spitzer. The Louisiana Folklife Society in cooperation with the State Folklife Program has recently produced three initial albums illustrative of the blues and hillbilly traditions.

In radio, the picture is much the same. A growing proportion of programming is being devoted to the exploration of traditional music. According to a recent survey, French-language programs, most presenting music, can be heard in sixteen Louisiana cities, amounting to approximately one hundred hours of airtime per week.[55] Of special note are the remote broadcasts of Revon Reed's programs from Mamou over Eunice's station KEUN. College and public broadcasting stations are some of the most reliable sources for broadcasting folk music. One of the latest to enter the field is WWOZ-FM of New Orleans, with regular programs which explore in remarkable detail various indigenous styles and substyles. Among country music programs, the Louisiana Hayride stands out. The show is presently syndicated to thirteen radio stations, throughout the region.

In sum, the opportunities for experiencing the state's rich musical heritage through the media of recordings and radio are quite numerous, even to an unprecedented degree. One need not pine in antiquarian angst for the good old times played in the good old ways. The traditions live on, entwining one with the other in unpredictable ways, creating new sounds, but with powerful echoes from the past.

---

[55] Theodore C. Grame, *Ethnic Broadcasting in the United States* (Washington, DC, 1980).

# "Colinda:" Mysterious Origins of a Cajun Folksong[1]

## Shane Bernard and Julia Frederick

Like the Cajuns themselves, south Louisiana's Cajun music is the synthetic product of ethnic cultural interaction.[2] Cajun musicians learned new dance rhythms and a "terraced" singing style from Native Americans. They embraced the syncopative, percussive, and improvisational styles of black Creoles and were later greatly influenced by the blues. While borrowing tunes from the Spanish and the diatonic accordion from Jewish-German immigrants, the Cajuns also composed French lyrics to Anglo-American times, which they reinterpreted in their own musical style. Folklorist Barry Jean Ancelet, referring to Cajun musician Dennis McGee's "Valse du Vacher," notes that "the singer, whose name reflects Irish roots and whose facial features reflect American Indian origins, describes the loneliness of a cowboy's life in French to the time of a European mazurka clearly influenced by the blues." Many Cajun songs share a similarly diverse background, but "Colinda," also known as "Danser Colinda" or "Allons Danser Colinda," is perhaps most illustrative of Cajun music's complex genealogy.[3]

"Colinda," an extremely popular traditional Cajun dance song, has been recorded by numerous musicians—Cajun and otherwise—over the past half-century. The most notable renditions are Rod Bernard's 1962 bilingual "swamp pop" version, which reinterpreted the old Cajun standard using electric instruments and a rock 'n' roll beat; Louisiana governor, Jimmie Davis' 1949 country version, the first to adapt English lyrics to the tune; and Leroy "Happy Fats" LeBlanc, Oran "Doc" Guidry, Sr., and the Boys' 1946 Cajun French version, the earliest known recording of "Colinda." Like many Cajun songs, the lyrics and tune of "Colinda" vary slightly among renditions, even among renditions by the same performers.

Although many musicians call themselves the composers of "Colinda," the original composer or composers—as with many Cajun songs—will probably remain unknown. Enough historical evidence survives, however, to es-

---

[1] This article first appeared in the *Journal of Folklore Research* 29 (1992): 37-52. For their assistance, the authors would like to thank Professors Frans Amelinckx, Barry Ancelet, and Carl Brasseaux of the University of Louisiana at Lafayette, as well as Rod Bernard, Michael Doucet, Ms. Lou Gabus, Dr. Robert C. and Jeanne LeBlanc Gilmore, Mr. And Mrs. Oran "Doc" Guidry, Richard Guidry, and J.D. Miller.
[2] In this paper Cajun music refers to the folk music of southwest Louisiana's white Francophones; black Creole music, to the folk music of that region's black Francophones, which has become present-day zydeco music; and "swamp pop," to the rhythm and blues/rock'n'roll music of mostly young Cajuns and a few black Creoles in the late 1950s and early 1960s, which was heavily influenced traditional Cajun and Creole music and by the New Orleans Fats Domino sound.
[3] Barry Jean Ancelet, *Cajun Music: Its Origins and Developrnent* (Lafayette, 1989), 17, 19.

tablish that "Colinda" and its sources extend much deeper into the past than post-World War II south Louisiana. It is known to have existed within the Cajun community shortly after the turn of the century, when the word *Colinda* applied to both a Cajun song and a Cajun dance. Prior to the twentieth century, however, the word referred strictly to a black Creole dance, the song's inspiration. The lyrics *"Allons danser, Colinda"* thus originally meant "Let's dance *the* Colinda" (a dance of African origin), not "Let's dance, Colinda" (a girl's name).

"Colinda" remained largely unknown outside the French-speaking communities of south Louisiana and east Texas before Rod Bernard released his swamp pop version in 1962. According to Bernard, his version, recorded in Beaumont, Texas, sold about eighty to one hundred thousand copies, mainly along the Gulf Coast and in Canada.[4] It attracted enough attention nationally, however, to prompt an invitation from Dick Clark's "American Bandstand," which Bernard reluctantly turned down because of his recent induction into the military.[5]

Bernard's recording owes much of its popularity to its bilingual lyrics, which caught the attention not only of French-speaking audiences in south Louisiana, east Texas, and Canada, but also of an Anglo-American audience, who found the alternating English and Cajun French lyrics too exotic to ignore. Bernard grew up at a time, however, when Cajun children were punished at school for speaking French. Although he never learned to speak the dialect, Bernard sings in French on "Colinda" and a few other swamp pop songs. The second stanza of his version reflects the period's prevailing anti-Cajun sentiment.

> *Allons danser, Colinda,* (2)
> *Pendant ta mère n'est pas la,*
> *Pour faire fâcher les vielles femmes.*
> *C'est pas tout le monde à danser*
> *Toutes les vieilles valses à deux temps.*
> *Pendant ta mère n'est pas la,*
> *Allons Danser, Colinda.*
>
> [trans.: Let's dance, Colinda,
> While your mother isn't around,
> to make the old women mad.
> Not everyone can dance
> All the old two-step waltzes.
> While your mother isn't around,
> Let's dance, Colinda.]

---

[4] John Broven, *South to Louisiana: The Music of the Cajun Bayous* (Gretna, 1983), 208-09.
[5] Rod Bernard, interview by Shane Bernard, October 19, 1991, Lafayette, Louisiana, tape recording, Archives of Cajun & Creole Folklore, Center for Louisiana Studies, University of Louisiana at Lafayette (hereafter ACCF).

> 'Linda was the sweetest girl
> In all the bayou land.
> And all the boys who danced with her
> Tried to win her hand.
> Her mother always chaperoned
> With 'Linda every night.
> She didn't want no Cajun boys
> To hold her daughter tight.[6]

Bernard's recording seems to have been influenced equally by Jimmie Davis' 1949 English version of "Colinda" and Happy, Doc, and the Boys' 1946 French version. Bernard undoubtedly became familiar with the latter while performing as a child on Happy and Doc's talent show, held every Saturday morning from about 1948 to 1950 at the old Rose Theater in Opelousas, Louisiana, and broadcast live on KSLO, the local radio station. Beyond this period, however, Bernard provides little information regarding the origin of "Colinda." "All I know," he says, "it's just an old song that was handed down from generation to generation.... Jimmie Davis sang it and Doc Guidry played fiddle and I think they put their name down as writers...they really didn't write it. It's an old, old, old song. They stole it first and I stole it second."[7]

As Bernard indicates, Jimmie Davis' 1949 English version of "Colinda" features Oran "Doc" Guidry, Sr., on fiddle. Guidry, co-leader of Happy, Doc, and the Boys, also appears on the 1946 Cajun French version, recorded for J.D. Miller's Fais Do Do label of Crowley, Louisiana. Miller was not involved with the production of Davis' version, but recalls: "Doc Guidry recorded that with Governor Davis and they put some English words [to it].... And Governor Davis and Doc, I think, wrote the English words, I believe Doc told me, while they were flying to Nashville or wherever they recorded."[8]

Happy, Doc, and the Boys' classic 1946 version is largely instrumental. Its lyrics, however, correspond to those in the French stanza of Bernard's version.[9] In *Yé Yaille, Chère!: Traditional Cajun Dance Music*, Raymond E. François notes that "the tune is an old one, but J.D. Miller gives 'Doc' credit for the words."[10] During a recent interview, however, Miller states that Fats and Guidry merely added lyrics to an existing song. Miller explains: "Let me tell

---

[6] Transcribed and translated by Carl Brasseaux. Rod Bernard's version of "Colinda" can be heard on *Swamp Gold vol. 2* (Jin CD-107), 1991.
[7] Rod Bernard interview.
[8] J.D. "Jay" Miller, interview by Shane Bernard, February 21, 1991, Crowley, Louisiana, tape recording, ACCF. Gov. Jimmie Davis confirms Miller's account. Telephone interview by Ms. Lou Gabus, January 15, 1992, Lafayette to Baton Rouge, Louisiana.
[9] Happy, Doc, and the Boys' version of "Colinda" appears on *Fais Do Do Breakdown, vol 1., The Late 1940s*, Flyright FLY609, 1986. A 1962 recording of "Colinda" by Doc Guidry can be heard on *The Best of La Louisianne Records*, La Louisianne LLCD-1001, 1990.
[10] Raymond E. François, col., trans. and anno., *Yé Yaille, Chère!: Traditional Cajun Dance Music* (Lafayette, 1990), 325.

you something about 'Colinda.' Doc and Fats remembered something of that old song, but didn't remember it all and actually they added words to it in New Orleans.... I don't know where its roots were, but just like a lot of these Cajun things, nobody knows who wrote them."[11] But in John Broven's *South To Louisiana: The Music of the Cajun Bayous*, Fats shares with Guidry the credit for composing the entire tune and lyrics, stating:

> We took the name from a song called 'Danse Colinda,' we got it from a book in a library at Southwestern University, Lafayette [i.e., Southwestern Louisiana Institute, now the University of Southwestern Louisiana]. Actually, it was a Haitian song, so we just took down the name, the tune is not the same, or the lyric[s]. Doc Guidry and I just sat down and we wrote a French song, a two- or three-chord song that is pretty easy to write.[12]

A thorough search of the University of Southwestern Louisiana's library holdings failed to uncover any publications corresponding to Fat's description. In addition, the idea of traditional Cajun musicians hunting for song material in a university library seems uncharacteristic. After all, they could easily pick up new songs from other musicians on records, on the radio, or at live performances. Miller, who accompanied Happy, Doc, and the Boys to Cosimo Matassa's studio in New Orleans to record "Colinda," states:

> I don't know of anybody [who] went over to USL to find out about French music, being honest with you...that [song] was done in the same manner as the others were done. They'd come up with, 'Look, let's do this.' We made up our minds the night before what we were going to record, because at that time these boys knew a bunch of Cajun songs. They [the songs] hadn't been recorded before or they had been recorded years and years before, but in this particular instance, this was just brought up and they tried to record all the song, all the words, and they couldn't. So they put words to [the tune], made the words up themselves.[13]

Miller again observes that Fats and Guidry wrote only a portion of the lyrics. They didn't know who was the original writer," he adds, "and I doubt if anybody knows."[14]

An interview with seventy-three-year-old Doc Guidry cleared up much confusion about the authorship of "Colinda." When asked about the origin of the song, he initially replied: "I'm telling you, we didn't have nothing to do about writing it—except the words."[15] Further questioning, however, helped to restore his memory and was most revealing.

---

[11] Miller interview.
[12] Broven, *South to Louisiana*, 39.
[13] Ibid.
[14] Ibid.
[15] Oran "Doc" Guidry, Sr., interview by Shane Bernard, November 2, 1991, Lafayette, tape recording, ACCF.

*Shane Bernard*: You think that the song, the tune was around already.
*Doc Guidry*: Oh, sure.
*SB*: The melody already existed before you recorded it?
*DG*: That's right. That's why I said that's our rendition of it.
*SB*: And what about the French lyrics?
*DG*: That's the original lyrics,
*SB*: You didn't write it?
*DG*: No.
*SB*: Okay—Happy Fats didn't? So you think he [Fats] was just mistaken here [in Broven's book] when he said that?
*DG*: It was a mistake when they put 'Words and music by Happy and Doc.'[16]

Guidry added that he and Fats didn't locate "Colinda" in the library at Southwestern Louisiana Institute [now University of Louisiana at Lafayette], but in a song book belonging to Guidry's cousin. He also noted that the songbook included both the time and lyrics of "Colinda."[17]

Fats and Guidry thus did not write the lyrics or nine of "Colinda," and Guidry simply confirms what other sources already imply. For instance, Dennis McGee's "Madame Young Donnez Moi Votre Plus Jolie Blonde," recorded in 1929 for the Vocalion label, borrows the tune of "Colinda."[18] Ann Allen Savoy notes in her *Cajun Music: A Reflection of a People* that "Madame Young" is: "a plea to Mrs. Ulysses Young, mother of Dennis's first wife, Maria Young, to give him her beautiful blonde daughter. Maria's sister, Néta Young, taught him the tune and he recorded it for her."[19]

Oran "Doc" Guidry fused Cajun and country fiddling styles, ca. 1957.
Photo courtesy of Johnnie Allan.

Savoy does not mention the similarity of the songs, but her account of "Madame Young's origin suggests that Néta Young probably taught McGee the tune of "Colinda."[20] In fact, "Colinda" is known to predate "Madame Young" by several years. In a 1962 interview by folklorist Lauren Post, pioneer

---

[16] Ibid.
[17] Guidry, Sr. interview, November 2, 1991; Oran "Doc" Guidry, Sr., interview by Shane Bernard, December 26, 1991, Lafayette.
[18] McGee's recording of "Madame Young" can be heard on *Louisiana Cajun Music, Volume Five, the Early Years, 1928-1938*, Old Timey Records 114, 1973; Ann Allen Savoy, comp. and ed., *Cajun Music: A Reflection of a People*, 3rd ed. (Eunice, 1988), 54, 62-3; François, *Yé Yaille, Chère!*, 209-11.
[19] Savoy, *Cajun Music*, 63.
[20] The modern Cajun group Beausoleil has recorded a medley entitled "Kolinda," which combines the lyrics of "Colinda" and "Madame Young." See Beausoleil, "Kolinda," *Bayou Boogie*, Rounder C-6015, 1986.

Cajun accordionist Joseph Falcon states "'Allons danser Colinda'—I knew that tune since I was a little boy. I played it many times...." Born in 1900, Falcon thus confirms that "Colinda" existed shortly after the turn of the century.[21] Falcon also makes the only known reference to "Colinda" as both a Cajun song and a Cajun dance. "That 'Colinda,'" he says, "that's what the old folks call a 'two-step waltz.' He adds: "I had one of my musicians say that there wasn't no such thing as that. I said, 'Hold it brother, I'm older than you.' He said 'There ain't no such thing as a two-step waltz. What number could it be?' I said, 'Allons danser Colinda.' That's a two-step waltz from the old times."[22] "Colinda's" lyrics actually mention the "two-step waltzes" referred to by Falcon: "*C'est pas tout le monde qu'à danser/Toutes les vieilles valses à deux temps*" ("Not everyone can dance/All the old two-step waltzes"). Some versions of "Colinda," however, delete this reference.

Falcon also agrees with Post that "Colinda" may derive from a black Creole source.[23] Surprisingly, a 1956 field recording exists of a black Creole song called "Allons au Bal Colinda." Although its tune clearly is related to the traditional Cajun "Colinda," its black Creole lyrics bear no resemblance to the Cajun lyrics.

*Allons au bal, Colinda. (3)*
*Ti vas matin dans le brouilard.*
*Ta robe était déchirée.*

*Allons au bal, Colinda. (3)*
*Pourquoi, ti me dis pas, Colinda,*
*Où t'a été hier au soir?*

*Allons au bal, Colinda. (3)*
*Alle y va matin dans le petit jour.*
*Sa robe était déchirée.*[24]

Let's go to the dance, Colinda.
You go in the morning fog.
Your dress was torn.

Let's go to the dance, Colinda.
Why won't you tell me, Colinda,
Where you were last night?

Lets go to the dance, Colinda.
She left at the break of dawn.
Her dress was torn.

The lyrics of "Allons au Bal Colinda" closely resemble those of Cajun musician Nathan Abshire's "Pine Grove Blues," recorded for the Old Timey label in 1949, which derives from fellow Cajun musician Columbus Frugé's earlier song "Tite Negresse." Whether "Allons au Bal Colinda" or "'Tite Negresse" appeared first is unknown, but the question to be asked is: could "Allons au Bal Colinda" be the melodic source for the Cajun "Colinda," or could both songs have derived from a third, much earlier song? Both the Cajun and Creole songs interpret *Colinda* as a girl's name. They also refer to dancing and exhibit an underlying sexual theme, both of which appear to be remnants of

---

[21] Savoy, *Cajun Music*, 96, 92.
[22] Ibid., 96.
[23] Ibid.
[24] Performed by Godar Chalvin, 1956, Abbeville, Louisiana, field recording in the possession of Michael Doucet, Lafayette. This translation is closely bassed on Doucet's.

an almost forgotten source—namely, the *Calinda*, a dance of African origin, banned repeatedly by white authorities because of its lascivious nature.[25]

The Calinda dance survives in several Caribbean locations, including Haiti, Bequia, Carriacou, and Trinidad.[26] Contrary to Harold Courlander's assertion in *Negro Folk Music, U.S.A.*, the dance no longer exists in Louisiana, having disappeared, apparently, in the mid- to late nineteenth century.[27] Prior to this period, however, the dance flourished in Louisiana and is mentioned in at least three Creole songs from that region, all of which include a variation of the phrase *"Danser Colinda."* Perhaps the latest example is "Michié Préval," a favorite of the slaves who gathered in New Orleans' Congo Square on Sundays to dance the Calinda. Its first verse reads:

| | |
|---|---|
| *Michié Préval li donnain grand bal,* | Monsieur Préval gave a big dance, |
| *Li fé nég payé sauté in pé.* | He made the Negroes pay to stomp their feet. |
| *Dansez Calinda, baudjoum, boudjoum!* | Dance the Calinda, boudjoum, boudjoum! |
| *Dansez Calinda, boudjoum, boudjoum!*[28] | Dance the Calinda, boudjoum, boudjoum! |

Several more verses—each ending with the refrain "Dance the Calinda, boudjoum, boudjoum!"—document the riotous events of Préval's dance, which concludes with his imprisonment by the master jailor. The slaves then rejoice that "they put him in prison/Because he gave a dance to steal our money." Later the lyrics state that Préval was imprisoned for holding a slave dance without official permission.[29]

The song satirizes members of New Orleans' upper class, its public figures in particular. Préval has been identified as a prominent New Orleans judge and a certain Michié Mazuro—who in the fourth verse is likened "in his big office" to a "bullfrog in a bucket of water"—has been identified as Atty. Gen. Etienne Mazureau (1772-1849).[30] Frequent alteration of "Michié Préval's"

---

[25] See François, *Yé Yaille, Chère!*: 443-45; and Broven, *South to Louisiana*, 33. Calinda possesses a variable orthography. Other spellings are "Kalinda," "Calenda," "Kalenda," "Calendoe," "Calineda," "Calenida," and even the familiar "Colinda." See Harold Courlander, *Negro Folk Music, U.S.A.* (New York, 1963), 165-67; J.D. Elder, "Kalinda—Song of the Battling Troubadours of Trinidad," *Journal of the Folklore Institute* 3 (1966): 192; Dena J. Epstein, *Sinful Tunes and Spirituals: Black Folk Music to the Civil War* (Urbana, 1977), 24, 28, 30, 31-32; and Henry Edward Krehbiel, *Afro-American Folksongs: A Study in Racial and National Music* (New York, 1914), 66, 116.

[26] Elder, "Kalinda—Song of the Battling Troubadours of Trinidad," 192.

[27] Courlander, *Negro Folk Music, U.S.A.*, 191.

[28] Mina Monroe, comp. and ed., *Bayou Ballads: Twelve Folk-Songs from Louisiana*, Schirmer's American Folk-Song Series, set. 2. (New York, 1921), 40-55.

[29] "Yé metté li prison/Pasqué li donnain bal pou volé nous l'arzent." Monroe, *Bayou Ballads*, 49. "Michié Préval" appears under the title "Dansé Calinda" on the De Paur Chorus, *Dansé, Calinda! Creole Songs, Work Songs, Spirituals* (n.d.).

[30] He resembles "*dans so gros biro...crapaud dans in baille d'ollo,*" Irène Thérèse Whitfield, *Louisiana French Folk Songs* (Baton Rouge, 1939); George Washinton Cable, "Dance in Place Congo," *The Century Magazine* 31 (1886): 528; Glenn R. Conrad, ed., *A Dictionary of Louisiana Biography* (Lafayette, 1988), s.v. "Mazureau, Etienne."

title and lyrics permitted the dancers to satirize other New Orleans public figures. George Washington Cable mentions "Michié Préval" in "The Dance in Place Congo," noting that "for generations the man of municipal politics was fortunate who escaped entirely a lampooning set to its air" and that "a page might be covered by the roll of [its] victims."[31]

A related song, "Michié Baziro," also mentions the Calinda. Although its tune closely resembles that of "Michié Préval," its lyrics are largely original. Its first verse, however, mimics the fourth verse of "Michié Préval."

| | |
|---|---|
| *Michié Baziro don so vié biro,* | Monsieur Baziro in his old office, |
| *Li semblé crapaud dans baille do l'eau* | Looks like a bullfrog in a bucket of water. |
| *Dansez Calinda, Boudoum, Boudoum.* | Dance the Calinda, Boudoum, Boudoum. |
| *Dansez Calinda, Boudoum, Boudoum.*[32] | Dance the Calinda, Boudoum, Boudoum. |

Research fails to uncover Michié Baziro's exact identity or occupation, but to assume that he was a public figure in New Orleans would not be absurd. *Baziro* also may be a corruption of *Mazuro*, the song, merely one of numerous offshoots of "Michié Préval."

The Creole song "Lizette to Quité la Plaine" also refers to the Calinda dance. First published in Louisiana in 1859, the song earlier appeared under the title "Chanson Nègre," which was published in Philadelphia in 1811. The song appeared even earlier as "Chanson Creole" in a circa 1740 treatise by Jean Jacques Rousseau concerning his invention of a new system of musical notation. The first quatrain of the third stanza mentions the dance:

| | |
|---|---|
| *Dipo mo perdi Lizette,* | Since I lost Lizette, |
| *Mo pa batte Bambaula,* | I don't beat the Bamboula, |
| *Bauche a moi tourni muette,* | My mouth has become mute. |
| *Mo pa dansi Calinda.*[33] | And I don't dance the Calinda. |

"The Love Song," sketch by E.W. Kemble.
From George Washington Cable, "Creole Slave Dances: The Dance in Place Congo," Century Magazine 31 (November 1885-April 1886): 525.

Although this is the earliest known reference in song to the Calinda, many first-hand accounts of the dance itself survive. One of the latest is found in Mina Monroe's *Bayou Ballads*, first published in 1921, in which the author relates a

---

[31] Cable, "Dance in Place Congo," 527, 528.
[32] Whitfield, *Louisiana French Folk Songs*, 135-37.
[33] Translated by Richard Guidry. The bamboula was a drum of African origin. See Epstein, *Sinful Tunes and Sirituals*, 94.

description of the dance by "an old darkey once an expert at the Calinda." Monroe writes:

> In Louisiana, the Calinda was a war-dance in which men alone took part, stripped to the waist and brandishing sticks in a mock fight, while at the same time balancing upon their heads bottles filled with water from which one drop spilled put the participant *hors de combant*.... there was much sport in it at the stage of dancing with water-filled bottles, and...the last remaining dancer well deserved to have the water in his bottle replaced by good 'tafia' (whiskey) to celebrate his victory.

The main characteristic of the Calinda according to Monroe is stick-fighting, which corresponds to present-day descriptions of the dance in Trinidad. Monroe's account, however, contains the only known reference to the Calinda as a war-dance in Louisiana.[34]

Another late description dates from March 1885, when author and editor Charles Dudley Warner visited New Orleans. Entering a house near the former site of Congo Square, Warner observed "an incantation rather than a dance." He writes:

> A colored woman at the side of the altar began a chant in a low, melodious voice. It was the weird and strange 'Danse Calinda.'... The chant grew, the single line was enunciated in stronger pulsations, and other voices joined in the wild refrain.... The singing became wilder and more impassioned, a strange minor strain, full of savage pathos and longing.... the chant had been changed for the wild *canga*, more rapid in movement than the *chanson africaine*....[35]

Other sources also connect the Calinda with voodoo or similar cults. Cable states in his "Creole Slave Songs" that

> In Louisiana, as I have been told by that learned Creole scholar the late Alexander Dimitry, Voodoo bore as a title of greater solemnity the additional title of Maignan, and that even in the Calinda dance, which he had witnessed innumerable times, was sometimes heard, at the height of its frenzy, the invocation—
>
> 'Aïe! Aïe!
> Voodoo, Magnan! [sic][36]

In addition, Courlander claims that the Calinda survives in present-day Haiti not as a dance associated with voodooism, but with zombiism. According to the author,

> There is a secret society called *Société Vinbindingue* which is dedicated to what might be called 'zombiism.' A person who has been 'killed' has been buried, and now the *zaubaups*, members of the society, are digging the body up.... The zaubaups

---

[34] Monroe, *Bayou Ballads*, vii; Elder, "Kalinda—Song of the Battling Troubadours of Trinidad," 192-203.
[35] Epstein, *Sinful Tunes and Spirituals*, 135.
[36] George Washington Cable, "Creole Slave Songs," *The Century Magazine* 31 (1886): 815-17.

"The Bamboula," sketch by E.W. Kemble.
*From George Washington Cable, "Creole Slave Dances: The Dance in Place Congo," Century Magazine 31 (November 1885-April 1886): 524.*

have their own dance, the Calinda, which is in no way associated with Vodoun [Voodoo] religious practices.[37]

Moreau de Saint-Méry of Saint-Domingue (now Haiti) suggested in 1797 that the Calinda functioned as a social gathering reminiscent of a fertility ritual.

> This dance has an air which is specially consecrated to it and wherein the measure is strongly marked. The proficiency in that dancer consists in the perfection with which she can move her hips and the lower part of her back while preserving the rest of her body in a kind of immobility, that even the slightest movement of the arms that balance the two ends of a handkerchief on her petticoat does not make her lose. A dancer approaches her; all of the sudden he makes a leap into the air and lands in measured time so as almost to touch her. He draws back, he jumps again, and excites her by the most seductive play. The dance becomes enlivened and soon it presents a tableau, of which the entire action, at first voluptuous, afterwards becomes lascivious.[38]

Thirty-seven years earlier English cartographer Thomas Jefferys mentions "the *Calendoe*" in a study of French colonies in the Americas. He also provides a rare reference to the geographical origin of the dance, calling it "a sport brought from the coast of Guinea, and attended with gestures which are not entirely consistent with modesty, whence it is forbidden by the public laws of the islands." In 1758 historian and Louisiana planter Le Page du Pratz observed that "Nothing is more to be dreaded than to see the Negroes assemble together on Sundays, since, under the pretense of Calinda, or the dance, they

---

[37] Harold Courlander, *Haiti Singing* (Chapel Hill, 1939), 71-72, 88.
[38] R. Nettel, "Historical Introduction to 'La Calinda,'" *Music and Letters* 27 (1946): 60.

sometimes get together to the number of three or four hundred, and make it a kind of Sabbath, which it is always prudent to avoid; for it is in those tumultuous meetings that they...plot their rebellions."[39]

From Martinique in 1698 Prejean Baptiste Labat wrote a description of the dance, giving the earliest known reference to its place of origin.

> The one [dance] in which they take the greatest pleasure, which is the usual one, is the Calenda. It came from the Guinea Coast and to all appearances from Ardra. The Spaniards have learned it from the Negroes and throughout America dance it in the same way as do the Negroes. [40]

Labat regarded all the African dances as *"dèshonnêtes," "indécentes," "lascives,"* and *"infame,"* but took more interest in the Calinda than other observers. Indeed, his account provides greater detail than Moreau de Saint-Méry's. Labat writes:

> The dancers are drawn up in two lines, one before the other, the men all one side and the women on the other. Those who are waiting their turns, and the spectators, make a circle round the dancers and the drums. The more adept chants a song which he composes on the spur of the moment, on some subject which he deems appropriate, the refrain of which, chanted by all spectators, is accompanied by a great clapping of hands. As regards the dancers, they hold their arms a little after the manner of those who dance while playing the castanets. They skip, make a turn right and left, approach within two or three feet of each other, draw back in cadence until the sound of the drum directs them to draw together again, striking the thighs one against the other, that is to say, the man against the woman. To all appearance it seems that the stomachs are hitting, while as a matter of fact it is the thighs that carry the blows. They retire at once in a pirouette, to begin again the same movement with altogether lascivious gestures, as often as the drum gives them the signal, as it often does several times in succession. From time to time they interlock arms and make two or three turns, always striking the thighs and kissing. One easily sees from this abbreviated description how the dance is opposed to decency.

He adds that "As the postures and movements of the dance are most indecent, the masters who live in an ordinary way forbid it to their own people, and take care that they do not dance it..."[41] Not only master,s but also civil authorities often prohibited the Calinda. For instance, the colonial government of Martinique outlawed the dance on May 23, 1772, reinforcing an earlier ban enacted on August 5, 1758. These prohibitions, however, merely strengthened a 1678 prohibition of the "Kalinda" by the Conseil Souverain de Martinique. This initial ban resulted from the indictment of a planter named Greny, who had permitted a day-long Calinda to be performed at a slave wedding. (Note a resemblance to the theme of "Michié Préval.") According to civil records,

---

[39] Epstein, *Sinful Tunes and Spirituals*, 31-32.
[40] Nettel, "Historical Introduction to 'La Calinda,'" 60; also see Epstein, *Sinful Tunes and Spirituals*, 30, 32.
[41] Nettel, "Historical Introduction to 'La Calinda,'" 60.

a soldier sent to disperse the slaves on Greny's plantation was forced by the dancers to flee on horseback. Needless to say, Labat's own plan to replace the Calinda with the more civilized minuet and courante failed completely.[42]

The precise time of the Calinda's arrival in the New World is unknown, but Labat's description—the earliest known reference to the dance—proves that it was already established in the Caribbean before the close of the seventeenth century. Labat and Thomas Jefferys, however, both cite Guinea, which began to supply slaves to the New World in 1562, as the Calinda's place of origin.[43] Labat even pinpoints Ardra, a region near the mouth of the Volta River on the Gold and Slave Coast of Guinea.[44] Lee Warren, in *The Dance of Africa: An Introduction*, also traces the dance from Guinea to the New World, claiming that it similarly made its way into the African interior, where, in the vicinity of present-day Chad, it became the *Yuka* dance. Warren states that the Yuka later appeared in Cuba and eventually became the American Rumba, first popularized at the 1932 World's Fair in Chicago. In addition, he suggests that other American dances—like the Shimmy, the Black Bottom, the Charleston, and the Foxtrot—descend from the Calinda. Warren also argues that several older popular dances evolved from the Calinda. For instance, Arab invaders carried it to medieval Spain as the *Zarabanda*; it later became the ever-popular *Fandango*, which in Haiti was later transformed into a religious dance called the *Loaloachi*. The Zarabanda also crossed the Pyrennes, becoming the popular Sarabande of the French nobility. All these dances, insists Warren, derive from the Calinda.[45]

Warren's research confirms the Calinda's existence between 711 and 1236 A.D., the period of the Arab occupation of Spain.[46] Oddly, the Provençal troubadour Raimbault de Vaqueiras composed a mildly erotic medieval dance song entitled "Calenda Maya" about 1200 A.D.[47] This title translates as "The First of May," because in this instance *calenda* derives from the Latin *calendae*,

---

[42] See Adrien Dessales, "Histoire générale des antilles," in Epstein, *Sinful Tunes and Spirituals*, 28. Three descriptions of the Calinda in Diderot's *Encyclopédie* are based on Labat's report. See *Encyclopédie, ou dictionarire raissoné des sciences, des arts et des métiers* (1777), s.v. "Calinda," "Negres," and "taboula;" Epstein, *Sinful Tunes and Spirituals*, 27-28.

[43] Bernard Grun and Werner Stein, *The Timetables of History: A Horizontal Linkage of People and Events*, 3rd rev. ed. (New York, 1991), 249.

[44] I.A. Akinjogbin, *Dahomey and Its Neighbors, 1708-1818* (Cambridge, 1967), 214.

[45] Lee Warren, *The Dance of Africa: An Introduction* (Englewood Cliffs, 1972), 45-46.

[46] Grun and Stein, *The Timetables of History*, 70, 171.

[47] "Calenda Maya" (also spelled "Kalenda Maya") appears in numerous sources on medieval music. Excellent tranlations, however, are provided in William E. Burgwinkle, *Razos and Troubadour Songs* (New York, 1990), 286-91; and Archibald T. Davison and Willi Apel, *Historical Anthology of Music: Oriental, Medieval and Renaissance Music*, rev. ed. (Cambridge, 1950), 241. A recording of "Calenda Maya" appears on The Boston Camerata, *New Britain: The Roots of American Folksong (Les racines du folksong Américain)* (1990). (The compilers of this compact disk do not associate "Calenda Maya" with "Allons Danser Colinda" but with "Cuando Por el Oriente," a Christmas processional heard among the Spanish inhabitants of New Mexico.)

meaning "the first of the month." (Hence the English *calendar* and *calends*.[48]) The Romanian *Colinda* (or *colinde*) also derives from this source. These are traditional rustic Christmas carols, many of which, however, are secular in nature and borrow frequently from pagan mythology."[49] The colinda descended from the ancient Roman New Year festival called the *Calendae*, which persisted in Eastern Europe several centuries after the downfall of Rome. In the fourth century A.D. St. John Chrysostom wrote an entire sermon on the evils of the Calendae. The Byzantine church repeatedly denounced the Calendae because of its pagan origin and in 692 A.D. the Council *in Trullo*, an ecclesiastical assembly, banned the celebration "once and for all...from the association of the faithful."[50]

Whether or not "Calenda Maya," the Colinda of Romania, and the Calendae of ancient Rome actually are linked to the Calinda dance, and therefore to the Cajun song "Colinda," is presently unclear. Four of these folk traditions—the Calinda dance, Vaqueiras' "Calinda Maya," the Colindâ of Romania, and the Calendae of ancient Rome—are associated with themes of fertility and regeneration. Although the Cajun "Colinda" does not possess this trait, it exhibits a sexual theme, which suggests a link to the older traditions. An etymological link may also exist between *Colinda/Calinda* and the other Old World traditions. W.W. Newell first suggested a link between Calinda and the Latin Calendae in 1891. William A. Read, who suggests a Congo source in his *Louisiana-French*, regards Newell's idea as "even more preposterous" than Lafcadio Hearn's statement that it derives from the Spanish *que linda*, meaning "how beautiful." Courlander, however, suggests that the Calinda could be "an African dance with an African name, or a European dance taken over in part and adapted by the slaves, or *a European name attached to a number of dances traditional among slaves*." The above evidence indicates the latter theory; namely, *Calinda* is a term of Latin origin applied to an African dance or dances.[51]

Speculation aside, the Calinda originated in Guinea prior to the late-seventeenth century. It traveled to the New World on slave ships and arrived as several dances or as a single dance that evolved into many related dances in the Caribbean and Louisiana. For example, it became an occult dance associated with Voodooism in New Orleans and Zombiism in Haiti; a stick dance associated with warfare in Trinidad and also in New Orleans; and a purely social-oriented dance in many locations, with overtones of a fertility ritual. The

---

[48] *Oxford English Dictionary*, s.v. "calendar," "calends."
[49] See also Louise B. Dyer, *Onze colindes et cinq chants populaires roumains* (Paris, 1933), n.p.; Béla Bartók, "Romanian Folk Music," in *Béla Bartók Essays*, comp. and ed., by Benjamin Suchoff (New York, 1931), 115, 118, 120-21, 126; Courlander, *Negro Folk Music, U.S.A.*, 191.
[50] Egon Wellesz, *A History of Byzantine Music and Hymnograph* (Oxford, 1949) 68, 74, 79-80.
[51] W.W. Newell, "Waste-Basket of Words," *Journal of American Folklore* 4 (1891): 70; Lafcadio Hearn, *Gombo Zhèbes: Little Dictionary of Creole Proverbs* (New York, 1885), 32; William A. Read, *Louisiana-French* (Baton Rouge, 1939), 121; Courlander, *Negro Folk Music, U.S.A.*, 191.

dance survives to the present in scattered areas of the Caribbean, but in Louisiana it disappeared in the nineteenth century. Its name persisted, however, in songs like "Michié Préval" and "Michié Baziro." Here further speculation is required: Cajuns and black Creoles in the late-nineteenth century forgot or never experienced the Calinda. They thus mistook the phrase "Dansez Calinda" (a dance) for "*Danser* Colinda" (a girl's name). Cajuns or black Creoles then composed a new song around this refrain or merely adapted an older song to new meaning. While "Allons au Bal Colinda" is a candidate, "Michié Préval" and "Michié Baziro" also present themselves as possible sources for "Colinda." Indeed, the traditional Cajun "Colinda" exhibits two characteristics suggesting a link to "Michié Préval" and "Michié Baziro." First, the lyrics of all three songs express disregard for authority figures. "Michié Préval" and "Michié Baziro" satirize upper-class and even well-known citizens of New Orleans; and the voice of "Colinda" wants to dance "to make the old ladies mad." Second, a "forbidden dance" theme is prominent in both "Colinda" and "Michié Preval." The police break up Préval's dance and Préval is thrown in jail for sponsoring the event "*sans permis;*" and the voice of "Colinda" urges his partner to "dance all the old two-step waltzes.... While your mother isn't around," apparently because the dances are considered indecent.

All three songs thus appear to have been influenced by the irreverent and lascivious nature of the Calinda dance and its frequent prohibition by authority figures. The result of this ethnic cultural interaction, "Colinda," became, a traditional Cajun standard, recorded in French by Happy, Doc, and the Boys in 1946, in English by Jimmie Davis in 1949, and in French and English by Rod Bernard in 1962. Other artists also recorded versions of "Colinda" over the past half-century. "Colinda" thus possesses an extremely complex genealogy, a trait shared by numerous Cajun songs. Although "Colinda" stands apart because of its African influence and extensive evolution, it also serves as an additional example of the numerous influences on Cajun music.

# How Y'all Are:
# Justin Wilson, Comedy, and Ethnic Identity

*Kevin S. Fontenot*

At the time of his death in 2001, Justin Wilson was likely the most famous Cajun in the world. His popularity rested on years of exposure as a humorist on both the southern and national stages and as the man most instrumental in bringing Cajun cooking to the world outside southern Louisiana. While his national and international reputation grew, Wilson remained tied to the South, particularly his native Louisiana, and retained his strong fan base among the white southern and Cajun working class. The majority of his fans would have expressed shock that the genial, gently humorous old man in the string tie, plantation hat, belt and suspenders (because he was a safety man first) was reviled by the Cajun cultural elite.

Attorney and cultural activist Paul Tate branded Wilson "a redneck telling jokes for rednecks." James Domengeaux, founder of CODOFIL, routinely called the humorist a degrader of the Cajun people, someone who cared little for cultural survival. The critics routinely questioned Wilson's Cajun credentials, saying that he was born in Mississippi, could not speak French, and deliberately drew pictures of Cajuns as ignorant, lazy, and unable to speak proper English. Wilson's Cajuns, they snorted, were perplexed by the modern world, uneducated oafs unwilling (or worse, unable) to cope with the likes of airplanes and flush toilets. To his middle class, upwardly mobile Cajun critics, Wilson was an embarrassment who needed to go away.[1] But did their claims have any basis in fact, and if so, why did Wilson gain and maintain such great popularity among the Cajun working class?

Justin Wilson was born near Amite City, Louisiana, in 1914.[2] A farming family, the Wilsons all worked in the fields and helped run the farm. Harry Wilson, Justin's father, also built a career with the Illinois Central Railroad and served in several public offices. In 1916 Harry Wilson was elected Commissioner of Agriculture and held the office until he died in 1948. During that period Wilson cemented ties to the Long machine, a relationship that his son Justin reinforced by campaigning for Earl K. Long in 1948. The race pitted Long against ex-governor Sam Jones. Jones suffered an accident near Alexandria, following which Uncle Earl hired Justin to travel the state telling audi-

---

[1] For an excellent example of the criticism, see Chris Drew, "Justin Wilson, Humorist," *New Orleans Magazine* (June 1979). The Tate quote is from this article.
[2] Wilson biographical information from Mark Lorando, "Justin Wilson Seasons Dishes with Humor," *Times Picayune*, August 11, 1989; Chris Drew, "Justin Wilson, Humorist;" and Will McDonald, "Au Revoir, Mister Wilson," *Chili Pepper Magazine* (February 2002), 78-79.

ences that the veterinarians of Alexandria were suing Jones' doctor for "treating a jackass without a license."[3]

Wilson's mother, Olivet Toadvin, was a Cajun, justifying his claim to be a "half-bleed" Cajun. Wilson recalled his mother as "a wonderful, creative cook" and the main inspiration for his own culinary talents. She also taught Wilson some French, but it was not until he began to travel as an after dinner speaker that the started to collect and tell Cajun jokes. His parents also ignited his talent for humor and Wilson grew especially fond of Will Rogers, the famed humorist of the 1920s and 1930s. Shortly before Rogers died in 1935, the two met and Rogers passed along some advice to Wilson, namely to always include something positive. Wilson held to that advice, usually including material on patriotism and voting during his routine.

Wilson attended, but did not graduate, Louisiana State University. Leaving college during the Depression, Wilson "hoboed" around the United States, working at odd jobs. He soon settled into a career as a safety engineer, traveling extensively through Louisiana and the South. His natural gregariousness led to a career as a speaker on safety issues and Wilson started using humor to break

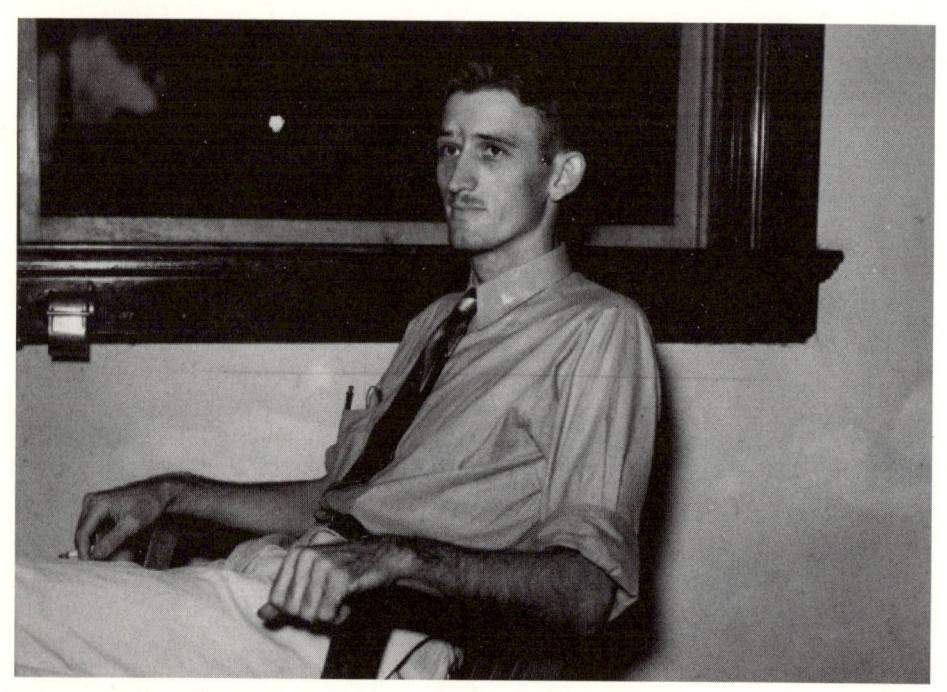

Justin Wilson at the Rice Festival, Crowley, Louisiana, date unknown. Photo courtesy of Freeland Archive, Acadia Parish Library.

---

[3] Harry Wilson biography drawn from the *Dictionary of Louisiana Biography*, ten year supplement, Carl A. Brasseaux and James D. Wilson, eds. (Lafayette, 1998), 244. Wilson quote from the LPB documentary "Uncle Earl."

up his speeches. As his reputation as a humorist grew in Louisiana, Wilson began to record albums of his comedy, the first appearing in 1961 on the Project label. Titled "I Gawr-On-Tee," the album set the stage for future Wilson material with his fractured English and tales of Cajuns trying to retain some resemblance of themselves in a quickly modernizing world. Tony Guillory, a naval serviceman stationed at Guam, remembered buying Wilson albums at the PX. "They were like going home," recalled Guillory.[4] Over the next thirty years Wilson would record and release at least twenty-seven studio albums and live performances occasionally are still released.

As his reputation as a humorist grew, Wilson found a second performance venue as an early "celebrity chef." At the urging of friends, Wilson published *The Justin Wilson Cook Book* in 1965. The book was filled mostly with family recipes. Its success led to a long running cooking show produced for public broadcasting. In various incarnations, Wilson's program has aired continually since the early 1970s and has been broadcast throughout the nation. Long before Paul Prudhomme, John Folse, or Lucy Zaunbrecher, Justin Wilson popularized Cajun food beyond Louisiana. Prudhomme openly expressed his admiration for Wilson's popularizing of Cajun cuisine and said people outside Louisiana, particularly men, remark on enjoying Wilson's shows. "He made a lot of people happy," remarked Prudhomme, "The culture he was talking about was my culture. Some of the things he said in a humorous way really did happen. We appreciated it. It was good fun."[5] But not everyone was as enthusiastic as Prudhomme. Wilson's humor rankled sensitive Cajun culturalists intent on smoothing out rough edges and showing the world that Cajuns were not backward rustics out of touch with the modern world.

Wilson's humor was based in the broad tradition of southern working class humor. The tradition emphasized storytelling over the punch line. Jerry Clower defined his style in this way: "I tell about something funny that happened to real folks; and the funniest things in the world actually happened. I don't think I'm necessarily a comic; I think I'm a humorist. A comic tells funny stories, and a humorist tells stories funny." Wilson always insisted that he was a humorist, not a stand-up comic. Wilson drew images in his audience's mind, familiarizing them with his characters—often characters with whom the audience could identify. And that identification formed an important basis of southern humor.[6]

---

[4] Tony Guillory, the author's granduncle, related this to the author in the mid-1980s following my attendance at a Wilson performance in Kinder, La.
[5] Prudhomme quote from Ron Thibodeaux, "Louisiana Chef, Humorist Justin Wilson dies at 87," *Times Picayune*, September 7, 2001, A1.
[6] I do not differentiate between southern and Cajun humor, rather I view the later as a version of the former, in much the same way as Cajun music is tied to country music.

Southern working class humor has been largely ignored by historians. Bill C. Malone, however, recently outlined the basic premises of the style in *Don't Get Above Your Raisin'.* "Country humor at its best asserted the humanity of working people's lives, exposed the hypocrisies that lay around them, brought the pompous and mighty down to size, served as a painless way of calling up bittersweet memories of the past, eased the pain of lives that were often hard and lonely, and of course, added the healing balm of laughter to spirits in need of relief. Humor also served as a populist defense mechanism in southern folk culture, attacking pretension and sham, and striving to keep people from becoming too self-important—admonishing them with the unspoken command not to get above their raising."[7]

One of the most common stock jokes used in country humor was the "Arkansas Traveler" routine in which a city "dude" tries to outsmart a "rube" by asking obvious questions and is unable to ruffle the feathers of the country boy. Wilson used this routine to great effect in "Little Boy Not Lost."

Wilson drew often on the stock of southern humor for material. He himself insisted that many of his jokes came from Cajuns themselves, who volunteered them at performances or sent them in letters.[8]

One category of stock southern jokes that Wilson utilized to great lengths can be described as "Cajuns confronting the modern world." In these jokes, a Cajun finds himself in a new situation usually brought on by modern technology—such as an elevator or airplane—with humor ensuing. This category was extremely common among southern comedians of the 1940s, '50s and '60s, exactly the time frame that southerners (including Cajuns) began to confront technology. Though often dismissed as derogatory material, these jokes actually function as "defense mechanisms" turning embarrassing situations into humorous events in order for the "rube" to gain control. Indeed, the rube often turns the tables by pointing out the uselessness of modern inventions or their inherent comedy. In a world of machinery, the southern folk assert individual identity by controlling the laugh. The embarrassment many felt at being baffled by technology on first encounter is diffused.[9] Wilson's "confronting technology" tales must be understood in this light to be fully appreciated.

The stock southern repertoire that Wilson used so effectively has been mined by other Cajun comedians. Dave Petitjean, often praised by Cajun cultural elites as a "good" Cajun comedian, drew upon the repertoire for his "Counterfeiting Texans," "Furniture Disease," and "Texas Hunting." Petitjean owes a

---

[7] Bill C. Malone, *"Don't Get Above Your Raisin'": Country Music and the Southern Working Class* (Urbana, 2002), 172.

[8] See Drew, "Justin Wilson, Humorist."

[9] Wilson is heavily criticized for this type of material by Barry Ancelet, but the material is extremely common among many humorists in the South. It has reasserted itself in the form of some "Boudreaux and Thibodeaux" jokes—jokes usually told by Cajuns.

deep debt to Wilson, one perhaps not acknowledged—that of the mangled English language. Petitjean, who speaks in a heavily accented English, refers to himself as a "full bleed Cajun" and in "Texas Hunting" rattles off a litany of Wilsonian mispronunciations: cataract for Cadillac, once hole shot gun etc.[10] Thus the darling of modern Cajun critics (and Petitjean is very funny) is a direct descendant of Wilson. If his Cajuns come off better in encounters with the modern world (as some critics would suggest), their success is because they are living thirty years after Wilson's Cajuns first encountered technology.

But Wilson and Petitjean were not the first Cajun humorists to engage in the use of fractured English. The tradition extends at least as far back as 1929 when Walter Coquille cut the very first Cajun comedy records. As the "Mayor of Bayou Pom Pom," Coquille, in a heavy accent, railed against politicians who blacktopped the roads—not because of the expense or for fear of the outside world—but because it would burn the bare feet of Cajuns in the summer. He also extolled the virtues of the crawfish as a symbol of Cajun culture—"he would rather die than back down."

So Wilson's use of fractured English which bothers his critics so intensely is not exclusive to him. The tradition is old and continues today. Again, the use of fractured English fits into the self-defense mechanism because fractured English is used to state the obvious and deflate pomposity.

Wilson's critics also asserted that he offered a negative portrayal of Cajuns. This critique does not hold up under scrutiny. First, Wilson always expressed a deep admiration for the Cajun people and identified with them. His "Definition of Cajun," a standard opening for his routines even when performed for Cajuns, sketches a defiant and proud people unwilling to swear allegiance to the English king, but quick to "swear at him" for violating their lives. By asserting this positive image at the beginning of his routine, Wilson could then relate humorous stories in a context of an honorable people. His use of stock jokes with Cajun characters then acted as markers identifying Cajuns with the broader southern culture. Cajuns were not that different than other southerners, they had trouble with modernity as well. They had old men who hung out on the courthouse steps or in barrooms. People outside of Acadiana thus connected with the Cajuns. "After listening to Justin Wilson," recalled a transplant to Louisiana, "I saw the Cajuns as clearly as I could see my own people, warm, humorous, filled with the ability to laugh at themselves as well as other, lovers of good food and a completely likable people who had retained their special qualities and remained Cajuns to the last."[11] Wilson said in 1979, "People come up to me and ask me how they can become Cajuns."[12]

---

[10] Listen to Petitjean on "Cajun Kings of Comedy" and "Favorites."
[11] Mrs. Charles Fowlkes of Slidell quoted in *Times Picayune*, July 7, 1974, sec. 2, p. 4.
[12] Drew, "Justin Wilson, Humorist."

**In Her Embarrassment, the Bashful Marie Upset a Chair and Stepped On a Sleeping Cat's Tail.**

Mayor Boudreaux's wife Marie is escorted to the podium so that she can share her gumbo recipe.
From Walter Coquille, *The Mayor of Bayou Pom Pom Speaks, by the Mayor Heemself* (New Orleans, 1954), 38.

So if Wilson did not deviate greatly from mainstream style of Cajun humor when he used fractured English, if his stories may be read as self-defensive texts or even as strong statements about Cajunness, especially when placed in the context of an overall performance, if people outside the region generally seem to have a good opinion of him, what made him the particular target of the Cajun cultural elite, particularly the Council for the Development of French in Louisiana?

The strongest response must lie in Wilson's great popularity and the timing of his popularity. Wilson came to national attention during the 1960s and 1970s, during which CODOFIL also reached its height. The organization desperately wanted to improve the image of Cajuns and that meant teaching continental French in the schools and carefully managing perceptions of Cajuns to the outside world. Wilson's fractured English was embarrassing to the doctors, lawyers, and college professors interested in showing that Cajuns were just like everyone else, just with a proper French accent. His stories of Cajuns in the modern world were misinterpreted and taken out of context, thus being viewed as derogatory and not part of a broader complex tradition of rural people trying to retain their cultural identity by organic means—by their humor, their music. CODOFIL was imposed from above, and its greatest success was when it nurtured the culture by encouraging musicians, storytellers, cooks and others. But the cultural elite that led the movement failed to understand the popularity of Wilson and the role he played in popularizing Cajun cooking and humor.

CODOFIL's dissatisfaction with Wilson might also have a political connection. James Domengeaux was an active member of the anti-Huey Long faction of state politics, and the Wilson family strongly supported both Huey and Earl Long. Justin Wilson had campaigned for Earl Long, attacking the former Sam Jones during the 1948 campaign that marked the return of Longism to power on the state level. Wilson had also forged enough of an alliance with Cajun boss Dudley LeBlanc to be invited to speak as an example of a Cajun storyteller at several 1950s festivals celebrating Cajun culture. LeBlanc was not a member of the Long faction, but he also did not court the Genteel Acadian groups led by Domengeaux. For the Genteel Acadians, Wilson represented not only backward and embarrassing culture, but populist and unruly politics.

If the cultural leaders of Acadiana failed to appreciate Wilson, the working people embraced him and his humor. No systematic study was ever conducted of the typical Wilson fan, but claims that his base was strongest among "upwardly mobile Cajuns" remain to be demonstrated. On the contrary my experience with Wilson's fans is exactly the opposite. At the three or four performances that I personally attended, the audience was composed largely of working-class Cajuns, people I knew from my home area. Among the people I know who purchased his records, all are from the working class. The people who criticize Wilson are almost exclusively from the educated elite—doctors, lawyers, college professors, upwardly mobile groups if I ever knew them. Ultimately the questions they ask about Wilson are best not asked about him, but rather themselves. Attacking Wilson might just be their defense mechanism

*CODOFIL founder James Domengeaux led the charge in criticizing Justin Wilson's portrayal of Cajuns.*
*Photo courtesy of Center for Louisiana Studies, University of Louisiana at Lafayette, accession number 272.*

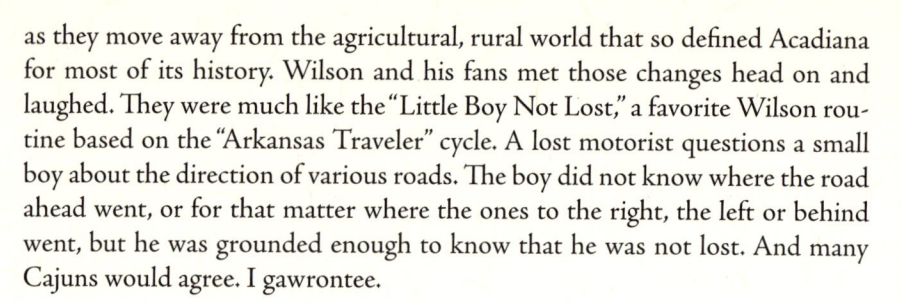

as they move away from the agricultural, rural world that so defined Acadiana for most of its history. Wilson and his fans met those changes head on and laughed. They were much like the "Little Boy Not Lost," a favorite Wilson routine based on the "Arkansas Traveler" cycle. A lost motorist questions a small boy about the direction of various roads. The boy did not know where the road ahead went, or for that matter where the ones to the right, the left or behind went, but he was grounded enough to know that he was not lost. And many Cajuns would agree. I gawrontee.

# Country Chameleons:
# Cajuns on the Louisiana Hayride[1]

*Tracey E.W. Laird*

Cajun musicians and country musicians have exchanged musical ideas at least as early as the late 1920s, when records by both first became widely available. Both Cajun and country artists began incorporating elements from the other style into their own musical repertoires. For example, the early 1930s recordings of Cajun musicians Joe and Cléoma Falcon include Cajun French translations of Carter Family songs like "I'm Thinking Tonight of My Blue Eyes" and "Lu Lu's Back in Town." Leo Soileau recorded "Personne m'aime pas," translated from the song by Jimmie Davis, "Nobody's Darlin' But Mine." Some Cajun bands began adapting country instruments like the electric steel guitar and the trap drum set, which by the 1940s were standard alongside the traditional fiddles, guitars, accordions, and assorted percussion.

Cajun music gradually made its way to the ears of mainstream country musicians, beginning with the first commercial Cajun release, the Falcons' "Allons à Lafayette" in 1928. But it would take nearly two decades before a south Louisiana musician received wide notice. Guitarist, fiddler, and singer Harry Choates was born near Rayne, Louisiana, but lived much of his life in Port Arthur, Texas, where he moved to work in the oil industry. There he became a regional favorite in honky-tonks throughout southwest Louisiana and in the Texas region known as the "lapland" (for the overlap of Cajun culture there). Choates' 1946 version of "Jole Blon" was a huge regional hit, and his influence extended up into north Louisiana and beyond. (The earliest version of this song, called "Ma Blonde est partie," appeared on record in 1928 by the Breaux brothers, Amédé, Ophé, and Cléopha, in-laws of Joe Falcon.)

Choates inspired other country artists, including the late Roy Acuff and the legendary pianist and singer Moon Mullican, who was also from the lapland. Later in 1946 Mullican released "New Jole Blon." This song was based on the Choates version, but because Mullican did not understand French, he replaced the original lyrics with things like "possum up a gum stump." Mullican tried to build on the popularity of this song with the lesser-known follow-up, "Jole Blon's Sister."

This process of musical borrowing and exchange continued in 1948 with the beginning of the Louisiana Hayride in Shreveport, Louisiana. The Hayride was north Louisiana's forum for country music during the postwar era. Broadcast from the Municipal Auditorium over the 50,000-watt station KWKH, the Louisiana Hayride launched some of the greatest careers in country music

---

[1] This article first appeared in the 1999 Louisiana Folklife Festival booklet.

from 1948 until 1960. It blasted throughout north and south Louisiana, as well as more than twenty-five other states, and gave numerous musicians their first national exposure. In fact, KWKH nurtured so many successful country music careers that it came to be called the "Cradle of the Stars."

Known for its experimental attitude and its openness to artists who stretched the boundaries of country music, the Hayride introduced to the nation some of country music's most unique and influential voices: Hank Williams, Webb Pierce, Kitty Wells, Elvis Presley, George Jones, Johnny Cash, Jim Reeves, and Johnny Horton. A wide variety of artists appeared on the Hayride stage—from honky-tonkers to crooners to rockabillies—so that KWKH played a part in shaping or popularizing a number of styles, all within the context of a country music radio show. Among the variety of artists who appeared on the Hayride were musicians from south Louisiana who played pure Cajun songs or country songs that reflected the musician's Cajun roots.

A handful of highly-respected Cajun musicians graced the Louisiana Hayride stage from time to time. One of the most commercially successful of these south Louisiana musicians was Jimmy C. Newman, who first appeared on the Hayride in June 1954 and went on to spend forty-three years on the Grand Ole Opry. Born in 1927 on the prairies of Big Mamou, Louisiana, Newman began his professional music career in 1946, as singer in a band that played country and some Cajun music in clubs around Bunkie, Louisiana. With this band, led by fiddler Chuck Guillory, Newman made his first recordings in 1946, singing mostly Cajun songs in his native French patois.

Country songs influenced Newman from his early childhood, when he and his brother Walter listened to old phonograph records by the Carter Family and Jimmie Rodgers, and to the Grand Ole Opry on the radio on Saturday nights. By the late 1940s and early 1950s Newman started experimenting with a mainstream country sound. He acquired a songwriting contract from Acuff-Rose, which led to a deal with Dot Records. Newman's first major hit, "Cry, Cry, Darling'" in 1954 reached the top five on the country chart and led to an invitation to join the Louisiana Hayride. Newman's country hits continued, including "Daydreamin'," "Blue Darlin'," and "God Was So Good" in 1955, and "Seasons of My Heart" in 1956. Like so many Hayride artists before him, he left Shreveport to join the Grand Ole Opry in 1956, and continued to chart songs, the biggest of which, "A Fallen Star," crossed over to the pop chart as well.

During his two-year stint at the Hayride, most of Newman's repertoire was mainstream country; the one exception was the song "Diggy Diggy Lo," which was a Cajun melody given words in English. After switching from Dot to MGM Records in 1958, Newman began experimenting with blending Cajun and country styles. In 1961 and 1962, respectively, he recorded "Alligator Man" and "Bayou Talk," both country songs that recalled the singer's Cajun roots. In 1964, Newman recorded for Decca his first album of Cajun music in almost fifteen years, called "Folk Songs of the Bayou Country," which featured acoustic instruments only, and included Rufus Thibodeaux on fiddle and Shorty LeBlanc on accordion. Since that album, Newman has performed as an ambassador of Cajun musical culture in places like the Wembley Festival in London and the Smithsonian Festival in Washington DC. At the same time, Newman continued to excel as a performer of mainstream country, with hits like "DJ for a Day," "Artificial Rose," "Back Pocket Money," and "Louisiana Saturday Night."

In 1970, Newman recorded an album for the small label La Louisianne, which included the first song in Cajun French to become a gold record, "Lâche Pas La Patate" ("Don't drop the potato"). Largely ignored in most of the United States, this song was a hit in south Louisiana and French Canada, especially Quebec. In the late 1970s, Newman put together a band called Cajun Country that included his son Gary Newman, fiddler Rufus Thibodeaux, and accordionist Bessyl Duhon. His band still performs on the Grand Ole Opry today. And his repertoire has come full circle. With the exception of his biggest country hits, Newman's band performs "about 99 percent Cajun" these days.

Another Cajun musician who made waves throughout the world of country music was fiddler Doug Kershaw. Along with his brother Rusty, Doug Kershaw appeared on the Hayride from 1955-56. Together, the Kershaws created a frenetic blend of Cajun and rockabilly, which they carried to the Wheeling Jamboree in West Virginia in 1956 and to the Grand Ole Opry in 1957. The brothers then joined the Army for a couple of years, and returned in 1960 to record their biggest hit as a duo, "Louisiana Man." They recorded a few more hits together in the early 1960s, including a version of "Diggy Diggy Lo" and "Cajun Stripper." In 1964, they decided to split up their partnership.

Doug Kershaw emerged as a solo performer, beginning with an appearance on the television debut of the Johnny Cash Show in 1969. Throughout the 1970s, Kershaw, alternately known as "the Ra-

Fiddler Doug Kershaw, progenitor of the Cajun-country sound, and accordionist Iry LeJeune, champion of the post-World War II accordion revival, 1951.
Photo courtesy of Johnnie Allan.

gin' Cajun" and "the Cajun hippie," continued melding together Cajun music and rock 'n' roll through his fierce fiddle style—with the instrument cradled in his armpit—that delighted audiences as much as his velvet suits and wild stage antics.

Other Cajun musicians appeared on the Louisiana Hayride, each concentrating for the most part on mainstream country, but sometimes recalling their south Louisiana roots. These artists attest to the long-standing rapport between Cajun and country musical styles, both vital genres that easily adapt to one another. Singer Thibodeaux "Tibby" Edwards, for example, appeared on the Hayride from 1952 until 1958, when he joined the Army. Despite Edwards's Cajun ancestry, he most often performed honky-tonk music more reminiscent of Hank Williams or Lefty Frizzell. Yet, he demonstrated his flexibility while on the Hayride, recording in several styles during the 1950s-honky-tonk, rockabilly, and Cajun. Commercial success came with two rockabilly releases in 1955, "Flip, Flop, and Fly," and "Play It Cool, Man, Play It Cool." Edwards's Cajun release also sold well, "C'est Si Tout," which was co-written by Leon Tassin.

The late singer/guitarist Allison Theriot, better known as Al Terry, was raised near Kaplan, Louisiana, immersed in the country records of Jimmie Rodgers, the Carters, Riley Puckett, Jimmie Davis, Gene Autry, alongside the early jazz of Django Reinhart. Country music made the deepest impression on Terry, especially the smooth style of Western singers like Autry or the Sons of the Pioneers. Though never a Hayride cast member, Terry was a featured guest during the mid-1950s, performing in a crooning style reminiscent of Eddy Arnold. Terry's biggest hit was "Good Deal Lucille"—a song that reflected his Cajun roots in its mixture of French and English lyrics.

Oddly enough, the performer who probably did the most to introduce Cajun musical style to mainstream country music was not Cajun at all. Hank Williams gained his first major exposure on the Louisiana Hayride, and he had a deep affection for Cajun culture. Even before he rose to national prominence in 1949 with "Lovesick Blues," south Louisiana audiences loved his music, especially ribald songs like "Move It On Over." Jimmy C. Newman spoke with me about the appeal of Hank Williams to French Acadian audiences:

> With Cajun people, he hit. He was telling it the way it was, you know, and the Cajun people love that real sincere story in a song. "Jole Blon" proved that—"Jole Blon" was a heartbreak song. And a lot of other Cajun songs, songs I've done through the years.

When Williams released "Jambalaya (On The Bayou)" in 1952, it was immediately popular not only with Cajun audiences, but all over the country. The song was taken from the 1946 Cajun melody "Gran Texas" by Chuck Guillory (with whom Newman played). Williams then wrote lyrics with Moon Mulli-

Left to right: Herman Durbin, Jimmy C. Newman, Chuck Guillory, Pork Chop Roy, KSIG announcer, and Julius A. "Papa Cairo" Lamperez. *Courtesy of the Margie Lamperez Breaux Collection, Center for Louisiana Studies, University of Louisiana at Lafayette, accession number 4027.*

can. Like Terry's later hit, "Jambalaya" was a hodgepodge of French and English lyrics set to an Acadian groove, intended to evoke the spirit and aesthetic of Cajun music while remaining friendly to a mainstream country audience. The song became immensely popular and was eventually recorded successfully by artists as divergent as Fats Domino and John Fogerty.

Not only was one of Williams's best-known tunes derived from a Cajun song, but fellow KWKH-Louisiana Hayride star Kitty Wells, the "Queen of Country Music," is also popularly known for a song written by a Cajun. Crowley-based producer and songwriter J.D. Miller, who recorded Cajun artists like Newman, Kershaw, and Terry on his Feature Records, wrote "It Wasn't God Who Made Honky-Tonk Angels," which Wells popularized in 1952. That same year, Wells left Louisiana and the Hayride, as so many eventually did, for Tennessee and the Opry. Eminent Cajun-country artists came into their fame via the Louisiana Hayride, and other regionally popular performers appeared on the show, including south Louisianians Happy Fats (guitar) and Oran "Doc" Guidry (mandolin and fiddle), as well as fiddler Buddy Attaway, a Shreveport native who performed Cajun classics such as "Poor Hobo," and his own Cajun-style compositions such as "I'm Going Back to Cloutiersville." Even so, the songs "Jambalaya" and "It Wasn't God Who Made Honky-Tonk Angels" just may be the most far-reaching contributions of Cajun culture to mainstream country music by way of Shreveport's Hayride stage.

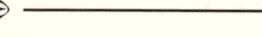

For more information see the following: Bill C. Malone, *Country Music, U.S.A.: A Fifty-Year History*, 2nd rev. ed. (Austin, 1985); Steven R. Tucker, "Louisiana Saturday Night: A History of Louisiana Country Music" (Ph.D. dissertation, Tulane University, 1995); Barry Jean Ancelet, *Cajun Music: Its Origins and Development* (Lafayette, LA, 1989); John Broven, *South to Louisiana: The Music of the Cajun Bayous* (Gretna, LA, 1987); Barry McCloud, *Definitive Country: The Ultimate Encyclopedia of Country Music and Its Performers* (New York, 1995); Colin Escott, *Hank Williams: The Biography* (Toronto, 1994, 1995); Douglas B. Green, "Jimmy C. Newman and his Cajun Country Roots," *Country Music* 7 (1979): 20, 66, 68. Information for the article was also drawn from a personal telephone interview with Jimmy C. Newman, July 27, 1999.

# J.D. Miller and Floyd Soileau: A Comparison of Two Small-Town Recordmen of Acadiana[1]

### Shane K. Bernard

The south Louisiana region known as Acadiana—a twenty-two parish area recognized by the state for its large Cajun population—is renowned for its ethnic musical tradition; Cajun, zydeco, and swamp pop originated in this region, which also fostered a number of great rhythm & blues musicians.[2] South Louisiana music has influenced, and continues to influence, American pop music (though it is actually more popular in Europe than in the United States). The credit for recording, preserving, and promoting south Louisiana music belongs to a handful of producers who have operated for almost a half-century between New Orleans and Houston, including several in smaller cities like Baton Rouge, Lafayette, Lake Charles, and Beaumont. But the most dynamic producers of Cajun, zydeco, swamp pop, and to a lesser extent, rhythm & blues music are the small-town producers who have operated their studios in, and promoted their labels from, the heart of the Acadiana region. Jake Graffagnino's short-lived, often overlooked studio and record labels (Carl, High-Up, and Jag) provided a springboard for several Opelousas area artists, including rhythm-and-blues/zydeco musician Rockin' Sidney and swamp pop musician Rod Bernard.[3] Lee Lavergne's obscure Lanor label had regional hits with Cajun musicians Shirley Bergeron ("J'ai Fait Mon Idée") and Bill Matte ("Parlez-Vous L'Francais") and swamp pop musician Charles Mann ("Keep Your Arms Around Me" and "Red Red Wine"). Lavergne even had a national hit with black swamp pop musician Elton Anderson ("Life Problem").[4] J.D. "Jay" Miller of Crowley and Floyd Soileau of Ville Platte, however, are the most successful by far of these small-town producers.

---

[1] This article first appeared in *Louisiana Folklife Journal* 15 (December 1991): 12-20.
[2] In discussions of south Louisiana music, Cajun is generally used to describe traditional, white French music played by descendants of the original Acadians who immigrated to Louisiana. Zydeco music is a hybrid form played with a heavy blues beat. This music first gained popularity in the Creole community on the southwest Louisiana prairies and is usually associated with Clifton Chenier, now deceased. Swamp pop describes French music heavily influenced somewhat by Elvis Presley and the rock & roll sound of the 1950s, but more so by the sounds and innovations of Fats Domino. (Editor's Note)
[3] Jake Graffagnino, interview by author, February 5, 1991, Opelousas, Louisiana, tape recording, Archives of Cajun and Creole Folklore, Center for Louisiana Studies, University of Louisiana at Lafayette (hereafter ACCF).
[4] Lee Lavergne, interview by author, January 30, 1991, Church Point, Louisiana, tape recording, ACCF, cited as Lavergne. "Life Problem" was written and originally recorded by south Louisiana rhythm-and-blues artist Bernard "King Karl" Jolivette, who also wrote and recorded the classic swamp pop hit "This Should Go On Forever."

Miller's studio has attracted such mainstream American artists as Paul Simon and John Fogerty, but it is best known for its Cajun and swamp pop releases and its recording of Louisiana blues artists for the Nashville-based Excello label. Soileau's Jin, Swallow, and Maison de Soul labels are the home of numerous Cajun, zydeco, and swamp pop artists, and his famous Floyd's Record Shop brings in visitors and mail-order business from around the world. These two business-wise producers were among the pioneers of the Louisiana recording industry and were instrumental in marketing and preserving south Louisiana's ethnic music tradition. Although they resided in towns several miles apart, a number of similarities can be identified through a comparison of these small-town producers.

Miller, born in Iota, Louisiana, in 1922, and Soileau, born in Grand Prairie, Louisiana, in 1938, were both interested in music as children and wanted to play and sing in Cajun and country music bands. Miller's parents were supportive: they bought an eight dollar guitar and a twenty-nine cent Gene Autry songbook from Sears-Roebuck for him.[5] As soon as the thirteen year old Miller had learned enough chords to perform in public, his parents entered him in a talent contest sponsored by the Dairyland Ice Cream Company of Lake Charles. (Oddly, the contest was held in Bat Gormley's Nightclub near Lake Charles, where the Miller family had relocated in 1933 after about a ten-year sojourn in El Campo, Texas.) Miller performed Huey P. Long's anthem, "Every Man A King." "I won," says Miller, "not because I was that good, but because the competition was so bad."[6] The prize was a fifteen-minute radio broadcast each Saturday morning at eleven o'clock. Miller strummed his guitar and sang cowboy tunes like "Red River Valley" and Strawberry Rum."

Miller notes that he also made five dollars per show, a sizable amount of money for a teenager at the time. He was inspired by this early success, and when his family settled in Crowley in 1937, Miller began to play professionally in local groups. He played his first dance with Joseph Falcon and his Silver Bell Band which was playing at the Cow Island nightclub that lacked an electrified sound system. Although the group was billed as a "string" band, Miller recalls that it featured the Breaux Brothers, traditional Cajun musicians. "I'd never seen an accordion before," admits Miller. "When [Amidie Breaux] pulled that thing out of the box, I didn't know what I'd gotten into!"[7] Miller went from one band to another over the next few years—the Four Aces, the Rice City Ramblers, the Daylight Creepers. However, he stopped playing the night before his marriage to Georgia Sonnier, daughter of accordionist Lee Sonnier (of Lee Sonnier and the Acadian Stars).[8]

---

[5] John Broven, *South to Louisiana: The Music of the Cajun Bayous* (Gretna, LA, 1983) 37.
[6] J.D. Miller, interview by author, February 21, 1991, Crowley Louisiana. tape recording, ACCF.
[7] Ibid.
[8] Broven, *South to Louisiana*, 36-38.

Soileau was not so fortunate with his wish to be a musician. Surprisingly, Soileau, who spoke only French until the age of six, when he entered school, came from a family of traditional Cajun musicians. "My dad played the fiddle," says Soileau, "and my grandfather—his father—played the fiddle, and his father before him played the fiddle. My brother...played the fiddle and accordion." Soileau appreciated Cajun and country music, however, and finally became professionally involved in music when he graduated from high school in 1956. At this time, he began to work as a part-time disc jockey at KVPI, a local pop-oriented radio station, which, operating at a mere 250 watts, stopped broadcasting at nightfall because of interference with stronger stations.[9]

> It was there that I really honed my interest in music and various forms of music. I was exposed to country and Cajun French before that time, then, at the radio station, rhythm and blues was just starting to make a big impact on the area and I got exposed to pop music. I remember the first time we got a sample of 'Sixteen Tons' by Tennessee Ernie Ford, and I said to my partner at the radio station.... I said, 'I don't know why Capitol would put a record like that out—that'll never sell.' So that's how much I knew about the record business back then. But I learned a lot about the music and got more interested in the music business working at that radio station.[10]

When the station manager suggested that Soileau find a second job, possibly in record sales, to supplement his income as a deejay, Soileau went to his parents, who approved the idea. With a loan of five hundred dollars, Soileau traveled to New Orleans, where he spent fifty dollars on a phonograph and three hundred dollars on records. He also rented a one-room office on the first floor of the old bank building in Ville Platte, just below KVPI's second-floor offices. As word began to spread about Soileau's new business, he became accustomed to running up and down the stairs between the station and his record shop, which had turned out to be a modest success. However, when Soileau, in his haste to return to the busy shop, mistakenly played a fifteen-minute Christmas program in the middle of summer, he was told by his manager to give up the business or quit the station. Soileau chose to keep his record shop, and as he noticed the local demand for Cajun records, which were always in short supply, he considered becoming a producer.[11]

Miller entered the record business for a similar reason. Traveling around the country with his father, he worked as an electrician at several defense plans. When war broke out in 1941, Miller, a pilot, was drafted into the navy as an aviator. His company had already received their uniforms when they were transferred into the army without explanation. Due to a recurring bout with malar-

---
[9] Ibid., 193.
[10] Floyd Soileau, interview by author, February 15, 1991, Ville Platte, Louisiana, tape recording, ACCF.
[11] Broven, *South to Louisiana*, 193.

ia, however, Miller never went overseas, but served at Forts Walter and Hood as a communications instructor in a tank destroyer unit.[12] When he returned from the Army, Miller and his father opened the M&S Electric Company at 218 North Parkerson Avenue in Crowley. They did extremely well wiring the local rice dryers and mills which were just beginning to convert to electricity. According to Miller, M&S had no local competitors with the amount of experience or expertise, so the income was steady and very good; but Miller did not like the work. In 1946, he decided to open a small record shop in a corner of the M&S building. "Had a building and didn't have much money to put stock in there," he says, "so I diversified a little bit."

Just as Soileau would discover ten years later in Ville Platte, Miller's customers wanted Cajun records, which were not as readily available as they had been years before. "Well, at that time, we had hardly anything," he explains. "Harry Choates had 'Jole Blond' and three and four others out.... So they kept wanting them and we could only order the same thing over and over, so I said, 'Heck with it, I'm gonna make some!'" Miller learned that the only recording studio in Louisiana belonged to producer Cosimo Matassa of New Orleans. Recording Happy Fats, Doc Guidry, and the Boys at Matassa's studio in June, 1946, Miller released the cuts on his own 78 rpm label, Fais Do-Do.[13]

The songs were a mixture of Cajun and country: "Colinda" and "Chere Cherie" were accompanied by songs like "My Sweetheart's My Buddy's Wife" and Miller's own "Don't Hang Around." They were followed by cuts like "Fais Do-Do Breakdown," "New Jolie Blond," "La Valse de Hadacol," and "Crowley Two-Step."[14] The response from Crowley consumers was positive, and by October of that year, Miller had opened his own studio, first located in his house and later in the M&S building. "I went to Gates' Electric [i.e., Gates' Radio Supply] in Houston and they had just received three Magnacorders...I think it was [Model] P-56, a little portable player, and that's what we started with."[15] Miller notes that these were some of the earliest tape recorders available to the public and that his studio was the first in the state to use the devices.

About a dozen Fais Do-Do 78s were released before Miller replaced this label with the new Feature label, which was also issued in a 78 rpm format.[16] A few of the artists recorded by Miller for Feature were Amidie Breaux, Jimmie Choates, Chuck Guillory, Austin Pete (Pitre), and Happy Doc, and the Boys. Miller's father-in-law, Lee Sonnier, and his Acadian Stars also recorded for Feature, yielding Miller's biggest success of the period, "The War Widow Waltz." Miller also released a number of country and hillbilly tunes on Feature, such as

---

[12] Miller interview.
[13] Broven, *South to Louisiana*, 38-39.
[14] Ibid., 39.
[15] Miller interview.
[16] Ibid.

Bill Hutto's "Some of These Days," Lou Millet's "That's Me Without You," and (female vocalist) Al Montgomery's "It Wasn't God Who Made Honky-Tonk Angels," which was written by Miller. The later two were respectively covered by Webb Pierce and Kitty Wells and both went to number one on the country charts, which "improved Jay Miller's status with the Nashville country music hierarchy...[and] led to a song writing contract with influential music publishers Acuff-Rose—and a firm friendship with co-owner Fred Rose."[17]

Like Miller, Soileau began with a short-lived Cajun-oriented label and then began to break out quickly with new labels that were directed toward wider audiences. Soileau's first label, Big Mamou, was formed in partnership with Ed Manuel, a Mamou, Louisiana, jukebox operator, nightclub owner, and regular customer of Floyd's Record Shop, who had the financial backing to assist the young entrepreneur. Manuel had also taped Cajun musicians Milton Molitor and Austin Pete at a party where they performed "Manuel Bar Waltz" and "Midway Two-Step." Although these songs were recorded merely to advertise a couple of Manuel's nightclubs, Soileau shipped the masters to Don Pierce's Starday Records in Nashville.[18] During his days at KVPI, Soileau had often run across promotional fliers from Starday, which read "If you've got a tape, we can press a record for you." The Big Mamou releases sold encouragingly and began to revive interest in Cajun music around Ville Platte. "We put our first record out and started selling it," says Soileau.

> And then when word got out that somebody in Ville Platte was releasing French records again.... I say again because most—in fact, I think everybody had stopped, they weren't selling enough French records.... Country music had come through and sorta swept around here and there was nobody interested in doing Cajun records anymore. I didn't know any better, people kept asking for Cajun records and they wanted to know if there was anything in a 45 available. So the jukeboxes were coming out; they were playing 45 rpm records. So we put that first record out. It sent the message that there was somebody releasing that kind of music again.[19]

Several local artists began to ask Soileau to release their work. Among these were Lawrence Walker and Aldus Roger. In fact, Walker offered to sell Soileau four taped songs; Soileau bought two for sixty dollars and optioned the others for forty. However, when he told his Mamou partner Ed Manuel the news, Manuel stated that he was no longer interested in the record business. Manuel offered to back Soileau with loans, but the record business, he said, would belong entirely to Soileau.[20]

---

[17] Broven, *South to Louisiana*, 61.
[18] Ibid., 193-94.
[19] Soileau interview.
[20] Ibid.

Floyd Soileau's Swallow label. Image courtesy of Cajun and Creole Music Collection, Edith Garland Dupré Library Special Collections, University of Louisiana at Lafayette.

Now on his own, Soileau changed Big Mamou to Vee-Pee (i.e., Ville Platte) label and founded two new labels, Jin, named after his wife Jinver, and Swallow, a play on the pronunciation of his name as well as on RCA's popular Bluebird label. "I knew damn well I couldn't put S-O-I-L-E-A-U on there," he says. "They wouldn't be able to pronounce it in most places out of here." Soileau's father, however, was not pleased with the spelling of the label's name. "When my dad saw that, he said [with a thick Cajun accent] 'What's the matter! You 'shame of your name?' I said 'It's not gonna fit.... Besides, that's the bird,... it's not necessarily my name.' And he had a hard time—I don't know if he ever bought that entirely."[21]

A few Cajun songs were released on Jin before Soileau decided to reserve the label entirely for pop music; on the other hand, he reserved the Swallow label for Cajun music. Soileau segregated the labels because he suspected that his pop releases were discriminated against by consumers and promoters who disliked Cajun music.

> At that time Cajun was not cool.... You had those who liked it and thought it was okay and you had those who thought it stunk and they wouldn't get within ten feet of it. So I started figuring out, I thought I maybe was having trouble getting anything on my label.... Maybe it was just crazy, but I decided maybe it might be a good idea to sorta split that, segregate that music and keep the English stuff on Jin, have the French stuff with the Swallow logo.[22]

In 1957, Floyd Soileau rented Miller's studio to record Roger's "The Cajun Special" and continued to use the Crowley studio (and Miller's skill as a producer) when he recorded the swamp pop group Doug Ardoin and Boogie Kings in 1958. Their song "Southland"[23] was closely followed by "This Should Go on Forever" by Rod Bernard and the Twisters. This recording reached number twenty on the *Billboard Hot 100* in March 1959, and became the first national hit released by Soileau. (The record was first put out on Jin and then leased to Leonard Chess' Argo label of Chicago, which could better distribute it nationally.) In 1959, Soileau recorded Jivin' Gene's "Breaking Up Is Hard To

---

[21] Ibid.
[22] Ibid.
[23] This song is mistakenly referred to in Broven's *South to Louisiana* as "Southland Blues;" it is in fact an extremely upbeat rockabilly tune.

Do" (leased to Mercury) and Johnnie Allan's "Lonely Days and Lonely Nights" (leased to MGM), both of which became swamp pop classics.[24]

Around this time, Soileau and Miller had a "falling out," and, as a result, Soileau set up his own studio equipped with a single-track Magnacoder unit in a small one-room building next to the old Platte Theater. The earliest notable song cut in this studio was Rockin' Sidney's "No Good Woman," which was followed by a few successful Cajun records by various artists. When Soileau's five-year lease expired, he moved his studio to a new building that also accommodated his record shop, music store, offices, and warehouse.[25] Although he had purchased an Ampex two-track unit for this studio, Soileau decided to use Matassa's studio in New Orleans to records Joe Barry's "I'm a Fool To Care," which, leased to the new Smash label, a division of Mercury, reached number twenty-four on the *Billboard Hot 100* in April 1961. He later recorded Tommy McLain's "Sweet Dreams," which climbed to number fifteen in June 1966.[26]

Expanding his business into electronics sales and wholesale distribution, Soileau lost interest in recording in the late 1960s and converted his studio into office and warehouse space. He opened another studio in the early seventies, however, which, in an unusual arrangement was connected to a men's private health club." "These guys would come in at all hours to sweat out a drunk or whatever," says Soileau. "But we had [the building] well insulated enough to where we didn't hear their racket and they didn't bother us at all." This studio shut down in 1975, and Soileau sold its contents to New Orleans jazz musician Ronnie Kole, who started his own small-town studio (The Studio) in Slidell, Louisiana, near New Orleans.[27]

In addition to the Big Mamou, Vee-Pee, Jin, and Swallow Labels, Soileau founded several other labels, including Fame, which was used exclusively for Rockin' Sidney's releases, but was discontinued to prevent confusion with the renowned Fame studio of Muscle Shoals, Alabama. Sidney and Cajun musicians Gene Rodrigue and Nathan Menard each recorded at least one 45 for the short-lived Rod label, which was named for swamp pop musician Rod Bernard. Soileau canceled this label because he was dissatisfied with the logo art work.[28] Another short-lived label was

Floyd Soileau's Jin label produced music such as this biracial recording featuring Rod Bernard and Clifton Chenier. Image courtesy of Cajun and Creole Music Collection, Edith Garland Dupré Library Special Collections, University of Louisiana at Lafayette.

---

[24] Broven, *South to Louisiana*, 195-96, 213-14.
[25] Soileau interview.
[26] Broven, *South to Louisiana*, 217-18, 335-36, 228.
[27] Soileau interview.
[28] Ibid.

MSL, representing a partnership between Soileau, Houston-based producer Huey Meaux, and Harold Lipsius of Philadelphia's Jamie records which handled the nationwide release of McLain's "Sweet Dreams" and an unsuccessful follow-up.[29] More successful labels, however, were Kom-a-day (a play on the pronunciation of the French word *comédie*), reserved for Cajun humorists like Dave Petitjean, and Maison de Soul, reserved for zydeco artists like Clifton Chenier and Rockin' Sidney.[30]

J.D. Miller also issued a number of labels. In addition to Fais Do-Do and Feature, he put out Rocko (originally Rocket), which was reserved for rock'n'roll, as well as Zynn (a name chosen by Miller to assure that it would fall last in the phone book) and Showtime, which featured a variety of artists and musical styles.[31] In the mid-1960s, Miller issued the Rebel label, which specialized in anti-desegregation and anti-Lyndon B. Johnson political humor.[32] He also issued the Kajun, Cajun Classics, and Blues Unlimited labels, as well as several short-lived labels (such as the Swade label).[33] Besides recording several Louisiana bluesmen (Lazy Lester, Lightnin' Slim, and Slim Harpo) for the Excello label of Nashville, Miller also recorded Warren Storm's "Prisoner's Song," which, released on Nasco, Excello's sister label, reached number eighty-one on the *Billboard Hot 100* in August 1958.[34]

Soileau, on the other hand, never opened another studio although he admits that he has "itchy fingers" for yet another one. "I'd like it as my hobby, just to work on my own projects, experiment with some group that's coming around, maybe have a song idea or something they'd like to piddle around with." Occasionally, he still produces an album using local studios like Carol Rachou's La Louisianne Studio of Lafayette. Encouraged by such musicians as the Balfa Brothers and Clifton Chenier, Soileau attempts to salvage and preserve traditional Cajun, zydeco, and swamp pop music. Soileau recently purchased tapes of Rockin'

Jay Miller's Feature label showcased such artists as Amidie Breaux singing "Jole Blon."
*Image courtesy of Cajun and Creole Music Collection, Edith Garland Dupré Library Special Collections, University of Louisiana at Lafayette.*

---

[29] Ibid., Broven, *South to Louisiana*, 228-31.
[30] Soileau, interview, ACCF.
[31] Miller interview.
[32] Broven, *South to Louisiana*, 43, 252-53.
[33] Miller interview.
[34] Ibid., 337.

Sidney's misplaced Fame releases from a European record collector.[35] He also salvaged three Boogie King albums originally released on S.J. Montalbano's Montel label of Baton Rouge. According to Soileau, Montalbano had completely misplaced the Boogie King masters. "I had to salvage the sound and those album jackets from several collectors," he says.

> One collector had a jacket that was in mint condition on the front but the back was bad, so I had to borrow a jacket from another person to get the back photographed. The records, one collector might have had a pretty good record except the last two cuts had a big scratch on it, on one side. So we'd get another record and pick up the next two cuts. And we salvaged those three albums from record collectors in the best shape we could get them in. Other than that, there would be none of that Boogie King stuff out right now.[36]

Soileau points out that he does not own the salvaged Boogie King albums but that he merely leases the distribution rights from Montalbano. Soileau has also leased music from other south Louisiana labels, such as George Khoury's Lyric and Khoury labels. These acquisitions, however, excluded titles assigned to other labels already, such as Phil Phillips' swamp pop classic, "Sea of Love," which is leased by Mercury (currently a division of Polygram). Soileau did manage to lease the rights to Cookie and the Cupcakes' "Mathilda," recorded by Khoury in 1958; many fans and artists still consider this song the undisputed anthem of swamp pop. Soileau is also slowly transferring his musical catalog to compact disc (CD) to help ensure preservation of south Louisiana music.[37]

Miller is also releasing music on CD. "Zydecajun" musician Wayne Toups, managed and produced by Miller and his son Mark, enjoys impressive CD sales. Miller has also invested a small fortune in his present studio, possibly the most technologically advanced in Louisiana. Established in 1967 at a cost of 300,000 dollars, the Master-Trak Studio of Crowley has been upgraded several times and currently possesses twenty-four-track analogue and digital capabilities. Miller also stores his masters on digital

J.D. Miller's Kajun label produced Wayne Toups' "Zydecajun" sound as well as classics like Nathan Abshire singing the "Mardi Gras Song." Image courtesy of *Cajun and Creole Music Collection, Edith Garland Dupré Library Special Collections, University of Louisiana at Lafayette.*

---
[35] Soileau interview.
[36] Ibid.
[37] Ibid. Soileau's most recent and perhaps most ambitious CD release is the two-volume swamp pop anthology, *Swamp Gold*, which contains thirty-two songs by various south Louisiana artists.

audio tape (DAT) cassettes.[38] Despite the technological advances in production, Miller misses the days when four microphones, a two-track recorder, and an echo room were sufficient to produce a best-selling record. In fact, he openly scoffs at the gadgets and techniques used by today's producers, even those used by his son who now operates the Master-Trak studio. Miller explains: "The norm way back there even in Nashville or anywhere you went...you were shooting for at least four songs in a three-hour session. Now maybe they work for a couple days on one song to get it down.... You may get a better product, but you take a lot of the purity out of it, believe me.... Hell, they've got eleven mics on the damn drum over there...to me that's the most ridiculous thing."

Today, J.D. Miller owns the rights to an impressive repertoire of music produced in his studio over the last forty-five years. Much of this music has been leased to the Flyright label of England.[39] During the day and late into the night, musicians record in his state-of-the-art Master-Trak studio, adding to his enormous library of masters, which, stored on the DAT cassettes, occupy a fraction of the spaced used by old masters. Indeed, Miller appears to find a degree of amusement in the present state of his archaic reel-to-reel library consisting of thousands of tapes stored on the floor. (Miller, however, is currently reorganizing the entire reel-to-reel library, which he has moved to a newly renovated storeroom on the second floor of his studio.) Miller also owns the Jamil and Whitewing music publishing companies. He named Whitewing for legendary steel guitarist Pee Wee Whitewing.[40] Miller also operated the Modern Music Record Shop and Music Store, which adjoins his studio on North Parkerson Avenue in Crowley.[41]

Soileau, on the other hand, continues to thrive mainly on the reissue of Jin, Swallow, and Maison de Soul records; these form the core of the extensive stock of records marketed through the storefront and mail-order facilities of Floyd's

Floyd Soileau's Maison de Soul label recorded zydeco greats such as Clifton Chenier.
*Image courtesy of Cajun and Creole Music Collection, Edith Garland Dupré Library Special Collections, University of Louisiana at Lafayette.*

---

[38] Miller interview.
[39] Ibid. The Rhino label recently issued eighteen Miller-produced songs on its CD anthology, *South of the Swamp: The Best of Excello Records, Volume One*. Rhino has also released a single track produced by Miller on its CD entitled *Hellooo Baby! The Best of the Big Bopper, 1954-1959*; this previously unreleased production–the ad-libbed "Bopper's Boogie Woogie"–is the earliest known recording of J.P. Richardson as the legendary Big Bopper.
[40] Ibid. Miller wrote numerous songs for his blues artists; however, these were published by Miller under the pseudonym "Jay West" because many black deejays refused to play anything written by a white songwriter.
[41] Ibid.

Record Shop. His record pressing plant, print shop, publishing, and distribution companies work to spread his musical products world-wide. Soileau's various labels and companies, now organized under the corporate umbrella of the Flat Town Music Company,[42] will, like Miller's, no doubt continue to prosper as long as the demand exists for south Louisiana music.

The comparison of recordmen J.D. Miller of Crowley and Floyd Soileau of Ville Platte reveals a number of similarities; indeed, their careers seem to have followed almost the same pattern. Both chose to remain in the small Louisiana towns near which they were born. Both wanted to play Cajun or country music as children and finally entered the music business because of their love for music. They both began by selling records and soon after established their own labels in response to a local demand for recorded Cajun music. They opened recording studios in their hometown, and they operated these studios in conjunction with record and music stores and other music-oriented businesses. Then branching out into other forms of south Louisiana music, Soileau and Miller began to establish new labels to promote zydeco, blues, and swamp pop music.

A few obvious differences, however, do separate the two small-town producers. Miller has focused more on production, while Soileau on marketing his diverse music-oriented products. In addition, Miller is best known for his recording of blues musicians for the Excello label of Nashville; Soileau, on the other hand, is noted for his recording of Cajun, zydeco, and swamp pop musicians for his own labels.

These minor differences aside, Miller and Soileau are both extremely successful small-town businessmen with almost legendary reputations for the distinctive sound of their recordings. In fact, they have each received numerous awards and citations in recognition of their over seventy-five years of combined experience in the field. Miller has both a gold record and a platinum record for his contributions to Paul Simon's acclaimed *Graceland* album. He has also received nine BMI awards (presented by Broadcast Music, Incorporated, a professional song writers' organization). Soileau has received one BMI award, but in 1985 three of his artists, Rockin' Sidney, Cajun fiddler Dewey Balfa, and the Cajun

J.D. Miller's Excello label recorded blues musicians such as Slim Harpo. Image courtesy of *Cajun and Creole Music Collection, Edith Garland Dupré Library Special Collections, University of Louisiana at Lafayette.*

---

[42] Soileau interview.

group Beausoleil, were nominated for Grammy awards. Unfortunately these nominations were confined to the same category (Best Ethnic or Traditional Folk Recording), so, at most, only one of his artists could walk away with an award. (Sidney won for his zydeco hit, "My Toot Toot").[43] While these two small-town producers are certainly interested in profit, they have also exhibited a concern for the preservation of south Louisiana' ethnic musical tradition. Without their efforts, this music might not have been heard beyond the nightclubs and dancehalls of the Acadiana region.

---

[43] Ibid. Soileau can also boast of leasing the Sundown Playboys' "Saturday Night Special" to the Beatles' Apple label in 1972; he still proudly bears the contract signed by George Harrison and himself.

# Twistin' at the Fais Do-do: The Roots of South Louisiana's Swamp Pop Music[1]

## Shane K. Bernard

Swamp pop music is a rhythm and blues idiom that combines elements of New Orleans rhythm and blues, country and western, and Cajun and black Creole music. Highly emotional, colorful lyrics, tripleting honky-tonk pianos, bellowing horn sections, and a strong rhythm and blues backbeat typify the genre's sound. Swamp pop standards include such national hits as Bobby Charles's "Later Alligator," Dale and Grace's "I'm Leaving It Up to You," Freddy Fender's "Wasted Days and Wasted Nights," Phil Phillips's "Sea of Love;" and Jimmy Clanton's "Just a Dream." In south Louisiana, however—the birthplace of swamp pop—numerous songs less popular nationally are embraced as even more essential to the basic swamp pop repertoire. These include such regional hits as Cookie and the Cupcakes'"Mathilda," Tommy McLain's "Sweet Dreams," Randy and the Rockets'"Let's Do the Cajun Twist;" Clint West's "Big Blue Diamonds;" Rufus Jagneaux's "Opelousas Sostan;" and Johnnie Allan's "South To Louisiana."[2]

### What is Swamp Pop?

Swamp pop music hails almost exclusively from Acadiana, a twenty-two parish region of south Louisiana recognized for its large Cajun and rural black Creole population; however, swamp pop also originates in the Beaumont-Port Arthur area of southeast Texas, where Cajuns and black Creoles migrated in sizable numbers around World War II. Often misunderstood and even ignored by many enthusiasts of south Louisiana's music, swamp pop deserves recognition and preservation as the region's third major indigenous genre (along with Cajun and zydeco music)—not only because it once thrived in the region and even attracted a national audience, but

Swamp poppers Dale Houston and Grace Broussard garnered national attention. with their number one hit "I'm Leaving it Up to You."
Photo courtesy of Johnnie Allan.

---
[1] First published in *Southern Cultures* 2 (1996): 314-28.
[2] The term "south Louisiana" denotes the Cajun and rural black Creole region of the state—i.e., the twenty-two parish Acadiana region, which excludes the major metropolitan areas of Baton Rouge and New Orleans.

because it descends from traditional Cajun and black Creole sources through a blending process similar to that which produced rock, blues, and jazz music.

Swamp pop goes by many alternate titles: swamp rock, Cajun rock, Cajun pop, bayou rock 'n' roll, bayou boogie, even the Gulf Coast sound. The terms "south Louisiana music" and "south Louisiana rock 'n' roll," however, appear more frequently, as does the more generic "swamp music." But among fans and artists the most popular moniker by far is "swamp pop music" or simply "swamp pop." Surprisingly, the term "swamp pop" originated not in south Louisiana nor even in the United States, but in England, where young music enthusiasts stumbled on the imported sound shortly after its American inception. Englishman John Broven often is cited as the term's inventor; however, he attributes the term to his compatriot, music writer Bill Millar, who states he probably coined "swamp pop" in the late 1960s. Millar recalls using the term informally until it first appeared in 1971 in his ground-breaking article "Swamp Pop-Music [sic] from Cajun Country."[3]

Despite widespread usage of the term "swamp pop," the question remains: just what is it? Music writers often cite two competing views, the most popular of which derives from New Orleans rhythm and blues artist Mac Rebennack, better known as "Dr. John." This view holds that swamp pop consists only of slow ballads with E-flat, B-flat progressions. A glance at the original source, however—the liner notes of Rebennack's 1972 *Gumbo* album—reveals that the performer makes no reference to swamp pop nor attempts to define any musical genre. Rather, he merely describes one of the album's tracks, a re-recording of a New Orleans rhythm and blues ballad, as "a classic south Louisiana two-chord [E-flat, B-flat] slow ballad"—a far cry from declaring all swamp pop songs slow ballads. Based on misquoted data, this alleged definition of swamp pop must be dismissed as groundless. A second, more obscure view, however, issues from acclaimed swamp pop saxman Harry Simoneaux. His clever, highly quotable definition—"half Domino and half fais do-do"—correctly implies the important influence of New Orleans rhythm and blues (Fats Domino) and traditional Cajun music (*fais do-do*, the name for a communal Cajun dance) on swamp pop's de-

Swamp pop pioneer Rod Bernard.
Photo courtesy of Shane K. Bernard.

---

[3] Bill Millar, "Johnnie Allan: A Swamp-Pop Special," *New Kommotion* (Summer 1978), 15; Interview with Bill Millar, February 24, 1992; Millar, "Swamp Pop-Music from Cajun Country," *Record Mirror*, June 12, 1971, n.p.; John Broven, *South to Louisiana: The Music of the Cajun Bayous* (Gretna, LA, 1983), xi, 179; Kurt Loder, "Sound of the Swamp," *Esquire*, November 1991, 64.

velopment. Inevitably, his witticism neglects several other vital influences, such as country and western and black Creole music.[4]

The definition of swamp pop actually hinges on the question of which cultural forces created and influenced the genre and inevitably concerns the ballad/rocker controversy: that is, does swamp pop consist only of slow, usually melancholy ballads like T.K. Hulin's "Graduation Night," Rod Bernard's "This Should Go on Forever;" and Bobby Page and the Riff Raffs' "Loneliness," or does it also include more upbeat rockers like Johnnie Allan's "Promised Land;" Gene Terry and the Downbeats' "Cindy Lou;" and Lil' Bob and the Lollipops' "I Got Loaded?" Music writers tend to fall into one of two camps, supporting either a narrow or broad interpretation of swamp pop.

Weighing the merits and shortcomings of these diverse, sometimes irreconcilable views on swamp pop music, I suggest a different definition of swamp pop (albeit a working definition merely for the purposes of this study): a rhythm-and-blues hybrid, influenced mainly by New Orleans rhythm and blues, country and western, and Cajun and black Creole music indigenous to southeast Texas and the Acadiana region of south Louisiana. This definition embraces the broad interpretation of swamp pop and recognizes the obvious influences of New Orleans rhythm-and-blues and country-and-western music; it also acknowledges the often subtle yet nonetheless vital role of Cajun and black Creole music.

## *The Origin and Development of Swamp Pop Music*

In *Memories: A Pictorial History of South Louisiana Music*, swamp pop artist-turned-researcher Johnnie Allan compiled vital statistics for hundreds of south Louisiana performers, including swamp pop musicians. Allan's data reveal that 87 percent of swamp pop artists hail from south Louisiana and southeast Texas, regions that have embraced swamp pop since its inception. His data also indicate that 78 percent of swamp pop artists hail from Acadiana and that of these, 73 percent were born in a central seven-parish area consisting of Acadia, Evangeline, Iberia, Lafayette, St. Landry, St. Martin, and Vermilion parishes. Notably, this central region (largely composing the "Cajun Heartland" district) also produced 82 percent of traditional Cajun and black Creole musicians, of whom 42 percent were born in a northern prairie area roughly bounded by the towns of Church Point, Sunset, Opelousas, Ville Platte, Mamou, and Eunice—the same region that appears to have given rise to swamp pop music.[5]

---

[4] Dr. John, liner notes, *Dr. John's Gumbo*, Atco 1972; Larry Benicewicz, "Rod Bernard and Swamp Pop," *Newsletter of the Baltimore Blues Society* (February 1992), 2; Broven, *South to Louisiana*, 180; Millar, "Rockin' on the Bayou;" 51; Interview with Harry Simoneaux, May 3, 1992.

[5] Johnnie Allan, comp. and ed., *Memories: A Pictorial History of South Louisiana Music, 1920s-1980s*, vol. 1, *South Louisiana and East Texas Musicians* (Lafayette, 1988), 2-7, 84, 89, 102-3, 160-61, 202, 207, 232; Barry Jean Ancelet and Elemore Morgan, Jr., *Makers of Cajun Music/Musiciens cadiens et créoles* (Austin, 1984), 21; Interview with Carl A. Brasseaux, July 13, 1992; Alan Lomax, prod. and dir., *Cajun Country: Don't Drop*

Conditions that directly precipitated the birth of swamp pop first appeared during the 1920s and 1930s, when south Louisiana's Cajuns and black Creoles experienced a period of rapid Americanization. Responding to the influence of more mainstream African American music, for instance, black Creole accordionists adopted a "blusier" sound. Cajun musicians, on the other hand, emulated Anglo-American string-band music, reinstating the fiddle as lead instrument and advancing the role of the guitar—at the expense of the accordion. Cajuns also added the steel guitar, upright bass, drums, and, on occasion, even banjos and mandolins. By the early 1950s, however, the accordion again dominated Cajun music, resurrected by the popularity of accordionists like Iry LeJeune and by World War II and Korean War veterans seeking comfort in "old-time" music.[6]

Ironically, the accordion's return coincided with the advent of an increasingly popular national genre—rhythm and blues. Although the accordion—particularly the double-row, triple-row, and piano-key accordions favored by black Creole accordionists—could accommodate the rhythm and blues sound (as demonstrated by zydeco pioneer Clifton Chenier), teenage Cajuns and black Creoles took up the piano, sax, and electric guitar, instruments closely associated with the alluring music from seemingly distant places like Memphis and especially New Orleans. Experimenting with the new instrumentations, rhythms, melodies, and vocal arrangements of the rhythm-and-blues sound, they combined these elements with more familiar influences to create a fusion of rhythm and blues, country and western, and Cajun and black Creole music. Lacking a better term, they called it south Louisiana music, the genre now known as swamp pop.[7]

Some music writers and artists have downplayed the accordion's influence on swamp pop, claiming the limited range of the single-row diatonic accordion precluded any impact on the genre. This view begs reconsideration not only because it overlooks the popularity of the more versatile, multi-row diatonic and piano-key accordions favored by black Creole artists, but because it ignores the music of Cajun musicians like Belton Richard and Blackie Forestier, who have successfully captured the "triplety" swamp pop ballad sound on the single-row diatonic accordion. In addition, Cajun groups have covered swamp pop tunes like Johnnie Allan's "Your Picture" and Cookie and the Cupcakes' "Mathilda!" So accordions *can* accommodate the swamp pop sound—and swamp pop can draw in turn on accordion music. Music writer Kurt Loder thus correctly de-

---

the Potato, American Patchwork: Songs and Stories about America, (1990), videocassette; Lauren C. Post, *Cajun Sketches: From the Prairies of Southwest Louisiana* (Baton Rouge, 1990), 159.

[6] Barry Jean Ancelet, *Cajun Music: Its Origins and Development* (Lafayette, 1989), 26-31; Ann Allen Savoy, comp. and ed., *Cajun Music: A Reflection of a People*, 3rd ed. (Eunice, 1988), 14.

[7] Ancelet, *Origins and Development*, 31-36; Broven, *South to Louisiana*, 79; Savoy, *Reflection of a People*, 14.

The premier swamp pop ensemble, the Boogie Kings.
*Photo courtesy of Ryan A. Brasseaux.*

scribes swamp pop as "black rhythm and blues rendered with dense textures of accordion-based Cajun country music (but—the genius part—*without the accordions*)!" (Emphasis added.)[8]

Those who minimize the influence of Cajun and black Creole music on swamp pop also ignore the more important fact that swamp pop draws not so heavily on accordion music as on Cajun string-band music. Allan's biographical data reveal that the median year of birth for swamp poppers is 1939, which falls squarely in the string-band era (ca. 1935-50). Most swamp pop artists were born to parents who courted during the height of the string-band era and who after marriage probably continued to appreciate, purchase, and perhaps even perform Cajun string-band music, a sound future swamp pop artists naturally absorbed growing up in their parents' homes. In fact, many swamp pop artists performed in Cajun string bands during the late 1940s and early to mid-1950s, and although a few did perform with accordion groups, they almost exclusively wielded instruments brought to Cajun music during the string-band era.[9]

---

[8] Broven, *South to Louisiana*, 237, 289; Loder, "Sound of the Swamp," 64.
[9] Allan, *Memories*, 160-61, 202, 207, 232; Ancelet, *Origins and Development*, 28-32; Interview with Barry Jean Ancelet, October 29, 1992; Savoy, *Reflection of a People*, 14; Broven, *South to Louisiana*, 197, 214, 218-19, 231, 246-47.

Although the precise time and place of swamp pop's birth no doubt will remain a mystery, evidence suggests an early 1950s origin in the northern prairie region of Acadiana, a region that occupies a cultural crossroads where heavy interaction (musical and otherwise) occurred between Cajuns and black Creoles. An important clue concerning swamp pop's origin on the northern prairie issues unexpectedly from New Orleans rhythm-and-blues musician Earl King, whose "Those Lonely Lonely Nights:" recorded in 1955, is often cited as a proto-swamp pop song and even is mistakenly viewed by some as the first swamp pop recording. King states that his inspiration for "Those Lonely Lonely Nights" came from the northern prairie: "I was beginning to formulate a different style [after early 1954]…I had been around Eunice and Opelousas and I began to get a feel for that ballad sound that those people liked to hear. If you listen closely to 'Lonely Lonely Nights,' you can hear that turn around right after the break. I wanted that to be my trademark and put it on all my records. I wanted people to associate that with me."[10]

In addition to suggesting the northern prairie region as the birthplace of swamp pop, King narrows the time of the genre's birth to 1954 or 1955 at the latest. He also implies that swamp pop exerted a small but detectable influence on New Orleans rhythm and blues (which, of course, exerted a *major* influence on swamp pop). Strangely, in the mid-1950s Opelousas and Eunice boasted populations of roughly 15,000 and 10,000 respectively, in contrast with greater New Orleans' 598,000. Again, the musical importance of this small rural area springs from its locale, which promoted ethnic interaction among local musicians and in turn created a demand for innovative music, attracting rhythm-and-blues artists from New Orleans to its numerous—perhaps at the time even legendary—live-music nightclubs.[11]

Although a bi-racial genre, swamp pop appears to have been invented on the northern prairie by young black Creole rhythm-and-blues musicians. Allan's work supports this hypothesis: while the median year of birth for Cajun swamp pop artists is 1940, the median year for black Creole swamp poppers is 1936. Black Creole swamp pop musicians thus matured earlier than their Cajun counterparts, a four-year gap widened by the tendency of black Creole swamp poppers to begin performing in nightclubs at younger ages than Cajun swamp poppers. Black Creole swamp pop artists like Guitar Gable and the Musical Kings featuring King Karl, the Boogie Ramblers (later Cookie and the Cupcakes), Guitar Jr., Elton Anderson, and Lil' Bob and the Lollipops are

---

[10] Ancelet and Morgan, Jr., *Makers of Cajun Music*, 21; Interview with Brasseaux; Lomax, *Don't Drop the Potato*, videocassette; Post, *Cajun Sketches*, 159; Benicewicz, "Rod Bernard and Swamp Pop," 2; John Broven, *Rhythm and Blues in New Orleans* [*Walking to New Orleans: The Story or New Orleans Rhythm and Blues*] (Gretna, 1988), 118; Bill Millar, "Rockin' on the Bayou," *Melody Maker*, February 17, 1979, 51; Jeff Hannusch [Almost Slim], *I Hear You Knockin': The Sound of New Orleans Rhythm and Blues* (Swallow, 1989), 190, 197.

[11] Milburn Calhoun, ed., *Louisiana Almanac, 1988-89* (Gretna, LA, 1988), 138, 142.

known to have performed in Cajun and black Creole clubs in the northern prairie region during the early to mid-1950s.[12]

Although today few south Louisiana and southeast Texas nightclubs sponsor live swamp pop music, the scene thrived in the late 1950s and early 1960s. Most of these nightclubs, however, were Cajun swamp pop clubs in which appeared both black Creole and Cajun swamp pop groups. Lafayette, for instance, boasted Landry's Palladium, the Roof Garden, Whit's Lounge, and the Bayou Club; Lake Charles, the Bamboo Club and the Golden Rocket; Lawtell, the Step Inn and the Green Lantern; and Opelousas, Raphael's Inn, the Moonlight Inn, and the Southern Club. Many were rough-and-tumble clubs, often exposing even the performers to violence. Still, a few rarely saw violence—in fact, some operated as respectable dinner clubs.

Swamp pop quickly spread from nightspots like these to recording studios, and although a few swamp poppers conducted early sessions in New Orleans (at studios like Cosimo Matassa's), most utilized local Acadiana and east Texas studios. The earliest of these were operated by Eddie Shuler of Lake Charles and J.D. Miller of Crowley. Shuler yielded swamp pop hits not only for his Goldband label but also for George Khoury's local Lyric and Khoury labels. He produced such well-known swamp pop recordings as Gene Terry's "Cindy Lou," Guitar Jr.'s "Family Rules," and Phil Phillips's "Sea of Love." Similarly, Miller directed sessions for Dago Redlich's Viking label of Crowley, Lee Lavergne's Lanor label of Church Point, and Floyd Soileau's Jin label of Ville Platte, as well as for his own labels, including Zynn, Rocko, and Showtime. He also licensed swamp pop songs to Ernie Young's Nashville-based Excello and Nasco labels, which issued his many swamp blues recordings during the late 1950s and early 1960s. Miller oversaw sessions yielding classics like Rod Bernard's "This Should Go on Forever," Warren Storm's "Prisoner's Song," and King Karl and Guitar Gable's "Irene," "Life Problem," and "Congo Mombo."[13]

Southern Club in Opelousas hosted many swamp pop performers.
*Photo courtesy of Paul Harris Photography.*

---

[12] Allan, *Memories*, 160-61, 202, 207, 232; Interview with Lil' Bob, July 9, 1991; Benicewicz, "Rod Bernard and Swamp Pop," 2; Interview with Guitar Gable, November 1, 1991; Interview with King Karl, December 11, 1991; Interview with Little Alfred, September 8, 1991; Interview with Lionel "Chick" Vidrine, February 5, 1991.

[13] Interview with Eddie Shuler, September 25, 1991; Interview with George Khoury, September 25, 1991;

Subsequent swamp pop producers emulated recording techniques pioneered by Shuler and Miller. By 1958 renowned south Louisiana producer Floyd Soileau was recording swamp pop artists for his successful Jin label. Other producers—including Carol Rachou, Bill Hall, Lee Martin, Stan Lewis, Roland "Rocky" Robin, Jake Graffagnino, Myra Smith, Huey Meaux, and S.J. "Sam Montel" Montalbano—were also busily recording swamp pop music. These producers turned to deejays like south Louisiana's Buddy King, J.P. "The Big Bopper" Richardson of Beaumont, and Jack the Cat of New Orleans to promote swamp pop over the airwaves. The combination of these artistic, technical, and promotional entities converted swamp pop from a rough-hewn, fledgling genre performed by Cajun and black Creole teenagers in rural and small-town nightclubs into a commercially viable sound that captured fans worldwide. Swamp pop has always maintained its rough edge, however, a quality that Johnnie Allan attributes to the influence of Cajun music, but which may be equally attributable to the influence of black Creole music.[14]

Popular swamp pop crooner Warren Storm.
Photo courtesy of Al Harris.

### The Uncertain Future of Swamp Pop

Today the genre remains largely a regional phenomenon. To experience live swamp pop music usually requires a visit to its natural habitat—the smoky nightclubs of south Louisiana and southeast Texas, where swamp poppers still gather to play old favorites for devotees. Some swamp poppers have ventured overseas, however, to perform at international folk and blues festivals. And in recent years numerous overseas record companies have secured distribution rights to swamp pop recordings. Major American compact disc labels, on the other hand, have tended to ignore swamp pop while promoting Cajun and zydeco music (although small south Louisiana labels like Jin and Goldband are now issuing swamp pop compilations on compact disc). And the American folk and music festival scene continues to neglect swamp pop, excluding it from their venues while actively promoting Cajun and zydeco music.[15]

---

Interview with J.D. Miller, February 21, 1991; Broven, *South to Louisiana*, 36, 48, 189, 199, 270; Interview with Floyd Soileau, February 15, 1991.

[14] Interview with Shuler; Interview with Miller; Broven, *South to Louisiana*, 78, 154, 158, 189, 199, 201, 246-48; Broven, *Rhythm and Blues in New Orleans*, 104-5.

[15] Interview with Johnnie Allan, June 12, 1991; Allan, "South Louisiana—The Promised Land: Johnnie Allan," interview by Paul Harris, part 2 (England, 1986), *Now Dig This*, April 1987, 10-11; Allan, "South Louisiana—The Promised Land: Johnnie Allan," interview by Paul Harris, part 3, (England, 1986), *Now Dig*

Despite such unfavorable treatment, swamp pop preservationists have achieved moderate success in recent years thanks largely to the popularity of Broven's *South to Louisiana* and the activism of swamp pop artists like Johnnie Allan. Nevertheless, many enthusiasts striving to preserve Cajun and zydeco music may be condemning a third major indigenous south Louisiana genre to extinction. Cajun music has its Roddie Romeros and zydeco its Geno Delafoses, but swamp pop—still rarely featured outside south Louisiana and southeast Texas nightclubs—today boasts few performers under the age of fifty. "I'm just a little afraid," confides Rod Bernard, "that these beautiful songs might all die with us."[16]

Bernard's fear is not unfounded—swamp poppers are appearing in public much less frequently, in part because festival organizers, who could provide comfortable venues for these middle-aged performers, overlook their contributions. Authors, filmmakers, and photographers also ignore the genre, usually examining zydeco and Cajun music without reference to swamp pop. Perhaps they reason that these types of music are traditional genres and swamp pop is not. But how accurate is this assessment? Cajun music continues to evolve, and as folklorist Barry Jean Ancelet states, "Purists who would resist new instrumentation, styles and compositions neglect to consider that change and innovation have always been an integral part of Cajun music." As for zydeco, it appeared only when pioneers of the genre like Clifton Chenier and Boozoo Chavis mixed traditional black Creole music with rhythm-and-blues elements. Zydeco's appearance could not have preceded the rise of rhythm and blues between 1945 and 1950, only a few years prior to swamp pop's own advent around 1954. (In fact, although Clarence Garlow recorded the zydeco-ish "Bon Ton Roula" in 1950, Chenier and Chavis did not record until 1954, *only one year* before the Boogie Ramblers, Bobby Charles, and Roy Perkins yielded the first swamp pop recordings.) Today zydeco increasingly is performed not in the black Creole dialect, but in English, and often sounds much like mainstream soul or rhythm and blues merely fronted by an accordion.[17]

At best it can be argued that Cajun and zydeco are merely *more* traditional than swamp pop music. Yet that impression does not merit swamp pop's dismissal as a musical form unworthy of equal footing with its antecedents. Once it is regarded as a major indigenous genre of south Louisiana music descending in part from traditional Cajun and black Creole music—and once it is recognized as a positive expression of the entire Cajun and black Creole experience—swamp pop at last may receive the recognition it deserves, and perhaps

---

*This*, May 1987, 7-8; Broven, *South to Louisiana*, 215-16, 292.
[16] Rico [Rick Olivier], "Putting the Fizz in Swamp Pop," *Wavelength*, April 1984, 22.
[17] Ancelet, *Origins and Development*, 51; Ancelet, "Blues, Beans and Beyond," *Black Music Research Journal* 8 (1988): 48; Savoy, *Reflection of a People*, 305-6; Broven, *South to Louisiana*, 101-2, 104-5, 108-10, 185-86.

even benefit from preservation efforts similar to those that rescued Cajun and black Creole music from extinction.

## *Suggested Listening on Compact Disc*

Allan, Johnnie. Promised Land. CDCHD 380. Ace (UK), 1992.

Bernard, Rod. Swamp Rock 'n' Roller. CDCHD 488. Ace (UK), 1994.

Broussard, Van. The Early Years. CSP 1007-2. CSP Records, 1993.

Cookie and the Cupcakes. By Request. Compact disc 9037-2. Jin, 1993.

McLain, Tommy. Sweet Dreams. CDCH 285. Ace (UK), 1990.

Storm, Warren. Night After Night. Compact disc 90363-2. Jin, 1992.

Various Artists. Another Saturday Night. CDCH 288. Ace (UK), 1990.

--Eddie's House of Hits: The Story of Goldband Records. CDCHD 424. Ace (UK), 1992.

--Lafayette Saturday Night. CDCHD 371. Ace (UK), 1992.

--Louisiana Saturday Night. CDCHD 490. Ace (UK), 1993.

--Louisiana Swamp Pop. FLY CD 21. Flyright (UK), 1990.

Swamp Gold, Vol. 1. CD-106. Jin, 1991.

Swamp Gold, Vol. 2. CD-107. Jin, 1991.

Swamp Gold, Vol 3. CD-108. Jin, 1994.

Swamp Gold, Vol. 4. CD-109. Jin, 1994.

# The Cajun Music Festival: Genesis And Legacy[1]

## Barry Jean Ancelet

The story begins during a critical transitional period in the mid-1970s, when a festival helped to proclaim what became known as the Louisiana French renaissance movement. The date was March 26, 1974. The occasion was the first Tribute to Cajun Music festival in Lafayette. More than twelve thousand people gathered to celebrate music that was widely dismissed, even by some Cajuns, as "nothing but chanky-chank." The moment proved to be a pivotal one in the effort to revitalize Louisiana's French culture and language. The event turned into a mass rally, but instead of politicians and ideologues, it was musicians who took the stage to express a subtle but powerful message of cultural pride. Over the years we all have come to understand more about the phenomenon of that stormy night and what has happened since.

The idea of a festival honoring Cajun and Creole music was conceived in 1973. My own involvement in the project came as a result of a personal exile experience in France. Toward the end of what seemed to be an interminable academic year there, I was feeling out of place and I didn't understand why. I spoke the language fluently—although my French friends often interrupted our conversations to comment on how cute my accent and expressions were. I had studied French culture and civilization for four years in high school and three years in college, so I was familiar with the place and the people even before I arrived. Yet I was homesick. Something was missing and I didn't know what or why.

One afternoon while walking back from the marketplace in Nice, I saw a poster announcing "Roger Mason joue la musique de la Louisiane" (Roger Mason plays music from Louisiana). I was curious and decided to see what this was all about. The evening of the concert, I arrived just in time to hear the strains of "The Crowley Two-step" drift up from the basement where Mason was performing. The music washed over me like a warm tide. This was what was missing. Like the rest of my generation, I had grown up on rock and roll, but I had heard Cajun music on local television on Saturday afternoons when the choice was between that and golf, and on the record player during barbecues or crawfish boils when Daddy got to choose the records. It was something that we all heard, but rarely really listened to. That night, Cajun music was the most comforting sound I had heard in a year.

---

[1] Reprinted by permission of Louisiana State University Press from *Cajun Music and Zydeco* photographs by Philip Gould and with an introduction by Barry Jean Ancelet. Copyright © 1992 by Louisiana State University Press.

After the performance I headed backstage to tell Mason what his music had done for me. I learned that he was an American air force brat who spoke French fluently, having grown up in Europe. In no way a Cajun himself, he had encountered Cajun music through the American folk music revival movement and had fallen in love with it. Living now in Paris, he had discovered that the French enjoyed this profoundly American folk music with lyrics they could understand, and he was making a modest living playing it on the coffeehouse circuit throughout France. I told him I was from south Louisiana myself and that the evening had chased away my blues. "Oh, so you're from Cajun country," he said. "Then you must know all the great people I learned from: Dewey Balfa, Nathan Abshire..." I didn't know any of them, and it occurred to me that something was wrong. I knew about the châteaux along the Loire in France, but virtually nothing about the cultures along the Bayou Teche in my native state. I knew about French artists and authors and wines and cheeses from books, yet I had grown up and lived all my life in south Louisiana and didn't know anything about the Cajun musicians whom this American in Paris considered heroes. "If you want to know something about all this," Mason suggested with a grin, "talk to Dewey Balfa. He lives near Basile, Louisiana."

When I returned home a couple of months later, I immediately borrowed my father's pickup truck, drove to Basile, got directions to Dewey Balfa's house, and knocked on the door. When he answered I blurted out: "Mr. Balfa? My name is Barry Ancelet from Lafayette, and I need to know who you are." Dewey was obviously puzzled. When I told him about my evening with Roger Mason, he laughed and invited me in. He immediately accepted me as a sort of cultural godchild and began filling in the gaps in my formal education.

One of the first things Dewey suggested was that I start a collection project. He had worked with Ralph Rinzler (a folklorist with the Newport Folk Festival in the 1960s and the Smithsonian Institution since 1967) and had learned much about his own culture by considering the questions Rinzler asked. Several folklorists had made field recordings in south Louisiana, including John and Alan Lomax in the 1930s, Bill Owens in the 1940s, Harry Oster in the 1950s, and Rinzler in the 1960s, but no one had found a place to leave copies of any of these collections within the state. Dewey reasoned that we ought to develop our own information bank. When I protested that I didn't have that kind of money, he countered: "You have enough for one reel of tape? Buy it and record. When it's full, buy another one. When it's full, you'll have two, and that's the beginning of a collection." Embarrassed by the brutal simplicity of his logic, I went straightway to the electronics store. In January 1974, I began my "collection," recording stories and songs with Barbara Ryder, who was majoring in French at Colby College in Maine.

Toward the end of 1973, Dewey had attended an informal meeting with James Domengeaux, founder and chairman of the Council for the Development of French in Louisiana (CODOFIL). Dewey had been warned that although Domengeaux was fighting passionately for the survival of the French language in Louisiana, he saw no value in Cajun music, and not to bring up the subject. But when Dewey was introduced, Domengeaux recognized the name and asked if he was one of those Balfa brothers who were playing Cajun music at folk festivals around the country. Since Domenageaux had opened the door, Dewey decided to walk in. Admitting that he was indeed one of these Balfas, he went on to say that he had been one of the first Cajun musicians to perform at the Newport Folk Festival, in 1964, and that he had seen how powerful Cajun music could be in such a setting; he insisted that Cajun music could galvanize the still-struggling Louisiana French movement. "You've got the power," Dewey dared. "If you put on a festival here, you'll see what the music can do for our people." Domengeaux let the conversation drift away from this uncomfortable track, but the seed had been sown.

Balfa and Domengeaux met again at the invitation of two National Endowment for the Arts fieldworkers, Ron and Fay Stanford, who wanted to establish a folklore program and were exploring ways to take advantage of a visit by Rinzler and the eminent French ethnomusicologist Claudie Marcel-Dubois. They thought that as a state agency established to preserve the French language and culture in Louisiana, CODOFIL might be a likely sponsor. By then, Domengeaux had begun to agree that language does not exist in a vacuum. Although he did not have a place for the folklore program in CODOFIL, he suggested that the University of Southwestern Louisiana, in Lafayette, might. He was also interested in the visit of so renowned a French scholar as Marcel-Dubois. CODOFIL had agreed to host an international convention of French-speaking journalists in March 1974, and Domengeaux was looking for newsworthy events for them to cover. I was working as a student aide at CODOFIL while waiting to graduate in May 1974, and Domengeaux invited me to attend a convention meeting. Dewey and I resuscitated the idea of a music festival and suggested that such an event might capture the attention of the visiting journalists. We also suggested that the visiting Rinzler and Marcel-Dubois might be most helpful in exerting a behind-the-scenes influence toward the establishment of a permanent folklore program at the university. Eventually, Rinzler's meeting with USL president, Ray Authement, spawned the creation of the Center for Acadian and Creole Folklore. CODOFIL and the French journalists, meanwhile, got a passionate display of reborn cultural pride at the first Tribute to Cajun Music. And Dewey got his experiment.

Domengeaux appointed a committee to oversee the organization of the concert. Chaired by a Mamou attorney and cultural activist, Paul Tate, the committee met several times to discuss philosophy and establish basic guidelines, but the actual planning of the event took place on a much smaller scale in the CODOFIL office. Domengeaux asked Carol Rachou, a Lafayette-based record producer, to help with arrangements, and Rachou placed his catalogue of musicians at our disposal. Rachou also sent his student aide, Keith Cravey, to assist with the technical aspects of the preparations. Cravey, a hard-core pragmatist, wandered into our den of dreamers and asked about what was under way. I explained our intent to pay tribute to Cajun and Creole music in a grand concert. He listened patiently. When I finished my pitch, he looked me in the eye, said, "You're crazy," and walked out. Twenty minutes later he was back. His boss had told him that even if he thought we were crazy, his job was to help produce the tribute. "So let's get started," he said as he sat down next to a telephone and began calling for amplifiers and speakers, stages and locations; we were finally moving from philosophy to action.

As things began to fall into place, the stakes were raised. At Dewey's suggestion, Rinzler became involved in the festival's production, lending the prestige of the Smithsonian Institution to the project. He served as a programming consultant by phone and agreed to come to Lafayette to help host the concert.

We knew almost nothing about what we were so enthusiastically doing. We had no idea who might be interested in attending such an event. At first, the proposed location for our little academic exercise was the USL Student Union theater, which seats a few hundred. Then we began to receive feedback from the public, and there seemed to be more community interest than we had thought. So we upgraded our expectations and moved across the hall to the Union ballroom, which holds a thousand. Our expectations continued to grow, and we raised our sights first to Lafayette's Municipal Auditorium, which a capacity of around three thousand, then to Blackham Coliseum, with eight thousand seats. We panicked and backtracked several times along the way, but eventually decided to go for broke: we announced that the Tribute to Cajun Music would be held in Blackham Coliseum.

Domengeaux was especially nervous. Following his original plan, he had tied the event to the visit of more than 150 French-language journalists from all over the world. The concert was to showcase the vitality of Louisiana's French culture and language. But what if no one comes? Or what if only a few thousand come? The coliseum would appear half empty. Many people went to weekend dances, but a concert? Cajuns were notoriously suspicious of such new affairs. And what if only older people came? That certainly would not appear vital to 150 perceptive journalists.

To make things worse, the afternoon of the concert the skies opened, dumping nearly a foot of rain on most of south Louisiana, accompanied by a spectacular display of lightning. At that point we weren't even sure that the musicians would come. After all, no one was being paid a cent, not even travel money. The concert was scheduled to start at seven-thirty. By four o'clock the sound system was set up and ready. Fiddler Lionel Leleux had arrived early, pants rolled above his knees and instrument case held high and dry. His sound check sounded great—but what if no one came? Around four-thirty a family showed up, three generations strong, and we began to feel better. Soon enough, the coliseum started to fill, mostly with the same sort of folks—whole families. To our surprise and relief, a great many people were coming—the young ones, too. And every musician showed up; we even got a few extras who were added to the program literally at the last minute.

By seven-thirty, the coliseum was not only filled, but overflowing. Every seat was taken except for the 150 chairs reserved for the journalists, on the floor directly in front of the stage. When the show didn't start right on time, the crowd correctly guessed that we were waiting for whoever was supposed to sit in those empty chairs. The journalists had been delayed by the weather and the incredible traffic jam outside the coliseum. As soon as they arrived, they were escorted to the reserved seats. The crowd, knowing the show could now begin, erupted in applause. The journalists assumed the clapping was for them and gratefully acknowledged the warm "reception." Meanwhile, several thousand people stranded outside because of the fire code limits remained under their umbrellas, asking only that the doors be left open so that they might listen. One CODOFIL official reopened the doors and let them in, reasoning that there was a worse risk outside than in. The fire marshal came to me frantic, wanting to know how this happened. I didn't know, but I was reasonably sure he wouldn't shut us down: his father was playing in the second group.

From the outset it was obvious to everyone that it was a magic moment. We all felt it, organizers, musicians, audience, and journalists alike. Area newspapers reported on the event with a newly discovered pride. For example, the Opelousas *Daily World*, which only a few years earlier had run an editorial entitled "They Call That Music??!!" maligning Cajun music, now described the festival in glowing terms in a story headlined "Coliseum Shivers Under Impact of Music Rally."

The program was carefully designed to demonstrate, with living musicians, the history and development of Cajun music and zydeco as we understood them at the time. Ballad singers Inez Catalon and Marcus Landry represented the oldest, unaccompanied tradition, with songs traceable all the way back to France. Twin fiddlers Dennis McGee and Sady Courville played tunes from the earliest instrumental days, before the accordion came to dominate Cajun music. Marc Savoy, Lionel Leleux, Varise Conner, and Don Montoucet reproduced the sound of early accordion-driven house-dance bands from around the turn of the century. The Balfa Brothers recapitulated the message of the whole festival, demonstrating the evolution of Cajun music with the resources of their own band. Nathan Abshire and the latest version of his often-reconstituted Pine Grove Boys performed in the style of Cajun music's revival period ushered in by Iry LeJeune following World War II. Blackie Forestier and this Cajun Aces, one of the hottest dance-hall bands at the time, provided the modern sound of Cajun music. The Ardoin Family Band, featuring Alphonse "Bois Sec" Ardion and Canray Fontenot, demonstrated early black Creole music in the tradition of their legendary cousin, Amédé Ardoin. Clifton Chenier dazzled the crowd with his sometimes bluesy, sometimes rocking urban zydeco. And erstwhile Cajun crooner Jimmy C. Newman came home from Nashville to perform a few country-influenced classics and his then current hit, "Lâche pas la patate," the title of which (literally "Don't let go of the potato," but figuratively "Hang in there") came to serve as a motto for both the festival and the entire Louisiana French renaissance movement.

There was a spirit of elegance and formality unusual among a people famed for their informal approach to life. The evening was hosted by Rinzler and USL Hebrard Professor of French Hosea Phillips. Most in the audience who had heard Cajun music before had done so in dark, smoke-filled dancehalls, paying only enough attention to know when to put the next foot down. The concert format was deliberately designed to prevent people from dancing. As they found themselves sitting and listening closely to the music for the first time, many discovered that it was actually quite beautiful. Domengeaux himself realized that he apparently had only heard Cajun music poorly performed until then, and he soon mobilized CODOFIL's state-funded forces on the cultural front, announcing that "music and language are inseparable in Louisiana."

The festival was a powerful medium. Afterward, I realized that I had understood only the second part of Dewey's message. He had said, "You'll see what the music can do for our people." We were aiming the message out to the audience. But Dewey had meant the first part, too: that we, the producers, would see. His message was aimed backstage as well, and indeed, we saw.

Another thing we saw, however, was that Louisiana French music did not seem to be renewing itself. Of the musicians who performed that first year, the youngest was Marc Savoy, born in 1940, and he was an anomaly. The rest were in their fifties, sixties, seventies, and eighties. But as improbable as it may have seemed that night, within a very few years the situation began to change. The CODOFIL movement regenerated pride among the Cajuns in general. Its festival and others brought much positive attention to Cajun and zydeco music. Outside the area, local musicians were showered in glory at such prestigious events as the Chicago Folk Festival, the Smithsonian's Festival of American Folklife, and the national Folk Festival. Closer to home, the New Orleans Jazz and Heritage Festival added Louisiana French music to its statewide focus.

Even closer, events such as the Church Point Cajun Days and the Mamou Cajun Music Festival celebrated local traditions and encouraged young musicians. Meanwhile, Dewey Balfa's Folk Artists in the Schools project, funded by the Southern Folk Revival Project, the Acadiana Arts Council, and the National Endowment for the Arts, invaded what had been hostile territory, taking the message of cultural pride into the classrooms. Soon enough, young musicians began to emerge.

Some of them first appeared at the grass-roots level in response to an ongoing effort to revive Cajun music in the countryside. Since 1965, the Newport Folk Festival Foundation, in cooperation with the Louisiana Folk Foundation, had sponsored contests and performances throughout south Louisiana to discover new talent and encourage the preservation of the tradition. By the early 1970s, these contests included categories for emerging young musicians. The roll of winners of the Church Point Cajun Days accordion contests from 1974, 1975, and 1976, for example, reads like a who's who of contemporary Cajun music: Danny Brasseaux, Paul Daigle, and Wayne Toups. About the same time, accordionist Nathan Abshire took on a class of apprentices, among them Robert Jardell. Other old masters began to get the same idea. Marc Savoy, whose music store is nicknamed "The Bunker" and whose motto is "I don't go to work; I go to war!" virtually reinvented the diatonic accordion from the inside out, building on the earlier work of craftsmen such as Sidney Brown and Shine Mouton. Savoy in turn inspired a new corps of accordion builders, whose instruments were needed to meet an ever-increasing demand.

Some musicians, rather than simply coming up in the genre, made a conscious intellectual choice to enter (or reenter) it. Michael Doucet and Zachary Richard had undergone what could be thought of as exile experiences, Doucet while a student at Louisiana State University in nearby but basically un-Cajun Baton Rouge, and Richard while on a quest to become a folk singer in New York City. Both were inspired to rediscover the language and culture of their heritage. The two knew each other from high school, and joined forced with other young singers such as Roy Harrington and Kenneth Richard in the Bayou des Mystères Band, bringing a youthful, rock-oriented approach to performing and arranging Cajun music. At the same time, they discovered and studied the old masters. Doucet apprenticed himself to a pantheon of great Cajun and Creole fiddlers, including Dennis McGee, Dewey Balfa, Canray Fontenot, Lionel Leleux, and Varise Conner. Zachary Richard revived old ballads with crystal-clear vocals and haunting, intricate harmonies. He also apprenticed himself to the master accordionist Felix Richard.

The Bayou des Mystères Band also found eager and enthusiastic audiences in Quebec and in the Acadian community in New Brunswick and Nova Scotia. Trained in history at Tulane, Zachary Richard was especially inspired by the moving story of his own people and by the activist nature of French Canadian politics. He was among the first to compose songs that reflected both the Acadian exile and the more recent acculturation and assimilation of the Cajuns. Many of his lyrics served as miniature history lessons for a people who had never had the opportunity to learn about their own past.

Richard's compositions did not always sound like traditional dance music. He wanted Cajuns to take a break from dancing and to listen seriously. The combination of emotional Cajun music with French lyrics and contemporary rock-oriented arrangements made Richard an overnight sensation in Quebec and even in France, where he has had several huge hits and gold records.

Richard and Doucet performed at the second Tribute to Cajun Music in 1975. Their performance was laden with passion and politics and was completely misunderstood. As Richard sang his emotional complaint "Réveille" through clenched teeth, many older members of the crowd probably wondered why Eddie Richard's boy was so mad. On the other hand, the contemporary arrangement of Richard's Bayou des Mystères Band and of Coteau, a group brought together by Doucet shortly afterward, began to attract the attention of the young hip crowds around Lafayette.

In Coteau, Doucet and another young Cajun musician, Bessyl Duhon, joined forces with rockers Bruce McDonald and Dana Breaux on electric guitars, Kenny Blevins on drums, and Gary Newman, son of Jimmy C. Newman, on bass. These eclectic resources made for a rich but volatile blend, highly original and inspired yet charged with personality clashes that threatened to blow the band apart. Before it indeed did blow apart, Coteau succeeded in attracting a young audience for its souped-up version of Cajun music. Once Coteau got them that far, many were hooked.

Coteau was Doucet's money band. When it broke up around 1976, he turned his attention to his hobby band, Beausoleil, a much more traditionally oriented group originally built around Duhon and the Richard brothers, Kenneth and Sterling. It is through Beausoleil that Doucet's influence has been most strongly felt in the Cajun community. The group accompanied the award-winning Louisiane Bien Aimée Bicentennial Exhibition on a trip France and cut its first album, *Beausoleil la nuit*, in Paris during an all-night session at the famed Pathé-Marconi studios. Ironically, Bruce McDonald, the rocking lead guitarist from the now-defunct Coteau, accompanied Beausoleil on the trip to France. Thus, although the record has its traditional side, it also includes a hint of the wonderful creative tension that fueled Coteau, whose one live session has not been released.

Beausoleil gained momentum, earning regular slots on the Lafayette nightclub scene and an enthusiastic following among the college crowd. Doucet deftly blended rock, jazz, and classical styles into the carefully researched traditional base of the group. An expanded version of Beausoleil played at the third Tribute to Cajun Music, now moved outdoors to Girard Park, in 1976. The group's performance proved to many doubting traditionalists that young people with long hair and jeans could play Cajun music. Later that year, during the weeks surrounding the Fourth of July, Cajun and Creole musicians were prominently featured at the Smithsonian's three-month-long bicentennial run of its annual Festival of American Folklife. This event made the national news and echoed back home to Louisiana. Now the local media were pointing to Cajun music as a source of pride, not shame.

It was beginning to appear that Cajun music had a chance of passing to at least one more generation. In January 1977, Beausoleil was invited by the Smithsonian's Office of Folklife Programs to perform at Jimmy Carter's inaugural festivities, largely on the strength of sixteen-year-old Sterling Richard vocals, which were clearly inspired by the legendary Iry LeJeune. Later that year at the Tribute to Cajun Music, a teenager named Marc Boudreaux joined veterans Octa Clark, Hector Duhon, and the Dixie Ramblers for a couple of songs. His energetic yet respectful performance was impressive. One member of the large audience, a young bluegrass musician named Bruce Daigrepont, whose family had moved from Avoyelles Parish to the New Orleans area, decided that he wanted to play Cajun music, too. He traded his banjo for an accordion and within a few months formed a band. Daigrepont quickly established himself as an important innovator in the genre, composing new songs that soon became part of the tradition. His "Valse de la Rivière Rouge," pointing out the difference between money and happiness, struck a resonant chord among Cajuns in the throes of the depression caused by the oil bust of the 1980s. In "Two-step de Marksville," Daigrepont described the founding of his hometown, and in "Disco et fais do-do," he faced his own rebellious past and the subsequent cultural reawakening of an entire generation.

Other young Cajun musicians were similarly inspired. At the 1978 Tribute to Cajun Music, eight of the twenty-two groups invited to perform consisted entirely of musicians under the age of thirty. Two of those, Tim Broussard and the Cajun Ramblers and the black Creole Sam Brothers, consisted entirely of musicians under twenty. Their approach was distinctly nontraditional, reflecting years of influence by country, rock, blues, and soul music. Of course, earlier innovators, such as Joseph Falcon, Lawrence Walker, Aldus Roger, and Belton Richard, had initially sounded just as new and surprising.

The young troops took their places alongside the old guard on festival stages and dance-hall bandstands, and especially in the new breed of music venues—restaurants such as Mulate's, Préjean's, Bélizaire's, and Randol's, where one does not have to be of legal drinking age to hear the music, and where children can learn to dance from their grandparents. In later years, musicians such as Doucet, Daigrepont, and Zachary Richard were among the cultural heroes who inspired a new wave of recruits, including Steve Riley, Richard LeBoeuf, and Blake Mouton. Many young musicians who came up through the ranks—Robert Jardell, Johnny Sonnier, Terry Huval, Reggie Matte, and Paul Daigle, to name a few—have emerged as the leaders of today's Cajun music. A few who have been willing to take the interstates, such as Doucet, Zachary Richard, and Wayne Toups, have made names for themselves beyond Louisiana. Others, such as Walter Mouton, have preferred to stick to the parish roads closer to home, emulating earlier musicians like Octa Clark, who never wandered farther than a few hours' drive from his native Judice.

Although women generally have avoided the bandstand, many have helped to preserve Cajun music in subtler ways. Some sang ballads and folksong to their children. Other played instruments. Prominent Cajun musicians such as Nathan Abshire, Eddie LeJeune, and Don Montoucet reported learning from their mothers and grandmothers at home. And recently a few women musicians, such as Sheryl Cormier and Becky Richard, have emerged, following the lead of Cléoma Falcon, who performed with her husband, Joseph, on the very first recording of Cajun music in 1928. Jane Grosby Vidrine, Ann Allen Savoy, and Sharon Arms Doucet married Cajun musicians (John Vidrine, Marc Savoy, and Michael Doucet) and have joined their husbands in their bands.

Steve Riley and Wayne Toups, who both fell in love with Cajun music at an early age, exemplify the two main directions in which contemporary Cajun music seems to be moving. Toups grew up accompanying his parents to Saturday night French dances around his native Crowley. He quit school before his teen years to work in the rice fields, so he missed out on the high-school scene, steeped in rock and roll, of the sixties and seventies. His brother inspired him to try the accordion, and he quickly excelled, studying the styles of masters such as Iry LeJeune, Lawrence Walker, and Walter Mouton. Toups's father squired him around to the local dancehalls to sit in with the bands; finally, Milton Adams gave the young musician a break, lending Wayne his Midnight Playboys Band to back him at a Christmas Day dance in the mid-1970s. Toups soon organized his own Crowley Aces and recorded several local hits with singer Camey Doucet. By the late seventies, however, Toups had become disenchanted because of a lack of interest in his chosen musical form, especially among the young people in the rural areas. He quit playing to work on the oil rigs, ironically just as Cajun music was beginning to hit stride both in Lafayette and on the national festival circuit. Toups came back a few years later, playing the dancehalls again. His performance at the 1984 Cajun Music Festival electrified the crowd, and he quickly became a major figure. His highly innovative style has inspired a legion of admirers, young and old. Toups has jacked the musical level up a few notches with complex arrangements and daring new uses of the accordion, making some strict traditionalists nervous, but it is obvious that he has done his homework. He can and still does play acoustic sets in the old style. Despite the purists' fears, Toups' new material is simply a well-placed next step, in the spirit of earlier innovators such as Joseph Falcon, Nathan Abshire, Belton Richard, and Aldus Roger, each of whom changed the course of Cajun music in his day.

Steve Riley grew up in Mamou, a southwestern Louisiana prairie town long famous for its great Cajun musicians. Unlike most of his generation, he was enamored of Cajun music as a child. By the time Riley was five, his grandfather Burke Guillory had already taught him to sing a few Cajun French songs. Guillory also helped his grandson meet the musical heroes who lived in his own neighborhood: it is evident from Riley's music that Dewey Balfa and Marc Savoy were his mentors. Young Steve listened to Cajun music whenever he could, hanging onto the edge of festival stages like a star-struck groupie. He has pushed the accordion to new limits while carefully respecting the traditional style that first interested him. He is also an accomplished fiddler. Less an iconoclast than Toups, Riley creates a sound that is a careful blend of the rich resources available in his band, the Mamou Playboys, which features Kevin Barzas on guitar, David Greely on fiddle, Mike Chapman on drums, and Dewey's daughter Christine Balfa on triangle. Together the band puts a high-gloss shine on old standards, sometimes tinkering with them, reaching for the edge, speeding them up or modulating them to different keys. This is experimental Cajun music, too, but well within what most consider to be the cultural boundaries.

From its very beginnings, the so-called Louisiana French renaissance suffered from an identity crisis. The word *Cajun* itself, which had been rehabilitated only since the mid-1970s, posed a problem for many, especially in its English pronunciation and connotation. For many upwardly mobile whites, the world essentially meant "poor-white, French-speaking trash." For black Creoles, *Cajun* was the insult used to respond to *nigger*. Yet now the effort to reclaim anomaly was that although CODOFIL's Tribute to *Cajun* Music regularly featured black Creole performers, and their rich musical tradition was honored in the detailed descriptions of the groups, the word *Creole* did not appear in the festival's name. In fact, Chairman Domengeaux fought hard to keep black Creole musicians off the annual poster because he claimed their presence on it "would hopelessly confuse the ethnic issue." At the same time, prominent Creole musicians—Clifton Chenier for one—resisted being lumped into the Cajun music category.

In 1980 Domengeaux moved on to other projects, and he discontinued CODOFIL's sponsorship of the Tribute to Cajun Music. Rubber Boots, the team that actually produced the festival each year as part of the larger Festivals

Acadiens, renamed it Festival de Musicque Acadienne/Cajun Music Festival, found an eager new sponsor in the Lafayette Jaycees, and immediately arranged to have Creole fiddler Canray Fontenot on the poster. A few years later the festival was dedicated to the legendary Creole accordion player, singer, and composer Amédé Ardoin and focused on the important contributions of black Creole musicians to the development of Cajun music. These were steps in the right direction, but the black community rightly continued to resist getting lost in the Cajun fad, insisting on its own identity. As zydeco accordionist Stanley "Buckwheat" Dural explains, "Instead of one culture, what we have here is two. And both of them are good. We have two good things going."

Cajun music and zydeco have joined Cajun and Creole food as major cultural exports. Displaced Cajuns and Creoles stay in touch. The Cajun Music Festival now gets demo tapes from groups as widely dispersed as the Edinburgh (Scotland) Playboys, who went to work offshore in the North Sea, and the California Cajun Orchestra, who moved to the Bay Area for economic opportunity. Creole musicians such as Queen Ida and Danny Poulard also stay in touch from the West Coast. Some non-Cajun and non-Creole groups and individuals, such as Bayou Seco from New Mexico and Jim McDonald from New York, are opening a new front—and raising new issues of authenticity—by becoming interested in these heretofore quintessentially vocal music forms and learning to play them. California's Arhoolie Records and Massachusetts' Rounder Records are among the leading producers of Cajun and zydeco recordings, along with Louisiana's own Swallow Records. But even while Cajun and Creole musicians are making inroads on the national and international scenes, the real heart of the music continues to beat in the dancehalls and church halls throughout south Louisiana and southeast Texas.

The Lafayette festival, which helped to rejuvenate the Louisiana French music scene in 1974, is still around, keeping in touch with what seems to be important today, following new trends, new developments, and new players. It also still brings together old masters and Young Turks in an ongoing effort to both water the roots and throw light on the new branches. The Festival de Musique Acadienne now has plenty of company. Many other festivals, special concerts, restaurants, dancehalls, and radio and television shows in south Louisiana and beyond regularly feature Cajun music and zydeco. For just one example, the Jean Lafitte National Historical Park's Acadian Culture Center features a permanent exhibition on the development of Cajun music and zydeco and presents a weekly interpretive concert and live radio show in the Liberty Theater in Eunice. Offerings such as this give the local population new chances to understand and appreciate their heritage and its music.

Meanwhile, with their growing acceptance and popularity, Louisiana French musicians now perform in places that would once have been considered highly unlikely, from presidential inaugurations to Carnegie Hall, and perhaps most important, in many south Louisiana schools. Yet beneath all the flash and glitter, today's performers are simply doing what Cajun and zydeco musicians have always done: creating new songs and finding new directions for growth, all the while drawing on the deep roots of their traditions. That is how music is made when a culture is alive and well.

Of course, nothing is ever certain. Ongoing cultural and linguistic conservation efforts will affect the future of both traditions. And important questions remain. Is "Jolie Blonde" sung in English still Cajun music? And just what is the dividing line between zydeco and soul? The next generation will have to fight at least as hard as the last to preserve the culture in and beyond themselves. In the words of Dewey Balfa, "A culture is preserved one generation at a time."

# "HE DECIDED A SONG ABOUT THAT"

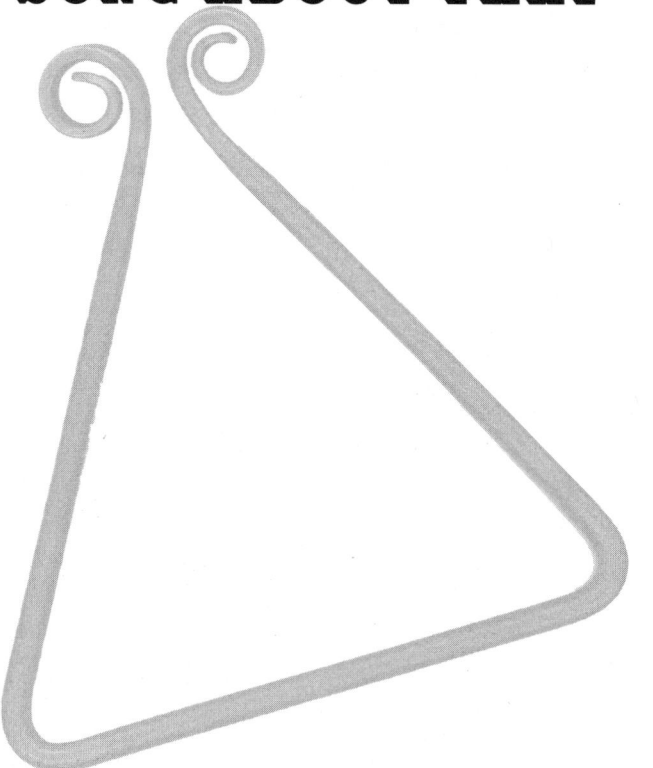

## Profiles of Cajun Artists

With the rise of radio performance and recordings, Cajun musicians moved from being next door neighbors who happened to play music to regional stars. Some, such as Dewey Balfa, even achieved cult status as they willingly accepted the mantle of cultural crusader. What type of person was driven to music as a profession? The following essays provide a composite portrait of the Cajun musician.

First, Cajun musicians tend to be male. While some women, like Cléoma Breaux Falcon, actively participated in the music, the number of women performing Cajun music in the public arena has always been small. Even fewer have left a lasting impact on the field. Exactly why this is so has never been adequately addressed. Perhaps it is because playing music professionally is a public activity and women have been traditionally relegated to the private sphere. The very nature of the honky tonks in which Cajun music has mainly been performed since the 1930s might also play a role. Respectable women just did not enter "those places." Honky tonks were male spaces and the modern Cajun music that emerged there addressed male questions and experiences. Even with the expanding public role of women in Acadiana, few women play music publicly and the genre remains overwhelmingly male.

Successful Cajun musicians seem to view music as a career from an early age. Obscure performers such as Adam Trahan or Dewey Segura tended to see music as yet another way to make money, in addition to performing work varying from farming to moonshine running. For Joe Falcon, Leo Soileau, Jimmy C. Newman, and Vin Bruce, music was a career in itself and they fine tuned their skills so they could earn a living playing music. That meant learning to appeal to a broad audience. As musicians they soaked in sounds from other groups, particularly country music. They looked to Jimmie Rodgers, Bob Wills, and Hank Williams as musical idols and eagerly incorporated their influence to broaden their own base. That tradition continued into the rock era as swamp poppers emulated Elvis Presley and Fats Domino. Zachary Richard fused Cajun music and sensibility with a rock-singer-songwriter ethos to open a new world of musical exploration, one which found a greater audience outside of Louisiana.

Historian Carl Brasseaux identified family as one of the enduring themes of Cajun society and musicians reflect family's ongoing importance. Professional musicians often emerged from musical families. Bands were often family based. The sprawling Breaux-Falcon family complex included siblings Cléoma, Amede, and Ophy, Joe Falcon, and Johnnie Allan. The Michot family has operated a family band for generations, the latest installment being the Lost Bayou Ramblers.

Cajun musicians, no matter how experimental or fusionist, tend also to recognize the importance of the genres' roots. Leo Soileau and Cléoma Falcon both embraced country music but often translated the lyrics into French for their audience. Belton Richard fused accordions into swamp pop. Jimmy C. Newman and Rufus Thibodeaux collaborated on modern collection of Cajun classics after diverse careers in country music and studio work. Beausoleil and Zachary Richard continually return to roots sounds even in the midst of fusionist pieces. No artist was more careful to tend the roots of Cajun music than Dewey Balfa, who turned his music career into an grassroots activist campaign to save the culture. There seems to be a realization, perhaps often unstated, that the musicians act as Cajun cultural guardians. Thus the irony of young Cajun musicians writing lyrics in English and having college-educated friends translate them into French.

It was once true that Cajun musicians came from rural or small town backgrounds. That is no longer true. Reflective of changes in Acadiana, Cajuns musicians and their fans are as likely to be urban as rural and often have received educations at institutions of higher learning. But like their country music kin, Cajun musicians still cling to rural images and harken back to a Jeffersonian world.

Thus the Cajun musician is reflective of his world at the time he is active. He is a member of a community of individuals, a community that allows a great deal of experimentation within a certain set of boundaries that flows with the times.

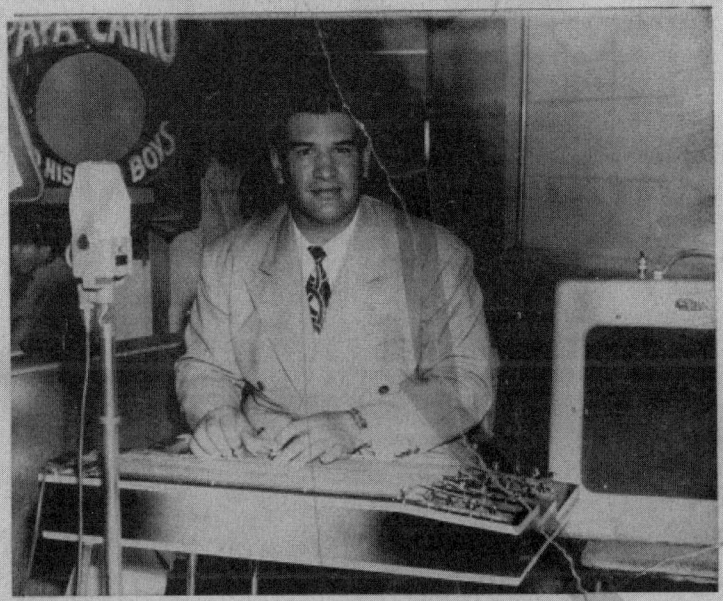

Handbills and posters were common methods of advertising dances. During the post-war era, the most successful Cajun musicians, such as Papa Cairo, performed a range of musical styles for dancing and listening enjoyment. *Image courtesy of Margie Lamperez Breaux Collection, Center for Louisiana Studies, University of Louisiana at Lafayette, accession number 4037.*

# Joseph C. Falcon, Accordion Player and Singer: A Biographical Sketch[1]

### Lauren C. Post

### Joseph C. Falcon

Born near Bayou Plaquemine Brulé
in Acadia Parish
September 28, 1900

Died in Crowley
in Acadia Parish
November 19, 1965

It was appropriate that Joe Falcon was the first Acadian to make a commercial recording of any of the instrumental and vocal music of the French speaking and fun-loving Cajuns of southwest Louisiana. First, Joe lived in the heart of that part of Louisiana that seemed to have the greatest number of Cajun musicians and bands, and second, he was one of the best and no doubt had the greatest following for the longest time. His playing years covered a full half century.

Joe played his last dance in July of 1963, and by that time many other folk musicians had followed in his footsteps and recorded hundreds of folksongs in Louisiana Cajun French. By a stroke of good fortune, this writer who had always admired Joe Falcon, felt the desirability of taping an interview with him for the record and possibly for this very article. Five months later Joe passed away.

Let us now turn to the content of the taped interview and let Joe speak through these pages.

### The Recording Session

POST: Here we are at Joe Falcon's home in Crowley, and it is July 2, 1965. We have just had a wonderful crawfish dinner that was cooked by Joe's wife, Theresa, and we are sitting around talking about the old days. He decided that we should tape our comments. Joe, when were you born?

JOE: I was born in 1900, on September 28, three and a half miles north of Rayne, close to the German Cove.

POST: That was a few miles to the west of where most of the other Falcons lived.

JOE: Yes, John Falcon, Abel Falcon, Frank Falcon, and Sosthene Falcon, that's all uncles.

POST: And nearly every one of them had a syrup mill.

---
[1] This article first appeared in the journal *Louisiana History* 11 (1970): 63-88.

Cléoma, Lulu, and Joe Falcon pose outside their home in Rayne, Louisiana, for Lauren C. Post, ca. 1934.
*Photo courtesy of Malcolm L. Comeaux.*

JOE: Yeah. John Falcon and Abel and also my Daddy and Pierre Falcon. They all had syrup mills.

POST: They all raised sugarcane. And they would cut the cane and haul it to the mill and boil it out with wood. They didn't have coal or oil in those days.

JOE: No! No!

POST: I suppose you also raised cotton. How much did cotton-picking pay then, Joe?

JOE: Oh, around fifty cents a hundred.

POST: You told me about a big event that happened in your life when you were seven years old.

JOE: When I was seven years old, we begged our Daddy to go to Lafayette. First we begged him to get us an accordion. They didn't have any in Rayne so he went to Lafayette. But about the time he left to go there, we had bad luck. We lost some of our family so when he got back, we couldn't play it in the house so we went to the barn and started playing it in the barn. We had the biggest trouble over there with the cattle. They wanted to come in with us.

I kept hanging on the accordion until I struck a tune. It was so many years ago I forgot what tune it was. But I stayed with it and before I turned it loose I kinda started something.

Post: You continued to practice, and you played pick-up dances, and you kept going to dances. Then one day Onéziphone Guidry needed a band. Will you tell us what happened then?

Joe: Well, I didn't know nothing about it. I had just took my accordion when I left with my sister with the horse and buggy to go to the dance. And when I got there, his band didn't show up. So he asked me, "How about you coming in and playing my dance? I'll pay you." I said "Oh, no. I just play like that. I just play for fun."

He said, "Come on. I ain't got no music." So I got up on the bandstand and I started playing, and I played until twelve o'clock, and at twelve o'clock he come there and he paid me four dollars. Boy, I mean, I was glad with them four dollars.

Post: Four dollars would buy something in those days.

Joe: In them days you could buy plenty with four dollars.

Post: What was the price of steak then?

Joe: In them days you could go to the meat market and buy first class round steak for eight cents a pound.

Post: And you continued to play for dances here and there, and they paid you for it from there on.

Joe: Yes.

Post: And you tied up with the Breaux family. I remember the names of Amadée Breaux and Cléoma Breaux.

Joe: Yes, they was brother and sister. And they also had Ophy Breaux and Clifford Breaux.

Accordion champion Amadée Breaux poses, after winning the 1960 Crowley Rice Festival accordion contest, with two unidentified women, ca. 1960. *Photo courtesy of Freeland Archive, Acadia Parish Library.*

Post: And Amadée had his band and in time you had your band. And the connection with Cléoma Breaux was a fortunate one for you. She sang for you and in time you married her.

Joe: Yes, that's right.

### Commercial Recording

Post: Then the next big thing that happened, of course, was the recording of that first disc.

Joe: That's right.

Post: And that was in New Orleans. And who was your manager then?

Joe: George Burr.

Post: Who was supposed to sing that first song?

Joe: Well, the one supposed to sing *Allons à Lafayette* was a man by the name of Leon Meche from Bosco. He got all ready, and he buttoned up his coat and this and that, and he was getting pale as a sheet, and he looked at me and said, "You better sing it yourself, I might make a mistake." So I took over.

Post: And that was an historic occasion. Because he clammed up, you became the first to sing an Acadian song for a recording and that was in 1928.

Joe: Yes. That's right.

Post: Now tell us about the arrangements and the need to convince those people in New Orleans that this should be done.

Joe: Well, I'll tell you just how it happened. When he [Burr] went to talk to them, they asked him where the band was. Burr pointed to me and Cléoma and Meche.

    The man said that in those days they wasn't making no records otherwise than with big orchestras, you understand. That's not enough music. He said, "I can't use them." Then Burr started talking with them again, and he let them cool off a little. And they decided that they would let us make one record. But it's not going to be on the market. It's just going to be for us to hear. When they get through with it, we are going to play it.

    So when I got through with the record, *Allons à Lafayette*, they put it on the Victrola. In those days, them records was about a couple of inches thick, and they just could record on one side, you understand. It was some wax, but you couldn't use those records to play on your Victrola. They just used them to stamp the other records. So they played it. And they started going around the machine. All them high bucks listened and listened and listened. And they came over to where we recorded and they said, "Pardner, get ready, we're going for good now. We are going to make it. It sounds good." And that's when we made it and it went over big.

Post: So that was your first one. What did they put on the back of that?

Joe: *The Waltz That Carried Me to My Grave*.

Post: And after that, other Cajun bands picked it up and here and there they would make recordings.

Joe: Yes, some of my friends did. But before it came out, let me tell you something. Leo Soileau and Mayuse LaFleur went and recorded for a company—I don't know if it was in New Orleans or where. In just a month their record came out, but mine came out eight days before. And I had recorded three months before.

Post: So Leo Soileau had a band. Who else had a band, Amadée Breaux?

Joe: Yes, and by the way, a lot of people don't know it, but Amadée Breaux made the first recording of that waltz, *Jolie Blonde*. I personally took him to Atlanta, Georgia, and that's where he made that recording. A lot of people said I made it, but pardner, let me tell you the God's truth, it was Amadée Breaux that made the first record of that waltz, *Jolie Blonde*.

Post: And since then, other people made other versions of it. They changed it to *Jole Blonde's Sister* and this and that, but there was only one real *Jolie Blonde*.

Joe: Then Harry Choates came to Crowley for the Rice Festival, and he made it, and he sang it a little different, but he made a good record of it.

Post: And when did Happy Fats [LeBlanc] come into the picture?

Joe: You mean when he first started, I wouldn't know, that was quite a few years ago.

Post: In 1936 he was playing with Louis and Eric Arceneaux. I took their picture then, Happy Fats was not the leader. I think Louis was the leader then. [Louis Arceneaux passed away many years ago.]

Joe: Yes, in those days, I believe Louis was the bandleader.

Post: And all those little bands played the dances from New Iberia to Lake Charles.

## Origin of Cajun Folksongs

Post: And now something about the songs they sang. Where did those songs really come from? Who really made up *Allons à Lafayette*?

Joe: Well, since I was a young little kid—I knew the time of it.

Post: It was played by other people before you knew it, wasn't it?

Joe: Yes, yes.

Post: That's one of the oldest songs that you knew, isn't it?

Joe: Well, pretty close to it.

Post: Now every song has to be made up by somebody.

Joe: Well, I guess so. It has to come from somewhere.

Post: Did you ever make up a song yourself—a song that nobody ever made up before you made it up?

Joe: Yes, it was *When I Left Home for Texas*. I picked up my accordion and fooled around with it until I struck the tune. And I made that especially for my old mother.

Post: You made it up in French.

Joe: Yes, in French.

Post: Tell us more about the circumstances for the occasion. What was the condition of your mother?

Joe: She was very ill. You know, she was sitting down in a rocking chair, poor old lady, for seventeen years, and she wasn't able to walk. And she died soon after I made the song.

Post: So it was for her memory.

Joe: Yes.

Post: That's one that no one else ever did before. What else did you do that no one else had ever done?

Joe: Well, after I made them, other people went copycat on them.

Post: No, I mean the songs, not the records.

Joe: You mean the song; I made only one, and that was *When I Left Home to Go to Texas*.

Post: Do you know of anyone else who made up a song—a song that you were sure he was the first to ever play it?

Joe: Not for sure.

### Negro Contributions

Post: Did you know that you play three songs that are supposed to be Negro folksongs? One of them is *Hip et Taiaut*.

Joe: That's one that I just picked up like that and played it. I recorded it in San Antonio, Texas.

Post: How much of that did you learn from someone else?

Joe: I just picked it up like that. They wasn't playing no public dances. I just heard the tune.

Post: Was it from a white person or a colored person?

Joe: Colored. It was a Babineaux.

Post: Not Oscar Babineaux?

Joe: It was Oscar Babineaux's son, and then there was Sidney Babineaux, the accordion player—and he could play, too!

Post: Was Oscar Babineaux light complexioned?

Joe: Yes, kinda like that. [At this point it might be noted that when the author was about seven years old, Oscar Babineaux lived on his father's farm as a sharecropper in about 1906. The author remembers him quite clearly. While working he occasionally sang some kind of blues songs, and the writer once heard him playing the fiddle at his house. The writer never saw Oscar after he moved away in about 1908.]

Post: So they were playing *Hip et Taiaut* before you got hold of it?

Joe: Yes, that's how I heard it.

Post: And you developed it your way?

Joe: Well, I played it a little different.

Post: And you were the first to record it?

Joe: Yes, as far as the recording goes, I was the first to record it.

Post: Do you feel that there is a little different swing in that one from regular Cajun music?

Joe: Yes, there's a little different swing to it. That's right.

Post: That one is always sung in French. One of the others that I have heard many times is *Corinne Corinna*. I heard that is of Negro origin. It is always sung in English.

Joe: Yes, all the time in English. That is all the time that I heard it. The first time I heard it, it was played by the "Hackberry Ramblers." [That was a band from Rayne in Acadia Parish in the 1930s.]

Post: And who was in that band?

Joe: Luderin, and there was just three of them, but *you talk about music*. They played it so good it was like you could see Corinne. They was real musicians!

Post: That's what it takes. The other song was *Colinda*.

Joe: *Allons danser Colinda*—I knew that tune since I was a little boy. 1 I played it many times, but I never recorded it. Years back somebody went and recorded it. It came out pretty big. Everybody liked it.

Post: The first people you ever heard play that, were they white or colored?

Joe: White. That *Colinda*, that's what the old folks call a "two step waltz." I had one of my musicians say that there wasn't no such thing as that. I said, "Hold it brother, I'm older than you." He said "There ain't no such thing as a two step waltz. What number could it be?"

I said "*Allons Danser Colinda*. That's a two step waltz from the old times."

Post: So those are the three songs that are supposed to have Negro origins. But the Cajuns took them and dressed them up in their own way and made them popular.

Joe: Yes, we gave them a little extra swing, you know.

Post: I have a recording by a colored man named Amadée Ardoin. Do you remember him?

Joe: Yes, I know the man good.

Post: Was he colored or white?

Joe: He was colored, and he was colored black, too.

Post: Was he good?

Joe: Oh, yes. I took Amadée Ardoin myself on a bus, way down to New York, me and my wife, and he recorded by himself.

Post: He recorded by himself in New York?

Joe: Yes, he recorded by himself.

*Lawrence Walker and Others*

Post: You know Lawrence Walker, don't you?

Joe: I know him good, personally.

Post: He played the accordion and the fiddle, and he would sing. He has been at it for more than forty years or more.

Joe: Oh yes.

Post: I took him to Dallas back in 1936 to the National Folk Festival. He played the accordion, and he sang. He had only a little pickup band at that time. We also took "Pop Eye," [Aldus Broussard from Rayne, who played the fiddle] and some people from Lake Arthur. They were Sidney Broussard, Sidney Broussard, Jr., and Evelyn Broussard. We also took Norris Mire who played the triangle and Elmore Sonnier. He was a very good Cajun tenor from Scott.

Although Lawrence was what some people call "American," some of his family were Cajun and he spoke Cajun French perfectly. He made quite a few recordings.

[Sidney Broussard, Sr., passed away nearly twenty years ago; Aldus Broussard passed away two years ago; and Lawrence Walker passed away during the summer of 1968. Thus, four of the better known old time Cajun musicians have left us.]

POST: And Aldus Roger, do you know him?

JOE: *Yes, I know him good!*

POST: And he plays the accordion.

JOE: Yes, he plays the accordion and he plays it good.

POST: And he is still playing.

JOE: Yes, he's still playing.

POST: Who are some of the others who are still playing?

JOE: They have a new band that just came out a few years ago, Belton Richard. He's got his own band.

POST: About four pieces?

JOE: No, about five or six.

### Fais-dodo Dancehalls

POST: I notice that for quite a while they have used electric amplifiers on their accordions and other instruments.

JOE: Yes, they got them all electric now.

POST: And they just plug them in and it gives them a lot more sound.

JOE: Yes, with a good mike and everything, there is a lot more sound and less strain.

POST: In the old days you had to do it all yourself.

JOE: It had to come out of your own system.

POST: If there were drunk people out there, you needed something.

JOE: You needed something to quiet them down a little bit.

POST: In those *fais-dodo* dancehalls they didn't have enough windows and it was hot.

JOE: It was hot as hell, and they was dancing like nobody's business.

POST: Sweating and dancing.

JOE: They even had some gasoline lamps and they were smoking. And the next day, I mean, you couldn't blow your nose enough. They didn't have no electric light then, you know.

POST: I went to a dance in Abbeville with some people from Louisiana State University, and you know what I saw? They had the musicians on a built-in platform in the side of the dancehall with chicken wire in front of them. They had that so no one could throw pop bottles at that.

JOE: That's right.

POST: Anyway, they were protected by that wire netting.

JOE: It protected them to not get hurt.

POST: They had a rule in the old days. If a girl left the dancehall, she couldn't come back in.

JOE: Oh, no! It was good night Irene, and she couldn't come back.

POST: Not that night or any other night.

JOE: Well, not that night for sure. If she stayed out, she was out for good. If they hadn't seen her.

POST: The mothers would come, and they had a room on the side for the babies.

JOE: Yes, and the girls would come with their mothers and fathers, and they would go home with their mothers and fathers.

POST: Sometimes they would bring the whole family in a wagon.

JOE: Yes, and they would come in buggies.

POST: And sometimes they would come on foot.

JOE: If it wasn't too far.

POST: And when they walked home, sometimes they would take off their shoes.

JOE: Why sure, they wasn't used to shoes.

POST: And that dust felt good on their feet.

JOE: They was used to that.

**Mrs. Joe Falcon, the First and the Second**
POST: Joe, you might tell us a little about Cléoma. [Cléoma Breaux Falcon, Joe's first wife, who was a singer and guitar player.] She passed away many years ago, didn't she?

Joe: Yes, she did. It was just after the high water we had in Crowley. That was in 1940, and she died in 1941. The doctors never could find out exactly what she had.

Post: And some years later you married Theresa. And what was Theresa's full name? She had been married before, hadn't she?

Joe: Yes, she was a Moore, and she was married with a Cormier.

Post: And you have been married to her quite a few years now, and one time when you needed a drummer, you made a drummer out of her.

Joe: Yes, one night—and let me tell you just how it happened. I was waiting for my drummer, and he didn't show up. And I had my drums all set up to go, and I was ready to start my dance. And no drummer. She said, "I think I can play those drums." I said, "Well, go ahead. Sit down and watch me and do your best."

And from there on, she played and she kept on playing until I had to quit two years ago. On the Fourth of July, that was my last dance two years ago.

Post: I remember [and it's on the tape] she sang *Les traces de mon boogy* (*My Buggy Tracks*).

Joe: Yes.

Post: That was about a fellow who was cutting up a little, and he rode around.

Joe: And he got caught doing something that he shouldn't do, and it was by the tracks of his buggy they caught him.

Post: Tell me a little about that song. Where did Theresa learn it?

Joe: Well, she heard the record. And from that she picked it up and she sung it.

Post: And that record, the one she learned it from, is it available commercially now?

Joe: Yes.

Post: What is something else that she sang that night in Scott?

Joe: *J'ai Passé Devant ta porte*. And she sang another waltz, the *War Widow Waltz*.

Post: Allen Richard sang *Les Pistaches a Tante Nana*. Yes, that was Allen Richard from Gueydan, Louisiana. Joe, where did you learn that song, *Cinq pieds Deux* (*The Old Drunkard and His Wife*)?

JOE: *The Old Drunkard and His Wife*, well, I learned that from one of my old friends from Duson. He was staying on the Whitfield place. He was Emile Trahan, and he was a son of Rouge Trahan.

[As a matter of interest, this was the farm where Irène Thérèse Whitfield, author of the book, *Louisiana French Folk Songs*, was born, and next door to the Post farm. Lawrence Walker, previously mentioned, once lived on the same farm.]

Emile had a horse and buggy, and he would pass and get me when I was coming to play my dance here at old man Ferjus Bernard's place here in Crowley. And that's where I learned that dance with him, *The Old Drunkard and His Wife*.

POST: Joe, that was *Ou te Parti, Mon bonne vieux mari*. And Cléoma would ask the questions and you would answer. [That was the way it was on the recording.]

It was like a duet, back and forth between you.

JOE: Yes, it was.

**Sundry Songs**

POST: What was some other song you had fun doing? How about *Les flames d'enfer*?

JOE: Oh, yes. *Les flames d'enfer*. That's *The Flames of Hell*. That's all I can tell you.

POST: It has some pretty lively words. Did you sing them all that night in Scott?

JOE: Yes, I believe I did.

POST: And the *St. Landry Waltz*. You must like that one; you played it first.

JOE: Yes, I remember that. It's a nice waltz.

POST: And the *Tennessee Waltz*. Do you like that one?

JOE: Yes, but its "American." Allen Richard sang it that night.

POST: The *Tennessee Waltz*, have you done that one much?

JOE: Yes, but Allen Richard must have done that one too.

POST: Did you do the old *Casey Jones*?

JOE: I didn't play it that night, but I used to play it. That's an old number. I used to play it. I was wearing short pants when that came out.

POST: So was I. We are about the same age.

JOE: A man by the name of Jim Coon knew it all, he would haul some cane to Daddy's mill to make syrup, and every time he would come with a load of cane, I would say, come on Jim Coon, put that *Casey Jones* down and let me hear it.

POST: One of the things the Cajuns learned long ago was to take a regular American song and make up French words for it.

JOE: Well, some of them do.

POST: Take *Aloha*, the Hawaiian song, they put French words to it, and they did the same for *Bonnie Blue Eyes*, but it would be the same tune.

JOE: The same tune, yes.

### Reminiscing

POST: I'm awfully glad that we recorded that last dance that you played at the Triangle Dancehall in Scott. There are thirty-two dances on those tapes.

JOE: I'm glad myself. I was flattered.

POST: We got a good recording of it. It took from 8:00 until 1:00 or 1:30, but we got it all.

JOE: It took a long time, but we had a good crowd, you remember.

POST: Yes, and it was a nice crowd, very congenial. That was the first time I had been to a *fais-dodo* in quite a while. It brought back old times a little. You know, I missed out on a lot of that. About the time that I was big enough to go to dances, I left Acadia Parish to join the Navy; so I have been away a lot of the time in the last forty-eight years.

POST: What else is there you think that we ought to put down here? Or do you think we ought to quit while we are ahead.

JOE: If we don't want to lose.

Joe was an excellent *raconteur*, especially in French. The writer asked him to tell a few jokes in French—just for old time's sake. He told several and then was asked to tell the World War I joke about the Cajun soldier who spoke only French before he was drafted and only English when he returned from France. The soldier asked what this was and what that was, pretending to understand only when the answer was given in English. There was a rake leaning against the the barn with the teeth outward. He stepped on the projecting teeth and asked what they called that thing. The handle swung over and cracked him on the forehead, and he gave his own answer (in French), "*Mon fuit putin de rateau.*"

## Commercial Recording

A prized portion of the author's greatly varied collection of old Cajun-French records consists of sixteen discs made by Joe Falcon and Cléoma Breaux Falcon, mostly in collaboration with the Breaux brothers, Amadée, Clifford, and Ophy. Joe and Cléoma both sang, but always as soloists except in one song, *The Old Drunkard and His Wife*, in which the singing takes the form of a dialogue. But of course, this was an Anglo American song put to Cajun-French words. The recordings have no dates on them, but most of them were made in the 1930s. Other discs in the collection made by Cajun folk musicians run into the dozens and most of them are of early vintage. Here are the sixteen mentioned above:

Joseph F. Falcon–Allons à Lafayette (Let's Go to Lafayette). Vocal Cajun-French Song 15275-D (146217) 16588 Columbia Phonograph company, Inc., NY.

Joseph F. Falcon–La valse qui ma porter à ma fosse (The Waltz that Carried Me to My Grave). Vocal Acadian French Song. Columbia 15275 (146216).

Joseph F. Falcon and Cléoma Breaux–Fe Fe Ponchaux. Instrumental. Made in USA by Columbia Phonograph company, Inc., NY. 15301-D (140908) 16588.

Cléoma and Joseph Falcon–Le vieux soulard et sa femme (The Old Drunkard and His Wife). Sung in Cajun-French as a dialogue, with accompaniment. Made in USA by Columbia Phonograph Company, Inc., NY. 15301-D (140908) 16588.

Joe Falcon–Ossun One-Step. Sung in Cajun-French with accompaniment by Cléoma and Ophy Breaux. Made in USA by Columbia Phonograph company, Inc., NY. 40506-F (110553) 16588 and 1702564.

Joe Falcon–Posché town Waltz. Sung in Cajun-French with accompaniment by Cléoma and Ophy Breaux. Made by Columbia Phonograph Company, Inc., NY. 40506-F (110552) 16588 and 1702564.

Joe Falcon–La marche de la noce (The Wedding March). Sung in Cajun-French with accompaniment by Cléoma Breaux. Made in USA by Columbia Phonograph Company, Inc., NY. 15325-D (146906).

Joseph F. Falcon–Vieux Airs (Old Tunes). Instrumental with Cléoma Breaux. Made in USA by Columbia Phonograph Company, Inc., NY. 15325-D (146906).

Joe Falcon–Elle m'a oublié (She Has Forgotten Me). Sung in Cajun French with accompaniment by Cléoma and Ophy Breaux. Made in USA by Columbia Phonograph Company, Inc., NY. 40508-F (110554) 16588 and 1702564.

Cléoma Breaux—C'est si triste sans lui (It Is So Sad Without Him). Sung in Cajun-French with accompaniment by Joe Flacon and Ophy Breaux. Made in USA by Coumbia Phonograph Company, Inc., NY. 40508-F (110554) 16588 and 1702564.

Joseph Falcon—C'est Tard et le Temps Partir (It's Late and Time to Go). Cajun one-step with singing. Manufactured in USA by Decca Records, Inc. 61905 and 17034 A.

Cléoma Breaux—Bonnie Blue Eyes. Cajun singing with guitar and fiddle. Manufactured in USA by Decca Records Inc. 61909 and 17034 B.

Joseph Falcon—La Valse de Madame Sosten (Madam Sosthene's Waltz). Cajun singing with accordion and guitar. Manufactured in USA by Decca Records, Inc. 17000 A.

Cléoma Falcon—Mes Yeux Bleux (My Blue Eyes). Cajun singing with accordion and guitar. Manufactured in USA by Decca Records, Inc. 17000 B.

Joseph Falcon—Step on It. Sung in Cajun French. Manufactured in USA by Decca Records, Inc. 61907 and 17030 B.

Cléoma Falcon—Lulu's Back in Town. One-step sung in Cajun-French. Manufactured in USA by Decca Records, Inc. 61911 and 17030 A.

Joseph Falcon—Au revoir, Cherie (Bye Bye, Sweetheart). Two-step sung in Cajun-French with accordion and guitar. Manufactured by Decca Records, Inc. 17001 A.

Cléoma Falcon—Ouvrez grand ma fenetre (Raise High My Window). Cajun singing with accordion and guitar. Manufactured by Decca Records, Inc. 17001 B.

Cléoma Falcon—Pas la belle de personne que moi (Nobody's Darling But Mine). Sung in Cajun-French with guitar and violin. Manufactured in USA by Decca Records, Inc. 17015 A.

Cléoma Falcon—Juste parceque (Just Because). One-step sung in Cajun-French with guitar and violin. Manufactured in USA by Decca Records, Inc. 17015 B.

Joseph Falcon—La jolie fille n'en veut plue de moi (The Nice Girl don't Want Me Anymore). Sung in Cajun-French with accordion and guitar accompaniment. Manufactured in USA by Decca Records, Inc. 11011 A.

Joseph Falcon—Ne buvez plus jamais (Never Drink No More). Sung in Cajun-French with accordion and guitar accompaniment. Manufactured in USA by Decca Records, Inc. 17011 B.

Joseph Falcon–Ils ont volé mon traineaux (They Stole My Sled). Joseph Falcon singing with his accordion and Mrs. Falcon's guitar. Bluebird, RCA Victor Company, Inc. Camden, NJ. B-2191-B.

Joe Flacon–La Fille à Oncle Elair (Uncle Elair's Daughter). Joseph Falcon singing with his accordion and Mrs. Falcon's guitar. Bluebird, RCA Victor Company, Inc. Camden, NJ. B-2191-A.

Joseph Falcon–La valse de mon reve (The Waltz of My Dream). Sung in Cajun-French with accordion and with guitar by Mrs. Falcon. Bluebird, RCA Victor Company, Inc. Camden NJ. B-2188-A.

Joseph Falcon–Vous etres si douce (You are So Sweet). Sung in Cajun-French with accordion accompaniment and guitar by Mrs. Falcon. Bluebird, RCA Victor Company, Inc. Camden N.J., B-2188-B.

Cléoma Falcon–Mon Coeur t'appelle (My Heart Aches for You). Also known as "I Passed by Your Gate." Cajun-French singing. Okeh Phonograph Corporation, New York. Accompaniment by Joe Falcon and Ophy Breaux, 90004 (110561). Made and patented USA 16588 and 1702564.

Amadée Breaux–Les tracas du hobo blues (The Worried Hobo Blues). Accompaniment by Cléoma Breaux and Ophy Breaux. Okeh Phonograph Corporation, New York 90004 and (110560). Made and patented USA, 16588 and 1702564.

Joe Falcon–Elle m'a oublié (She Has Forgotten Me). Acadian-French Vocal with Cléoma and Ophy Breaux. Okeh Phonograph Corporation, New York. 90008 (110554). Made and patented USA, 16588 and 1702564.

Cléoma Falcon–C'est si triste sans lui (It's So Sad Without Him). With Joe Falcon and Ophy Breaux. Okeh Phonograph Corporoation, New York, 90008 (110551). Made and patented USA, 16588 and 1702564.

Joe Falcon–Quand je suis partir pour le Texas (When I Left Home for Texas). Joe Falcon with Cléoma and Ophy Breaux, Cajun-French Vocal. Okeh Phonograph Corporation, New York, 90003 (110556). Made and Patented in USA, RE. 16588 and 1702564.

Cléoma Breaux–Prenez courage (Take Courage). Cajun-French with Joe Falcon and Ophy Breaux, 90003 and (110550). Okeh Phonograph Corporation, New York, 16588 and 1702526.

In the old days the recordings were made only on single discs. Now most of them appear in album form. From the dance mentioned previously which Joe Falcon and his band played in Scott, Louisiana, an album of eight songs was published by Arhoolie Records, Berkeley, California. In the band were Joe Falcon (vocals and accordion), Theresa Falcon (drums), Lionel Leleux (fiddle), and Allen Richard (guitar). The recording was done by Valerie Post, and the notes of the album were written by Lauren C. Post.

The eight songs included from the tape of thirty-two songs are the following: *Les flames d'enfer* (The Flames of Hell), a song in which the singer is seeking pity because of his cruel fate; *Le tortillage* (The Cajun Twist), which is played to the tune of "Keep a Knocking, but You Can't Come In;" *Lacassine Special*; *Osson Two-Step*; *Hip et Taiaut*; *Creole Stomp*; *Allons danser Colinda*, and Joe's famous previous recording, *Allons à Lafayette*.

The uniqueness of this album lies in the fact that it was recorded live at an actual *fais-dodo* and that it was Joe's last recording and the next-to-last dance that he ever played.

Joseph C. Falcon's career and the world of Cajun music were one and the same; indeed, Joe was "Mr. Cajun Musician" himself. It was a great talent that Joe carried to his grave on November 19, 1965. The old order passeth.

# "Mama, Where You At?"
# The Chronicle of Maius LaFleur[1]

## Donald Lee Nelson[2]

"Misfortune nursed me as her child/And loved me fondly too...." When Sara Carter recorded this plaintive sentiment in 1936, Maius LaFleur, a man whom she'd probably never heard of, had been dead for nearly eight years. The two lines, however, seem to graphically sum up the sadness which was his life perhaps better than any similar verse ever written.

Maius was born August 14, 1906, at Mamou, a town in what is now Evangeline Parish, in the very heart of Cajun Louisiana. His parents, Henry and Zola (Bourque) LaFleur, were farm people. In February 1907 Zola LaFleur left her husband and infant son; Maius was never to see his mother again.

Henry, barely nineteen at the time, could not care for the baby, and brought him on horseback to his widowed mother, Marie Elvena Manuel LaFleur, who lived near Ville Platte. It was she who raised Maius. In 1912 Henry married Dina Soileau, but his son preferred to remain with his grandmother, who herself had remarried. Her new husband was John Vidrine, a local farmer. Their home to this day remains in the Vidrine family.

Henry was an accomplished accordion player, and well known locally. It is doubtful, however, that it was he who taught Maius the instrument, as they were seldom together.

One of Maius's closest boyhood friends was a distant relative and violin enthusiast, Leo Soileau. Although the two may have played some music together as youngsters, there is little to show that their career partnership was formed at an early age. Both lived in a little village three or so miles south of Ville Platte called La Sopi.

Like most boys in an agrarian community, Maius spent his youth working at odd jobs, most of which were farm related. His music was becoming an avocation, and a good singing voice added impetus to this interest. By the mid to late teens he was being asked to perform at a number of house parties.

Physically he had grown to a full six feet in height, had green eyes, a dark complexion, and was well built and handsome, with the wide mouth which characterized the LaFleur family. Maius was shy around strangers, but friendly and fiercely loyal to those whom he knew.

---

[1] This article first appeared in the *John Edwards Memorial Foundation Quarterly* 19 (Summer 1983): 76-79.
[2] The author wishes to thank the following persons for their kindness and time in sharing information and data, making the article possible: Mrs. Percy Perrodin, Mr. and Mrs. Wade Soileau, Mrs. Lou (Soileau) DeRouen, Mrs. Winnie (Soileau) Chapman, Mrs. Ramona (Soileau) Launey, Paul Sandau, Moise Robin, Luderin Darbone, Crawford Vincent, and Walter Lee, Clerk of the Court of Evangeline Parish.

Sometime during this period in his life he met Hazel Brunet, a young lady from Mamou, who was three years his junior. The two fell in love but encountered objections from her parents, who felt Maius would not be a suitable husband. In rural Louisiana, as in most places at that time, musicians were not highly rated as prospective sons-in-law. The itinerant lifestyle such a profession molded was inconducive to the security parents wanted for their daughters. Maius, deeply troubled, presented the problem to his dad and was simply told, "Take her and marry her." He followed through, and he and Hazel were married on April 22, 1926, by Reverend A. Viel, a Catholic priest, before two witnesses.

Friend Leo was less able to settle into farming than Maius. He found work as a fiddler at a dancehall in Basile owned by one Maxine Ledoux. Ledoux was a first cousin to Leo's wife, Joyce, and played accordion to Leo's fiddle. Business increased sufficiently to force Ledoux to retire from the stage in order to manage the hall on a full-time basis. Leo asked Maius to replace him. The new accordion-fiddle duet, combined with Maius's superb vocals, brought in even more customers.

In the Evangaline and St. Landry parish areas the names of Soileau and LaFleur were beginning to be hailed as synonymous with good times, large crowds, and fine music. In addition to their regular job at Ledoux's, they were hired for dances, house parties, and weddings. Most everyone spoke French in the area, and the vast majority of their repertoire was in that language, but Maius always included such hillbilly favorites as "Casey Jones" and "Roving Gambler." Surprisingly with all their popularity they never appeared on radio.

By the mid-twenties the automobile had become the normal mode of travel in most areas of the nation, but not so in central Louisiana. Bad roads and worse maintenance would keep the horse in business for another decade. Most often Maius and Leo traversed the byways of their locale in this fashion.

Despite strong objections about the marriage, Hazel LaFleur's parents, J.M. and Eve (Fontenot) Brunet gave the newlyweds a plot of ground adjacent to their own in Mamou. The couple built a home and commenced housekeeping, and a son was born to them. Everything looked quite promising for the young LaFleurs.

Henry and Dina LaFleur had begun raising a family and Maius often visited. He was good natured and took a kindly interest in his young half-brothers and sisters. Though not apparent at the time, he brooded heavily about his mother. He almost never spoke of her, but subsequent events, examined in retrospect by those who knew him, show a great longing to see her.

The fact that Maius was constantly on the go, performing wherever Leo booked them, added substance to his in-laws' objections to him. Finally they told him to leave the home he had built on the property they had given him and his wife. Their infant son had died. He and Hazel then separated. A short time later the house burned down.

In the late summer of 1928 the Victor Recording Company, making a field recording swing through the South and Midwest, advertised for local performers to contact them regarding a session to be held in Atlanta in mid-October. Under the aegis of Frank Dreitlein, an Opelousas jeweler, Leo made the arrangements, and the second week in October they began the nearly five-hundred-mile journey.

Conceding the impracticality of travel by horse, Leo persuaded his cousin "Cat" Doucet, then sheriff of St. Landry Parish, to carry them to Georgia in his automobile. Since neither musician had ever been very far from Cajun homeland, it was a trip of great revelation.

Unbelievably, the original recording studio had been set up near the railroad station. Each time an artist began performing, a bell would clang, a whistle would scream, or a blast of steam would accompany the screeching of air brakes. Victor engineers saw the error of working under such conditions, and recording ceased until the portable studio could be moved out into an old home in the woods, several miles from town. This fiasco occurred about the ninth of the month.

By the time Leo and Maius arrived, the session was in full swing. Most performers, including Jimmie Rodgers, had been ensconced in a local hotel. The two Louisianians met the famously affable Rodgers, who knew where to secure a supply of moonshine of such high quality and refinement that it would produce even more conviviality; the trio chatted and drank the night away.

The following day, October 19, Maius and Leo were driven to the makeshift studio. The home was the local Ku Klux Klan hall. Years later, Leo recalled robes and artifacts were everywhere.

When it came time to record, both men were extremely nervous and quite without concept of the equipment surrounding them. Since the dancehalls of the 1920s did not have microphones, the single one suspended above their heads had no significance for them. They began their first number with all the gusto and volume of a live performance and almost demolished the recording engineer, his control panel, and his makeshift booth. After several less cacaphonic but still unsatisfactory starts, it became obvious that the duet was too jittery to do their best. It was determined that one of the local citizenry who had been employed to assist the Victor officials should go to the nearest pharmacy and obtain a pint of prescription liquor. The idea met with success. While awaiting the relaxant, Maius walked out into the yard and discovered a large number of squirrels about. He good-naturedly located some peanuts and whiled away the time feeding the little denizens.

The liquor arrived, and after the dispensing of calming-sized portions, the recording began again. "Basile Waltz," also known as "Grand Basile," was their initial offering. The second piece had been composed by Maius, but never performed by him in public. "Mama, Where You At?" spoke directly to the one person who most filled his thoughts. "The Criminal," which is sometimes called "Criminal Waltz," followed. The final side, another which could only have been authored by Maius, was titled "Your Father Put Me Out." This piece of autobiography is spoken to someone else whom he dearly loved, and, like "Mama," it was performed with a dignity which allowed nothing maudlin to enter either the music, lyrics, or delivery. Even today many people in southern Louisiana know both songs and the stories behind them, speaking of each with great respect.

Thus Leo and Maius (whom Victor and many others spelled "Mayuse") became the first Cajun duet to record. Joseph Falcon, the initial artist to record in French, had performed "Lafayette" for the Columbia microphones earlier in the year. Proof of the recording companies' belief in the Cajun market is evidenced by the inclusion by them of many such performers in subsequent field recording forays. Victor alone recorded ten different groups in its next two such junkets.

Maius and Leo were each paid $100.00 for the four songs they recorded. It was then that Maius confided to his partner that with this windfall he hoped to locate his mother, whom he believed lived somewhere between Lafayette and Crowley.

Before going back to Louisiana, the young men went to see *The Jazz Singer*. The Al Jolson movie had been playing for about a year when they saw it. Such a tremendous impression was created that either man would discuss it with great enthusiasm at any opportunity.

After returning to Ville Platte the two musicians took up where they had left off, both at Ledoux's and with any side jobs. On Sunday evening, October 28, some nine days after their recording session, Leo and Maius played a house party in Basile. Afterwards they stopped at the home of a friend, Alexander Bellon. The Bellon house was supposedly a "Blind Tiger," and the two men were relaxing with a drink of moonshine when tragedy descended.

Earlier in the day two brothers from the town of Jennings, Aurelian and Clarence Crochet, had gone to see Bellon, supposedly to peddle five gallons of illegal whiskey. For whatever reason, their pick-up truck went out of control and struck Bellon's porch, doing considerable damage. The homeowner demanded immediate reparation in the amount of ten dollars. Aurelian Crochet said he had only seven dollars, offering it to Bellon, who roughly refused it. He told the two men they could not remove their truck until he was paid in full. When Clarence Crochet attempted to get to the truck, Bellon struck him forcefully, allowing him to see his pistol in the process.

The brothers departed and went to the home of a friend, Kossuth Manuel, whom they asked to intercede on their behalf. Manuel, a large blond man in his mid-forties, was well known in the community. According to the testimony of a guest in the Manuel home, after his interview with the two Jennings men, Kossuth asked his wife for his pistol. One of the brothers also requested one, but Manuel said his would be sufficient. They then went to the Bellon home in which Maius and Leo were guests.

There were several eyewitness accounts to what occurred, some at variance with others, but in the main the court accepted the following facts: As Manuel, who supposedly had been drinking, approached, Bellon, who had been drinking with his two musician friends, came out of the house and on to the gallery. He had a pistol with him. Manuel said the Crochets were friends of his and meant no harm, asking for the return of the truck. Bellon refused, and both parties became increasingly belligerent. Finally, Bellon struck or pushed Manuel off the gallery. Manuel said, "Bellon, whatever you do, don't hit me again!" Accepting the veiled threat as a challenge, Alexander Bellon knocked his unwelcome visitor down. Manuel draw his pistol and fired either two or three times (accounts differ) striking Bellon, who went down. As the severely wounded man crawled under the truck, Manuel fired again.

Hearing the disturbance from the kitchen, Maius ran outside. Seeing his friend in danger, he leaped the gallery rail and ran to his side. Manuel, seeing this, fired one shot at Maius, killing him instantly. Manuel then mounted the truck and shot Bellon a final time.

Leo had followed out of the house within seconds of Maius, and Manuel pointed his pistol at him as if to fire. Leo was able to wheel quickly around and get back inside; this quick reflex quite probably saved his life.

Seeing that Bellon was mortally wounded, Kossuth Manuel left the scene. He first went to the town marshal and handed over his pistol, then traveled to Ville Platte to surrender himself to authorities.

When word reached Henry LaFleur about his son's death, he contacted a friend, Calbert Douis, who owned a pickup truck. The two men went to Basile to claim Maius's body, and returned him to Ville Platte in the back of the truck. He was taken to the home of his grandmother (who sometime earlier had removed from the farm and now lived in town) for wake and services. He was interred in the city's Catholic cemetery in a family plot which has since accepted his father, step-mother, four half-brothers, and his beloved grandmother.

Seven weeks later the *Weekly Gazette* of Ville Platte had two stories of connecting interest on the front page. The first concern the finding by the state that Kossuth Manuel was sane and able to stand trial for the killings with which he was charged. The other announced the arrival of a sample record by Maius and Leo at the Evangeline Pharmacy. The *Gazette* noted that Victor had shipped several hundred of the discs which would soon arrive in the area for distribution by local dealers.

In early 1929 Kossuth Manuel, who some years earlier had been tried and acquitted for the killing of another man, was convicted of manslaughter in the death of Alex Bellon, and murder without capital punishment in the case of Maius. He was sentenced to a life term in Angola Prison, but served only a few years. Talk of political influence in securing his early release angered many in the community.

When the long-awaited records arrived in Ville Platte the Evangeline Pharmacy placed a phonograph in the middle of the street, with the volume turned up; the voice of Maius LaFleur sang hauntingly for all to hear. His heartsick father was later to secure copies of the recordings and close himself in the family parlor to listen to them in solitude.

It is vividly recalled by many long-time residents that J.M. Brunet had a filling station in Mamou. A rival station was just across the street. The owner of that station bought several copies of each record and played them loudly to infuriate Brunet. Brunet would forever after break any copy of his son-in-law's record which he could get his hands on, whether he owned them or not.

Leo Soileau was deeply injured by the senseless death of his friend. He seldom spoke of the incident, preferring to discuss Maius's musical ability and fine character. With no partner now, he asked Maxine Ledoux to take over accordion duties again at the dancehall. Ledoux did so for a few nights until Leo arrived with a seventeen-year-old prodigy from nearby Arnaudville, Moise Robin. Moise had known his predecessor slightly and had patterned his accordion technique after him. Leo and Moise would be partners for the next three or so years.

In assessing Maius LaFleur's standing as an artist, Moise has often referred to him as "the flower of the corn," calling him the best accordionist he has ever heard. He rates Joseph Falcon second, Ambrose Thibodeaux third, and Angelas LeJeune[3] fourth. The Robin list does not include Lawrence Walker because he never heard him play. The largest portion of people who heard each of these men perform in person feel that Moise's listing is just about right, most especially in placing Maius at the top.

An often-noted coincidence, included here for completeness, tells that Iry LeJeune, another great Cajun accordionist, the nephew of Angelas, was born October 28, 1928—the very day that Maius died.

---

[3] *Editor's note*: Many names mentioned here and elsewhere in the reader have variant spellings, based on phonetic versus standard French spelling; for instance, LeJeune is also spelled Lejeune, Lejune, and LeJune. Anjalais is also spelled Angelas.

What may be the final note to the entire story occurred many years later when two ladies, who were sharing a hospital room in the Crowley area, some thirty miles south of Ville Platte, became friendly. They chatted about a variety of subjects, and the topic of music finally arose. After some hesitation one lady confided that she was, indeed, Maius LaFleur's mother. She had remarried and had a family and lived in the general vicinity. Although she did not greatly elaborate, her hospital roommate was absolutely convinced of the authenticity of her statement.

# Playing in the Shadows: Obscure Early Cajun Recording Artists[1]

*Ron Brown*

The last frontier of American traditional music is perhaps only a slight exaggeration to confer on what otherwise could be considered fertile ground for research—Cajun music's earliest recorded artists. Folklorists in Louisiana and elsewhere have added considerably to the expanding body of knowledge about many of the more prominent early-day musicians; yet precious little has been published regarding a majority of the lesser-known Cajun artists who recorded prior to 1931.

The sketches that follow are intended to bring into sharper focus the lives and music of a small yet representative group of these obscure 1920s-era Cajun musicians. They are presented chronologically, based upon their respective recording dates. Although these performers resided in different parishes and had varying musical styles, they shared a common bond—for a variety of reasons these musicians were destined to remain in the shadows of some of their better-known contemporaries. While the artists featured below have never been regarded as the standard bearers of Cajun music's earliest era, their repertoires, collectively, provide a significant contribution to the dimensions of Cajun music appreciation and scholarship.

## Adam Trahan[2]

By July of 1928, it had become quite apparent to Columbia's record company executives that an intriguing development was taking place. Their new experiment with Cajun music, which began a few months earlier when they recorded accordionist Joe Falcon, was proving to be an unexpected success. The bayou and prairie country of Cajun Louisiana, almost totally ignored by record companies up to this point, had overnight become a potential hotbed for record sales.

Falcon was back in the Columbia studios the following month for a second recording session. By this time news of his debut "Allons à Lafayette/The Waltz That Carried Me to My Grave" had swept throughout the entire Cajun region. Columbia agents were combing the area for additional talent—as were competing record companies—all now keenly aware of the lucrative possibilities that lay ahead. Many Cajun musicians at that time began to hone their skills in preparation for an opportunity to record their songs and gain widespread

---

[1] © Ron Brown, Athens, Tennessee, 2005.
[2] The author would like to gratefully acknowledge the following informants for their kind generosity and assistance: Adam Trahan, Dalfares Trahan, David Trahan, and Maxie Trahan.

recognition. Against this backdrop, nineteen-year-old Adam Trahan had been practicing intently. He was by his own admission "a fast learner" having developed his accordion skills a few years earlier. As December 1928 approached, Adam felt confident that he was as competent an accordionist as Joe Falcon. In the meantime Columbia was becoming well established in Cajun Louisiana, and over the next few years, records by their featured Cajun artists, most notably Falcon, would sell quite well.

It is interesting to note that although the two records recorded by Adam Trahan, released in December 1928, sold fairly well, details concerning his personal background were virtually unknown for more than sixty years. Trahan was "rediscovered" purely by chance in 1989 at which time this author interviewed him regarding his life and music.

Born in 1909, Adam Trahan was the son of Felix and Elizabeth Hebert Trahan. Adam was raised near the outskirts of Abbeville and had four brothers—Alexis, Columbus, Alexandre, and Edward, as well as two sisters—Azalie and Victoria. Adam began learning the accordion well before he was eighteen. His brother Columbus had an accordion secured under lock and key. Adam would "borrow" it often to practice. He felt that the instrument, taken without permission, was put to good use given that Columbus never developed any real playing skill.

Once Adam had mastered the basics, one of his uncles took him to Rayne where he purchased a Monarch accordion for $22.50. Inspired by Cajun-area musicians such as Joe Falcon, he kept practicing until, in his own words, "I got to be pretty good." He further stated, "I learned the accordion by myself—on my own—no one ever really taught me how to play it."[3] At some point Adam also become quite adept at playing the fiddle. He felt as competent at playing fiddle as he was on the accordion.

While still living with his parents, he formed his own band, which consisted of fiddler Obrey Clark and guitarist Otis Monceau, both of whom were Gueydan residents. Whitney Mouton, their promoter and sponsor, transported Adam and his band around to dancehalls and private homes throughout the local region—as far away as Orange, Texas. Adam also played dances with his brother Edward after teaching him to fiddle.

In 1928 Paul Brook, a local phonograph machine and record dealer, owned a furniture store on State Street in Abbeville. He had heard Adam's music and concluded that this young accordionist played well enough to be given the opportunity to make some records. A successful outcome by this budding local talent could mean a virtual windfall in profits with a boost in phonograph machine and record sales. Brook talked with his Columbia agent who, in turn, arranged a recording session for Adam.

---

[3] Interview with Adam Trahan conducted by Ron Brown on July 4, 1989 near Kaplan, Louisiana.

Trahan's personal account of the chain of events leading up to this session is as follows: While still unmarried and living at his parents' home, Trahan received a telegram from F. Mackey, a Columbia Record Company representative. The telegram directed him to "hop on the next train to New Orleans," where he would meet with the Columbia record contacts. Adam was most likely informed of the possibility he might be invited to record but was obviously taken aback by the suddenness of Columbia's decision to actually select him, coupled with the abruptness of his departure time. With no time to lose, Adam went first to the Gueydan rice mill where Obrey Clark and Otise Monceau worked, only to find that his two fellow bandmembers employed there were unable to take off work for the necessary amount of time needed to make the trip. Trahan then contacted a guitar player he knew in Kaplan who owned a shoe shop. The owner could not leave, but he did locate his brother, Edney Broussard, also a guitarist, who was willing to travel to New Orleans and record with Adam.

Trahan and his new accompanist journeyed alone to Columbia's recording studios located in a New Orleans hotel on Canal Street. On December 14, 1928, while the duo waited to record, a large orchestra arrived and set up their instruments for the next session following the two Cajun musicians. That day Adam Trahan and Edney Broussard recorded four songs. Two sides were instrumental—"The Waltz of Our Little Town" and "The Acadian Waltz." On the other two selections, Adam sang the vocals, which he learned from others living in his locale. One of these pieces, "The Pretty Girls Don't Want Me," is an intense fast-paced song that demonstrates Trahan's expertise on the accordion. The second title, "Do You Think Work Is Hard," is played at a slower pace. Unfortunately, Broussard's guitar chords on the four recordings are out of musical phase with Trahan's accordion much of the time. Broussard's limitations stemmed from his unfamiliarity with Adam's repertoire and their lack of available preparation time prior to the actual recording session. In spite of this, Trahan's vocals and accordion playing are well executed, and his records are a lasting tribute to his abilities.

Adam was paid $100 plus trip expenses for his recordings. Columbia probably released one of his two records fairly soon thereafter. The second release was made available some months later. Maxie Trahan vividly recalled his Uncle Adam's first release. The accordionist arrived at the family home late one night with one of his new records in hand. It was a proud and exciting moment when they heard his recording being played on their Victrola.

Predictably Trahan's popularity increased upon his return, and requests to perform from fans and club owners surged. He had been living with his parents and siblings, but his life was to undergo a significant change. Adam decided to abandon his musical career for the next several years and sold his accordion some months after his recording session. The excessive demands upon his time musically conflicted with his plans to marry and get a "responsible" job. The Columbia Record Company invited Trahan back for a second recording session, but he declined, having already sold his accordion.

Adam married Ophelia Guidry, and together they had two sons—Dalfares and John. Upon getting married, Trahan lived and worked on the Guidry farm with his father-in-law for several years. A tornado later destroyed the homestead in 1941 and the couple rebuilt north of Kaplan. Trahan began playing music again in the early to mid-1930s. Adam recalled taking part in a New Deal-sponsored parade and concert in downtown Abbeville during the Great Depression. He performed the entire day as a public service. According to his son Dalfares, Trahan continued with his music until the late 1940s.

Adam Trahan was multi-faceted with regard to his occupational talents. He had drive and ambition, yet enjoyed change, as reflected by the variety of job experiences he had during his lifetime. Before he married, Adam was a professional jockey and raced horses in Gueydan as well as at Jefferson Downs in New Orleans. Afterward, he farmed during the first few years of his marriage. Additionally, he was a surveyor, rural route mail carrier, and a teller at the Bank of Abbeville for eighteen years. Finally, along with his two sons, he owned and operated a farm supply and feed store in Kaplan from 1957 until 1986.

Adam knew and heard many prominent musicians throughout the years and considered Joseph Falcon the "best-known" early-day accordionist. He regarded Amédé Breaux and Lawrence Walker as "good players" and attended their dances. Even so, Adam considered his own accordion playing to be on a par with that of his better-known contemporaries. It is regrettable that Adam Trahan's repertoire was not more extensively recorded. Nonetheless, we are fortunate to have the fine musical legacy that Adam has provided on record. Trahan's advice to those learning to play the Cajun accordion: "One of the best things to do is to play alone—you will learn much faster than playing along with others."

Indeed, Adam was one to know—he truly was a "fast learner," both in terms of his musical talents as well as his many occupational skills. A fine musician, he was well-loved by his family and highly regarded by his community and beyond. Adam Trahan died in 1994 and is buried in the Holy Rosary Cemetery in Kaplan.

*Blind Uncle Gaspard, Delma Lachney, and John Bertrand*[4]
The names Blind Uncle Gaspard and Delma Lachney are little known outside of their locale. Yet for those whose good fortune it has been to hear their music, this reissue project is long overdue.

Avoyelles Parish, Louisiana, is located along the part of the northern fringe of what might generally be considered "Cajun" country. This area has been poorly documented in terms of its musical heritage. The Gaspard-Lachney recordings are the only examples known to exist from this locale prior to the 1940s.

Gaspard played guitar and Lachney the fiddle on their records. Both musicians, whose repertoires included ballad-style songs as well as dance-oriented instrumentals, were extraordinary singers in the rural tradition. Indeed, the ethereal and haunting quality of Gaspard's voice is in distinct contrast to Lachney's evocative and intense singing style. Yet both men project a strong sense of drama and musical presence.

John Bertrand, an accordion player and singer from the Opelousas, Louisiana, area, is also featured on this musical anthology. Bertrand's repertoire ranged from dance music to old ballads originating from France. When singing the French ballads, Betrand's vocals are reminiscent of Gaspard's. This hint of musical exchange between these two musicians was not coincidental.

A common link shared by Gaspard, Lachney, and Bertrand was the relatively late arrival of several of their ancestors into Louisiana during the late 1700s and early 1800s. Collectively, the impact that their comparatively recent French/French-Canadian heritage had upon their music is unclear. What is known is that several of the ballads sung by Bertrand and Gaspard are of French origin.

Although these and other similar old ballads had been sung by Cajuns in Louisiana for generations, they were generally neglected by the record companies of that time period in favor of dance-oriented repertoires.

It should be noted that Delma Lachney wrote most of the songs he sang that were recorded. Bertrand also composed at least one recorded song, "Miserable."

Regardless of source, the recordings of Gaspard, Lachney and Bertrand allow a rare glimpse through the window of Cajun balladry as sung during the 1920s and before.

---

[4] This article first appeared as the liner notes to the 1999 Yazoo Records' release Blind *Uncle Gaspard, Delma Lachney, John Bertrand: Early American Cajun Music, Classic Recordings from the 1920s* (Yazoo, 2042). The author would like to gratefully thank for their kind assistance and invaluable contributions: Dr. Barry Ancelet, Gerald Bertrand, Randy DeCuir, Gerard Dole, Hartman Firmin, Effie Guillory, Gertrude Guillot, Benno Haüpl, Chester Lachney, Percy Lachney, Bobby Michot, Jules Moreau, Wils Moreau, Katie Pierrote, Milton Pitre, Tony Russell, Ann Savoy, Dr. David Smith, Betty Torneo, and Evelyn Vige.

Alcide Gaspard was born in 1880 at Dupont in Avoyelles Parish to Genoise Gaspard, a Civil War veteran, and his wife, Pauline (Joffrion). Alcide had five brothers—some of whom were also—musicians, and one sister.

When he was about seven years old his eyes were afflicted by a nerve disease which resulted in near-total blindness. An additional handicap occurred many years later when he cut his right index finger, part of which required amputation due to blood poisoning.

Alcide learned to play several instruments, possibly from family members. These reportedly included guitar, violin, accordion, and bass fiddle. At times he played with his brothers, Amadie, a violin player, and Victor (Jeb), who played bass. In addition to house parties, the Gaspard brothers occasionally played at Joe Guillory's dancehall in Dupont.

Alcide became known as 'Blind Uncle' Gaspard and was also nick-named 'Bos' by many.

Gaspard was noted mainly for his singing and guitar playing. He entertained at many social gatherings, usually performing alone. Donations on these occasions were his main source of income. Gaspard is said to have owned a Montgomery Ward guitar which he kept in immaculate condition. In addition to French/Cajun music, he liked cowboy-oriented songs such as "Rolling Gambler" and "Cowboy Jack."

By all accounts, Gaspard compensated for his visual impairment in several remarkable ways. He had extraordinary senses of smell and hearing—abilities which served him unusually well when traveling alone on the local roads. He invariably knew whose house he was walking past even when several miles from his own home and could also identify the type and location of various objects ahead of him on the road such as parked automobiles, etc.

Alcide fell in love but never married. It is said that he wrote the song "Baoille" for his sweetheart he could never have. Other sources, however, dispute this claim and attribute the song to his musical partner, Delma Lachney.

Well-loved by his community, he was a gregarious and good-natured man who enjoyed visiting friends. He liked young people and was renowned for his numerous stories and anecdotes. Blind Uncle Alcide Gaspard died in 1937 and is buried at the Placheville Cemetery near Dupont.

Delma Lachney was born in 1896 at Egg Bend in what is now called Fifth Ward, Avoyelles Parish, near Marksville. Lachney's great-grandfather had migrated to this area from Quebec, Canada, sometime in the early 1800s. The family surname in an earlier time was spelled "Lachenaye."

Delma's father, Lorena, married Virgilie Dauzat and they, in turn, raised a family of eleven or twelve children. Delma, along with his brother, Philogene, were their only children known to play music. Philogene beat straws on the fiddle and played spoons—a practice often associated with Anglo-American fiddling.

Reportedly, Lorena was a fiddler who played quadrilles and other older types of dance tunes. Delma's fiddle repertoire differed significantly from that of his father's. Delma, a left-handed fiddler, composed most of his own songs that were recorded. The source of his distinctive fiddle style, however, is unknown. He reportedly had the ability to sing and play fiddle simultaneously.

Lachney had a deep emotional attachment towards his mother whose death in 1928 he grieved. The song "L'Aurevoire d'une Mere" (Mother's Farewell) reflects his sentiments for her.

Delma's first marriage was to Estelle Gaspard, a relative of Alcide's. They had four children: Rena, Raymond, Silton, and Betty Aline. Delma and Estelle separated sometime before his recording session in 1929.

A small family-related band formed during the mid-1920s and consisted of Delma (fiddle), his nephew, Philmore Lachney, on guitar, and Clifton Mayeux, also a fiddle player. They played music together as a group for four or five years and performed at house parties around Marksville as well as at Percy Boulette's dancehall in the Fifth Ward.

Delma organized another group about 1939 which included his sons, Raymond (Mandolin) and Silton (lead guitar), a cousin, Chester Lachney (rhythm guitar), and a drummer. This band frequently played for dances at the Black Cat Club in Marksville. By this time Delma was playing Cajun standards such as "Joli Blonde" and "Allons à Lafayette" as well as Anglo-American fiddle tunes such as "Ragtime Annie." The group disbanded about 1943.

Delma last participated in a band in 1946 or 1947. This group's repertoire consisted of country music typical of that time. The band played at a Mansura night club and featured Delma (fiddle), Silton (lead guitar), Wils Moreau (rhythm guitar and vocals), and Hudson Dauzat (drums). This group was short-lived, however, and remained intact for only about six months.

Lachney married his second wife, Clara, sometime in the early 1930s. They had three children: Robert, Margie, and Ruby.

Delma worked a farm in the Fifth Ward most of his life and traveled locally by wagon selling the meat of animals he raised. During the 1940s he also worked at a defense plant in New Orleans.

Lachney loved his music and shared it with all who would listen. Often he would sit on his front porch and play his fiddle for passers-by. Delma Lachney died in 1949 and is buried in the Marksville Cemetery.

It was early in 1929 when Guy Goudeau, a Marksville furniture and record storeowner, learned that a young man named Jules Moreau had just acquired a brand new Pontiac.

Shortly before, Goudeau had contacted and made arrangements with the Brunswick-Balke-Collender Company for two local musicians, Blind Uncle Gaspard and Delma Lachney, to travel to Chicago and have phonograph records made of their songs.

Sixty-four years later, Jules Moreau, eighty-six years old in 1993, gave his recollection of the events that follow: Guy Goudeau offered Moreau $100 plus expenses to drive Gaspard and Lachney to Chicago and back. In addition to the two musicians and Moreau, the group included Goudeau's son, Harry, and a friend, Charles Bordelon. The five men traveled north through Memphis and Cape Giradeau. As they approached Cairo, Illinois, the weather turned very cold and icy. They drove straight through to Chicago with Gaspard playing guitar and singing during part of the trip.

After their arrival in Chicago, Moreau recalled that Gaspard dropped his guitar on the ice before the recording session—fortunately it remained intact. While there, the musicians made some extra money singing and playing on a street corner.

Lachney had caught a cold during the trip and sneezed some during the recording session, which took place in late January 1929.

After they recorded their songs, the company was at first reluctant to pay them at all, but finally wrote out a check to Guy Goudeau, their sponsor. The musicians each received about $150 for their efforts.

Lachney and Gaspard recorded ten titles while in Chicago, including "Baoille," perhaps their best-known song. Although a debatable topic, it is likely that Delma Lachney composed it—he sings the song on the record and, according to several sources, reference in the lyrics is made to his mother and to his first wife, Estelle.

About a month after their Chicago session, Gaspard and Lachney recorded an additional six titles for the same company in New Orleans. There were a total of sixteen songs and tunes released from the combined sessions on Brunswick's Vocalion label. At least two songs that Blind Uncle Gaspard sang and recorded alone, "Sur le Borde de l'eau" and "Natchitoches" originated in France.

John Bertrand was born in 1891 at Prairie Ronde in St. Landry Parish, a tiny community near Opelousas, Louisiana. John was the oldest child of Homer and Nora (Boone) Bertrand and had two brothers and four sisters as well as several half-brothers and sisters.

Although none of his immediate family played any musical instruments, an older half-brother had an accordion that John taught himself to play when he was in his late teens. Bertrand's overall repertoire ranged from dance-oriented pieces to ballads.

John married Agnes Andrepont about 1911. Agnes could play the accordion but put it aside after getting married. They had seven children: Evelyn, Anthony, Gertrude, John Willie, Jounious, Gerald, and Gordon.

Bertrand was a blacksmith by trade but also repaired wagons and carriages at various times and once operated a gristmill.

The Bertrand family remained in the Opelousas area for several years, but about 1919 they moved first to a location near Big Cane, then to Rosa, and finally to Morrow. These villages are located near the northern edge of St. Landry Parish, which borders Avoyelles Parish.

A road from Big Cane leads fifteen miles or so northeast to Cottonport, a town frequented by Blind Uncle Gaspard and near his residence. It is likely that the two musicians met and established their friendship during the five-year period Bertrand was living in this area.

In 1924 the Bertrand family returned to the Opelousas area to live in the little community of L'Anse Aux Pailles. A young man named Milton Pitre lived there next door to the Bertrands. Evelyn, John's daughter, described Pitre as being tall, quiet, with blond hair, and having very little if any formal education.

Milton Pitre, a son of Oras and Adeline (Marcantel) Pitre, had one brother, Eaise. Eaise was known to have played accordion during the 1940s.

Milton reportedly was able to play the fiddle but was better known for his guitar backup when he recorded with Bertrand.

Pitre was about twenty years old in January 1929, when he and John Bertrand traveled to Paramount's recording studio in Chicago. Winter LeMoine, an Opelousas insurance agent, who was also a sewing machine and record dealer, was responsible for arranging their recording session.

Bertrand and Pitre recorded three records (six sides), a mixture of two steps and waltzes. In addition to playing accordion, Bertrand sang all the vocals at this session. A few weeks after their return, Milton Pitre was shot and killed in a dispute over a woman.

Bertrand composed at least one song, "Miserable," that was recorded with Pitre. Its lyrics are autobiographical and pertain to his wish at one time to wed Clotille Andrepont, a first cousin to his future wife, Agnes. Clotille's family, however, did not approve of the relationship, and John's request to marry her was turned down.

Later, when Agnes was of age to marry, Bertrand proposed to her.

Another song recorded with Pitre, "Cousinne Lilly" is the probable source for the better known "Pointe au Pins."

A month later, another recording opportunity with Paramount presented itself. Pitre had recently died, so John traveled to Chicago with his son, Anthony, then fifteen years old, and Roy Gonzales, a guitarist and singer.

Anthony Bertrand's index finger was partially severed when he was younger. Despite this handicap, he learned to play the violin and did so at the second recording session while his father played accordion and sang most of the vocals.

Roy Gonzales, a Jimmie Rodgers-style singer, played guitar and sang. He recorded two songs, one a French version of Rodger's "Waiting for a Train."

Bertrand's repertoire for this session consisted of old ballads, most or all of which had come from France. They were a part of his mother's collection of old songs that had been kept in her family and sung by her. Nora Boone Bertrand taught Evelyn, her granddaughter, several songs who, in turn, helped her father learn them for the recording session.

Evelyn recalled that about 1930, Blind Uncle Gaspard came to their house and stayed for at least a month. Gaspard, her father, and her brother, Anthony, would sit and play music on the front porch.

In addition to their repertoires of old French ballads, Gaspard and Bertrand also had in common the inclination, while playing, to whistle the melodies of various songs. Gaspard provides an example during his recording, "Natchitoches."

By the early 1930s Bertrand was playing his accordion less frequently. He developed an interest in playing the fiddle as well as assisting his wife's uncle with making fiddles.

John Bertrand was an affable man and a popular musician who was much in demand at many private parties and dancehalls throughout the Opelousas area. He died in 1942 at the age of fifty-one and is buried at Prairie Ronde.

This account featuring the recordings of Gaspard, Lachney, and Bertrand, is one of many anthologies issued within the framework of Louisiana's musical heritage.

Yet, even within the context of early traditional Cajun music, it would be difficult to overstate the beautiful and dramatic sense of eloquence conveyed by these men through their songs. Occasionally, we have the opportunity to embark upon a unique musical journey...one that transcends time and culture. This is just such an occasion.

A detailed study of the songs and tunes included here is beyond the scope of this anthology; however, some observations should be noted.

Traditional Cajun music as we know it is fairly inclusive, having been shaped by a variety of cultural influences, yet—remarkably, it has retained a distinct and identifiable sense of musical style.

Delma Lachney's fiddle style, as demonstrated on his dance instrumental recordings, differs considerably from earlier forms utilized by Cajun fiddlers as well as those styles recorded later and in greater abundance during the 1920s and 1930s. Although Lachney and Gaspard were exceptional French-speaking rural Louisiana musicians, are we able to conclude that their recorded repertoire was part of the Cajun musical tradition? Certainly, in terms of their balladry...but regarding the dance instrumentals? Perhaps, uniquely so.

## Julian Crader and Adlar Conner[5]

There are many little-known 1920s and 1930s-era Cajun musicians who made a handful of recordings for prominent record labels before slipping into anonymity. Among the most obscure have been Julian "Bee" Crader[6] and Adlar Conner, an accordion and fiddle duo, who recorded two songs for the Brunswick-Balke-Collender Company on October 1, 1929, in New Orleans. Within the larger framework of early-day Cajun music, the single record made by Crader and Conner would, on the surface, seem to barely warrant a footnote. However, one needs to hear "Lake Arthur Two-Step" and "La Valse de Boscoville" only once to recognize their musical significance.

According to Levodie Conner, his father Adlar and Bee regularly played music together. Levodie added that in the late 1920s a Brunswick agent approached Bee, who had been living in New Orleans since 1924, about making a record. Bee, in turn, then asked Adlar to record with him in the company's New Orleans studios. Bee Crader sang and played accordion on both pieces while Adlar Conner seconded him on fiddle. In "Lake Arthur Two-Step," Adlar provided a subtle yet effective counterpoint to Bee's sustained and plaintive style of vocal delivery through the use of repetitive alternate noting. Bee's expertise on accordion and his strong and expressive voice are quite evident on the two recordings. Their songs were probably released in December 1929, just after the onset on the Great Depression. In addition to the dire economic situation, the fact that Crader and Conner were unknown outside the Lake Arthur area contributed significantly to their disappointing record sales.

Julian Crader was born in 1891 in Rayne, the son of Alcée and Azema Mire Credeur. Bee had two brothers—Vilmond "Red" and Amelian "Jack"—as well as seven sisters—Regina, Alma, Lea, Leonie, Amelia, Agnes, and Ezola. Alcée moved his family to the Lake Arthur area when Bee was about sixteen years

---

[5] The author would like to gratefully acknowledge the following informants for their kind generosity and assistance: Marie Allemand, Merie Broussard, George Conner, Levodie Conner, Margie Conner, Varise Conner, Pearl Friedrichsen, Kathryn Green, Mabel Hebert, Gladys Ogea, and Martha Trahan.

[6] Like Cajun fiddler Will Bolfa, who spelled his surname differently from the rest of the Balfa clan, Julian "Bee" Crader used an alternative appellation of the common south Louisiana family name Credeur. Reportedly, the Crader family line is originally from the British Isles and upon settling in Louisiana, was assimilated into the Cajun-French culture. The name "Crader/Credeur" is a Cajun modification of their original surname "Caruthers/Carruthers."

old. Alcée worked in New Orleans for the Southern Pacific Railroad while his wife remained with the children in Lake Arthur.

Bee's mother Azema was a member of the Mire family, well known for its number of talented musicians. Azema was a proficient accordionist and fiddler in her own right. Her brother Erise Mire had seven sons, all of whom were also musicians. One of those sons, accordionist Cleveland Mire, had a band which was recorded circa 1950 by famed Crowley record producer J. D. Miller on the Feature label. Given his mother's musical influence, Bee probably learned to play the accordion at a fairly early age and later played dances at the Red Hall in Lake Arthur.

In 1915 Bee married Estelle Guidry, and the couple had two children—Mabel and Doris. Mabel stated that in 1924 the family moved to New Orleans, where Bee found employment for many years as a chef in one of the city's upscale restaurants. Crader died in New Orleans in 1945 and is buried in the Adrus Cove Cemetery near Lake Arthur. Julian Crader was a highly regarded musician whose two beautiful recordings with Adlar Conner are a lasting tribute to Cajun musical heritage.

Within the context of traditional Cajun music, the surname Conner is most often associated with Varise Conner, a celebrated fiddler from Lake Arthur. However, Varise had an older cousin, Adlar Conner—virtually unknown today—who was among the earliest Cajun musicians to record during the late 1920s.[7]

During a 1970s interview with Barry Ancelet, Varise mentioned that he bought his first fiddle from Adlar. Varise also noted that several members of his extended family were fiddlers, including Adlar and a first cousin who played in Varise Conner's family band.[8] Born in 1887, Adlar Conner was the son of Alcée and Alice Landry Conner. Alcée and his brother Arsin, Varise's father, were native to the Lake Arthur area. Adlar, too, was born and raised near Lake Arthur area, along with his nine siblings: brothers—Edward, Abra, Amada, Cleopha, and Gabriel and sisters—Fenilla, Marie, Clara, Laura, and Alicia. Like Bee, Adlar grew up in a musical environment. His grandfather Octave, uncle Arsin, and cousin Varise were all excellent fiddlers. In addition, Adlar's mother and brother Amada played the accordion, and his brother Edward was a fiddler. Varise Conner noted, "Adlar's brother, Eddie, played fiddle as well—[he was a] good fiddler...first-class lead fiddler—played hornpipes [too]."[9]

Around 1924 or 1925 Varise formed a musical group that included his two brothers, Valsin and Murphy, who played fiddle and guitar respectively. Adlar completed the group and accompanied Varise's lead fiddle role. Accord-

---

[7] For an example of Varise Conner's style see Louisiana Folk Masters, Varise Conner, 1975-1977, Louisiana Crossroads Records, LCR CD 2001.
[8] Barry Jean Ancelet, *The Makers of Cajun Music* (Austin, 1984), 68.
[9] Interview with Varise Conner conducted by Ron Brown in July 1989 at Lake Arthur, Louisiana.

ing to Varise, "Adlar wasn't much to play lead—he played second fiddle." He added that the Conner family band played throughout the local area for about two or three years. However, after Joe Falcon made his recordings, accordion music became much more popular than the Conners' fiddle-dominated musical style; so their group disbanded.

It is likely that Adlar and Bee Crader were well acquainted and had played music together prior to Crader's move to New Orleans about 1924. Apparently Adlar and Bee resumed playing music again at some point after the Conner family band dissolved, perhaps with the October 1929 recording session in mind.

Adlar married Edmonia McNeal about 1908 and had nine children—Pauline, Hortense, Octave, Levodie, Edovic, Alcée, Estelle, Louella, and Laura. Adlar and his family remained in Lake Arthur for several years following the 1929 recording session. During the mid-to-late 1930s, they moved to Sweet Lake, southwest of Lake Arthur. There Conner was a sharecropper on the Gayle Farm which employed many families in that coastal area.

While living at Sweet Lake, Adlar kept his musical ability intact by playing at local house parties. A skilled carpenter, he was adept at building houses as well as pirogues and other boats. Adlar was an avid outdoor enthusiast who often went hunting in the rice fields and was considered excellent at training dogs to retrieve game.

In the early 1940s he moved to Morse where he worked as a carpenter and bartender. Levodie Conner recalled that his father continued to play fiddle until the late 1940s. An active and energetic man, Adlar enjoyed life and had many interests. He was well-loved by his family and fondly remembered by those who heard his music. Adlar Conner died in 1957 and is buried in the Andrus Cove Cemetery near Lake Arthur.

Today Bee Crader and Adlar Conner's recordings are unfortunately not easily accessible to the general public. After many decades of almost total obscurity, Crader and Conner's music is long overdue to receive the recognition and appreciation it so well deserves.

### *Delin Guillory and Lewis LaFleur*[10]

When older Cajuns today reminisce about the legendary early-day musicians who made records during the 1920s and 1930s, the names Delin Guillory and Lewis LaFleur are not among those likely to be remembered and discussed. In fact, Guillory and LaFleur's four commercial recordings were little known beyond their respective communities—even in the days when their records were readily available for purchase. Consequently, it is hardly surprising that

---

[10] The author would like to gratefully acknowledge the following informants for their kind generosity and assistance: Carrie Guillory, Sherman Guillory, Henry Lee Manuel, and Cecile Theisen.

Lewis LaFleur and Delin Guillory,
early recording duo.
Photo courtesy of Ron Brown.

fifty years later the collective memory of their songs has all but disappeared from the Cajun musical landscape.

Accordionist Delin Guillory and fiddler Lewis LaFleur reportedly met around 1927 and began playing music together. The two men were born and raised in separate yet neighboring rural communities in the vicinity of Ville Platte. Popular throughout the general area, Guillory and LaFleur played in private homes as well as in local dancehalls—including the Soileau, Fais-Do-Do, and Fuselier, all in Ville Platte, and the Ardoin Club in Basile. They also played for dances in Lafayette. Delin was regarded as a spirited singer and by all accounts played his accordion "hard." Lewis' fiddle style, while somewhat softer and less intense, was just as expressive. Both musicians were considered quite adept in conveying their feelings and emotions through their music.

As their musical reputation grew, in all likelihood, it was Guillory who had an interest in recording and encouraged LaFleur to join him. Although details regarding their initial record contact are unclear, Delin and Lewis traveled to New Orleans on November 7, 1929, and recorded four songs for the Victor Record Company. Two of these sides, "Ma Petitie Blonde" (My Little Blonde) and "Quelqu' un Est Jalous" (Somebody Is Jealous), were released in February of 1930.

By this time the Great Depression had descended upon the nation's economy. This sobering development, coupled with the fact that Guillory and LaFleur were not well known musically beyond their local area, cast a long shadow across what might otherwise have been a bright and promising recording career. The steep economic slide hit home all too quickly for the duo as their first release sold quite poorly.

Guillory and LaFleur's second disc, "Stop That" backed with "Alone at Home," while also recorded in 1929, was not actually issued and distributed until 1940. Victor (RCA Victor by this time) had introduced a discount label in 1933 called Bluebird to compete with the less expensive "dime store" record companies prevalent during that area. It was this Bluebird subsidiary which released Delin and Lewis' second recording.

By 1940 the effects of the Great Depression had virtually disappeared. Nonetheless, vestiges of its impact remained—especially in some poor and isolated areas of the American South. However, record sales for this release were very low due to an entirely different development. In the mid-1930s fiddle-dominated Cajun string bands, many of which were influenced by American popular and western swing music, began to displace the traditionally oriented accordion-led groups. The accordion—which had been a popular musical instrument in 1929 when the record was made—had almost completely fallen out of public favor by the late 1930s.

All four of Guillory and LaFleur's recordings are well-executed pieces that readily display the range of musical skills possessed by each artist. "Quelqu' un Est Jalous," a highly energetic piece, is one of the earliest recorded renditions of the popular dance number "Bosco Stomp." The reverse side, "Ma Petite Blonde," is a wistfully expressive waltz with the softer touches of LaFleur's fiddle being much in evidence. "Stop That" is an animated and intense piece that aptly demonstrates Guillory's accordion ability. "Alone at Home" is an early version of "Love Bridge Waltz," popularized by accordionist Iry LeJeune in 1948. Guillory and LaFleur played music together from around 1927 until 1932 when Lewis LaFleur met with an untimely death.

Born in 1904, Delin Guillory was the oldest child of Laurent T. Guillory and his wife Deah Miller. Delin had two brothers—Daley and Vernel, as well as three sisters—Lela, Bernie, and Anna Bell. Delin was born and raised in the small rural community of Tit Mamou, three or four miles southwest of Ville Platte. At least two generations of the Guillorys were living and farming in the community prior to Delin's birth.

Delin's first accordion was homemade. After he developed a degree of proficiency on it, his father bought him a new one from a local store for twenty-five dollars. This may have been the "large Monarch" that Delin is remembered playing. According to his son Sherman, Delin learned to play the instrument from a black accordion player living in the local area. In addition to Delin, family members with musical ability included his brother, Vernel, a good fiddler in his own right. Vernel headed his own string for four or five years during the 1930s. Delin's sister, Lela, could sing and play harmonica.

Delin married Anna Reed in 1924, and together they had three children—Bertha, Sherman, and John. Guillory was a sharecropper. About 1927 he began to supplement his income as a farmer by performing at night with his musical partner, Lewis LaFleur, until the fiddler's accidental death five years later. Tragedy stuck again when Guillory's health began to fail. He began to have seizures one or two years after LaFleur died, and, by the mid-1930s, Delin had stopped playing music completely. His physical condition continued to deteriorate until his death in 1948. He is buried in the old Mamou (St. Ann's) Cemetery. Delin

Guillory's spirited mastery of the accordion is an excellent contribution to the annals of early traditional Cajun music.

Lewis LaFleur was one of five children born to Dorville and Cora Hardy LaFleur. Lewis, born in 1885, had three brothers—Leonard, Charles, and Edward, and one sister—Blanche. "Lew," as his family and friends called him, was born and raised in the vicinity of Chataignier, a rural community about ten miles south of Ville Platte. Evidently Lew's parents lived in this immediate area for five years at most, as the 1880 census shows Dorville (newly married) and Dorville's father Dorsan residing that year in L'Anse Aux Paille.[11] In 1907 LaFleur married Eva Ardoin with whom he had five children—Ewell Ollie, Wallace, Thelma, and Betty (Bess). As an adult, Lew remained primarily in the Chataignier area and farmed for a livelihood.

Lewis LaFleur's earliest musical influences are unknown; however, it is likely that he learned to play the fiddle while still living at home. Lew's younger brother Leonard, also a fiddler, was the only other member of his immediate family known to play music. Prior to 1927 Lew's associations with fellow musicians other than Leonard are unknown. But about that time, LaFleur began playing music with accordionist Delin Guillory. Together they developed an audience by playing throughout the local area for about five years. Their musical career, however, was cut short in 1932 by LaFleur's accidental death. He is buried in Mount Carmel Cemetery in Chataignier. Lewis LaFleur, well-loved by family and friends, has been described as a quiet, pleasant, and mild-mannered family man whose expertise on the fiddle is well appreciated.

External events well beyond Guillory and LaFleur's control seemed to deny them the opportunity they needed to gain musical prominence in their own day. Indeed, more than fifty years would pass before this duo's long submerged legacy would surface. During the early 1990s the Country Music Foundation reissued three of their four recordings on a series of compact disk anthologies,[12] making available to all, the spirit of Guillory and LaFleur's brilliant music performed so long ago.

---

[11] Since the close of the French and Indian War in 1763, Lewis LaFleur's family ancestors had settled and lived on sizeable tracts of land within the "Grand Prairie" region northwest of Opelousas. These land tracts encompassed portions of present-day St. Landry and Evangeline parishes.

[12] Various Artists, *Le Grand Mamou: A Cajun Music Anthology, The Historic Victor/Bluebird Sessions 1928-1941*, Country Music Foundation CMF-013-D. Various Artists, *Raise Your Window: A Cajun Music Anthology, The Historic Victor/Bluebird Sessions 1928-1941*, Country Music Foundation CMF017-D.

# Acadian Fiddler Dennis McGee and Acadian Dances[1]

## Brenda Daigle

As Lauren C. Post points out, "Dancing has always been the favorite amusement of the Acadians. Throughout most of their stay in Louisiana, they have held private dances in their homes...as well as the public county dance which they call the *"fais-dodo."*[2] The Cajuns, however, have not always danced to "chank-a-chank" music, as it is sometimes called today. On the contrary,

> ...the great mansions along the Mississippi and other rivers and bayous in Northeast Louisiana echoed on wedding nights and at balls to the strains of European waltzes, gallops, polkas, and cotillions, though the boisterous reels, ancestors of the square dance of the back country were more solidly in the native tradition.[3]

Cajun dance types and Cajun music evolved from European country and ballroom dances. As Marie Ruef Hofer points out that every wave of immigration brought its social conventions and its dance types.[4] The colonial minuet survives in the Southern states; traditional English ballads and country dances continue among mountaineers. As she emphasizes, American dance types and dance music were produced through a blend of Irish, Dutch, German, Spanish elements as well as contributions from Puritans and cowboys.

Dancing was central to early social life. John Q. Anderson describes the northeast Louisiana "frolic:"

> The most general form of entertainment or "pleasurin'" as it was called, was the frolic, whether it was a barn dance, wedding, shivarre, or "hop." This custom was brought to Northeast Louisiana by settlers from the Southern states, where, since 1775, people had gathered to raise houses, clear land, shuck corn, or cord cotton, tasks for which many hands were quicker than a few. After the work was done, a dance inevitably followed because social dancing was the most popular form of entertainment. Dances were held both in the daytime and at night and always on holidays. In the early days, dances were sometimes held outside in a clearing where the ground was smoothed and sprinkled with corn bran to keep down the dust. Such gatherings were called *barn dances*, later corrupted to barn dances. More often dances were held in double log cabins, and the celebration lasted all day and all night.

---

[1] This article first appeared in the journal *Attakapas Gazette* 7 (1972): 124-43. Erik Charpentier kindly translated the French-language interview for publication here.
[2] Lauren C. Post, *Cajun Sketches* (Baton Rouge, 1962), 152.
[3] John Q. Anderson, "Folkways in Writing About Northeast Louisiana Before 1865," *Louisiana Folklore Miscellany* 1 (1960): 21-22.
[4] Marie Ruef Hofer, *Polite and Social Dances* (Chicago, 1917), 14.

Records show such frolics were common all over the South.[5] The Cajun counterpart of the "frolic", the *fais-dodo*,[6] was held either in a private home or in a public dancehall. George Cable's Zosephine recalls "the great clean-swept seed cotton room of a cotton gin house belonging to a cousin of the ex-governor."[7] The "frolic" and the *fais-dodo* have many characteristics in common. The most popular type of frolic was the wedding frolic.

> Wedding frolics were usually more elaborate and boisterous than the ordinary "hop." The dance began after the wedding supper, though the bride and groom were not allowed to dance. About nine o'clock the ladies "stole off" the bride and put her to bed in the loft; later the young men "stole off" the bridegroom and put him in bed beside his bride. Dancing was resumed until daybreak.[8]

The most popular type of *fais-dodo* was also the *bal de noce* or wedding dance which was considered such an attraction that the operators of the *fais-dodo* strove "to have the *bal de noce* of a popular couple at his hall. Some couples pointed with pride to the fact that they had been paid to have their wedding ball at a certain dancehall."[9] At a "bal de noce," unlike a wedding frolic, the bride and groom dance. In fact the dancing began and centered around the new couple. "Le bal commence, comme d'habitude, par une marche reservée au cortège nuptial." Then the dancing continued for a day and two nights. "Le cortège nuptial dansait une série de sept dances, valse, valse à deux temps, polka, mazurka, 'jig-a line,' 'glide,' et les lanciers. Il ya avait une promenade entre chaque danse."[10] After, everyone joined in the dancing.

An excellent description of a northeast Louisiana wedding frolic can be found in the *Richmond Compile*, a weekly newspaper published in Madison Parish.

> After the supper the dance began. In deference to the ladies, the group danced cotillions first, but,...the forrest [sic] boys don't fancy cotillions, they must have the reel— tall doings, and rapture to the full heart brimming...[to the tunes of] "Roaring River," "Sick a Gettin Up Stairs," "Leather Breeches," "Mal the Wad," "The Devil Among the Tailors," "Dance All Night," etc...which they "heel and toe" more rapid than horses seized with the stampede."[11]

---

[5] Anderson, "Folkways," 19.

[6] As soon as they [the babies] dropped off to sleep, they were put on big beds, in a room in the back. There they either slept or cried, usually with less attention than they were accustomed to at home. The term *fais-dodo*, go to sleep, is said to have originated this way. Post, *Cajun Sketches*, 153.

[7] George W. Cable, *Creoles and Cajuns* (Massachusetts, 1965), 289.

[8] Anderson, "Folkways," 19.

[9] Post, *Cajun Sketches*, 156.

[10] Elizabeth Brandon, "Moeurs et Langue de la Parouisse Vermillion en Louisiane" (Ph.D. dissertation, Laval Universite, 1955), 1, 149, 152.

[11] Anderson, "Folkways," 19.

For the *bal de noce*, the "young folks occupied the floor," with the girls subjected to the strictest supervision and chaperoning from their mothers and the older women.[12] Mr. Dennis McGee recalls how "the old lady was sitting near and she watched with big eyes. And when one left the dance with one's intended, the mother-in-law-to-be followed right at your heels with a lantern."[13]

Lauren Post relates:

> No girl could ever leave the dancehall, once she had entered, until she left with her parents after the last waltz. "If a girl ever leaves a dance without her mother, she can never come back in." That was the unwritten law, more strictly enforced than almost any of the written laws. Some of the old folks tell regretfully of the passing of that custom.[14]

Mr. McGee agrees: "That is how young girls were raised in those days and it was a good thing. It was much better than it is now. Nowadays, the boy blows the horn and she kisses me on the run and yells: 'good-bye Mom!'"

At both frolic and *fais-dodo* the men were held to a strict code of dress and behavior. Mr. McGee recalls "We danced holding close, but we had to have a handkerchief tied around our hand. You had to have a handkerchief tied around your hand because the girls used to wear corsets and out of respect for them the man wrapped a handkerchief around his hand so she would know no man had felt her corset bones through her dress." When asked if men were required to wear coats, Mr. McGee answered: "Absolutely. If one didn't have a tie, one had to tie a handkerchief around one's neck." The frolic required similarly formal conduct and attire: "Some have their shirt collars of so extensive dimensions and stiff, you can only discern that portion of the cranium above the upper extremities of the ears—some have scarfs or cravets (cravats) of a deep red hue.... The coat sleeves of some reach a little below the elbow."[15]

There are no references to the musical instruments used at frolics, but one can assume that the musicians used the fiddle as they did at the early *fais-dodo*. At some time, however the accordion entered Cajun music. Since the accordion was invented in 1822 in Germany, it seems likely that the instrument was brought to Louisiana by "a group of mid-western wheat farmers of German

---

[12] Post, *Cajun Sketches*, 153.
[13] Dennis McGee, the seventy-eight-year-old fiddle player from Eunice, Louisiana, is the father of twelve children, four of whom play musical instruments. He speaks French most of the time, but he does speak and understand English. He is a barber by profession, working now only three days out of the week and enjoying his fishing hobby when the occasion presents itself. He has played the violin since he was fourteen years old and has performed with Amédée Ardoin and Angelas LeJeune. On July 4, 1971, he played along with Alphonse Ardoin in Canada. He recorded with his brother-in-law Sady Courville.
[14] Post, *Cajun Sketches*, 154.
[15] Quoted by Anderson, "Folkways," 21.

extraction [who] came into South Louisiana in the latter part of the nineteenth century when rice farming became economically practical."[16]

The accordion quickly replaced the fiddle:

> Although twenty years ago most people could name someone who used to play the fiddle (le violin) it was already becoming a thing of the past to play the violin at home for one's own pleasure. The Acadian instrumental music which is now performed at home is played either on the accordion or the guitar.[17]

As interest in the "violin" diminished, so did interest in the dances and dance steps associated with fiddle music. The mazurkas, polkas, reels, cotillions, gallops, and waltzes that the older folks thoroughly enjoyed are only remembered by a few. As Lauren Post states: "Only the oldest of the Acadians can now remember when anything but the modern dances such as waltzes, one-steps, and two steps were danced."[18]

Dennis McGee is old enough to remember these dances and their steps, and because he is a violin player he also remembers the tunes. When asked about the Lancers he said, "This was not a dance nor a piece of music." Yet Post describes, "Les Lanciers or Lancier Acadien" as "a dignified square dance" which consisted of:

> ...five different moods of music for the five parts which likewise were danced differently, as indicated by their names or titles:
>
> Premiere Partie .........................................L'Avance
>
> Seconde Partie ..................................... Petit Salut
>
> Troisieme Partie ............................. Grand Salut
>
> Quatrieme Partie ............................... Les Visites
>
> Cinquieme Partie .....................Grand Chaine[19]

The Lancers described by Post closely resembles the contra-dance described by Mr. McGee. The fiddler was not familiar with the Lancers, but he was most eager to talk about other dances. He remembered well the "dance of the four corners of the handkerchief:"

> this dance was for the best dancer that walked. You see each man would dance each turn so that they could choose the best, of them all. The best would then be the King of the dancers. Each one would spread a handkerchief on the floor, a white handkerchief about 24 inches square, on which he danced. The man would start dancing in

---

[16] Catherine Blanchet, "Louisiana French Folk Songs Among Children in Vermilion Parish" (M.A. thesis, University of Southwestern Louisiana, 1970), 167.
[17] Ibid.
[18] Post, *Cajun Sketches*, 155.
[19] Ibid.

one corner of the, handkerchief [the one nearest] and then progress to a leap into the opposite corner. He continued to dance this way until the judge allowed him to stop. Then they would decide upon who had made up the most artistic and beautiful steps.

The jig, he said, was actually a reel. When asked if he had known any jiggers, he replied, "Yes, I knew the best dancers around here. They would stand face to face and when a jig was played they jigged 'all the way.'"

The waltz in two times he recalled quite clearly:

> They danced in couples for a while, then they would move away from one another and turn in one direction, then in the other direction...that is why it is called the waltz in two times, because they turned in alternating directions.

About the mazurka, he reminisced: "I have danced the mazurka in the past, but I could no longer dance it. It is kind of like a buzzard when it begins to fly, or when it is attempting to get off the ground. It is a kind of lunging motion forward. Like a buzzard." This description may sound strange, but is not unlike the directions given by Miriam D. Lidater and Dorothy H. Tamburini, for teaching the mazurka:

> Stand in place and rock forward onto the right foot on count one, letting the left foot come slightly off the floor; rock back in place on the left foot, count two, lifting the right foot, with the knee bent; on count three, brush or swing the left foot over the right instep and directly toward the shinbone.[20]

Mr. McGee also described the polka:

> The position is like the mazurka [but] the steps are not exactly alike. The varsouvienne, polka, mazurka, it's a different step. I couldn't do it [polka] if I wanted to. I can't anymore. They held the same position as for the [mazurka] dancing and turning three or four times together. Then the individuals within the three or four couples would come together and begin to seemingly scold one another and then they would move away from each other. At this time they would move away from each other. At this time they would hit their feet in back.

Here again the similarity between the Cajun dance and its European counterpart in striking. The directions given by Richard Kraus for teaching children the polka even included the "scolding" effect Mr. McGee mentions.[21]

---

[20] Miriam D. Lidster and Dorothy H. Tamburini, *Folk Dance Progressions* (Wadsworth, CA, 1965).
[21] Richard G. Kraus, *Folk Dancing* (New York, 1962).
Formation: Form a single circle of couples, with each girl on the right of her partner as they face the center (the girl is *always* on the right, unless otherwise specified). Partners face each other and join hands, with arms extended to the side at shoulder height.

Part One. (Music A)
Meas. 1—2. Moving to boy's left and girl's right, couples take two-draws toward the center (step-close, step-close) and then three light stamps in place.

In the gallop, as Mr. McGee remembers it,

> The couples would move in one direction and then change direction [opposite direction]. They danced, four or five couples together. They called it the gallop you know "'Ti gallop, Ti gallop." It is hard to explain because I have not seen it performed in sixty years.

Mr. McGee has not seen this dance performed in "sixty years," and, unfortunately, we have never seen it. As Marie Ruef Hofer deplores

> The introduction of modern dancing into country inevitably forces out the old fiddlers (who cannot play the new dance music, though they play the old dance-music irresistibly), and the older people, who can dance only the contradances.

The country folk dances, evolved from European dance types, have been driven by modern dances which appeal more to the young people, and the country musicians have be en displaced by the juke-box and transistor radio.

### Interview with Mr. McGee

PIERRE VARMAN DAIGLE (the author's father, hereafter identified as VARMAN): What did you say about this fiddle?

DENNIS MCGEE (hereafter identified as MCGEE): I said it was crazy.

(Played *La valse de la Bamboche* – *The Drunkard's Waltz*)

VARMAN: How old is that song?

MCGEE: The waltz is eighty years old.

VARMAN: How did you learn this song?

MCGEE: From my old father.

VARMAN: Oh yeah.

MCGEE: And when he died, he was eighty-six.

VARMAN: So the song is probably as old as your father.

MCGEE: It is eighty to one hundred years old.

---

Meas. 3—4. They repeat this, away from the center, starting with the boy's right and the girl's left: step-close, step-close, stamp-stamp-stamp.

Meas. 5—8. Action of Meas. 1-4 is repeated.

Part Two. (Music B)

Meas. 1—4. Each child claps his own thighs once with both hands, claps his own hands together once, and claps both hands against his partner's hands three times. The count is: *knees* and *hands* and *one-two-three*. This entire action is repeated.

Meas. 5—6. Each child lightly springs on the left foot in place, at the same time placing his right heel forward and shaking his right forefinger at his partner three times with a "scolding" in motion. The action is repeated with the left heel and forefinger.

Meas. 7—8. Each child turns to the right, in place, with four steps, faces his partner and stamps three times.

Varman: And your old father played the fiddle?

McGee: Yes, he played the fiddle? It sounds alright now, but it could be a lot better, you know. If we could add another fiddle, it would sound much better. It'd be more open.

Varman: We know. But, as we told you, this is just for a study. It's just for...

Brenda Daigle (hereafter identified as Brenda): I would like to know how old he is?

McGee: Who?

Brenda: You.

McGee: Seventy-eight.

Brenda: How long have you been playing the fiddle?

McGee: Well, I was fourteen and I am now seventy-eight.

Brenda: Fourteen.

McGee: I was fourteen when I started. Sixty-four years. You want to hear another one?

Varman: Yes. Do you know some really old songs, mazurkas for example? Can you play some of those?

McGee: I don't know.

Varman: Let's try one.

McGee: A mazurka?

Varman: Or a polka if you know a little bit of a polka.

McGee: Let's see. Turn your machine on (tape recorder). I'm going to see if I can get it. This one is pretty, but it's much older. It's very old (he plays the mazurka). I can't get it. I don't play those well (he plays a polka and a gallop). This is how I do it. It's changed though, everything's changed.

Varman: It's not played the same anymore.

McGee: You played the other dance before?

Brenda: No, you want to hear it?

McGee: Everything I did, it's all changed.

Varman: How about a reel?

McGee: Yes. A reel—it's a cotillion, it's not a reel

Varman: Cotillion (plays the cotillion).

McGee: It's a cotillion. They used to dance it in a contradance. I don't know how they danced the cotillions.

Varman: How did you call a contradance?

McGee: A cotillion.

Varman: Yes, yes, but they dance it in a contradance.

McGee: You know how they did the contradance? People would get together in groups of eight. The dancehalls were pretty small back then, with room for only six to eight people. So you took a girl and you'd place yourself in a couple pair with another couple across, and a pair at each center. You see, one pair at each end. They did "family in a circle" [famille en ronde]. When the band started to play, everybody screamed "famille en ronde!" Ha! Ha! They made "famille." Then, they go to one end, where the girl was, they'd come back, they'd go around and you'd come where the girl was. Two pairs would go forward, facing one another, a girl would go between two other girls and she would come back. She would come and turn with her padna [partner]. They would grab each other's hand, he would spin her around two or three times and she would go back to the other end. Then, she'd take the boy at the other end and come back. She would then turn over there and then turn with another boy, one at the time.

Brenda: Boy! It was complicated!

McGee: It'd be nice if I could show you this dance. If only they were some older people around. They are no elders left that could teach this dance.

Varman: You know one. Would you mind going to college to teach the young people how to do it? You could do it. The young people could do it if you explain it to them.

McGee: Yeah, you'd need a man that knows the dance, that would know the steps, that would know how many families it takes for a dance, you see. You need two families. They should both step forward at the same time. They should step forward three times, the two families.

Varman: You have danced those dances?

McGee: Oh, yeah!

Varman: How about the dances that we know today, the ones we dance. When did they come about? Later? Do you know how to waltz?

McGee: It began in those days. Well, we used to waltz back then.

Varman: Y'all would waltz?

McGee: We'd grab each other, but you needed a handkerchief on your hand.

Varman: So that you wouldn't touch the lady?

McGee: So that you wouldn't touch the lady.

Varman: You couldn't rub against her?

McGee: Oh, no, no! There was always an old lady watching you with her big eye. No, no, you couldn't stand too close.

Varman: Could you get away without the handkerchief?

McGee: Oh, no, no. You had to have your handkerchief. You'd wrap it around your hand because the girls wore corsets. Do you understand? You were not allowed to touch their corsets. So you had to put a handkerchief on your hand.

Varman: Didn't the boy also have to wear a coat [or jacket]?

McGee: Absolutely. You needed to be wearing your coat and a tie to dance. If you didn't have a tie, you had to wear your handkerchief around your neck. And when you started dancing with your partner, the old lady would stand in your way with a lantern, and she would follow you. That's how the girls were raised and it was a good thing. A lot better than it is today.

Varman: It wasn't bad.

McGee: Nowadays, the girls corner you and they kiss you on the fly. They say "Good-bye Mom!"

Varman: No need for a handkerchief!

Brenda: Your parents, were they French?

McGee: They were Irish, Irish-French.

Varman: McGee, that's not a French name. Did you learn from your father? And your grandfather spoke French. Do you remember your grandfather not speaking French? They were Irish?

McGee: They were Irish and Irish-French. They came from Ireland and from France. See, it's all mixed. You see, I don't think that my grandfather spoke a word of English. He was pure French and Irish. My father's father, you see, that would have been two hundred years ago. I never knew my old grandfather. He died, I think, before I was born.

Varman: And your name is Denis?

McGee: Dennis. D-E-N-N-I-S.

Varman: This is what I thought. On the records, it's Dennis. And you are the son of?

McGee: John McGee. You got it on? (the tape recorder)

Brenda: Yes.

McGee: Now they're going to hear everything we say.

Varman: This is what we want. We want the story.

McGee: I'm going to play a little waltz that goes back a hundred and ten years. La valse de Guilbeau Pilloquin [Guilbeau Pilloquin's Waltz], a man of war. He went to the Civil War and he later deserted, he was a maroon. They caught them though. In those days, They would kill deserters. And they took him. They dug his grave and they put his coffin on the ground. He sat on it and he played. He asked him if he could play a song before going.

Varman: Which song did he play?

McGee: A fiddle waltz. So, they let him play and when he was done, they shot him and they put him in the ground. The song is called Guilbeau Pilloquin.

Varman: Pilloquin. You are a real treasure, you know?

McGee: I know all these things by ear, you know; but I forgot a lot because I don't talk about it.

Varman: I don't think so.

McGee: Nobody asks me anything because nobody knows anything about this. What's left, I'm the one who knows about it. They are no old folks left like me to talk about this; the ones left, in my family, don't know about this. Nothing. I'm the one who knows about this. And I'm going to play this waltz.

Varman: Who's waltz?

McGee: Guilbeau Pilloquin's. (He plays the waltz)

Brenda: That was pretty.

McGee: It's a pretty waltz, a pretty old waltz. Nobody dances these waltzes anymore. In those days, you would go a turn or two and you would take your partner and you'd shake around. They called it the "ballotage." The old lady would be in the back standing on her dress. Sometimes she'd stepped on it as she danced.

Varman: Yes, La valse à Guilbeau Pilloquin. He was a Confederate, I believe.

McGee: He was a Confederate, yes, during the Civil War. He went maroon, but they caught him and they shot him. They called the man who shot you a "fusiller."

Varman: Do you know of any other stories that are related to your music?

McGee: Hum! I don't know. Maybe if I think about it a lot. I forget, you know? When you get to be sixty-eight, you sort of lose it.

Brenda: Oh! No! Maybe he knows the story of La valse à Ti't Dame Hanks [Ti't Dame Hanks Waltz]?

McGee: Ah Ti't Dame? Let me see. (Dad sang and whistled the tune and after a short while Mr. McGee recalled the tune and then not completely or fluently.)

Varman: That was the story. Do you know Ti't Dame's story?

Brenda: Why is it called like this?

Varman: There was a Ti't Dame Hanks.

McGee: Yes, yes! I played that song with Angelas LeJeune. I don't remember the story. The mother would say "Alice, get ready, I can see him going, Grand Rex on Henri with the jug on the saddle horn and his hat by his side." The song, I can't carry it the way I used to....

Varman: The story I heard, and it might not be true. Somebody told me that on the night before Angelas went out to record, that Ti't Dame went and that he sang the way she wanted him to sing it, but maybe it's not true. Somebody told me that.

McGee: No.... Because went left from Opelousas when we went to record. Angelas knew the song because we played it often. I don't know. I can play a lot of songs, but I don't know all the stories. There's that song called "The Lost Indian Song." I can play this song (He began retuning his fiddle for this particular tune.)

Varman: Why is it called "The Lost Indian Song?"

McGee: He learned to play this song in the woods. He was an Indian.

Varman: An Indian?

McGee: He learned how to play it. He played it until he wasn't lost. He got lost and he played until someone found him. He was sitting on a stump and he played that song. This is why the song is called "The Lost Indian Reel."

Varman: Oh! It's a reel?

McGee: A reel.... It's very difficult to play. Two songs are played in this key (He plays the song.)

(Questioned about his opinion of an accordion player heard earlier at Fred's Lounge in Mamou, he said)

McGee: I can't tell you, ma'am. I don't know. I don't like the way he plays. His accordion sounds too low, two keys lower. It's too loud.

Varman: Who is the best accordion player you've ever heard?

McGee: This man in Lafayette, Aldus Roger. I like his style. Marc Savoy is good, but he's playing too fast. His timing is off.

Varman: How was Angelas LeJeune?

McGee: Now I'm going to play this waltz. And I don't know if I can play. I'm going to play my old deceased father's waltz. His father played it too, Eraste Courville and John McGee. They liked this waltz very much. When my father was dying, I went over to see him and he asked me to play this waltz. Afterwards, I promised that I would never play this waltz for anybody dying. He started to cry, the old man. It broke my heart. I played the waltz for him, and I said "Pop, I can't play if you cry." And he said, "It's alright, play it. I know that I'm not going to be here for long. It's old yeah, 'Valse à Pop'" (Mr. McGee cried when he told us about this tune.)

*Second Interview with Mr. McGee*

Varman: Have you ever seen people dance on the four corners of a handkerchief?

McGee: Yes.

Varman: What is it? A jig, eh? What was the melody like?

McGee: It's a reel.

Varman: A reel?

McGee: It's just for one, that.

Varman: Did you know any good jiggers?

McGee: Yes. I've known the best ones around here. Angelas Frugé, his grandfather, both deceased, he was a jigger. His grandmother, both were jiggers. They would stand there, face to face, and they jigged all the way.

Varman: Mr. Who?

McGee: David Courville. There was another around here, at Bayou des Cannes, his name was Ti' Xénon Darbone. He danced, he would raise his foot and hit it with his hand. He was the best dancer. And Oscar Comeaux. He's dead now but he was also a good dancer. We have a lot of good dancers; jiggers, reel dancers, breakdowns, various steps. The steps were difference you see. One went like this and with a reel, you had to click your heels (alternating finger and heel of the feet in the heel and toe action). And it sounded good; they would follow the fiddle with their heel and the tip of their feet.

Varman: Sort of like tap dancing.

McGee: Yes, sort of like tap dancing, but faster. It was pretty. Yeah, you can dance all sorts of ways.

Varman: What about the "valse à deux temps" [Double-time Waltz]?

McGee: People would dance in pairs, boy-girl. Then, they'd let go of each other and they would turn on one side, then another. This is why it's called "valse à deux temps" because they were turn on each side. One time on one side for one, and then the other; "deux temps." There were all sorts of dances back then.

Brenda: Was there a dance called the "Colinda?" Or is it just a name?

McGee: That is only a name, Colinda. Crazy people recorded the song. It's the same a that song I did, "Madame Young." They're both the same. I recorded "My Creole Sweet Mama" at the same time. Those were the first two songs I recorded.

Brenda: "My Creole Sweet Mama," was it with Amédé Ardoin?

McGee: No, with Sady Courville. It was a twin fiddle tune.

Brenda: Only the fiddle? Just like the songs you played for me? Do you know how people danced the mazurka?

McGee: I danced some mazurkas, but when I was young. I couldn't do it anymore. The dance goes like a carencro who wants to stand. Have you ever seen a carencro stand? Well, the dance is the same, stretching.

Brenda: Side by side?

McGee: No. Boy and girl, just like a waltz.

Brenda: Face to face?

McGee: Yes, yes.

Varman: They do that in square dancing.

McGee: Well, square dancing, you have to hold it constantly.

Varman: No, at times.

McGee: Yes, when they saw you come forward, they came forward. There's one pair stepping forward. Then, one girl went between the other boy and the girl, and she goes to the other end where the other girl is standing. She comes back and she steps between the others. And again, they come back, the same boy who is on this side with the girl. He came back to make two or three turns with the girl, you see, by the hand (he indicated that the hands were held level with the shoulder when turning while holding hands.) And they go at it again. Before they are done, they have come forward three times.

Brenda: This is what you called a contradance last time.

McGee: That is a contradance.

Brenda: But the mazurka was different?

McGee: Yes, the mazurka and the contradance, that's a different case; they wouldn't let go of each other. The mazurka is a lot like a waltz. You waltz with someone. But not anymore, nobody knows what waltzing is. Today, they "cocobille."

Brenda: And polka?

McGee: Same thing. You hold your partner as if it were a mazurka.

Brenda: Same steps?

McGee: No, it's different. The varsouvienne, the polka, the mazurka; it's different steps.

Brenda: And how do you polka?

McGee: Ah, I couldn't do it even if I wanted to. I can't anymore. And I don't remember much about the polka. They would dance and turn two or three times together. And then they would step forward, a little, they were two or three together, you see, three or four pairs together. They'd step forward as if they were teasing one another. Then, they'd step back. And they'd click their heels together. This is how I remember how it went. And with the polka, you "put your little foot right there," you see? You'd step forward a little and you'd hit you foot on the floor. You'd step back and same thing with the foot. That was the varsovienne, "put your foot right there."

Brenda: And the gallop?

McGee: They'd come and they'd go, from far in one corner to the other end. They were four or five pairs dancing together, you know. They called it the gallop. "Ti galo, ti galo." It's hard to explain. I haven't seen these dances in sixty years. But I still remember how they danced.

Brenda: And the reel?

McGee: It was only for men. Only one man danced.

Brenda: A reel?

McGee: Yes, that's for the best dancer, you know. So, a man danced. Each of them would dance a turn and the best one would often become the king of the dancers. They'd come, get in place and dance. They'd place a large white handkerchief on the floor. It was square. A man would then dance on the corner of the handkerchief. Here (indicating the nearest corner), then he'd jump to the other corner without missing a step. He'd do his steps on the other side and come to the corner (indicating first corner.) He'd dance for a while until the judge would tell him to stop, you see.

Varman: They were judging who…

McGee: They would judge three or four dancers, who had the best steps, some pretty nice steps because people back then knew how to dance. Tap dancing is nothing compared to this. There was an old man around here, in Mowata, his name was Bet Miller (Millair). He died many years ago but he was a good dancer. He knew what to do with his feet. I often played reels for him so that he could dance.

BRENDA: The "Lost Indian Reel" that you played for me last time, they could dance this reel—-

McGEE: Oh, yeah! It was the same as the other reels, except that it was strange [or foreign]. It came from that Indian. He was in the woods, he invented it. He played until his fiddle ran out of tune. And when they found him, this is what he was playing. His fiddle was tuned like this. That's "The Lost Indian Reel." You have to tune your fiddle in a way to play it.

BRENDA: Have you ever heard of the lancers?

McGEE: The lancers, yes. They weren't musicians, it wasn't a dance. They were hunters, deer hunters.

BRENDA: Is there a song or a dance about the lancers?

McGEE: No, not that I know of.

BRENDA: The mazurka you played the last time, does it have a name?

McGEE: No, I don't know. It's called the French Mazurka.

# Moonshine and Mosquitoes: The Story of Dewey Segura[1]

*John H. Cowley*

Dewey Segura was born on February 12, 1902, and is one of twelve children, six girls, and six boys. His father was of Spanish origin, his mother French. French is in fact his first language and, although he learned a little English at school, his knowledge of it comes mainly from his working experiences.

His mother and an older sister, Anita, both played accordion, as did most of his brothers and sisters (some also played harmonica), though none became committed fulltime musicians like Dewey. Dewey wasn't greatly influenced by them, however, and taught himself to play music, first the harmonica and then the accordion—the latter by sneaking practice sessions on Anita's instrument, which, at first, he was "ashamed to play."

By the time he was eight, Dewey was given his own accordion and was experienced enough to play at Saturday night dances run by his father, where he "used to play most anything."

During the next few years Dewey presumably kept up with his musical activities, but in 1925 he became involved in the hazardous and (especially in those days of prohibition) profitable occupation of moonshining. This provided his fulltime employment for the next three years or so, and he transported bootleg liquor as far afield as Lake Charles and east Texas. Dewey's exploits of whiskey-running, in a converted Chandler sedan, with a fifty-gallon accompanied by his wife and their several children "asleep" on a blanket at the back to avoid detection, make colorful and hair-raising tales.

It was in 1928, whilst on a whiskey run, at Port Arthur, just across the Louisiana-Texas border, that Dewey read in a local newspaper about French records being made in New Orleans. His uncle's son-in-law, a photographer, had some connections with these record manufacturers—Columbia—who at the time Dewey recalls, visited New Orleans every six months or so for recording sessions. Through his relative, Dewey and his brother Eddie managed to contact Columbia, and their session, he remembers, was a last-minute affair, made just prior to Columbia's departure from New Orleans. At that session, on Sunday, December 16, 1928, Dewey just played the accordion, his brother singing and playing the triangle.

Following this first session Dewey must have attained some local fame, and he gave up his risky moonshining business for the safer occupation of playing music. He formed several bands, some of which included two more of his

---

[1] This article first appeared in the British magazine *Old Time Music*, 12-14.

Brothers Dewey and Eddie Segura.
Photo courtesy of Johnnie Allan.

brothers; one played fiddle and the other, Joseph, was apparently aged only five when he joined Dewey's group.

In 1929 Dewey made two or three trips to New Orleans to try and make further recordings, deciding on hunches when the record company might be in town. On the first trip he hoboed to New Orleans by rail with his brother

Eddie. They missed the record people, but their uncle was successful in arranging a broadcast for them. The radio station, very probably WWL, ran an anyone-can-play show on which the Seguras played two numbers. The reception to their act, Dewey remembers, was so great—telephone calls and telegrams being received by the station—that the other acts were postponed while he and his brother played "all night."

In December 1929 Dewey did manage to catch up with the record people again. This trip to New Orleans was made not with his brother, who had lost interest in singing, but with guitarist Didier Hebert, and, apparently because of a very cold winter, they had a rather adventurous journey in a Dodge. Four recordings were made: on three Dewey sang and played accordion with Hebert accompanying on guitar, whilst Hebert sang and played by himself on the other.

Columbia credited Dewey's recordings to E. Segura, probably confusing him with his brother. They also misspelled Hebert's surname as Herbert. Neither Dewey nor Didier wrote many songs but they did contribute two to this session: Dewey wrote *You're Small and Sweet*, and Didier his solo *I Woke Up One Morning in May*. Dewey remembers that the recording team did not understand the words to his songs and his uncle had to give simple explanations of what he was singing. They warned that he shouldn't sing songs with "dirty" lyrics.

His reputation made by his recordings, Dewey remained a fulltime musician for the next couple of years, playing mainly in the Delcambre area but occasionally as far away as New Orleans or Texas. By about 1931, however, he found that the income from his music wouldn't support him, possibly because of the effects of the Depression, and he managed to find employment on a tugboat—a job he held for the next nineteen years, while continuing with music part-time.

Dewey's wife Euphemie often accompanied him on the guitar during this period, though she was "too ashamed" to sing. Percy Babineaux, a fiddler, also played with Dewey at some time during the '30s. Babineaux apparently asked to join Dewey at a function he was playing near Lafayette, a social at a local backwoods farm. Up to this time Dewey's brother had been accompanying him on the fiddle. Other accordionists Dewey played with were Amadie Breaux, Joe Falcon, and Iry LeJune, all of whom he used to meet at dances.

In the summer of 1934, John and Alan Lomax and Irène Whitfield came to southern Louisiana to record Louisiana-French folksongs for the Library of Congress. They recorded the singing of one of Dewey's brothers, probably Eddie or possibly Joe, who may have been accompanied by their fiddle-playing brother (whose name is unknown to us).

By 1950 Dewey had tired of his tugboat job and opted for employment nearer home. He found a suitable appointment operating the swing bridge that carried Louisiana State Highway 14 over the bayou at Delcambre. (The waterway is used for boat traffic.) This stable occupation, which gave him greater financial security and took up most of his time, meant he need not supplement his income by playing music, and in 1952 he gave up playing for dances. In 1957 he retired from the bridge job with a pension and since then has been living quietly with his wife in his native Delcambre.

# Leo Soileau[1]

## Tony Russell

Through the summer of 1928, record dealers in southern Louisiana rubbed their hands at the success of one of the latest Columbia's—Joseph Falcon, an accordion player from Rayne, singing and playing "Lafayette" and "The Waltz That Carried Me to My Grave," the first commercial record of Acadian French-Cajun-music. By late August Columbia had got the message and summoned Falcon for a second session of those quaint Old World dance-tunes and songs which were so evidently pleasing a valuable (and hitherto undiscerned) minority market in the bayou country. The word was getting out, and it could be only a matter of months, maybe weeks, before Columbia's chief rival got in on the act. Victor's first Cajun signing, in October, was the two-man band of accordionist/singer Mayuse LaFleur and fiddler Leo Soileau.

Falcon's success had reverberated among musicians' circles in Louisiana as well as in New York offices. Though a well-liked figure, Joe Falcon was not held in the highest regard by many musicians, and several may have felt, as we know Ernest Stoneman did upon hearing the records of Henry Whitter, that they could do at least as well themselves. Local businessmen boosted favored artists to visiting record-company agents, and before the spring of '29 was out several more companies (Paramount, Brunswick/Vocalian, Okeh) had joined the Cajun bandwagon.

This was how Soileau and LaFleur made it. An Opelousas acquaintance of Soileau, one Frank Dietlein, who had a jewellery store and sold records on the side, contacted the Victor agent and said he knew of an act that could match Falcon. The Victor man went to visit the musicians in their hometown of Basile. A week later, they in turn came up to Opelousas to meet him, and were put on their way to Atlanta, where Victor was holding a field session. On Friday, October 19, the duo cut four magnificent records. They were Victor's first venture into Acadian music, and the first recordings to feature a Cajun fiddler.

One of those remarkable performances, "Mama, Where You At?," can be heard on the second of Old Timey's reissues of early Cajun music (OT 109). LaFleur's accordion-playing is almost painfully exciting, pressing upon and almost hurrying the beat, a perfect match for the true Cajun plaintiveness of his singing. Soileau's fiddle weaves round the vocal and accordion melody. Joe Falcon came first, but he never approached this sort of playing. These are the first recordings that hint at the power of Cajun music.

---

[1] This article first appeared in *Old Time Music* 27 (1977): 5-9. Information for this essay was chiefly gained from an interview with Leo Soileau in Ville Platte, Louisiana, September 25, 1977, conducted by the author, who would like to thank to Mr. and Mrs. Soileau for their hospitality.

It was lucky LaFleur got to make that trip, for nine days later he was dead, victim of a shooting in a Basile bar.

Soileau now teamed up with another box-player, Moise Robin of Arnaudville (southeast of Opelousas), and together they recorded for three different companies in the summer of 1929. Paramount had dipped a toe into Cajun waters by recording the accordion-player John H. Bertrand, also of Arnaudville, about January 1929, and these sides, which include the first recording of what was later to be a hit for Soileau, "La Valse de Gueydan," had evidently whetted an appetite for more, which the company satisfied in July by bringing a party of Cajun musicians to the Richmond, Indiana, studios of Gennett, who often recorded material on their behalf. Bertrand was on this trip too, with Soileau, Robin and a singer and tenor guitarist from Crowley named Roy Gonzales, who made some fascinating sides translating Jimmie Rodgers songs into Acadian. Soileau and Robin cut the fine "Easy Rider Blues" and "Ma Cherie Tite Fille" (reissued on the fifth in Old Timey's series mentioned above) and a couple of others. Soileau may also have played fiddle on one or two of Gonzales' sides.

Two months later, in Memphis, there was a Victor date, and a month or so afterwards one for Vocalion in New Orleans. Typically these sessions would consist of two waltzes and two two steps, cross-coupled when released. The Vocalion performance "Le Cleuses de Negre Francaise" stands out as a loose bluesy piece (the correct spelling should perhaps be "Les Blues du Negre Francais") with a lovely relaxed vocal by Robin.

Soon after that, in early November, Victor held a session in New Orleans, recording Cajun bands solidly for the best part of a week. Though most of the material was issued, it is fantastically rare, and, so far as I know, nobody in collecting circles has ever heard what sound highly promising, the four sides by Leo Soileau twin fiddling with his cousin Alius Soileau from Eunice.

In the same week Leo recorded some duets with accordionist Wilfred Frugé, which were never released. (He has, however, no recollection of these sides.) Alius joined the accordion-player Oscar (Slim) Doucet, thought to be from Opelousas, for four sides, but this is his last appearance in known Cajun discography.

Cajun business lost the record companies' interest quite quickly, and after Brunswick's New Orleans session of winter 1930 (a date of extraordinary musical value, but financially unrewarding), there was no Cajun recording for nearly four years. As a seasoned dance musician, who on a good night could draw 350 or 400 couples, Soileau probably felt the pinch as little as anyone. Also, he was less conservative than many of his fellows, and old-fashioned Acadian music did not wholly satisfy him. Finding accordionists always too slow for him, he played his fiddle as a lead instrument, and when, towards the middle '30s, the accordion began to go out of fashion, he was scarcely one to bewail its loss. He formed a mainly stringed group, with Floyd Shreve on lead guitar, Bill (Dewey) Landry on tenor guitar, and a drummer. As the "Three Aces" they recorded for Bluebird in 1935, scoring an instant success with "La Valse de Gueydan"/ "Hackberry Hop," twice issued in the label's Cajun (B-2000) series.

There were further recordings on Bluebird, but they stayed in the Cajun list, not breaking out into the general southern market as the Hackberry Ramblers did. Possibly Bluebird didn't see the potential of Soileau's new band; maybe it didn't seem different enough from the string groups already on the label.

At any rate, Soileau took his services to Decca, signing a contract to begin an association that was to last, he says, eight years. The band—now Four Aces—piled into a Ford Model A and drove all the way from Crowley (where Soileau was now living) to Chicago for their first session.

Decca's first move in the Cajun field had been in the winter of the previous year, 1934, when two established recording artists, Joseph Falcon and the accordion-player Amedie Ardoin, were brought to New York to lay the foundation of a Cajun catalogue, the 17000 series. Soileau's Four Aces were the next to be recorded. Logs of the May 1935 Chicago session mention two names

The Four Aces Orchestra, led by legendary fiddler Leo Soileau, Crowley, Louisiana, ca. 1934. From left to right, Bill Landry, Soileau, O.P. Shreve, Tony Gonzales, and Floyd Shreve.
*Photo courtesy of Johnnie Allan.*

that are hard to fit in, O. P. Shreve and Johnny Roberts; possibly they played bass and drums. (A Johnny Roberts later recorded a couple of country songs for Decca in Dallas; I have no idea if it was the same man.) At any rate, the dominant sounds of the Four Aces' records were the angular, often very bluesy fiddle of Soileau, and the singing of Floyd Shreve. The first sides recorded were Cajun tunes for the 17000 series, but Decca wanted hillbilly material, too, for the regular (5000) series, and the band came up with Acadian-flavored renderings of "My Brown Eyed Texas Rose," "Little Dutch Mill," "Birmingham Jail," "My Wild Irish Rose," and other country and pop favorites of the day. If not then, certainly later, Soileau would listen to contemporary bands' records for possible material, and among his favorites were Milton Brown's Brownies.

An anecdote of Soileau's about this session testifies to the new ground that he was crossing. The Decca engineer, seeing a drum kit being set up in the studio, asked Soileau what he was doing. "Making records," came the answer. There were problems, sure enough, and pillows had to be stacked round the kit (which consisted of bass drum, snare and foot cymbal) to absorb some of the sound. But on playback it seemed to be going down all right. "Well," said the engineer, "I'm learning something."

The roster of pop and hillbilly tunes at this first session seems to imply manipulation, but in fact it was very much to taste. He had grown rather tired of traditional Cajun tunes, and welcomed the opportunity of playing "English" material, which he felt had "more music" in it—more chord changes, more interesting melodies. Like many musicians who play for varied audiences, he prided himself on being able to draw from several traditions—polkas, Mexican music, square-dances and so forth. He worked extensively in Louisiana and parts of southeast Texas, and met many of the Texas band musicians, like Cliff Bruner, the Raleys, Bob Dunn and Moon Mullican. Often they would run into each other at the Dallas recording sessions which Decca held in the later '30s. Soileau remembers that there might be as many as sixty musicians staying at one hotel while recordings were going on.

The Four Aces, now apparently consisting of Soileau, Shreve, Landry and drummer Tony Gonzales (a brother of Roy), had another long session for Decca in New Orleans in March 1936. Again, pop and country material predominated over Cajun, particularly the former. Numbers like "Painting the Clouds with Sunshine" and "Love Letters in the Sand" were taken on as readily as "Wreck of Old No 97." The abilities of the musicians were not always equal to the more sophisticated tunes—one can sometimes hear the guitarists messing up the changes—but all through the session there was a solid, danceable rhythm, typical of the band's background.

Embracing all this "foreign" material, Soileau might have been expected to turn his band into something more like a western swing unit, and a nod in this direction may be detected at the next recording date, in February 1937, when the group changed its name to Leo Soileau's Rhythm Boys. But there was not much alteration in their style, and all the sides were issued exclusively in the Cajun series. This did not mean, however, a return to traditional Acadian material: a lot of what was coming out in the 17000s was simply current pop or hillbilly songs with their lyrics translated into French.

Soileau's last recordings were made in December of that year, with a lineup (still called the Rhythm Boys) of fiddle, piano, electric guitar, rhythm guitar, and bass. At dances of this period, Soileau says, he was using pickups on all the instruments in the band. Again, the sides were kept for the Cajun series, which ran for another year or so but seems to have stopped releasing material around 1940.

During the war years Soileau had a variety of nightclub jobs, for example in Orange, Texas and Lake Charles, Louisiana. While at the Silver Star in Lake Charles he would often meet up with Cliff Bruner's band, then active around the Beaumont-Port Arthur area. At the end of the war he was on a long engagement (fourteen months) at the Showboat in Orange, with a band of fiddle, steel guitar, electric mandolin, piano, rhythm guitar, bass and drums. (The only musician whose name he recalls is drummer Crawford Vincent. The picture alongside may be from this period; the steel player is Papa Cairo, the others unidentified.)

He also had broadcasting spots on KVOL Lafayette, KPLC Lake Charles, KWKH Shreveport, and a Port Arthur station. "Under the Double Eagle" was the band's theme song. He cut some transcriptions for the Lafayette and Lake Charles stations, sponsored by Community Coffee, but did not participate in the revived Cajun recording scene of the late '40s and '50s, though he played with some of its luminaries, like Iry LeJune.

He retired from music—which had always been his fulltime occupation—in 1953, and spent the next six years working at an oil refinery in Lake Charles, where he had lived since the '30s. Then he moved to Ville Platte to work as a janitor, finally retiring about 1968. He still lives in that town, a few stonesthrows from the well-known store of Floyd Soileau (no relation), one of the centers of present-day Cajun record-making and selling.

The old Aces are mostly gone; Floyd Shreve and Dewey Landry died in the early postwar years, and Soileau has lost touch with Gonzales (who may still be around Crowley). Moise Robin is still around, though, and indeed he cut a record not so long ago, for the local Cajun Classics label owned by Jay Miller: "Poor Me" and "Chere Petite Filles de Louisianne" (2007). His singing had weakened but the accordion-playing was strong, and it was pleasant to hear so old-fashioned a style on a new 45. There was quite unobtrusive backing (fiddle, guitar, and triangles), and a churning repetitiveness that was reminiscent of some bluesy Nathan Abshire sides of the day. An odd occurrence, however, and one would like to know what motivated it.

Leo Soileau plays no more, but is glad to discuss the old days, and has been visited by several interested parties in recent years. A few of his recordings have come out on anthologies (though the Aces and Rhythm Boys sides have been largely neglected), and Morning Star Records hopes to assemble the best early material, with Lafleur and Robin, for an LP in the near future. It will be wonderful music, but it will not, on its own, demonstrate the most remarkable quality of Soileau's musical career—his ability to move with the times, and the unusually long recording life this talent permitted.

# The Hackberry Ramblers

*Ben Sandmel*

Back in 1933, during the depths of the Depression, two young men named Luderin Darbone and Edwin Duhon formed a dance band called the Hackberry Ramblers. The group remained in almost continuous existence for more than seven subsequent decades, performing only in Louisiana, for the most part. A late-career resurgence that began in 1991 and lasted a dozen years saw the Ramblers play all over America and make three trips to Europe. Due to advancing age, such travels are limited once again to Louisiana. Edwin Duhon passed away on February 26, 2006, at age 95, and long-time bandmembers Johnny Faulk, Johnny Farque, and Crawford Vincent, who played with the Ramblers during the 1990s, are gone now, as well. But at this writing (May 2006) Luderin Darbone remains in good health at age 93, and he is eager to keep playing. Future engagements, in-state, may yet occur.

In the course of seventy-three years, the Hackberry Ramblers' instrumentation has changed, their repertoire has expanded greatly, and numerous musicians have come and gone. Yet with all these changes, Darbone and Duhon's original *raison d'être* remained the same—to make people dance. Persevering through thick and thin, these handsome young hit-makers of the 1930s evolved into revered elder statesmen of Cajun music. Until quite recently, the Hackberry Ramblers were lauded for their remarkable longevity and undiminished appeal to dancers.

From an historical perspective, however, the Ramblers are best known for two major contributions to the evolution of Cajun music. The Ramblers were the first band to blend the traditional Cajun repertoire, sung in French, with Anglo-American country music sung in English. They were also the first musicians to bring electronic amplification to area dancehalls. Such innovations did not occur in a vacuum. The Ramblers' rich saga is inextricably linked with the cultural, social and political history of Louisiana—both as the product of such forces, and as musical innovators in their own right. Before discussing this legacy in further detail, it must be mentioned that this writer combines several different perspectives. In addition to my work as a folklorist and journalist, I have also worked with the Hackberry Ramblers since 1987 as the band's drummer, manager, and record producer. The primary purpose of my contribution here is to introduce and contextualize Luderin Darbone's remarkable essay about the history of the band.

Profound changes swept southwest Louisiana during the 1930s, as a once-isolated, agrarian, and primarily French-speaking society felt the growing pains of industrialization. Development of the area's oil fields, which began at the turn of the century, was accompanied by the rapid advance of mainstream American culture and the English language. The latter was reinforced by a ban on speaking French in Louisiana's public schools, enacted in 1921. This edict reflected a prevailing sentiment that was memorably expressed by Theodore Roosevelt: "There is room for but one language in this country, and that is the English language, for we must assure that the crucible turns out Americans and not some random dwellers in a polyglot boarding house." Roosevelt also railed against the concept of "hyphenated Americans."

Modernization accelerated rapidly with Huey Long's aggressive program of Depression-era highway construction. These new thoroughfares made Cajun/Creole country infinitely more accessible to the outside world, especially to an influx of oil field workers from neighboring Texas and Oklahoma. Aural highways made significant inroads as well, thanks to the burgeoning popularity of radio and records. Before the advent of these new inventions, early twentieth-century Cajun music was primarily characterized by medieval French fiddle tunes and *a capella* ballads that had been brought to Louisiana via Acadie after *le Grand Dérangement*. Along with this distinct ethnic identity, Cajun music interacted with some other genres. In particular, many Cajuns lived in close contact with black people whose African American and Afro-Caribbean traditions such as *juré* and blues became important aspects of the Cajun-music aesthetic. And the raucous sound of the accordion—regarded today as the archetypal instrument of both Cajun music and zydeco—is, in fact, a cultural contribution from Austria and Germany, its region of origin.

During the latter half of the nineteenth century, Austrian and German peddlers began selling accordions around America. The accordion was durable, portable, and loud enough, in the days before electricity, to cut through the noise of a crowd. It caught on quickly in many parts of the nation, Louisiana included, and was still popular when the first recordings of Cajun and Creole music were made in the 1920s. By the next decade, however, the accordion dwindled out of fashion in Cajun music, and the 1930s came to be known as the Cajun string-band era. The growing influence and popularity of fiddle-dominated country music contributed to this phenomenon. So did the advent of electronic amplification, which allowed acoustic instruments such as fiddles and guitars to be heard clearly for the first time. The accordion virtually disappeared from the Cajun music of this period; Barry Ancelet aptly notes that it temporarily became an *instrumenta non grata*. After World War Two, however, the accordion ascended again, thanks to such great players as Iry LeJeune, Lawrence Walker, and Nathan Abshire. Eventually, Edwin Duhon resumed playing his accordion with the Hackberry Ramblers, among various other instruments.

During the 1930s, the dissemination of new musical ideas advanced at ever-increasing speed with the ever-expanding installation of electricity. Among the many fresh styles introduced to Louisiana via the new media of radio and records, the two sounds that resonated the most were country music and jazz. Coincidentally, these two genres were then forming a unique synthesis known as western swing, thus disproving the stereotype that country and jazz are mutually exclusive. This lilting hybrid caught the ear of young Luderin Darbone.

Significantly, Darbone had not learned to play fiddle via folk tradition within an ethnic community. Quite the contrary—in a move that personified the era's social changes, he took a correspondence course in violin from a music school based in New York City. With the ability to read musical notation, Darbone bought the published sheet music to various popular songs. Once he memorized a song, Darbone did not need to read the score again, and his keen memory also allowed him to learn traditional material by ear.

Darbone was born in Evangeline, Louisiana, in 1913, but spent much of his childhood in east Texas. He grew up listening mainly to Anglo-American string-bands. Darbone's father moved the family frequently in search of oil field work and eventually brought them to the small Cameron Parish town of Hackberry. There young Darbone encountered Cajun music in general, and a neighboring youth named Edwin Duhon who played both accordion and guitar. The two started working up some numbers together, retreating to the Duhon's tool shed after "my old man threw us out of the house, we sounded so goddamn bad!" Significantly, the duo's efforts mirrored the growing regional trend of the string-band era when Duhon set aside his accordion to play guitar exclusively. "We had a radio," Darbone explained to writer, researcher, and musician Ann Savoy, "and we'd start listening to this hillbilly music from Nashville and other parts of the country, and there were no accordions in it. So we started playing fiddle and guitar."

Darbone and Duhon brought a second guitarist into their new group, and started playing at dances and parties. When the threesome was hired to make live weekly radio broadcasts in Lake Charles, Darbone formalized the band's existence by naming it the Hackberry Ramblers. Air-time brought more bookings, and soon the Ramblers were playing five nights a week in different clubs, and continuing to broadcast on Mondays. Life on the road was tough, as it is for most young bands; the threesome slept on dancehall floors, survived on sardines and crackers, and spent hours on rutted gravel roads where the maximum possible cruising speed was thirty-five miles per hour. "The first time we flew from Louisiana to New York, in 1991," Darbone points out, "it took less time to get there than driving seventy-five miles from Hackberry to Basile, back in the '30s. That was an all-day trip."

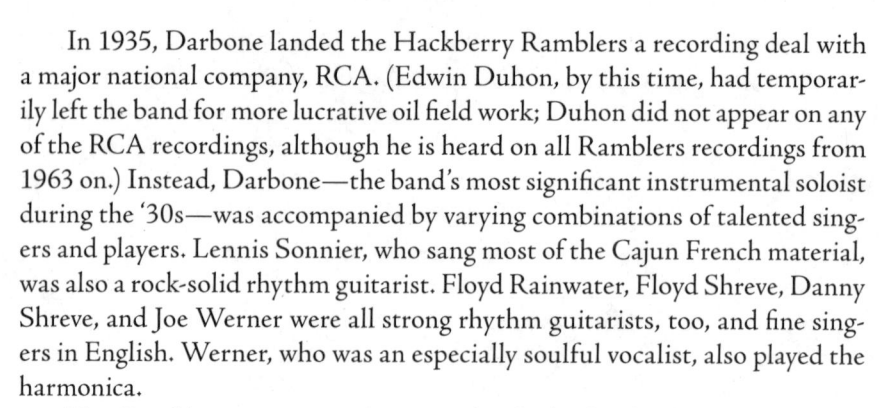

In 1935, Darbone landed the Hackberry Ramblers a recording deal with a major national company, RCA. (Edwin Duhon, by this time, had temporarily left the band for more lucrative oil field work; Duhon did not appear on any of the RCA recordings, although he is heard on all Ramblers recordings from 1963 on.) Instead, Darbone—the band's most significant instrumental soloist during the '30s—was accompanied by varying combinations of talented singers and players. Lennis Sonnier, who sang most of the Cajun French material, was also a rock-solid rhythm guitarist. Floyd Rainwater, Floyd Shreve, Danny Shreve, and Joe Werner were all strong rhythm guitarists, too, and fine singers in English. Werner, who was an especially soulful vocalist, also played the harmonica.

The Ramblers were signed to RCA's Bluebird subsidiary. During the 1930s and '40s, RCA-Bluebird also recorded other fellow Cajun musicians; prominent jazz artists including Louis Armstrong, Jelly Roll Morton, and Benny Goodman; rural blues stylists Leadbelly and Memphis Minnie; early country stars the Carter Family and Jimmie Rodgers; and the suave crooner Frank Sinatra.

RCA-Bluebird's vast, eclectic catalogue embraced many ethnic genres and documented a wealth of fine traditional music that might otherwise have never been recorded. The company's role as cultural preservationists was purely coincidental, however. Its sole mission was to sell records and make money and, in microcosm, the same can be said of the Hackberry Ramblers. The Ramblers were young, ambitious, forward-thinkers who scrambled to make a living during the depths of the Great Depression. Although many of their '30s recordings sound somewhat dated today, they functioned then as cutting-edge modernists. Unabashedly commercial, with nary a thought of folkloric legacies, the Ramblers wanted to record hits.

By the time the Ramblers signed with RCA-Bluebird they were performing an improbably eclectic repertoire that seamlessly encompassed Cajun material, sung in

The Hackberry Ramblers, ca. 1941. From left to right Minos Broussard, Crawford Vincent, Luderin Darbone, and Jack Theriot.
*Photo courtesy of Luderin Darbone.*

French, and a wide variety of material sung in English: country, blues, adaptations of New Orleans jazz, popular songs, and songs reflecting ephemeral fads such as Hawaiian novelty numbers. This stylistic blend was quite unique; heretofore, bands that played Cajun music rarely played little if any songs from other styles, or sang in English. In retrospect, such diversity has aptly come to be recognized as a major cultural milestone. At the time, however, it was simply a canny move to sell more records and get more bookings.

Accordingly, the Ramblers' sessions for Bluebird, recorded between 1935 and '38, in New Orleans, touched on the entire spectrum of what they played at dances. The best known number was the first version of *"Jolie Blonde,"* under that title. The song, which later came to be informally known as "the Cajun national anthem," was first recorded as *"Ma Blonde Est Parti"* by Amédée Breaux. But the band also recorded such jazz songs as "You've Got to Hi-De-Hi" and "Ain't Gonna Give You None of My Jellyroll," with vocal jive reminiscent of Cab Calloway, and "Vinton High Society," an instrumental spin-off of Johnny Dodd's famous clarinet solo from the King Oliver recording of "High Society." This jazz standard has its origins in turn-of-the-century military marches, and has been covered and claimed by countless other artists. Darbone confined his interpretation to the clarinet solo only, rather than the complete ragtime arrangement from Oliver's record. Darbone's solo draws on a masterful mixed bag of tricks, including nimble stop-time runs, percussive passages, and seamless shifts between bowing and plucking.

The jazz element in Darbone's playing is due, in part, to his move to Crowley, Louisiana, in 1935, where that he met an African American trumpeter named Ike Jenkins. "Oh, he was a nice fellow," Darbone recollects, "and a smart fellow, too. He led a big band, and I wish I'd thought to ask him for some of his charts and lead sheets—he wrote some great arrangements, and all of his bandmembers could read sheet music. I used to go hear them play at different places, and Jenkins would hang around my service station in Crowley. Sometimes we'd sit and talk for two or three hours at a time."

Darbone absorbed many jazz and blues concepts from Jenkins' live performances, as well as from the jazz-infused western swing recordings of artists such as Bob Wills. It was Wills' recording of "Trouble in Mind," for instance, that inspired Darbone's *"Fais Pas Ça,"* a blues tune that the Ramblers still perform today. The same goes for "[Sitting] On Top of the World," a song that was popularized again the '50s by the great blues singer Howlin' Wolf. But the Ramblers' Cajun roots remained evident on such songs as the waltz: *"J'ai Passe Devonde Ta Porte,"* (which first appeared as *"Mon coeur t'appelle,"* a 1929 recording by Cléoma Falcon) and the rollicking two steps "Mermentau Stomp," *"J'ai Pres Parley,"* One-Step De L'Amour" and "Hackberry Trot." Note that the French titles cited here reflect the hit-or-miss spellings that appeared on the original record labels.

"Dissatisfied," "Drifting Along" and "One Sweet Letter" are squarely in the western-swing camp, with infectious grooves and powerful vocals by Joe Werner. "One Sweet Letter," like many of the group's English songs, was released under the name "Riverside Ramblers"—because Darbone had made a sponsorship deal with Montgomery Ward, a national chain of department stores and mail-order merchants. "Montgomery Ward was the advertiser for one our radio programs in '36 and '37," Darbone explains. "They were pushing a house brand of tires called 'Riverside.' We cut sixteen sides as 'The Riverside Ramblers.'" Such commercial endorsements were common at the time; one popular western swing band of the era was known as The Light Crust Doughboys. Then, as now, sponsorship helped offset the considerable expenses of keeping a band on the road.

One of the Riverside Ramblers' biggest hits was an English number entitled "Wondering." The song introduced Darbone to the seamy side of the music business. "Decca Records asked us to re-record "Wondering" for them," Darbone recalls, "and I didn't want to mess up our deal with RCA. Next thing you know, Joe Werner splits off and records it for Decca as 'Joe Werner and the Ramblers.' He took out a copyright on the song, too. We were disappointed that he did that." In 1951, "Wondering" was a hit, once again, for the great north Louisiana country singer Webb Pierce, and it has also been recorded by such contemporary artists as Emmylou Harris and Elvis Costello.

In a similar spirit of commercialism, RCA's Eli Oberstein asked Darbone to record the Hawaiian novelty song "A Little Rendezvous in Honolulu." "I wrote back to him and said we'd give it a try," Darbone says. "Eli sent me the sheet music, and we worked it up with Floyd Rainwater singing lead. I think it came out pretty good. It was different for us in several ways, because RCA usually wanted us to record peppy numbers."

The Ramblers' forward-looking approach forged another important innovation. Darbone grew frustrated with the limited volume of his acoustic trio, which was drowned out by dancing feet at the Ramblers' increasingly well-attended engagements. With the fiddle's increased popularity and the temporary decline of the accordion, Darbone wanted people to really hear him. Noticing that politicians were amplifying their stump speeches by using newly-invented public address systems, Darbone decided to order one from Sears & Roebuck. He was the first bandleader in southwest Louisiana to do so. But this presented another challenge, because some places where the Ramblers played still did not have electricity. Undaunted, Darbone powered his primitive sound system with the engine of his car, which idled throughout the length of the Ramblers' dances.

Amplification constituted a truly quantum leap. For the first time, musicians who played acoustic instruments could make themselves clearly heard by simply stepping up to the microphone. This new audibility encouraged dramatic improvement in instrumental technique; up until then one's level of skill didn't matter much since they couldn't be heard anyway. Amplification also offered up the concept of soloing for players who had previously been limited to playing rhythm parts and keeping time for dancers. Luderin Darbone, in particular, emerged as a deft and sophisticated fiddle soloist on a par with such noted contemporaries as Bob Wills, Joe Venuti, and Stephane Grappelli. In addition to the pioneering contributions of the band as a whole, Darbone's style has influenced such stellar Louisiana fiddlers as Harry Choates, Hadley Castille, and Michael Doucet.

By the mid-1940s, Darbone had moved to Sulphur, and the Hackberry Ramblers were based in Calcasieu Parish, in the western suburbs of Lake Charles. Darbone's acoustic trio had evolved into a nine-piece western swing orchestra with horn players, a drummer, and a hot electric guitar soloist named Grover Heard. With this configuration the Ramblers settled into a decade-long tenure at an area dancehall called the Silver Star. Many prominent country artists also played there, including T. Texas Tyler and Moon Mullican. At times these stars were co-billed with the Ramblers and engaged them in friendly competitions known as "a battle of the bands."

Ten years was a good run, even by the Hackberry Ramblers' standards of longevity, but by the early 1960s there was little demand for their unique brand of Cajun swing. Rock and roll had ascended, country had grown self-consciously slick and orchestrated, and Cajun culture was still scorned in the assimilationist atmosphere of the Eisenhower era. All of the Ramblers had day jobs, to use musicians' parlance, and Luderin Darbone seriously considered retiring the band.

It was at this critical juncture that opportunity—in the form of one Chris Strachwitz—came knocking, quite literally, on Darbone's door. Strachwitz ran a then-fledgling record label, Arhoolie Records, that focused on a wide variety of esoteric ethnic music. Arhoolie produced new recordings and also reissued vintage material, specializing in music that major record labels dismissed as obscure and commercially unviable. The newly formed company had already changed the course of Louisiana music by introducing Clifton Chenier's zydeco to discerning listeners around the world. Arhoolie remains gloriously active today and Chris Strachwitz, like Luderin Darbone and Edwin Duhon, is justly revered as a trailblazer.

In 1963 Strachwitz was on the road in Louisiana, buying old 78 rpm records and looking for artists to record. He drove to Hackberry in search of Luderin Darbone and was directed instead to Darbone's current home in the town of Sulphur. Strachwitz rapped on the door, introduced himself, and soon convinced Darbone to keep the Ramblers together because Arhoolie wanted to record them anew. The importance of this meeting cannot be overstated, because without it Darbone would quite likely have dissolved the band.

In addition to longtime members Darbone, Duhon, and Lennis Sonnier—lead singer on the original *"Jolie Blonde"*—the album that Strachwitz recorded in '63 featured a young steel guitarist named Glen Croker. Croker joined the Ramblers in 1959 and is still with them today. He now plays electric guitar and also serves as the emcee and principal lead singer. Today, Croker's steel sound is reprised on some Ramblers shows by Terry Huval. Huval, best known as the fiddler and lead singer for the Jambalaya Cajun Band, is also a fine steel guitarist.

A generation younger than the Ramblers' founders, Croker expanded the band's repertoire by introducing rhythm & blues, rockabilly, and swamp pop. With his input, the Ramblers' chronological repertoire extends to such late-'60s songs as Merle Haggard's "Today I Started Loving You Again" and Credence Clearwater Revival's "Proud Mary." The latter is a romanticized depiction of Southern culture that the Ramblers have reinvented, full-circle, as authentic folk art. Besides Croker, the current line-up also includes this writer as drummer/record producer. In the years since Luderin Darbone wrote the annotated history of the band, below, rhythm guitarist Johnny Farque and bassist Johnny Faulk have both passed away, and Crawford Vincent has retired.

In 1984 I saw the Hackberry Ramblers perform at the World's Fair in New Orleans, and I was astounded. Their music was obviously out of the past, but the joy that it emanated—along with the compelling power to make people dance—was timeless and undiminished. I noted these qualities in an article about traditional music at the World's Fair for the *Times-Picayune*, having no idea that I would cross the Ramblers' path again. Then in 1987 I programmed the music for the Louisiana Folklife Festival, which was held that year in Baton Rouge. Remembering their hot set from 1984 I immediately booked the Hackberry Ramblers. For some reason they arrived to perform without a drummer; we got to talking, I sat in, and the music clicked as if we'd played together for years.

This marked the inception of the band's comeback. The Cajun/Creole cultural renaissance was in full swing as was the Cajun chic fad—fueled by the parallel success of Chef Paul Prudhomme and the popular film *The Big Easy*, with its south Louisiana soundtrack. The Ramblers had been working infrequently, in Louisiana only, and it was an auspicious time to bring them wider circulation. After rave reviews from a 1991 performance in New York, the band went on to cut two new albums. *Cajun Boogie*, released in 1993, marked the first recording in thirty years, while *Deep Water* followed in 1997. These 1990s albums featured guest artists Marcia Ball, Rodney Crowell, Michael Doucet, and Jimmie Dale Gilmore. As performers of original, innovative material that is grounded in tradition, all have an organic connection with the music of the Hackberry Ramblers.

*Deep Water* was nominated for a Grammy Award as the Best Traditional Folk Album of 1997. Attending the Grammy ceremonies in New York, the Hackberry Ramblers also made an unlikely but well-received appearance on MTV—alongside a teen band called Hanson, on a broadcast that celebrated the year's oldest and youngest nominees.

Since then the Ramblers have graced far-flung venues all around America, festival concert stages in France and Holland, and national television and radio programs such as *Fresh Air*, *All Things Considered*, and even *Entertainment Tonight*. A life-long dream was fulfilled by performing on the Grand Ole Opry, in December 1999; in September 2002, Luderin Darbone and Edwin Duhon were jointly awarded a prestigious National Heritage Fellowship by the Folk Arts Panel of the National Endowment for the Arts. In January 2004, the hour-long documentary *Make 'Em Dance: The Hackberry Ramblers' Story*, aired on the PBS series *Independent Lens*. Through all of this commotion, and no small amount of culture shock, both the Ramblers' music and stage persona have both remained remarkably unchanged. Age has taken its toll in terms of precision but there has been no loss of passion or the power to get couples a-twirling.

In performance, songs are chosen spontaneously, based on what seems to best suit the crowd. The eclectic program is augmented by Croker's classic corny jokes and country platitudes. These factors are constant whether the Ramblers play for their elderly peers or at grunge bars where the youthful patrons sport green hair, body piercings, and florid tattoos. There have been initial moments of mutual consternation with such young crowds, but it dissipates instantly when they hit the floor. Sometimes their moves seem best suited to mosh pits, and even the most enthusiastic may know or care nothing about the Hackberry Ramblers' venerable résumé. They simply respond to the songs—"Jolie Blonde," "Take Me Back to Tulsa," "C.C. Rider," "J'étais au bal," "Whole Lotta Shakin' Going On"—and accept the band on its own terms. Seventy-two years later, Luderin Darbone still maintains that "the best compliment you can pay the Hackberry Ramblers is to dance to our music."

Luderin Darbone is a meticulous man. For most of his musical career Darbone played on weekends only, after working every Monday through Friday as a bookkeeper and accountant. This profession calls for precise record-keeping, obviously, and Darbone extended a similar approach towards the details, names and dates of his avocation. In addition, Darbone remains intellectually curious and well-informed, to this day. Accordingly, his chronicle of the Hackberry Ramblers reflects an understanding of the broader social, cultural, and musical contexts in which the band emerged. Many musicians do not possess such a broad perspective. We are fortunate, indeed, that Luderin Darbone does.

# Brief History of the Hackberry Ramblers[1]

## *Luderin Darbone*

The Hackberry Ramblers string band was organized in Hackberry, Louisiana, by Luderin Darbone and Edwin Duhon in March of 1933.[2] Darbone played fiddle and Duhon played accordion and guitar, a third member, Alvin Ellender played guitar also.[3] On several occasions he returned to find there were other string groups who played for house parties, but the Hackberry Ramblers decided to seek more fertile grounds and decided to go professional and play their type of music in dancehalls located in towns and country localities. Dancehall owners in most towns used orchestras.[4] On Saturday nights while the country dancehall owners used the traditional Cajun band, which consisted of an accordion player, fiddle player, and a triangle player; later a rhythm guitar player was added. The triangle, or "little iron" as it was called, was used to sustain the rhythm of the band. As stated above the Hackberry

---

[1] This first hand account of the band's history was written in 1991.
[2] Neither Darbone nor Duhon was born and raised in Hackberry; both moved with their families, as teenagers, when their fathers found oil field work.
[3] Duhon soon set his accordion aside to concentrate on guitar. In doing so he reflected a broader trend that saw the accordion fall from favor in the Cajun music of the 1930s, although it returned to prominence after World War Two. In addition, Duhon left the band frequently to pursue lucrative oil field work and electrical engineering jobs in central and south America. Each time he returned to Louisiana he had to learn a new instrument in order to rejoin the band, because each successive instrument was assigned to someone else in his absence. Over the years Duhon played piano, acoustic bass, harmonica (which he called "French harp"), and drums; when I joined the Ramblers, in 1987, he played electric guitar almost exclusively. By 1993, however, he set this instrument aside to focus on the accordion.

In a 1993 letter to this writer, Duhon recalled his varied roles in the band:

> the first I met the kid [Darbone], which at the time he was a teenager, I was 23 years old, just come back from Broussard, just out of Lafayette. I was working at my uncle's meat market every Sat. nite we played at St. Martin [this may refer to neighboring St. Martin Parish or the town of St. Martinville] at a dancehall, he played the accordion and I played the guitar. When I moved at Hackberry, LA, my daddy run an oil lease and I wanted to find someone that played some kind of instrument to practice [with.] My mother told me that Mr. Darbone [sic] that run the oil lease across the street had a boy learning to play fiddle. I visited with Ludrin [sic] and at the time he was taking music lesson[s] mail order. So we started to practice every evening and that's how the band started. I was an oil-field worker but was out of work at the time. We decided to give a name to our band and we came up with the name the Hackberry Ramblers...

> "We done good for a few years, I played rhythm guitar. I left for the oil field for awhile, when I came back someone had took my place so I played lead then I left for a job in South America. When I came back we had a lead guitar player so I bought me a brand new bull-fiddle stand-up bass with [a] pick-up on it and all, I played about six months and then I had to leave. When I came back we had an electric bass so I played piano for five years. We played three nights a week at the Silver Star Club for nine or ten years. I was chief of police of Westlake, then.

[4] Darbone's use of the term "orchestras" here is a general term for bands that were popular at the time. It does not refer to performances of formal, classical compositions that required the ability to read music.

Ramblers originated the band, using only a fiddle and two rhythm guitars.[5] Ellender did not play too long [due to his work in the oil fields] and he was replaced with Floyd Rainwater who played rhythm guitar and was a gifted singer and yodeler.[6] Rainwater added tremendously to the band.

To go professional the Hackberry Ramblers realized they had to become well known. Luck was with the band, because at that time, there were no radio stations in southwest Louisiana and the only radio station that covered southwest Louisiana was KFDM located in Beaumont, Texas. The owners of KFDM decided to set up a radio station in the Majestic Hotel in Lake Charles at the same time the Hackberry Ramblers organized, to be operated by remote control from Beaumont. The band obtained radio time from the new station, the call letters were the same as the station located in Beaumont, which was KFDM but it was operated by the Lake Charles Broadcasting Co. The band started broadcasting once per week in March of 1933 on Monday mornings at 7:00 a.m. for fifteen minutes. The band played an assortment of hillbilly (now country) and popular selections, with an occasional Cajun waltz or two step per session.

The listeners were tired of the accordion bands because most of them at that time were limited to a repertoire of Cajun waltz and breakdown tunes only, whereas the Hackberry Ramblers played hillbilly numbers, such as "Bonnie Blue Eyes," "Just Because," "Corrine Corrina," etc., popular numbers, such as "Diana," "Tiger Rag," "The Waltz You Saved for Me," etc. plus Cajun tunes.

The band began receiving requests by the score and were hired to play their first country dancehall engagement in Basile, Louisiana in April of 1933 and were an instant success. The band started getting bookings at other country dancehalls throughout southwest Louisiana.

It wasn't long before the accordion bands began fading out. The sound of the string bands was not as loud as the music of the accordion bands and that caused hesitancy of some of the dancers to regularly attend the string band dances. In the fall of 1933, the Hackberry Ramblers remedied that situation by being the first string band to acquire and use a sound amplification system in southwest Louisiana. Of course, this created a sensation and the popularity of the band was assured. It wasn't too long before other string bands started popping up and the accordion bands took a back seat for several years. About

---

[5] While the Hackberry Ramblers are justly renowned for the innovations mentioned above, it seems unlikely that they literally originated the format of one fiddle and two guitars as Darbone asserts here. This configuration was one of many that were commonly used in string bands. Perhaps, however, this first incarnation of the Ramblers was also the first band with such a line-up on the Cameron/Calcasieu Parish circuit.

[6] This refers to the "blue yodeling" style popularized by Jimmie Rodgers during the 1920s. Country music's first recording star, Rodgers interspersed many of the verses of his songs with non-verbal, falsetto yodels.

80 per cent of the new string bands formed and named themselves Ramblers also.

The Hackberry Ramblers became so well known they were asked by RCA Victor to record for them on their Bluebird label. The first session was in August of 1935 when ten selections were recorded; they continued to record for RCA until the fall of 1938. The band was under contract and would travel to New Orleans every six months for the recording session. For the first recording session, the musicians were Luderin Darbone, fiddle; Lennis Sonnier, guitar; Floyd Rainwater, guitar; Joe Werner, guitar and harmonic; Johnny Puderer, bass fiddle; Floyd Shreve, guitar; Danny Shreve, guitar; and Pete Duhon, bass fiddle. An average of four musicians were used at each recording session. A total of eighty-two selections were recorded for RCA.

In 1936 the Hackberry Ramblers band was hired by Montgomery Ward, located in downtown Lafayette, to broadcast over KVOL, a new Lafayette radio station, three times a week direct from the store by remote control. The band broadcast from the store for one year. For broadcasting and advertising purposes while playing for Montgomery Ward, the band was renamed the Riverside Ramblers in a contest conducted by the store. After hundreds of suggestions, the band was renamed Riverside Ramblers to advertise Montgomery Ward's most popular tire at that time, "the Riverside Rambler."

When the band would be called for a recording session after the first session, twelve selections would be recorded each time; eight Cajun selections would be shown as being recorded by the Hackberry Ramblers and four English selections would be shown as being recorded by the Riverside Ramblers. That is why the song "Wondering" which was one of the most popular hits by the band is shown as being recorded by the Riverside Ramblers. Other popular Riverside Rambler songs were "There'll Come a Time," "One Sweet Letter," "Right or Wrong," and "Little Acadian Girl." The Hackberry Ramblers was the first band to record Louisiana's most popular Cajun tune and song using the title "Jolie Blonde." The tune had been previously recorded by

*Ramblers' guitarist Floyd Rainwater, sporting a cowboy stage outfit. ca. 1944. Photo courtesy of Luderin Darbone.*

an accordion band with a different title.[7] Other popular Hackberry Rambler Cajun songs were "Une Pias Ici, Une Pias La Bas," "La Breakdown à Pete," "Mermentau Stomp," and "Faux Pas tu Brai Cherie." In early 1939, Darbone and the band quit playing music for a while when Darbone's father was killed in an oil field accident in Hackberry, Louisiana.

In early 1940 the Hackberry Ramblers reorganized with Darbone playing fiddle, Jack Theriot playing steel guitar, Minos Broussard playing rhythm guitar, and Crawford Vincent playing drums. This band played every weekend in Creole, Louisiana for two years until World War II caused the drafting of all members of the band except Darbone. Again the band had to disband temporarily. Darbone, who was the oldest of the group we[n]t to work for Swift & Company, a meat packing firm which was an essential industry necessary for the war effort, soon joined another band in the Lake Charles area which was immediately renamed the Hackberry Ramblers, due to the name being well known. Members of this band were Luderin Darbone, fiddle; Edwin Duhon, guitar; Eddie Schuler, guitar; Chink Widcamp, bass fiddle; Jim Gentry, mandolin.[8] All the members were gainfully employed and were using money made from playing dances as supplemental income. The band played an average of three nights per week at night clubs in the Lake Charles area during the war years.

In 1946 the Hackberry Ramblers were hired to play music for dancing at the Silver Star Club, located between Sulphur and Lake Charles, and played there until 1956; the first two years the band played on Friday, Saturday, and Sunday nights, the next two years, the band played on Saturday nights. While playing at the Silver Star Club the band used many different musicians. Featured at different times were: on saxophone, Gary Major, LeRoy Girolla and Don Wimberly; on trumpet, Neil Roberts; on piano and bass fiddle, Edwin Duhon; on lead guitar, Grover Heard and Jack Lawson; on steel guitar, L. D. Whitlow; on rhythm guitar, Lennis Sonnier and Boley Thibodeaux; on

---

[7] The rendition of "Jolie Blonde" that elevated it to anthemic stature was recorded by Harry Choates in 1946. In a 1991 interview, Crawford Vincent discussed different versions of the song. Over the years Vincent played both drums and guitar with Leo Soileau, the Hackberry Ramblers, and Choates, among others: While I was [living] here in Lake Charles I was jobbing around, I was working at City Service at Kellogg's for the construction of City Service Highway and City Service refinery, and I met up and started playing with Harry Choates and Leo Soileau here, at that time, in the 1940s, and then played different times with the Hackberry Ramblers...when you have a name—[people] knew that I had been playing wit the Hackberry Ramblers, so there wasn't a problem when you establish a name like that, well you always...get calls to play with different bands, and from there on I played on weekend jobs, mostly around Lake Charles.... Harry Choates was not known like he is now, like he was when he died, he went on and got famous with "*Jolie Blonde*," in 1946, it became an instant his worldwide, I'd say that he made the best version of "Jolie Blonde."...

[8] Eddie Schuler went on to form Goldband Records, a Lake Charles-based album that was quite active and successful in Cajun music, zydeco, swamp pop, and rhythm & blues.

drums, Lefty Boggs. Luderin Darbone played fiddle and did not miss a Saturday night.[9]

In 1963 Chris Strachwitz of Berkeley, California, came to this area looking for the Hackberry Ramblers to record an album for the Arhoolie Record Company. The album was recorded in April of 1963. Members of the band at that time were Luderin Darbone, fiddle; Edwin Duhon, accordion and rhythm guitar; Lennis Sonnier, rhythm guitar; Glen Croker, steel guitar; Crawford Vincent, drums; Johnny Parker, bass fiddle. A picture of this group hangs in the Cajun section of the Music Hall of Fame in Nashville, Tennessee.[10]

In 1965 the Hackberry Ramblers accepted an invitation to play their style music at the Berkeley Folk Music Festival scheduled by the University of California in Berkeley, California. Members who were in the band at the time were Luderin Darbone on fiddle, Edwin Duhon on bass fiddle and accordion, Lennis Sonnier on rhythm guitar, Butch Ogea on lead guitar, and Maxie Sonnier on drums.[11] This group continued playing for dances until Lennis Sonnier fell sick and became unable to play his instrument anymore. The band discontinued playing professionally but Darbone continued playing the fiddle more or less as a hobby until 1982.

In 1982, when it was learned that some of the members of the band were still active, they were booked for a concert at McNeese State University, and for an appearance at the Acadian Cajun Festival in Lafayette; in 1983 they played at the Fan Fair in Nashville by invitation of Jimmy C. Newman. In 1984 the Hackberry Ramblers played a week's engagement at the World's Fair in New Orleans, and also played at the final three days performance; in 1985 the band was hired to play at the Northwestern State University Music Festival held in Natchitoches, Louisiana. In 1986 the band played a recreation of a 1930' radio broadcast at the liberty Theatre in Eunice, Louisiana for the Jean LaFitte National Historical Park of New Orleans.

Members who played from 1982 are Luderin Darbone, fiddle; Edwin Duhon, rhythm guitar; Crawford Vincent, drums and rhythm guitar; Roy Morgan, rhythm guitar; Pierre Crader, accordion; Tim Dugas, mandolin; L.D. Whitlow, bass guitar and steel guitar; James Dupree, rhythm guitar;

---

[9] With this configuration, the Hackberry Ramblers recorded some fine Cajun swing material for a New Jersey-based label, DeLuxe, in 1949. "Unfortunately," Darbone comments, "there was a problem with DeLuxe's pressings. The volume was really low, and you could barely hear them on a jukebox, compared to the other records." Nevertheless, the Cajun/country swing orchestra format on these hot numbers reflects the Hackberry Ramblers' ability to stay on top of changing trends. "Whatever the public wants," Darbone says, "whatever they enjoy dancing to, that's what we give them. We always have."

[10] In 1999, the Hackberry Ramblers returned to the Country Music Hall of Fame, where Darbone and Duhon donated instruments in a ceremony, followed by a performance.

[11] A brief excerpt from this performance is seen in the documentary *Make 'Em Dance*, directed by John Whitehead.

The Hackberry Ramblers, with their electronic amplification set up at the front of the stage at the Silver Star Club between Sulphur and Lake Charles, ca. late-1940s. From left to right, Edwin Duhon, Neal Roberts, Lefty Boggs, Luderin Darbone, Lennis Sonnier.
*Photo courtesy of Luderin Darbone.*

Johnny Faulk, bass fiddle; Johnny Farque, rhythm guitar; Glen Croker, lead guitar; and Ben Sandmel, drums.[12]

Since 1988, the Hackberry Ramblers have played at the New Orleans Jazz and Heritage Festival for six consecutive years; the Louisiana Folklife Festival five consecutive years; Liberty Theatre in Eunice several times. The Hackberry Ramblers received the Big Easy Entertainment Award in New Orleans for best Country/Folk 1990 in April 1991. The band also played at the Festival de International in Lafayette in April 1991; in August and September the band took a tour and played at 'The Tramps' Club in New York City and at the Stepping Stone Ranch Cajun and Bluegrass Festival in Escoheag, Rhode Island.

The Hackberry Ramblers have been mentioned in stories in several books since the origin of the band. Two of these books are John Broven's *South to Louisiana* and Ann Allen Savoy's *Cajun Music—A Reflection of a People*. The band also received international recognition in September 1990 with a story about the band in *Manner Vogue* a German magazine published in Munich,

---

[12] Sandmel first sat in with the band in 1987, and performed as a bandmember in 1988.

Germany. The band was also featured in a national radio broadcast on public broadcasting in February 1991. Several leading newspapers in the nation have published stories about the Hackberry Ramblers; namely, *New Orleans Times-Picayune*, *New York Times*, *New York Post*, *New York Daily News*, *Boston Herald*, and *Providence Journal*.

Darbone is the only fiddler the Hackberry Ramblers have had and he has missed only two scheduled engagement since the band organized in 1933, once due to death in the family and once due to employer-related activity.

Present members of the Hackberry Ramblers are Luderin Darbone, fiddle; Edwin Duhon, lead guitar and accordion; Glen Croker, lead guitar; Johnny Farque, rhythm guitar; Johnny Faulk, bass fiddle and electric bass; Ben Sandmel, drums.

## Update

The above was written in 1991. Since then the band has been across the United States to play music at concerts, festivals, and dances in Boston, Mass., Providence, R.I., Manhatton [sic], New York, Chicago, Illinois, Yosemite National Park near Sacramento, California, Valparaiso, Indiana, Austin, San Antonio and Dallas, Texas, Nashville, Tennessee, Birmingham [sic], Alabama, Kansas City Missouri, and New Orleans, Louisiana.

Four of the members are retired from their regular occupations and when not travelling [sic], donate their time to playing music at area nursing homes. This gives the members a feeling of accomplishment, knowing that their music is bringing back memories of their youth to some, and to others it is a form of therapy.

# The Bayou Buckaroo:
# LeRoy "Happy Fats" LeBlanc[1]

*John Broven*

*Introduction*

It was more than a quarter-century ago that I visited south Louisiana to conduct the primary interviews for my book *South To Louisiana: The Music Of The Cajun Bayous*. I had already targeted the active local record men and artists but felt I needed to speak to an old-time musician to get a first hand portrait of the early Cajun music recording scene. Leroy "Happy Fats" LeBlanc seemed to be the ideal person, and he did not disappoint.

As I wrote in my book: "A major Cajun personality since his days with the Rayne-Bo Ramblers in the thirties, Happy Fats has been a great popularizer of Cajun music. He has remained loyal to his sentimental form of Cajun-country music—and to the Cajun heritage—through many different trends."

LeBlanc was an unashamed hustler with political connections, seemingly able to land sponsors at will. But he hustled for the Cajun tradition as well as for himself. He did not mince words. In his self-published book *What Has Made South Louisiana God's Special Country* he stated forthrightly "If anyone is glorified in this book 'they deserve it;' if anyone is belittled 'they deserve it too.'"

The interview was conducted at his neat mobile home on Swan Street, Rayne. At the time he seemed to be an old man, and it is something of a shock now to find that he was only sixty-four years old. Accompanying me was a party of British music fans that had crossed the Atlantic for the New Orleans Jazz Festival. LeBlanc took all this attention in his stride as I started the interview by asking about his early recording career. Then we embraced a variety of topics including Cajun dances, his radio shows, his later records (including the controversial Rebel releases) and the equally controversial—to his mind—CODOFIL organization. Not long after, his health declined due to diabetes. He died on February 23, 1988.

I am proud to have conducted this interview, which documents an era long gone—even in the later years. The text has been edited only modestly and rearranged in better chronological order; extra data has been added in brackets. But the content has stood up well to factual verification.

Happy Fats's country style of Cajun music may not be fashionable today but it is worth revisiting and reassessing—especially through the remarkable

---
[1] This article is based on an interview with LeRoy "Happy Fats" LeBlanc conducted by John Broven in Rayne, Louisiana, on May 1, 1979.

series of recordings by the Rayne-Bo Ramblers. This is where we began the interview.

### The Victor Sessions

We were contacted by RCA Victor through a fellow here in Rayne by the name of Hillman Bailey, who now has a radio station in Natchitoches, Louisiana. And we were brought to New Orleans for the first time, we recorded there at the old St. Charles Hotel. That was in 1935 [August 10]. Then we had several other sessions. We were brought to Dallas, Texas and to Atlanta, Georgia and to Chicago.

In those days they recorded on wax and it was very interesting for a Cajun that had never seen anything like that. But since then I went on to record (many times), I recorded for RCA Victor the last time immediately after World War II. At that time they wanted "Jole Blonde" and then I talked them out of it because it had already ran its course—I believed. But I made a mistake there because if I had recorded that thing I would have gained some of the royalties that would have come from "Jole Blonde."

We recorded for Eli Oberstein most of the time, he was in charge. Eli was a very jolly man, I'd call him a jolly giant. I'd say he was a man about six feet five inches tall, a Jewish man. He was a stormy type of fellow, one of these if you didn't get things done right, he'd get awful mad for a few seconds. Then he'd come back and say, "Let's cut a good one."

The latter few we had Steve Sholes in command. Now RCA have become far more centralized since then, most people are sent to Nashville or possibly Camden, New Jersey, to record. In those days they were traveling units. And they'd come in, and they'd hire probably a floor of a hotel and put all of their equipment in it. They were very bulky in those days, you can imagine with all the equipment to run. Then they'd come in to record with a little tape recorder.

This fellow Hillman Bailey, he had a radio shop here and a music store and they had contact with the Werlein's of New Orleans. Through him and one of the fellows working at Werlein's we got the first recording session for RCA. The first ones weren't on the RCA label, they were on their subsidiary Bluebird. Towards the end they put us on the regular RCA Victor black label.

We had one good one we recorded, in those days there was no Top Ten or anything like that, but they did have *Hit of the Week*, and in the 1942 edition of some big radio book they put out we had an ad. In there, our picture came out along with people like the Sons of the Pioneers. We had the hit of the week, which was a song we recorded called "La Veuve de la Coulee," that I had recorded in Dallas. *The Hit of the Week* I understand in those days was a record that had sold 10,000 in the first week. We had no way of knowing the amount of records we sold. As a matter of fact we were doing them for cash. There were no royalty deals in those days at all.

We got $25 a song for the whole band. That wasn't much if you look at it nowadays but in them days during the Depression $25 was a good bit of money. We'd make up to 300 a session [for a generous twelve songs], they'd pay our expenses too, of course. We were drinking whiskey, all we needed.

*Early Years*
I was born right here in Rayne, Louisiana, in 1915, January 30th [to Gilbert and Carrie LeBlanc]. In my young days I always wanted to buy a guitar, I loved music. So my mother—we were always poor people, my daddy was a rice farmer—one rice season she gave me a sack of rice and I traded it to a druggist for a guitar. I bought it from a sales rep. or somebody, and I learnt myself.

My guitar style was based on Jimmie Rodgers. I taught myself, and if I'd see a hobo or something with a guitar, I'd go pick him up and bring him home, give him dinner. Maybe learn a few chords with him. Then there was a colored boy here in town that I learned a lot from, a fellow by the name of [Clarence] Locksley, he's still living, I see him the other day. He's much older than me, because he was a man when I was a little kid. He knew some chords, he'd play this black blues stuff, I didn't like it too much, I like Jimmie Rodgers stuff.

When I started it was right on the end of the Depression—it was still the Depression. I won't say the Depression hurt me, in fact I think the music helped me. It gave me something to do because for a fellow of my age at the time, it was hard to find a job. There was nothing to do. So playing music gave us an outlet. But back in them days we'd play dances for $10 for the whole band—two dollars a piece and two dollars for traveling expenses. We were poor, you see. But you could get a plate lunch for fifteen cents then, meat was about fifteen to twenty cents a pound and playing three or four dances a week you made, you could make eight or ten dollars a week. That was good money in them days.

Just before I started my band I was working at a rice mill here for fifteen cents an hour, ten hours a day. Stacking rice, that's a dollar-and-a-half for ten hours of work. It was hard work, sure.

I went into it seriously in '35 when we organized a little band and got a recording contract. I kept at it since then. I was influenced by Jimmie Rodgers, people like Bradley Kincaid and all the old ones. The western swing came in, I'd say, in the thirties, Bob Wills and the Light Crust Doughboys [prior to being the Texas Playboys] I liked a lot. During those years I more or less copied them. We started out with mostly Cajun but Cajun died out a lot during the late thirties, early forties. I don't know why that was so, I guess the people just dropped it. Right around this section here [in Rayne] they'd have a few accordion dances and things like that.

The Rayne-Bo Ramblers finished when World War II started, we had disbanded then. We were playing jobs around here, so I disbanded and went to Lake Charles. Then I came back and started calling it something else. I've had different names, the Bayou Buckeroos, the Cajun Storytellers, but the Rayne-Bo Ramblers was the first band, it went from 1935 till 1941.

During the war I played with Leo Soileau in Lake Charles. He was playing for a fellow by the name of Mr. Davies who had the old club there [the Silver Star]. He was a wrestler. I led the band, they had a daily program on Radio Station KPLC, Lake Charles. That's mostly why they hired me, to do the radio announcing. I led the band, Leo had become quite a drinker and he

Rayne-Bo Ramblers, an early string band, ca. 1935. From left to right:
Eric Arceneaux, Louis Arceneaux, and Happy Fats LeBlanc.
*Photo courtesy of Center for Louisiana Studies, University of Louisiana at Lafayette, accession number 580.*

couldn't take care of things. He was a good musician but I had to take care of him.

## "Jole Blonde"

Leo had quite a few records, you've seen some of these Old Timey [LP] records, he's on some of these. He had some pretty good hits like "Le Gran' Mamou" and I believe at one time he recorded a version of "Jole Blonde." Incidentally it had become a hit through him, myself, and Harry Choates who recorded it. I was at this club in Lake Charles, they had a lot of soldiers that had come there from Camp Polk, from the Lake Charles airbase and other places on a Saturday night. And they loved this "Jole Blonde."

So I wrote to Steve Sholes, and told him, "We ought to record this." And he wrote back and said, "Well there's a shortage of shellac during the war" and all that stuff, and he gave me all that. [See LeBlanc's previous comments when he himself rejected recording "Jole Blonde" after the war].

In the meantime Harry Choates went off to Houston, he left the band and went to Houston and got in with a fellow by the name of Quinn, Bill Quinn [of Gold Star Records]. And he made "Jole Blonde" and it was a million seller. Harry played with me in 1938-39, I've got some records on RCA that he cut with me, in fact this record "La Veuve de la Coulee," Harry played the fiddle on that. He was a very good fiddle player.

In a way, he just lost his mind. He was a very bad alcoholic, when he wanted whiskey or a drink, he had to have it. But they put him in jail there, Waco, Texas, or somewhere, he just killed himself, hitting the bars with his head. At least that's the story I heard, there is a possibility that the police killed him, I don't know. There was a big question about that when it happened, but we all knew him, we knew how he was, he'd do anything. I've seen him break, right on Main Street in Lake Charles, a (shop window) glass with his elbow and crack it open and reach in and get a fifth. A liquor store on Main Street, he just had to have it, that's all he took, one little bottle of whiskey.

Then Moon Mullican recorded "Jole Blonde," they played it on Nashville radio. Uncle Dave Macon at one time, he tried to get us to work, in fact he insisted but the brass didn't want it. But he wanted a Cajun band back in the fifties on the Grand Ole Opry, and he corresponded with me and he come down. We played a show with him in Lafayette, he said "I want to get y'all on, this Cajun music should be represented there." He always had that idea, then he died [in 1952].

## The 1940s

So I stayed two years there [in Lake Charles with Leo Soileau], and I came back here and reorganized. I played at only one club here, which was the old Hollywood Club in Rayne. I had Al Terry [guitar] playing with me, Ambrose

Thibodeaux [fiddle] played with me still, and we played there two or three nights a week at the Hollywood Club. You couldn't travel, no cars, no gasoline so we just played at one place.

Al Terry has always been a crippled boy, he had polio when he was young. Two of his brothers had a little band out of Kaplan. I brought them in, I had a radio program, I brought them on my radio program and he eventually got a job announcing on KVOL radio station in Lafayette. Then he played with me for a few years off and on before he organized his own band. Al's had a lot of good English records, he hasn't made any Cajun—he had a lot of country and western which sold like "Good Deal Lucille."

Cajun music became popular in the forties, I think it was because Cajun musicians came out of the cracks. It was hard to find musicians because everybody was in the army, fighting overseas and the older people were the Cajun music players. So they came out and started playing, and it was Cajun music.

Iry LeJeune got really big after he died, Eddie Shuler [of Goldband Records] in Lake Charles had a bunch of his records, but Iry was I guess one of the greatest accordion players from around here. He's still remembered. Things got kinda tough playing and things like that, so I booked a couple of sponsors that I was just singing and playing the guitar for. [Oran] "Doc" Guidry was a very good violin player, very good fiddle player. I thought he would add a little something to it so I got Doc.

Doc Guidry was born below Scott, Louisiana, I must be about four years older than him. The way I come to meet him, he was still going to school, he was in the seventh or eighth grade, and the fiddle player comes up missing. So they told me there was a young fellow at Scott that played fiddle and I waited outside the school for him. But he comes out and I hired him there, and he played with me for two or three years. His brother played with me too, he had a brother that played [Nathan Guidry, a guitarist and bassist]. Then they went together, they organized their own band, then he came back with me the years I was talking about on the radio. We played mostly just radio, no dance jobs. I was playing more dance jobs than him just off and on, but he played with another band.

We had a lot of sponsors, at one time we were on seven radio stations. Most of it was live, we did a lot of traveling. Like on a Saturday we would play Opelousas, Lafayette, and Abbeville, three stations. Two of them were live from the stage of theatres they had linked with the radio stations and we stayed together during the forties and early fifties. We appeared on Louisiana Hayride a few times.

I had a connection with Mr. Murphy, who owns the Shreveport Syrup Company. I worked down here for him, and Jay Miller had a boy by the name of Bill Hutto whom he was pushing. So Jay got him on the Louisiana Hayride and he got us to go back him up in a group. When we got there to put on Bill Hutto, Mr. Murphy was there and he told the station manager "I wanna hear Happy and Doc." He bought a lot of time with that station so his word was pretty strong on that station.

So O.K., he fixed us up on the network program which was a half hour that went on the network but they wasn't supposed to take any repeats on it. He kinda sniggered so we played "Jole Blonde," there was a tremendous crowd that night—Hank Williams was there playing—we got on and we played "Jole Blonde" and when we got through playing it they started clapping. Horace Logan the station manager was there so I thought he wanted us to quit. "No," he said, "play it again!" "Well, you said no repeats." We had to repeat on that network program three times!

And, after that we stayed on the whole show. We stayed on the show in place of poor Bill Hutto which I wasn't glad of 'cos he was a nice boy and everything, and Jay too. But they invited us back and we went back several times. It was good, we had some pretty lean times, which at that time gave me the feeling that Cajun music was graduating up, up to north Louisiana and all we'd play was Cajun songs.

Hank Williams had a lot of influence down here; he was on the Louisiana Hayride. It covered about a quarter of the nation, it was a 50,000 watt station. And Hank, you've got to give him that, he was good; he was really good. He was on like I was for Johnny Fair's Syrup, he left to go to the Grand Ole Opry. He gave me the job, the Old Syrup Sopper; you would sop up the syrup.

*Cajun Dances*
The Cajun dance, we just started playing and they started dancing. Then about ten o'clock they'd have what they call a "Treat Your Lady" intermission, and then they'd get back and get out 'til twelve or one o'clock. And play "Home Sweet Home" and they all went home.

Now it was different when there was a wedding dance. They had a wedding dance, the wedding couple and their attendants would come in, and they had possession of the floor for the march. They'd make a march around the hall for a couple of times, the music they'd play would be the wedding march and the first two dances were theirs, just them and their attendants. And they'd dance a waltz and a two step. Then their mothers would come in.

Back then, there was no television, very little radio, that was their opportunity to blow off steam. And here in the Cajun country, this town here [Rayne] during this time was five or six thousand people and there were three big dancehalls, weekends, Friday, Saturday, and Sunday they'd have dancing, they'd all be full. People would come in, they'd bring them in by school buses from out of the country, everyone of them would be full of people, they'd dance all night long.

The club I played the longest at was the old O.S.T Club here in Rayne, over in Ville Platte was the Club Rendezvous and we played at Mermentau, there was a club called the Colonial Club. T[it] Maurice, you've heard of Te Maurice, in fact one of my records is called "La Valse De Te Maurice," it was a club, that was during the thirties, it was near the Bosco oil field about twelve miles north of Rayne. I'd say that club had the biggest attendance of any for eight or ten years. Now they're trying to revive it, the fellow that owned it is making a trail ride this week, they're having a dance. The old place is down but he's built another smaller place.

But this old one, the dance floor was about 100 [feet] by 100 [feet] so it was a pretty big dance floor. The bandstand was at one end with the bar the other end. They had chicken wire on the windows so they wouldn't come in. In some places they had chicken wire in the front of the band. In fact they had chicken wire at a dancehall in the country here; they had a shooting in the middle of the floor, and the chicken wire didn't stop them from getting out of that place! In fact the chicken wire in front of our bandstand, they broke through that and the one in the back. You can imagine it, about 600 people there and somebody starts shooting, got a pile (of bodies) right in the middle of the floor, and you think "I'm gonna get out of here!"

### More Recording Sessions

The De Luxe session came about when a fellow in New Orleans by the name of Al Young who was an agent, he contacted me and brought us to New Orleans. This was a subsidiary of King called De Luxe, so he brought us to New Orleans; we made it. He was supposed to have paid us there, and he didn't pay us. So I contacted King Records, and they come back, and I was told they didn't know nothing about this fellow Al Young. [Young ran The Bop Shop on Rampart and Dumaine, and was soon involved with Imperial Records in New Orleans, notably with Fats Domino.] So I told them, "I've got a contract which is co-signed by the union and everything else." "I hate to admit it, but they say he's not working for us anymore." "Well," I say, "somebody's gonna pay me, you're gonna release this record or something." So they released one, they paid me through the union, we got $50. I can't remember the record, it wasn't Cajun, it was country ["Happy Birthday (This Is Your Day)"/"I Loved You Once Before" on De Luxe 5066 around August 1949]. It was in an old warehouse, they set up a studio down on Louisiana Avenue, somewhere back there.

Most of the records in the forties were made for Jay Miller, we went to New Orleans in the studios in the beginning and made a bunch of records which came out on the label called Fais-Do-Do. The studio was on North Rampart, J&M [run by Cosimo Matassa].

We had one that we made there that has become quite a (success), I've been collecting royalties on it ever since [Governor] Jimmie Davis recorded it,

Nathan Abshire (left) and Happy Fats (right) flank an unknown man and the young unidentified 1958 Rice Festival accordion winner.
*Photo courtesy of Freeland Archive, Acadia Parish Library.*

"Colinda" [in 1953]. We recorded that for a session, ours never did make much of an impression [in the name of Happy, Doc, and the Boys, with Doc Guidry on vocal]. When Jimmie took it over I've been getting royalties off it, from all over, overseas, England, Belgium, West Germany, South Africa, New Zealand. It's selling good there. In fact the last [BMI] check I got there must have been someone on it in Holland.

We took the name from a song called "Danse Calinda" which was from a book in a library at the South Western University[University of Louisiana at Lafayette]; actually it was a Haitian song. So we just took the name, the tune is not the same or the lyric. Doc Guidry and I just sat down we wrote a French song, a two- or three-chord song that is pretty easy to write. On [last] Friday night I played for the Confederate Air Force at Acadiana Regional Airport, and if we played that once we had to play that five or six times during the night. They enjoyed it very much, they liked it. It's a perky tune.

Me and Alex Broussard made some records for La Louisianne, they did not make a very big impression. La Louisianne never...Jay Miller got out more, you know what I mean. Better promoter than [Carol Rachou], they didn't promote them too much.

### "Dear Mr. President"

We had some fair sellers for J.D. [Miller], none of them made a great big impression. Except one I cut for him called "Dear Mr. President" which was a controversial record. It's a civil rights thing, when they were pushing us down here. We made "Dear Mr. President," another fellow made "Fight NAACP 105" [by Son of Mississippi]. Mine sold 250,000 copies, it sold more than that actually, and when it sold 250,000 Miller gave me a gold record.

We didn't have any problems with that, not at all. There wasn't anything violent about it, it was just a joke. I had a car of black people run me down on the highway one time coming into Lafayette and they said "Are you the fellow that made 'Dear Mr. President'?" I said "Yeah." They said, "We'd like to buy some records, they bought about fifteen records." There was a big van full of black people and they loved it.

Actually when all this was happening we always got along well with the black people down here. That's with the Cajun people. And either side, at that time, they didn't want it very much, they wanted to go each their own way. And if you notice nowadays it's getting back to where they wanted to go their own way.

### The 1970s

I got a little business, record racks around the country. Of the Cajun records, Iry LeJeune is the top seller; Camay Doucet sells well; he's from Crowley on Swallow, and then Belton Richard sells. That's about the biggest sellers. Nathan Abshire did sell for a while but it's dropped off, I don't know why; they tell me he went to drinking; he had stopped drinking for sixteen years, fouled it up quite a bit. Jimmy Newman is playing Cajun music on the Grand Ole Opry now. Jimmy is very well thought of down here; people think of him well because Jimmy has been of pretty much help; and he hasn't forgotten his Cajun traditions. This makes them think a lot of him. I do myself, and he's a good artist; he's a good singer.

I'm still going strong, I've got an album coming out this week [May 1979], I've got a [45 rpm] record that's out now, that's gonna be on it called "Cajun Heaven" [on Swallow]. You've heard "Hillbilly Heaven," it's a French version of that. I named all the French artists through the years who are up in heaven.

I'm sixty-four years old now; I can't stand up there every night and play, I've got to sit down some. But God's with me, in the music business there's no retiring. You don't have no social security or nothing like that. If you don't save none you're in bad shape. Besides the racks I have a radio program which brings me the bulk of my income, on KSIG in Crowley. I had a television show in Lafayette for about twelve years [first KLFY-TV] then the station I was on [KLNI] closed down so I went back to radio. Went on KXKW, I stayed there about eight or nine years, at Lafayette. Then I went on KSIG in Crowley. It goes out six to seven on Saturday morning and twelve o'clock on Sunday afternoons for two hours. I record it here at my house, and I just bring in the tapes. I've always had a little studio back there that I do my recording.

During the past several years Cajun music has come into its own. And that's why I keep a Cajun accordion in my band, all the time. We play pretty big shot jobs like the year before last we went to Newport and California, Los Angeles, even played Beverly Hills.

In my band I have a fellow playing fiddle for me by the name of Ambrose Thibodeaux; we've been together since I started over forty years ago. I've got one of my cousins, Smilin' Jack LeBlanc who's a real estate man in Lafayette; he plays electric guitar. I've got Ambrose's son, Merton, who plays the electric piano and his son who plays the drums with us. One side of it is almost a family band. Merton worked with Lefty Frizzell, Bob Wills, and people like when he was young. He had the misfortune of breaking his back, he's a paraplegic now, he has to stay around home so I carry him around with us, he's a very, very good musician.

I don't play too much right around here, I keep a big band I try to pick pretty big jobs. We play Houston, like the Petroleum Club of Houston and places like Conroe, Texas. This month we're going to Canton, Mississippi. It shows you the Cajun influence, they all insist on Cajun music. The Cajun music and the crawfish go together, one has helped the other! I'd like to add this too, I say Cajun, I don't say French, I don't like to be called a Frenchman, I'm a Cajun.

We've got some people here who are pushing the French influence. We've got a fellow who's written us a schoolbook in Cajun language and they got it put in the schools, in the schoolrooms. And this CODOFIL got it thrown out because it's not the true language. But I think it's the true language.

Now you're from England and I'm an American Cajun. And around here in the United States since you (English) were here, we don't speak the same anymore. Is that right? That's the same thing with the French. You get the French kids here, the Cajun kids, they try to teach them Parisian French. And it's a mess because it's all different. In England you've got a lot of dialects too, and here we've got our dialects, and I believe they should leave it alone. Seeing that you're down here writing and talking about us, there must be something to it.

# Harry Choates: Cajun Fiddle Ace[1]

## Mike Leadbitter

Remembered by some as a "no good, wine-head, son-of-a-bitch," Harry Choates is perhaps the best known of all the Cajun (French Acadian) fiddlers. He may not have been the greatest, but he was certainly the most successful during his short life. He may not have even been a Cajun, for Choates (pronounced Shoats) is not a French name, but it is hard to be certain because, from all accounts, his command of the French patois of southwestern Louisiana was as bad as that of his English. Whatever, we all need to know a great deal more about his life and the very fine bayou music he was famous for.

Choates was born and raised on a farm near New Iberia, Louisiana. A passably handsome man of slight build, he was possessed of a great deal of nervous energy, preferring to wander the countryside, drink, chase women and hang around musicians, rather than sweat in the fields. From an early age he played steel guitar, influenced by the western swing bands of Texas, but switched to fiddle when he found employment with Leo Soileau's band in Ville Platte during the late '30s.

Soileau much impressed Choates and with the band he really learned his fiddle technique, adopting the shouted "Eh...ha, ha!" trademark that would later serve him well. When he left Ville Platte he'd already got a reputation as an entertainer and was especially popular with the ladies. From Soileau he moved on to work with bands led by Papa Cairo, Jimmy Foster, and Crawford Vincent, playing fiddle or steel guitar as required, but by the time war was over he'd got his own little combo together.

Johnnie Smirle, a young girl pianist, "Te" Joe Manuel, a guitarist and banjo-player, and bassist B.D. Williams were the first members of the Choates band. They became extremely popular in Texas and Oklahoma with their mixture of Cajun, hillbilly, and western swing music, but desperately wanted a record to help promote live appearances. The only local independent recordman in 1946 was Bill Quinn, who operated the Gold Star studio at Houston. It was to Quinn that Harry turned and though the man hadn't the faintest idea what Cajun music was; "Jole Blon" was recorded, after a lot of attempts, that same year.

"Jole Blon" was a traditional French song, but it was soon to become Harry's own property. Though nothing happened for weeks, Quinn managed to persuade a DJ in Houston to play the record, and suddenly orders were pouring in. The tiny Gold Star pressing plant could not keep up with the tremendous

---
[1] This article first appeared in *Old Time Music* 6 (1972): 20-22.

The string band at its height, the great Harry Choates and his band, ca. 1945. From left to right, B.D. Williams, Kersey "Pork Chop" Ray, Mrs. Joe Manuel, Choates, Joe Manuel, Eddy Pursley, Pee Wee Lyons.
*Photo courtesy of Johnnie Allan.*

demand and work was farmed out in all directions. Eventually the large Modern company took over, distributing the disc nationally. Few could understand what Harry was singing, but the song's wistful quality got through to people everywhere. Covered by many other artists it eventually became the biggest selling Cajun record ever produced, and even today—twenty-six years later—it is still being re-pressed and regularly played.

For five years Harry went berserk. When he wasn't on the road, someone would want to record him. When he wasn't in the studio or on stage, he was usually in an alcoholic daze. He fell in and out of love rapidly—Johnnie Smirle was his until he lost her to Joe Manuel; then he married a girl called Helen, fathered some children and vanished in search of new prey. By 1950 he was in a terrible mess, demanding more and more money from record companies and nightclub owners, then letting them down by being in no fit state to record or play, or spending weeks in a drunken stupor.

Throughout, all his public stayed faithful, flocking to the dancehalls to hear "Jole Blon" for the thousandth time, but his wife filed a non-support charge in 1951 and took him to court. He never got around to paying the maintenance order that was slapped on him, so a warrant was taken out for his arrest. Picked up by the Austin, Texas, police, he was thrown in jail overnight, pending a move to Beaumont for trial. Now a chronic alcoholic, Choates suffered an attack of DTs, keeping both the guards and the prisoners awake. To make him be quiet, he was brutally beaten, and fell into a coma and died. On July 17, 1951, Choates was buried at Port Arthur, Texas, by a much neglected wife. He was just twenty-eight years old.

# Iry LeJune[1]

## Mike Leadbitter

Iry LeJune's music was, and still is, loved and known by everyone in the Cajun belt, and he was easily the most popular artist of the postwar period of French music. He was born and raised on his father's small farm on the outskirts of Church Point, Louisiana, October 28, 1928, and he grew up in a music-loving family. At an early age he began playing accordion, helped by his father, Agnus LeJune, who taught him the rudiments of music. Suffering from near-blindness, young Iry came to rely on music as his sole enjoyment from life; and as he grew older he was forced to rely on it for his living. His greatest influence was a very much respected black musician named Amédé Ardoin, who was well represented on record. From Amédé he picked up his crying style of singing as well as his basic accordion sound, which Iry, with nimbler fingers, played in a faster and more complicated manner.

He soon became a well known figure at local dances, but couldn't make much of himself for in the '40s the accordion was out and fiddle music was in. The Cajuns didn't want accordion music, they wanted stringbands. Happy Fats, Leo Soileau, Harry Choates, and the Hackberry Ramblers were the stars. In desperation, Iry tried to learn the fiddle but soon quit and relied on his strong self-confidence to win the day. He moved to Lacassine, a small town near Lake Charles, and began to sit in with bigger bands. In 1948, after a lot of pleading, Floyd LeBlanc took him to Houston, to record for the Opera label with Virgil Bozman's Oklahoma Tornadoes. His recording of "Love Bridge Waltz" was the turning-point in his life and in French music. That record was a big seller and for the first time in ten years the accordion wailed from jukeboxes in Cajun country! With Floyd, Iry stayed in Houston for six months playing the bars and small dances before returning to Louisiana.

On his return he went straight to KPLC Lake Charles and asked to play on the Eddie Shuler show. The station didn't like his music, but Eddie did. Signing the mutual contract with a shake of the hand, the pair began to put out a string of Iry LeJune records on Goldband, Folk Star and TNT. The "Calcasieu Waltz" and "Teche Special" really established Iry and suddenly fiddles were on the way out.

With musicians like Duckhead Cormier, Wilson Grainger, Robert Bertrand, and sometimes Eddie Shuler himself, Iry traveled all over southwestern Louisiana filling dates and recording. Eddie would cut records at local radio stations or in his studios and sometimes even took his tape recorder to Lacas-

---
[1] This article first appeared in the British magazine *Old Time Music* 14 (1974): 21-22.

sine and put it on the kitchen table. From this kitchen-table recording came the beautiful "Duraldo Waltz," the only recording of Iry's on which no accordion was featured.

On October 8, 1954, at the peak of his career, Iry was killed. He was returning home from Eunice with J.B. Fusilier, and their car had a flat. Without pulling off the highway (the shoulders of the highway were in repair), the pair set to work, and a passing car knocked them into a field. J.B. was a hospital case; Iry died instantly.

Iry LeJune and his Accordion Band, ca. 1947. From left to right, Robert Betrand, Wilson Granger, Iry LeJune, Alfred Cormier.
*Photo courtesy of Johnnie Allan.*

# King of the Dancehalls:
# Accordionist Lawrence Walker

*Kevin S. Fontenot and Ryan A. Brasseaux*

Cajun music's early commercial era launched the careers of several young musicians who would later become fixtures in south Louisiana's dancehall pantheon. Fiddler Leo Soileau left the sound of the accordion behind to become the grandfather of Cajun swing in south Louisiana. Nathan Abshire's blues-laden accordion chops made him a local favorite in south Louisiana honky tonks after World War II. The period also introduced young upstart Lawrence Walker, who would later share the spotlight with Abshire as a major proponent of the "dancehall sound."[1] Walker's approach, however, was radically different from most Cajun musicians recording during the early commercial era. He experimented with the foundation of Cajun music, mixing and matching elements of American popular culture with Louisiana's musical traditions in his dancehall laboratory. His formula often paralleled the rock and roll recipe that white Southern musicians would employ two decades later.

Lawrence's musical proficiency allowed the fiddler and accordionist to filter and concentrate all of his musical influences into one song. His affinity for southern popular music, particularly the blues, hillbilly, and Anglo string band compositions, are evident in the ten innovative recordings he waxed between 1929 and 1935. Adept and attuned Cajun audiences embraced Walker's efforts, notably after World War II during the dancehall era, when the Cajun community bestowed the title "King of the Dancehalls" upon the multi-instrumentalist.

Lawrence Walker was born near Duson, Louisiana, into a musical family on September 1, 1907.[2] Although reared in the heart of French Louisiana, Lawrence straddled the Anglo and Franco American worlds. Like Louisiana's convoluted cultural and historical make up, the accordionist's genealogy touched his Anglo American, French, and Acadian heritage. "Although Lawrence was what some people call 'American,'" denotes Ann Savoy, "some of his family were Cajun and he spoke Cajun French perfectly."[3] Lawrence was perfectly bilingual which allowed him to negotiate his way through both Anglo and Cajun social circles. According to the 1910 United States census, his father, fiddler

---

[1] Small-amplified rhythm sections fronted by an accordionist defined the dancehall sound after World War II. Electric bass, electric guitar, steel guitar, and drums all factored into this style.
[2] There are conflicting dates for Walker's birth. Ann Savoy argues that the accordionist was born in 1908, while Pierre Daigle concludes that September 1, 1907, is the precise date. Pierre Daigle, *Tears, Love and Laughter: The Story of the Cajuns and Their Music*, 4th ed. (Ville Platte, LA, 1987), 140; Ann Allen Savoy, *Cajun Music: A Reflection of a People* (Eunice, 1984), 206.
[3] Savoy, *Cajun Music: A Reflection of a People*, 206.

Allen Walker, was an educated and literate Anglophone tenant farmer. Allen presumably also spoke French. Alicia Leger Walker, Lawrence's Cajun mother, spoke both English and French.[4] When the family relocated to Orange, Texas, in 1915, the move was facilitated by the Walkers' linguistic flexibility.

The Lone Star State's oil fields offered many Cajuns a chance at economic prosperity. Louisianians left in droves in hopes of finding a better life. During his stint in Texas, Lawrence formed his first musical ensemble, "The Walker Brother's Group" with his brother Elton. The duet absorbed the sounds of east Texas, and fused elements of Anglo American blues and hillbilly with Cajun music. Lawrence's accordion and Elton's fiddle later formed the foundation of the trio that recorded for the Brunswick record label on October 30, 1929 in Dallas, Texas, where the brothers and an unknown guitarist recorded only two sides.[5] Walker and Elton captured the classic Cajun string band sound with their twin fiddle arrangement "La Breakdown La Louisiane," which reflected their father's musical influence. Lawrence picked up the accordion for the record's flip side "La Vie Malheureuse." Six years later, Lawrence Walker stepped into the studio again and waxed a handful of tunes that reflected the pending shifts in the Cajun repertoire. On January 18, 1935, the multi-instrumentalist recorded eight more sides that drew heavily from the blues and hillbilly traditions on his English renditions of songs like "Alberta," "What's the Matter Now," and while fiddling behind Tony Alleman's hillbilly influenced string band music performed in French. Walker's fiddle work on Alleman's sides preempted the first Cajun swing records released by string band ensembles like the Hackberry Ramblers and the Rayne-Bo Ramblers.[6]

In 1936, Lawrence teamed up with his childhood acquaintance and cultural geographer Lauren Post at the National Folk Festival in Dallas, Texas, the site of Walker's first commercial recordings. Post exercised his position as the chairman of the festival's Louisiana component by escorting members of the same ensemble that recorded with Walker in 1935: fiddlers Aldus "Pop Eye" Broussard and Sidney Broussard; guitarists Junior Broussard and Norris Mire; and twelve-year-old triangle player and vocalist Evelyn Broussard. The combo's instrumentation reflected the contemporary trends in Cajun music. Aldus Broussard shared the vocal responsibilities as twin guitars, often used by Cajun swing bands to reinforce the rhythm section, provided a rhythmic wall of sound behind Lawrence's accordion. The band enjoyed critical success, even by the standards of the nation's top folk music authorities. Lauren Post

---

[4] 12th Decennial Census of the United States, 1910, Louisiana, Acadia Parish, Ward 2, Household 99.
[5] Lawrence Walker, accordion and vocal, Elton Walker, fiddle, and an unknown guitarist recorded the two sides on October 30, 1929 in Dallas, Texas. Brunswick released the record as Brunswick 381.
[6] Pat Harrison, *Cajun: Early Recordings*, CD C (London, 2004), JSP7726; Robert Sacré, *Musiques cajun, créole et zydeco* (Paris, 1995), 37-39. Daigle, *Tears, Love and Laughter*, 140. Savoy, *Cajun Music: A Reflection of a People*, 206.

recalled the festival in *Cajun Sketches*: "No less an authority on folk music than Alan Lomax commented that 'Aldus was the best example of folk talent in the whole festival.'"[7] The band's performance in Dallas, is yet another example of Cajun music intersecting with Americana. According to Post, the group enjoyed a warm reception wherever they performed at the festival, denoting that the American audiences recognized the viability of Cajun music as a peripheral piece of American culture. Elmore Sonnier, an educated and formally trained tenor from Scott, Louisiana, also performed in Dallas as an example of Cajun proficiency in the American influenced arts.[8]

A burning desire to forge new ground with Cajun music consumed Walker. His 1930s recordings presaged the dancehall sound of the post-war era with their pulsating rhythm and heavy guitar use. Walker managed to ride out the string band era using his skills as a fiddler. As the Second World War wound down, Walker was one of the first accordionists to return the instrument to

Lawrence Walker and his band the Wandering Aces were staples of the Cajun radio scene. Walker is seated on the left.
*Photo courtesy of Johnnie Allan.*

---

[7] Lauren C. Post, *Cajun Sketches: From the Prairies of Southwest Louisiana* (Baton Rouge, 1974), 159-60; Savoy, *Cajun Music: A Reflection of a People*, 206.
[8] Post, *Cajun Sketches*, 159-60.

prominence—but not in the old style. His band, the Wandering Aces, fused the string band format with a heavy steel guitar sound with the drive of the accordion. The result was a brash new sound that came to be labeled "dancehall."

A highly creative musician, Walker exhibited a strong desire to record and perform on radio. His life as a rice farmer permitted a certain flexibility with regards to a music career and his post war recordings reveal a strongly talented intellect eager to experiment with new styles. He also demanded absolute perfection from his bandmembers, both in performance and presentation. Guitarist Shelton Manuel recalled, "Lawrence Walker was a very good musician. He was precise in his music, especially on his tune-ups. He made sure everything was tuned right, and we wore uniforms back then. We wore white shirts with ties. We'd travel around in a station wagon. We had a local broadcast at KPLC in Lake Charles once a week. We'd do the broadcast at the same time that we had a dance in the vicinity. The broadcast was on the route to the dance. He was working pretty much back then. He had two dances at the O.S.T. in Rayne, one in Lake Charles at the South Street Club. I spent about a year doing that."[9] Future swamp pop icon Johnnie Allan played steel guitar with Walker for five years in the mid-1950s. "He played about four or five country and western songs, but the majority of the job was strictly Cajun-French songs," Allan told writer John Broven. "Lawrence was a very proud man, he took pride in his music and always strove to get a good sound."[10]

Walker's post-war recording career began with Lake Charles producer George Khoury and continued in Ville Platte with Floyd Soileau. Generally Walker initiated contact with the recordmen, certain of his ability to sell records. And he cut many jukebox hits for Khoury and Soileau including "Reno Waltz," "Evangeline Waltz," and "Bosco Stomp." Always willing to try new styles, Walker cut some of the earliest Cajun rock and roll tunes. "Allons Rock and Roll" and "Lena Mae." Walker's recording success reinforced demand for his band on the dancehall circuit and he soon laid claim to the title "King of the Dancehalls." Walker's 1950s band was a stellar group of young instrumentalists led by a seasoned veteran. But musical styles were changing and the young band, led by Johnnie Allan, defected in 1958 to create the Krazy Kats, one of the earliest swamp pop groups. Walker was deeply hurt by the abandonment, saying to Allan, "So that's what happens when you put an old horse out to grass."[11] Despite the injury, it is a tribute to Walker that his band was a breeding ground for some of the most adventuresome and talented young Cajuns. The "old horse" continued to record in the 1960s but age began to take its toll.

---

[9] As quoted in Raymond François, *Yé Yaille, Chère: Traditional Cajun Dance Music* (Ville Platte, 1990), 459.

[10] John Broven, *South to Louisiana: The Music of the Cajun Bayous* (Gretna, 1983), 48.

[11] Ibid., 214.

On August 15, 1968, he suffered a heart attack while painting his house near Rayne, falling from a ladder dead.[12]

Lawrence Walker was one of the most talented and driven of Cajun musicians. He demanded perfectionism and precision in his bandmembers, and held himself to a very high standard. He also mastered the presentation of his music, keeping his musicians well dressed and using his natural handsomeness to good advantage. His lyrics were vivid and deeply memorable. Lawrence Walker was the first Cajun to take his band to a national folk festival and anticipated the powerful dancehall sound by nearly ten years. One of the great ironies of Cajun music history is that this seminal figure remains largely forgotten and still awaits a systematic reissue of his important work.

---

[12] *Crowley Daily Signal*, August 16, 1968.

# Aldus Roger:
# King of the French Accordion

*Ann Allen Savoy*

Aldus Roger, a young man dressed in a crisp white shirt with a white felt hat, peers smilingly from an old photograph. In his hands is posed the black, classic "Sterling" diatonic accordion. Standing around him are other smiling, youthful musicians who would make an indelible stamp on Cajun music. Philippe Alleman, Rodney Miller, Raymond Cormier, "Man" Abshire, Doc Guidry, Aldus "Pop-Eye" Broussard, Tony Thibodeaux, and Louis Foreman are the core of excellent musicians with whom Roger always surrounded himself. There were others, too, and chosen by Roger and his vision of excellence in Cajun dancehall music. For perhaps twenty years Aldus Roger ruled Cajun music from the dancehall to the channel 10 KLFY TV screen. He was the inspiration of hoard of young Cajuns, white and black, who heard his fine danceable music coming over the air waves.

His early story is much like the story of many Cajun musicians. Born in Carencro in 1915 into a heyday of local great music, Roger began playing his father's accordion at the age of eight. Inspired by his cousin Ivy Roger, Aldus continued to play, and when he was old enough he would frequently go to the dances of the late Lawrence Walker. Roger remembers watching Lawrence Walker play and imitating his style. He quickly moved from the simple fingering style to the "playing double" (two notes at the same time), also citing the playing of Amede Breaux as being very influential to him.

In the mid 1940s Roger put together a band of top notch musicians and started to play dances all over southwest Louisiana. By day he was a carpenter, by night he and his band played music at the 'Tit Maurice, the Midway Club, the Bon Ton Rouley, the Four Roses, the Belvedere, the Chinaball Club, the OST club...Every important club featured "Aldus Roger and the Lafayette Playboys."

There were several factors that contributed to the success of the Lafayette Playboys. Their music, like Lawrence Walker's band, was very smooth and danceable, but Roger liked his band to be loud and forceful. Though they produced a loud and forceful sound, this effect wasn't achieved by an excess of notes; rather their style was clean, succinct and tight, always enough but never too much.

Their force came from the cumulative effect of being together on each neatly played beat. They dressed neatly and behaved in a professional manner. Aldus composed some exciting accordion tunes that became their theme songs, such as "Johnny Can't Dance," "The Mardi Gras Jig," and "The Lafayette Playboy

Waltz." Also, Roger would hire young musicians who were in touch with what songs were regional hits (such as "One Scotch, One Bourbon, One Beer" and "Mean Woman") so the bands could stay in touch with what the crowds liked. Popular vocalists Man Abshire, Philippe Alleman, Johnny Credeur, and Roy Morgan were featured. Aldus attributes some of his success to the fact that the band played their music "straight," no tricks, no performance, just plain good musicianship.

After the Lafayette Playboys band established themselves on the dancehall scene, they became the house band on Lafayette's Channel 10 Saturday afternoon TV program. For years, most Cajun households that owned TVs were tuned in, every Saturday afternoon, to Aldus Roger and the Lafayette Playboys. The impact this had on the Cajun culture was enormous. People could enjoy watching a great Cajun band without going to the dancehall. Young people not only had an available accordionist role model in Aldus Roger, "the King of the French Accordion," but also modeled themselves on the other fine bandmembers. In actuality, the Lafayette Playboys set the standards for future Cajun bands.

Aldus Roger and his band, the Lafayette Playboys. From left to right, Phillip Alleman, Dunice "Bee" Abshire, Roger, Harry Lee Bart, Doc Guidry, Louis Foreman, David Abshire.
*Photo courtesy of Johnnie Allan.*

Today, Aldus still lives in Scott and still plays an occasional dance or tribute. His musicianship at age seventy-six remains undaunted by the passing years. For most of his life, Aldus played his old "Sterling" accordion, insisting that the old reeds sound the best. The recordings he made between 1947-1965 are being reissued by English companies and local labels. Never before have his recordings been available in such excellent conditions.

Aldus Roger, the legend, lives on in the hearts of all who have been living in Louisiana over the years. If fame is measured by the impact of the artists upon that culture, then we must acknowledge him as the most famous. If talent is judged by the amount of respect an artist is paid by his own people, then we must truly hand Aldus Roger the plaque bearing the title "King of the French Accordion."

# Jimmy C. Newman and His Cajun Country Roots[1]

## Douglas B. Green

Talk about coping with mid-life crises: Jimmy C. Newman must be the national champ. A couple of years ago he had just turned fifty, and surveyed the options before him: a star of the Grand Ole Opry since 1956, he could continue to grind out those one-nighters with unfamiliar bands, many of which contained members who were infants when Jimmy had his biggest hits (*Cry, Cry, Darling* in 1954 and *A Fallen Star* in 1957).

He could, of course, have tried the country-pop approach, though his unusual Cajun-accented tenor voice made that an unlikely avenue. Or he could simply retire to his 670-acre horse (Appaloosa) and cattle farm fifty miles southeast of Nashville.

It's a tough time in a performer's career: the salad days are gone, and, as Jimmy himself said. "I had been in country music a long time, and there's a lot of great new talent, and the business is changing a whole lot, and the young ones were taking over, and it was time to make a change, *very much* time to make a change!"

The change he made, the approach he took, surprised everybody: instead of simplifying and streamlining operations he hired a six-piece band; instead of heading for an increasingly general and widely appealing approach, he returned to the exciting and compelling music of his roots, Cajun music, and he hasn't looked back since. He hasn't needed to. His formerly stagnant career has rocketed forward with the creation of one of the most distinctive groups in the country.

It began with his long-time friend and frequent co-worker, a hulking, mustachioed fiddler named Rufus Thihodeaux, who is a show unto himself. With the breakup of his successful Cajun-rock band, Jimmy's son Gary moved back to Nashville from Lafayette, Louisiana, to play bass in the emerging hand. Convinced that they were on the right track, they hired a drummer and a steel player (currently Burt Hoffman and Larry Stewart, respectively), and country singer, guitarist, and banjo player Ray Kirkland as front man and bandleader.

The final ingredient was the addition of accordionist Bessyl Duhon in January of 1978: suddenly Rufus' fiddle was complimented by the authentic sound of the accordion, lending the music both authenticity and excitement: "It was a different sound. Immediately, on the Opry, people really liked the sound, because it was so different. Now this is a different type of accordion

---

[1] This article first appeared in the magazine *Country Music* 7 (1979).

than the piano accordion, and they say that the accordion is dead, that people don't want to hear the accordion sound, but they like this sound!" Jimmy said with a laugh.

Jimmy Newman is no poseur when it comes to Cajun music: a full-blooded Cajun, he was born in Big Mamou, Louisiana, on August 27, 1927. He was playing and singing with bands in his teens. and recorded his first record as a vocalist with another band in 1946, sung strictly in French. "Some people down home think I'm a Nashville Cat: they don't consider me a purist, but little do they know that for a long time I couldn't get a record contract because of my French accent!"

In the early 1950s Jimmy finally did get a contract, with Dot Records, and joined the prestigious Louisiana Hayride. He became one of country music's bright young stars when *Cry, Cry, Darling* became a hit in 1951 and he moved to the Grand Ole Opry in 1956. His next hit, *A Fallen Star*, was his biggest, but he continued to put out a series of hit records for Dot, MGM, and Decca for the next decade, including *You're Making a Fool Out of Me* (1958), *Grin and Bear It* (1959), *Alligator Man* (1961), *Bayou Talk* (1962), *DJ for a Day* (1963); (this was the first hit record written by a young Tom T. Hall); *Artificial Rose* (1965), *Back Pocket Money* (1966), *Blue Lonely Winter* (1967), and *Born to Love You* (1968).

But the hits began to dwindle, and the road became a grueling experience: frustrating as well, for few of the bands he was given to work with knew anything but the straight-ahead hits of the day: "It was a tough battle: but I had to do it rather than get out of the business. I would still do it. But it is really rough when you do the type of music we do, because

Jimmy C. Newman poses with his guitar during an NBC recording session, ca. 1954.
*Photo courtesy of Johnnie Allan.*

most of your country bands know the current country songs, and consequently, since I wasn't even recording any more, it was getting harder and harder. And, too, I couldn't get up and do traditional Cajun songs—they'd never heard them! We do a lot of songs now that no one's ever heard before because they're traditional Cajun songs There are a lot of those, a lot of those we haven't done yet!"

Jimmy yearned to do straightforward Cajun music for some time; in 1964 he even recorded an album for Decca called *Folk Songs of the Bayou Country*: "His most talked about album, and you can't even buy it any more." Although the spoken parts (done with "host" T. Tommy Cutrer), seem a little hokey today, the music is pure, old-fashioned Cajun. "I brought the late Shorty LeBlanc from Lake Charles, Louisiana, and of course I had Rufus Thibodeaux—he's my number one man—and it was a thing that was very good for us. *Very* traditional. Then I wouldn't use *any* electrical instruments. I used Dobro—Shot Jackson played some and Jackie Phelps played some—but no electrical instruments. It was a very good album and it is still talked about." *Folk Songs of the Bayou Country* featured Jimmy in top voice, and some of the songs included the Cajun evergreen *Jole Blon* as well as *Jean Lafitte, Grand Chenier, Angeline, Grand Basile,* and others. It was a fine, interesting experiment, but did not sell in significant numbers to justify another like it, and Jimmy remained a single and an Opry act, for the time being.

Having lost his major label affiliation, Jimmy signed briefly with La Louisianne for a time in the early 1970s, and, by an unusual circumstance, obtained his first gold record on the little label: going back to his roots, he recorded a number of new and old Cajun songs for La Louisianne, among them a new ditty called *Lâche Pas La Patate*. The record went virtually unheard in the standard country music market, but took off in Canada, particularly French-speaking Québec, and became the first song in Cajun French to earn gold-record status. "They weren't sure of some of the words, and at the time they didn't accept Cajun music—but they do now! They have a hard time understanding the sound, because, you see, much of Cajun French is slang."

This success, the fact that his career was in a treading-water phase, and his longing to return to his Cajun roots all prompted him, his son, and Rufus Thibodeaux to put together their band, Cajun Country. It was a bold and daring step, and a risky one, but it may turn out to be the best move Jimmy Newman has made, for in this era of bland sound-alike singers with facile, formulaic bands. Cajun music is different, vibrant, visually and aurally exciting, and a tribute to one of the country music's great subcultures.

Jimmy Newman and Cajun Country went through a rough spell for a time—it's hard to suddenly book a six-piece band where you'd been working for much less as a single—but Jimmy credits the Grand Ole Opry for sticking with his late-blooming decision to form a band. "They were very nice about it. I don't know if they were receptive, but they were tolerant of it, you know, and then people started liking the sound, and I think they're very happy with us. They really gave us the opportunity; if it hadn't been for the Opry, we wouldn't have been able to survive or even do this, because we weren't working much at first on the road, and this gave the boys an income."

Jimmy and Cajun Country played at the Talent Buyers Seminar last fall, and the response was overwhelming. There was genuine excitement rarely seen among these hard-bitten businessmen and women, and Tandy Rice, who ran the seminar, knew a good thing when he saw it, and signed Jimmy to his growing roster at Top Billing. The dates have been coming in with gratifying regularity.

Jimmy is especially proud of the versatility of the band. He says "In a normal show Ray Kirkland comes out and does about fifteen minutes of hard country; he also is a fine banjo player, and we can do a bit of bluegrass too. If we have time, our drummer, Burt Hoffman, is just great at doing the rock of the fifties, and we can do a little of the big band era, with me singing *Stardust* or all of us playing *In The Mood*. With a little work we can do the real cowboy and western songs, and western swing is a natural for us too. For my part, if I do a half hour, I'll do 25 minutes of pure Cajun music, traditional and modern. Of course I always have to do *A Fallen Star* and *Cry, Cry, Darling*."

But the success of Jimmy Newman and Cajun Country transcends the career of one man and one band—it is an affirmation of the potential popularity of one of country music's most exciting substyles. Cajun music is, as Jimmy says, "true Americana," and its enthusiasm crosses barriers of language and culture to appeal to the modern country music audience. Like many musical styles which do not fit a Top-40 radio format, it sometimes appears in danger of withering away, but the success of Cajun Country proves that interest in ethnic music, music of tradition and character, is still there.

Jimmy Newman and Cajun Country are carriers of a proud tradition, practitioners of a music which is rich and hearty as Cajun gumbo, and as real.

"It's a great advantage to us, whenever we are introduced, wherever we are. It doesn't matter who's been on, we don't have to worry about sounding like them. We don't! And for those who follow us," Jimmy concluded, with his infectious laugh, "no matter how big a super star he is, he's got his work cut out, too, after those crazy Cajuns been out there!"

# People Buy the Feel:
# Cajun Fiddle Master Rufus Thibodeaux

*Kevin S. Fontenot*

Of all the great Cajun musicians, few have enjoyed as diverse a career as fiddler Rufus Thibodeaux. He performed and recorded with George Jones, Jimmy C. Newman, Lefty Frizzell, Jim Reeves, and a host of other great country musicians. Alone among Cajun fiddlers he played with the legendary Bob Wills and the Texas Playboys for a brief stint in the late 1950s. Thibodeaux also contributed his fiddling talent to several records by rocker Neil Young during the 1970s and 1980s. "I consider myself all around" as a musician, he has stated, "but being Cajun that is number one." Despite this wide ranging career, Thibodeaux's status as a sideman has kept one of the best fiddlers largely in the shadows when it comes to public knowledge of his talent.

Rufus Thibodeaux was born in Ridge, Louisiana, on January 5, 1934. Three years later his family moved to Hayes. Thibodeaux first learned to play the guitar around the age of six and later the fiddle, of which he became a master. By thirteen he was playing professionally with the Rayne Playboys in the honky tonks of southwest Louisiana and on the radio with Happy Fats LeBlanc. By 1949 he was good enough to join Papa Cairo's stringband where he met the up and coming singer Jimmy C. Newman. Thibodeaux became Newman's fiddler for a series of sessions in Nashville that brought the Cajun stringband tradition to the Country Music capital. Newman's success provided further exposure to Cajun music when he and his band began to regularly perform on the Grand Ole Opry.

Newman's music was a Cajun-country fusion, and Thibodeaux's fiddling contributed to the forging of that style. Though a fan of Harry Choates' hard driving Cajun honky tonk sound, Thibodeaux's style was always more sophisticated, and demonstrated a lighter touch more reminiscent of Luderin Darbone at his best. But a major influence came from the great western swing fiddler and bandleader Bob Wills. Thibodeaux took the driving sound of Cajun fiddle and tempered out the rough edges on the Wills anvil. As a result, Thibodeaux's style is uniquely his own among Cajun fiddlers and allowed him to easily move between the various Cajun and country styles. This flexibility led to Thibodeaux being in constant demand by bandleaders on the Gulf Coast circuit. He gigged with legends Lefty Frizzell and Jim Reeves. Thibodeaux also appears on a rare George Jones live recording from the Dancetown USA ballroom outside of Houston. Thibodeaux performed a solo rendition of "Jole Blon" that refers to Choates' classic recording but is much smoother in its execution and swing.

In 1958 Rufus received an invitation from the great Bob Wills to join the Texas Playboys. Cajuns held Wills in high regard and Thibodeaux jumped at the opportunity to play with the master. His stint as a Playboy lasted about a year and a half, "the most beautiful experience I ever had. [Bob] was the greatest bandleader that ever lived."

But Thibodeaux was in demand for more than live dates. Starting in the 1950s he became a regular house musician at Jay Miller's studio in Crowley. He played on a wide range of recordings cut by Miller, including playing guitar on blues tracks behind Slim Harpo. He backed George Jones on the singer's first recordings and later performed on sides by the Everly Brothers and Porter Waggoner. Thibodeaux's diversity and his ability to adapt made him a premier sideman, but it did not always work. During the 1970s he backed accordionist Nathan Abshire on several cuts for La Louisianne. Though all the musicians sounded fantastic, the rough barrelhouse accordion of Abshire clashed with Thibodeaux's smooth lines. In 1974 he reunited with old friend Jimmy C. Newman on the "Lâche Pas La Patate" album marking Newman's re-embracing of straight Cajun music after a successful mainstream country career.

In 1975 Thibodeaux's career took another turn when he was asked to perform on Neil Young's International Harvesters. Thibodeaux added an authentic feel to Young's search for a more folksy sound on such albums as "Comes a Time," "Hawks and Doves," and "Old Ways." He also toured with Young, playing a memorable performance at the New Orleans World Fair in 1984.

Though best known for his work with others, Thibodeaux produced a number of his own projects. He recorded for the D label in the 1950s, releasing the singles "Mean Autry" and "Cameron Memorial Waltz." He cut a tribute album to his heroes Choates and Wills, with a side dedicated to each. In 1987 he released "The Cajun Country Fiddle of Rufus Thibodeaux" on La Louisianne.

Thibodeaux's career represented a rare moment in Cajun music history. An artist was able to parlay his talent into a paying vocation that crossed genre lines. Rufus Thibodeaux succeeded by using that age-old Cajun ability to adapt to new circumstances and still keep his feet grounded in his culture. "Lâche Pas La Patate" was not just a tune for him, it was a way of life.

*Sources:*

Chris Hall, liner notes to Jimmy 'C' Newman, "Sings Cajun," Ace CDCHD 501.

George Jones, "Live at Dancetown USA," Ace CDCHM 156.

Jimmy McDonough, *Shakey: Neil Young's* Biography, New York, 2002.

Todd Mouton, "Rufus Thibodeaux, Forever Fiddling," *Offbeat.*

Rufus Thibodeaux plays the fiddle on the Grand Ole Opry, ca. 1973.
*Photo courtesy of Johnnie Allan.*

# Vin Bruce

*Michael Hurtt*

Justifiably called "The King of Cajun Music," Vin Bruce was born in Cut Off, Louisiana, in 1932 and first picked up the guitar at age seven. By the mid-'40s he was playing with Dudley Barnard's Southern Serenaders, an underheralded string band that launched the careers of many Cajun, country and rock 'n' roll musicians from the Bayou Lafourche area. It's a musical tragedy that the Serenaders never recorded, as drummer Pott Folse, steel guitarist Harry Anselmi and guitarists Luke "Smokey" Charpentier and Leroy Martin all passed through the band's ranks.

"I played with them for a few months," remembers Vin, "not long. They fired me. I don't want to tell you why! Then they took Leroy with them and I went with Gene Rodrigue." Rodrigue, who, like Barnard, would eventually record for New Orleans' Meladee label, specialized in an accordion-less strain of Cajun music injected with a heavy hillbilly influence. Rodrigue's band went by the suave handle of the Louisiana Troubadours (and later the Hillbilly Swing Kings).

"At that time it wasn't country," stresses Bruce, "it was hillbilly music. I did Cajun and English. We used to play night dances at honky-tonks and we used to go on the radio and advertise the places we would play. They would buy time on a Saturday morning show that we would broadcast from the old Jung Hotel in New Orleans.

"Henry Hildebrand worked with Columbia Records," Vin continues, "So the big man from Columbia, Don Law, come over, and he signed me." It's hardly surprising that Bruce's talent was recognized by Law, who had recorded Robert Johnson during the '30s and would go on to produce Johnny Cash's superb '60s material. Law went to work before Vin had even cut his first record.

"Columbia started pushing me before my record came out; they wanted the people to know about me so I went on the Louisiana Hayride. Gene didn't want me to go, so he fired me. And then I formed my band before my record came out."

When Vin went to Nashville to record, a chance meeting with his hero Hank Williams led to a lasting friendship. "I met Hank at Hank and Audrey's Corral in Nashville, a gift shop. I was buying a buckle for my belt and I had it in my hand. And then he walked in from a back room, he didn't come from the front door. Hank Williams, on the street, he couldn't have walked ten feet; he was the biggest at that time. Ernest Tubb, Eddy Arnold; they were big, but when he came out with 'Lovesick Blues,' that was it.

"And then he saw me. He said, 'Hey there, son, what you have?' I couldn't talk. He says, 'Where you from?' I said, 'Louisiana.' 'What brings you here?' I say, 'I'm recording.' He didn't believe me, you know? Seventeen, eighteen years old, recording, from Louisiana. He said, 'What company?' 'Columbia.' At that time we only had MGM, Columbia, Decca, Capitol, a handful of recording companies. He says, 'You got songs?' I told him I go to Acuff and Rose [a publishing firm], and he wrote songs for Acuff and Rose. Then I told him the musicians—Chet Atkins, Grady Martin, Tommy Jackson—that were playing on my recordings."

In a highly-publicized public ceremony, Hank married Billie Jean Jones at New Orleans' Municipal Auditorium in the Autumn of 1952 and Bruce and his band played the reception. "It was fun while it lasted," he remembers. "I stayed with Hank for a couple of days at the Roosevelt Hotel after. He sent Billie back to Bossier City, so man, here I was with the big guys; I was a small dog with the big dogs. I'd have stayed a month if he'd have stayed a month, I was living high."

Vin's tenure with Columbia represented the first time that a Cajun artist was marketed to the general public by a major label, an occurrence that his cousin, Joe Barry, calls "A miracle." His recordings, sung in both French and English, were uniformly excellent, seamlessly blending his Acadian roots with the Bayou Lafourche hillbilly and western swing tradition. Hits such as "Dans la Louisianne" led to appearances on the Grand Ole Opry before but as Vin puts it, "rock 'n' roll came along and wiped us out." He says the last few words as if it was an overnight occurrence. Was it? "Oh yeah. I didn't hate rock 'n' roll but it took my contract away from me. Columbia wasn't selling. Carl Smith wasn't selling no more, Ray Price wasn't selling; Vin Bruce wasn't selling at all. I mean, I was just starting out. I think I lasted about five years."

Returning to Cut Off to raise cattle, he cut his first album in 1961 for Swallow Records under the super-

Popular vocalist Vin Bruce brought polished country-style singing into Cajun music.
*Photo courtesy Johnnie Allan.*

vision of his old friend Leroy Martin, who by then was playing bass in Joe Barry's band the Vikings. Martin wasn't the only former Southern Serenader involved in the album; Harry Anselmi was on steel and Luke Charpentier was on lead guitar. The icing on the cake, however, was legendary fiddler Doc Guidry. Martin began playing bass with Vin and his band, the Acadians, shortly thereafter, a position that he occupies to this day, while Anselmi still wields the steel guitar in the group.

*Interview With Vin Bruce:*

HURTT: Your father was a musician, right?

BRUCE: My dad was a great fiddle player. I wish I'd have had a tape recorder to tape…him and I used to go trapping back in the marsh and I'd bring my guitar and he'd bring his fiddle. That was our radio, that was our music.

HURTT: Did you learn a lot of songs from your dad?

BRUCE: He used to play the waltz and the two steps and the quadrilles, what do you call it, or something else and I'd follow him with the guitar. And I learned a lot by just watching him. My mama bought me a guitar when I was seven years old. She paid ten dollars for the guitar. It was a dobro-style guitar. It was kind of hard to play. That was second hand now, when she bought it.

HURTT: Were you listening to a lot of hillbilly music when you were young?

BRUCE: That's all we listened to. We started on Jimmie Rodgers. My grandmother was a Jimmie Rodgers number one fan. She had a record player with one of those crystal heads you called it. You'd put a needle in there, a sharp needle. She had to crack it, change the needle, then they had that brush. You'd brush it before playing it so that needle wouldn't get too dirty. And she did it herself. Maybe twice a month we could go sit down around that old record player and play those Jimmie Rodgers songs. Then Ernest Tubb came out with some old stuff before "Walking the Floor Over You" and we'd listen to that. We had some other singers. But that's the way I learned and I heard. I said, "I wish someday I'd be one of them."

HURTT: And then you were.

BRUCE: And then I almost was. Well, I was. Yeah.

HURTT: Did you listen to any local hillbilly or Cajun musicians on the radio back then?

BRUCE: Oh yeah. Man, I used to hear Johnny Bonvillian on the radio station from New Orleans. In those days we didn't hear too many steel guitar players, and Johnny was one of the top. Johnny's a little older than me. I said, "Boy, I'd like to play with that man one day!"

HURTT: And Johnny later joined your band.

BRUCE: Yeah, when I recorded for Columbia I formed a band afterwards with Johnny on steel guitar. I had a small band before.

HURTT: Were you listening to Johnny on WWL?

BRUCE: I guess so. They were good. It was like a hillbilly band, it wasn't no country band in those days, you know? We had a battery radio at that time; one wire from one roof to the other. That was the good old days to me. Nobody had cars, we didn't have to pay no notes, you know? We didn't finance nothing. We didn't have no money, but we didn't owe nobody. I wonder if people think about that. And we made an honest living. I'm not saying nobody was dishonest, but if we needed a cup of sugar you'd go to your neighbor to borrow a cup of sugar. People would trade until the wagon would pass on that gravel road. I remember when they had a rolling store pulled with a horse with everything on it. Part of it was open so you could see what you wanted. Mama would sew her own dresses, so she'd say "I want two yards of that material." And he had the scissors, he'd cut the material off and he'd always give you about a foot extra lagniappe. I can still see that scissor. Oh, I could tell you some stories....

HURTT: How did you begin playing music professionally?

BRUCE: I grew a little older, I was say about fifteen, and I was—we used to go trapping with—you've heard of Gene Rodrigue? We were good buddies so I went to see Gene play one night in Grand Isle. I had an old '38 Ford, second hand you know, and I sang with Gene. The owner of the place, Mr. Joe Caulfield or Garfield, he wasn't from here but he had the place. He came to the bandstand and asked me, "Son, where you from?" I told him. He said, "Gene, come see. I want you to hire that boy when you come here." I thought I had wings on me and was ready to fly. So Gene hired me and that's how it started. His band was the Louisiana Troubadours. Dudley Barnard had let me sing with him a few times, I probably started first with him but I didn't stay long. So I stayed with Gene quite a while til the big man called me from Nashville.

HURTT: How did that come about?

BRUCE: Gene and I were playing every Saturday morning on the radio station in New Orleans from the Jung Hotel. We'd have to find our own sponsors. So we played there for awhile until Henry Hildebrand heard me. He got in touch with the radio station and the next Saturday we went and the disc jockey said, "Vin, I've got this number here you've gotta call. It's a man from Columbia Records." I said, "What does he want, he want to sell me some records?!" And so we called and he told me, "Look, I'm a representative from Columbia Records. I heard your voice and I like it. I spoke to Don Law already, I called him up." So then he called me back. I didn't have no telephone so he told me the date that he was gonna call back. I was at Rex Ice Cream after Johnny Souest became my manager. (Souest was the owner of Rex Ice Cream, a Raceland Drive-Inn). So Johnny talked to him and he made arrangements to come meet us. He wanted me to sing a few songs. I had wrote "Dans la Louisianne" and they were interested in recording a French song. So they came over. Johnny was living in a trailer and we got in that trailer and I sang the song. I didn't sing it all and he said, "That's enough." We signed a three-year contract plus a two year option, I believe a year, I forgot. He said, "Well, you got any songs? Bring 'em over. If we don't have enough we'll find some songs for you." So we packed and went to Nashville.

Hurtt: In Nashville you were paired with some of country's top session players.

Bruce: Oh yeah. Chet Atkins, Grady Martin, Tommy Jackson. We recorded in the Andrew Jackson Hotel, they had a studio on the third floor I believe. We were staying at the Sam Davis. So I recorded, let's see, four songs I believe, two French and two English. "Dans la Louisianne," "Fais de la Ville," and then "I Trusted You." I was missing on the third song so we went to Acuff and Rose. They had two million songs I believe. I've never seen so many songs in my life. Fred (Rose) said, "Here's a tape recorder." Wesley was young at the time. Autry someone—it wasn't Autry Inman—wrote "Sweet Love." It sounded like one of Lefty Frizzell's songs and Lefty was pretty hot at the time. Don said, "I like that Lefty Frizzell sound and I think this one would fit you." Well, I'm not about to tell the man no, you know? I said, "I love it too." (Laughs). I was kind of green too; country boy had barely ever been to New Orleans and at seventeen, eighteen years old I landed in Nashville. That's a pretty big jump for me.

Hurtt: Tell me about appearing on the Grand Ole Opry.

Bruce: When Don Law came and signed me up he brought Troy Martin with him. I kind of liked old Troy so every time we'd go to Nashville he'd come meet us. He liked his whiskey so we'd bring him whiskey. When we got there one Friday we recorded and he didn't want to tell me before I finished recording but afterwards he said, "You've gotta stay Saturday and see the Opry." It was like counting how much money we had to see if we could afford another night! Then he says, "I wish you don't refuse this, it's gonna help you out. I've got a spot for you on the Grand Ole Opry." I said, "Repeat that." He says, "I got you on the Grand Ole Opry with Ernest Tubb." So he had a half a pint of VO. He said, "Have a little snort of that; that's gonna make you feel good!" I had a little snort and we went and rehearsed Saturday evening with Ernest

Tubb. But I had met Ernest Tubb before, back in the early '40s, and he remembered.

HURTT: You'd met him in New Orleans?

BRUCE: At the Municipal Auditorium. Let me tell you what I asked Ernest Tubb when I first met him. I'm going back five or six years now. Johnny Souest brought me. Johnny knew his way around and he [Tubb] came at the Municipal Auditorium. So we went back stage—Johnny knew the big man to get in back stage—and Tubb was on a break. But Tubb was so much of a nice guy. So Johnny said, "This is the boy that wants to meet you, he's been dreaming every night of you, he wants to meet you…" and this and that; a lot of bull you know? Tubb said, "Where you from, kid?" He had a voice. He got up, I think that man was ten feet tall. By looking at him I was so scared and I said, "You know what? I want to sing like you." Boy, that man stooped down, and he let it out. He said, "Son, let me tell you. You want to sing?" I said, "I'd like to." He says, "There's only one Ernest Tubb. When I see you again you're going to be the one and only Vin Bruce. You don't sing like Tubb; you sing like Vin Bruce." And he was so right. 'Cause anyone who wants to sing like the other guy never makes it. You can't imitate; there's only one of anybody and you maybe can come close to take his place but you'll never do it.

So OK now, back again with Troy Martin at the Grand Ole Opry. We went and rehearsed and I had recorded "I'll Stay Single;" Chet Atkins wrote that song. That was a good song for me. So Chet was at the Opry that night and he had just worked with me the Friday night cutting that record. And Troy says, "Why don't we do 'I'll Stay Single.' Here's the man that wrote it, here's the man that plays on your record." So Chet sat in with the Ernest Tubb band and we did "Dans la Louisianne" and "I'll Stay Single." In fact, "I'll Stay Single," I had to sing it twice. And when I pulled away from the mike on the second time that I sang, Minnie Pearl and June Carter both kissed me on the cheek. I'll never, never, never forget that. That was an honor.

HURTT: Speaking of honors, you and your band played at Hank Williams' wedding in New Orleans when he married Billie Jean Jones. How did you come to meet Hank?

BRUCE: Well, Hank had that gift shop, Hank and Audrey's Corral. And I was recording in Nashville. I told Johnny, "Man, I've got to go take a walk." I had heard of Hank and Audrey's Corral so I passed right in front and I said, "Here I am, right here." I walked in and said, I'm gonna buy me a gift. I think the Lord was giving me a little hint there. So I bought a belt and they could print your name on the back of the belt. The guy said, "Go in that little room there," and he put my name down. When I came out to pay, they had a side door. And don't Hank Williams come out of that door? I said, "This is Jesus Christ. This is my day. 'Mansion On The Hill!!'" He looked at me. I had my mouth open and I was shaking. He says, "What you got, boy?" I said, "Well, I got me a-a-a-a belt." Then I guess he talked to me because I had bought that belt; that saved my life. So he said, "Where you from?" I said, "I'm from Louisiana." He said, "What part of Louisiana?" I said, "Cajun country, below New Orleans." That hit him. He says, "What you doing here, you visiting?" I said, "No, I'm recording here." That didn't ring a bell. He was probably thinking "That boy's lying." "Recording? Do you have any songs? Do you write songs?" I said, "I write a few songs—but not like you!" (Laughs). He says, "What songs do you write?" "French, English." "You write French songs?" "Yeah. I recorded some over here in Nashville." "*You* record here in Nashville? What place?" He's questioning me. I'm thinking, "Let me define myself here; I can talk here." I said, "The Andrew Jackson Hotel." He says, "I record there. Where you get your songs?" "Fred Rose." "Oh Lord, well you're not lying!" I said, "No!" And then he asked me who I recorded with; whether it was some people from down where I was from. "No, Chet Atkins." "Chet Atkins?!" (Laughs). "Yeah, I just finished recording a song he wrote. Then I told him Owen Bradley played piano. Well, that cut the cake right there. That broke the cake! He said, "Let's sit down a while, we're going to talk a while. I like you." "Mister Hank," I say..."No, no, no. No *Mister* Hank. I'm Hank Williams, you call me Hank. I want to know what part of Louisiana you're from." I said, "Cut Off, Louisiana." "Cut Off, Louisiana? I think I'm going to be doing a job around that part at the Bellevue. I'm going to give you some information. You got a manager?" "Yeah, he's in my room." He knew I was kind of green, he could see that. "You tell your manager to call my office and I want to see you there." We shook hands and in fact I didn't pay for the belt. I was so nervous I forgot to pay. I said, "Johnny, I didn't pay for the belt." He said, "We're going to get put in jail!" "Well, let's call Hank and Audrey's Corral. I said, "I'm the boy who walked out with the belt." The man said, "It's your belt, don't worry. You were talking to the big man and you're not paying for no belt!" Boy, I wish Johnny would have heard that. So I got a free belt by meeting Hank Williams—I wore that belt for a long time when I played music. So I told Johnny and he said, "But why? If they did that for every customer they gonna close up." "Yeah," but I said, "Let me tell you the rest. I met the owner." "What's his name?" "Hank Williams." "Look," he said, "you didn't meet Hank Williams. It can't be. And you didn't come get me?" "Well, I was too busy." "It can't be, man...well I'm glad for you."

So we came back home and we called the office and found out the date. At that time I hadn't hit the road yet with my big band, I was still with Gene Rodrigue. I said, "Gene, Hank Williams is coming and he invited me to go." He says, "Ernest Tubb invited me to go too," like he didn't believe me. I said, "Well, you watch me." He said, "If you go, you're fired." I had a month before

Gene would fire me but I was going! At that time, Don Law called Johnny up and had a place for me at the Hayride to promote my song. So I was going out with my wife, and we didn't play that Saturday. So we took off, me, Johnny and another guy to the Louisiana Hayride. I had never seen Webb Pierce, Johnny Horton, Faron Young; they were all there at that time. Here I was with the big ones. So I went a couple of Saturdays. I took off the Friday because we had to leave early and when I told Gene he said, "Don't come back." Instead of being proud of a hometown boy trying to make it...I'd have been proud, me. And then when we got in the Sunday night, me and my wife, we met him on the highway. I said, "Hey, Gene, we're back. Are we playing?" "No, no, no," he says. "*I'm* playing. You're not. You're fired!" OK, well, no hard feelings. So I lost my job with Gene, and Hank Williams came to the Bellevue. We went and ate with him at a little restaurant down the bayou, and he invited me for his wedding. Municipal Auditorium. On a Sunday in October 1952.

HURTT: Now, that wedding was really a concert and they got married in the middle of it, right? Your guitarist at the time, Gene Dusenberry, told me that Red Sovine also played.

BRUCE: Yeah. And Billy Walker. Johnny Bonvillian was also with me.

HURTT: Is it true that they wound up having to do two shows back to back because so many people were waiting to get in to the first one?

BRUCE: Yeah, two shows. Oh, man, they had a lot of people. I had bought me a Martin. And I had that Martin on the bandstand and Hank Williams saw it and said, "I want to play on the Martin," you know? I think he had a Gibson if I'm not mistaken. I said, "If you want it, take it." So he played on that Martin. And we had pictures taken. John and I kind of separated and he had a lot of stuff for me in the attic at the Rex, but the Rex burnt. They found a few pictures, one of Hank with my guitar and one of he and Billie but there's none of me and him with the band.

HURTT: Did you take Hank around New Orleans after the show that night?

BRUCE: Yeah. He was at the Roosevelt Hotel I believe. And I didn't know much about New Orleans but Hank wanted to see the town. So I stayed and I came back the next day. He sent Billie back to Bossier City, so man, here I was with the big guys; I was a small dog with the big dogs. I'd have stayed a month if he'd have stayed a month, I was living high! It was fun while it lasted but that was the end of Hank Williams with me. He died not long after that.

HURTT: You really broke new ground when you were on Columbia, cutting records in French that actually sold outside of Louisiana. At the time that was unprecedented. The only one who'd been able to do it was Harry Choates and he was on an independent label.

Bruce: Harry Choates come out before me with "Jole Blonde" and boy, when I heard that I said, "That's what I want to be." The poor man died young. Didn't take care of himself. I never met him and I wish I would've.

Hurtt: Did you play out of state much?

Bruce: Yeah. We would travel to Texas, Mississippi…we didn't go too far North. We traveled pretty far, like to Lubbock, Texas, but we were so busy down here [in South Louisiana] and around New Orleans. Johnny Bonvillian can tell you. For awhile we had a bus, but some of the guys wanted to drive back to see Mama after the show so we decided OK, we're going to leave the bus alone, everybody drive their own vehicles.

Hurtt: So things were going well for you and then…

Bruce: I was selling pretty good and then rock 'n' roll hit. Elvis rocked the world you know? So they didn't renew my contract because I wasn't selling. Guys like Carl Smith, Lefty Frizzell, Ray Price, Marty Robbins was all on the same label as me, they wasn't selling. They didn't hardly have any bookings left. Rock 'n' roll took over, man, over night. It came along and just wiped us out.

Hurtt: Was it that much of an overnight occurrence?

Bruce: Oh yeah. I didn't hate rock 'n' roll but it took my contract away from me. I mean, I was just starting out. I think I lasted about five years. I cut eighteen sides; nine 78s. So we came back home and I formed a little band and kept on playing and it kept me alive until I ran into Leroy Martin.

Hurtt: Leroy had taken your place ten years before in Dudley Barnard's band the Southern Serenaders.

Bruce: I knew Leroy Martin all my life. So Leroy says, "I can get you a contract with Floyd Soileau." So Floyd says, "I'll record Vin anytime." So we cut a 45 and then we cut an album for Floyd at the old KLFT radio station in Golden Meadow. We had one mike for me and one mike for the rest of the band. It came out pretty good.

Hurtt: Leroy told me that the fiddle player you had on the 45 wasn't working out for the album [Jolie Blonde] so you all went to have a few drinks.

Bruce: Yes, at the old Theriot's Lounge in Golden Meadow. I said, "I know who I can get? I can try Doc Guidry." Leroy says, "You know Doc Guidry?" I said, "We gotta call him." "Well," he says, "if you can call Doc Guidry I can call Ernest Tubb!" We called Doc in Lafayette and Doc was there. He said, "Well, what time do you need me?" Just like that.

Hurtt: Leroy told me you recorded that album from about three o'clock in the afternoon til about two in the morning.

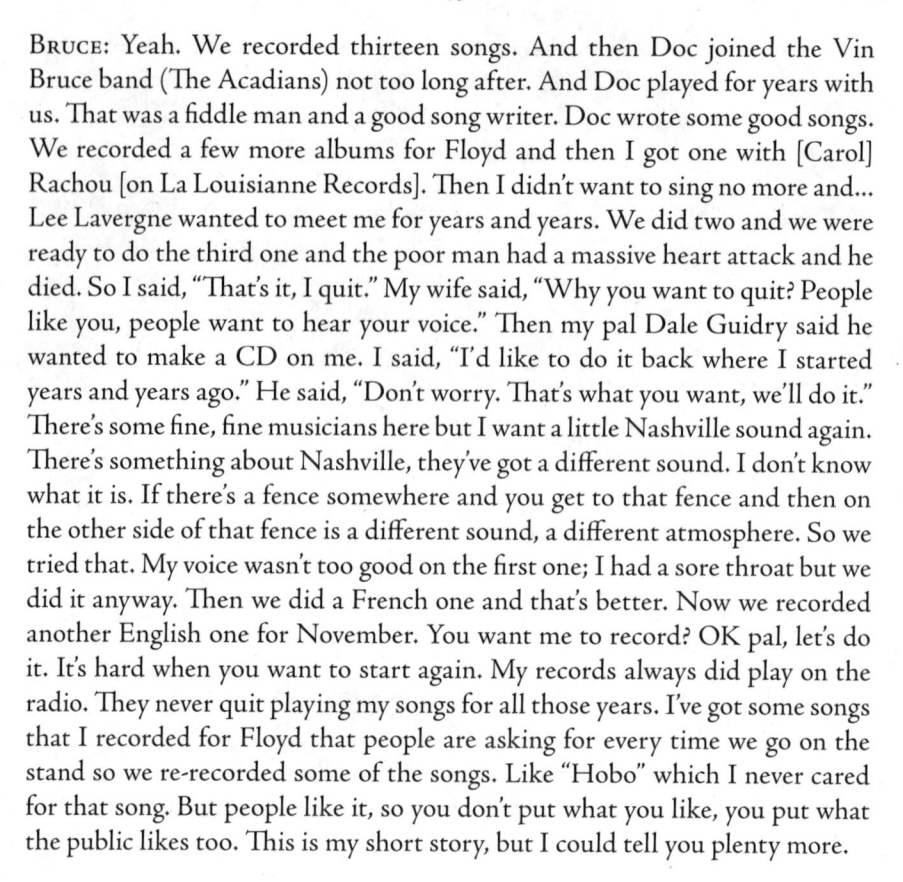

BRUCE: Yeah. We recorded thirteen songs. And then Doc joined the Vin Bruce band (The Acadians) not too long after. And Doc played for years with us. That was a fiddle man and a good song writer. Doc wrote some good songs. We recorded a few more albums for Floyd and then I got one with [Carol] Rachou [on La Louisianne Records]. Then I didn't want to sing no more and… Lee Lavergne wanted to meet me for years and years. We did two and we were ready to do the third one and the poor man had a massive heart attack and he died. So I said, "That's it, I quit." My wife said, "Why you want to quit? People like you, people want to hear your voice." Then my pal Dale Guidry said he wanted to make a CD on me. I said, "I'd like to do it back where I started years and years ago." He said, "Don't worry. That's what you want, we'll do it." There's some fine, fine musicians here but I want a little Nashville sound again. There's something about Nashville, they've got a different sound. I don't know what it is. If there's a fence somewhere and you get to that fence and then on the other side of that fence is a different sound, a different atmosphere. So we tried that. My voice wasn't too good on the first one; I had a sore throat but we did it anyway. Then we did a French one and that's better. Now we recorded another English one for November. You want me to record? OK pal, let's do it. It's hard when you want to start again. My records always did play on the radio. They never quit playing my songs for all those years. I've got some songs that I recorded for Floyd that people are asking for every time we go on the stand so we re-recorded some of the songs. Like "Hobo" which I never cared for that song. But people like it, so you don't put what you like, you put what the public likes too. This is my short story, but I could tell you plenty more.

# Dewey Balfa: A Cultural Ambassador[1]

*Barry Jean Ancelet*

Each school day in Basile, a few dozen children pile into Acadia Parish School Bus No. 3. Their driver is Dewey Balfa, a friendly middle-aged man who owns a local furniture store and does a weekly Cajun music program over KEUN radio in nearby Eunice. With one exception—his daughter Christine—these children are unaware that Dewey is one of the most widely respected folk musicians and cultural activists in America today. Few of their parents, in fact, are aware of the impact Dewey has had on their own children.

Dewey's calm, homespun eloquence and sincerity have made him a recognized spokesman for traditional culture in circles outside Louisiana, such as the Smithsonian Institute and the Library of Congress. He sits on the Folk Arts Advisory Panel of the National Endowment for the Arts and is a member of the National Council for the Traditional Arts. Most of his battles to save his own Cajun French culture, however, are fought with a fiddle in south Louisiana, his home.

Dewey's soulful music reflects the sorrowful history of his exiled Acadian ancestors. More than that, it echoes the tragedies of his own personal life. The recent loss of several close family members has only intensified his determination to win his cultural battles.

"My culture is not better than anybody else's culture," Dewey says. "My people were no better than anybody else. And yet I will not accept it as a second-class culture. It's my culture. It's the best culture for me. Now, I would expect, if you have a different culture, that you would feel the same about yours as I feel about mine."

Dewey Balfa's rich musical heritage is a family affair. "My father, grandfather, great-grandfather, they all played the fiddle, and, you see, through my music, I feel they are all still alive."

His father, Charles, was a sharecropper on Bayou Grand Louis in rural Evangeline Parish near Mamou. He instilled his great love of life and music in his children. Will Burkeman, Harry, Dewey and later Rodney grew up making music for their own entertainment in the days before television. Many musicians must learn to play against the wishes of their parents, but the Balfa brothers did not have to sneak behind the armoire to play the accordion or unravel window screen for wire to make cigar-box fiddles. The Balfa household

---

[1] This article first appeared in the magazine *Louisiana Life* (September-October, 1981), 78-85.

often was filled with music after the day's work, and children were encouraged to participate with anything they wanted to try to play. Spoons, triangles and fiddlesticks were an important first step in the learning of rhythm. Mastering fiddles, however, took time.

"I remember when I was a little boy, when I first started playing," Dewey says, "my mama would say 'It sounds like when you catch a cat by the tail. Get out of the house.' So I had to go in the barn. I was about thirteen when I started playing the fiddle."

Dewey had many models to follow, some outside the family, some even outside the culture. "I learned songs from my daddy and also from some other musicians too," he says. "You know, I was influenced by J.B. Fusilier, Leo Soileau, Harry Choates, and I think Bob Wills and the Texas Playboys had a little effect on my fiddling. And I can play a song and tell you whose influence is showing. This has developed to be my style from different influences."

Soon enough, Dewey and his brothers were playing together for family gatherings and house dances. In the 1940s, when dancehalls were at the height of their popularity, the Balfa Brothers band stayed busy. "We sometimes played eight dances a week. Sunday afternoon, Sunday night, and Monday through Saturday nights. Some of the places we played were very small and couldn't afford a full band. And Mr. Hadley Fontenot, who was our accordion player at the time, was farming and couldn't play every night, so Will and Harry and I would just go as a string band."

Cajun music in the '40s was characterized by the string band sound. Heavily influenced by western swing, bluegrass and American country music, the traditional music of French Louisiana was drifting toward Americanization along with the rest of the culture. The melting-pot movement, fueled in south Louisiana by an Anglo American minority with oil-based new money and compulsory English language education, forced traditional Cajun music underground along with most of the French language and culture.

Then, in the years following World War II, interest in cultural heritage began to resurface. Musicians like Iry Lejeune, Nathan Absire, Alphé Bergeron, and Lawrence Walker dusted off their long-abandoned accordions to perform again and to record traditional Louisiana Cajun French music. Through the '50s, Cajun music styles continued to develop naturally, from within, narrowly avoiding the overwhelming influence of the rock years. Traditional dance bands again performed regularly, often several times a week.

Unfortunately, despite the traditional revival, several non-traditional elements of Cajun music that had been introduced in the 1940s survived—the use of steel guitar and drums, electrical amplification and the practice that musicians call "successive instrumental rides" (bandmembers taking turns dominating in a song.) Moreover, in seeking more generally palatable sounds,

Cajun groups began to stray from traditional sources toward pop and country styles, as was the case with the Nashville sounds of Louisiana's Jimmy C. Newman and the later music of Doug Kershaw. If the reborn traditional Cajun music was to remain a legitimate expression of Louisiana French society, some people were convinced that deliberate efforts would have to be made to encourage the maintenance of the music's traditional form.

In 1964, the Newport Folk Festival sent folk musicologist Ralph Rinzler to scout for talent in French Louisiana. The Newport Folk Foundation board planned to present traditional musicians at the festival, alongside such popular revivalists as Joan Baez, Bob Dylan, and Buffy St. Marie, to illustrate the importance and impact of roots music.

Dewey Balfa served as a last-minute replacement on guitar, and he accompanied accordionist Gladius Thibodeaux and Louis "Vinesse" LeJeune at the New Port Folk Festival in 1964. In an Opelousas *Daily World* editorial of October 20, 1965, Burton Grindstaff commented condescendingly about the notion of finding talent among Cajun musicians. His opinion represented the

The Balfa Brothers on stage with Ray Abshire, ca. 1974. From left to right, Will Bolfa, Dewey Balfa, Ray Abshire, Rodney Balfa, Ray Abshire.
*Photo courtesy of Ray Abshire.*

opinions of many who, at the time, had predicted embarrassing consequences if, indeed, Louisiana were so represented in Newport.

As Dewey tells the story, events took quite another turn. "I had no idea what a festival was. They were talking about workshops, about concerts, and I didn't have the slightest idea what those were. I always loved to play music as a pastime. I've always looked on music as a universal language. You can communicate with one, or you can communicate with a whole audience at one time. But then, here I was going to Newport, Rhode Island, for a festival. I had played in house dances, family gatherings, maybe a dancehall where you might have seen 200 people at once. In fact, I doubt that I ever seen 200 people at once. And in Newport, there were 17,000—17,000 people who wouldn't let us get off the stage. I can remember some of the bigger names were Peter, Paul, and Mary, Johnny Cash, Mississippi John Hurt, and many other very well-known people. I'll tell you the truth, I was kind of embarrassed to go up there and play. I was there with Vinesse and Gladius and Revon Reed on triangle. Mr. Paul Tate (a Mamou lawyer and folk-culture activist) was there, too, as a dignitary. And the crowd gave us a standing ovation for playing traditional Cajun music.

"After I saw that reception, I came back, and I couldn't get that off of my mind. I said, 'Something has to be done, but what can a poor fellow like me do about a whole culture?' I remember writing to Mr. Rinzler and thanking him for the opportunity and that I would never forget it as long as I lived. From there, it led to another festival and another and another."

In 1965, when Ralph Rinzler came back to south Louisiana to record musicians, he also brought Newport Folk Foundation money to plow back into the culture through the newly formed Louisiana Folk Foundation. Traditional music contests with attractive cash prizes were organized at local festivals to flush out talented, unknown musicians and to show outside and inside support for this venerable folk-art form. Clearly the Newport board was playing to politics of culture. In spite of his distaste for the contest tactic, Dewey stayed close to this early activity and began to learn from the fieldworkers how to approach the personal "mission" he had undertaken at that first experience in Newport. He turned inward to ponder his own culture with an arsenal of new questions.

"You know, a lot of times I had questions," he remembers, "and I didn't know the answer, but something would happen that I would have a logical answer. Now don't ask me how or why or where I got it. I guess I had some kind of mission to do.

"A little girl once asked me, 'Mr. Balfa, how can you play music by ear?' And I didn't know how to answer her, but it came to me all of a sudden. I said, 'Honey, how did you learn to talk before you could write? Didn't you learn from your parents?' She said, 'Yes.' I said, 'Well, I learned to play music the same way I learned to talk. The only difference between my playing music by ear and you talking is that later you learned to read and write. I've always only depended on my ear and my memory...and my feelings.'"

In 1967, Dewey told Ralph Rinzler that he felt it was important to present his family tradition. And that year, the Balfa Brothers band was invited to perform at the Newport Folk Festival.

"When we first started going to the festivals," Dewey says, "I can remember people saying, 'They're going out there to get laughed at.' But when the echo came back, I think it put an alert to people that there were great efforts being made by people who were interested in preserving the culture. But a lot of people don't realize that they have a good cornbread on the table until somebody else tells them that they have one."

Dewey's timing was perfect. The creation of the Council for the Development of French in Louisiana in 1968 testified to a changed cultural climate.

In 1974, Lafayette had its first "Tribute to Cajun Music," sponsored by the council, and Dewey recalls that "even though it had rained for three days, Blackham Coliseum couldn't hold all the people who came."

As a result of the overwhelming response, the Cajun music festival has become an annual outdoor event, the largest mass rally for Cajun culture to date. Dewey saw the festival all along as being more than entertainment; the festival has made cultural heroes of its performers, thus attracting new, young musicians to Cajun music and offering an alternative to popular music. The existence of this alternative and the message of Dewey's mission gained even more recognition in 1977, when Dewey received a "Folk Artists in the Schools" grant from the National Endowment for the Arts.

"I can remember doing workshops away from home, people were so amazed at the music, and when I'd tell them about the culture, they just couldn't believe it. And the question would always come up: 'Do you think that this music, language and culture will survive?' And I had my doubts, because there was nobody who would work in the fields and who would come back and sit on the back porch or sit by the fireplace and play their instruments and tell stories from grandmother and grandfather. Instead, kids would come back from school and do their homework and watch television. A lot of artificial things, instead of the real down-to-earth values. And I thought that the only way it would survive, could survive, was to bring this music into the schools for the children."

Dewey's message was heard by many young Cajuns who began to perform the music of their heritage, often with a few new wrinkles. Although considered a purist by many, Dewey sees legitimate change as a vital necessity. "Things have to change," he says. "When things stop changing, they die. The culture and the music have to breathe and grow, but they have to stay within certain guidelines to be true. And those guidelines are pureness and sincerity. Some young musicians are playing Cajun music. Others are using it."

In 1978, Dewey's brothers Will and Rodney were killed in an automobile accident in Avoyelles Parish near Bunkie while on a family visit. Last year his wife, Hilda, who always provided him with a secure home base from which to work, died of trichinosis. Though these personal tragedies in Dewey's life affected him very deeply, cultural heroes, like all public figures, must be larger than life. After a period of mourning for each, Dewey resumed his work with an even stronger sense of mission, marked by a certain feeling of urgency and a concern to preserve the ground they had gained together. He carried the spirit of the Balfa Brothers with Rodney's son, Tony, now, and he never finds the load too heavy. It is a banner of pride for his culture.

"Mr. Rinzler asked me at a festival one time, 'Do you realize how many lives, how many people the Balfa Brothers have affected through the years of music?' I said, 'No.' And I really had no idea until my two brothers passed away. Only then did I realize the tremendous power we had and didn't know. We never thought of promoting the group. We were promoting the culture. We never thought that we were bringing the music to different people and different places. We always thought that the music was bringing us.

"We had many of our friends come with us on trips away from Louisiana, and we always really enjoyed that, because they were the Balfa Brothers, too. Will and Rodney were my blood brothers and my musical brothers. So were these other people my musical brothers. I think of the Balfa Brothers band as a brotherhood of musicians, not just as the three or four blood brothers. Dick Richard, Marc Savoy, Robert Jardell, Ally Young and many others...I have a big family."

# The Cajun Mick Jagger[1]

## Richard Baudoin

The third Saturday in September is one of those near-sacred events at the Grant Street Dancehall, a warehouse turned honky tonk in a slightly seedy section of Lafayette, Louisiana. After a day of dancing, eating and drinking, the rowdy throng whooping it up at the Festivals Acadiens in nearby Girard Park somehow finds its way down to Grant Street, where the party continues and intensifies.

On this particular third Saturday in September, however, the crowd at Grant Street is somewhat thinner than usual. Hurricane Gilbert has so rattled everyone that the festival has been canceled and the tourists have vanished. But no threat of a hurricane is going to diminish the enthusiasm of the acolytes who are lining up to see their hero, the performer who always occupies center stage on this most special of evenings, the man they call "the Cajun Mick Jagger," the crown prince of Cajun rock 'n roll, Zachary Richard.

By 10 p.m., the crowd is beginning to squirm in anticipation of Richard's appearance. The energy level, not surprisingly, is high. After all, this assembly is composed not of intellectual devotees of folk music, but rather of kids who look like they would be more at home at a Sting concert. Finally, Richard bursts onto the stage, whirling among the amplifiers, wrapping his accordion around himself like a boa constrictor. The small, wispy musician is belting out his trademark version of *Lacassine Special*, a classic of the Cajun repertoire. A frenzy ensues.

"They dig it because it rocks," says Richard, as he pours coffee on the back porch of his neo-Acadian cottage in a soybean field northwest of Lafayette. This rather simplistic self-evaluation of his music is an accurate one, but it belies the true complexity of the man who utters it. While Richard insists that his true goal in life is "to make popular tunes in south Louisiana" and "to be played on KVPI [a small Cajun-oriented radio station in Ville Platte, Louisiana]," in reality his artistic mission has been a much more expansive and rich one.

He is an accomplished songwriter and arranger with a huge following in Canada and France. He has been a political activist who tried to import the militance of the French separatist movement in Quebec to south Louisiana. He is a poet who has published work in both English and French. And he has inevitably been at the center of controversy—spurned by other Cajun musicians; banished from the Cajun music festival for three years; locked in a complicated feud with another giant of the genre, Michael Doucet of the band Beauso-

---

[1] This article first appeared in the Tulane University magazine the *Tulanian* 59 (1988): 22-27.

leil. Not a bad resume for someone with a degree in history which he jokingly claims "qualified me for nothing."

Ralph Zachary Richard is not, as he puts it, "one of those kids from Church Point [a small town in southwest Louisiana] who grew up playing the accordion." He is Cajun by birth, to be sure, but he was raised in a comfortable middle-class home in the small town of Scott just west of Lafayette. His father, a local politico, is a member of the Rotary Club. He attended the premier Catholic boys high school in Lafayette. And he went to Tulane, an atypical choice for south Louisiana Cajuns who have usually gravitated to the University of Southwestern Louisiana or LSU in Baton Rouge.

Zachary Richard live on *Le Ranch à Willie*, a television variety show, Québec, Canada, ca. 1974. This was his first exposure in Canada. Note also his cousin Michael Doucet at right.
*Photo courtesy of Zachary Richard.*

Richard cites his years at Tulane, both inside and outside the classroom, as a major contributing factor to his artistic development. At Tulane, he was exposed to a liberal arts curriculum "which gave me a cultural experience that I never would have had." He went Junior Year Abroad to Edinburgh, Scotland, where he took courses in African studies and formed a band consisting of himself, two Czech refugees and "a drummer who was into the Grateful Dead." When the Tulane Liberation Front took over the University Center in 1970, he hung out with the rest of the erstwhile revolutionaries. Out of these experiences grew many of his musical and political ideas.

But no academic gave Richard the musical training that would propel him to pop stardom. Back home in Lafayette after graduation, he plunged into a rigorous program of self-education, devoting eight hours a day to practice on the guitar, piano, and French accordion—which would eventually become his hallmark instrument. He integrated a newly acquired appreciation for traditional Cajun music with his natural rock'n roll instincts and formed a hot band of local musicians which included his cousin Michael Doucet. Soon they were Canada bound.

In the early 1970s, the provinces of Quebec and New Brunswick were seething with revolt. Activists were challenging the society's historic repression of Francophone culture, and the movement toward autonomy was gathering momentum. In this superheated environment, Richard and his Bayou Drifter Band were an immediate hit. "Fiery music from a long-forgotten vestige of North American French culture was just what Quebeckers wanted to hear," wrote USL professor Barry Jean Ancelet, an expert on Cajun culture, in his 1984 book *The Makers of Cajun Music*.

One constant throughout Richard's frenetic career has been his tremendous acceptance in the Francophone world, especially in Canada and France. Two of his records have gone gold in Canada and he earned enough money from arranging the traditional Cajun song *Travailier, C'est trop dur* for a French pop singer to build a home. During the mid-1970s, when his career was just beginning to develop, he could always count on being hired to play at Canadian music festivals or appear on television. In 1980, his tremendous popularity was confirmed when he received the *Prix de la Jeune Chanson* from France, given annually to the outstanding young French language singer. To this day, he remains a *phenomenon* abroad.

It is a peculiar irony that Richard, as well as other musicians of Acadian heritage, have often enjoyed their greatest success in the countries from which their forefathers were forced to leave. But the adulation he has received in foreign countries was not enough for Richard. Although he could have carved out a successful career as an expatriate rock'n roller, he has always chosen to return to Louisiana. Ancelet suggests that Richard, like other young people of his generation who spent time outside of their native region, underwent "an exile experience" which made them identify more intensely with Louisiana. That experience of separation allows artists like Richard to identify more closely with the historical experience of the Acadian people, who knew all too well the reality of leaving their native land. The poignancy of this separation resounds through much of Richard's early music:

> La Louisiane est si loin
> De ce pays
> que mon coeuer
> est distant de l'amour.[2]

But the experience of homecoming has not always been as successful for the young Cajun as his decision to leave. In 1975, Richard and his band were featured in the second annual *Hommage à la Musique Acadienne*, a showcase for the revival of traditional south Louisiana music which was then in its early stages. Richard and his youthful, long-haired Cajun rockers were an odd counterpoint to the other bands on the stage that day, which were composed mostly of older men who played music part-time while holding down day jobs as barbers, furniture makers, or store managers.

The differences became clear as the Bayou Drifter Band concluded its set. His face clouded with a righteous anger, Richard raised his fist in a militant salute as friends of the band unfurled a homemade banner emblazoned with an oak tree and a gold star on which had been stitched the message *Solidarite et Fierté* ("Solidarity and Pride"). As these theatrics were taking place, another of the band's retainers read a manifesto composed by Richard which described the oppression of the Cajuns in south Louisiana and urged the speaking of French.

There was only one problem: nobody got it. It was bad enough that few people in south Louisiana had ever been exposed to or even cared about the kind of militant language politics that had enflamed *Québecois*. The confusion was compounded by the individual chosen to present the revolutionary message, a Canadian school teacher then living in Lafayette. He read the statement in a flat, strangely accented voice that the Cajun French speakers in the audience had difficulty understanding. "That was a very critical mistake that I made," says Richard some thirteen years later. "We muffed it, we missed it, we blew it."

But the message was not lost on James Domengeaux, the conservative Lafayette attorney who was the political godfather of the French renaissance movement in Louisiana. Domengeaux was livid at Richard's attempt to inject revolutionary politics into what he saw as a purely cultural initiative. He banned the musician from the festival for several years and thus denied him a major source of exposure to the increasing audience for Cajun music.

---

[2] "Louisiana is so far! from this land! as my heart is distant from love," *C'est Dur a Croire* (Copyright, Editions du Marais Bouleur; used by permission).

Despite his early disagreements with Domengeaux, who died earlier this year after two decades as president of the Council for the Development of French in Louisiana, Richard has today come to terms with his contribution to the promotion of Cajun identity. And like most individuals of his generation, his youthful anger has diminished over the years. "I still have the uncompromising militancy that I had when I went to Canada in 1974," he says. "It's been tempered somewhat by society."

But political differences have not been the only source of controversy for Richard in south Louisiana. Despite his early musical success in Canada, Richard has often been scorned by other musicians playing Cajun music. Part of the problem is his need to perform radical experiments with the music, to push what has been a rather conservative regional folk idiom toward new frontiers. The result, however, is often a hybrid form which critics and other musicians have trouble assimilating. "It's not Cajun, it's not country, it's not rock 'n roll. It's a bunch of b.s. that doesn't have a thing to do with anything," another Cajun musician was reported to have said in the early 1980s when one of Richard's albums was released.

Richard's early fame in Canada and France may also have caused resentment among other aspiring musicians. While they were still playing the south Louisiana club circuit with an occasional national folk festival gig thrown in, he was a superstar who performed before thousands of adoring fans. Furthermore, his willing incorporation of commercial rock elements into his music was resisted by cultural purists who wanted to see the Cajun style preserved as it is rather than adapted to the time. "Other Cajun musicians resented Zachary Richard, seeing him as a turncoat using the shell of Cajun music to promote himself as a rock star," wrote James Edmunds in a 1981 profile of Richard.

Gaining acceptance in the United States outside of Louisiana has also been a frustrating experience for Richard at times. He was hailed as a sensation by San Francisco papers last year when he played at a trendy Mann County club, even if they didn't know exactly what to make of his music. "This is a show band, a dance band, a blues band, a jazz band—a rock band, too," *San Francisco Examiner* music critic Philip Elwood wrote of Richard's current unit, the Zydeco Rockers. But *Rolling Stone* writer Steve Pounds dismissed Richard's current efforts as "flashy, crowd-pleasing and distressingly shallow zydeco-rock."

(That cut was deepened by the context in which it appeared: a glowing profile of Michael Doucet. Although Richard and Doucet are cousins and high school classmates, the relationship between them is strained. The source of their differences is very murky, but Ancelet, who is close to both of them, says that the feud is "due to the fact that you have two giants who are too close to each other.")

Richard himself acknowledges the sometimes negative effect his musical experiments have had on his acceptance by critics and the American public. "I think my real fault is a tendency toward eclecticism pulling from everything I've ever heard," he said in an introspective interview published in 1987.

And so after decades of tinkering and adjustments, Richard has set his course on refining and distilling his music into the essence of what he says he has always wanted it to be—simple tunes which drive south Louisiana people onto the dance floor. "Essentially, after having tried out different ways of doing it, after having had some escapades through funk and Afro-Caribbean and all kinds of different influences, I got back to what I think is the real essence of my music," he says. "And that is, without want of a better word, heavily zydeco-influenced. Which is not to necessarily say that it is everything that the zydeco players are doing. But it's more zydeco in the sense of rock'n roll."

Richard also seems less eaten up with the need to "make it" on the national scene. He is comfortable playing about 100 concerts a year, whether in Boston, Massachusetts, or Chenier, Louisiana. "I don't have this thing where I'm going to have a Top 10 hit in the United States or my career's a failure. I still have a huge following in two foreign countries," he said in the 1987 interview.

Richard's spread in the country is his refuge from the pandemonium of the dancehall and the controversies among the music brotherhood. There he practices the craft he is best at—composing songs—and the one he cares most about—writing poetry.

"I'm a songwriter. That's where I make my income," says Richard. Today, he has about 120 songs in publication around the world. The royalties he receives from artists who perform and record these songs allow him to avoid the insanity of the musical road, where playing every night can soon burn a bright talent out.

Richard's songwriting has expanded in recent years to include collaboration, a process he learned while in France in the early 1980s. Among his collaborators today are Claude Michel Schoenberg, composer of the Broadway smash *Les Misérables*.

But if performing feeds his ego and songwriting puts *baguettes* on his table, it is poetry which provides his inner spiritual nourishment. Richard has been publishing poetry since his college years, when two of his works appeared in the inaugural number of *Nunc Dimittis*, a now defunct Tulane literary journal. USL's Center for Louisiana Studies has published a volume of his French poems, *Voyage de nuit*, and he was a contributor to *Cris sur le bayou*, an anthology of contemporary Louisiana French poetry which was released in Montreal in 1980.

Richard divides his poetry into two streams: so-called poetry of contemplation, which is heavily influenced by Gary Snyder, and what he calls "American night hero poems" in the tradition of Jack Kerouac and friends. "Spiritually, I'm a son of the beat generation," he says.

His French poetry is more simple, almost primitive. (He calls himself the "Clementine Hunter of French poetry.") Still, the act of writing in French is important to him, just as singing in the language of his forebears is a significant personal, political and cultural statement, in the introduction to *Voyage de nuit*, Richard told interviewer David Wetzel (in French, translated by this writer), "I am a Louisiana Acadian, and that's part of my personality that needs to be revealed. I have a chance to do something that is absolutely unique, thanks to a set of circumstances. I come from an oral tradition which is extremely interesting. I can bring to the contemporary French language an older French, conceived by an American, spoken by an Acadian and expressed today."

But Richard has no real illusions about a south Louisiana of the future where French is spoken as often as English; those dreams vanished with the passing of his militant phase a decade or more ago. But he insists that the language will retain a sacred quality for the Cajun people of south Louisiana. "It will remain as important as Hebrew to the Jews, as Gaelic to the Irish," he says.

Richard's poetry is not confined to the printed page. Ancelet says that one of Richard's greatest contributions to Cajun music is the quality of his lyrics. "He expanded the possibility of themes in Cajun music," says Ancelet of Richard. "He has a certain social and historical consciousness."

Particularly in the early stages of his career, Richard's music resonated with a revolutionary fervor, much of it inspired by his experiences in Canada during the early 1970s. Perhaps his most famous song of the period is *Réveille*, a dramatic recreation of the destruction of Acadia by the English in the eighteenth century:

*Zachary Richard's influence outside of the United States is more political than the cultural icon he has become for southern Louisianians.*
*Photo courtesy of Zachary Richard.*

*Réveille! Réveille!*
*C'est les goddams qui viennent*
*Voler les enfants*
*Réveille! Réveille!*
*Hommes Acadiens*
*Pour sauver l'heritage.*[3]

Today, Richard's songs are more simple and rollicking. He willingly discards French lyrics in order to achieve a broader audience. But he hasn't abandoned his mission. While those young kids are rocking out on Grant Street, they are being exposed to a gradually maturing message from their idol. The means of communicating it may be different, but the end point is the same: "Awaken! Awaken! Men of Acadia, to save the heritage."

---

[3] "Awaken! Awaken! The English are coming to steal the children. Awaken! Awaken! Men of Acadia, to save the heritage." *Réveille* by R. Zachary Richard. Copyright, Editions du Marais-Bouleur. Used by permission. Translation by Barry Jean Ancelet, copyright, *The Makers of Cajun Music*, University of Texas Press.

# Hawaiian Shirts and Cajun Power: Basking in the Sunshine of Michael Doucet and Beausoleil

*Ryan A. Brasseaux and Erik Charpentier*

During the late 1960s and 1970s, certain Cajun attitudes coincided with the ebb and flow of the nation's increasingly acute ethnic consciousness, spurred in large part by the Civil Rights Movement. While Cajuns had always straddled the traditional and mainstream currents shaping south Louisiana's cultural landscape, a handful of politicians, activists, scholars, artists, poets, and musicians joined forces in a unified effort to emphasize the linguistic and ethnic component of the Cajun equation through a cultural movement known as the Cajun Renaissance. Like other musical ambassadors of the Renaissance, French lyrics became a defining characteristic of Beausoleil's repertoire.[1] This youthful Cajun band worked to make traditional Cajun music palatable for contemporary audiences who cut their teeth on the Beatles, Rolling Stones, and Elvis. "Cajun music is wrapped up in emotion," maintains fiddler and Beausoleil bandleader Michael Doucet. "Maybe some of the emotions, the more modern emotions, aren't adequately covered by the old songs. So that's what we try to do through our new compositions. In many ways we're the same individuals our ancestors were 300 years ago, but the times around us have changed. If the music captures where we are now, it just adds to the preservation of Cajun music."[2]

Beausoleil is one the premier interpreters of Cajun music. No band before or since has maintained the level of international notoriety that Michael Doucet and his colleagues have enjoyed for over twenty-five years. The group helped stimulate the national Cajun craze of the 1980s by transcending south Louisiana's dancehalls and honky tonks for fertile pastures in New York City and beyond. From sold out concerts at Carnegie Hall, opening for the Grateful Dead, and winning a Grammy Award, to appearances on Garrison Keillor's "Prairie Home Companion" and at Pres. Jimmy Carter's Inaugural reception, Beausoleil has brought Cajun music to a global audience without compromising their artistic vision and integrity. This Beausoleil retrospective chronicles the twists and turns of Cajun music's most celebrated ensemble and the underlying motivations and cultural currents that shaped bandleader Michael Doucet's approach to the band and Cajun music.

---

[1] Other Cajun Renaissance bands included the Balfa Brothers band, various ensembles led by Dewey Balfa, and Zachary Richard's Bayou des Mystere band. All of these groups, whether performing traditional tunes or new compositions, emphasized French lyrics.

[2] As quoted in http://www.lsue.edu/acadgate/music/mdoucet.htm, accessed June 10, 2005.

Michael Doucet was born into a musical family in 1951 in Scott, Louisiana. As a child, Doucet absorbed all of the music around him—Tennessee Ernie Ford and Elvis Presley from the radio, his clarinetist mother's penchant for early jazz, and traditional Cajun fiddling from his paternal uncle, Will Knight, who gave the youngster his first music lessons. Michael began lessons on banjo and guitar. At fourteen, he learned his first fiddle tunes—"Allons à Lafayette," "Jolie Blon," and "St. Louis Blues"—from his uncle, though the developing musician did not take up the violin seriously until 1974. His training also included formal musical instruction, first as a trumpet player at Lafayette's exclusive Catholic institution Cathedral Carmel, then folklore and musicology in Baton Rouge at the Louisiana State University (LSU).[3]

In an ironic twist of fate, three of the most visible members of the Cajun Renaissance attended Cathedral Carmel together in the late 1960s—Ralph Zachary Richard, Barry Jean Ancelet, and Michael Doucet. These three stalwarts of Louisiana's Francophone culture came of age at the tail end of the America's counter culture movement when the Civil Rights movement, youth and drug cultures collided. Indirectly informed by "black power," alternative hippie lifestyles, the context surrounding the counterculture and the Vietnam war—and in reaction to the erosion of traditional customs in Louisiana by the encroachment of American mainstream culture—Richard, Ancelet, and Doucet carved out separate but complementary niches for themselves in music and scholarship. Their collective work helped to forge an introspective "Cajun power" movement that promoted an alternative lifestyle—not the social utopia endorsed by hippies, but an idealized Francophone utopia based on activists' perceptions of the pre-industrialized, agrarian Cajun lifestyle during the first half of the twentieth century. "We noticed that people of our parents' and grandparents' generation were going," remembered Doucet, "and with them our culture."[4] The fiddler's college experience further developed his fascination with his cultural roots.

In 1969, Doucet enrolled at LSU, where he became acquainted with folklore methodology and Cajun music scholarship by means of professor George Foss' Anglo-Saxon Folk Music course. When the freshman inquired why Louisiana French music was not part of the curriculum, Foss replied, "because Cajun songs were just translated English songs."[5] Dissatisfied with his instructor's response, Doucet retreated to the library stacks, uncovered works by LSU's

---

[3] Barry Jean Ancelet and Elemore Morgan Jr., *The Makers of Cajun Music* (Austin, 1984), 141-45.
[4] The widespread industrialization and Americanization of south Louisiana began during the early twentieth century, and accelerated after World War II, shortly before Michael Doucet was born. As quoted in Michael Simmons, "Michael Doucet: A Fiddler's Education," *Fiddler Magazine* 8 (2001): 4; Shane K. Bernard, *The Cajuns: Americanization of a People* (Jackson, 2003).
[5] As quoted in Simmons, "Michael Doucet: A Fiddler's Education," 4.

Cajun music scholars Irène Whitfield and Harry Oster, and began his quest to understand the region's cultural memory, oral history, and musical legacy.

In 1971, Michael Doucet realized his interest in Louisiana music and joined a trio that would forever solidify his musical direction and cultural awareness. He became the guitarist in a three-piece ensemble featuring mandolin player Kenneth Richard and Doucet's first cousin Ralph Zachary Richard. The band reinvigorated Cajun music with a rock 'n' roll energy that attracted a small, eclectic crowd of young Cajuns and Québecois French teachers in clubs and dancehalls around Lafayette, Louisiana. As Doucet explained to Ancelet in *The Makers of Cajun Music*,

> Whenever I had dealt with Cajun music before, it had always related to older people and how things were. Here were serious musicians, in their twenties, playing and relating to Cajun music in terms of what it could be. In Louisiana around that time, Cajun music was being displaced by Cajun country sounds which didn't ring true. I began to understand what we had and what we stood for. What we really had here in Louisiana was underneath the surface. That's where Ralph and I began to part ways.[6]

The band drifted apart when Doucet and Zachary Richard could not reconcile their musical approaches. Michael gravitated toward traditional Cajun musical expression while Richard realized that the frontier of commercial Cajun music expanded as far as France and French Canada, where he established himself as a pop phenomenon in the late 1970s.

In 1975, Doucet applied his ethnographic skills, with the help of a National Endowment for the Humanities Folk Arts Apprenticeship grant, to document those extant musicians versed in Louisiana's varied fiddle styles. Throughout the late 1970s and 1980s, Doucet sat for hours playing with master musicians from both sides of the racial divide, including Cajun fiddlers like Varise Conner, Dewey Balfa, Dennis McGee, Luderin Darbone, Oran "Doc" Guidry, and Creole fiddlers like Canray Fontenot, Bébé and Calvin Carriére. As musical performance became less of a hobby and more of a preoccupation, he then applied the understanding and repertoire he accumulated towards his varied musical endeavors.

Between 1975 and 1977, Doucet fronted Beausoleil's alter ego, the Cajun fusion group Coteau. The experimental band synthesized traditional Cajun with psychedelia, folk rock, jazz, and country. The fiddler remembered, "This was a group with a lot of different influences: rock, from Bruce MacDonald and Dana Breaux; Nashville Cajun country, from Jimmy C. Newman's son Gary; and Cajun from Bessyl [Duhon] and me."[7] Their musical experiment sounded something like Sergeant Pepper's Lonely Harts Club Band playing Joe Falcon's repertoire, a sound that connected with a youthful audience. Coteau was sur-

---

[6] From Ancelet, *The Makers of Cajun Music*, 143.
[7] Ibid., 146.

Michael Doucet and his early band Coteau expressed a Cajun-hippie aesthetic, ca. 1975. Back row, from left to right, Michael Doucet, Kenny Blevins. Front row, from left to right, Danny Kimble, Bessyl Duhon, Gary Newman, Dana Breaux, Bruce McDonald.
*Photo courtesy of Johnnie Allan.*

prisingly influential considering the groups' short lifespan. They were featured in André Gladu's 1976 documentary *Réveille*, and blew the crowd away at The Barns at Wolftrap, in Virginia.[8]

Michael Doucet's most famous musical project, Beausoleil, organized in 1976 along Cameron Parish's Gulf Coast. Doucet, Kenneth Richard, and Bessyl Duhon gathered at the Duhon family camp in Holly Beach to hone their repertoire before a free acoustic performance at a blue-collar honky tonk called the Bon Temps Rouler Club. The bandleader christened the group "Beausoleil," consciously referencing guerrilla fighter and leader of Acadian resistance movement during the *Grand Dérangement*, Joseph Broussard *dit* Beausoleil. The group's membership remained somewhat fluid even as the fiddler continued to front Coteau in 1976, when the French government invited Beausoleil to perform at the *Louisiana Bien-Aimée American Bicentennial* exhibition in Paris.[9]

---

[8] The only available footage of Coteau is French Canadian filmmaker André Gladu's *Réveille* (Montreal: National Film Board of Canada, VHS color, 28 minutes, March 1976). The documentary also features footage of Zachary Richard performing with Kenneth Richard, Doucet's band mates from the early 1970s.

[9] Back in Lafayette, the new outfit evolved to feature François Schaubert, Bessyl Duhon, David Doucet, Gary Hernandez, Steven Conn, Billy Ware, Harold Bernard, and Tommy Comeaux.

After attending the band's performance on a bateau-mouche on the Seine, a producer from Pathé-Marconi records booked the band in the studio and recorded its first album, which was never officially released in the United States until EMI records subsidiary Hemisphere issued the record in Europe as *La Nuit*.[10] Doucet explains that Beausoleil spent their first years "just trying to find songs. We didn't play in public at first. Lafayette wasn't ready for that yet. Those were the beginnings of Beausoleil. The identity of the group was always connected with a search for the spirit of Cajun music."[11]

Throughout the late seventies and the early eighties, Beausoleil released an array of recordings with an assortment of musicians who interpreted early fieldwork materials collected by ethnographers like Harry Oster, French ballads, jazz and blues, and early commercial releases from Cajun music's past. The group issued its first American release *Spirit of Cajun Music* (1977) on the Swallow record label and an album entitled *Les Amis Cadjins* (1980) in Quebec, Canada, before reaching a national audience with *Michael Doucet dit Beausoleil* (1981), the ensemble's first Arhoolie project. By the late 1980s, the band's commercial success included film soundtracks for the locally produced feature film *Belizaire the Cajun* and the Cajun-flavored Hollywood murder-mystery *The Big Easy*. The majority of the compositions featured on Beausoleil's early releases reflected the bandleader's attraction to traditional and early commercial issues from Cajun music's past.

The group's repertoire was profoundly influenced by their bandleader's interest in Cajun music's historical roots and his penchant for archival research. In 1979, Michael Doucet traveled to the Library of Congress in Washington, DC, where he uncovered John and Alan Lomax's 1934 Louisiana field recordings. The musicians first learned about the collection from an Alan Jabbour release that contained a couple of examples of fiddle virtuoso Wayne Perry's Depression-era performances recorded by the Lomaxes in the vicinity of Crowley, Louisiana. The music captured in the grooved faces of the Lomaxes' aluminum discs left an indelible mark on the music of Beausoleil. Doucet recalled fondly his experience in the Archive of Folk Songs:

> It was amazing, an old kind of cluttered building.... [The archivist inquired] "What do you want to listen to?" I said, "Well, I'm looking for the stuff in Louisiana." He brought out like all these things. I said, "Well, I'll just start at the beginning." And I said, "Let me hear the first one he recorded." And so he brought out the tape and I had to go in this little room. And I was in shock! I could not believe the quality. I could not believe the quantity. I could not believe that these things existed and no one had ever heard

---

[10] The record, originally issued in 1976, was reissued on CD as *Arc de Triomphe Two Step* in 1997. Beausoleil, *Arc de Triomphe Two Step* (Hollywood: EMI Hemisphere CD 7243 59272 2 5, 1997).
[11] Ancelet, *Makers of Cajun Music*, 147.

of these things...[after] almost fifty years. And it just opened up an amazing world to me.[12]

The band recorded tunes from the collection like Mr. Bornu's "Belle," Wilfred Charles'"Dago" reframed as "Boudreaux," and Jesse Stafford's "Je m'endors."[13]

Later, the band adopted a less academic and esoteric approach to their sound, focusing instead "on a very mobile style with influences from each member's origins."[14] With the release of its fifth album, the seminal classic *Parlez-nous à boire*, the group solidified its reputation as Acadiana's funkiest purveyor of sophisticated Cajun roots music. Beausoleil also helped to stir interest in the Cajun restaurant-dancehall phenomenon, performing French music weekly in two Lafayette area restaurants, Mulate's and Prejean's. In early 1986, the bandmembers quit their respective day jobs and became full-time musicians. "This was especially difficult for me," remembers Doucet. Cajuns traditionally equated work with manual labor and music with leisure and entertainment. "In Louisiana, unless you went to Nashville and played country-Cajun the idea of sustaining a family on music was an unheard-of occupation."[15]

In the 1980s, several cultural factors converged and stimulated a national Cajun and zydeco craze. Chef Paul Prudhomme became one of America's most recognizable culinary figures. Rockin' Sidney won a Grammy Award for his 1984 zydeco hit, "Don't Mess With My Toot Toot." Riding on the crest of the south Louisiana wave sweeping the nation, Beausoleil embarked on a career path that led them out of the Bayou country. In 1985, Doucet and his cohorts wrote a lucrative thirty-second jingle for Frito Lay's "Crunch Taters" and filmed a nationally syndicated commercial for the snack company that helped to disseminate the group's music and image across the United States. In 1986 and 1987, the band performed a series of concerts in New York City that ultimately solidified the group's reputation as a world-class American roots ensemble. As the group's visibility grew, Doucet developed a persona that embodied Jimmy Buffett's easy-going and laissez-faire attitude, which included a uniform consisting of bright floral patterned Hawaiian shirts, while Beausoleil traversed the Gulf Coast's varied musicals traditions. Audiences imbibed the band's assorted repertoire, appealed to the group's refined musicianship, and Beausoleil's intoxicating sound that was simultaneously wildly exotic and uniquely American.

---

[12] Michael Doucet interviewed by Ryan A. Brasseaux and Erik Charpentier, September 7, 2004.
[13] Beausoleil's interpretations of the Lomax collection can be heard on released like *Déjà vu* ("Belle" and "Je m'endors"), *Vintage Beausoleil* (live version of "Belle"), *L'Amour ou la Follie* ("Boudreaux"). The original field recordings are featured on the Rounder Records release *Cajun and Creole Music Vol. I & II: The Classic Louisiana Recordings, 1934/1937* (Cambridge, MA: Rounder Records 11661-1843-2, 1999).
[14] Ancelet, *The Makers of Cajun Music*, 147.
[15] Michael Doucet, *Vintage Beausoleil* liner notes, Chapel Hill: Music of the World, Ltd. CDC-213.

Cousins Zachary Richard and Michael Doucet played and performed together before their careers took different directions. Note also that they are both playing guitar, not the signature fiddle of Doucet's mature career, nor the accordion that brought Richard such wide acclaim.
*Photo courtesy of Zachary Richard.*

Beausoleil's music fluctuated thematically and stylistically until the late 1980s, as the groups rotated personnel on a regular basis. Doucet drew from the Lafayette area's pool of accomplished musicians, each of whom brought their individual idiosyncratic interpretations of Cajun music to the bandstand and recording studio. Errol Verret, the band's accordionist until the mid-eighties, provided the ensemble with a smooth accordion style based on his delicate melodic touch. His replacement, Pat Breaux, of the famed Breaux family who helped pioneer early commercial Cajun music, added saxophone and triple row accordion to the ensemble's mix of swamp-party music and thoughtfully updated arrangements of archaic compositions. A second member of the Breaux family, Pat's brother Jimmy, became full-time accordionist in the late 1980s. Jimmy Breaux's highly percussive, melodically driven, accordion style altered Beausoleil's musical personality with a technical prowess reminiscent of Creole accordion master Amédé Ardoin. The only non-native player of the band, banjoist-bassist and fiddle player Al Tharp, began performing with the group in the late 1980s and officially joined the band in the 1990s. "I was attracted to them because the band had this kind of hard, in-your-face and, in a way, sort of older, pre-country feel to it," Tharp explained to music writer Todd Mouton.[16] The multi-instrumentalist meshed well with the core members of Beausoleil, some of whom performed regularly with the ensemble since the mid-1970s.

The Beausoleil regulars shared a similar vision that allowed the band to evolve with a fair amount of consistency over time. Percussionist Billy Ware, who has been with the band since its inception, was a student of rhythmic structures from the Cajun, zydeco, and world music traditions when he joined the outfit. He embellished the group's already dynamic sound with the different colors provided by his *ti-fer* (triangle), *frottoir* (washboard), vibraphone, timbale, cowbells, congas and shakers. Drummer Tommy Alesi, another early fixture in the Beausoleil lineup, held the band together with a relaxed yet precise and syncopated backbeat. Mandolin and bass player Tommy Comeaux and Michael's guitar picking brother David Doucet brought a bluegrass and old time country string band sensibility to the table. David Doucet carved a unique niche for himself in contemporary Cajun music. He escaped the confinement of the typical Cajun rhythm section by embellishing on traditional and original melodies with his Doc Watson-styled finger picking.

Michael Doucet's fiddle playing lies at the heart of Beausoleil's sound. His furious syncopated short-bow movements churn traditional melodies into a musical hurricane that periodically jolts listeners with mad, seizure-like, cascading frills. His fiddling transcends the Cajun genre, opening traditional song structures to broader, more diverse musical possibilities in the tradition of innovative Cajun luminaries like Leo Soileau, who, like Michael Doucet, reinvented Cajun music in the mid-1930s.

During the 1990s, Doucet and Beausoleil served as the local model of success. The band traveled to across the United States, Canada, Europe and beyond performing along the folk circuit, at festivals, for national movie soundtracks and the like. Doucet's session work also proved lucrative. Mary Chapin Carpenter highlighted his fiddling on the smash hit "Down and Out at the Twist and Shout." In 1997, six-time Grammy nominee Beausoleil received its first award from the Recording Academy for the album *L'Amour ou la Folie*. This outside validation reinforced the super-group's status at home. Up-and-coming artists like Steve Riley and the Mamou Playboys followed the same avenues paved by Beausoleil by making older compositions and traditional music available to younger generations. The Playboys eventually made their way out of Bayou Country into America.

---

[16] Todd Mouton, "Love or Folly: Cajun Trailblazers Beausoleil Celebrate 20 Years Together," *OffBeat* (1997): 45.

Beausoleil is recognized around the world as the quintessential Cajun band. On stage, Doucet's manic and exuberant fiddling and the group's tightly woven grooves dazzle audiences and dancers. At home, the bandmembers resume their quiet unassuming lives, occasionally sitting in with local ensembles at performances around Lafayette. For thirty years, the band has remained hip, upwardly mobile, and uncompromising in a ruthless business known for cutthroat politics. They have successfully negotiated the boundaries separating ethnic, roots, and mainstream music and culture while singing French compositions from a bygone era. Their formula for success equates to emotional honesty. Beausoleil emerged as a vital force in south Louisiana that, like Zachary Richard's music, gave voice to the region's self-consciousness Cajun Renaissance movement. Doucet and his band mates made Cajun music come into a youthful animation that has sustained the ensemble and the genre for three decades. They were respectful of Cajun music's past, but were not afraid to experiment with traditional arrangements in a way that spoke to their contemporaries. Young Cajuns who frequented the band's performances in the Lafayette area during the 1970s were adamant in their abhorrence of what they labeled as "chanky chank" music. These twenty-somethings embraced rock and roll, swamp pop, and the music of the 1960s, and would not have listened to Cajun music if they did not identify with Beausoleil's contemporary interpretations of old standards. "Had it not been for Beausoleil's presence on the scene in the 1970s," explained Carl Brasseaux, a historian who witnessed the band convert hundreds of young locals, "I wonder if Cajun music would have been embraced by another generation, even with the beginning of the cultural revival that was going on all around them."[17] Indeed, Cajun music's first super group has fashioned a legacy that has given the world a reason to dance.

---

[17] Carl Brasseaux interviewed by Ryan A. Brasseaux and Erik Charpentier, September 7, 2004.

# Never Mind the Bowties—
# Here's the Bluerunners[1]

## Michael Tisserand

It was admittedly not the best idea for a photo shoot. The day was already on shaky footing. Three of the Bluerunners had driven into New Orleans from their homes in Lafayette. Their van had broken down, another van loan fell through, and they couldn't find a car to transport themselves, a guitar, a fiddle, and an old, beat-up accordion.

So they were forced to rent one, depleting the last of an already strained band budget. But not before suggesting to bassist Rob Savoy, who lives in New Orleans, that maybe he could go down alone and *OffBeat* could just take his picture.

By the time the studio lights were up and a couple practice shots taken of drummer Mike McBane giving the finger, everyone seemed ready. The four musicians shambled over to the set. The concept was explained: we wanted to capture the experimental nature of the Bluerunners, who merge Cajun and zydeco music with punk-edged rock. How about a shot of Steve LeBlanc smashing his accordion? Maybe something like the cover of the classic LONDON CALLING album by the Clash, a band often cited as a major Bluerunners influence? Nobody was making any sudden moves, and McBane offered an explanation. "Maybe you got the wrong band," he said. "We're not exactly extroverts. Maybe you should have gotten Cowboy Mouth."

But we pushed on. We tried playing a Sex Pistols album for ambiance. We hauled over a bucket of tools that was sitting in the corner: saws, hammers, crowbars. Hey, we asked, what if you guys could all pretend to be tearing apart your instruments? And so, at 4 p.m. on a Thursday in a photo studio in Mid-City New Orleans, with Sid Vicious droning *God save the Queen/She ain't no human bein'*, the Bluerunners found themselves three hours from home, significantly poorer, shuffling around in a little circle under hot lights, holding woodworking equipment and wondering what the hell they were doing.

It was guitarist, chief songwriter and vocalist Mark Meaux who finally erupted. "What am I doing with this saw?" he wondered, his voice rising. "This is *stupid*!" Then he walked.

He walked the way he wanted to walk during a Bluerunners show at Tipitina's in May, when the band opened with a Giant Sand song and nailed it. "You could have heard a pin drop," Meaux says, recalling the audience's less-then-enthusiastic response. "I thought we might get at least a smatter—it was a free

---

[1] This article was originally published in *OffBeat*, August, 1994 © Michael Tisserand.

show." The band next played a more traditional tune, and the floor filled with dancers. That made it even worse.

Then there are those tour dates, when the Bluerunners enter a club and see tables with candles, and people start requesting Cajun chestnuts like "Jambalaya" and "Jolie Blonde." That's when Meaux realizes that the band got that particular gig only because people had seen some good-time Cajun band in a movie like *The Big Easy* and assumed that this Lafayette accordion ensemble would follow suit. That's not when the band walks, though. That's when the band, in Savoy's words, decides to "fucking crank it up to eleven and show that there's something else, too."

There was another night in New York, at a disco. A man was leaning against the stage, with his back to the band. Meaux took the microphone, went up to the man and screamed, "You mother-fucker!" Steve LeBlanc kicked some drums over, and everyone felt better.

But the Bluerunners agree that their favorite memory is San Francisco, September 1991. LeBlanc was feeling lonely and far from home, and he was trying to pump a dying accordion. "It was losing a lot of air and stuff," he remembers. "We were on the last song of the show, and the bellow cracks, and there's nothing. I was at the end of my ropes, so I just swung it over my heard and bashed it against the wall. It didn't break the first time, so I took about three swipes at it, and it was in pieces on the ground." Savoy saw the splinters, and turned away and kept playing. Meaux remembers, "I knew we were fucked—we were in San Francisco and he's got no accordion. I was so proud of him, and proud of being in the band at that point."

There is, of course, nothing new about smashing an instrument. Since Jerry Lee Lewis and Pete Townshend, it's turned into something of a rock & roll cliché. But it's definitely not a Cajun cliche, or an accordion cliché. Which is why we had thought it might make a great image of the Bluerunners. It would illustrate something that Meaux says about his band: "We're not trying to destroy Cajun culture, we're trying to destroy the stereotypes."

As it turned out, when Meaux took off during the photo shoot, it was only to walk around the block. By the time he returned, the bucket of tools had been quietly returned to its corner. Concept abandoned, the rest of the afternoon proceeded relatively well.

"Oh, I was pissed too," McBane later says. "Steve has smashed things, and I've broken a few things, Mark's broken some guitars. You do it when it's the end of your gig and you have this thing in your stomach: How can you make it mean more? How far can you take it? It's only valid at that point. It's not valid at a photo shoot. I don't want to make you guys feel bad, but it's really pretty humiliating. Having to get directed to do things is pretty bad." The whole point of the band," he explains, "is that it feels weird taking pictures."

During a recent Friday night gig at the Grant Street Dancehall in Lafayette, a piece of paper turns up on stage, begging the band to play "Go On Get Out," a honky-tonk tune featured on the band's new release, *The Chateau Chuck*. The band ignores it.

There's a social geography at play when the Bluerunners are performing in this area. At Grant Street's fringes are groups of two stepping couples, many older and well-dressed. In the center are college kids in T-shirts, slamming. Two frat boys are waltzing together. One clean-shaven young man in a striped shirt can later be heard singing a French ballad to some admiring friends. But right now he's at the front of the stage, headbanging between the monitors.

The Bluerunners' new album, with distorted guitar work that often buries the accordion and fiddle, has been labeled the band's rock statement. "It's a harsh listen," admits Meaux. "These songs are so angry." Originally, *The Chateau Chuck* was more balanced: a couple of acoustic, accordion-driven tunes were left off the final cut. The first draft even included sound bites from Cajun fiddle pioneer Dewey Balfa. When the Bluerunners perform live, most songs continue to pivot around LeBlanc's fierce accordion and fiddle playing.

But Meaux is right: this is an angry record, including the song "Coming Down," which succinctly describes the band's experience of signing—and being dropped from—the major label Island Records. *This is your birthday party, smile don't look so tense/It's two words, music business, and it don't make no sense.* "All I really remember from that whole period is just being confused all the time," says Meaux. "When they first started talking about signing us, our train of thought was to get some guy to give us 2,000 bucks and we'd have a record."

Instead, Island threw around six-digit numbers. Meaux recalls going to his dad, a businessman, for advice. "He had this look on his face like, what the fuck happened. I knew right there that this wasn't the little garage band thing, where you just go around and put up fliers for your show. It's a most strange feeling. We really didn't get a dime. It's money that we never had, so I don't feel like I lost it—a lot of money just went right around us. It's a weird form of stealing."

The band's stay at Island produced a single, self-titled album in 1991. The band also became a footnote in electoral politics when "Lame Pretender," a song mocking David Duke, was released as a single. *USA Today* and wire service reports noted the song, and Phil Donahue featured it on his TV show.

For Meaux, it was just another example of losing creative control over his work. "The guys at the label just fucking jumped all over it—wanted to exploit it," he says. At first, Meaux refused to let Island release "Lame Pretender" as a single, so the label convinced him to let it go out as a b-side. When Meaux rejected the idea of putting Duke's picture on the cover, Island talked him into a tiny image of a burning cross. The label then issued a fabricated quote from Meaux talking about artistic responsibility, along the lines of, "I wrote "Lame

Pretender" as my contribution in the fight against these poisonous characters...." In the end, Meaux says, "they just lost sight of what they hell they were doing, and they were giving him more publicity."

After Island dropped the Bluerunners, the band went through a series of personnel and business changes, finally stripping themselves down to a quartet. *The Chateau Chuck*, their first album in three years, was actually recorded almost two years ago, and the delay further stressed relations within the band.

Little wonder that even the little caricature of Napoleon that graces the cover of the new album has a tooth knocked out. The cartoon is actually a former logo for a hotel in Lake Charles that inspired the album's title. The band saw the hotel (which, incidentally, is now under new management) as a metaphor for all that's gone wrong in the over-commercialization of French Louisiana. It's a frequent theme for the Bluerunners.

Meaux explains: "Our first ten minutes in this hotel, a rat had already taken a shit in the bed. It's a dump—obviously a dump. And it had been, maybe a few years ago, this really great-for-Lake Charles hotel, and it had gone to crap. And on the sign there's this little Napoleon guy, and we thought it was just so fucking funny that that's their French influence with the culture. It couldn't have been more crass and stupid. "But I also knew nobody would get it, so it would just be a goofy little guy on the cover—so that was cool, because it wouldn't be us with our shirts open."

With the new album comes a new tour—the best they've seen in years. Not long ago, bandmembers were talking about quitting, and for a brief, unreported time the Bluerunners had *de facto* disbanded. But now they're speaking in terms of the long haul. "We've always talked about doing this when we're sixty," says Meaux. "In this part of the country, you have a lot of role models."

"We made it through a tough time and we're still kind of going through it," adds LeBlanc. "The whole thing just came to a grinding halt. You just kind of keep on playing and writing. It was hard going for three years without a record. And this time it'll be just a year. It'll be regular, the way it's supposed to be."

There's a folktale about the bluerunner snake and how it attacks by putting its tail in its mouth, rolling like a wheel and then letting go, whipping its victim. Meaux heard the story when he worked at a golf course and a drycleaners. When his then-rockabilly band needed a name, he thought of the snake. "If anybody thought we'd still have it, we would have put more thought into it," he now says. "It's kind of like a misnomer, because everyone thinks we're a blues band. And with the bean thing—a lot of people thought we were named after Bluerunner beans. I found out about that later."

Neither Meaux nor LeBlanc were musicians when they met up in a local Catholic high school. "In my family, the idea of being a musician was never encouraged," Meaux says. "In fact, they told me not to buy a guitar. When I was eighteen, I had my own money, and they made me promise I'd never get into a band."

LeBlanc recalls going with his mom to the first Tribute to Cajun Music, the 1974 event that would evolve into the annual Festivals Acadiens. But by high school, he was more into Neil Young and heavy metal. He and Meaux started getting together to figure out guitar chords. He tried college but quit to work for his brother-in-law in Port Arthur. That didn't last, and he and Meaux started talking seriously about playing rockabilly. LeBlanc bought a set of drums.

Savoy met his future bandmates when the Bluerunners opened for the Rockin' Shapes, a new wave band that included Savoy on bass. His earliest memories of Cajun music include Sunday afternoons after church, with chicken baking in the kitchen and the musician Happy Fats on TV. Savoy joined the orchestra in eighth grade and picked the bass because it was the biggest instrument. He started taking the school's electric bass home to jam on Lynyrd Skynyrd tunes.

At twenty-four, McBane is the youngest in the group. Until he met the Bluerunners, he says, he grew up thinking that Cajun music was crap. In high school, it was the punk-rock crowd that was the most accepting. "I look at Wayne Toups now," he says, "and the first thing I think is that he's the kind of guy who beat me up in high school." McBane, the son of a traveling lounge musician, played drums in the school band, when he wasn't getting disciplined for drawing on his jeans. "I always had a little gene inside me that fucks things up," he says with some satisfaction.

The first incarnation of the Bluerunners mostly performed rockabilly covers, until then-bandmate John Maloney brought a rubboard into the sound. Soon the band began experimenting with rubboard/drum zydeco breakdowns. One day LeBlanc asked Meaux's wife if he could borrow her accordion. Things started changing. "Once Steve started picking up a traditional instrument, you've got all these voices," Meaux says. "You've got thousands of people who came before you, and there's a heavy responsibility with that. I still take it to heart."

Cajuns have a "punk-rock mentality," insists McBane. "They just came here, they're like, 'Fuck all of y'all,' And when they tried to Americanize the Cajuns, you know, they're just like double-bird." McBane proudly raises his middle fingers.

The practice of blending traditional music with popular styles has a distinguished lineage in south Louisiana. The Hackberry Ramblers, Harry Choates, D.L. Menard and Clifton Chenier all did their share. The traditional/popular dichotomy forms the basis for swamp pop, a south Louisiana genre in which the Bluerunners are perhaps the most important and most unheralded practitioner. Most swamp pop blends Cajun and commercial styles—not Cajun and avowedly anti-commercial styles, like punk.

In south Louisiana, what the Bluerunners do with an accordion makes a lot of people uncomfortable. Many of the best-paying and most prestigious gigs in Lafayette—including Festivals Acadiens—have ignored the band, despite its strong local following. Zachary Richard, who broke some Cajun-rock barriers of his own, once said that he likes the Bluerunners because they're now catching all the flak.

"We kept being seen as these young punks who were saying 'fuck off' to their elders," Meaux says.

> It's the complete opposite. I look at bands that just cover 'The Back Door' as just totally ripping off their culture. If you want this shit to keep going, you better throw some more wood on the fire. That's not to say that you can't do cover tunes. But you see a band, they don't have a fucking thing original about them. And they're doing this pure thing, they pull this Cajun crap, and their big contribution is they wear matching hats and vests and play the restaurant circuit.
>
> The only thing we're trying to do is make an honest expression of our reality, of our situation. The way we grew up, the way we live now. There's no attempt at recreating the past, or any of that bullshit. And if they see that and think it's bullshit, well, they didn't grow up in the '70s and listen to AM radio on the school bus.

Then like the bluerunner itself, Meaux circles back in his argument. To accept the simple distinction between pure Cajun music and his music is to fall into a simplistic view of Lafayette culture in the '90s.

"I swear, just about every fucking interview I did during the whole Island thing was, 'Well, what do the purists think?' That's the first question. Who the fuck are the purists? And are they going to knock on my door or send me a letter: 'We're the purists and we think you suck.' It never happens in real life."

Performers like D.L. Menard and fiddler Michael Doucet have been encouraging—Doucet plays on both Bluerunners albums and occasionally sits in with the band. Yet Meaux admits that others in his community have turned their heads, hoping those feedback-laden accordion sounds would just go away. It pisses him off.

"I'm a Cajun, right?" he says. "I mean, my parents, I've got all the blood, the whole fucking thing. I speak English. I don't have an accent. Am I less a Cajun now? Is my culture less valid because it doesn't correspond with some stereotype?"

Adds Savoy: "I can't believe there's not twenty bands in Lafayette doing this right now. I guess if you're a rock band, you work hard to distance yourself from Cajun, and if you're Cajun, you distance yourself from rock."

The musicians in the Bluerunners find themselves in what Savoy calls the "middle, lost generation" of Cajuns. They know all the stories about their parents and grandparents being punished for speaking French in school. Meaux still remembers one day when he came home and said something like, "Mais, yeah," and was warned not to repeat the phrase in front of his father.

The Bluerunners play waltzes for rock crowds, and they play rock for Cajuns. It puzzles them, but it's the rock crowds who seem more open-minded. "It's tough," McBane says. "It really seems like nobody gets it. They're there to see Zach, or they're there to see Wayne Toups. When I look at these people, I see people that are way different from me. And I guess that's cool, but I think if they really knew who we were, they wouldn't like us."

Still, there is a certain Cajun spirit that haunts the house in Lafayette that serves as LeBlanc's home and the Bluerunners' rehearsal space. The building is set in a swampy, mosquito-infested one-acre parcel of land, right off a busy road in the middle of the city. An overgrown roots system bulging across the driveway and two large beehives hanging near the house insure privacy.

LeBlanc moved into the house following his grandmother's death. He says he still feels her presence at the place where she used to prepare *pain perdu*. Twice, he says, he has even woken up to the presence of a *couche mar* in his bed-

*The Bluerunners, ca. 2005. From left to right, Cal Stevenson, bass; Will Golden, steel guitar and rubboard; Zydeco Mike, percussion; Frank Kincel, drums; Mark Meaux, guitar, fiddle, and vocals; Adrian Huval, accordion. Promotional photo courtesy of The Bluerunners; © Rick Olivier.*

room, a strange presence holding him down with firm hands. There are ways to rid your house of such things, but he's not interested in trying. He'd rather co-exist.

Some Saturday mornings, LeBlanc rises at 7 o'clock to drive to Marc Savoy's Cajun jam session in Eunice. Most every Wednesday, he attends another traditional jam, at C'est Bon Pizza in Cecilia. So far, he is the only player at these places with a shaved head and tattoos, and who has smashed his accordion on stage.

Meaux sees his old high school friend as the soul of the band. "Steve inspires me all the time, because he's such a hard ass," he says. Savoy calls LeBlanc the *tête dur* ("hard head"). When asked why, he just points to the roots in the driveway.

LeBlanc sits in an overstuffed antique chair in his living room, surrounded by band instruments, monitors, speakers. He lightly strums a fiddle and explains that, musically, he lives somewhere between two points: Clifton Chenier and Jimi Hendrix. And he wonders if sometime, perhaps in the next ten or twenty years, a Bluerunners tune might find its way into the Cajun repertoire. "If we can make new songs, and get some kind of respect from the people around here, and add new songs to what's around, that would be enough for me," he says. Maybe, by then, you'll even be hearing that new standard in a local restaurant. But probably not.

## Afterward

After I profiled the Bluerunners, the band continued to move in surprising directions. Of the 1994 line-up, only Mark Meaux remains. Bassist Rob Savoy did a stint with New Orleans-based rockers Cowboy Mouth and now plays with Susan Cowsill in a band that also includes Cowsill's husband (and former Bluerunner) Russ Broussard. Mike McBane is making music in Austin, Texas. As for the *tête dur*, Steve LeBlanc, at least for now has largely given up music to devote himself to a career in computers. He passed the Bluerunners' fiddle over to Meaux.

Following the band's Island debut and *The Chateau Chuck*, the Bluerunners recorded *To the Country* in 1998 and *Le Grand Bleu* in 2001. Their most recent album is 2005's *Honey Slides*, which features the band's current roster: Meaux on guitar and fiddle, Will Golden on lap steel guitar and rubboard, Adrian Huval on accordion, Cal Stevenson on bass and Frank Kincel on drums. On *Honey Slides*, the Lafayette band stirs in more of everything—zydeco bounce, voodoo blues, the rugged poetry of Cajun living and loving—in perfect, original proportion," enthused *Rolling Stone*.

As for Meaux in 2005, things couldn't be going much better. "In terms of the future, I know I have a lot of music in me," he says. Looking back over the past decade, he says the biggest change for him is that he's tried to stop worrying about the future. His attitude is reflected in the band's recent music, which, in addition to Cajun and zydeco, rock and punk, also includes more introspective, alt-country sounds.

"We were doing so many gigs and working so much, I don't think many of the guys were happy at that point," Meaux recalls of 1994. "I was so influenced by punk rock and I felt we had to go in and be harder than anything else, just to prove our worth. Now, we tend to value the audience, which for us now is a lot better than viewing them as the enemy."

There are signs that the decision-makers in the Cajun community have calmed a bit, as well. In late summer 2005, the Bluerunners were preparing for their third consecutive appearance at Festivals Acadiens.

One last note: in 1994, I briefly described a fan at a Bluerunners show who was headbanging between the monitors and later singing a French ballad in a small circle of friends. That fan, Horace Trahan, is now well-known in south Louisiana as a gifted musician whose career in Cajun and zydeco music is as individualistic as that of the Bluerunners themselves.

# Fabricating Authenticity: The Cajun Renaissance and Steve Riley & the Mamou Playboys

*Ryan A. Brasseaux and Erik Charpentier*

Since the band's inception in 1987, Steve Riley and the Mamou Playboys have emerged as a leading proponent of Cajun music both in south Louisiana and abroad. The group initially embarked on a traditionalist crusade to preserve and perpetuate Cajun music. By the mid-1990s, the dance band became a favorite among Cajun audiences after expanding the parameters of its vision by incorporating modern influences into its repertoire. In addition, the Playboys belong to an elite class of Cajun bands who, like Beausoleil, have amassed an international following by transcending the regional dancehall circuit that sustains Cajun music in Bayou Country. The group has toured extensively in the United States and Europe—from New York to Norway, the Toronto Jazz Festival to Tokyo, Japan. Steve Riley and the Mamou Playboys have also appeared on internationally syndicated radio broadcasts such as Public Radio International's World Café, American Routes, and Afro Pop Worldwide programs, on the Prairie Home Companion and the British Broadcasting Corporation.

The Mamou Playboys are the product of the complex cultural milieu that corresponds with the late twentieth-century Cajun experience. While the band has forged a sound unique to Cajun music, its career path has been illuminated by the trailblazing legacies of Wayne Toups and Beausoleil who in effect modernized the genre by synthesizing French Louisiana's musical traditions with the contemporary sounds of rock and roll, jazz, zydeco, and rhythm and blues. Ideologically, Steve Riley and the Mamou Playboys stand at the point of impact where the Cajun Renaissance's[1] interpretation of authenticity and America's vision of traditional music collide. This study raises questions about a neglected issue currently facing young Anglophone Cajuns—the criteria of authenticity during the post-modern era—as viewed through the career and music of Steve Riley and the Mamou Playboys.[2]

---

[1] The Cajun Renaissance (1964-present) is an ethnic and linguistic movement that sought to revitalize the group's image and declining native tongue. The Renaissance was a multifaceted phenomenon that included political, scholarly, literary, and musical components. Shane K. Bernard, *The Cajuns: Americanization of a People* (Jackson, 2003), 85-145.

[2] Two book-length studies published by historian Bernard, *The Cajuns: Americanization of a People*, and social scientists Jacques Henry and Carl Bankston, *Blue Collar Bayou: Louisiana Cajuns in the New Economy of Ethnicity* (West Port and London, 2002) are the only two substantial works to address the Cajun identity, ethnicity, and authentic cultural expression at the end of the twentieth century. This study refers to modern Cajuns as Anglophones to denote the ethnic group's linguistic orientation in the twenty-first century, rather than their cultural pedigree or affiliation.

Steve Riley came of age at the end of the twentieth century during a period when the number of monolingual and bilingual Francophones in the Bayou Country was on a dramatic downward spiral.[3] Like most of his small town contemporaries, Riley grew up speaking English in Mamou (pronounced "Ma Moo"), a culturally rich commercial center that served as both part of the Cajun frontier and as a historic cradle for Cajun music along the northern fringe of Acadiana. The Mamou Steve Riley knew was a far cry from the setting musicologist Harry Oster encountered during his field expeditions during the late 1950s.[4]

In the late 1960s, the town's youth emerged from its sleepy, regional doldrums and embraced the counter-culture movement sweeping the nation. The subsequent cultural diversification that ensued generated a spectrum of musical expression within the community that ranged from French ballad traditions maintained by town elders to youth-oriented American popular culture that embraced the likes of the Beatles, the Rolling Stones, Iron Butterfly, and Led Zeppelin. Cajuns changed with the times and interpreted hippie and rock and roll culture. Youngsters allowed their beards and hair to grow in defiance of the community's traditional clean-cut appearance and supplemented the region's alcohol culture with marijuana and hallucinogens.

"In the 1970s," remembers former Mamou resident Cecil Doyle, "There wasn't much to do. What you did on a typical day was get up, go to the middle of [town], hang out."[5] Some residents cruised around the Mamou city limits (approximately one square mile) for amusement. "You [rode] all day long in the seventies," remembered singer-songwriter and leader of Cajun-Rock band Mamou Steve LaFleur. "[You rode] around and [caught] a buzz. That was always the objective."[6] The Vietnam era transformed small town life in Mamou by opening the discourse between south Louisiana and America. By the 1980s town residents, including Steve Riley, synthesized cultural information derived from traditional frontier-life and modern American pop culture along with the rest of Acadiana.

During the 1990s, the Mamou Playboys became known as one of the top purveyors of "authentic" traditional Cajun music. This portrayal, however, ignores the sometimes-conflicting musical and cultural tendencies at play within the band and their music. A deepening gap between measures of authenticity, as defined by Cajun activists and roots record labels, and the reality of life in south Louisiana culturally constrained the Playboys' capacity for expression. "Sometimes we do these concerts, people are all sitting there, looking at us, listening, hanging on every word, and they don't understand a single one of

---
[3] See Bernard, *The Cajuns*, 18, 83-84, 148.
[4] Harry Oster, *Folksongs of the Louisiana Acadians* (El Cerrito, CA, 1994).
[5] Interview Cecil Doyle and Steve LaFleur by Ryan A. Brasseaux and Erik Charpentier, September 7, 2004.
[6] Ibid.

them," maintains the band's fiddler, co-founder and singer-songwriter David Greely. "And it frustrates me a little bit, you know? I wish that I was communicating with those people."[7] The French language stymied the range of lyrical possibilities for the group's songwriters while simultaneously conferring upon the ensemble the mantle of authenticity in the eyes of roots music aficionados, traditionalists, and south Louisiana's Franco-centric cultural activists.

Authenticity is defined as genuineness—original as opposed to reproduction, not pretended. The Renaissance identified French as the criteria for authenticity within the Cajun community despite the ever-decreasing number of native Francophones in the Bayou Country.[8] The Playboys and the Renaissance developed a symbiotic relationship. Activists embraced the group for their penchant for historic Louisiana French music. These cultural middlemen promptly validated the band's efforts by decreeing that their music was an authentic expression generated within the bounds of tradition. This endorsement ensured the Mamou Playboys' marketability as a legitimate Cajun band on their roots record label Rounder Records. In return, the band became the poster children movement's pro-French agenda. Steve Riley expounded, "Our first three records were all traditional Cajun music; then we started writing our own music, which was in the tradition—you know, Cajun French."[9] The catch phrase "creating within the tradition" has followed the English-speaking bandmembers throughout their career, as the ensemble has consciously performed French material.[10] Folklorist and French language activist Barry Jean Ancelet writes in the liner notes to the Playboys' 2003 release *Bon Rêve*, "They improvise and create within the tradition, finding poetry in historical manuscripts and in the language of real life, and they manage to do this in a way that both innovates and preserves at the same time."[11] Despite the claim that the French album speaks to the listener "in the language of real life," there are, ironically, no English songs on the release, further illustrating the gap between the linguistic reality of south Louisiana and the Francophone utopia depicted by the Renaissance. On the other hand, without their French orientation, the band would lose its traditional/authentic status. This brand of folk music is as much a careful and deliberate recreation of the past as a lingering cultural influence. For several members of the bands, including co-founders Steve Riley and David Greely, and former bassist-manager Peter Schwarz, their indoctrination into the gospel of the Renaissance came at the hands of the one of the movements

---

[7] http://www.dirtynelson.com/linen/feature/67riley.html, accessed June 20, 2005.
[8] Bernard, *The Cajuns: Americanization of a People*.
[9] http://www.rootsworld.com/rw/feature/riley.html, accessed June 20, 2005.
[10] In recent years, particular bandmembers have made successful strides to immerse themselves in the French language. Todd Mouton, "Steve Riley and the Mamou Playboys: Creating Within The Tradition," *OffBeat* (1995): 39-44.
[11] Barry Jean Ancelet, liner notes, *Bon Rêve*, Steve Riley and the Mamou Playboys (Cambridge, MA, 2003).

most visible figure heads, Dewey Balfa. All three Playboys studied under the master fiddler as each developed his skills as a Cajun musician.

John Stephen Riley II was born in Mamou, Louisiana, on June 14, 1969. The accordion prodigy began playing the squeezebox at age seven under the tutelage of his grandfather Burke Guillory, and promptly developed a technical prowess eclipsing that of older, more experienced musicians. By age twenty-three, Riley had won so many regional talent contests that local coordinators unanimously imposed a lifetime ban to block his entry. His proficiency stemmed partially from the accordionist's experience as a member of the Fred's Lounge band in Mamou and Hadley Castille's Cajun Swing show band. In 1986, Riley also performed with the world-renowned fiddler and grassroots Cajun activist Dewey Balfa and the Balfa Brotherhood. Balfa's brand of fiddling and activism would dramatically shape the young musician's direction and affiliation with the Cajun Renaissance after Riley and a seasoned fiddler named David Greely formed the Mamou Playboys, styled after a defunct group by the same name originally headed by Maurice and Vorance Barzas.

David Greely hailed from Denham Springs, Louisiana, a working-class Anglo-Protestant enclave east of Baton Rouge. During the late 1970s, the fiddler toured with a bluegrass ensemble, Cornbread, before delving into Cajun music. Greely first met Riley in the late 1980s in Eunice, Louisiana, at accordion-maker Marc Savoy's Saturday morning Cajun music jam sessions. The two musicians quickly realized that they shared a mutual love for traditional Cajun music and a coincidental connection to Louisiana's capital city. Greely made extra money playing solo lunchtime gigs at the Baton Rouge branch of the famous Cajun restaurant Mulate's. Riley, then enrolled at Louisiana State University, began to skip class to sit in with his new band mate and thus began the Mamou Playboys' career. The duo imported the rhythm section from the Fred's Lounge house band for their first substantial performances at the Baton Rouge Mulate's before transferring to the restaurant's original Cajun Country location in Breaux Bridge, after Beausoleil relinquished their regular Thursday night spot in order to take advantage of more lucrative opportunites resulting from their rising national profile. In Breaux Bridge, drummer Mike "Chop" Chapman and guitarist Kevin Barzas (whose father and grandfather headed the original Mamou Playboys) joined the fold and became the Playboys' regular rhythm section. Their stripped down old-timey sound became the focus of the group's first two commercial releases on Rounder Records *Steve Riley and the Mamou Playboys* (1990) and *'Tit Galop Pour Mamou* (1992), produced respectively by Cajun Renaissance champions Zachary Richard and Al Tharp (of Beausoleil fame).[12]

---

[12] Both releases also feature Dewey's daughter Christine Balfa on triangle. Steve Riley and the Mamou Playboys, *Steve Riley and the Mamou Playboys* (Cambridge, MA, 1990); Steve Riley and the Mamou Playboys,

The Mamou Playboys retooled their sound several times following their first two studio appearances by hiring different personnel. Between 1993 and 1999, the band became increasingly more sophisticated as the new talent surrounding Riley and Greely gelled. These six years, the band's most creative and productive, were marked by the release of five distinct albums documenting the evolution of the Playboys' sound: *Trace of Time* (1993), *Live* (1994), *La Toussaint* (1995), *Friday at Last* (1997), and *Bayou Ruler* (1998). Drummer Kevin Dugas, a veteran of Belton Richard's outfit and Danny Brasseaux's Wandering Aces, replaced Chop Chapman in the early 1990s to become the Playboys' permanent full-time drummer. Guitarist Jimmy Domengeaux joined in the mid-1990s and electrified the group's sound with rock licks and extended solos until 1999, when the musician succumbed to a fatal motorcycle accident. A number of guitarists—including swamp blues/rocker Charles "C.C." Adcock, slide specialist Roddie Romero, and singer-songwriter Sam Broussard—entered the line-up to fill Domengeaux's shoes. Over the years, several bass players such as Kyle Hebert and, recently, Brazos Huval, have toured and recorded with the band. The most influential member of the early-to-late nineties, however, was bassist, fiddler, vocalist, and arranger Peter Schwarz, whom Riley met while playing on the back of a Mamou Mardi Gras wagon.

The son of New Lost City Rambler Tracy Schwarz—who performed and recorded with Dewey Balfa after the two met at the 1964 Newport Folk Festival—Peter's entree into Cajun music came when he moved into the Balfa home at age fifteen to complete a six-week National Endowment for the Arts apprenticeship. He joined the Playboys in the early 1990s after receiving a baccalaureate in anthropology from Harvard University, and he soon assumed the group's managerial reins. Schwarz's arrangements and dynamic bass and fiddle playing brought a particular sophistication to the group's performances and recordings. He helped put what folklorist Barry Ancelet called a "high gloss spit shine on old standards, sometimes tinkering with them, reaching for the edge speeding them up or modulating to different keys, conjuring haunting harmonies. This is experimental Cajun music, but well within what most would consider the culture's boundaries."[13]

Steve Riley and the Mamou Playboys began as traditionalists in the mold of the Cajun Renaissance's perception of authenticity before exploring more experimental avenues with their album *Bayou Ruler*. While the bilingual album was frowned upon by the Renaissance's talking heads, the recording was ironically the band's most accurate portrayal of the modern Cajun experience. The album was in many ways a departure, as the band stepped outside of the realm of the Renaissance and challenged the invisible lines delineating local cultural

---

*'Tit Galop Pour Mamou* (Cambridge, MA, 1992).
[13] As quoted in Pete Bergeron's unpublished manuscript, in the authors' possession.

boundaries. Up to the 1997 release *Friday at Last*, Barry Ancelet played a key role in guiding the band through their formative years. His absence in the *Bayou Ruler* liner notes clearly indicated a riff between the rigid constraints of Renaissance ideologies and the late twentieth-century artistic yearnings of a south Louisiana band. The band's musical pendulum reached its extreme dynamic polarity with the release, before the group's disposition reverted in a decidedly conservative direction.

With the passing of Jimmy Domengeaux and Peter Schwarz's departure from the outfit after *Bayou Ruler*, the Playboys struggled to put the pieces of their artistic vision back together. Residual effects of the experimental album were still apparent on the band's 2001 release, *Happytown*. However, the band found solace by retreating to French compositions in the traditional vein. The group's 2003 release, *Bon Rêve*, marked Ancelet's return in the band's first set of completely bilingual liner notes, as the Mamou Playboys set out to revisit sonically terrain reminiscent of their 1995 issue *La Toussaint*.

Over the years, the band has amassed a devoted following. The Playboys have also had a tremendous influence on the development of up-and-coming artists like Kevin Naquin & the Ossun Playboys and *La Bande Feu Follet*. A mentor to these bands' accordionists, Steve Riley's dedication to the continuity of the musical process within the cultural boundaries paralleled Dewey Balfa's efforts to salvage the echoes of the past. The Playboys now stand as the established point of reference as newcomers like *Feu Follet's* young members—most of whom are products of the movement's French immersion program[14]—serve as the new examples of the effectiveness of the Renaissance's agenda.[15]

Like academic theory, authenticity is a philosophical construct used to comprehend cultural phenomena. However, the synthetic and heterogeneous nature of Cajun culture and musical expression complicates any notion of legitimacy within the theoretical "traditions" and "cultural boundaries" fabricated by scholars and activists in Louisiana, particularly as the community's realities perpetually fluctuate. The socio-economic, cultural, and linguistic factors that inform and shape the Cajun experience evolved dramatically over the course of the twentieth century. As sociologists Jacques Henry and Carl Bankston note, "Many of the Cajuns's social structures and practices came to be indistinguishable from those other Louisianians, and from those of other Americans."[16] The shifting cultural climate brought new implications for the

---

[14] French immersion programs became part of south Louisiana's elementary and middle school curriculum largely through the machinations of the Cajun Renaissance's political manifestation the Council for the Development of French in Louisiana (CODOFIL). Students follow the same prescribed courses as other students, only instruction is rendered completely in French. Bernard, *The Cajuns*, 130-31, 143-44.

[15] *Against the Tide: The Story of the Cajun People of Louisiana*, directed by Pat Mire, DVD, color, 56 minutes (Baton Rouge, 2004).

[16] Henry and Bankston, *Blue Collar Bayou: Louisiana Cajuns in the New Economy of Ethnicity*, 139.

Cajuns. Musical expression in the post-modern period took on new meaning, particularly as the linguistic foundation of the community shifted and French became "increasingly rare."[17] Young English-speaking Cajun bands, who perform old and new material in a second language, clearly indicate how Cajun French music has shifted from the late nineteenth-early twentieth century's mainstream form of cultural expression to a more marginalized cultural arena within the context of a new millennium. A dialogue between the increasingly self-conscious Cajun French music tradition and mainstream popular culture has produced a sort of multifaceted, post-modern cultural hybrid, which, like the song selection of a jukebox, comes in a variety of local and imported sonic textures or emotions. While commercialization implanted Cajun music into the American consciousness as a unique form of indigenous artistic

Steve Riley & the Mamou Playboys, ca. 2006. From left to right, Kevin Dugas, drums; David Greely, fiddle; Steve Riley, accordion and volcals; Brazos Huval, bass; Sam Broussard, guitar. Photo courtesy of Steve Riley & the Mamou Playboys, © Rick Olivier.

expression, this form of modernization also transformed radically the historic contexts that once informed the very nature of the traditional. Cajun music, then, is a legitimate article of consumption with great entertainment value both within and beyond the boundaries of south Louisiana.

Today, young musicians apply a new meaning to French material that is informed by both the historic implications interwoven into themes, motifs, lyrical components of French songs, fragments of the tradition, technology and the post-modern context surrounding a Cajun artist's contemporary experience. Youthful French expression in south Louisiana is veiled by a cloak of authenticity. Budding Cajun musicians are betwixt the English-speaking world they comfortably engage everyday and a body of French compositions that harkens to the ephemeral traces of Francophone Louisiana lingering in the community's

---

[17] Ibid.

collective memory. Their French musical expression, however, is not representative of south Louisiana's mainstream linguistic landscape. As David Greely laments in his composition "Entre l'amour et l'avenir" (Between Love and the Future), the Mamou Playboys are sitting on the edge of post-modernity, somewhere between their love for the music, language, the legacy of the past and the new horizons calling south Louisiana communities into the twenty-first century.

# Get Lost: The Lost Bayou Ramblers

*Erik Charpentier*

Many profound changes have shaped the evolution of Cajun music in the last thirty years. From the genre's humble beginnings as a regional folk music on the periphery of mainstream cultural and artistic expression, the music now stands as a form of popular culture embraced by national and global communities. While every band draws from the same traditional materials, some ensembles have embraced mainstream America's current conservative attitudes. Others have adopted a more ethnically-driven, indigenously-based approach to their environment's post-9/11 social and cultural realities. The Lost Bayou Ramblers fall into the latter category.

Propelled by its swinging train-like cadences, the Ramblers' rhythm section—Chris "Oscar" Courville on bass drum, cymbal, and snare, guitarist Jon Bertrand, and Alan LaFleur on upright bassist—wrecks into a crudely soulful bounce, as brothers Louis (fiddle and vocals) and André Michot (lap steel and accordion) salvage antiquated melodies and 1930s-inspired original compositions out of the collision. Formed in the late 1990s, the Lost Bayou Ramblers are known for their high energy, *fond de culotte*[1] approach to the genre—bringing its brand of "pre-commercial fiddle music and early accordion dancehall tunes [and] Cajun-inflected western swing popularized during the late 1930s and 1940s"[2] to the somewhat homogenous field of contemporary Cajun music.

The band's two front men—Louis and André Michot—are simultaneously an organic extension of south Louisiana's rich musical heritage and the product of American popular culture. In the tradition of the Breaux Family Band and the Balfa Brothers ensemble, the Michot brothers were born into a musical family. They were constantly exposed to acoustic Cajun jams, French language radio, and Cajun music concerts hosted by their relatives. By their early teens, André and Louis had become part of the phenomenon, performing on guitar (André) and upright bass (Louis) with their father and uncles' band, Les Frères Michot. During the family's five-year stint in Baton Rouge (1988-1993), André pick up the electric blues guitar and attended weekend jam sessions at Tabby's Blues Box, a locally famous African American nightclub, chaperoned by his father Tommy Michot, who sometimes sat in on harmonica. Louis also learned guitar. Together, the brothers spent countless hours locked in André's bedroom practicing, learning licks, and listening to classic blues records by Muddy Waters Howling Wolf, Johnny Winter, and the Allman Brothers Band, as well as

---

[1] *Fond de culotte*: "by the seat of your pants."
[2] Ryan A. Brasseaux, liner notes, Lost Bayou Ramblers, *Pilette Breakdown* (Ville Platte: Swallow Records 6177, 2003).

vintage Cajun music. "Cajun music has a bluesy foundation," explained André, acknowledging the inherent connections between improvisation, themes of heartbreak, and working class ethnic links in both the Cajun and American Blues traditions.[3] When the family moved back to Lafayette in 1993, André took up the accordion and Louis began fiddling after receiving a violin as a gift from his maternal grandfather, "Papeaux" Pierce Meleton. Upon graduating from St. Thomas More Catholic High School, a local private school, Louis hitchhiked and traveled extensively across North America, supporting himself by playing traditional Cajun songs on the street corners of America. André settled into carpentry work, property management, and various family business endeavors until music reunited the brothers.

The Lost Bayou Ramblers began in 1999 as a loosely organized ensemble of friends who performed at house parties, Cajun music jam sessions, and small, but well-attended gigs around Lafayette, Louisiana. The late Ryan Domingue, an avid Grateful Dead bootleg collector and cognitive science lab technician at the University of Louisiana at Lafayette, bequeathed the nickname "Lost Bayou Ramblers" to the Michots, who employed the moniker at their first official gig at the now defunct Café Rue Vermilion in downtown Lafayette. Fronted by a dreadlocked, twenty-year-old Louis Michot, the group consisted of André (accordion), Oscar (drums), family friend Adam Cohen (guitar), the brothers' uncle David "Dav" Michot (upright bass), and Thad Duplechain, of Sampy and the Bad Habits, on rubboard. Gary Hernandez, of early Beausoleil fame, sat in on a few songs, blowing his clarinet. As anthropologist, sometime band contributor and *ti-fer*[4] wizard Ryan Brasseaux remembers,

> It was a weird crowd. I remember that one guy was wearing a sarong. Most of the folks attending were Louis' people, hippies—Lafayette's alternative scene. It was cold outside so it must have been wintertime. During the break, André went to his car and got some Red Dog [beer] that he brought inside the coffeehouse. He gave me one and I ended up playing triangle during the second set. I remember that at one point, we all went outside, including the whole audience, and paraded down Vermilion Street all the way to Antler's [bar and restaurant] on Jefferson Street. We were playing the "Mardi Gras Song," so it must have been before carnival season.[5]

The coffee house could not contain the band's enthusiasm, as the Ramblers led a parade-like promenade through the streets and bars of downtown Lafayette, thus generating an overnight sensation. The Lost Bayou Ramblers injected a fresh energy into the pre-World War II compositions André and Louis learned as members of Les Frères Michot. The Café Rue Vermilion performance

---

[3] André Michot, personal communication, phone call, July 20, 2005.
[4] *ti-fer*: triangle.
[5] Ryan Brasseaux, informal conversation with author, June 2005.

brought these historic compositions into a youthful aliveness and gave voice to a new faction in Cajun music.

André and Louis Michot and the rock-solid drumming of Chris "Oscar" Courville formed the ensemble's core as several eclectic musicians drifted in and out of the group. David Michot is the most influential Rambler alum. While his steady guitar and upright bass plucking helped provide rhythmic stability within the ensemble, his simple and poignant songwriting radically shaped the band's dynamic. The elder Michot's compositions maintain the sensibility of old-time Cajun music, even when the arrangements incorporate elements of country and western. Lyrically, Dav weaves his personal philosophy and experiences rambling around North America into chestnuts like "Moi, Je Connais Pas" (I Don't Know), a song that scoffs at the pervasive fanaticism clouding the judgment of America's polarized political factions. In March 2004, David Michot left to band to pursue his wandering ways and to spend more time with his wife and ten-year old daughter living in a New Orleans suburb. Nonetheless, Dav, a convivial, yet elusive figure, remains a constant source of inspiration to his nephews and former bandmates.

Longtime Austinite Cavan Carruth came into the fold to fill in for David. The solid rhythm guitarist and talented vocalist in the tradition of Hank Williams' piercing high and lonesome singing and fiddler Matthew "The Deuce" Doucet contributed their individual style to the development of the group's musical personality before moving on. In March 2004, the Michots hired two new bandmates to accommodate their musical needs: a twenty-four-year-old cowboy and guitarist from Elton named Jon Bertrand, who graduated from the French program at the University of Louisiana at Lafayette; and a tattooed, chain-smoking slap-bass talent named Alan LaFleur. Bertrand and LaFleur respectively brought a rock and roll attitude and rockabilly sensibility to the rhythm section. This new approach remains at the heart of the Lost Bayou Ramblers' sound. The band's latest approach avoids the mainstream "cradle of traditionalism" endorsed by the Cajun Renaissance and by the Nashville-polish of contemporary Cajun bands. Rather, the band embraces older, indigenous musical approaches (rhythmically-complex, minimalist arrangements) of the early days of Cajun music in both spirit and creativity.

In early 2003, the Ramblers released the self-made *Un 'Tit Goût* [A Little Taste], a twelve-song album recorded at the Michot family camp in Milton, Louisiana and at KRVS 88.7 FM, Lafayette's National Public Radio affiliate. The previous summer, Louis had issued some of those KRVS recordings while living in Brooklyn as a way to support himself. As he remembers,

> I was basically burning CDs on my laptop at night and selling them by day. I was busking the streets and playing my fiddle. One day, I was on the street and this dude hunched under a trash bag walked by. He stopped for a while, listened, looked at me

and took his cell phone out. It turns out that it was this guy Tony Garnier [Bob Dylan's bassist and musical director], and he was calling his brother in Lafayette [D'Jalma, a respected Creole fiddler] to tell him how you can find Cajun music everywhere, even in Brooklyn! That was a trip. One time, I walked into a restaurant and I made $150 in forty-five minutes. I was pretty psyched so I walked over to this other place, a pizza joint I believe. I started playing and less than five minutes into it, I realized that nobody was giving a shit. New York, man, that's how it is.[6]

In September 2003, the Lost Bayou Ramblers released its first "official" album, *Pilette Breakdown* on Swallow Records. By then, the band had become quite adept at "stripping traditional songs to their emotional cores, then reconstructing unique contemporary arrangements [that revisit] the golden age of the *bals de maison* (house dances), when music was equated with community and social interaction."[7] Since the release of the album, the band has toured extensively in front of an ever-growing number of local and national fans, building over the previous two years' gigging experience on both coasts. The Ramblers' first tour, a few gigs in and around New York City, convinced the band that there was a demand for traditional south Louisiana music outside of Acadiana. Monthly gigs in New Orleans further solidified the group's intuition that a fresh take on historic music would appeal to hip, young, alternative audiences in addition to the obvious "Cajunite" and "Zydeholic" crowds who attend dances outside of Cajun Country. Over time the band began to broaden the scope of their touring. On their first trip after the New York tour, the band traveled to St. Louis, Missouri, and performed to an enthusiastic crowd at a worm grower convention, to a collection of eclectic oddballs who shared similar eccentricities with the some of the Lost Bayou Ramblers' personnel. At the 2004 Festivals Acadiens, the Ramblers' performance under the Heritage Tent generated a Beatles-like reaction from female members of the crowd. Monthly concerts at the Blue Moon Saloon—a Lafayette youth hostel, saloon, and live music venue—have also generated a buzz, some serious dancing and a strong sense of community amidst the fans.

Currently, the band travels the nation three to four times a year with an occasional European gig to supplement the already vast landscape covered by the Ramblers' dynamic performances. A growing cottage industry, the band provides crowds with high intensity performances, CDs, t-shirts, as well as six different kinds of hot sauce including the popular garlic-based concoction *L'ail Ya Yaille*—a take on the French word "ail" [garlic] and the Cajun expression "O yé yaille." Peach and strawberry flavored Lost Bayou Ramblers love rubs are also in the works. To date, the band has toured extensively in Texas, Louisiana and the Gulf Coast. They have traveled to the West Coast, the Pacific Northwest, Wyoming, Nevada, Colorado, Chicago, Wisconsin, Missouri, Arkansas,

---

[6] Louis Michot, informal conversation with author, May 2005.
[7] Brasseaux, liner notes, *Pilette Breakdown*.

The Lost Bayou Ramblers in a 2006 promotional picture.
*Photo courtesy of Zack Smith.*

the East Coast, and New York City, where the group received considerable attention—performing annually at the Brooklyn Botanical Gardens' Chili Festival.

In addition to playing on the national dance and festival circuit sustaining many Cajun and zydeco bands today, the Lost Bayou Ramblers employ their talents at universities around the United States. The band has developed an hour-long multimedia and interactive presentation that highlights the European, African, and North American cultural contributions that molded south Louisiana's diverse musical traditions. The Ramblers demonstrate their profound understanding of the nuances shaping historic Cajun music by taking audiences on an ethnomusical tour of the cultural forces acting on the genre through live musical illustrations. In 2004, the Ramblers were featured keynote presenters at Nashville's International Country Music Conference, the world's premier symposium for country music scholarship. Later that year, the group brought the history of Cajun music to life in front of a standing-room-only auditorium at the Brooklyn Botanic Gardens. In late-September 2005, the Lost Bayou Ramblers were invited guests at Yale University.

In a post-9/11 environment, the Lost Bayou Ramblers are reaching back to the blueprint of recorded Cajun music documented in the late 1920s and early 1930s as a reconsideration of the Cajun experience at the dawn of the twenty-first century. While the band's music can be included in the latest swing revival—interpreted locally by such luminaries as the Red Stick Ramblers, original Renaissance visionaries Michael Doucet and Beausoleil, and the Magnolia Sisters—their swing repertoire recycles fragments of the past with a modern ethnic flair.

The Lost Bayou Ramblers are currently mixing their upcoming album, *Bayou Perdu*—from the title track penned by David Michot, his second contribution to the band's growing list of original material after the often requested "Moi Je Connais Pas." As well, the group is developing a side project with help of occasional bandmate Ryan Brasseaux and accordionist extraordinaire and piano prodigy Wilson Savoy of the famed, Eunice-based Savoy musical family. Dubbed the Mello Joy Boys project—after a popular brand of south Louisiana coffee—the band is developing a concept album that revisits and reinterprets with youthful vigor the nostalgic 1936 Louisiana soundscape. The material is inspired by or taken directly from compositions popular in Cajun Country during the 1930s. The band has developed a Mello Joy theme song loosely based on the jingle used by the Light Crust Doughboys (1934), a pioneer western swing outfit and spokesmen for Fort Worth-based Burrus Flour Mill. The Mello Joy Boys also recall the legendary Cajun swing ensemble the Hackberry Ramblers, who changed their name to the Riverside Ramblers in 1937 to market Montgomery Ward's Riverside tires in a historically accurate and culturally appropriate way.

In the meantime, the Lost Bayou Ramblers continue to solidify and balance their internal structure by gigging extensively, planning their own upcoming video game, sharing tall tales—and low ones—on the road and by reaffirming the non–musical bond they commonly share, carpentry, which is applied to the construction of Louis' Acadian-inspired cottage and the renovation of André's historic home in Broussard.

# Saving Culture with a Song:
# Cajun Music and the Twenty-First Century

Where in the world is Cajun music at the dawn of the twenty-first century? The simple answer is everywhere. At the premiere of Warner Brothers' motion picture the *Divine Secrets of the Ya-Ya Sisterhood*, the theater's speaker system came alive with strains of Blind Uncle Gaspard's sweet melancholy tenor and strumming guitar. The film further conjured the nostalgia for Depression-era Louisiana during a scene featuring music writer and guitarist Ann Savoy, backed by her son Joel's fiddling, reenacting the sounds of Cléoma Falcon's late-1930s swing stylings. Cajun music also wafts from radio speakers around the country tuned to folklorist Nick Spitzer's nationally-syndicated public radio program *American Routes*. In Europe, dancers flock to performances by Cajun music bandleaders and Louisiana aficionados like Englishmen Chris Hall and Chris Jagger, whose famous brother fronts the Rolling Stones. Furthermore, if music promoter Cynthia Simien—wife of zydeco artist Terrance Simien—has her way, the world may also one day see a Zydeco-Cajun category at the Grammy Awards. Cajun music has transcended the indigenous Bayou Country contexts from whence it came and now plays to a global audience. Cajun-styled bands now exist in California, New York, Europe, Japan, and beyond.

Although the genre has found receptive audiences beyond the Gulf Coast, the actual battle for the future of Cajun music is still fought on Louisiana soil between the Sabine and Mississippi rivers, where a broad range of contexts inform and shape the expression in ways that reflect the state's contemporary cultural landscape. At least three distinctive musical aesthetics form the basis of a continuum through which Louisiana's Cajun bands flourish at the dawn of the twenty-first century. Local ensembles perform to the three primary audiences—the Cajun Renaissance/French Movement, the Cajun French Music Association (CFMA), and the blue-collar Cajun community—whose tastes and values define the region's musical aesthetics. While bands with particular inclinations may primarily occupy particular niches, they are by no means confined exclusively to them. The boundaries associated with these musical strains are fluid, and ensembles cross aesthetical boundaries as circumstances dictate. For instance, a musician may frequently access field recordings at the Archives of Cajun and Creole Folklore[1] (assembled and maintained by the members of Louisiana's French movement) at the University of Louisiana at Lafayette, sometimes sing *a cappella* ballads on music festival stages, and, on occasion,

---

[1] The University of Louisiana at Lafayette's Archives of Cajun and Creole Folklore houses the world's largest collection of Cajun/Creole field recordings, with a particular emphasis on folk music.

play in exchange for a bar tab at blue-collar hangouts and/or at the CFMA awards ceremonies.[2]

Renaissance bands are those groups affiliated with Lafayette, Louisiana's politically-charged French movement, an organization of middle-class, university-educated activists with working-class roots who seek to cultivate French speakers in Cajun Country while simultaneously purging the region's Anglophone tendencies. These groups perform almost exclusively in French, embrace innovation (particularly by drawing inspiration from historic field recordings by ethnographers like Alan Lomax, Harry Oster, and Barry Ancelet) and cater to a culturally conscious audience.[3] These bands—Feufollet and Balfa Toujours, for instance—are generally artists featured on the main stage at the Festivals Acadiens—the movement's most visible musical manifestation. From its inception, the festival drew inspiration from the Newport Folk Festival, where folklorists devised programming featuring both older vernacular musical acts and younger contemporary artists like Bob Dylan and Joan Baez, who interpreted, drew inspiration from, and built upon the foundation established by the working-class musicians of earlier generations. Likewise, some young Cajun acts associated with the French Movement are following a trajectory similar to that of a young Bob Dylan. For instance, Steve Riley and the Mamou Playboys began as an acoustic Cajun band modeled after early dancehall ensembles, before "going electric"—and more radically going English—with the release of *Bayou Ruler* (1998), a record that shocked the sensibilities of Festivals Acadiens' coordinators.[4] Festival organizers promote innovation "within the tradition," provided that "innovation" includes French lyrics. In 1984, ten years after the festival began, working-class Cajuns decided to create their own organization that interpreted and promoted local linguistic and musical traditions.

If the French Movement serves as the impetus for a sort of cultural Reformation, the Cajun French Music Association is the musical Counter-Reformation. The CFMA is comprised of "grass roots Cajuns who want to preserve their heritage by teaching the authentic Cajun language and the traditions of their Acadian ancestry."[5] This group's definition of "authentic Cajun language" rails against the tendency of CODOFIL and the Cajun Renaissance toward

---

[2] Accordionist Kristi Guillory, the archivist at the Archives of Cajun and Creole Folklore, frequently traverses all three aesthetics and plays to the diverse audiences that fill dancehall floors, festival grounds, and CFMA award ceremonies. Kristi Guillory, personal communication, June 13, 2006.

[3] Young bands like the Pine Leaf Boys, featuring accordionist Wilson Savoy (son of Renaissance proponents Marc and Ann Savoy), and the Lost Bayou Ramblers are by-products of the Renaissance, who consciously operate outside of the movement's parameters. These groups are frequent performers at Lafayette, Louisiana's Blue Moon Saloon, an open-air honky tonk that caters to audiences following this rebellious faction.

[4] Editor Ryan A. Brasseaux worked backstage at the Festivals Acadiens' main stage between 1996 and 2000 and witnessed first hand the reaction of the programmers when the Mamou Playboys issued *Bayou Rouler*. The record sent shock waves reminiscent of Bob Dylan's *Bring It All Back Home* and his first electric performance at the Newport Folk Festival in 1965.

[5] http://www.cajunfrenchmusic.org/cfma.htm, accessed June 14, 2006.

standardized French, promoted locally by Jimmy Domengeaux and the University of Louisiana's educated elite respectively. Rather, the CFMA's political orientation centers on local patois and musical convention as defined by the group. While the organization's largely working-class contingency strives to develop a local cultural consciousness, it does not always coincide with the Renaissance's interpretation of genuine Cajun music, or the bawdy working-class aesthetic that prevails in honky-tonks and dives around south Louisiana. Rather, the CFMA is a sort of family-oriented and respectable network of organizations modeled after fraternal lodges like the Knights of Columbus and Woodmen of the World. Chapters sponsor language classes, dance and music lessons, and social dances for members. Association affiliates are recognized annually at the CFMA's "Le Cajun" award ceremony held at Blackham Coliseum, ironically, the site of the first Tribute to Cajun Music, an event sponsored in part by CODOFIL. Frequent award winners like Kevin Naquin and the Ossun Playboys and Jackie Callier and the Cajun Cousins are local artists who are in the organization's good graces. Past winners also include musicians affiliated with the Renaissance and select groups representing the working class aesthetic like various ensembles featuring fiddler Jason Frey.[6]

Blue-collar bands, on the other hand, play an eclectic, heterogeneous and linguistically flexible (French, bilingual, and English) repertoire that draws heavily from zydeco, swamp pop, popular music, and modern country. Groups like the Kickin' Cajuns, fronted by Acadian Ambulance paramedic Jamie Bergeron,[7] Travis Matte and the Zydeco Kingpins,[8] Junior Melancon and the Come Down Playboys,[9] and Damon Troy and Louisiana Beat[10] cater to the aesthetic of their primary audience, working-class Cajuns who spend their hard-earned dollars for entertainment value—not the cultural and historical agendas reflected in the official Cajun musical canon. If the music is performed well and danceable, it is good—better if cold beer is being served. The working-class aesthetic comes into clearer focus through anecdotal evidence suggesting that blue-collar folks attend dances to have a good time, not for intellectual stimulation or cultural appreciation. When the all-female band Bonsoir, Catin, comprised of musicians affiliated with the Cajun Renaissance, performed an outdoor concert in Parks, Louisiana in the spring of 2006, a middle-aged working class woman with a thick bayou Cajun accent approached bandleader Kristi Guillory and inquired, "Why y'all playing that French shit?!" Guillory replied, "You don't talk French?" To which the woman retorted, "*Mais*, non" before re-

---

[6] http://www.cajunfrenchmusic.org/music/pastwinners.htm, accessed June 15, 2006.
[7] http://www.kickincajuns.com/, accessed June 14, 2006.
[8] http://www.travismatte.com/us.htm, accessed June 14, 2006.
[9] http://www.lsue.edu/acadgate/music/jrmelancon.htm, accessed June 14, 2006.
[10] http://www.damontroy.com/, accessed June 14, 2006.

questing the group's best rendition of Van Morrison's "Brown-Eyed Girl."[11] The traditional musical eclecticism that pervades contemporary working-class attitudes sustained the careers of dynamic musicians like Harry Choates, Leo Soileau, Nathan Abshire, J.B. Fusilier, Lawrence Walker, and Belton Richard. This eclecticism is now clearly heard in radio programming on locally supported stations like KBON (101.1 FM, Eunice) and KROF (960 AM, Lafayette), which cater to blue-collar Cajun audiences. For bands that emerge from within the working class context, the fine line separating the artist from their audience can be blurred. For instance, during a December 2004 performance, accordionist and emergency medical technician, Jamie Bergeron leaped off stage to resuscitate a dancer who collapsed during a Kickin' Cajun performance in Gueydan. Yet, despite its significance and pervasiveness, the contemporary blue-collar ethos is almost entirely ignored by scholarly literature on Cajun music.

Other gapping holes exist in Cajun music scholarship, leaving plenty of room for discourse. For instance, the role of Louisiana radio in the dissemination and popularization of local musical traditions has not been fully realized. Scholars have neglected the influence of modern stations like the University of Louisiana at Lafayette's National Public Radio affiliate KRVS, which features a significant amount of locally-generated and French language programming. KRVS broadcasts a variety of programs that play to the Renaissance[12] and CFMA[13] crowds. The eclectic non-French programming available on the university station is an intellectual interpretation of the mix-and-matched musical genres comprising the formats featured on blue-collar stations—in particular KBON and KROF—which offer listeners the opportunity to hear amazingly diverse selections—for example, recordings of Iry LeJeune, Merle Haggard, Cookie and the Cupcakes, and Hank Williams Sr. in consecutive order. The long-running *Rendezvous des Cajuns*, a weekly live radio broadcast generating from the Liberty Theater in Eunice, Louisiana—a show that is part Louisiana Hayride, part Prairie Home Companion—must also be analyzed for its influential role in contemporary Cajun music. Likewise, other grass-roots organizations working to promote Louisiana French music—namely Louisiana Folk Roots and their Dewey Balfa Heritage Camp—are due scholarly attention.

According to Louisiana Folk Roots president Gilbert "Winky" Aucoin, the Dewey Balfa Heritage Camp is designed to sustain some of the unique cultural traits associated with south Louisiana. Aucoin asserts, "we need to preserve the

---

[11] Kristi Guillory, personal communication, June 15, 2006.

[12] "Rendezvous des Cajuns," "Lacouture Lagniappe," "Demain C'est Pas Dimanche," and live remote broadcasting of Festivals Acadiens are categorized here as representative examples of musical programming appealing to the Renaissance aesthetic.

[13] "Dimanche Matin," "Bal de Dimanche après midi," and "Bonjour Louisiane," the latter hosted by disc jockey Pete Bergeron (a fervent CFMA supporter), are regarded in this study as appealing to the CFMA aesthetic.

music, and preserve the language, and preserve the dance."[14] In essence, the nonprofit organization interprets fiddler and cultural activist Dewey Balfa's vision to nurture Cajun culture, particularly musical traditions, one generation at a time. The Dewey Balfa Heritage Camp began in 2001 at Iberia Parish's Lake Fausse Pointe State Park, before relocating to Chicot State Park near Ville Platte. Aucoin observed that the camp also serves as a vehicle for Louisianians to promote their culture on their own terms, noting:

> other folks, primarily those in Washington state, the state of California, the state of New York and the state of Georgia were coming to Louisiana to Cajun and Creole Country and taking our musicians, taking our cooks, taking our dancers and bringing them to their respective states and were conducting Cajun and Creole camps to teach people about Cajun and Creole culture. Christine Balfa Powell, the wife of Dirk Powell, was often a player and/or instructor along with her husband at these camps, along with many other of our instructors. So we realized there was only one place that we didn't have a camp like that to immerse the people and/or re-immerse and, that was in Louisiana.[15]

The camp offers instruction in Cajun accordion traditions, fiddling, and French vocal delivery to both locals and a large number of Cajun music aficionados from the continental United States and Europe. "Yankee-chanks," "Zydeholics," "Cajunites," and "Balfites"—as locals refer to the Cajun enthusiasts from beyond Louisiana—have not been recognized for their role in sustaining (at least through economic support) festivals, traveling Cajun bands, music preservation efforts, and locally owned and operated record producers and retailers. Cultural tourism is but one pressing topic in a long list of challenges facing modern Cajun music.

Scholars have yet to explore adequately the evolving dancehall scene, the role of jam sessions as interactive spaces where musicians develop technique and forge new ensembles, or themes and motifs within the respective ballad and dance repertoires. The current literature also fails to address the Cajun swing revival led by bands like the Red Stick Ramblers, the impact of evacuees from other musically rich sections of Louisiana who now call Acadiana home, the status of Cajun music in Europe, Cajun music festivals beyond Cajun Country and other current issues affecting the direction of modern Cajun musical expression. We hope this collection of essays will stimulate a new generation of researchers to document shifts within the local, regional, even global soundscapes. Perhaps this collection of essays, and the investigations will encourage budding scholars and established humanists alike to document a bit of culture for posterity one song at a time.

---

[14] Gilbert Aucoin interviewed by Ryan A. Brasseaux, Chicot State Park, Louisiana, April 24, 2006.
[15] Ibid.

# An Evolutionary Chronology of Cajun Music

| | |
|---|---|
| *1604* | French colonists establish Acadian colony in Maritime Canada. |
| *1755* | *Le Grand Dérangement*, the Acadian deportation, scatters thousands of Acadians around the globe. |
| *1764* | First Acadian refugees arrive in Louisiana. |
| *1782* | Documentary record provides the first mention of Acadians owning instruments in Louisiana—clarinet and fiddle. |
| *1803* | Travel writer C.C. Robin provides the first documentation of *bals de maison* (house dances). |
| *1861* | Alexandre Barde publishes the first mention of dancehalls frequented by the Cajun community. |
| *1871* | Ralph Keeler and A.R. Waud publish an illustration of an accordionist at the mouth of the Mississippi River corroborating the claim that the instrument was available to musicians in Louisiana before the end of the nineteenth century. |
| *1928* | Joe Falcon and Cléoma Breaux record the first commercial Cajun recording "Lafayette (Allons a Laufette)" [sic]/"The Waltz that Carried Me To My Grave" on Columbia Records; Dennis McGee and Sady Courville broadcast from KWKH in Shreveport, Louisiana, becoming some of the earliest vernacular Cajun musicians to perform on radio. |
| *1929* | The Breaux Family Band records the first rendition of "Jole Blonde," under the title "Ma Blonde est Parti;" Douglas Bellard and Kirby Riley become the first rural black Creole musicians to record; white Cajun fiddler Dennis McGee and black Creole accordionist Amédé Ardoin make the first interracial Cajun/Creole recordings. |
| *1930* | The Great Depression halts all Cajun recording sessions between 1930 and 1934; Irene Petitjean submits her Master's thesis "Cajun Folk Songs of Southwest Louisiana," the first substantial academic study of Cajun music, to the faculty at Columbia University. |

| | |
|---|---|
| 1933 | Fiddler Luderin Darbone and guitarist Edwin Duhon form the Hackberry Ramblers and begin broadcasting on Beaumont's KFDM radio relay housed in Lake Charles' Majestic Hotel. |
| 1934 | John and Alan Lomax, with the help of Acadia Parish native Irène Thérèse Whitfield, collect an extensive Cajun and Creole folksong collection during their music survey of the American South. |
| 1935 | Leo Soileau and the Four Aces record the first Cajun swing sides on the Bluebird record label; the Cajun string band era (1935-1947) begins. |
| 1936 | Southwest Louisiana's first locally operated radio station, KVOL goes on air in Lafayette; cultural geographer Lauren Chester Post leads the Louisiana delegation—including a Cajun dance band led by accordionist Lawrence Walker and a musical/dance "Evangeline" troupe from St. Martinville and New Iberia—to the National Folk Festival in Dallas Texas. |
| 1937 | Crowley, Louisiana, hosts the first annual National Rice Festival (later the International Rice Festival) and features live musical performances by Cajun artists. |
| 1939 | Irène Thérèse Whitfield publishes the first book length academic study of Cajun music, *Louisiana French Folk Songs*. |
| 1942 | LeRoy "Happy Fats" LeBlanc and the Rayne-Bo Ramblers sell 10,000 copies of their RCA/Victor release "La Veuve de la Coulee" in one week and receive national attention after being proclaimed *Hit of the Week* in a nationally syndicated publication. |
| 1946 | Cajun fiddler Harry Choates records "Jole Blon" on the Gold Star record label in Houston, Texas. The release reached number four on "Billboard's Most Played Juke Box Hits" in 1947 and spurred remakes by Bob Wills and the Texas Playboys, Moon Mullican, Roy Acuff, and Waylon Jennings; J.D. Miller forms Cajun Country's first independent record label, Fais Do Do, after issuing Happy, Doc and the Boys'"Colinda." He is followed by Eddie Schuler (Goldband), George Khoury (Khoury), Floyd Soileau (Swallow), and Carol Rachon (La Louisianne). |

| | |
|---|---|
| 1948 | Accordionist Iry LeJeune records the "Love Bridge Waltz" for the Opera record label in Houston, Texas. The release simultaneously solidified the viability of independent record labels along the Texas-Louisiana corridor and swung the commercial musical pendulum toward a new form of Cajun accordion music that combined early accordion compositions with Cajun swing instrumentation; Dewey Balfa forms the Balfa Brothers band with his siblings Will, Rodney, and Harry. |
| 1949 | Accordionist Nathan Abshire ensures the viability of accordion-based music on local record labels with his recording "Pine Grove Blues." |
| 1952 | Hank Williams Sr. releases his Cajun anthem "Jambalaya," based on steel guitarist Julius "Papa Cairo" Lamperez's composition "Grand Texas," itself based on a traditional tune, "L'Anse Couche-Couche." |
| 1955 | Doug and Rusty Kershaw debut on the Louisiana Hayride radio program in Shreveport, Louisiana. |
| 1956 | Jimmy C. Newman begins performing on the Grand Ole Opry; ethnomusicologist Harry Oster starts collecting Cajun music field recordings (1956-1959). |
| 1959 | Arhoolie records issues Harry Oster's Cajun field recordings as *Folksongs of the Louisiana Acadians*. |
| 1963 | KRVS goes on air from the University of Southwestern Louisiana (now the University of Louisiana at Lafayette). |
| 1964 | Gladius Thibodeaux, Louis "Vinesse" LeJeune, Dewey Balfa, and Revon Reed perform at the Newport Folk Festival after an invitation from the Smithsonian's Ralph Rinzler; Rinzler begins collecting Cajun music field recordings (1964-1966). |
| 1965 | Swallow Records issues *The Balfa Brothers Play Traditional Cajun Music, Volume 1*; Accordionist and accordion maker Marc Savoy opens the Savoy Music Center in Eunice, Louisiana. |
| 1968 | Louisiana State Legislature creates the Council for the Development of French in Louisiana (CODOFIL). |
| 1969 | NASA's Apollo 12 moon mission broadcast Doug Kershaw's "Louisiana Man" back to earth from outer space. |

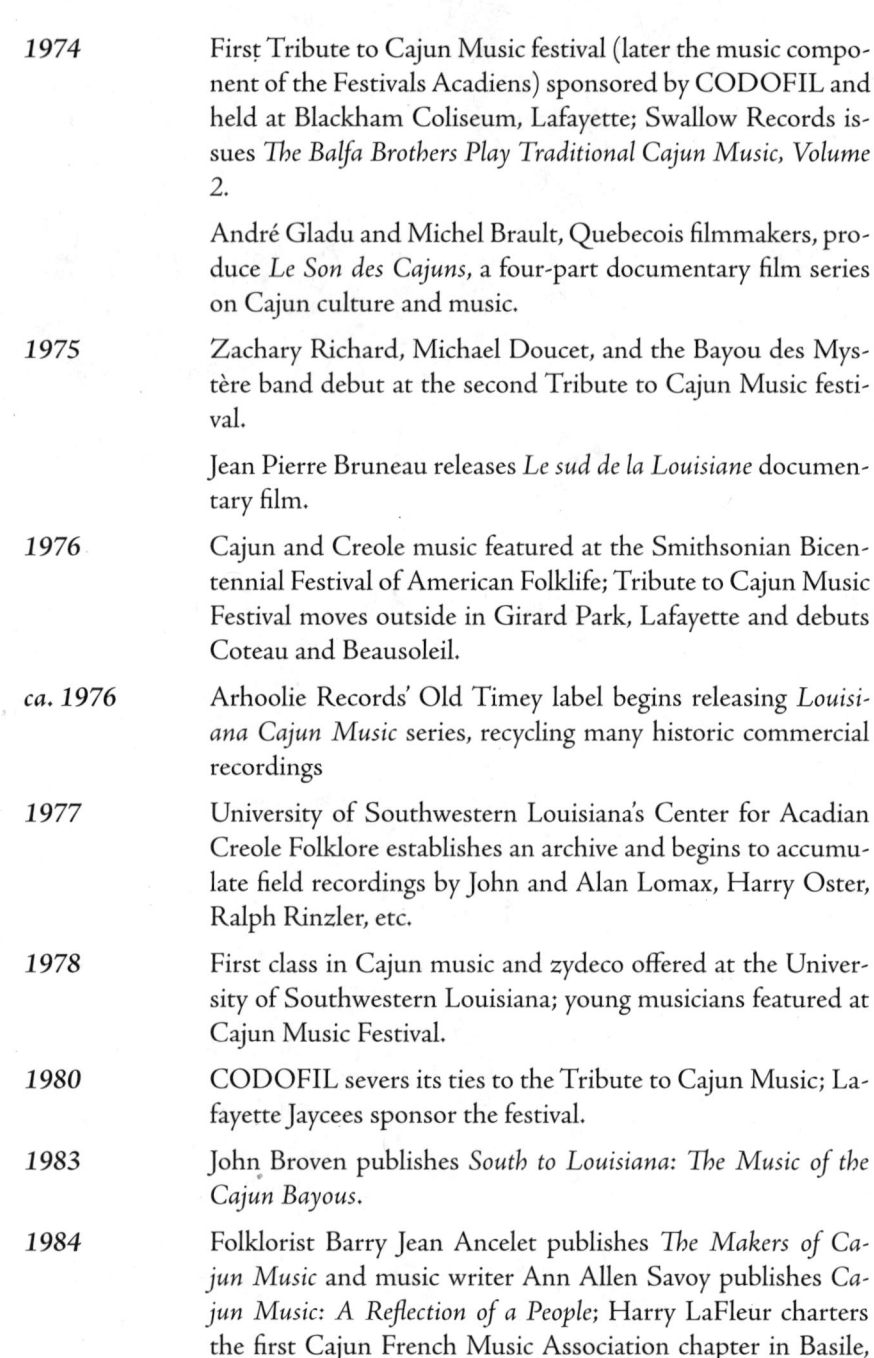

| | |
|---|---|
| *1974* | First Tribute to Cajun Music festival (later the music component of the Festivals Acadiens) sponsored by CODOFIL and held at Blackham Coliseum, Lafayette; Swallow Records issues *The Balfa Brothers Play Traditional Cajun Music, Volume 2*. |
| | André Gladu and Michel Brault, Quebecois filmmakers, produce *Le Son des Cajuns*, a four-part documentary film series on Cajun culture and music. |
| *1975* | Zachary Richard, Michael Doucet, and the Bayou des Mystère band debut at the second Tribute to Cajun Music festival. |
| | Jean Pierre Bruneau releases *Le sud de la Louisiane* documentary film. |
| *1976* | Cajun and Creole music featured at the Smithsonian Bicentennial Festival of American Folklife; Tribute to Cajun Music Festival moves outside in Girard Park, Lafayette and debuts Coteau and Beausoleil. |
| *ca. 1976* | Arhoolie Records' Old Timey label begins releasing *Louisiana Cajun Music* series, recycling many historic commercial recordings |
| *1977* | University of Southwestern Louisiana's Center for Acadian Creole Folklore establishes an archive and begins to accumulate field recordings by John and Alan Lomax, Harry Oster, Ralph Rinzler, etc. |
| *1978* | First class in Cajun music and zydeco offered at the University of Southwestern Louisiana; young musicians featured at Cajun Music Festival. |
| *1980* | CODOFIL severs its ties to the Tribute to Cajun Music; Lafayette Jaycees sponsor the festival. |
| *1983* | John Broven publishes *South to Louisiana: The Music of the Cajun Bayous*. |
| *1984* | Folklorist Barry Jean Ancelet publishes *The Makers of Cajun Music* and music writer Ann Allen Savoy publishes *Cajun Music: A Reflection of a People*; Harry LaFleur charters the first Cajun French Music Association chapter in Basile, Louisiana; accordionist Wayne Toups makes his debut at the Tribute to Cajun Music festival. |

# An Evolutionary Chronology of Cajun Music

|      |   |
|------|---|
|      | Clifton Chenier wins a Grammy Award for his zydeco album *I'm Here*. |
| 1987 | *Rendezvous des Cajuns*, a live weekly radio broadcast from the Liberty Theater in Eunice, Louisiana (hosted by Barry Jean Ancelet) goes on air. |
|      | Swallow Records releases *Louisiana Cajun and Creole Music, 1934: The Lomax Recordings*, reissuing many of his historic field recordings. |
| 1988 | Steve Riley and the Mamou Playboys debut at Cajun Music Festival. |
| 1989 | Barry Jean Ancelet publishes *The Origins and Development of Cajun Music* and expands the available literature with an inquiry into the evolution of the genre. |
|      | Chris Strachwitz and Les Blank release *J'ai été au bal: The Cajun and Zydeco Music of Louisiana* documentary film. |
| 1993 | Kristi Guillory's Réveille and Christine Balfa's Balfa Toujours debut at Cajun Music Festival. |
| 1996 | Cajun singer-songwriter Zachary Richard releases *Cap Enragé*, an album that achieves multi-platinum status in Quebec and France; Shane K. Bernard publishes *Swamp Pop: Cajun and Creole Rhythm and Blues*, the first substantial study of the genre. |
| 1997 | Beausoleil wins a Grammy Award for their album *L'Amour ou la folie*; independently owned and operated radio station KBON goes on air from Eunice, Louisiana and presents an eclectic mix of Louisiana music with a particular emphasis on Cajun and Creole stylings. |
| 2005 | The National Endowment for the Arts awards Michael Doucet of Beausoleil with a National Heritage Fellowship. |

# Recommended Readings

*Documentary Films*

Blank, Les, and Chris Strachwitz. *J'ai été au bal (I Went To The Dance Last Night): The Cajun and Zydeco Music of Louisiana*. Brazos Films, 1989.

Lomax, Alan. *Cajun Country: Don't Drop the Potato*. Pacific Arts Video, 1990.

Whitehead, John, and Ben Sandmel. "*Make 'Em Dance*": *The Hackberry Ramblers' Story*. VHS, Fretless Pictures, 2003.

*Articles*

Blanchet, Catherine. "Acadian Instrumental Music." *Louisiana Folklore Miscellany* 3 (1970): 70-74.

Brandon, Elizabeth. "Chanson folklorique et les Acadiens." *Revue de Louisiane/ Louisiana Revue* 5 (1976): 5-33.

———. "'L'Alouette'—A Functional Song." *Louisiana Folklore Miscellany* 4 (1976-1980): 116-21.

Comeaux, Malcolm. "The Cajun Accordion." *Revue de Louisiane/Louisiana Revue* 7 (1978): 117-28.

Del Sesto, Steven L. "Cajun Music and Zydeco: Notes on the Music of Southern Louisiana." *Louisiana Folklore Miscellany* 4 (1976-1980): 88-101.

———. "Traditional Social Institutions in Southwest Louisiana: A Sociological Note on the Study of Culture." *Attakapas Gazette* 10 (1974): 72-75.

Holmes, Irène Thérèse Whitfield. "Acadian Folk Song." *Attakapas Gazette* 15 (1980): 165.

———. "Acadian Music and Dances." *Attakapas Gazette* (1976): 181-85.

———, and Gayle Calais Guidry. "Le Marin Breton: An Acadian French Song." *Attakapas Gazette* 14 (1979): 110-11.

Lagarde, Marie-Louise, William S. Chute, and George F. Reinecke, eds. "Six Avoyelles Songs from the Saucier Collection." *Louisiana Folklore Miscellany* 2 (1965): 1-26.

Mattern, Mark. "Cajun Music, Cultural Revival: Theorizing Political Action in Popular Music." *Popular Music and Society* 22 (1998): 31-48.

Norwood, Beth. "French Radio Broadcasting in Louisiana." *Southern Speech Journal* 30 (1964): 46-54.

O'Neal, Jim. "Louisiana Wax Facts: The Blues and Cajun Record Scene 1973." *Living Blues* (1973): 9-12.

Pittman, Nick. "Johnny Rebel Speaks." *Gambit Weekly*, June 10, 2003, 9-12.

Reed, Revon, Paul Tate, and Kathy Bihm. "The Voice in the Soul of Cajun Music." *Louisiana Heritage* 1 (1969): 14-15.

Reinecke, George F. "The Wandering Jew in French Louisiana." *Louisiana Folklore Miscellany* 3 (1970): 46-54.

Savoy, Ann. "Cajun Music: Alive and Well in Louisiana." 1990 Louisiana Folklife Festival booklet.

Simmons, Michael. "Doug Kershaw: The 'Real Deal' in Cajun Fiddle." *Fiddler Magazine* 10 (2003): 4-6.

———. "Michael Doucet: A Fiddler's Education." *Fiddler Magazine* 8 (2001): 4-5.

Ware, Carolyn. "Cajun Music as Oral Poetry." www.louisianavoices.org/creole_art_oral_poetry_caj.html, accessed 1/28/03. First appeared in the Festival Internationale de Louisiane book (1990).

Westbrook, Laura. "Pretty, Little, and Fickle: Images of Women in Cajun Music." *Louisiana Folklore Miscellany* 11 (1996): 41-52.

Whatley, Randy. "Cajun Fiddler Harry Choates." Baton Rouge *Sunday Advocate Magazine*, February 4, 1983, 32.

Wilgus, D. K. "Country-Western Music and the Urban Hillbilly." *Journal of American Folklore* 83 (1970): 157-79.

## Books/Chapters in Edited Volumes

Allan, Johnnie. *Memories: A Pictorial History of South Louisiana Music Volume 1 & 2 Combined 1910s-1990s*. Lafayette, LA, 1995.

American Folklife Center. "Ethnic Recordings in America: A Neglected Heritage," *Studies in American Folklife, No. 1*, Washington D.C., 1982.

Ancelet, Barry Jean. *The Origins and Development of Cajun Music*. Lafayette, 1989.

Ancelet, Barry Jean, and Elemore Morgan Jr. *The Makers of Cajun Music*. Austin: University of Texas Press, 1984.

Ancelet, Barry Jean, Jay Edwards, and Glen Pitre. *Cajun Country*. Jackson: University Press of Mississippi, 1991.

Bernard, Shane K. *Swamp Pop: Cajun and Creole Rhythm & Blues*. Jackson: University Press of Mississippi, 1996.

# Recommended Readings

Blanchet, Catherine Brookshire. "Louisiana French folk song among children in Vermilion Parish, 1942-1954." M.A. thesis, University of Southwestern Louisiana, 1970.

Brandon, Elizabeth. "Acadian Folk Songs as Reflected in 'La Délaissée,'" in Glenn R. Conrad ed., *The Cajuns: Essays on Their History and Culture*, 185-211. Lafayette: Center for Louisiana Studies, 1978.

Broven, John. *South to Louisiana: The Music of the Cajun Bayous*. Gretna, Pelican Publishing Co. 1983.

Comber, Chris, and Mike Paris. "Jimmie Rogers," in Bill C. Malone and Judith McCulloh ed., *Stars of Country Music: Uncle Dave Macon to Johnny Rodriguez*, 121-41. Urbana: University of Illinois Press, 1975.

Conrad, Glenn R. and Vaughan B. Baker. *Louisiana Gothic: Recollections of the 1930s*. Lafayette: Center for Louisiana Studies, 1984.

Coquille, Walter. *The Mayor of Bayou Pom Pom Speaks (By The Mayor Heemself)*. New Orleans: Coquille Publishing, 1954.

Daigle, Pierre. *Tears, Love and Laughter: The Story of the Cajuns and Their Music*. Ville Platte: Swallow Publishing, 1987.

Escott, Colin. *Hank Williams: The Biography*. Boston: Little, Brown, 1994.

François, Raymond. *Yé Yaille, Chère!: Traditional Cajun Dance Music*. Ville Platte: Swallow Publications, 1990.

Gilmore, Jeanne, Robert C. Gilmore, et al. *Chantez Encore: South Louisiana French Folk Songs*. Lafayette: Acadiana Music, 1977.

Lomax, John A., and Alan Lomax. *Our Singing Country: A Second Volume of American Ballads and Folk Songs*. New York: Macmillan, 1941.

Malone, Bill C. *Country Music U.S.A.*, 2d rev. ed. Austin: University of Texas Press, 2002.

Malone, Bill C., and David Stricklin. *Southern Music/American Music*. Lexington: University Press of Kentucky, 2003.

Petitjean, Irene M. "Cajun Folk Songs of Southwest Louisiana." M.A. thesis, Columbia University, 1930.

Porterfield, Nolan. *Jimmie Rodgers*. Urbana: University of Illinois Press, 1979.

Post, Lauren C. *Cajun Sketches: From the Prairies of Southwest Louisiana*. Baton Rouge: Louisiana State University Press, 1974.

Reed, Revon. *Lâche pas la patate: Portrait des Acadiens de la Louisiane*. Montreal: Édition Parti Pris, 1976.

Russell, Tony. *Blacks, Whites and Blues*. New York: Stein and Day, 1970.

Savoy, Ann Allen. *Cajun Music: A Reflection of a People*. Eunice: Bluebird Press, 1984.

Sonnier Jr., Austin. *Second Linin': Jazzmen of Southwest Louisiana, 1900-1950*. Lafayette: Center for Louisiana Studies, 1989.

Spottswood, Richard Keith. *Ethnic Music on Records: A Discography of Ethnic Recordings Produced in the United States, 1893 to 1942*. Urbana: University of Illinois Press, 1990.

Stivale, Charles. *Disenchanting Les Bons Temps: Identity and Authenticity in Cajun Music and Dance*. Durham: Duke University Press, 2003.

Thériot, Marie del Norte, and Catherine Brookshire Blanchet. *Les Danses Rondes: Louisiana French Folk Dances*. Abbeville: R.E. Blanchet, 1955.

Townsend, Charles. *San Antonio Rose: The Life and Music of Bob Wills*. Urbana: University of Illinois Press, 1986.

Wolfe, Charles K. *The Devil's Box*. Nashville: Vanderbilt University Press, 1997.

### Compact Disks Linernotes

Ancelet, Barry. *Alan and John A. Lomax: The Classic Louisiana Recordings, Cajun & Creole Music 1934/1937*. Rounder 11661-1842-2, 1999.

Brasseaux, Ryan A. *Pilette Breakdown (Lost Bayou Ramblers)*. Swallow SW-6177, 2003.

Broven, John. *Floyd's Early Cajun Singles*. Ace, 1999.

———. *The Goldband Story: Eddie's House of Hits*. Ace CDCHD 424, 1994.

———. *Louisiana Roots: The Jay Miller R&B Legacy*. Ace CDCHD 682, 1998.

Brown, Andrew. *Harry Choates: Devil in the Bayou, The Gold Star Recordings*. Bear Family Records BCD 16355, 2002.

Brown, Roy. *Blind Uncle Gaspard, Delma Lachney, John Bertrand: Early American Cajun Music*. Yazoo 2042, 1999.

Buzelin, Jean. *Cajun: Louisiane 1928-1939*. Frémeaux & Associés, 1994.

Coffey, Kevin. *Harry Choates: Five-Time Loser 1940-1951*. Interstate Music LTD, Krazy Kat KK CD 22, 1998.

———. *Jole Blon: 23 Artists One Theme*. Bear Family Records BCD 16618 AJ, 2003.

Cohn, Lawrence. *Cajun Vol. 1.: Abbeville Breakdown 1929-1939*. COLUMBIA Records CK 46220, 1990.

Crumb, R. *Hot Women: Women Singers from the Torrid Regions*. Kein and Aber Records, 2003.

Harrison, Pat. *Cajun: Early Recordings, Important Swamp Sides Remastered*. JSP Records JSP7726, 2004.

Humphrey, Mark. *Cajun Dance Party: Fais Do-Do*. Roots n' Blues, 1994.

Oster, Harry. *Folksongs of the Louisiana Acadians*. Arhoolie CD 359, 1994.

Rinzler, Ralph. *Louisiana Cajun French Music from the Southwest Prairies, 1964-1967*, vols. 1 and 2. Rounder CD 6001, 1989.

Savoy, Ann Allen. "Dennis McGee," *The Complete Early Recordings of Dennis McGee 1929-1930*. Yazoo 2012, 1994.

———. *Edius Naquin: Ballad Master*. Audio cassette produced for New Orleans Jazz and Heritage Foundation.

———. *Iry LeJeune, Cajun's Greatest: The Definitive Collection*. Ace Records CDCHD 428, 1992.

———. "Leo Soileau: From Cajun Classic to Innovator," *Early American Cajun Music: The Early Recordings of Leo Soileau, Classic Recordings from the 1920s*. Yazoo 2041, 1999.

Sandmel, Ben. *Luderin Darbone's Hackberry Ramblers Early Recordings: 1935-1950*. Arhoolie CD 7050, 2003.

Seemann, Charlie. *Le Gran Mamou: A Cajun Music Anthology, The Historic Victor/Bluebird Sessions 1928-1941*. Country Music Foundation, 1990.

Seemann, Charlie. *Raise Your Window: A Cajun Music Anthology, The Historic Victor/Bluebird Sessions 1928-1941*. Country Music Foundation, 1990.

Seemann, Charlie. *Le Grand Prairie: A Cajun Music Anthology, The Historic Victor/Bluebird Sessions 1928-1941*. Country Music Foundation, 1990.

Strachwitz, Chris. *Luderin Darbone's Hackberry Ramblers: "Jolie Blonde."* Arhoolie CD 399, 1993.

Strachwitz, Chris. *Cajun Breakdown: Cajun String Bands of the 1930s*. Arhoolie Records, 1997.

Various artists. *Cajun Honky Tonk: The Khoury Recordings*. Arhoolie 427, 1995.

# Index

Abbeville, LA, 48-49, 79, 330, 348, 350
Abshire, Man, 431
Abshire, Nathan, 4, 24, 90, 193, 198, 201, 204-205, 217, 256, 302, 306-07, 310-311, 388, 390, 416, 425, 440, 454
Acadia (Acadie), 31, 48, 77, 156-157, 174, 225, 293, 465-466
Acadia Parish, 11, 15-16, 157, 219, 321, 327, 333
Acadiana, viii, 80, 184-85, 188, 193-94, 291, 293, 296-97, 317-18
Acadians, 3, 15-21, 43, 55-60, 77, 83, 86, 97-98, 101, 108, 139, 140-143, 151, 153, 157, 161-164, 167, 172-174, 176, 180-182, 208, 212, 216-218, 244, 276-277, 303, 307, 321, 324, 334, 336, 363, 366, 383-384, 386-387, 444-445, 453, 459, 461, 465; Acadian-Cajun Festival, 403; Acadian French music, 383; audiences, 276; music, 383; refugees, 108; resistance movement, 470; Acadian Stars, 282
Acadians, Genteel, 180, 271
accordionists, 21-22, 80, 109, 198, 208-209, 234-235, 240, 243, 275, 344, 347-350, 358, 360-362, 381, 383, 384, 427, 435, 440, 473, 490, 492, 500
accordions, 3-4, 12-13, 16, 19, 21, 31, 35, 37, 40-43, 80-114, 107-114, 125, 179, 181, 185-186, 199, 200, 201-202, 204, 206, 208-209, 211-215, 218-226, 273, 275, 280-281, 294-295, 299, 305, 307, 309, 310-311, 322-329, 335-366, 373, 379, 381, 383-385, 387, 390, 391, 394, 399, 400-401, 403, 405, 409, 412, 417, 423-426, 428, 431, 433, 435, 440, 443, 453-454, 459-473, 477, 478, 479, 481, 482, 484, 490, 495, 496; accordion-based bands 186, 305, 400; contests, 185; Creole accordions, 312, 473; diatonic, 19, 85, 99-100, 102, 111, 113, 223, 251, 294, 431; fall in and out of favor, 114; in Texas, 89; triple row button, 102, 113; tunings, 112
accordions, piano, 113
acculturation, 17, 47, 54, 57, 59, 63, 308
Aces, 386-388
activists (see also Cajun Renaissance), 22, 318, 467-468, 490
Acuff, Roy, 273
Acuff-Rose Publishing Company, 244, 274, 283, 444, 447
Adams, Milton, 310
Adcock, Charles "C.C.," 491
African Americans, 58, 59, 60-64, 72, 97, 99, 171, 326, 390; blues, 244; influence of, on Cajun music 63, 73, 97-99, 103, 108-109, 158,
171, 239, 252, 257, 258, 261, 262-264, 294, 390, 393, 408-409, 416, 423, 468; Afro-Caribbean influences, 73, 244, 390, 464, 496; Afro-Creoles, 4, 12, 25, 186; blues tradition, 49; folk music, 47, 49; French-speaking blacks, 92; jazz and blues, 59
alcohol, 41-42, 45, 51-52, 58, 68, 119, 124, 142-43, 145-147, 153-175, 285, 309, 329, 341, 343, 409, 411, 416, 419-420, 459, 488
Alesi, Tommy, 209, 474
Alexandria, LA, 231, 241, 265
Allan, Johnnie, 25, 203, 285, 291-294, 298-299, 317, 428
Alleman, Philip, 202, 222, 431-432
Alleman, Tony, 426
Allman Brothers Band, 496
"Allons à Lafayette," 14, 234, 273, 324-325, 337, 347, 353, 468
All-Star Revelers, 243
Amelia, LA, 239
American, folk music, 302, revival movement, 302; Folklore Society, 21
Americanization, 18, 20, 47, 57, 200, 202, 212, 454, 481
Amite City, LA, 265
amplification, 394, 400; electrical, 89, 114, 150, 168, 199, 280, 329, 389-390, 454
Ancelet, Barry Jean, viii, ix, 6, 9, 13, 20-24, 84, 90, 102, 117, 120, 128-129, 131, 251, 293-295, 299, 302, 351, 358, 390, 461, 463, 465-466, 468-469, 471-472, 489, 491-92
Anglo American, 63, 83, 334, blues and hillbilly music, 426; fiddling, 353; fiddle tunes, 353; folk-song style, 247; minority, 454; string bands, 391, 425
Anglo-Celtic music, 230
Angola State Penitentiary, 239-240
*Anse aux Pailles*, LA, 355, 362
*Anse Prien Noire*, LA, 153, 168, 170-171
Anselmi, Harry, 443, 445
anthropology, 9, 17, 19-20, 24
Archive of Folk Songs, 471
Archives of Cajun and Creole Folklore, 23
Ardoin Family Band, 216
Ardoin, Alphonse "Bois Sec," 99-100, 102, 205, 306
Ardoin, Amédé, 6, 99-100, 102, 109, 198-201, 235, 243, 273, 306, 312, 317, 328, 375, 385, 423, 473
Ardoin, Doug, and Boogie Kings, 284
Argo record company, 284
Arhoolie record company 6, 102, 197, 213, 246, 248, 312, 336, 395, 403, 471
Armstrong, Louis, 392

# Index

520

Arnaudville, LA, 344, 384
assimilation, 57, 88-89, 92, 179, 308, 395
Atchafalaya, 206, 215
Atkins, Chet, 444, 447-449
Atlanta, GA, 230, 233-234, 325, 341, 383, 408
Austin, TX, 421
Authement, Ray, 303
authenticity, issues involving, 125, 128-130, 132, 134-135, 225, 396, 487-489, 491-493
Autry, Gene, 245, 276, 280
Avoyelles Parish, 15, 309, 351-352, 355, 458

**B**abin, Erwin, see, Miller, J.D.
Badeaux, Eliard, 205
Baez, Joan, 455
Balfa Brothers, 21, 199, 201, 204, 209, 216, 246, 286, 453-54, 458, 490, 495,
Balfa, Christine, 223
Balfa, Dewey, 20-21, 23-24, 83, 84, 100, 199, 201, 204, 209, 211, 216-217, 223-226, 246, 289, 302-307, 305, 311, 313, 317-18, 379, 380-382, 453-458, 467, 469, 479, 490-492
Balfa, Tony, 205
ballads (see also women and Cajun music; home music), 1, 3, 9, 11-17, 19, 21-22, 24, 31, 60, 69, 73, 77-78, 85, 210-212, 216-217, 223, 305, 307, 310, 351, 354, 356, 390; French, 479, 485, 488
ballads, occupational, 64
*bals de maison*, 31, 46, 128, 141, 143, 498
banjo, 109, 224, 435, 438, 468, 474
Barnard, Dudley, and the Southern Serenaders, 443
barrooms, 94, 95, 134, 137, 146, 147, 148, 150, 151, 198, 222, 269, 359, 496
Barry, Joe, 203, 285, 444-445
Barzas, Kevin, 311, 490
Barzas, Maurice and Vorance, 490
Basile, LA, 168, 171, 174, 182, 246, 302, 340, 342-343, 360, 383, 391, 400, 453
Basin Brothers, 224
bass, 202, 209-210, 215, 221, 222, 223, 308, 352, 386, 387, 399, 401, 402, 403, 405, 481, 484, 491, 495, 497; upright bass, 495, 496-497
Baton Rouge, LA, 11, 16, 18, 19, 20, 183, 188, 229, 231, 239, 240, 241, 247, 279, 287, 307, 460, 468, 490, 492, 495
Bayou Buckeroos, see LeBlanc, LeRoy "Happy Fats"
*Bayou des Mystéres*, 212, 307-08
Bayou Drifter Band, 461, 462
*Bayou Ruler*, 491, 492
Bayous, des Cannes, 374; Lafourche, 443-444; Teche, 47, 55, 65, 113, 302
Beatles, 467, 469, 488, 498

Beaumont, TX, 13, 86, 89, 93, 238, 252, 279, 291, 298, 400, 421
Beausoleil, 13, 20, 26, 100, 208-211, 217, 224, 290, 308-309, 318, 460, 467, 469-475, 487, 490, 496, 500
beer, 131, 143, 148
Beethoven Miller's Merrymakers, see, Cajun swing
*Belizaire the Cajun*, 86, 471
Belizaire's, 309
Bellard, Douglas, 234
Bergeron, Alphé, 202, 214, 454
Bergeron, Shirley, 202, 224, 279
Berkeley, CA, 117, 121, 126, 133, 136-137, 336, 403; Folk Music Festival, 403
Bernard, Rod, 26, 194, 203, 251-253, 264, 279, 284-285, 292-293, 296-297, 299
Bernard, Shane K., 3, 5, 26
Bertrand, Hobo, 244
Bertrand, John, 351, 354, 355, 356, 384
Bertrand, Jon, 495, 497
Big Cane, 355
"Big Mamou," 274, 283, 284, 285
Biograph and Folkways, 239
Black Cat Club, 353
Blackham Coliseum, 105, 185, 304, 457
Blanchet, Catherine, 9
Blank, Les, 205, 225
Blevins, Kenny, 209, 308
Blue Moon Saloon, 498
Bluebird record company, 235, 236, 284, 360, 362, 385, 408, 418
bluegrass (see also country music), 200, 202, 209, 215, 218, 224-226, 247, 309, 404, 438, 454, 474, 490
Bluerunners, 27, 477-485
blues (see also Cajun swing), 93, 98-100, 103, 117, 126, 193, 199, 202, 230, 232-236, 238, 239, 240, 243-249, 251, 279, 280, 281, 286, 288, 289, 291, 292, 293, 294, 295, 296, 297, 298, 299, 302, 306, 309, 327, 336, 384, 386, 388, 390, 392, 393, 396, 402, 425, 426, 440, 463, 471, 480, 484, 491, 495, 496; classic, 496
*Blues Unlimited*, 25, 286
Bon Temps Rouler Club, 470
Bon Ton Roula, 103
"Bon Ton Rouley," 431
Bonsall, Joe, 88
Boogie Kings, 287
Bornu, Mr., 472
Bosco, LA, 324, 414
Bossier City, LA, 444
Boudreaux, Marc, 309
*bourré*, 145, 147, 149
Bozman, Virgil, 200

Brandon, Elizabeth, 9, 14, 21, 23
Brasseaux, Carl, 317, 475
Brasseaux, Danny, 307, 491
Brasseaux, Ryan A., 11, 23, 26, 496, 500
Brassieur, Ray, 19
Breaux Bridge, LA, 132, 490
Breaux Brothers (see also Falcon, Cléoma Breaux; Breaux, Amédé; Breaux, Ophy; Breaux, Clifford), 198, 235, 273, 280, 334, 473, 495
Breaux, Amédé (sometimes Amadée, Amidie), 193, 280, 282, 323, 325, 350, 352, 381, 393, 431
Breaux, Clifford, 323, 334
Breaux, Dana, 308, 469
Breaux, Jimmy, 209-211, 473
Breaux, Ophy, 317, 323, 334-336
Breaux, Pat, 209, 473
Brittany, France, 172
broadcasting, 281, 391, 397, 400-404, 428
Brooklyn, NY, 497-500
Broussard *dit* Beausoleil, Joseph, 470
Broussard, Aldus "Pop-Eye," 328-329, 426, 431, 433
Broussard, Alex, 202, 415, 418
Broussard, Ardus, 16
Broussard, Evelyn, 328
Broussard, Leroy, 244
Broussard, Minos, 402
Broussard, Russ, 484
Broussard, Sam, 491
Broussard, Sidney, Jr., 328
Broussard, Sidney, Sr., 16, 329
Broven, John, ix, 5, 25-26, 102, 292, 296, 404, 428
Brown, Milton, 238; and his Musical Brownies, 238, 386
Brown, Sidney, 290, 307
Bruce, Vin, ix, 27, 194, 215, 317, 443-444, 448, 451
Bruner, Cliff, 386-387
Brunot, Jean-Pierre, 205
Brunswick/Vocalian, 354, 383
Brunswick-Balke-Collender Company, 233, 235, 354, 357, 426
bull pens (see also dancehalls), 146
Bunkie, LA, 274, 458
Burke, Frenchie, 88
Burr, George, 324
Burton, James, 247, 248

C*age aux chiens*, see dancehalls
Cajun French Music Association (CFMA), 179, 182-189, 223
*Cajun Music: A Reflection of a People* (see also Savoy, Ann Allen), 255, 294
Cajun Ramblers, 309
*Cajun Sketches* (see also Post, Lauren C.), 427
Cajun, Le, awards 183, 185
Cajuns, viii, 9, 13, 18, 20-22, 43-44, 47, 50, 57-58, 60, 68, 83, 84-105, 139, 140, 142, 149, 150-151, 193, 194, 200, 210, 212-213, 220, 224, 226, 251, 264, 291, 294, 296; accordion revival, 85; and zydeco music, relation between genres, 121, 126, 130, 134, 477, 485; anti-Cajun sentiment, 252; Cajun Day Festival, 184, 185; Cajun Swing (see also Hackberry Ramblers; LeBlanc, LeRoy "Happy Fats;" Guidry, Oran "Doc;" Choates, Harry), 200, 214, 395, 425-26, 439, 490, 500; classics, 286, 387; Cajun Country, 10, 12-15, 17, 19, 22, 24, 84, 103; Cajun French Music Association (CFMA), 27, 95, 179, 182, 187, 220, 223; Cajun Grass Band, 215; Cajun Heartland, 293; Cajun Music Festival, 224, 310, 312, 475; confront the modern world, 268; country/bluegrass bands, 202; culturalists, 267; dances, 407; dancing, 413; *Folk Songs of Southwest Louisiana*, 11; folklore, 131; French music, 454, 493; French songs, 311; French language, 179, 180, 181, 183, 184, 186, 187, 321, 329, 334, 335, 417, 425, 428, 437, 453; honky tonk sound, 439, 469; humorists, 267, 268, 269, 286; jokes, 266; migration to Texas, 86; music, 3-6, 9-11, 14-27, 31-32, 43, 54, 58, 98-102, 109, 111, 112, 114-115, 139, 145, 150-151, 179, 181-182, 184-187, 193-194, 197, 199, 202-209, 212-26, 235, 246, 249, 251, 264, 273-277, 283-284, 289, 292, 294-295, 298-299, 301-313, 317-318, 327, 337, 347, 356-358, 362-363, 365, 383, 389, 390-392, 399, 402, 407, 411-413, 416-417, 425-427, 429, 431, 435-440, 443, 453, 454, 456, 458-459, 461-463, 465, 467, 468, 469, 471, 473-475, 481-482, 487-491, 493, 495-500; music characteristics, 43; music fans, 220, 225; music festival, 457; music history, 221; music programming, 184; music revival, 306; music studies, 3, 9, 10, 16, 17, 18, 19, 21-26; musical themes of the, 80; musical traditions, 11; musical ideas exchanged with country and western musicians, 273; recording artists, 25; Renaissance, 20-22, 25-26, 157, 396, 467-468, 475, 488, 490, 491-492, 497; renaissance (cultural and linguistic), 487, 490; restaurant-dancehalls, 472; Spanish influences, 140; storytellers, 271, 410; string band era (see also Cajun swing), 390; tunes, 400; weddings, 48;

working class, 265
Cajun Gold, 219
Calcasieu Parish, 395, 400
California, 31-32, 115-122, 124, 126, 127, 128, 129, 130-137, 215, 225, 417; Cajun Orchestra, 126, 312
California, Northern (see also Berkeley, CA), 117-19, 122, 126, 130, 136, 312
"Calinda" (see also "Colinda," "Danser Colinda"), 257-264, 415
call and response, 77, 171
Calloway, Cab, 393
Camden, NJ, 235, 408
Cameron Parish, 391, 470
Canada, 48, 55, 58, 60, 63-69, 71-72, 74, 83-84, 108, 139-140, 151, 183, 252, 459, 461, 463, 465; maritime provinces of, 108, 139, 140-141, 155-156, 163, 173, 212; music festivals, 461; variants of Canadian music, 74
Cane River, 109
Cankton, LA, 80
Canray Fontenot, 99, 100, 102, 205, 208, 209, 211, 216, 306, 307, 312, 469
canticles (sometimes *cantiques*) 61-63, 65
*Capitaine, capitaine, voyage ton flag*, 171
Capitol record company, 281, 444
Carencro, LA, 431
Caribbean influences, 55, 59, 73, 118-119, 136, 154, 257, 262-263
Carnegie Hall, 313
carnival, see Mardi Gras
Carpenter, Mary Chapin, 211, 474
Carrier, Odgel, 240
Carriere, Calvin, 469
Carruth, Cavan, 497
Carter Family, 273-274, 276, 392
Carter, Jimmy (see also Beausoleil), inaugural reception, 309, 467
Carter, June, 448
Cash, Johnny, 274-275, 443, 456
Castille, Hadley, 214, 395, 490
Catalon, Inez, 79, 305
Catholics, 57, 60-62, 117, 154-155, 183, 239, 340, 343, 468, 480, 496; African American, 60; anti-clericalism, 65-67, 140; clergy, 139-140
CDs, see, compact discs
Cecilia, LA, 484
Celtic influences, 78
censorship, 68, 70
Center for Acadian and Creole Folklore, 303
*Chandeleur*, 155-157, 172-174
chank-a-chank music, 88, 112, 114, 363, 475
*Chanky-chank, Le*, 210
chaperones, function performed at dances by mothers and older women, 365

Chapman, Mike, 311, 490
Chapman, Chop, 491
Charles, Bobby, 248
Charpentier, Erik, 23, 26
Charpentier, Luke, 445
Charters, Samuel, 249
Chataignier, LA, 362
Chavis, Boozoo (see also zydeco; African American influence on Cajun music), 199, 243
Chenier, Clifton (see also zydeco; African American influence on Cajun music), 99-100, 102-103, 117, 199, 217, 246, 279, 286, 294, 299, 306, 311, 395, 481, 484
Chicago, IL, 235, 354, 355, 385, 408; Folk Festival, 306
Chinaball Club, 431
Choates, Harry, ix, 5, 88, 193, 199-200, 214, 273, 282, 325, 395, 401-402, 411, 419, 421, 423, 439, 440, 454, 481
Choates, Jimmie, 282
Christmas, 154-155
Church Point, LA, 80, 94, 168, 182, 184-185, 219, 293, 297, 460; Cajun Days, 307
Civil Rights, era, 181; Movement, 416, 467-468
Civil War, 157, 372
clarinetists, 468
Clark, Octa, 99, 218, 224, 309-310
Clash, The, 477
Clement, Terry, 248
Club Rendezvous, 413
"Colinda" (see also "Calinda," "Danser Colinda"), viii, 142, 193, 199, 251-257, 262-264, 282, 327, 328, 337, 375, 414
Coliseum record company, 304-305
Collette, Danny, 224
Colonial Club, 413
Columbia record company, 233-234, 342, 347-350, 379, 381, 383, 443-444, 446, 450; record company executives, 347; recording studios, 349
Comeaux, Malcolm, 5, 11, 19, 21
Comeaux, Tommy, 209, 470, 474
commercial era, early, 425
compact discs, 5, 6, 226
*complaintes*, 59
Congo, 257, 258, 259, 260, 263, 298
Conn, Steve, 208
Conner, Adlar, 357-359
Conner, Varise, 24, 208, 210, 223, 305, 307, 357, 358, 469
Continental Playboys, see Miller, J.D.
coonass, 83
Coquille, Walter, 269
Cormier, Lionel, 244
Cormier, Raymond, 431

# INDEX

Cormier, Sheryl, 80, 220, 310
corsets, 365, 371
costumes, 155
Coteau, 207, 209, 308, 469, 470
cotillions, 363-364, 366, 369, 370
cotton, 19, 322
*Cotton-Eyed Joe*, 88
Cottonport, LA, 355
Council for the Development of French in Louisiana (CODOFIL), 20-21, 58, 180, 182-183, 187, 265, 270-271, 303-306, 311, 407, 417, 457, 463
country music (see also bluegrass; Acuff, Roy; Autry, Gene; Brown, Milton; Carter Family; Carter, June; Cash, Johnny; Davis, Jimmie; Davis, Link; Harris, Emmylou; Horton, Johnny; Jones, George; Pierce, Webb; Presley, Elvis; Price, Ray; Robbins, Marty; Rodgers, Jimmie; Tubb, Ernest; Tyler, T. Texas; Waggoner, Porter; Wells, Kitty; Whitman, Slim; Williams, Hank; Wills, Bob), 3-4, 59, 89, 193, 199-201, 203-204, 206-207, 211-216, 218-222, 225-226, 230-233, 236, 239-245, 247-249, 273-274, 275-277, 280-283, 289, 302-303, 306, 309, 317, 389-392, 395, 397, 399, 400, 403, 412, 435-437, 439, 443, 446-447, 454, 463-464, 469, 472, 474, 497, 500; alternative country, 485; Foundation (CMF), 214, 362; musicians, 439; pop, 435; radio shows, 274; rock, 248; style singing, 215
*Country Music, U.S.A.*, 25
Country Playboys, 214
*Courir du Mardi Gras*, 154-55, 173
courtship, 49, 64, 91, 96, 141, 166
Courville, Chris "Oscar," 495, 497
Courville, Sady, 198, 211, 305, 365, 375
Cow Island, 280
Cowboy Mouth, 477, 484
cowboys, 280, 352, 363, 438
Cowley, John H., 5
Cowsill, Susan, 484
Crader, Julian "Bee," 357-359
crawfish, 269
Crawford, Vincent, 387, 396, 401-403, 419
Credence Clearwater Revivals, 396
Creoles, 3-4, 13, 18, 21, 23, 39, 43, 56, 60, 63-64, 79, 111, 113, 115-120, 124, 126, 130-131, 134, 153, 157, 168, 170-171, 201, 209, 211, 217, 221, 224, 226, 301, 303-304, 307, 309, 311-312, 375; black Creoles (see also African American influences on Cajun music), 4, 73, 93, 97-105, 109, 111, 113, 198, 201, 234, 251-252, 256, 264, 291-300, 306, 309, 311-312; fiddlers, 307, 469; French lessons, 105; French-speaking artists, 240; *gens de couleur libre*, 4; in Houston, 117; in Los Angeles, 117; Mardi Gras, 153, 170-171; music, 4, 113-114, 301, 304, 390; white, 4, 180
creolization, 93
Crochet, Cleveland, 224
Croker, Glen, 396, 403
Crowley, LA, 39, 42, 240-241, 243, 244-246, 253, 277, 279, 280, 282, 284, 287-289, 297, 301, 310, 321, 325, 331-332, 342, 345, 358, 384, 385, 387, 393, 416, 440, 471; Aces, 310; Rice Festival, 223
"Cry, Cry, Darling," 274, 435-436
Cuba, 56, 262
cultural, activists, 20-23, 265, 453, 489; assimilation, 97; preservation, 179, 182; renaissance, 216
Cut Off, LA, 443-444, 449

Daigle, Paul, 219, 307, 310
Daigle, Pierre Varmon, 219
Daigrepont, Bruce, 215, 224, 309-10
Dale and Grace, 203, 291
Dallas, TX, 230, 233-235, 240, 328, 386, 408, 426
dance (see also *bals de maison*; dancehalls), 9, 12-13, 16-17, 19, 26, 31-32, 35, 37, 41, 43, 57-58, 65, 68, 72, 77-79, 98, 103, 115-118, 120-127, 130-137, 140-151, 204, 240, 246, 251-252, 256-264, 292, 321-323, 330-331, 332, 333, 336-337, 351, 357, 361, 363-371, 374-377, 383-384, 389, 396-397, 412-414, 428, 487; *bal de noce*, 364, 365; Cajun jitterbug, 122; contradance, 368, 370, 375; dance music, 3, 4, 5, 308, 351, 363, 368; dance of the four corners of the handkerchief, 36; dancer-tourists, 119; dancing in California, 120; detailed description of a *bal de maison*, 141; *fais do-do*, 35, 39, 46, 142, 146, 253, 282, 286, 329, 309, 333, 337, 363, 364-365; formal dance competitions, 123; four corners of a handkerchief, 374; French, 310; gallops, 363, 366, 368, 369, 376; house-dance bands, 305; house dances, 108, 113, 128, 140-144, 146-151, 200, 456, 409; 115, 339, 340, 352, 353, 359; jigs, 364, 367, 374; lessons, 184; line dances, 122-125; music and courtship, 91; social context of, 124; street dances, 142; styles, 123; Sunday, 94; tap dancing, 374; troupes, 123, 184; two step dancing, 93, 98, 121-125, 132, 252, 256, 264, 400; waltzes, 98, 121-122, 125, 201, 219, 222, 256, 361, 365-368, 370, 372, 374-375, 384; wedding dances, 145, 364; wedding marches, 413

# Index

dancehalls, 5, 16, 19, 22, 31-32, 77-80, 88-89, 91, 93, 95, 99, 114-115, 117, 119, 130, 136, 139-140, 142-148, 150-151, 290, 306, 310, 312, 330, 341, 344, 353, 356, 364-365, 370, 391, 399, 400, 425, 427-429, 431-432, 464, 467, 469, 487, 495; combination dancehalls/restaurants, 150; country, 400; cover charges, 144, 147, 148; description of dancehall interior, 148; Ville Platte, LA, 360

dancers 35, 37, 41, 45, 58, 90-95, 104, 115, 117, 118, 120-25, 127, 130, 131, 133-37, 139-40, 142-43, 146-47, 149, 150-51, 154, 158, 163, 166, 168, 193, 198, 240, 258, 261, 262-64, 306, 308, 323, 325, 327, 329, 333, 340, 348, 350, 353, 358, 360, 363, 364, 366-68, 370-76, 379, 394, 381, 382, 387, 389, 400, 402, 403, 409, 413, 431, 443, 454, 459, 478, 498,

*Dans La Louisianne*, 444, 447-448
"Danser Colinda," 251, 257, 262, 264
Darbone, Luderin, 213, 237, 244, 389, 391, 393-397, 399-405, 439, 469
daughters, eldest, in Mardi Gras songs, 160, 162-163, 165-166, 168
Davis, Jimmie, 230-231, 233, 235, 238, 240, 248, 251, 253, 264, 273, 276, 414
Davis, Link, 238
Daylight Creepers, 280
Decca record company (see also Cajun swing), 235, 238, 240, 275, 385, 386, 394, 436-437, 444
deejays, 281
Deep Water, 396
Delcambre, LA, 240, 381-382
Delmore Brothers, 236
DeLuxe record company, 414
Denham Springs, LA, 490
Depression Era, 12, 14, 234-235, 266, 381, 389-390, 409, 471
desegregation, 286
Dietlein, Frank, 341, 383
"Diggy Liggy Lo," 274, 275
disc jockeys, 281
Disco, 309, 478
discount labels, 360
Dixie Ramblers, 217-218, 235, 309
dobro guitar, 210, 437, 445
Doctor John, 292-293
Dole, Gérard, 25, 249
Domengeaux, James, 20, 265, 271, 303, 462
Domengeaux, Jimmy (see also Council for the Development of French in Louisiana), 271, 303-304, 306, 311, 462-463, 491-492
Domino, Antoine "Fats," 203, 248, 277, 317, 414
Dot record company, 274, 436

Doucet Brothers, 211
Doucet, Camey, 310, 416
Doucet, Daly J. "Cat," 341
Doucet, David, 474
Doucet, Matthew "The Deuce," 497
Doucet, Michael, 13, 20, 26, 207, 209-211, 216-219, 222-223, 307, 310, 395-396, 459, 461, 463, 467-472, 474, 482, 500
Doucet, Oscar "Slim," 384
Doucet, Sharon Arms, 310
"Down and Out at the Twist and Shout," 474
Drifting Cowboys (see also Hank Williams), 206
drummers, 202, 209, 331, 353, 385-387, 396, 435, 438, 461, 491
drums, 114, 209-210, 221-222, 308, 311, 331, 336, 353, 386, 387, 399, 402-403, 405, 417, 454, 478, 481, 484, 495-496; foot cymbals, 386; snare drums, 386; trap sets, 273
Dugas, Kevin, 491
Duhon, Bessyl, 202, 208, 211, 275, 308, 435, 469-470
Duhon, Edwin, 389-391, 395, 397, 399, 402-403, 405
Duhon, Hector, 99, 217-218, 309
Duke, David, 479
Dunn, Bob, 386
Dupont, LA, 352
Dural, Stanley "Buckwheat Zydeco," 99, 312
Dusenberry, Gene, 450
Duson Playboys, 88
Duson, LA, 332
Dylan, Bob, 216, 455

East Texas, 83, 85, 88, 93-94, 145, 230, 252, 297, 379, 426
education, 179-181, 183
Egg Bend, LA, 352
El Cerrito, CA (see also Arhoolie record company), 137, 226
Elkins, Robert, 219
Elks Club, 89
Ellender, Alvin, 399
Elton, LA, 168, 497
EMI record company, 471
England, 160-162, 164, 169, 171, 173, 177, 288, 292, 299
English, and French lyrics, 223; ballads, 363; companies, 433; English-speaking Americans, 84, 223; language, 389; material, 213; record collectors, 232; records, 412; songs, 393
*Entre l'amour et l'avenir*, 494
Ethnic Music on Records series, 24
ethnographers, 20, 23, 471

# Index

Eunice, LA, 10, 18, 24, 80, 88, 97, 102, 199, 215, 218, 223, 235, 249, 293, 294, 296, 312, 384, 403, 424, 453, 484, 490, 500
European, dance types, 368; instruments, 107; waltzes, 363
Evangeline Parish, 18, 19, 22, 339, 453
Evangeline Playboys, 201
Evangeline, LA, 49, 88, 181, 293, 339, 340, 344, 391
Everly Brothers, 440
Excello, 280, 286, 288-289, 297

Fais Do Do record company, see, Miller, J.D.
*fais-do-do* (dances), see dance
Falcon, Cléoma Breaux, 80, 197-98, 220, 234-235, 273, 310, 317, 323-24, 330, 332-36, 393
Falcon, Joe, 14, 21, 24, 49, 80, 234, 246, 256, 273, 280, 309, 311, 317, 321, 330, 334, 336-337, 342, 344, 347-348, 350, 359, 381, 383, 385
Falcon, Theresa, 336
False River, LA, 239
Fame releases, 285, 287
*famille en ronde*, 370
Farque, Johnny, 396, 403, 405
Faulk, Johnny, 396, 403, 405
Feature record company (see also Miller, J.D.), 277, 282, 286, 358
Fernice, "Man," 202
Ferriday, LA, 248
Ferrier, Al, 244-45, 248
festivals, 13, 16, 20-21, 32, 58, 59, 73, 79-80, 97, 100, 102, 105, 115, 117-20, 130, 132, 142, 151, 182, 183, 185-87, 197, 204, 218, 271, 298, 301, 303-06, 309-12, 397, 403, 426, 456-57, 459, 462, 463, 474; Festival de Musique Acadienne, 222, 312; Festival International de Louisiane, 100, 404; Festival of American Folklife, 309; *Festivals Acadiens*, 21, 100, 102, 120, 459, 481-482, 485, 498
*Feufollet, La Bande*, 492
fiddles, 3, 13, 16, 19, 21-23, 31, 35, 41, 68, 80, 85, 88-89, 108-09, 112-14, 125-126, 141, 143, 149, 185-186, 198, 201-23, 231, 234-36, 238, 240, 246, 253, 273-77, 281, 294, 311-12, 327-328, 335-336, 339, 348-69, 372-77, 380-381, 383-384, 386, 387, 390-91, 394-395, 399-405, 411-412, 417, 419, 425-27, 439, 445, 451, 453-454, 467-71, 474-77, 479, 484, 489-91, 495-97; cigar-box, 453; fiddle styles, 218.; twin fiddlers, 305
field work and field recordings, 9, 10, 14, 17-18, 23-24, 42, 48, 204, 216-18, 222, 234, 238-240, 302, 383, 456; technology, 40

first, Cajun recording, 234; Cajun swing records, 426; recordings to feature a Cajun fiddler, 383; Tribute to Cajun Music festival, 101, 217, 481
flat-picking, 209, 211
Floyd's Record Shop, 280, 283, 289
Flying Fish record label
Flyright, 240, 244-245, 248, 288
Fogerty, John, 277, 280
Folk Artists in the Schools project, 307
Folk Arts Advisory Panel, 453
Folk Star, 423,
folk, arts, 216; cultural activists, 456; culture, 12; dances, 47; festival circuit, 205, 225, 306; literature, 15; music, 3, 9, 12, 14, 16, 197, 211, 224, 229, 230-232, 236, 239-246, 249, 459, 489, 495; revival, 129; rock, 469; tradition, 391
folklife, 133
folklorists, 12-13, 15, 21, 23, 31, 53, 56-59, 63-64, 72, 182, 216, 227, 229, 303, 347, 468, 489, 491
*Folksongs of the Louisiana Acadians*, 216
folksongs, 4, 11, 12, 15, 18, 31, 35, 37, 42, 43, 44, 46, 47, 49, 55, 57, 59, 64, 68, 74, 85, 93, 310, 321, 326
folktales, 23, 480
Fontenot, Freeman, 99
Fontenot, Hadley, 204, 214
Fontenot, Isom, 216
Fontenot, Kevin S., 26
Fontenot, Merlin, 201, 218-219
Ford, Tennessee Ernie, 281, 468
Foreman, Louis, 431
Foret, L.J., 215
Forrestier, Blackie, and his Cajun Aces, 204, 206, 306
Fort Worth, TX, 500
Fossé, George, 468
Four Aces, 213, 280, 385-386
"Four Roses," 431
France, 31, 43, 44, 47, 48, 55, 56, 58, 59, 60, 63, 64, 65, 66, 67, 68, 71, 72, 75, 83, 84, 139, 140, 153, 154, 155, 156, 157, 166, 172, 174, 208, 210, 211, 212, 301-302, 305, 308, 333, 351, 354, 356, 371, 459, 461, 463-464, 469; medieval, 71
Francophones, 11-13, 17, 19, 20-22, 24-25, 97, 179, 180-181, 187, 461, 468, 488-489, 493
Fred's Lounge, 373, 490
French (see also language; linguistic), vii, viii, 3, 4, 9, 10, 11, 12, 14, 15, 17, 18, 19, 20, 21, 22, 23, 24, 25, 27, 32, 35, 37, 38, 39, 42, 43, 44, 45, 46, 47, 48, 49, 50, 53, 55, 56, 57, 58, 59, 60, 61, 62, 63, 64, 65, 66, 67, 68, 69, 71, 72, 73, 74, 75, 77, 80, 83, 84, 85, 87,

# Index

88, 89, 90, 92, 93, 94, 95, 97, 98, 101, 103, 116, 117, 118, 119, 120, 121, 123, 124, 125, 126, 127, 129, 130, 131, 133, 134, 135, 137, 153, 154, 155, 156, 157, 158, 159, 163, 165, 166, 171, 172, 173, 174, 175, 176, 179, 180, 181, 182, 183, 186, 187, 201, 202, 203, 206, 208, 209, 212, 213, 214, 216, 217, 218, 220, 222, 223, 225, 234, 235, 237, 238, 239, 240, 245, 249, 251, 252, 253, 254, 255, 257, 258, 260, 262, 263, 264, 265, 266, 270, 273, 274, 275, 276, 277, 279, 281, 283, 284, 286, 301, 302, 303, 304, 306, 308, 310, 311, 312, 318, 321, 326, 327, 332, 333, 334, 335, 336, 340, 344, 351, 356, 357, 362, 365, 366, 371, 379, 389, 390, 392, 393, 399, 415, 416, 417, 419, 425, 426, 436, 447, 449, 452, 454, 459, 461, 462, 463, 464, 465, 466, 467, 468, 469, 470, 471, 472, 475, 479, 480, 483, 485, 487, 488, 489, 492, 49 Canadians, 3, 153-154, 163, 166, 172-174, 308; Creoles, 73; folk mores, 68; heritage, 98; immersion programs, 184, 492; in Cajun songs, 44; in the schools, 270; islands in the Caribbean, 73; language programs, 249; language radio, 495; Louisiana, 179, 181-182, 480, 487; lyrics, 251-252, 255; Mardi Gras songs, 172; mazurkas, 377; music, 116-117, 121, 126, 130, 133, 135, 137, 423; patois, 274, 419; program, 497; records, 283, 379; Renaissance, 20, 22, 462, 467, 487, 489, 491-492, 500; separatist movement in Quebec, 459; songs, 14, 38, 223; speakers, 165; traditions, 72; traits, 60; variants of folk songs, 67, 68, 69, 70, 71
*Frères Michot*, 495, 497
Frishberg, Jono, 209
Frizzell, Lefty, 276, 417, 439, 447, 451
frolics, 363-65
*frottoir*, 100, 226
Frugé, Ernest, 198
Frugé, Wade, 210
Fusilier, J.B., 199, 213, 424, 454

**G**ambling, 68, 119, 143-144, 148; rooms, 143
Gaspard, Alcide "Blind Uncle," 6, 351-56
Gennett, 384
Gentry, Jim, 402
German Americans, 111
German Cove, 321
Germans, 108, 110-111, 114; Jewish merchants, 110
Germany, 108, 111-112, 365
girls, 67, 69-72, 365, 367-368, 370-371, 374-375
Girolla, LeRoy, 402
Gladu, André, 470

Gold Star record company, 89, 411, 419
Goldband record company, 243-244, 248, 412, 423
Golden Meadow, LA, 451
Golden Triangle region of Texas, 13
Golden, Will, 484
Gonzales, Roy, 235, 355-356, 384, 386-387
Goodman, Benny, 392
gospel music, 232-235, 238, 239, 241
Goudeau, Guy, 353-354
Graffagnino, Jake, 279
Grammy Awards, 211, 224, 290, 396, 467, 472, 474
"Gran Texas," 276
*Grand Dérangement*, 55, 77, 390, 470
Grand Isle, LA, 446
"Grand Mamou," 158, 168-174
*Grand Marais*, 153, 158-159, 161-163, 165-168, 176
Grand Ole Opry, 236, 247, 274-275, 397, 411, 413, 416, 435-437, 439, 444, 447-448
Grand Prairie, LA, 280
*Grand Texas*, 85
Grant Street Dance Hall, 459, 466, 479
Grappelli, Stephane, 395
Grateful Dead, 461, 467, 496
Great Depression, 233, 357, 360-361, 392
Greely, David, 223, 311, 489, 490, 491, 494
Gueydan, LA, 331, 348, 349, 350
Guidry, Oran "Doc," 202, 210, 238, 251, 253-255, 277, 282, 412, 414, 415, 431, 445, 451, 469
*guignolée*, 153, 155-156, 165- 167, 171-174
Guilbeau, Gib, 248
Guillory, Chuck, 274, 276, 282
Guillory, Delin, 351-352, 359-362
Guinea, 260-263
Guitar, Jr., 244
guitars, 16, 18, 31, 80, 109, 114, 185-186, 202, 207, 209, 211, 213, 215, 218, 219, 221-223, 231, 238-240, 243, 273, 280, 311, 330, 335-337, 349, 351-356, 358, 366, 381, 385-387, 390-392, 399-403, 405, 409, 411-412, 426, 428, 435, 439-440, 443, 445, 461, 468, 474, 477-479, 480-481, 484, 491, 495-496, 497; bassists, 412; electric, 387, 395-396, 399, 417; electric blues, 495; electric lead, 222; electric rhythm, 202; electric steel, 273; electric, 308; lap-steel, 484, 495; lead guitar, 353, 399, 402-403, 405; rhythm, 353, 387, 396, 399, 402-403, 405; steel guitars, 114, 186, 202, 207, 210, 221, 238, 288, 294, 387, 396, 402-403, 419, 428, 435, 443, 445-46, 454; tenor guitars, 385
gumbo, 141-142, 149, 158-159, 169, 170-171, 173-175

# INDEX

Hackberry Ramblers, ix, 27, 193, 199, 213, 235, 237, 243, 246, 327, 385, 389, 390-392, 395-397, 399-405, 423, 426, 481, 500
Hackberry, LA, 389-393, 395-397, 399-403
Hadacol, 282
Haggard, Merle, 396
Haiti, 98, 257, 259-260, 262, 263; Haitian Revolution, 157
handkerchiefs, 365, 366, 370, 371, 376
Hank and Audrey's Corral, 443, 448
*haricots sont pas salé*, 103
harmonicas, 19, 361, 392, 399, 495
Harpo, Slim, 286, 440
Harrington, Roy, 307
Harris, Emmylou, 394
Hawaiian, 333; novelty numbers, 392
Hawkins, Dale, 247
Heard, Grover, 395, 402
heavy metal music, 481
Hebert, Adam, 214
Hebert, Didier, 381
Hebert, Kyle, 491
Helms, Don, 206
Henderson, W.K., 229-231
Hendrix, Jimi, 484
heritage, 116, 121-122, 126, 128-137
Hernandez, Gary, 496
Hickory record company, 244
"High Society," 393
High-Up, 279
hillbilly music (see also country music), 59, 229, 230, 231, 232, 233, 234, 235, 236, 240, 241, 244, 245, 247, 249, 282, 386, 387, 391, 400, 416, 419, 425, 426, 443, 444, 445, 446.
Hillbilly Swing Kings, 443
hippies, 468, 488, 496
Hit of the Week, 408
Hoffpauir family, 240
Hohner, 110, 112
Holly Beach, LA, 470
Hollywood Club, 411
home music, 24, 77, 78, 79
"Home Sweet Home," 413
*Hommage à la musique acadienne*, 21, 24, 212, 301, 303, 304, 308, 309, 311, 457, 462
honky tonks, 273, 274, 276, 317, 425, 439, 443, 459, 470, 479
Horton, Johnny, 247, 274, 449
Houma, LA, 182, 183, 185, 188
house dances, see dances
house parties, see dances
Houston, Dale, see Miller, J.D.
Houston, TX, 89, 91, 92, 93, 238, 243, 245, 246, 247, 279, 282, 286, 411, 417, 419, 423, 439
Howling Wolf, 496

Huddie Ledbetter, 239
Long, Huey P., 280, 390
Hulin, T.K., 293
humor, 266, 267, 268, 270, 271; humorists, 265, 266, 267
humor, working-class, 267
Hurt, Mississippi John 456
Huval, Terry, 221, 224, 310, 396

Iberia Parish, 293
illiteracy, 110
Imperial record company, 414
improvisation, 197, 199, 496
independent, producers, 246; record companies, 242; record men, 419
Indians, 373, 377
industrialization, 389
instrumental rides, 454
instrumentation, 125, 126
interaction, between white and black musicians, 109; blurred lines between Cajun and zydeco, 126
International Rice Festival 325
interracial bandmemberships, 118
Iota, LA, 280
Irish, 363, 371, 465
Island record company, 479, 480, 482, 484
isolation, 18, 47, 57, 361, 389
"It Wasn't God Who Made Honky-Tonk Angels," 277, 283

Jackson, Tommy, 444, 447
"J'ai été au bal," 222
jam sessions, 115, 130, 185, 283, 387, 412, 414, 415, 440, 484, 490, 495, 496
"Jambalaya (On The Bayou)," 276
Jambalaya, 220, 221, 224, 276, 277, 396, 478; translation of, 220
Jano, Johnny, 248
Jardell, Robert, 224, 307, 310, 458
Jayhawkers, 157
Jazz and Heritage Foundation, 217
jazz, 18, 49, 93, 99, 105, 193, 208, 232, 234, 235, 248, 285, 292, 308, 391, 392, 393, 463, 468, 469, 471, 487; records, 232
Jenkins, Ike, 393
Jennings, LA, 342, 343
Jews, merchants, 110, 465
JIN record company 246, 248, 280, 284-285, 288, 297-98
Jocque, Beau, 100
*John Edwards Memorial Foundation Quarterly*, 5, 25, 10
"Johnny Can't Dance," 207, 209

Johnson, Bunk, 210
Johnson, Robert, 443
jokes, 265, 268-269
"Jolie Blonde" (also rendered Jole Blon, Jole Blond, Jole Blonde, Joli Blon, Joli Blonde, Jolie Blond, Jolie Blonde), 35, 43, 44, 88-89, 193, 200, 214-215, 220, 273, 276, 282, 313, 325, 353, 393, 395, 397, 401-402, 408, 411, 413, 419-420, 437, 439, 451, 468, 478
Jolly Boys, 213
Jones, Billie Jean, 444, 448
Jones, George, 247, 248, 274, 439-440
*Journal of American Folklore*, 10, 18, 21, 24
*Jours Gras*, 156
JSP record company, 6
Judice, LA, 310
jukeboxes, 283, 423, 493
*juré*, 4, 12, 98, 239, 390

Kahn, Mervine, 110
Kajun Classics record company, see, Miller, J.D.
Kajun record company, 286
Kajun Rocket record company, see, Miller, J.D.
KALB (Alexandria), 241
Kaplan, LA, 79, 244, 276, 348, 349, 350, 412
Kershaw, Doug, 88, 215, 245, 248, 275, 277, 455
Kershaw, Rusty, 88, 215, 245, 248, 275, 455
KEUN radio station, 102, 249, 453
keyboards, 222
KFDM, 400
Khoury, George, 287, 297, 298, 428
Kincel, Frank, 484
King record company, 414
KLFT (Lafayette), 451
KLFY (Lafayette), 202, 417, 431
KMLB (Monroe), 241
"Kolinda," 210
Kom-a-day record company, 286
KPLC (Lake Charles), 241, 243, 387, 410, 423, 428
Krazy Kats, 428
KRVS (Lafayette), 497
KSIG (Crowley), 241
KSIG (Jennings), 416
KSLO (Opelousas), 253
KVOL (Lafayette), 241, 387, 401, 412
KVPI (Ville Platte), 281, 283, 459
KWKH (Shreveport), 229, 230, 231, 235, 241, 242, 247, 273, 274, 277, 387

Lacassine, LA, 159, 163, 423, 424
"Lâche Pas la Patate," 22, 275, 437, 440
Lachney, Delma, 351, 352-354, 356-357
Lafayette Parish, 162, 167; School Board, 184

Lafayette Playboys, 88, 202, 204, 431, 432
Lafayette, LA, 3-4, 9, 11, 13, 19, 20-21, 23-25, 86, 88, 93, 95, 100, 103-105, 120, 129, 139, 142, 149, 150, 179, 181-182, 184-185, 188, 197, 202, 204, 207, 209, 212, 217, 219, 222, 224, 238-239, 241, 243, 245, 248, 279, 286, 293-294, 297, 300-304, 308, 310, 312, 322, 334, 342, 347, 360, 373, 381, 383, 387, 399, 401, 403, 411, 412, 416, 417, 418, 435, 451, 459, 460, 461, 462, 468-469, 470-473, 475, 477-479, 482-484, 496-498; Girard Park 309, 459; nightclub, 308; radio stations, 401
LaFleur, Alan, 495, 497
LaFleur, Lewis, 359, 360, 361, 362
LaFleur, Mayuse (also rendered Maius), 198, 222, 325, 339-453, 383
LaFleur, Steve, 225
Lafourche, 47, 55
Laird, Tracey E.W., 5
"Laissez les bon temps roulez," 97
Lake Arthur, LA, 16, 239, 328, 357, 358, 359
Lake Charles, LA, 182, 188, 241, 243, 279-280, 297, 325, 379, 387, 391, 395, 400, 402, 410-412, 423, 428, 437, 480; Broadcasting Co, 400
la-la music, 4, 98, 103, 113
"Lame Pretender," 479
*L'Amour ou la Folie*, 474
Lamperez, "Papa Cairo," 387, 419, 439
*Lancier Acadien*, 366
Lanciers, 366, 377
Landreneau, Adam, 216
Landreneau, Cyprien, 216, 221
Landreth, Sonny, 210-211, 213, 224
Landry, Bill (Dewey), 385
Landry, Lula, 79, 223
language (see also French; linguistic), 57-59, 179-184, 187, 210, 212, 226, 301, 303-304, 306-307, 390, 438, 462, 465, 489, 493-494
Lanor label, 279
Lavergne, Lee, 279
Lawtell, LA, 100, 297
Leadbitter, Michael, 5, 25
LeBlanc, Dudley, 271
LeBlanc, Floyd, 423
LeBlanc, LeRoy "Happy Fats," ix, 26, 202, 213, 251, 253-255, 264, 277, 282, 325, 407, 410, 414, 418, 423, 439, 481
LeBlanc, Shorty, 275
LeBlanc, Steve, 477-478, 484
LeBoeuf, Richard, 310
Ledbetter, Huddy "Leadbelly," 239-240, 248, 392
LeJeune Cove, LA, Cajun Mardi Gras at, 166
LeJeune, 200-201, 204, 206-207, 222

# INDEX

LeJeune, Angelas, 198, 200-201, 211, 344, 365, 373-374
LeJeune, Eddie, 206-207, 310, 379, 381
LeJeune, Iry, 5, 24, 89-90, 199-201, 207, 212, 218-219, 222, 226, 243, 294, 306, 309-310, 344, 361, 381, 387, 390, 412, 416, 423, 424, 454
Leleux, Lionel, 207, 223, 305, 307
Lent, 61, 78, 154, 159, 173
Leo Soileau, ix, 5, 6, 18, 21, 193, 199, 213, 222, 234, 273, 317, 325, 339, 340-344, 383-384, 388, 410-411, 418-419, 423, 425, 454, 474; and the Rhythm Boys, 387
Lester, Lazy, 286
Lewis, Jerry Lee, 203, 248, 478
Liberty Theater, 312, 403
Library of Congress, 217, 239, 240, 381, 453
Light Crust Doughboys, 409, 500
Lightnin' Slim, 286
linguistic, 55-56, 63, 487, 489, 492, 494, discrimination, 215; survival, 212
Logan, Horace, 413
Lomax, Alan, 10, 12, 20-24, 39, 68, 72, 208, 216-17, 381, 427
Lomax, John, 11
Lomax, John and Alan, 12-14, 17, 19, 21, 39-42, 209, 217, 239-240, 246, 302, 471
Lomax, John and Ruby, 239-240
Lonesome Sundown, see, Miller, J.D.
Long, Earl K., 265-267, 271
Longfellow, Henry Wadsworth, 181
Lost Bayou Ramblers, 26, 317, 495-500
Louisiana, 229, 230-235, 237-249, 389-391, 394-396, 399, 400-401, 443, 444, 446, 448, 450, 455; Aces, 205; field recordings, 471; Folk Foundation, 307, 456; Folklife Festival, 10, 396, 403; Folklife Society, 249; Folklore Miscellany, 10, 15, 19; Folklore Society, 246; ; French folk songs, 9-12, 212, 332, 381; French movement, 303; French music, 306, 468; French musicians, 240; French population of, 301, 304; French renaissance movement, 301, 306; French renaissance, 311; French, 163, 166, 180, 181, 464; Hayride, 5, 247-249, 273-274, 276-277, 436, 443, 449; Phonograph Company, 232; recording industry, 280; State University, 9-11, 15-19, 24, 43, 216, 266, 301, 307, 330, 460, 468, 490; Troubadours, 443, 446
*Louisiane Bien Aimée* Bicentennial Exhibition, 308
Louisianne record company, 248, 275, 286, 415, 437, 440
"Love Bridge Waltz" (see also LeJeune, Iry), 361, 423
"Lovesick Blues," 443

Loyola University, 231
"Lu Lu's Back in Town," 273
Lyric record label, 287, 297

"Ma Blonde est parti," 273, 393
Macon, Uncle Dave, 236, 411
Maddox Brothers and Rose, 247
Magnolia Sisters, 500
mail-order catalogs, 110, 280, 288
*Maison de Soul* record company, 246, 280, 286, 288
Maitre, Hubert, 207
Majestic Hotel, 400
Major, Gary, 402
Maloney, John, 481
Mamou Playboys, 223, 311, 487, 488
Mamou, LA, x, 18, 22, 26, 180-181, 198, 214, 216, 223, 225, 244, 249, 274, 283-285, 293, 303, 311, 339-340, 344, 361-362, 436, 453, 456, 487-494; Cajun Music Festival, 307; Mardi Gras wagon, 491
mandolins, 31, 109, 209, 240, 402, 403
Mann, Charles, 279
Mansura, LA, night clubs, 353
Manuel-Dewey Balfa Fiddle Apprenticeship program, 185
Manuel, Joe, 419, 420
Manuel, Kossuth, 343, 344
Manuel, Preston, 218
Marais Bouleur, LA, 39, 40, 46
Marcel-Dubois, Claudie 303
Mardi Gras, 31, 35, 87, 119, 126, 134, 153-181, 212-213, 215, 223; *bal de*, 158, 159; beggars and begging quest, 153-58, 171-173, 175; begging song, 156, 166, 168, 171-75; blackface, 155, 158; Mardi Gras Jig, 431; Mardi Gras song, 153, 157, 159, 168, 171-72, 174, 496
Maritime Provinces, see Canada
Marksville, LA, 352, 353
marriage, 39, 44, 45, 64, 66, 67, 70-75, 92, 96
Martin, Grady, 444, 447
Martin, Leroy, 443, 445, 451
Martinique, 261
Master-Trak Studio, 287, 288
Matassa, Cosimo, studio in New Orleans, 246, 254, 282, 285, 297, 414
Matte, Bill, 279
Matte, Reggie, 218, 221, 310
Mayor of Bayou Pom Pom, 269
mazurka, 364, 366, 367, 369, 375, 376, 377
McBane, 477, 478, 481, 483, 484
McCauley, Cory, 214, 221, 222
McDonald, Bruce, 211, 308, 469
McGee, Dennis, 24, 99, 198-99, 208-11, 223,

# Index

235, 305, 307, 365-68, 371-74, 469
McLain, Tommy, 285
Meaux, Huey P., 286
Meaux, Mark, 477, 484
Meche, Leon, 324
medicine show traditions, 247
Meladee label, 443
Mello Joy Boys, 500
Melotone record company, 235
Memphis Minnie, 392
Memphis, TN, 235, 236, 294, 354
Menard, D.L., 205, 209, 219, 481, 482
Mercury record company, 285, 287
Mermentau, LA, 413
Merryville, LA, 239
MGM record company, 274, 285, 436, 444
Mi-Carême, 155, 156
"Michié Préval," 257, 258, 261, 263, 264
Michot brothers, 495-497
Michot, André, 495-500
Michot, David "Dav," 496, 497, 500
Michot, Rick, 213
Michot, Tommy, 495
microphones, 394
Midway Club, 431
Miller, J.D., viii, 194, 244, 246, 251, 253, 279, 297, 298, 416
Miller, Rodney, 431
Minnie Pearl, 448
minority market, 383
minstrel, 247
Mire, Norris, 328
Mississippi River, 108, 140, 141, 238
Mississippi Sheiks, 233, 236, 238
Mississippi Valley, 156, 157, 165, 166, 172
Mississippi, 363, 451
Modern Music Record Shop and Music Store, 288
Modern, 420
Molitor, Milton, 283
Monarch brand (see also accordion), 112, 348, 361
Monroe, Bill, 241, 247
Montalbano, 287
Montana, Patsy, 247
Montel, 287
Montgomery Ward, 352, 394, 401, 500
Montoucet, Don, 91, 305, 310
Montreal, Canada, 464
moonshine, 317, 341-42, 379,
Moreau, Jules, 351, 353, 354
Morgan, Elemore, 90
Morning Star record company, 388
Morse Playboys, 207
Morse, LA, 359
Morton, Ferdinand "Jelly Roll," 392

motion pictures, 49
Mouton, Blake, 310
Mouton, Shine, 307
Mouton, Todd, 474
Mouton, Walter, 210, 222, 223, 310; and the Scott Playboys, 210
movies, 18
Mowata, LA, 376
MSL, 286
MTV, 397
Muddy Waters, 496
Mulate's Cajun Restaurant, 132, 309, 472, 490
Mullican, Moon, 89, 238, 248, 273, 277, 386, 395, 411
Muscle Shoals, AL, studios 285
music, 154, 159, 273-276, 278, 363, 366, 368, 372, 431-432, 487-491, 493, 494; business, 281, 289; commercial, 473; fusion of Afro-American and French elements, 57, 60, 73; hillbilly, 53; in a family context, 91; in a family setting, 80; music-oriented businesses, 289; musical borrowing and exchange, 273; recordings, 193, 217, 232; stores, 289, 408; styles, 482
Musical Aces, 203-204
Musical Brownies, see Brown, Milton
"My Toot Toot," 290

Naquin, Edius, 216
Naquin, Kevin, and the Ossun Playboys, 492
Nashville, TN, 215, 231-232, 235-236, 244-245, 280, 283, 286, 288-289, 306, 391, 403, 408, 411, 435-436, 439, 443, 446-448, 452, 455, 469, 472, 497, 500; Excello label, 280
Natchitoches, LA, 241, 243-244, 354, 356, 408
National Association for the Advancement of Colored People (NAACP), 105, 416
National Council for the Traditional Arts, 453
National Endowment for the Arts, 303, 307, 397, 453, 457; fieldworkers, 303; programs, 216
National Endowment for the Humanities, Folk Arts Program, 469; youth grants, 217
National Folk Festival, 13, 16, 113, 328, 426, 429
National Heritage Fellowship, 216, 397
Native Americans, 251
Nederland, TX, 86
New Brunswick, 157, 307, 461
New Deal, sponsored parade and concert in downtown Abbeville during the Great Depression, 350
New Iberia, LA, 35, 182, 188, 239, 240, 241, 325, 419
New Orleans, LA, 3-4, 56, 60, 73, 87, 93, 108, 111-112, 182, 185, 188, 212-213, 217, 229-

236, 238-249, 251, 254, 257-259, 263, 264, 279, 281-282, 285, 291-294, 296-298, 306, 309, 324-325, 349-350, 353-354, 357-360, 379-381, 384, 386, 392-393, 396, 401, 403-404, 407-408, 414, 440, 443-451, 477, 484, 497-498; Congo Square, 60, 257, 259; jazz, 238, 392; Jazz and Heritage Festival, 306, 407; Werlein's of, 408
New York City, 328, 336, 383, 385, 391, 396, 404, 467, 472, 478, 487
Newcomers Festival, 185
Newman, Gary, 275, 308
Newman, Jimmy C., ix, 194, 244, 247, 274, 276, 278, 306, 308, 317, 318, 403, 416, 435-40, 455, 469
Newport Folk Festival, 20, 204, 216-17, 246, 302, 303, 307, 417, 455, 456-57; Festival of 1964, 491
nightclub, 280, 283, 296, 297, 298, 299, 387, 495
Northwestern State University, Music Festival, 403
Nova Scotia, 55, 58, 77, 91, 157, 208, 307

O.S.T Club, 413, 428, 431
Oberlin, LA, 78
Oberstein, Eli, 236, 394, 408
oil industry, 13, 31, 39, 93, 94, 144, 179, 181, 182, 273, 389, 400, 417; oil fields, 86, 390, 391, 399, 402
Okeh record company, 232, 383
Oklahoma, 390, 419
Oklahoma Tornadoes Band, 200
*Old Time Music*, 5, 10, 25
Old Timey record company, 255, 256, 383, 384, 411
Oliver, King, 393
one-steps, 366
Opelousas, LA, 100-111, 201, 215, 248, 253, 279, 291, 293, 296-297, 305, 341, 351, 354-356, 362, 373, 383-384, 455
Opera record label, 423
Opry, 274, 277, 435, 437-438, 447-448
Orange, TX, 13, 348, 387, 426
orchestras (see also jazz), 399
Oster, Harry, 5, 9, 17-19, 21, 23, 59-60, 216, 246, 249, 302, 469, 471, 488
*Our Singing Country*, 10, 12
Owens, Bill, 302

P T's (or Petit's) Cajun Bar-B-Q House, 92, 93
Page, Bobby, 203
"Paper in My Shoe," 244
Paramount record company, 234, 355, 383, 384

*parc aux petits* (see also dance; bals de maison; fais do do; dancehalls), 142, 143, 144, 147, 151
Paris, France, 211, 302, 308, 470
Pathé-Marconi record company, 308
Peer, Ralph, 235
pentatonic scale, 63
percussion, 209
Perry, Wayne, 240, 471
Peter, Paul, and Mary, 456
Petitjean, Dave, 268, 286
Petitjean, Irene, 11
Phillips, Phil, 287
phonographs, 18, 47-49, 79, 274, 281, 344, 348, 354
pianists, 238, 245
pianos, 208, 215, 232, 238, 248, 387, 399, 402, 449, 461
Pierce, Webb, 247, 274, 283, 394, 449
"Pine Grove Blues," 201
Pine Grove Boys, 306
Pitre, Austin, 201, 216, 282-83
Plaisance, LA, 105
Playboys, 487-492, 494
polkas, 363-364, 366-367, 369, 376, 386
pop music, 274, 281, 284, 386, 454, 469, 475
Port Arthur, TX, 13, 86, 89, 92-95, 273, 379, 387, 481
"Porte d'en arrière" (see Menard, D.L., The Back Door), 205
Post, Lauren C., 5, 9, 15, 17, 19, 146, 154, 162, 163-165, 167, 174, 255, 321, 332, 337, 363, 365-366, 426
Poullard, Danny, 117, 126, 312
Prairie du Rocher, IL, 153, 165, 167, 171
Prairie Home Companion, 225, 487
Prairie Ronde, LA, 354, 356
Préjean's Restaurant, 309
Presley, Elvis, 243-244, 247-248, 274, 317, 451, 467-468
Price, Ray, 444, 451
priests, 139-140
Prix Dehors, 186
professionalization of Cajun music, 193
prohibition (see also moonshine), 40
Prudhomme, Paul, 267
Puckett, Riley, 276
Puderer, Johnny, 401
punk rock, 477, 481-482, 485

Q uadrilles, 353
Québec City, Canada, 14, 352, 471
Québec Province, 14, 20, 22, 55, 64, 66, 139, 156-157, 163-166, 172, 208, 212, 224, 275, 307, 308, 437, 461
Quebedeaux, Gervis, 218

Queen Ida, 117-118, 121, 312; and the Bon Temps Band, 103
Quinn, Bill, 411, 419

R & B-influences, 212
race, racial and gender inversion, 158; race recordings, 234; divide, 469; tensions, 105
Raceland, LA, 447
Rachou, Carol (see also Record Men), 246, 286, 298, 304, 416, 451
radio, viii, 10, 12, 18, 22, 27, 47, 49, 53, 79, 94, 102, 105, 181, 184, 193, 194, 209-210, 213, 221, 225, 229-235, 240, 241, 242, 243, 247, 249, 253, 254, 274, 280, 281, 312, 317, 340, 368, 390, 391, 397, 400, 403, 407, 408, 410-413, 416, 428, 438, 443, 445-446, 452, 459, 468, 487; programs, 394; shows, 407; stations, 184, 281, 381, 445
railroads, 265
Rainwater, Floyd, 392, 394, 400, 401
Randol's Restaurant, 309
Rayne, LA, 11, 16, 88, 110, 273, 321-322, 327-328, 348, 357, 383, 407-409, 411, 413, 418, 426, 429
Rayne-Bo Ramblers, 213, 407, 408, 410, 418, 426
RCA record company, 233-236, 238, 284, 341-342, 344, 360, 383-384, 391-392, 394, 401, 408, 411; Bluebird subsidiary, 235, 392; label, 391, 408; Victor, 401, 408
Rebel label, 286, 407
Rebennack, Mac, see Doctor John
records, 10, 12, 14, 16, 18, 19, 27, 40, 42, 197, 204, 205, 207, 210, 212, 217, 218, 219, 220, 222, 226, 231, 232, 233, 234, 235, 236, 238, 239, 240, 242, 244, 246, 248, 267, 279, 281, 283, 284, 285, 287, 288, 289, 321, 324, 325, 327, 331, 341, 342, 344, 347, 348, 349, 350, 351, 353, 354, 355, 357, 358, 360, 361, 383, 384, 387, 392, 393, 394, 395, 397, 401, 403, 407, 408, 411, 414, 416, 417, 426, 428, 443, 449, 451, 452, 464, 479, 480; companies, 186, 232, 233, 234, 239, 242, 248, 281, 283, 347, 351, 360, 383; gold, 289, 416; platinum records, 289; record-making and selling, 387; reissued, 5; sales, 281, 347, 348, 357; shops, 281, 282, 285
Red Hall, 358
Red Stick Ramblers, 500
Reed, Revon, 18, 20- 22, 194, 214, 221, 249, 456
reeds, 107, 112
reels, 363-364, 366-367, 369, 373-374, 376, 377; à bouche, 78
Reeves, Jim, 247, 274, 439
Reinhart, Django, 276

religion, 57, 64-65, 68; religious songs, 63, 65
restaurants, 309, 312, 472; restaurant/dancehalls, 139, 150-151
"Réveille," 212, 308, 465-466, 470
*Revue de Louisiane* 10, 19, 21
Rhode Island, 456
rhythm and blues, 98-99, 199, 244-245, 248, 279, 291-296, 299, 487
Rhythm Boys, 387, 388
Rice Brothers, 230, 241
Rice City Ramblers, 280
rice, 19
Richard, Allen, 331-332, 337
Richard, Becky, 80, 220-221, 310
Richard, Belton, 203-204, 209, 220, 222, 309, 318, 329, 416, 491
Richard, Dick, 458
Richard, Felix, 90, 212, 307
Richard, Kenneth, 211, 307, 308, 469
Richard, Sterling, 211-212
Richard, Zachary (see also Cajun Renaissance activists), 20, 210-12, 216, 223, 307, 310, 317, 318, 459, 460, 463, 466, 468, 469, 482-83, 490; Fatras band, 95
Richard's Club, 100
Richmond, IN, 234, 384
Ridge, LA, 439
Riley, Kirby, 234
Riley, Steve, 26, 214, 223, 310, 311, 487, 488, 489, 490-492; and the Mamou Playboys, 474, 487, 489, 490-491
Rinzler, Ralph, 20-21, 23, 204, 216, 302-304, 306, 455-458
Rivers, Jerry, 206
Riverside Ramblers, 393, 401Robbins, Marty, 451
Roberts, Neil, 402
Robin, Moïse, 222, 339, 344, 384, 387
rock and roll and rockabilly 54, 203, 204, 207, 209, 212, 222, 225, 245, 242, 244, 247-48, 251, 274-76, 286, 292, 301, 307-10, 317, 395-96, 425, 428, 443-44, 451, 454, 459-64, 469, 475, 477-88, 497
Rocket record label, 286
Rockin' Sidney, 279, 285, 287, 289, 472
Rocko record company, 286
Rodair Club, 89, 92-96
Rodgers, Jimmie, 79, 194, 200, 231, 235, 240, 245, 274, 276, 317, 341, 356, 384, 392, 400, 409, 445
Rodrigue, Gene, 443, 446, 449
Roger, Aldus, 85, 202, 223, 244, 283, 309, 311, 329, 373, 431, 432, 433; and the Lafayette Playboys, 203, 431-432
Rogers, Will, 266
Rolling Stones, 467, 488

# INDEX

Romero, Roddie, 491
Roosevelt Hotel, 444, 450
Rose, Fred, 449
Rounder record company, 21, 312, 489, 490
Rousseau, Jean Jacques, 258
rubboards, 102, 125, 481, 484, 496
Russell, Tony, 5, 25, 230, 233, 234, 235, 238, 240

Sabine River, 83, 86, 91, 94
Sacré, Robert, 25
Saint Landry Parish, 293, 340, 341, 354, 355
Saint Louis, Mo., 498
Saint Martin Parish, 224, 293
Saint Martinville, LA, 16, 56
Saint Mary Parish, 183
Saint-Domingue, 56, 260
Sampy and the Bad Habits, 496
San Antonio, TX, 234, 240, 326
San Francisco, CA, 463, 478; Bay area, 26, 115, 118, 225
Sandmel, Ben, 27
Saucier, Corrine, 9, 14, 23
Savoy, Ann Allen, ix, 10, 20, 22, 24-25, 80, 102, 141, 144, 146-147, 149, 255, 294, 310, 391, 404
Savoy, Marc, 80, 89, 204-205, 207, 215, 223, 305-307, 310-311, 373, 458, 490
Savoy, Rob, 477, 484
Savoy, Wilson, 500
Savoy-Doucet Band, 207
Saxon, Lyle, 60
saxophones, 208, 473
Schwartz, Peter, 226
Schwartz, Tracy, 226, 491
Scott Playboys, 210, 222
Scott, LA, 14, 16, 91, 328, 331, 332, 333, 336, 412, 427, 460, 468
Sears-Roebuck, 280, 394
Seeger, Mike, 216
segregation, 284
Segura, Dewey, 5, 317, 379, 381
Segura, Eddie, 240, 381
Seven Years' War, 157
Sex Pistols, 477
Sexton, Rocky, 18-19, 21, 27
sharecroppers, 359, 361
Shelton Brothers, 230-231, 233, 241
Shelton, Bob and Joe, 230, 235
showboats, 387
Shreve, Danny, 386, 392, 401
Shreve, Floyd, 385-387, 392, 401
Shreve, O.P., 386
Shreveport, LA, 229-230, 233, 239-243, 247, 273, 274, 277; Syrup Company, 412

Shuler, Eddie (see also Lejeune, Iry), 243-244, 248, 297-298, 402, 412, 423; show, 423
Silver Star Club, 387, 395, 399, 402, 410
Simon, Paul, 280, 289
"Sitting on Top of the World," 233
Skynyrd, Lynyrd, 481
slavery, slave weddings, 261; slaves, 56, 60, 64, 66, 72, 73, 98, 257, 261-263
Slim's Y Ki Ki, 100
Smash record company, 285
Smith, Carl, 444, 451
Smith, Ken, 206, 219
Smithsonian Institution, 20, 246, 302, 304, 306, 309, 453; Festival of American Folklife, 132-133, 199, 275, 306; Office of Folklife Programs, 309
Snow, Hank, 201
Society for Ethnomusicology, 132
Soileau, Alius, 384
Soileau, Floyd (see also Swallow Records record company), viii, 194, 204, 246, 279, 281, 284, 289, 297-298, 387, 428, 451
Sonet record company, 244, 248
songs, drinking, 77, 164, 175; French Canadian begging, 153; French drinking, 153; French folksong performed by African Americans, 93
songwriters, 274, 477
Sonnier, Elmore, 328
Sonnier, Joel, 208
Sonnier, Johnny, 220, 310
Sonnier, Lee, 282; and the Acadian Stars, 280
Sonnier, Lennis, 237, 244, 392, 395, 401-403
Sons of the Pioneers, 276, 408
soul, 99, 309, 313
*South to Louisiana*, 25, 254, 291
Southern, Folk Revival Project, 307; humor, 267; market, 385; Pacific Railroad, 358; popular music, 425; Southern Serenader, 445, 451
Southwest Louisiana Zydeco Music Festival, 105
Southwestern Louisiana Institute, 254, 255
Sovine, Red, 247, 450
Spindletop oil field, 86
Spirit of Cajun Music, 471
spirituals, 63-64
Spitzer, Nicholas, 218, 249
spoons, 353, 454
Spottswood, Richard, 24, 205
square dancing, 363, 366, 375, 386
Stafford, Jesse, 472
Stanford, Ron and Fay, 217-218, 303
Starday Records record company, 283
Sterling, 112, 308, 309, 431, 433
Stevenson, Cal, 484
*Stir Up the Roux*, 224

Strachwitz, Chris (see also Arhoolie record company), 102, 222, 225, 234-235, 246, 249, 395, 403
string bands, 88, 213, 233, 235, 294, 295, 361, 400, 426, 443, 454; era, 199, 214, 218, 391, 427; old time country, 474; traditions, 215
studios, 279, 280, 282, 284, 285, 286, 287, 288, 386, 414, 419, 420, 447
Suarez, Roy "Boogie Boy Perkins," 248
sugarcane, 322
Sulphur, LA, 395, 402
Sunset, LA, 293
Swade record company, 286
Swallow Publications, 10
Swallow Records record company, 6, 199, 201-202, 204-205, 208, 211-212, 214-215, 217, 219, 221, 223, 226, 246, 248, 280, 284-285, 288, 312, 416, 418, 444, 471, 495, 498
swamp pop, 3, 5, 25-26, 32, 193, 203, 209, 211, 212, 217, 226, 251, 252, 279, 280, 284-287, 289, 291-300, 317-318, 396, 402, 428, 475, 481
Sweet Lake, 359
swing, 199, 214, 215, 218, 327, 328
syncopation, 49, 98, 123, 202; percussive, 221

Tabby's Blues Box, 495
tafia, 141
talent contests, 280
Tasso, 210, 222
Tate, Paul, 18, 265, 303, Paul, 456
Taylor-Griggs, 230, 231, 235
Tee Mamou, 153, 158, 159, 160, 162, 163, 165, 166, 167, 168, 176
tenant farmers, 99
Tennessee, 215
Terry, Al, 244, 245, 276, 411, 412
Terry, Gene, 244
Texas, 4, 10, 13-14, 16, 31-32, 43, 45-46, 58, 62, 83-89, 91-96, 109, 111-112, 115, 117, 124, 130, 179, 182, 201, 220, 229, 230, 237, 238, 243, 247, 268, 273, 276, 280, 312, 326, 336, 379, 381, 386, 390-391, 408-409, 411, 417, 419, 426, 451, 484, 498; Cajun migration to, 58, 87, 88, 92; southeast, 291, 293, 297-299; Texan-Cajun relationships, 83
Tharp, Al, 474, 490
"The Back Door," 205, 482
The Big Easy, 471, 478
The Makers of Cajun Music, 23, 90, 97, 100, 102, 461, 466
The Music of the Cajun Bayous, 102
"The Old Drunkard and His Wife," 331, 332, 334
The Origins and Development of Cajun Music, 24

The Spirit of Cajun Music, 208, 212
The Story of Cajuns and Their Music, 22
"The Waltz That Carried Me to My Grave," 325
Theriot, Jack, 402
Theriot's Lounge, 451
Thibodeaux, Ambrose, 218, 344, 411, 417
Thibodeaux, Gladdy, 204
Thibodeaux, Gladius, 455
Thibodeaux, Rufus, 201, 219, 275, 318, 435, 437, 439, 440
Thibodeaux, Tony, 431
"This Should Go on Forever," 284
Thompson, Suzy and Eric, 226
Three Aces, 385
Tin Pan Alley, 59, 230
Tipitina's, 477
Tisserand, Michael, 27, 108-109, 113, 116, 124-125
Tit Mamou, 361
Tit Maurice, 413, 431
TNT record company, 423
toasts, 166, 167
Toronto Jazz Festival, 487
Toups, Wayne, 90, 95, 222, 224, 287, 307, 310, 481, 483, 487
tourism, 115-116, 120-121, 129, 132-133, 137, 180, 182
trade songs, 64
Trahan, Adam, 317, 347-350
Trahan, Horace, 485
"Travailier, C'est trop dur," 461
Triangle Dance Hall, 333
triangle, 16, 21, 35, 41-42, 114, 223, 311, 387, 399, 426, 454, 496
Tribute to Cajun Music festival, see Hommage à la musique acadienne
Trinidad, 257, 259, 263
trumpets, 402
Tubb, Ernest, 443, 445, 447-449, 451
Tucker, Stephen, 6, 25
Tulane, University 212, 307, 459, 460, 464; Liberation Front, 461
Twisters, 284
Tyler, T. Texas, 395

"Un autre soir ennuyant," 203
"Une Pias' Ici, Une Pias' La Bas," 402
Ungar, Jay and Molly, 224
Université Laval, 9, 14, 15
University of Louisiana at Lafayette (see also University of Southwestern Louisiana), 496
University of Southwestern Louisiana, 9, 10, 21, 23, 24, 103, 217, 254, 303, 460, 461, 464

Vacaville Dance Ranch, 133, 137
*valse à deux temps*, 374-375
"Valse de Gueydan," 384, 385
"Valse du Pont d'Amour," 200
Vee-Pee record company, 284, 285
*veillées*, 57-58, 128
Venuti, Joe, 395
Vermilion Parish, 47, 55, 57, 62, 167, 216, 293
Verret, Errol, 209, 224, 473
Veteran Playboys, 202, 214
"Veuve de la Coulee, La," 408, 411
Victor record company, see RCA
Victrolas, 324, 349
Vidrine, Jane Grosby, 310
Vidrine, John, 310
Ville Platte, LA, 88, 234, 243, 246, 279, 281-284, 289, 293, 297, 339, 342, 343-345, 360-362, 383, 387, 413, 419, 425, 428, 459
"Vinton High Society," 393
violence, 46, 144
violins, see fiddles
Vocalion record company, 233-234, 240, 255, 384
*Voix des Cajuns*, 183
voodoo, 259
voyageurs, 55, 64

Waggoner, Porter, 440
Walker Brothers, 426
Walker, Billy, 450
Walker, Lawrence, 5, 16, 27, 198, 201, 202, 207, 209, 210, 222, 283, 309, 310, 328, 329, 332, 344, 350, 390, 425, 426, 428, 429, 431, 454
waltzes, see dance
Wandering Aces, 202, 207, 210, 428, 491
Ware, Billy, 209, 470, 474
Storm, Warren, 203, 286
Watson, Doc, 474
Thibodeaux, Waylon, 215
Webb's Neighborhood Lounge, 139
Webster, Katie, see Miller, J.D.
weddings, 41-42, 48, 71-72, 74, 145, 363-64, 413, 450; wedding songs, 74-75
Wells, Kitty, 247, 274, 277, 283
Wembley Festival (London), 275
Werner, Joe, 392, 393, 394, 401; and the Ramblers, 394

West, Clint, 203
western swing, 88-89, 193, 203, 214, 235, 238, 361, 386, 391, 393, 419, 438, 439, 444, 454, 495, 500; orchestras, 395
whiskey, 45, 168, 379, 409, 411, 447
Whitfield, Irène Thérèse, 9, 10, 11, 12, 13, 15, 16, 17, 19, 208, 332, 381, 469
Whitman, Slim, 247
Widcamp, Chink, 402
Williams, Hank, 194, 205, 206, 220, 274, 276, 278, 317, 413, 443, 444, 448, 449, 450, 497; wedding in New Orleans, 448
Wills, Bob, and his Texas Playboys, 88, 194, 317, 393, 395, 409, 417, 439-40, 454
Wilson, Justin, 26, 265-271
Wimberly, Don, 402
Wimmer, Kevin, 226
Winter, Johnny, 496
WJBO (Baton Rouge), 241
WNCE (New Orleans), 241
women, and Cajun music 10, 68, 77-80, 118-121, 127, 130, 213, 220, 310, 317
"Wondering," 394, 401
World War II, 427
WWL, 229, 230, 231, 232, 238, 241, 242, 381
WWOZ-FM, 249

Yazoo, 6
*Yé Yaille, Chère!*, 25, 253, 255, 257
yodelers, 400
"You're Small and Sweet," 381
Young, Ally, 458
Young, Faron, 449
Young, Neil, 439-440, 481

Zack Attack, 213
ZydeCajun, 90, 95, 100, 222, 287
zydeco, 4, 26, 32, 93, 97-100, 102-103, 105, 113, 115-116, 118-119, 120-126, 129, 130-133, 136-137, 186, 199, 208, 210-211, 216-217, 224, 244, 279-280, 286, 289-291, 294, 298-299, 305-306, 312-313, 390, 395, 402, 463-464, 472, 474, 484, 487, 499; Extravaganza, 105; Force, 100; Hi-Rollers, 100; music, origin of, 103; People's Choice Awards, 105; recordings, 312; Rockers, 463; zydeco-rock, 463
Zynn label, 286